TO BE
DISPOSED
BY
AUTHORITY

ENVIRONMENT AND STATECRAFT

Note about the cover:
The image on the cover is of the "ozone hole" over the Antarctic taken on September 17, 2001, the day that the hole was at its peak for this year. The hole, roughly the size of North America, is shown in blue. It is defined as the region with total ozone, measured as the thickness of the ozone layer in a vertical column, below 220 Dobson units. The areas in yellow are high in ozone. The ozone hole reached its all-time peak in 2000, when it was about 10 percent greater than the area shown on the cover. Image courtesy of NASA.

Environment and Statecraft

The Strategy of Environmental Treaty-making

SCOTT BARRETT

OXFORD

UNIVERSITY PRESS

OXFORD

UNIVERSITY PRESS

Great Clarendon Street, Oxford OX2 6DP

Oxford University Press is a department of the University of Oxford.
It furthers the University's objective of excellence in research, scholarship,
and education by publishing worldwide in

Oxford New York

Auckland Bangkok Buenos Aires Cape Town Chennai
Dar es Salaam Delhi Hong Kong Istanbul Karachi Kolkata
Kuala Lumpur Madrid Melbourne Mexico City Mumbai Nairobi
São Paulo Shanghai Taipei Tokyo Toronto

Oxford is a registered trade mark of Oxford University Press
in the UK and in certain other countries

Published in the United States
by Oxford University Press Inc., New York

© Scott Barrett, 2003

The moral rights of the author have been asserted
Database right Oxford University Press (maker)

First published 2003

British Library Cataloguing in Publication Data

Data available

Library of Congress Cataloging in Publication Data

Barrett, Scott.
Environment and statecraft: the strategy of environmental treaty-making / Scott Barrett.
p. cm.
Includes bibliographical references and index.
1. Treaties. 2. International cooperation. 3. Environmental law, International. I. Title.

KZ1318 .B37 2002   341.7′62–dc21   2002028262

ISBN 0–19–925733–7 (hbk)

1 3 5 7 9 10 8 6 4 2

Typeset by Newgen Imaging Systems (P) Ltd., Chennai, India
Printed in Great Britain
on acid-free paper by
T.J. International Ltd., Padstow, Cornwall

To Jackson and Kira who, along with Leah, get all my red cards.

Contents

List of Figures

List of Tables

Preface and Acknowledgments

This book develops a theory of how states can cooperate in protecting their shared environmental resources—resources like the ozone layer, the blue fin tuna, the Aral Sea, the entirety of the earth's biodiversity, and the global climate. The book explains why international treaties are the primary means for doing this, and why, if they are to succeed, treaties must strategically manipulate the incentives states have to exploit the environment.

Though the issues of concern to this book are very real, they are as much a conceptual as a practical challenge. It is not even easy to tell whether a particular treaty succeeds in protecting the environment. For we see only one thing: a world in which the treaty exists. To know whether the treaty has succeeded we would need to see more. We would need to know what would have happened had the treaty never existed. And we would need to know what would have happened in an idealized world, where states were unhampered by the constraint of sovereignty. These benchmark outcomes cannot be observed. They must instead be inferred. Such inferences, however, must be arrived at systematically. We need to structure our imaginations, and this is why we need a theory.

Indeed, a theory can do even more than evaluate a given treaty. It can tell us how we might write better treaties, agreements that really do improve the way we manage our shared environmental resources. A key aim of this book is to show how we might do this.

Transnational environmental problems are much harder to remedy than the domestic variety because of the principle of sovereignty. Under the rules of international law, states can pretty much act as they like, and there is no World Government, no Global Environmental Protection Agency, that can make states act differently. And yet, if all states acted just as they pleased, the consequences may well be awful all around. There may be no check on the amount of greenhouse gases emitted into the atmosphere, no restraint on the logging of unique rainforests, no easing in the pace of over-fishing. To do better, we have to restructure the incentive system. This is what treaties are meant to do.

Unfortunately, most treaties—and I list or discuss over 300 treaties in this book—fail to alter state behavior appreciably. The great exception to this rule is the Montreal Protocol on Substances that Deplete the Ozone Layer, and I use the theory to explain how and why this agreement succeeded. My view is that you cannot understand the more common failures of international cooperation until you have understood the reasons for Montreal's success.

I have heard many people say that the reasons for Montreal's success are obvious. Some are. But others are camouflaged, and analysis of this treaty, like others, requires a certain forbearance. To make sense of this problem requires breaking it down into manageable pieces, and studying them one at a time. This is how my own research has proceeded, and by and large this is how the literature on this subject has developed. This book proceeds in the same way, but goes farther. It pulls the different pieces of the puzzle together, and in so doing creates an image that we have not seen before. It is not a wholly pleasing picture. One of the main conclusions of this book is that we cannot expect to realize a first best outcome every time. The problem is not just that past agreements have been poorly crafted. The problem is more fundamental: first best outcomes are not always attainable. There are good reasons why Montreal is an exception.

More positively, the theory also shows how we could improve many of our other treaties. Negotiators of the Kyoto Protocol on climate change, for example, thought they could replicate Montreal's success by applying a similar formula (in particular, by incorporating targets and timetables). The theory developed in this book suggests that they were wrong. Climate change and ozone depletion are different problems. They require different solutions. There is no one-size-fits-all treaty remedy for global or regional environmental problems. Each problem has its own best treaty remedy, even if it is one that falls short of supporting the ideal outcome.

This insight emerges not just from the theory, but from an examination of a large number of treaties. Though Montreal and Kyoto are among the best known agreements, other, lesser known treaties have as much to teach us. These include the North Pacific Fur Seal Treaty, the International Convention for the Prevention of Pollution from Ships, and the International Convention for the Conservation of Atlantic Tunas. Indeed, we can even learn from the failures of international cooperation. The entire body of treaty experience helps to illuminate the theory. It also gave me clues for how the theory needed to be further developed. This is important. I have been amazed to discover how little many treaty negotiators know of the experiences of earlier negotiations, and of the lessons that could and should be drawn from them. It is not just the lack of a theory that explains why negotiations so often fall short of potential. Ignorance of history is also to blame.

Before starting work on this book, some people urged me to write a different book: an analysis of the climate change negotiations. My feeling, however, was that it would be a mistake to write *only* on these negotiations. Much more could be learned, I thought, even about the climate change problem, by looking at other agreements and thinking more broadly about the challenge. In the event, my hunch proved right (at least to my satisfaction). The last chapter of this book contains my analysis of the climate change negotiations, and it is a chapter I couldn't have written had I not completed the 14 chapters that precede it first—proof, to me at least, that the effort that went into writing this book was worthwhile.

There is an old debate in the international relations literature about whether international regimes make any difference. I find that some do and that some do not, and that the success of a treaty depends partly on the nature of the underlying problem—something that is given and that cannot be changed by diplomacy or policy. Success also depends on the acumen of the negotiators. Some problems are easier to correct than others, but for any given problem some treaty designs are more helpful than others. The nature of the ozone depletion problem was favorable to a cooperative outcome, but the negotiators in Montreal could have negotiated a bad treaty. They did not. Climate change is a much harder challenge, but the negotiators in Kyoto could have done better.

These are the book's main conclusions. I do not arrive at them directly. They are rather implied by the theory developed here, a theory built upon the following foundations.

I adopt the realist perspective that countries care only about their self-interests, but I focus on situations in which unilateralism fails to sustain a mutually satisfying outcome. The most important of these involve mixed motives. Every country wants to avoid paying to protect the environment, but each recognizes that if every country did this the result would be bad overall. Each country would therefore prefer that every country behaved differently, even if that meant that its own behavior had to be bridled, too. So countries come to the negotiating table hoping to agree to mutual restraint.

They find it easy enough to negotiate a treaty that instructs every country to reduce its pollution. But self-interest combined with sovereignty may mean that few countries, if any, will sign such a treaty. Or it may mean that the parties to such an agreement will not honor their obligations. Or it may mean that every country will sign and comply fully with the treaty but only because the treaty asks them to behave the same as they would had the treaty never existed. The problem is that treaties seeking to improve on unilateralism must be self-enforcing.

Self-enforcement finds a particular expression in the theory. In particular, it must satisfy three conditions.

First, a treaty must be *individually rational*. This means that no party to the treaty can gain by withdrawing, given the choices made by every other country, and that no non-party (if any) can gain by acceding—again, given the decisions made by every other country. It also means that no party can gain by failing to comply, given the treaty's design. And it means that no non-party (again, if any) can gain by changing its behavior (by polluting more or less, say), given every other country's behavior. The assumption of individual rationality is made necessary by the principle of sovereignty.

Second, a treaty must be *collectively rational*. This assumption recognizes negotiation to be a collective activity, and requires that it not be possible for parties to gain collectively by changing their treaty. Collective rationality is similar to the concept of a "renegotiation-proof equilibrium" from game theory, but it is not exactly the same thing. It applies to static as well as dynamic games, and to N-player as well as 2-player repeated games. Importantly, it ignores coalition formation. It looks at matters from the perspective of the entire group of cooperating countries, and is self-enforcing only with respect to unilateral deviations. This, to my mind, is satisfactory, but it is a distinction worth underlining (and possibly in need of further refinement).

Since negotiators can anticipate how a treaty will restructure their relationship, they can use the treaty as a device for strategy. They can incorporate different instruments (technology standards rather than emission limits, say), or a minimum participation clause, or financial transfers, or trade restrictions of some kind—any feasible strategy that succeeds in restructuring the incentive system. The catch is that countries are constrained in making these choices. The promises and threats embodied in a treaty must be credible—and this is where the assumptions about rationality matter. They define what credibility means in the context of treaty-making. For example, a restriction on trade might deter every country from not participating, but if the restriction harmed the treaty's parties (collectively), given the decision by others not to participate, then the threat would not be credible. Making threats and promises credible turns out to be the greatest challenge to international cooperation. Writing a treaty that tells parties to reduce their emissions is easy. Making countries want to participate in such a treaty, and making participants want to comply with it, is much harder.

Finally, a self-enforcing treaty must be "fair." Put differently, it must be perceived by the parties as being legitimate. My approach here is light-handed. I do not let concerns for fairness override the demands of individual and collective rationality. I rather let it interact with, and sometimes reinforce, these requirements.

Fair agreements are focal. They are also the only agreements likely to be self-enforcing—in the long run, anyway. To take an example, the current regime for Antarctica excludes most of the world's countries from having any say in how the last continent is managed. The regime may be self-enforcing in a narrow sense (it has already lasted 40 years), but it is unlikely to endure in the long run. The regime can be sustained for now only because the parties to this treaty have yet to extract resources from Antarctica. If this situation were to change, non-parties to this treaty—the vast majority of the world's countries—will surely insist on having a voice in determining Antarctica's destiny, and the parties to the Antarctica Treaty will then have to listen to them, not least because their claims will have moral force. Indeed, as explained later in the book, the Antarctica treaty system has already had to bend to the wishes of non-party states.

At the same time, I do not assume that countries come to the negotiating table with the objective of writing a fair agreement. Each country is assumed rather to try to get the best deal for itself that it can. Some people have argued that a climate change treaty should allocate to each country the same entitlement to pollute per capita, possibly to allow for trading in these entitlements. This allocation might be fair in some abstract sense, but it disregards the status quo; if implemented, it would transfer billions or even trillions of dollars from the industrialized countries to the developing countries. This would only encourage the rich countries to walk out of the negotiations, leaving the poor with nothing at all—an outcome that is neither efficient nor fair.

To sum up, the theory developed in this book requires that agreements be self-enforcing that is, individually rational, collectively rational, and fair.

The main policy conclusions of this book are summarized in Chapter 14, and need not be repeated here. However, if I were to summarize in a single paragraph what the book teaches it would be this: The constraints imposed by sovereignty mean that a treaty has to restructure incentives in order to succeed in altering behavior. That is, a treaty is a strategic instrument of policy. Strategy has many means of effecting change, including the treaty's minimum participation clause, the use of sticks, including trade restrictions, and the use of carrots, especially side payments. Negotiators must also decide whether a treaty should be inclusive or exclusive, and whether it should demand a lot from every signatory, realizing that the consequence may be low participation, or whether it should demand little of every signatory for the sake of broadening participation. Again, every one of these choices will have an effect on behavior—an effect that can be analyzed using the theory. The theory doesn't say how a treaty should be written. But it does provide a framework for determining the consequences of various treaty designs. It therefore structures our thinking about the choices that negotiators can make.

Is the theory really useful? It is if it teaches something you didn't already know, or compels you to think differently about a familiar problem. I have tried to show that the theory developed here does both, by relating it to the existing literature and by holding it up to the light of real world experiences. This is not to claim that the theory developed here is "right." You can prove that a mathematical theorem is correct but you can't prove that a theory of social organization is right. You can only show that it is not wrong. The motive, rather, is to show that the theory is distinctive and compelling compared with the existing literature. I want also to show that more can be learned by shifting back and forth between the ivory tower of abstract models and the real world of international affairs than by residing in just one of these worlds. Up to now, the literature has tended to be more divided, with economists building elegant theories that often seem disconnected from the real world, and with political scientists writing detailed case studies that, to my mind view anyway, lack a coherent and consistent theoretical foundation.

Indeed, another feature of my approach is to try to connect these different literatures. Though scholars from both economics and political science have been writing on the same topic at the same time, there has been virtually no sharing of ideas between them. I have broken with this tradition, and tried to unify this much larger body of work. I have also made sure that the theory is compatible with international law, something which both of the literatures cited above have largely ignored.

My presentation of the theory is a little unusual. I make use of analytical game-theoretic models and classroom experiments, the recollections of real negotiators and histories told in case studies—any information that can help give a feel for the theory and what it has to tell us. The models may put off some readers, but they give structure to the analyses of the data. They are also very simple. Most can be solved using only algebra. Even more importantly, they yield valuable insights. They show, for example, that the usual 2×2 models studied in international relations distort the problems they intend to illuminate (the 2-player game is a very special case). The more technically inclined reader may feel differently—for this reader, the models may seem *too* simple. However, the results presented here can be shown to be reasonably robust. And simplicity has the virtue of allowing us to focus on essentials. My aim is to provide a framework, and rather than jump from model to model as is sometimes done in the literature, this book develops a unified approach that is sustained throughout. More importantly, the theory of international cooperation is an applied theory, and needs to be deeply rooted in its subject. A weakness of the existing theoretical literature is that assumptions are adopted with too little thought being given to their suitability. Here, the focus is very much on appropriateness—on connecting abstract models to the real world.

The book is also written in a somewhat unusual style—unusual, that is, for an academic audience. But my hope is that the book will appeal to a wider readership, to include present and especially future negotiators. Negotiation is often looked upon as an art, or perhaps as a craft to be learned by apprenticeship and perfected with experience—and it is this. But it is also much more. We expect domestic environmental policies today to be informed by cost-benefit analysis and to incorporate incentive mechanisms. We should expect no less of treaties. Negotiators trained in the strategy of environmental treaty-making will, I believe, negotiate more effective treaties, with the consequence that the environment is better safeguarded and peoples' lives improved. It was with this aim in mind that I wrote this book.

I have only come to understand this subject by discussing it with others, and especially by having others find fault in my arguments. By this process, I have reworked my thinking many times over.

Partha Dasgupta and Karl-Göran Mäler have left an indelible mark on me and my work, and their influence should show in these pages. When I would return home from seeing them in some far away place my productivity would jump—and then begin a long decline until we met again. This is how this book was written—in fits and starts. I must also thank Partha Dasgupta for urging me to write this book in the first place—and Karl-Göran Mäler for telling me to finish it.

Over the seven years it has taken me to write this book, I have also learned much from a great many other people. Individuals who have taught me something—and something that found a place somewhere in this book—include: Kenneth Arrow, Leah Barrett, Richard Benedick, Jagdish Bhagwati, Daniel Bodansky, Peter Bohm, Frances Cairncross, Carlo Carraro, Parkash Chander, Steve Charnovitz, Eileen Claussen, Brian Copeland, John Dixon, Brian Fisher, Henk Folmer, Lawrence Goulder, Kathryn Graddy, Robert Hahn, Geoffrey Heal, Michael Hoel, Tom Jones, Robert Keohane, Charles Kolstad, Marc Levy, William Nordhaus, David Pearce, Michael Rauscher, Philippe Sands, Todd Sandler, Anthony Scott, Dominico Siniscalco, Robert Stavins, Henry Tulkens, John Vickers, David Victor, Martin Weitzman, Jonathan Wiener, and Aart de Zeeuw. I am especially grateful to Richard Benedick, Daniel Bodansky, Partha Dasgupta, Robert Keohane, and Robert Stavins for reading the first complete draft, and for commenting on one or more chapters. The revised book is better for their advice. The support of Andrew Schuller, editors Gwendolen Booth and Sarah Dobson, and the readers for Oxford University Press is also much appreciated.

I must also thank my students at the Johns Hopkins University School of Advanced International Studies, on the Advanced Studies Program at the Kiel

Institute for World Economics, and at the teaching workshops organized by the Beijer Institute of the Royal Swedish Academy of Sciences—for reading drafts, giving me ideas for improvements, and letting me play games in the classroom.

My research assistants, Lara Marsiliani, David Michel, and Shlomi Dinar, found much of the data in the appendix to Chapter 6, and my administrative assistants, Christine Vandernoot, Bernadette Courtney, Patrick Gallagher, and Danielle Mesko, helped with numerous other tasks. I am grateful to them all.

Excerpts are reprinted by permission of the publisher from Ozone Diplomacy: New Directions in Safeguarding the Planet, by Richard Benedick, Cambridge, Mass.: Harvard University Press ©1991, 1998 by the President and Fellows of Harvard College.

My parents, Bruce and Nita Barrett, always thought I could do things, and their confidence in me rubbed off. It made *me* think I could do things. It made me think I could write this book. It certainly helped me to finish it, and I am especially grateful for that.

The inspiration for writing the book, and for everything else, came from the special people to whom I owe so much and to whom this book is dedicated: Leah, Jackson, and Kira. Thank you.

1

Introduction

We have moved beyond Cold War definitions of the United States' strategic interests. Our foreign policy must now address a broad range of threats—including damage to the world's environment—that transcend countries and require international cooperation to solve. Vice President Albert Gore, Jr., letter introducing the US State Department's first annual report on the environment and US foreign policy, *Environmental Diplomacy (1997).*

1.1. MONTREAL'S SUCCESS

I started thinking about the subject of this book on September 17, 1987, after reading in the London newspapers that an international agreement had been signed the previous day in Montreal. Twenty-three countries had agreed to cut their production and consumption of CFCs and other ozone-destroying chemicals by half before the end of the century, something I thought would never happen.

The ozone layer is not a layer at all. Ozone molecules, each consisting of three oxygen atoms, only sparsely pack the earth's stratosphere, where concentrations are typically less than one part per million. If you could bring all these molecules down to the earth, however, where they would be compressed by the weight of the atmosphere, they *would* form a layer—but only a very thin layer, less than a centimeter thick. Though not abundant, ozone is active. And it does something that no other gas in the atmosphere can do; it absorbs the sun's harmful ultraviolet radiation. If ozone became more scarce, more UV-B radiation would reach the earth's surface, damaging living cells. More people would get skin cancers and cataracts, agricultural yields would fall, and, by destroying phytoplankton near the ocean's surface, fish stocks further up the marine food chain would be thinned out. Every country would be harmed. And yet the process of depletion could possibly be halted and even reversed if all countries stopped releasing ozone-depleting chemicals into the atmosphere. This is why our diplomats traveled to Montreal in 1987. They were sent to negotiate an agreement that would control the release of CFCs.

My surprise was in learning that they had succeeded. For though every country would benefit from the protection of the ozone layer, each would benefit *whether it contributed to the protection effort or not,* and substituting away from CFCs would be costly. In the jargon of economics, ozone layer protection is a global public good. I had been taught, and had come to believe, that cooperation of the kind exhibited in Montreal could not be sustained because of the incentives to free ride.

I was not alone in thinking this way. When I asked colleagues at the LSE, where I was studying for a PhD at the time, what they thought of the agreement, the response was uniformly skeptical. Most of the professors and students I spoke to thought that the signatories would not do what they had pledged to do, that the agreement would eventually fall apart. I sensed that they were wrong, however—that the theory I had been taught and that had conditioned my thinking was wrong. Without knowing it, I had already begun to work on this book.

After doing a little research, I discovered that the Montreal Protocol kept company with over a hundred other multilateral agreements currently in force. Most of these received the smallest mention in the papers. A few, like the International Convention for the Regulation of Whaling and the Nuclear Test Ban Treaty, were well known— but they were famous for having failed. Recommendations by the International Whaling Commission were routinely flouted by whaling nations, and important nuclear powers like France and China had openly balked at signing the Test Ban Treaty. These behaviors conformed with the model I had been taught. The Montreal Protocol, however, *appeared* to be different.

As matters turned out, Montreal *was* different. Rather than fall apart, it entered into force on schedule. More importantly, the promised cuts in emissions were actually implemented. The agreement was also substantially strengthened. Periodic renegotiations brought many more substances under its control, and the initial 50 percent cut in emissions was extended to a total ban. Even the timing for emission reductions was accelerated. Remarkably, more countries ratified the agreement, even as it demanded more of its participants. Today, participation in this agreement is virtually full; only a few "rogue states" and countries lacking effective domestic government have yet to sign it. Montreal was not only different. It broke the mold. With hindsight, my original impression was correct. The chief US negotiator in Montreal, Richard Benedick, was justified in calling the treaty "unique in the annals of international diplomacy" (Benedick 1998: 1).

But since roughly the same forces act on all efforts to sustain international cooperation, it was not obvious in 1987, and nor is it obvious today, what made Montreal different. Why did Montreal succeed where so many other agreements had failed? Were the circumstances of ozone depletion uniquely favorable to international cooperation, or had the negotiators in Montreal discovered a formula that could remedy every cross border environmental problem? Ultimately, this is what I wanted to understand when I began this research, and this book contains the explanation I have arrived at.

When first negotiated, the Montreal Protocol seemed to have opened up new possibilities for diplomacy, prompting a British diplomat to call its entry into force "epoch-making" (Brenton 1994: 140). However, I believe that we have learned the wrong lessons from Montreal. The circumstances of this negotiation were unique, and it was a mistake to think—as so many did and still do—that the success at Montreal could be easily replicated. The Kyoto Protocol on global climate change, for example, negotiated ten years after Montreal and consciously fashioned after the Montreal Protocol, is a flawed agreement. Like the Montreal Protocol, the Kyoto Protocol establishes targets and timetables for reducing harmful emissions. But unlike Montreal, Kyoto fails to provide the supporting mechanisms needed to restructure the relations among the world's countries, to reverse the incentives to free ride.

This, ultimately, is what an international agreement to supply a global public good must do. It is a tall order, for sure, and the circumstances will not always be favorable to achieving full cooperation. But I will show that we could do much better than we have in the past—provided we learn the right lessons from Montreal.

1.2. A GAME OF CARDS

To appreciate the approach of this book, and the perspective it provides on these problems, you must first share my initial surprise in learning of the Montreal Protocol's apparent success in deterring free-riding. Here is how I motivate the problem in the classroom.

I distribute to each student two playing cards, one red and one black. I then ask each student to hand back to me one card. Each student is instructed to make this choice with a view to maximizing his own payoff. The payoff that any student gets depends on whether he hands back to me a red or a black card *and* the choices made by all the other students. These choices are private; none of the other students can tell which card a particular student has returned to me (that is why every student gets both a black and a red card).

Suppose there are twenty students in the classroom and that the rules of the game say that each student gets a payoff of $5 if she keeps her red card *plus* $1 for every red card handed in to me by *any* student. Then, if six students hand their red cards back to me, each of these students will get $6 while the fourteen students who kept their red cards will each get $11 ($5 for keeping their red cards plus $6 for the red cards handed in by others).

A student who hands in her red card supplies a public good—every student benefits from her choice, and none can be excluded from receiving this benefit. This is very different from the goods that you and I trade in every day. Private goods like this book are available only to the people who buy them (or who borrow them with permission from other people or institutions that buy them).

The problem with the supply of public goods is this: If every red card is handed in, each student gets $20. If no red cards are turned in, each student gets $5. However, students who hand in their red cards are penalized for their generosity; irrespective of how every other student has chosen, each student who hands in a red card loses $4 (in handing in her red card, a student sacrifices $5 and gains only $1). Each student thus has an incentive *not* to supply the public good—even though every student would be better off if the good were supplied. Note that I am careful not to tell the students this. I want them to discover the incentive problem for themselves.[1]

I have played this game about fifty times—with SAIS masters students in international affairs; with MBA and more mature Sloan students; with economics masters and PhD students; with non-economics PhD students only; with young academics

---

[1] You may recognize the card game as a variant of the prisoners' dilemma, discussed in detail in Chapter 3. I have found that if this game is first presented in its usual analytical form, students either take the Nash equilibrium to be a literal description of human behavior (which it is not) or they dismiss it as a mathematical artifact, yielding no insight into the incentives for collective action. Students who play the experiment are inclined to think more broadly about the incentive structure of the game.

from all around the world, and with academics from particular regions like West Africa, South Asia, and Central and South America; with undergraduate environmental studies students and with senior executives from the energy industry; with British diplomats and with Treasury mandarins. I have played the game with groups as small as six and as large as sixty, with groups whose members all knew each other and with groups whose members were strangers, with students who had previously been taught the prisoners' dilemma (the game after which the card game is styled; see Chapter 3) and with students who had never heard of it. Every time the result has been qualitatively the same. Only a fraction of the participants—ranging from about a third to two-thirds—hand in their red cards.[2] The collective result is never as good as it could be. Collectively, the class can do no better than to hand in every red card, but this has never happened in the fifty or so times I have played this game.

In a second round of play (and I do not announce in advance that there will be a second round), the students are invited to discuss their problem openly—that is, to negotiate—before making their choices. Again, the result is nearly always the same. One student will say something like, "We would all be better off if we all handed in our red cards, so let's agree to do it," and another will reply, "Yes, but how can I trust *you* to hand in *your* red card?" It is at this point—if any doubt remained—that all the students understand their predicament. Often after such a pre-play communication round the number of students who hand in their red cards increases slightly. But if I then allow students to communicate again and play a third round, cooperation typically drops, perhaps because the students who cooperated previously felt aggrieved that their benevolence was not returned.[3] Never in any round of any experiment have all students handed in their red cards, even on the occasions when all have pledged publicly to do so.[4]

I have also played different versions of this game. In one I pass out to each student two red cards and two black cards, and ask the students to hand back two cards. Typically, some students will keep both of their red cards, some will turn both in, and some will return just one red card. Once, I tried varying the marginal value to handing in a red card, telling each student that she would get $2 if she kept one red card and $6 if she kept both (suggesting increasing marginal costs). I have also played the game by assigning students different values. Handing out just numbered cards, I have told students that they would get the value of their red card if they kept it (e.g., $8 if a student kept her eight of hearts or eight of diamonds) but that each student would get $1 for every red card handed in by anyone. Every time, for all these variations of the game, the results have been qualitatively identical. Always, some students hold on to some of their red cards.

---

[2] This result is also pretty typical of "proper" public goods experiments. See Fehr and Schmidt (1999).

[3] For experimental evidence showing that people punish non-cooperators even when doing so is self-damaging, see Fehr and Gächter (2000*a*).

[4] In "proper" experiments, cooperation tends to deteriorate over time and typically reaches a low level in the final period. See Fehr and Schmidt (1999). For a possible explanation as to why this might happen, see Fischbacher *et al.* (2000).

However the game was set up previously, I conclude by asking the students to vote in a referendum (again, the students are not told in advance that this option will be available to them). I tell the students that a government stands ready to confiscate everyone's red card if given the authority by them, the electorate, to do so. All that is needed is for a simple majority to vote yes. As with the earlier choices, I require that this decision be made in private.[5] The students are instructed to write their votes on a slip of paper and to hand it in to me. I then count the votes without revealing how particular individuals have voted. Again, the result is always qualitatively the same: some participants vote no but the majority vote yes.[6] Collectively, the welfare of the entire group is thus maximized by the intervention.

The reason that international cooperation is a problem should now be obvious. There is no World Government authorized to tax the world's citizenry, no central fund to pay for the provision of transnational public goods. Supply of these goods must instead rely on self-enforcing, voluntary arrangements, and these are typically less effective than the strong and visible arm of government intervention. This is why the Montreal Protocol seemed so remarkable. It somehow got countries to hand in all their red cards.

1.3. THINKING ABSTRACTLY

The card game is a useful metaphor. But a classroom experiment with a deck of cards obviously cannot tell us precisely how countries actually behave in real situations. When playing the game, students are asked to consider seriously a hypothetical situation. And yet they know that no money will change hands (in "proper" experiments where money does change hands, free-riding is more prevalent), and so they can be generous at no personal cost. The amounts in any event are very small (interestingly, when the net benefits to free-riding are increased, I find that the level of free-riding increases too, even though the payoffs remain hypothetical). For all I know, a bias may be introduced simply by the way I pose the problem (some participants may give the answer that they think I want them to give or that they think I *do not* want them to give; who knows?). Most of all, the experiment abstracts from many important features of real situations. Countries are not individuals but collections of individuals,

[5] People often express views in public that contrast with their private preferences, which is why the private vote is so important to democracy. If a person's vote were public, intimidation could impel a person to vote for, or against, a particular party or individual or issue. The intimidation need not be brutal. It may not even be very obvious. I recall a meeting of my own institution's academic board. A motion was tabled that would have important and broad implications but that would have a more immediate and negative consequence for an admired colleague (who was not present). There seemed to be broad agreement on the issue as a principle, but when the discussion shifted to what the vote meant for our colleague, public support for the proposal waned. I motioned that our votes be recorded by private ballot, and this was seconded and approved by a majority of the faculty. When our votes were counted, the principle was endorsed. I cannot be sure, but I suspect that the vote might have been otherwise had the faculty's vote been public. For an absorbing discussion of "preference falsification," see Kuran (1998).

[6] To my amazement and amusement, of all the groups I have played this experiment on, the one having the slimmest yes majority was a group of British civil servants. I reminded them that taxation is confiscation. It also pays their salaries.

represented at treaty negotiations by their governments; payoffs are not known with certainty; provision of public goods is not usually binary; etc.

But upon a little reflection it becomes clear that *any* analysis of these issues must abstract. Whether you play a card game or conduct a proper experiment, whether you write a tight or discursive essay, whether you assemble a case study or interview participating negotiators, whether you estimate an econometric relation or construct a game-theoretic model—any of these approaches will abstract from certain details. The only difference is that in some cases the abstraction will be more or less appropriate and more or less explicit.

Abstraction is not only unavoidable; it also helps us to understand the real world better. For as mentioned in the Preface, if we look at the facts alone, we can only observe what actually happens. The card game showed us more. It showed us what would happen if every student kept his red card, and if every student handed his red card in. These outcomes are hidden in the telling of how the Montreal Protocol was negotiated. We have only observed a world in which this treaty exists. We cannot run a controlled experiment to determine what would have happened had a treaty never been negotiated, or what the world would have done had it been able to offer a referendum and enforce the will of the global electorate.

And yet these benchmarks are essential if we are to learn whether the Montreal Protocol really succeeded. For suppose that the real Montreal game differed from the card game examined earlier. Suppose that every player got $5 for keeping her red card and $10 (rather than $1, as in the earlier game) for every red card handed in by anyone. Then it would be in every player's interests to hand in her red card, whether any of the others did so or not. If Montreal merely codified this outcome, then it might appear to be a success, but really it would have achieved nothing. The same outcome would have been realized had Montreal never been negotiated. As we shall see in Chapter 8, the payoffs of ozone layer protection were favorable to cooperation—but the treaty exploited this situation, and was thus able to improve substantially on the non-cooperative outcome. This is important to know.

1.4. HELSINKI'S FAILURE

Though the Montreal Protocol has served as a kind of role model for the Kyoto Protocol and other treaties, Montreal and its associated agreements were themselves styled after a body of law developed years earlier to control acid rain in Europe (and, to a lesser extent, in North America). These earlier agreements achieved much less than Montreal, however, and it is just as important to know why these agreements failed as it is to know why Montreal succeeded.

Acid rain is caused by sulfur (and nitrogen) oxides emitted from the combustion of fossil fuels, especially sulfur-rich coal. Sulfur dioxide (SO_2), a member of the sulfur oxides family, is a potent urban pollutant: a cause of respiratory illnesses, and an aggravating factor in pulmonary and cardiovascular diseases. Usually a slow and invisible killer, its effects can sometimes be dramatic. In the Great London Smog of December 1952, an inversion trapped SO_2 and smoke emissions at ground level, killing about four thousand people.

Throughout the industrialized countries, measures were taken to limit this local pollution. In London, the use of coal (apart from the smokeless variety) as a domestic source of heating was banned; and everywhere in the United Kingdom and in many other countries, large combustion plants were made to build tall smokestacks to disperse the harmful oxides (and, in addition, particulates). The tall stacks worked as intended; they reduced pollution concentrations in urban areas. But they also had an unintended—indeed, a surprising—effect. Released from a high elevation, the pollution was carried by the prevailing winds, sometimes for hundreds or even thousands of miles. In the atmosphere, we now know, sulfur oxide particles react chemically with water vapor and are transformed into sulfuric acid (similarly, nitrogen oxides are transformed into nitric acid). When fused to precipitation, these acid compounds then fall to the earth as an acidic rain (they can also fall, and cause as much damage, in dry form). The result: acid deposition, which can damage lakes, forests, crops, and buildings.

Acid rain damage was first noticed in Scandinavia where the soils, lacking limestone, are especially vulnerable to acid deposition. Though the lakes appeared clean, fish kills in western Sweden indicated that something was terribly wrong. In the 1960s, a Swedish chemist, Svante Odén, showed that the pH level in the rain had dropped markedly. He also suggested a reason for the increase in acidity. The cause, he hypothesized, was air pollution transported from Britain and continental Europe—a claim that was disputed at first but subsequently proved correct.

Odén, called acid rain "an insidious chemical war" (Levy 1995: 59), but this was the wrong metaphor. In war, one state *tries* to harm another. The polluters in this case had no such intentions. Nevertheless, the Scandinavian countries were harmed by acidic emissions, and they remain victims of transboundary pollution today. (Figure 1.1, traces depositions of sulfur dioxide emissions in Sweden in 1997 to their original sources.) Sweden and Norway reacted as best as they could to the situation. They cut back their own emissions dramatically, and limed their most vulnerable lakes and rivers to restore pH levels. These unilateral actions could not eliminate the damage from acid rain, however, and nor did the Scandinavian countries believe it was their responsibility alone to do so. So they demanded that the pollution exporters cut their emissions, too, and thus started a process of negotiation that continues to this day.

The acid rain negotiations were, and still are, largely conducted under the auspices of the United Nations Economic Commission for Europe (ECE), an organization that conveniently includes member states from both Western and Eastern Europe (a substantial portion of sulfur imports to Scandinavia came from the Soviet bloc) and North America (where Canada was the victim of emissions exported by the United States).[7] A first treaty—the Convention on Long-Range Transboundary Air Pollution, or LRTAP—was negotiated in 1979, and protocols specifying emission reductions for the main acidic emissions (sulfur and nitrogen oxides) and for other transboundary air pollutants (including volatile organic compounds) were added in

---

[7] A number of European directives also address the acid rain problem, most especially the Large Combustion Plants Directive of 1988 that imposes limits on total sulfur emissions for existing large combustion plants and technical standards for new plants greater than 50 MW in size. As well, a bilateral treaty for North America was negotiated in 1991. Today, acid rain is an emerging problem in Asia where multilateral talks have been held but where a treaty has not yet been negotiated.

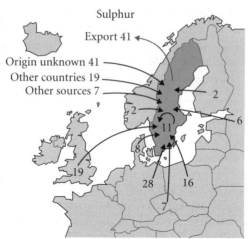

Sweden receives large quantities of acidifying sulphur dioxide from other countries. Figures for 1997, expressed as thousands of tonnes of sulphur. Source: EMEP Report 1/99.

Figure 1.1. *Flows of acidifying sulfur emissions to and from Sweden, 1997 (thousand tons of sulfur)*

Source: Swedish Environmental Protection Agency (1999).

later rounds of talks. This convention-protocol pattern later served as a template for the ozone negotiations. Montreal was the first protocol negotiated under an earlier, umbrella convention (the Convention for the Protection of the Ozone Layer). It is in many ways analogous to the first acid rain protocol, the Helsinki Protocol.

The Helsinki Protocol was adopted in 1985 and came into force just two weeks before the Montreal Protocol was ready for signing. Like Montreal, the Helsinki Protocol established targets and timetables for cutting atmospheric emissions. Specifically, it required that each party's sulfur emissions be reduced by at least 30 percent from the 1980 level by 1993.

Mandating specific emission cuts certainly made the Helsinki Protocol appear successful, but did the protocol really make a difference? The web page for the LRTAP Secretariat lists its achievements:[8]

As a result of this Protocol, substantial cuts in sulphur emissions have been recorded in Europe: Taken as a whole, the 21 Parties to the 1985 Sulphur Protocol reduced 1980 sulphur emissions by more than 50% by 1993 (using the latest available figure, where no data were available for 1993). Also individually, based on the latest available data, all Parties to the Protocol have reached the reduction target. Eleven Parties have achieved reductions of at least 60%. Given the target year 1993 for the 1985 Sulfur Protocol, it can be concluded that all Parties to that Protocol have reached the target of reducing emissions by at least 30%.

[8] See http://www.unece.org/env/lrtap/. The quote was obtained from this site in January 2002.

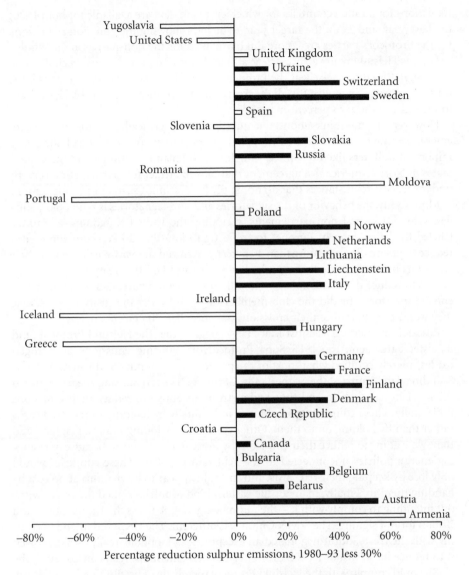

Figure 1.2. *"Compliance" with the Helsinki Protocol*

Source: http://www.unece.org/env/lrtap/sulf_h1.htm

Figure 1.2 summarizes this apparent "compliance" with the Helsinki Protocol, showing departures from the 30 percent level. Countries to the right of the vertical, zero percent line essentially over-complied with the Protocol, whereas countries to the left of this line fell short of the 30 percent reduction target. All members of the ECE were entitled to participate in this treaty, and Figure 1.2 shows the emission reductions for all such countries for which emission data are available for both 1980, the base year, and 1993, the target year.[9] The bars showing the emission reductions for the protocol's parties are colored in black; bars for the non-parties are in white.

So, was Helsinki really a success? At a first glance it appears to have been. Plainly, every signatory did precisely as the Protocol required and reduced its emissions by at least 30 percent—in Figure 1.2, all the treaty's parties, indicated by the black bars, are to the right of the zero percent marker.[10]

However, if you think about the question more critically, a different picture emerges. Some members of the ECE failed to sign and ratify the protocol, including important polluters like the United Kingdom and Poland in Europe and the United States in North America. An agreement that fails to attract full participation (except under special circumstances that do not apply here) cannot sustain full cooperation.

More subtly, the behavior of the signatories and non-signatories is remarkably similar. Why did several non-participants, including the United Kingdom—a country labeled the "dirty man of Europe" for refusing to join the "30 Percent Club"—also reduce their emissions by more than 30 percent? Why did so many parties reduce their emissions by much more than required by the treaty? Did the treaty really impel its parties to reduce their emissions by more than they would have, had the treaty never entered into force, or did the club members sign and ratify the treaty only because they were going to reduce their emissions by more than 30 percent anyway?

Research by political scientist Marc Levy suggests that the Helsinki Protocol (and its sister agreement, the 1988 Sofia Protocol on reducing emissions of nitrogen oxides) merely codified what most of the parties were planning to do anyway.[11] The Scandinavian countries, the Netherlands, Germany, Switzerland, and Austria suffered the most from acid rain and thus had a strong incentive to reduce their emissions unilaterally. These countries gained more individually by handing in their red cards rather than by holding on to them. Other countries, including France, Belgium, and Italy, were going to reduce their emissions by more than 30 percent because of changing energy policies unconnected to the acid rain problem. These countries would only lose by keeping their red cards, and so could appear to be virtuous at no cost by handing them in. Finally, many of the eastern bloc countries signed the treaty without intending to comply with it—their aim being to embarrass the United States and Britain for not signing. The Soviet Union was different. The USSR did intend to comply with the treaty, but it negotiated an exception—a loophole, really—that allowed it to reduce its "transborder fluxes" rather than its emissions. As a consequence, the USSR could comply with the Helsinki Protocol merely by redistributing its pollution, and not necessarily in a way favorable to the countries most harmed by acid rain.

---

[9] The data used to make up this figure are from the web site cited above. Members not represented in the figure include Bosnia and Herzegovina, Cyprus, Estonia, Georgia, Latvia, Luxembourg, Malta, Macedonia, and Turkey.

[10] As is customary with international agreements, these data were self-reported. Self-reporting is yet another expression of sovereignty.

[11] See Levy (1993, 1995). Note, however, that Levy adds a twist to this observation, discussed in the next section.

Levy's approach is qualitative, but his negative finding is also supported by the sophisticated econometric analyses of the Helsinki Protocol (see Murdoch and Sandler 1997; Murdoch *et al.* 1997, 2002). These studies also indicate that the actions of the Helsinki parties were not noticeably different from non-cooperative behavior. If the agreement had never been negotiated, the same amount of acid rain emissions would have fallen.

There is yet another way of determining whether the Helsinki Protocol made any difference: we can look at the treaty itself, at what it tells signatories they must do. A seminal analysis by the Swedish environmental economist Karl-Göran Mäler shows that full cooperation could only be sustained by a self-enforcing agreement if certain countries like the United Kingdom were compensated by others for reducing their emissions (Mäler 1990). The reason is that, in contrast to the card game discussed earlier, the acid rain game is highly asymmetric. Some countries lose when they hand in their red cards, even if all countries in the aggregate gain. Mäler also shows that all countries would gain most in the aggregate if different countries reduced their emissions by different amounts. Acid rain is more effectively controlled when the United Kingdom reduces its emissions than when Ireland does so. It is as if, when the United Kingdom hands in a red card, the aggregate payoff of Europe rises by more than when Ireland does so. However, the Helsinki Protocol is blind to these asymmetries. It does not compensate losers and it requires that all parties cut their emissions by the same percentage. Even if it improved on non-cooperation, these deficiencies mean that it would fall far short of full cooperation.

The protocol also lacks essential negative incentives. Countries that do not participate, or that fail to comply, are not punished by the treaty.[12] Indeed, the need for compliance is not even mentioned in the treaty. A theme of this book is that, to support real cooperation, treaties must incorporate mechanisms like carrots (positive incentives) and sticks (negative incentives) that make it attractive for countries to contribute to the greater good.

1.5. DID HELSINKI REALLY FAIL?

If treaties like Helsinki achieve so little, why do countries bother to negotiate them? After all, negotiation is costly. Surely *some* benefit must be gained to make the effort worthwhile.

One possible explanation is that countries go into a negotiation thinking that they can gain something substantive from it, only to discover later that they have to settle for an empty treaty. Another possibility, however, is that agreements like Helsinki really do achieve something—just something far short of full cooperation. Marc Levy argues that the Helsinki Protocol had an effect, "not in binding states to undertake measures they otherwise would not (as the Montreal Protocol does), but in helping shift states' perceptions of their self-interest" (Levy 1995: 61).

---

[12] Bulgaria fell short of the required emission reductions in 1994 and 1995, but so far as I know was never punished.

One of the important features of acid rain is that, while the transborder spillovers are substantial, a significant portion of a nation's own emissions fall domestically (as shown in Figure 1.1, a fifth of Sweden's emissions are deposited domestically). States harmed by acid rain thus have an incentive to cut their own emissions unilaterally, reducing pollution exports in the bargain.[13] A treaty is not needed to enforce such behavior, but Levy argues that the LRTAP programs for joint research helped identify the domestic sources of damage; that much of this information would not have become available were it not for the LRTAP; and that investigation of domestic damage intensified for the countries that chose not to join Helsinki, adding yet more pressure on them to join.

Levy also argues that political linkages influenced the decisions by some countries to participate in the Helsinki Protocol. As a member of the Nordic Council, for example, Denmark is obligated to internalize the harm that its own actions cause other Council members. But, though it is the Nordic connection that would ultimately compel Denmark to reduce its emissions, Levy (1993: 122) claims that "LRTAP served to signal precisely what Denmark's responsibilities were as a responsible Nordic Council member."

These are subtle arguments, to be sure, and they cannot be proved because we cannot observe how countries like Denmark would have behaved had the LRTAP not existed, a point Levy well understands. However, Levy's arguments are at the very least plausible. Helsinki may well have been better than nothing.

And yet Helsinki nonetheless falls far short of full cooperation, and "fails" in this sense. In defense of the Helsinki approach, Levy (1993: 132) claims that, "If [the LRTAP protocols] had been designed as regulatory rules, they would have been crippled by problems of free-riding and bickering over distributive gains." He could be right. For Montreal, however, this turned out not to be true. And Montreal did much better than Helsinki. It is important to know how it was able to do this.

1.6. OSLO'S REFORMATION

A further reason for supposing that Helsinki failed is that the parties themselves went on to negotiate a follow-on protocol in 1994 that deviated significantly from the Helsinki formula. If Helsinki had really been successful, why should the parties want to change it?

In contrast to Helsinki, the Oslo Protocol on Further Reductions of Sulphur Emissions specifies different emission ceilings for different countries. It focuses on the need to meet certain "critical loads" of depositions, and so is concerned much more with effects (damage) than with actions (emissions).[14] It allows parties to

---

[13] Research by Burtraw *et al.* (1997) shows that the benefits to the United States of Title IV acid rain controls exceed the costs by a large margin. That this policy helps Canada in the bargain is a bonus, but the fact that limiting emissions in this way benefits the United States implies that an agreement to implement Title IV (as in the 1991 United States–Canada Air Quality Agreement) need not include international enforcement mechanisms.

[14] Critical loads are estimates of the maximum pollution loadings that the environment can withstand on a sustained basis without material damage being caused.

implement their emission reduction obligations jointly by means of a mechanism called "joint implementation," provided doing so can save costs without worsening loadings. And, perhaps most importantly, it explicitly acknowledges the need for effective compliance.

And yet, despite these innovations and acknowledgments, Oslo may not improve much on Helsinki. First, the Oslo Protocol limits the emissions of just twenty countries. Polluters like the Baltic states in Europe and the United States in North America are not included. Moreover, of the countries that negotiated Oslo, several (Bulgaria, Hungary, Poland, Russia, and Ukraine) have yet to ratify it, and two others (Belarus and Portugal) have yet to sign it.

Second, and as shown in Figure 1.3, most of the parties to the Oslo Protocol have reduced their emissions by much more than required by this treaty.[15] For example, the United Kingdom (which joined Oslo at least partly because acid rain was identified as a domestic environmental problem and partly because of the removal of coal subsidies and electricity privatization) is allowed to emit 2449 thousand tons of sulfur dioxide (ktons SO_2) in 2000, and yet emitted just 1347 ktons the year before. Germany is prohibited from emitting more than 1300 ktons SO_2 in 2000, and yet its actual emissions were just 831 ktons in 1999. If the treaty were really constraining emissions, you would expect actual emissions to be closer to their limit values; few people drive 45 mph when the speed limit is 55. It is also interesting to note that the country most in danger of not complying with the agreement (Portugal) has also not signed or ratified it. An important theme of the book is that compliance and participation are linked problems.

Third, though non-uniform reductions are generally to be preferred, especially insofar as the treaty aims to meet critical loads of deposition in Europe, it is possible that the agreed emission reductions simply reflect the levels that the parties thought they would meet even in the absence of the treaty.[16] Favoring this hypothesis, the parties knew that emission reductions specified by the treaty would not actually meet the critical loads; the Oslo emission reductions were rather intended as a "first step."[17]

Fourth, though opportunities for cost savings are to be welcomed, the option of using joint implementation has not (yet) been taken up, and if it were the consequence may be to undermine the environmental effectiveness of the treaty. If, as suggested by

---

[15] Under the agreement, a party complies with the emission ceiling for any given year if the average of its emissions for that year, the year before, and the year after does not exceed the ceiling, and provided that the emission level for any single year is not more than 20% above the ceiling level. The US acid rain program, discussed in the next section, also experienced substantial over-compliance in its early years but this is because it allows utilities to "bank" allowances for future use (e.g., in 2000, allowances accumulated over the previous five years were used), and so provided an *incentive* for early over-compliance.

[16] Finus and Tjøtta (2001) carry out a game-theoretic analysis of Oslo and find that, for most parties, the Nash equilibrium emission levels are lower than the Oslo limits. That is, the Oslo constraints do not improve on unilateralism.

[17] See Article 2, paragraph 2. Note also that the web page for the treaty explicitly acknowledges that the "Protocol in itself is unlikely to yield the emission reductions necessary to fully achieve the aim of non-exceedance (sic) of critical loads, but implementation of the measures therein should make a significant contribution to achieving the aim." See http://www.unece.org/env/lrtap/conv/conclusi.htm.

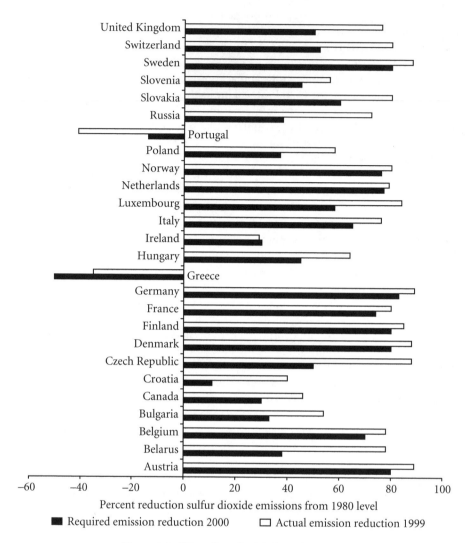

Figure 1.3. *"Compliance" with the Oslo Protocol*

Note: Greece and Portugal are required to reduce their emissions by 0% from their 2000 levels. Also, for these countries, the actual emission data are for 1998, the most recent year available (estimates of the 2000 ceilings come from Annex II of the agreement). Note also that recent emissions data were not available for Liechtenstein, Spain, and Ukraine, and so these countries were excluded from the table. Finally, note that emission ceilings for some countries are also specified for 2005 and 2010.

Source: Emission ceilings from Annex II of the treaty, available at http://www.unece.org/env/lrtap/protocol/94sulp_a/annex2.htm. Emissions data are from http://www.unece.org/env/lrtap/

Figure 1.3, the emission ceilings do not bind for many countries, allowing these countries to "trade" their excess emission reductions with other states may only reduce emissions on paper (a problem also for the Kyoto Protocol; see Chapter 15).

Fifth, the Oslo Protocol utterly ignores the need for side payments. As noted previously, if the winners of acid rain controls do not compensate the losers, the losers will have little incentive to participate or to reduce their emissions by more than they would have absent Oslo.

Finally, while the treaty acknowledges the need for compliance, it does not give enforcement any teeth. Article 7, which establishes an Implementation Committee to "decide upon and call for action to bring about full compliance," does not mention the kind of action that is needed. It refers to a possible need for "measures to assist a Party's compliance with the Protocol," but it declines even to acknowledge that punishments for non-compliance may also be needed.[18] Of course, it cannot be concluded from the wording of the treaty that the Committee will necessarily fail to enforce compliance, but, nor does the treaty reassure that the Committee will succeed.

1.7. DOMESTIC vs INTERNATIONAL ENFORCEMENT

This approach to enforcing international agreements stands in stark contrast to the way in which domestic law is enforced.

A useful example for reasons of comparison is Title IV of the Clean Air Act amendments of 1990, a US law intended to reduce acid rain depositions in the United States and, incidentally if not deliberately, in Canada.[19] In contrast to Oslo, which consciously avoids mention of an explicit penalty for non-compliance, Title IV imposes a fine, set by Congress, of $2000 per ton (to be adjusted by inflation; in 2000, the penalty was $2682 per ton[20]). Actual marginal costs for compliance have been about $187 per ton (Schmalensee *et al.* 1998), well below the penalty rate, giving polluters (electric utilities) a strong incentive to comply. Title IV also requires that polluters reduce their emissions in the year following a violation to make up for an earlier shortfall. This last requirement effectively reduces the polluter's benefit of non-compliance to the interest earned in one year on the $187 or so savings in expenditure—a value of less than $20. The combined effect of these two measures implies that, from the polluter's perspective, non-compliance is more than a hundred times as costly as compliance. But Title IV does not stop there; it gives polluters another reason to comply; it makes violation of the emission limits a felony, punishable by a prison sentence. Taken together, these measures offer an overwhelming incentive to comply, and they have had the expected effect: compliance has been virtually full. In 2000, excess allowances amounted to just 54 tons out of a total of about 10 million tons of allowances available

---

[18] Further details are given in Decision 1997/2 of the LRTAP Executive Body; see http://www.unece.org/env.lrtap/conv/report/eb53_a3.htm.

[19] See Stavins (1998) for a description of Title IV and an analysis of its adoption. Title IV also forms part of the commitments by the United States under a bilateral agreement between the United States and Canada on air quality.

[20] See http://www.epa.gov/airmarkets/cmprpt/arp00/index#allowdeduct.

that year. That is, the non-compliance rate has been about 0.00054 percent—a pretty good record by any standard.[21]

Two conclusions can be drawn from this comparison of domestic and international enforcement, one positive and one negative.

The positive conclusion is that frail international enforcement does not matter because international commitments can be enforced by means of municipal law. Indeed, the bilateral treaty between the United States and Canada on air quality actually incorporates Title IV as an air quality objective for the former country. Compliance with Title IV thus ensures compliance with, at least this provision, of the bilateral agreement.

Domestic enforcement *can* be useful to international cooperation, and I shall give an example of how it has been used effectively for this purpose in the next chapter. However, domestic law can only enforce the obligations that a country agrees to accept, and the decision to participate in a treaty is voluntary. As mentioned earlier, compliance and participation are linked problems and should be analyzed jointly. In the case of the bilateral treaty with Canada, Title IV became domestic law before this treaty was adopted, suggesting that the United States would have implemented Title IV whether or not this treaty entered into force.[22]

The negative conclusion that can be drawn from this comparison is that international agreements like Helsinki and Oslo cannot affect behavior materially. The United States could have enforced Title IV by the same means as the parties have chosen to enforce Helsinki and Oslo. And yet the US did not choose to do this—presumably because the heavy hand of compliance is more effective.

1.8. IS ENFORCEMENT REALLY A PROBLEM?

This gloomy assessment can be challenged from at least one other perspective. Free-riding at the local (sub-national) level, absent any centralized enforcement, has been shown, sometimes, to be less severe than the theory of collective action supposes—raising the hope that the same might be true at the international level. In particular, inspired and influential research by political scientist Elinor Ostrom has demonstrated that local communities can sometimes overcome the incentives to free ride when supplying local public goods like flood control and when managing common property resources like grazing lands (Ostrom 1990). Indeed, she argues that central intervention may do worse than decentralized cooperation.

It is certainly true that centralization, of the type exemplified by Title IV, cannot be relied upon to sustain first best outcomes. There are many reasons for this, but the most important as regards the issues discussed here is the organization of domestic government. As Arrow (1951) has shown, collective decisions taken democratically may lead to paradoxical outcomes. If sovereignty poses a problem for collective action at the international level, then so does democracy—and dictatorship, for that matter (see Olson 1993)—at the national level.

---

[21] Again, see: http://www.epa.gov/airmarkets/cmprpt/arp00/index#allowdeduct.
[22] This conclusion is further supported by the cost-benefit analysis discussed in note 13.

But decentralized regimes are not obviously superior to centralized ones as a general rule, and in practice the visible hand of the state plays an important supporting role in suppressing free-riding at the local level. Central government legally circumscribes the activities of institutions like cooperatives that organize collective action by community groups (think, e.g., of the anti-trust laws); it assigns property rights, even if only implicitly and even if to communities rather than individuals; and it enforces these rights, most especially by deterring the entry of community outsiders. As explained by Wade (1987: 232), rural groups rely on the state "to obtain legally enforceable recognition of their identity and rights," and they can also "call upon the state as an enforcer of last resort." This last observation, though subtle, may be more important than is usually recognized. Even if the state is not observed to intervene, the possibility that it might do so can influence behavior.

As well, local communities are made up of people who live near each other and who have intimate connections, shared values, common histories; groups that have managed their affairs effectively in related spheres, and that can leverage this success for managing their shared resources; communities that have few outside options and hence a strong need to make their collective endeavors succeed. It is one thing for members of a Turkish fishing village to regulate access to the best local fishing spots, or for a Swiss alpine community to restrict access to the common pasture. It is quite another thing for countries as diverse as the United States and Iran, Syria and Israel, and Iceland and Paraguay to cooperate in cutting their use of CFCs. Indeed, even neighboring communities find the need to call upon the state to resolve intercommunity conflict. Baland and Platteau (1996: 302) tell of how villagers in the higher rainfall areas of Burkino Faso "complain that they cannot control what they consider the abusive practices of migrants fleeing the drought-prone northern parts of the country because these new arrivals will not respect traditional authorities of the host community." Conflicts between nations can magnify these problems several fold. Though we may speak of the "community of nations," nations are distinguished by their differences, not their commonalities. Commonalities bind communities together to form a nation; differences keep nations apart.

1.9. THE EVOLUTION OF COOPERATION

A final counter-argument to the claim that Helsinki failed—and one that is not incompatible with my own interpretation of the treaty—is that Helsinki was but a first step. Helsinki may have failed by a narrow interpretation, but its failure created the incentive to negotiate Oslo; and, should Oslo also fail, an incentive will thereby be created for further institutional innovations. From this perspective, it may make little sense to put too great an emphasis on an individual treaty. Better to consider the evolution of the treaty process.

As in other endeavors, apart from the routine ones, learning *is* important to international cooperation. Indeed, it is inevitable. It simply will not be possible to construct a treaty that gets it all right from the start. And even if the treaty itself were flawless, knowledge about the environmental problem and the technologies that might be brought to bear on a remedy are likely to change. So a treaty needs to be flexible; it needs to be able to adapt to changing circumstances.

At the same time, however, being the first step should not be an excuse for falling so far short of potential. Even as a first step, Helsinki could have been better, and so, also, could Oslo have been improved. Montreal was also a first step, but Montreal created a platform on which even greater cooperation could be built. Seeing that this can be done—indeed, seeing that this *should* be done—is a lesson negotiators should learn.

1.10. TREATIES AS INSTRUMENTS OF STRATEGY

Recognition of the need for international enforcement and of the limitations of the Helsinki and Oslo approaches does not imply that international cooperation has to fail. It rather implies that enforcement at the international level needs to take a different approach. Being unable to apply the familiar domestic methods of enforcement, we need to discover another way to skin the cat, so to speak, of international enforcement. That is, we need to find another way to get countries to hand in their red cards. Finding this "other way" is a major aim of this book.

This is an unusual perspective. Negotiation is more often looked upon as a task of finding a formula acceptable to a large enough number of countries; or of agreeing on targets and timetables as was done in Helsinki, or targets and timetables coupled with "flexible mechanisms" as was done in Oslo and, later, Kyoto. But these are not really the most essential tasks. Since treaties must be self-enforcing, they must do more than simply tell countries what to do. Treaties must instead make it in the *interests* of countries to behave as every country would like them to behave. Treaties must somehow get countries to hand in their red cards.

To do this, treaties have to manipulate the incentive structure. They must, for example, make it more attractive for other countries to join when your country joins, and for others to reduce their pollution more when your country pollutes less. The underlying game will rarely make this behavior happen automatically. Successful environmental protection in the horizontal, anarchic international system will usually require a *strategic* manipulation of incentives. Treaties should therefore be seen as instruments of strategy.

Much of this book builds a theory explaining how and why Montreal was able to strategically manipulate incentives, but I can demonstrate both the power and the practicality of the theory even better (and certainly more succinctly) by telling another success story first—the story of how, by means of statecraft and especially international agreement, the northern Pacific fur seal was saved from extinction nearly a century ago. This story is told in the next chapter.

2

The North Pacific Fur Seal Treaty and the Theory of International Cooperation

[The North Pacific Fur Seal Treaty] furnishes an illustration of the feasibility of securing a general international game law for the protection of other mammals of the sea, the preservation of which is of importance to all the nations of the world.
President William Taft, State of the Union Address (1911)[1]

2.1. INTRODUCTION

Chapter 1 provided the motivation for the book. This chapter gives a glimpse of the book's essential lessons, as revealed by the telling of a very special story.[2]

The story concerns the northern fur seal (*Callorhinus ursinus*; see Figure 2.1), an animal that fills a special ecological niche, that has a distinctive morphology, that exhibits a remarkable social behavior—and that was hunted nearly to extinction about a century ago. The fur seal was saved by an ingenious treaty, the North Pacific Fur Seal Treaty of 1911, and this chapter explains how and why this treaty succeeded. As noted before, "success" is impossible to measure precisely. However, the fur seal case study comes as close to offering a counterfactual yardstick for success as we are ever likely to find.

2.2. DISCOVERY

Little is known about the early history of sealing, though Aleuts and other native peoples of the region probably hunted fur seals in the North Pacific and Bering Sea for centuries before Europeans began killing them for profit in the early 1700s, soon after Russia settled its eastern frontier. The seal's luxurious pelt, containing over 350,000 hairs per square inch, was a highly valued commodity, and a commercial market for the skins quickly developed.

At first, the seals were harvested at sea, close to the Siberian coast. But in 1741, the Russian explorer Vitus Bering discovered and was shipwrecked on the Commander Islands, where, by chance, he found one of the seal's main breeding grounds. Though Bering died near to where his ship foundered, on an island later named after him, other members of his expedition survived and returned to Siberia the next year. They

---

[1] Gay (1987: 129).
[2] An earlier version of this chapter was given as a keynote address to the conference of the European Association of Environmental and Resource Economists, held in Oslo in June 1999.

		Group of fur seals		Old male "roaring"
Young females	Old male	Young male	Mother seal	Young males
2 years	18 years	6 years	and pup nursing	2 years

Figure 2.1. *North Pacific fur seal (Callorhinus ursinus)*
Source: Elliot (1887: opposite 258)

arrived bearing a huge cargo of furs. They also told of how plentiful the seals were, and of how easily they could be slaughtered on land.

By this time a great fur trade had developed, financed by wealthy Moscow merchants and the Russian Imperial government. All sorts of furs were taken, not just seal skins. And the traders did more than take the furs they could find; as they depleted the stocks in one area they pushed on, exploring new sources of fur wealth. That quest ultimately led to the discovery of the entire Aleutian chain of islands.

The sea otter's pelt is even warmer than the fur seal's, and so the otter became the fur trade's main prey. The fur traders were too successful, however, and the population of sea otters fell quickly. By 1774 the catch "had dwindled from thousands and tens of thousands at first to hundreds and tens of hundreds at last," and so the fur-gatherers shifted their efforts, "to find new fields of gain when they had exhausted those last uncovered" (Elliot 1887: 191). Their new target was the fur seal.

Huge numbers of fur seals were observed to pass biannually through the Aleutian chain, heading north in the spring and returning south in the fall, indicating that an even larger breeding ground had yet to be discovered, somewhere in the distant sea. Russian ships pursued the herds in the hope of locating their main breeding grounds, but years of exploration turned up nothing. It is hard to imagine today just how hard the challenge was. The waters of the North Pacific and Bering Sea were uncharted, pulled in different directions by strong currents, and often fogbound. And yet the lure of fur wealth was irresistible, and so the search continued. Finally, in 1786, the main breeding grounds were discovered by a Russian sailor, Gerassim Pribilof—the son, it so happens, of a survivor of Bering's final expedition.

Like many details of history, the nature of Pribilof's discovery is disputed. By one Russian's account (reported in Fur Seal Arbitration vol. II, 1895: 23), Pribilof cruised an area of the sea for weeks in a dense fog without success until "fate, as if relenting, yielded to the untiring efforts of an enterprising man and lifted the curtain of fog, revealing the eastern part of the island nearest the Aleutian Archipelago ... " Elliot (1887: 193), by contrast, tells of how Pribilof's "old sloop" ran aground on the second largest of the islands, "and, though the fog was so thick that he could see scarce the length of his vessel, his ears were regaled by the sweet music of seal-rookeries wafted out to him on the heavy air."

However the discovery was made, Pribilof, whose five-year quest was financed by one of the leading trading companies, claimed the island for Russia and named it after his sloop, the *St George*. Upon returning the next year, Pribilof discovered an even larger island about 30 miles to the northwest (St Paul), and two very small islands in the same general vicinity (Otter and Walrus Islands). The entire chain was named after Pribilof, though they were also known as the Seal Islands.

Pribilof's discovery proved a turning point. Fur seals are an easy target on land. Like their sea lion cousins, the kind that perform tricks at the zoo, fur seals can bend their flippers forwards at the ankle and walk on all fours. This meant that they could be herded like cattle (see Figure 2.2). They were also easy to slaughter; a well-aimed

Natives driving "Holluschickie"
The drove passing over the lagoon flats to the killing grounds under the village of St Paul.
Looking SW over the village cove and the lagoon rookery.

Figure 2.2. *Herding immature males or "holluschickie" on St Paul*

Source: Elliot (1887: opposite 336)

The killing gang at work
Method of slaughtering fur seals on the grounds near the village of St Paul.
The drove in waiting   Sealers knocking down a "pod"   Natives skinning

Figure 2.3. *The Slaughter*

Source: Elliot (1887: opposite 339)

blow to the head would suffice (see Figure 2.3). So sealers rushed to the Pribilofs as to a gold rush. Indeed, news of Pribilof's discovery spread so fast that when he returned to St George the year after his first discovery, "a dozen vessels were watching him and trimming in his wake" (Elliot 1887: 193). Within a few years, uncontrolled harvesting had severely depleted the herd, which may have numbered five million at the time of their discovery. The much smaller local population of sea otters was extinguished within two years (Matthiessen 1978).

2.3. DOMESTIC MEASURES

Being the property of the Russian state, access to the seal rookeries could be regulated. A number of interventions would have sufficed to conserve the fur seal, but in 1799 Czar Paul granted a hunting and trading monopoly to the Russian–American Company, of which the czar's own family was the largest shareholder. The Company's license was subject to only two conditions: the seals had to be hunted on land, not at sea, and the harvest had to be restricted to surplus males.[3]

As shown in Figure 2.1, mature males, or "bulls," are much bigger than females. When they first arrive at the breeding grounds, males can weigh up to 600 pounds,

---

[3] Under its charter, the company paid no royalties to the government. However, "as its trade consisted chiefly in the exchange of furs for teas on the Chinese frontier, the Government received large sums through the duty collected on such teas" (Fur Seal Arbitration vol. II, 1895: 37).

six times as much as a mature female. The males need to be big. They have to establish their territories and defend their harems of 20–100 females from rival bulls. And they have to do this for around fifty days without entering the water to feed, during which time they can lose a quarter of their weight. Females mature when three to five years old, whereas males have little chance of breeding until they are at least nine or ten. Immature males are thus "surplus" to the population.

After the Russian–American Company acquired the monopoly, the fur seal population began to recover. Over the next several decades, the company harvested over 2.5 million seals without ever endangering the herd's survival (Gay 1987).

In 1821, the Imperial Government published an edict or ukase claiming a right both to the territories it had conquered and to the neighboring seas. The decree prohibited "all Foreign Vessels, not only to land on the Coasts and Islands belonging to Russia … ; but also to approach them within less than a Hundred Italian Miles." Moreover, the ukase declared that ships caught sailing in these waters were "subject to confiscation along with the whole Cargo" (Fur Seal Arbitration vol. II, 1895: 39).

The Governor-General of Siberia later explained to the US Minister in St Petersburg why the government had made the declaration. As the Minister relayed the message to the Secretary of State in a letter in 1822, the intent was to "secure to the Russian American Fur Company the monopoly of the very lucrative profit they carry on" (Fur Seal Arbitration vol. II, 1895: 40). Since the Pribilofs are within 200 miles of the Aleutians, the 100-mile limit would have given Russia, and its sealing monopoly, control of a vast territory.

Like any territorial claim, however, the Russian declaration had to be recognized as being lawful by other nations; otherwise, it would have no effect. As it happens, the claim was denounced by both the United States and Great Britain, and so failed to acquire legal recognition. That Russia should have made the attempt, however, is significant. Russia saw trouble on the horizon. Its territorial claim was intended as a preventative measure. Conflict would eventually come to the seas around the Pribilofs, and when it did, other approaches would be tried to suppress or contain it. As we shall see, most of these would fail too.

The Pribilofs were acquired by the United States under the Alaska Treaty of 1867, and uncontrolled harvesting resumed almost immediately after the handover; around 250,000 seals were taken in the summer of 1868 (see Figure 2.4).[4] Surprised by the scale of the slaughter, the US government imposed a temporary ban on sealing at the end of the breeding season. In 1870, a permanent arrangement was finally ready to be implemented. Fashioned after the earlier Russian regime, a monopoly was granted to the Alaska Commercial Company. The license was subject to a number of conditions. The annual harvest could not exceed 100,000 seals. Only mature males could be taken. Harvests had to be limited to land. Firearms were prohibited. The Company had further to pay the US Treasury an annual fee of $55,000, a tax of

---

[4] The Alaska purchase turned out to be a steal. The United States paid Russia $7.2 million for the whole of the territory, but the US Treasury netted $11 million in fur seal revenues alone between 1870 and 1891. See Behring Sea Arbitration (1893: 77).

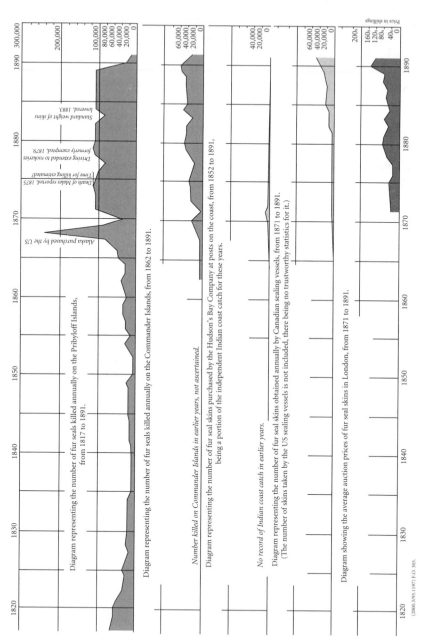

Figure 2.4. *Harvest rates and prices*

Source: Fur Seal Arbitration (1895), vol. VI, diagram after p. 218

$2.625 per seal skin, and a charge of $.55 per gallon of oil.[5] Finally, the Company had to give the native "inhabitants of the islands of St Paul and St George annually twenty-five thousand dried salmon, sixty cords of firewood, a sufficient quantity of salt and preserved meat; to maintain a school on each island for at least eight months in each year, and not to sell any distilled spirits or spiritous liquors" on the islands.[6]

Though Russia had now lost the fur seal's largest breeding ground, it retained control of smaller herds on the Robben and Commander Islands. Management of these herds was contracted out to the parent of the Alaska Commercial Company in 1871, earning Russia an annual rent of 5000 rubles and a tax of 2 rubles per pelt. As a condition of the monopoly, a supplementary payment of 50 kopecks per skin was also to be paid to the native inhabitants of the islands.

Both of the new arrangements proved as effective as the earlier regime. Over the duration of both twenty-year leases, more than 760,000 seals were killed on the Russian islands and more than 1.9 million on the Pribilofs. The seals on all these islands were never in danger of extinction.

2.4. INTERNATIONAL RIVALRY

Though domestic mismanagement was easily corrected, fur seals are an international resource. Like other pinnipeds, fur seals spend only about half the year at their breeding grounds; in the winter they live in the open sea. Even during the summer months, seals feed in the sea, up to 150 miles from shore and well outside the three-mile territorial limit that existed back then (Figure 2.5 shows the distribution of seals sampled by the *USS Mohican* in the summer of 1892). In these waters, the seals belonged to no one country; they were every nation's property.

Commercial sealing in the open sea—a practice known as pelagic sealing—began in earnest soon after the Alaska purchase (the timing was coincidental). It had a devastating effect. Pelagic sealing was wasteful; for every animal captured, around four or so were killed (see Paterson and Wilen 1977). Some seals escaped wounded, only to die later. Others died too quickly, sinking before they could be hauled on deck. Many were eaten by killer whales. The bigger problem, however, was the huge take of females.

Females give birth to a single pup almost as soon as they reach the rookeries, and within a week of giving birth they mate again. After this time, the females return to the sea to feed. Each feeding trip can take up to a week, and yet the pups need to be nursed for three to four months before being weaned. In the sea, females and immature males look alike (see again Figure 2.1), and in the main killing season, the majority of seals in the water were females; the adult males remained on shore, keeping

---

[5] It is not surprising that the Russian Czar would want to contract management of the seal to a monopoly owned by his relatives. But to the Americans, a monopoly also had advantages. In granting a monopoly, the US government could claim rents from the resource, and consumers' surplus would not have been an issue since all the skins were exported for processing.　　　　　[6] Behring Sea Arbitration (1893: 135).

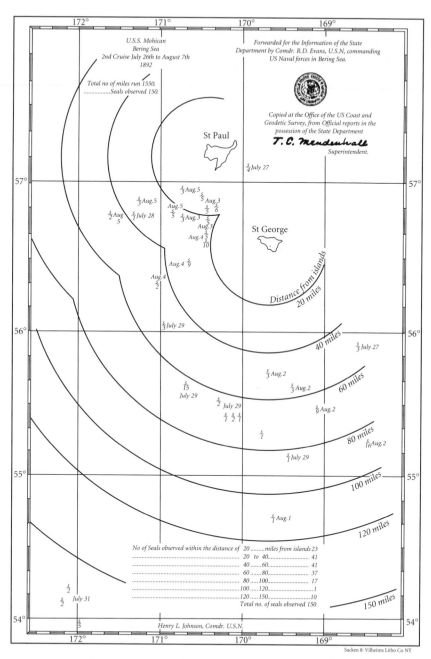

Figure 2.5. *Distribution of the fur seal beyond the territorial limit*

Source: Fur Seal Arbitration (1895), vol. VII, after p. 405

guard over their harems, and the immature males, needing only to feed themselves, did not have to be in the water as often. At a stroke, the killing of a single mature female would reduce the herd by two animals, since the female's pup would die without its mother's care.

Pelagic sealing, carried out mostly by Canadians at this time, robbed the Alaska Company of profits and stole rents from the US Treasury. The US government was furious and instinctively sought a unilateral solution. On August 1, 1886, US Treasury cutters seized two Canadian schooners working 75 miles from shore. The next day they captured another vessel operating 115 miles from the Pribilofs.

Though all three ships were sailing well outside the three-mile territorial limit, their crews were tried in a US court under the US law—Section 1956 of the Revised Statutes of the United States, which prohibited the killing of fur seals without the permission of the Secretary of the Treasury "within the limits of the Alaska Territory, or in the waters thereof." The US District Court in Sitka found the crews of all three ships guilty, and ordered that their schooners be sold and that their officers be fined and sentenced to a prison term. Great Britain, still representing Canadian diplomatic interests at this time, complained that the seizures were unlawful. The US officials also doubted the legality of the seizures, and in early 1887 the Secretary of State Thomas Bayard recommended to President Cleveland that the Canadian crews and property be released. A few days later the order was given.

The next year, more Canadian-registered schooners returned to the waters around the Seal Islands; a total of fifteen were detained by US cutters. As before, Britain protested at the seizures. This time, however, Secretary of State Bayard invited Britain to negotiate a treaty to ban pelagic sealing, and Britain accepted. Wanting to create a spirit of cooperation, Bayard told the Marquis of Salisbury, who was both Prime Minister and Foreign Secretary, that US revenue cutters had been given secret orders not to interfere with Canadian ships outside the three-mile limit. Pleased by this gesture, Salisbury urged the Canadian government to confine its sealers to port. Canada refused, however, and even insisted that it be compensated for the earlier seizures. Upon hearing Canada's position, the United States broke off the scheduled negotiations. The United States further amended its Revised Statutes in 1889 to provide for the seizure of all vessels found pelagic sealing anywhere "in the waters of the Behring Sea." Essentially, the United States was now claiming a property right to the Pribilof seals wherever they might be found.

The pelagic hunt resumed in the summer of 1889, and more Canadian vessels were seized by US cutters. Once again, British and American diplomats met to head off a confrontation, and, once again, they failed. The United States insisted that Canada stop pelagic sealing, while Great Britain proposed a temporary cessation, both at sea and on land. A compromise could not be found, and when the 1890 season opened, a violent encounter of some kind seemed inevitable. The US revenue cutters were once again instructed to patrol the region, and four British warships were ordered to meet them. The British order was deliberately leaked to the US officials, however, and the United States quietly withdrew its seizure instructions.

2.5. BILATERAL AGREEMENT

Negotiations resumed in 1891, and the United States and Great Britain agreed to prohibit pelagic sealing temporarily and to limit the land kill to 7500 seals for consumption by the native Indians only. A possible military encounter was thus avoided, but the agreement did nothing to resolve the underlying conflict.

Being unable to agree on a permanent regime for the seals, the parties formally agreed to disagree, and to let the matter be settled by arbitration. Seven arbitrators were appointed; two each from the United States and Great Britain, and one each from France, Italy, and Sweden/Norway. The Tribunal met in Paris in 1892, and, perhaps to signal the importance of the issue to the United States, John Foster resigned as Secretary of State to head the US delegation. In those days, secretaries of state did not travel abroad. This was well before the age of shuttle diplomacy.

The United States argued before the tribunal not only that it had jurisdiction over the Bering Sea, as Russia had proclaimed before, but also that it had a property right to the fur seal. Moreover, the US counsel stressed that having this right was instrumentally important to the protection of the fur seal, not only for the benefit of the United States but for the benefit of all nations. The British counsel disagreed, claiming that the United States only had "the right to kill on the islands exclusively; the right to kill within the territorial limits exclusively; [and] the right to compete on the high seas on terms of equality with all the rest of mankind ... " (Gay 1987: 84).

On this crucial point, the tribunal ruled for Britain. Jurisdiction in the Bering Sea, the tribunal reasoned, was restricted "to the reach of a cannon shot from shore," or the usual territorial limit of three miles; outside this limit, the tribunal ruled, the United States had no "right of protection of property in the fur-seals" (Gay 1987: 85–6).

However, under the 1892 Treaty of Arbitration, the tribunal also had to "determine what concurrent Regulations outside the jurisdictional limits of the respective Governments [were] necessary, and over what waters such Regulations should extend ... " In ruling on this matter the tribunal showed sympathy for the United States. In particular, it recommended that all harvesting be banned for at least one year, because of the "critical condition" of the herd; that pelagic sealing be prohibited within 60 miles of the Pribilofs; that the prohibition also extend, between May and July, to the Bering Sea and parts of the North Pacific, and that the use of nets, firearms, and explosives be forbidden. Native Indians, the tribunal decided, should be exempt from these regulations, provided they used canoes, were not transported to the sealing grounds by other vessels, and were not employed by others to take seals.[7]

Before going to Paris, both parties agreed that the country ruled to have acted illegally should pay the other compensation. The final ruling thus obligated the United States to pay damages to Britain for the seizure of its vessels. Britain submitted a claim for $542,169.26, but the United States refused to pay more than $425,000. To resolve this dispute, the parties once again appealed to an outside party; this time,

---

[7] A substantial amount of commercial sealing, both at land and at sea, was undertaken by native Indians on behalf of the commercial sealers.

an independent claims commission. In late 1897, the commission ruled that the United States owed Britain $473,151.26, and soon after the decision was rendered the United States sent Britain the money.

2.6. LEAKAGE ON THE HIGH SEAS

While the arbitration tribunal was in session and the joint British-American sealing ban was in effect, American and Canadian sealers relocated to the waters surrounding the Commander Islands. Russia seized a number of schooners outside its three-mile limit in 1892, and a new crisis loomed. This time, however, diplomacy succeeded. In an 1893 agreement, British (Canadian) sealers were prohibited from hunting within 30 miles of the Commander and Robben Islands and within 10 miles of the Russian continental coast, while Russia agreed to limit its annual land kill to 30,000 seals. A similar agreement was concluded between Russia and the United States the following year.

Laws implementing the Paris regulations were approved by the British Parliament and US Congress before the 1894 hunting season opened. However, the new laws proved hopelessly ineffective, and 55,000 skins were taken from the Pribilofs that year.

The problem was "leakage." After the Paris regulations were implemented, sealers who had been working on the Bering Sea moved to other areas—and not just to the Commander Islands, as happened when the ban was in effect. The Paris regulations only restricted harvests in the vicinity of the Pribilof Islands, and yet the Pribilof seals migrated in the winter months. Some of the seals traveled down the North American coast as far south as Baja, others traveled along the coast of Asia. In suspending sealing in the Bering Sea, the regulations only redirected pelagic sealers to these other waters. Moreover, the Paris regulations only applied to Great Britain and the United States. They failed to prevent entry by third parties or to stop US and Canadian sealers from flying the flag of a third party state in order to avoid the restrictions. Though the Paris regulations were intended to protect the Pribilof seals, they succeeded mainly in shifting the slaughter, not controlling it.

Indeed, the main consequence of all these bilateral arrangements was not to conserve the seal. The main effect was to encourage entry by Japan. Though Japan had its own small breeding population (which became extinct for a time) on the Kurile Islands, it began building a sizable pelagic fleet.

2.7. UNILATERAL FAILURE

By this time it was obvious that a comprehensive agreement was needed, one that included all the four sealing powers. The US Secretary of State Walter Gresham proposed extending the Paris regulations to the whole of the Bering Sea, and Russia and Japan agreed to negotiate on this basis. Great Britain, however, refused. An extension of the Paris regulations would further restrict Canadian access to the Commander Islands and to the sea adjacent to the Japanese coast; Canada could only lose from such a deal. After Gresham's sudden death in 1895, his successor, Richard Olney, tried again to persuade Britain to participate in a four power conference. His overture, however, was rejected. Upon hearing of the refusal to negotiate, the US ambassador in London, John Hay, complained, "I had always thought of English diplomacy as overbearing and pigheaded, but I never imagined it was tricky and tortuous" (Gay 1987: 103).

To try to bring Britain to the negotiating table, a frustrated US government contemplated a number of unilateral measures. The craziest of these was a threat to exterminate the Pribilof herd if Britain refused to cooperate. Sensibly, the Congress failed to endorse the threat. Were it ever carried out, the US would probably lose more than any country.[8]

Another proposal recommended branding female seals so as to render their skins worthless.[9] As noted earlier, however, females and immature males were indistinguishable in the water. Branding only females would probably not affect the pelagic hunt. At the same time, branding females *and* males would render all the skins worthless, and effectively kill the commercial enterprise. This proposal was also shelved.

Perhaps the most imaginative suggestion was to nationalize the Pribilof herd, not by claiming a right to the seals beyond the three-mile limit—that approach had already been tried and shown to be unlawful. The idea this time was to drive the seals to inland lakes, and to keep them there throughout the pelagic hunting season. Since females needed to feed in the sea, however, this plan was also scrapped.

Finally, in 1897, a desperate US government prohibited its own citizens from pelagic sealing and banned foreign imports of seal skins. The hope was that this action would serve as an example for others to follow. Unfortunately, it had no such effect. The pelagic hunt resumed as normal; the Pribilof herd continued to decline.

2.8. DECLINING RENTS

Japanese sealers had already entered the seas surrounding the Pribilofs to take up the slack created by the restrictions on Canadian sealers (imposed by the Paris regulations). The new ban on pelagic sealing by US nationals only encouraged further expansion by Japan, especially in the western Bering Sea. By 1898, Japan had become the dominant pelagic sealing nation in these waters.

As Japan's sealing fleet grew, the profits of Canadian sealers collapsed. In 1897, harvest rates per vessel were less than half their previous levels, and the price of skins also fell as huge inventories were accumulated (Paterson and Wilen 1977). Stocks recovered temporarily in 1898–99, in the wake of the cessation of the American pelagic hunt and the reduced quota allocated to the land kill. But the resulting growth in the herds only attracted vessels back into the business, as well as new entry by Japan, making a subsequent fall in profits inevitable.

By now, Canada could only lose by refusing to negotiate. As the Canadian Prime Minister, Sir Wilfrid Laurier, told a friend in 1899, "if pelagic sealing is allowed to continue for two or three years more, it will then come to an end by the gradual

---

[8] The Russians later threatened to exterminate their Commander Islands herd; see Mirovitskaya *et al.* (1993).
[9] The strategy of branding females is similar to the modern-day attempt to save African rhino from poachers by sawing off their horns.

destruction of the herds. Then the sealers would be left without any compensation, but with a fleet on their hands, and there would be much discontent in the country against us for having failed to do what we should do now" (Gay 1987: 108).

Just as the United States and Britain came close to an agreement, however, gold was discovered in the Klondike, and a new dispute arose between Canada and the United States—this time over the Alaskan boundary. Britain linked the two issues, refusing to negotiate a fur seal treaty until the United States recognized Canada's boundary claim. This effectively killed the sealing talks. The territorial dispute was not settled until 1903.[10]

While diplomacy was stalled, the pelagic hunt continued. The fur seal, however, was now very scarce. To maintain harvest rates, Japanese sealers became more aggressive. They even started to raid foreign rookeries. In 1901–02, nine Japanese poachers were killed by Russian officials on the Commander Islands; in 1906, 5 more were killed and 12 taken prisoner by the United States. Alarmed by these incidents, President Roosevelt reconsidered the strategy of threatening to exterminate the entire Pribilof herd if Japan continued to reject US overtures to negotiate.

Just at this time, however, Japan's interests shifted. As part of the settlement over the Russo-Japanese War, Japan took possession of Robben Island in 1906. Japan now had a sizable herd of its own to protect, and could see the advantage in a four-party treaty.

By this time, however, years of excessive harvesting had devastated the herds. In 1867 there were up to two million seals; by 1909 there were less than 150,000. Harvest rates had fallen, too. In peak years, Canada took 50,000 seals from the Bering Sea, and just as many from the Asiatic. In 1909, however, Canada harvested fewer than 4000 seals. There was no more money to be made from pelagic sealing. The Victoria Sealing Company, which controlled the majority of Canadian vessels, even offered to sell its entire fleet of sealing schooners to the United States.

2.9. MULTILATERAL SUCCESS

In 1910, the British Ambassador to Washington, James Bryce, informed the State Department that Canada would suspend pelagic sealing if given sufficient compensation. He suggested that the United States give Canada a share of its land kill or a minimum annual payment if the land kill were suspended. The offer was made, and accepted, and soon formalized in a bilateral pact. Knowing now that a bilateral agreement would make little difference—that a four-party agreement was what was really needed—the bilateral agreement would only come into force after all four sealing nations had agreed to a pelagic ban. Of course, once such a four-party agreement had entered into force, there would be no need for the Anglo-American agreement. This treaty was thus intended only to facilitate the more comprehensive talks.

---

[10] This is an example of how different issues can become linked in a negotiation. Later, other issues were brought to the negotiating table, including Canada's concerns about US tariffs on lumber and logs, and the conservation of shared fish stocks.

Multilateral talks commenced in 1910, and in July 1911 an agreement was ready to be signed. By the end of the year all of the parties had ratified the agreement, and the treaty came into immediate effect. Just as it did so, the British-American treaty was nullified.

The North Pacific Fur Seal Treaty of 1911 was an unqualified success. By 1917, only six years after the treaty entered into force, the Pribilof herd had more than tripled in size. By 1940, the total number of fur seals in the North Pacific once again exceeded two million.

The agreement was also remarkably stable. It survived the Bolshevik revolution, pleas by Canadian sealing interests to break from the treaty (after the seals had once again become abundant), and complaints by Japan that the growing fur seal population was depleting its fish stocks.

In 1940, however, Japan notified the other parties of its intention to withdraw from the agreement, and 12 months to the day after giving its notice, the treaty was nullified. No one seems to know the real reasons for Japan's withdrawal, though the treaty was probably a victim of the growing enmity between the United States and Japan. At the time Japan decided to withdraw from the treaty, war in the Pacific was just over a year away.

Fortunately, the demise of the treaty had little practical effect. During the war, Japan killed only a small number of seals—and these were killed close to its Pacific coast, not in the Bering Sea. The Soviet Union refrained from pelagic sealing entirely, and the United States and Canada entered into a bilateral agreement banning pelagic sealing (Britain was not a party to this treaty as Canada had become independent in 1931).

In 1957, the 1911 treaty was revived in a slightly altered form. This revised treaty was then amended in 1976 and the amended treaty remained in force until 1984, when the US Senate failed to extend its life, despite President Reagan's urging, because of protests by animal welfare activists. By this time, however, commercial interests in sealing had all but disappeared, and there was little need for the treaty. Only about 25,000 seals were harvested each year between 1980–84.[11] After failing to ratify the 1984 treaty, the United States banned commercial sealing on the Pribilofs. Only Indians, Aleuts, and Eskimos were allowed to kill fur seals, and they could only do so for subsistence purposes. The history of the fur seal had thus come full circle.

Native Americans still harvest fur seals today, but only in small amounts. In 1999, 1000 were killed on St Paul and 193 on St George (NOAA 2000). Despite the modest harvest, the US population of fur seals has declined. There are just over one million seals today, less than half the number that existed in the 1950s. The exact reasons for the decline are uncertain, though it is widely believed that the fur seal faces a different set of threats today. Many become entangled in plastic debris and discarded fishing gear, and their own food supply (mainly, pollock, herring, cappelin, and squid) has been depleted by over-fishing. Because of the population's decline, the fur seal is classified by the US government as a "depleted" species, but it is not in any danger of

---

[11] Alaska Department of Fish and Game's web page, wysiwyg://80/http://www.state.ak.us/local...ges/Fish.Game/notebook/marine/furseal.htm.

extinction. Healthy populations still congregate at the traditional rookeries every breeding season—and new rookeries have even been established on Bogoslof Island in the Aluetians and on San Miguel Island, off the coast of southern California.

2.10. CHANGING THE RULES OF THE GAME

The fur seal case illustrates the important themes of this book: resources that lie entirely within a nation's territorial borders can be effectively managed; shared resources are prone to overuse when countries pursue unilateral policies; an effective treaty can improve on unilateralism and make every party better off.

The case also provides examples of the many forms that statecraft can take: attempts to nationalize the resource, appeals to international law, threats to intervene militarily or to cause harm indirectly (in the fur seal case, by killing off the herd), technical fixes (as in the proposal to brand females), diplomatic interventions, petitions for arbitration, moral leadership (as when the United States prohibited its own citizens from pelagic sealing), the use of trade restrictions, and so on. Statecraft succeeded by one means only, however. It was the four-party agreement that saved the fur seal.

How was it able to do this? The theory developed in this book suggests that the treaty succeeded by changing the rules of the game, by restructuring the relationships among the countries. In particular, five tasks needed to be achieved, each necessary for success, but each also almost useless should any of the others fail. The treaty needed to: (1) create an aggregate gain, a reason for all countries to come to the bargaining table; (2) distribute this gain such that all countries would prefer that the agreement succeed; (3) ensure that each country would lose by not participating, given that all the others agreed to participate; (4) provide incentives for all the parties to comply with the treaty; and (5) deter entry by third parties. The strategies used to achieve these five tasks are explained below.

2.10.1. Creating an Aggregate Gain

Creating an aggregate gain was easy. The treaty only needed to ban pelagic sealing. The ban not only saved on the direct losses from pelagic sealing (recall how wasteful pelagic sealing was in comparison with the land kill), but it also saved on the losses from common property exploitation. In banning sealing at sea, exploitation of the herds could be determined solely by the governments having jurisdiction over the rookeries (Russia, you may recall, controlled the Commander Islands; Japan, Robben Island; and the United States, the Pribilofs). Essentially, the ban transformed the "open access" management regime that existed previously into a "sole owner" regime. A sole owner has every incentive to maximize the rents from the resource (see Scott 1955), and the history of sealing showed that the parties with breeding populations knew how to do this. So the aggregate gain created by the agreement was probably as large as the feasibility constraints would allow. There was no need for further regulation.

2.10.2. Distributing the Aggregate Gain

The ban on pelagic sealing may have maximized the aggregate gain, but it would also have left the pelagic sealing nations worse off. To encourage their participation, Canada and Japan had to be compensated.

The treaty did this by transferring both money and seal skins. Specifically, the United States agreed to pay Great Britain and Japan $200,000 each, as immediate compensation, to be credited against future side payments in seal skins; to supply each of these countries with 15 percent of its annual harvest or 1000 skins, whichever number was greater; and to pay $10,000 to each of these parties in any year when no skins were taken, provided the number of seals frequenting the United States islands in that year exceeded 100,000.

Russia and Japan also agreed to share their harvests, subject to certain restrictions meant to protect their breeding populations. Russia agreed to share 15 percent of its annual harvest each with Canada and Japan, while Japan pledged to transfer a 10 percent share of its annual harvest each to the United States, Canada, and Russia.

Canada, of course, did not have a breeding population of its own, but the treaty anticipated that it might acquire one in the future (and recall that two new populations have been established in recent times). In the event that a seal herd subsequently "resorts to any islands or shores of the waters … subject to the jurisdiction of Great Britain," Britain agreed to transfer 10 percent of the number of sealskins taken in any year to the United States, Japan, and Russia each.

Each country was thus required by the treaty to forfeit 30 percent of its annual harvest of sealskins, provided it had a population to exploit: a bargain that was symmetric, and for that reason, fair.

How were these particular numbers arrived at? Probably many allocations would have sufficed to redistribute the aggregate gain in a fashion acceptable to all the parties. However, we know something about how this particular allocation came to be chosen.

In the Anglo-American agreement that preceded the 1911 treaty, the United States agreed to transfer one-fifth of its annual harvest to Canada, and this served as the initial focal point for the multilateral negotiations.[12] At first, Britain insisted on retaining its 20 percent share; and Japan, naturally, argued that it should get the same quantity as Britain. This was too much for the United States, however, which countered by offering both countries a total of just 25 percent. Great Britain offered to meet the United States partway, accepting a 15 percent share, but Japan wanted more; it refused to accept less than 17.5 percent. After months of deadlock, President Taft appealed directly to the Emperor of Japan:

Your Majesty. It has been reported to me … that there is no prospect of reaching an agreement unless both the United States and Japan are willing to make some further concessions to each other. It appears that the United States has proposed to give up a twenty-five per cent gross interest in the American seal herd, which interest Great Britain and Japan would divide equally … .

---

[12] For a brilliant discussion of focal points and their importance in negotiation, see Schelling (1960).

Great Britain seems willing to accept fifteen per cent, but the Japanese Delegation refuses to consider less than seventeen and one-half per cent, which we cannot concede.... I am especially desirous that an agreement should be reached not alone because of the importance of preserving the fur seals but also because of the beneficial effect which a settlement of this question would have upon the friendly relations between the Japanese and American nations: and an agreement in this case will open the way for a general international game law for the protection of other mammals of the sea, the preservation of which is of importance to all the nations of the world. On the other hand a failure to reach an agreement in this case will inevitably result in the extermination of the fur seals ... (Gay 1987: 127.)

The President says that he could not concede 17.5 percent to Japan, perhaps not least because, with the total concession being divided equally between Great Britain and Japan (and fairness seemed to demand equal treatment in this case), that would mean giving 17.5 percent to Britain, and yet Britain had already said it would accept 15 percent. The letter strongly hints, but does not state explicitly, that the President would be willing to transfer 15 percent of its landings to both parties. Moreover, the 15 percent figure seems the most compelling compromise, being both mid-way between the 12.5 percent share offered by the United States and the 17.5 percent share demanded by Japan (that is, by "the Japanese Delegation," not the Emperor himself) and precisely equal to the British offer—for both reasons the obvious focal point. Having implicitly suggested a 15 percent share, the President is careful not to insist that the Emperor accept this amount; that would surely scupper the negotiations. Instead, he invites the Emperor to be magnanimous. The Emperor's reply came quickly:

Being all times anxious to strengthen the bonds of friendship and good understanding which unite our two countries and people, I am highly gratified to acquaint you that the last instructions to the Japanese delegates to the Conference will enable them to meet the American delegates half-way in adjusting the point at difference between them. (Gay 1987: 128.)

The offer was accepted at once. Three weeks later the treaty was signed by all four nations.

Negotiation is both an art and a science. This book emphasizes the science of negotiation, but President Taft's letter reminds us that there is more to negotiation than this.[13]

2.10.3. Deterring Non-participation

The offer to share the harvest ensures that every party is better off with the agreement than without it, but to succeed the treaty needed also to ensure that each country would lose by not participating, *given that the other three had agreed to participate.*

The history that preceded the four-party negotiation demonstrated that every country's participation was pivotal to the treaty's success. Failure by any of the four countries to participate would likely have spelled ruin for the entire industry. Since every country was sure to do much better with the treaty, each had a strong incentive to participate, given that all the others participated.

---

[13] See Raiffa (1982) for an engaging treatment of negotiation as both art and science. The letter by President Taft is an illustration of Riker's (1986) theory of "heresthetical maneuvers."

The treaty recognizes and exploits this situation by requiring ratification by all four countries to enter into force. Implicit in the original treaty is also a kind of "Grim" strategy calling for the complete dissolution of the agreement and, by implication, a reversion to the disastrous open access outcome, should any of its parties withdraw at a later date.[14] In its revised 1957 and 1976 versions, the fur seal treaty makes this threat more explicit. According to Article XII,

> Should any Party consider that … any … obligation undertaken by the Parties is not being carried out and notify the other Parties to that effect, all the Parties shall, within three months of the receipt of such notification, meet to consult together on the need for and nature of remedial measures. In the event that such consultation shall not lead to agreement as to the need for and nature of remedial measures, any Party may give written notice to the other Parties of [its] intention to terminate the Convention and … the Convention shall thereupon terminate as to *all* [emphasis added] the Parties nine months from the date of such notice.

The threat to terminate an agreement in the event of a single deviation is severe, and will not normally be credible. Usually, the countries called upon to impose a severe punishment harm themselves too much in the bargain for the threat to be credible. As Shaw (1991: 596), a legal scholar, has noted, "to render treaties revocable because one party has acted contrary to what might very well be only a minor provision in the agreement taken as a whole, would be to place the states participating in a treaty in rather a vulnerable position. There is a need for flexibility as well as certainty in such situations." This is true, of course, and the requirement for consultation suggests that the parties to this agreement recognized the problem. But a withdrawal from the treaty would not be a "minor" deviation, and the nature of sealing meant that the other three parties would probably do at least as well by terminating the agreement as they would by soldiering on with a weakened regime for cooperation. Indeed, the language of Article XII couldn't have been plainer: once one party withdraws, the treaty terminates for every party.

The credibility of the threat to dissolve the treaty in the event of a withdrawal was put to the test when Japan made its stunning announcement:

> In the early morning of October 26, 1940, a shocking blow came to the [US] State Department via a telegram from the American Embassy in Tokyo. As of October 23, 1940, the Imperial Government gave twelve months' notice of its intention to abrogate the Fur Seal Convention of 1911. Japanese Minister for Foreign Affairs Yosuke Matsuoka indicated Japan's preparedness to conclude a new accord, but the agreement was qualified by several proposals including controlled pelagic sealing and the restriction of the total number of seals in the North Pacific to 850,000. (Gay 1987: 150.)

Immediately upon receiving Japan's notice, the United States considered its response:

> Secretary of the Interior, Harold Ickes, in a long note to Secretary of State Cordell Hull, expressed the concern of the Interior Department that the Fur Seal Treaty might be abrogated. Ickes pointed out that since 1911, because of the effectiveness of the Treaty, the fur seal herd had grown from approximately 125,000 to 2,185,136 animals. An abrogation of the Treaty would mean the herd's possible destruction. Ickes urged a conference of the signatories be called immediately

---

[14] The Grim strategy is discussed in Chapter 10.

either to dissuade the Japanese from killing the Treaty or to conclude a new agreement which would continue the protection of the fur seals of the North Pacific. (Gay 1987: 150–1.)

The United States offered to renegotiate. It even made the crucial concession of allowing limited pelagic sealing as well as a progressive reduction in the herd. But the counter offer drew no response, and the agreement was terminated on October 22, 1941. Seven weeks later, Japan bombed Pearl Harbor.

Importantly, while the United States offered to renegotiate the terms of the agreement, suggesting that an alternative would have been acceptable to the United States from the beginning, once Japan had refused the offer, its withdrawal did indeed trigger the treaty's collapse. True, the United States and Britain negotiated a bilateral deal after this, but that deal was probably worth making because of special circumstances; war would have made pelagic sealing by Japan nearly impossible.

2.10.4. Deterring Non-compliance

Getting all the countries to participate was important, but the agreement also needed to provide incentives for the parties to behave as they promised they would when they ratified the treaty; non-compliance had to be deterred.

Article XII of the 1957 agreement applies to non-compliance with *any* obligation, implying that even small deviations from the agreement would trigger a response, and possibly an overwhelming response. However, enforcement of compliance is also addressed in other ways by the treaty.

Non-participation is easy to observe, but non-compliance need not be. Indeed, one of the main tasks of a treaty is to ensure that non-compliance *is* observed (or that it can be deduced with a high enough probability). If non-compliance cannot be observed, then it cannot be punished. Effective monitoring is a prerequisite for enforcing compliance.

The treaty made monitoring of the pelagic sealing ban a basic obligation of the states with breeding populations. The United States, Japan, and Russia were each required to "maintain a guard or patrol in the waters frequented by the seal herd in the protection of which it is especially interested, so far as may be necessary for the enforcement ... " of the pelagic sealing ban. Monitoring is sometimes a collective action problem of its own, but in this case each of the three countries with breeding populations had strong unilateral incentives to monitor. Recall that the United States patrolled the seas around the Pribilofs long before the treaty was negotiated.

The bigger challenge was to determine a way in which violations, once detected, could be punished. Britain and Canada certainly would not have let the United States punish *their* nationals, should any ever be caught cheating. After all, it was this trespass on Canadian sovereignty that led to the setting up of the Paris arbitration panel in 1892.

Instead, the agreement required that each of the parties "enact and enforce such legislation as may be necessary to make [the pelagic sealing ban] effective with appropriate penalties for violations thereof." Violations of the ban were thus to be made a domestic offense. If the United States found a Canadian ship sealing outside its territorial waters, say, the treaty would allow (indeed, obligate) the United States to seize the ship and to deliver it, its crew, and any evidence to the Canadian authorities, who would then be bound by their own domestic law to commit the crew of the impounded vessel to trial should the evidence warrant their arrest and conviction.

Why would Canada comply with the requirement that it pass and enforce such a law? One reason is that failure to do so would violate the treaty, possibly triggering the punishment made explicit in Article XII of the 1957 treaty. But there was also a more positive reason. Pelagic sealing would reduce the quantity of seals available to the land hunt, of which the treaty made Canada a significant beneficiary. As far as I have been able to determine, the agreement was never breached.

2.10.5. Deterring Entry

Deterring entry by non-parties was perhaps the treaty's greatest challenge. Rents were so low that entry by third parties was unprofitable before the signing of the 1911 agreement. But if the agreement succeeded, fur seals would become more plentiful, and entry by third parties would become profitable. Entry had been a problem before. And it was incredibly easy. When the United States and Canada entered into a bilateral agreement to limit fur seal harvests in 1891, the owners of US- and Canadian-registered sealing ships re-registered their vessels under the flags of other states in order to avoid being bound by the agreement (Birnie and Boyle 1992: 495). This could happen again, and yet international law did not give the four parties authority to seize vessels flying the flags of third party states in the high seas. The treaty thus had to make it in the *interests* of third parties not to want to engage in pelagic sealing.

This was the purpose of Article III, which banned imports of non-authenticated sealskins (the skins of seals killed by non-parties). The trade restriction deterred entry because the entire pelagic harvest of sealskins was processed and sold in London (Britain, of course, was a full signatory to the treaty), and London had an advantage that apparently could not be replicated:

First, London furriers maintained the secrecy of the dyeing process which precluded the emergence of other fur markets. In particular, the firm of Messrs. Martin and Company were reputed to be the finest dyers and dressers of fur sealskins and their close corporate connection with C.M. Lampson and Company, the principal auction house, ensured London's continuing dominance. Second, the method of selling furs depended on the buyers having trust in the auction house. Furs were baled into lots which contained a variety of qualities but one size—wigs, middlings and pups were the three main size categories—and then a few representative pelts were drawn from the bale for inspection by the potential buyers. Over time, the main auction houses had gained the confidence of the market. (Paterson and Wilen 1977: 97–8.)

As a Canadian delegate to the 1911 treaty negotiations observed, if seal skins were "... shut out of London, there would be no object in capturing them" (Mirovitskaya *et al.* 1993: 42). According to Gay (1987: 137), the strategy worked; entry was deterred:

During the first decade of the Convention there was some evidence that clandestine sealing might develop. Rumors were rife that non-signatories were preparing to enter the Bering Sea to seal. In general, the threat of commercial sealing in the North Pacific remained largely rumor. One case of pelagic sealing, however, gained notoriety. In the spring of 1913, Robert Whiteside, a cannery man, was fishing off Vancouver and was forced to club several seals which climbed into his boat. Whiteside's story so impressed customs officials at Vancouver that he was not prosecuted since 'he had acted in self defense.'"

As far as I have been able to determine, trade was never actually restricted. This is probably because the threat to restrict trade was credible.

2.11. CONCLUSIONS

The Fur Seal Treaty created the largest possible aggregate surplus, divided this among the parties such that each gained from cooperation, and deterred non-participation, non-compliance, and entry by third parties. It stands as a remarkable example of how international cooperation can succeed by restructuring the game of inter-state relations.

Indeed, its success was much celebrated at the time, and its potential as a role model for future agreements was widely recognized, as indicated by the quote that introduced this chapter. Sadly, however, this aspiration was never realized.

History seems determined to repeat this failure today. The Montreal Protocol is widely regarded as a model for success, and yet we seem not to have learned the right lessons from it.

Indeed, the Montreal Protocol is a more remarkable success than the Fur Seal Treaty. Fur seals are an international common property resource, but ozone protection is a global public good. Effective management of a common property resource requires that entry be deterred. For public goods, however, entry cannot be deterred—by definition. To the contrary, success in supplying a global public good requires that treaty participation be encouraged. And yet it is much harder to get 200 or so countries to cooperate than to get a handful to do so. That Montreal was able to do this is perhaps its greatest achievement.

My approach to understanding Montreal will be more rigorous than my analysis of the Fur Seal Treaty. For Montreal, the counterfactuals are less obvious, and important features of the problem more subtle. As well, we want to know what makes Montreal different. So we not only need a theory to interpret Montreal; we need a theory that shows why Montreal is a special case. Even better would be a theory that can show us how to negotiate more effective agreements. So our aim should be to develop a general theory of international cooperation—one that can be applied not just to Montreal but to other agreements, one that is relevant not just to ozone depletion but to other environmental problems. To meet this ambition, it is best to start from first principles. This is the subject of the next chapter.

Appendix 2.1. Preservation and Protection of Fur Seals

Convention signed at Washington July 7, 1911; exchange of notes of July 7, 1911, respecting a British reservation; note of July 18, 1911, withdrawing reservation

Senate advice and consent to ratification of the convention July 24, 1911

Ratified by the President of the United States November 24, 1911

Ratifications exchanged at Washington December 12, 1911

Proclaimed by the President of the United States December 14, 1911

Entered into force December 15, 1911

Terminated October 23, 1941[1]

> 37 Stat. 1542, Treaty Series 564 (convention); Department of State files, *Protocols of the International Fur Seal Conference, 1911*, p. 38 (notes)

CONVENTION

The United States of America, His Majesty the King of the United Kingdom of Great Britain and Ireland, and of the British Dominions beyond the Seas, Emperor of India, His Majesty the Emperor of Japan, and His Majesty the Emperor of all the Russias, being desirous of adopting effective means for the preservation and protection of the fur seals which frequent the waters of the North Pacific Ocean, have resolved to conclude a Convention for the purpose, and to that end have named as their Plenipotentiaries:

The President of the United States of America, the Honorable Charles Nagel, Secretary of Commerce and Labor of the United States, and the Honorable Chandler P. Anderson, Counselor of the Department of State of the United States;

His Britannic Majesty, the Right Honorable James Bryce, of the Order of Merit, his Ambassador Extraordinary and Plenipotentiary at Washington, and Joseph Pope, Esquire, Commander of the Royal Victorian Order and Companion of the Order of St. Michael and St. George, Under Secretary of State of Canada for External Affairs;

His Majesty the Emperor of Japan, Baron Yasuya Uchida, Jusammi, Grand Cordon of the Imperial Order of the Rising Sun, his Ambassador Extraordinary and Plenipotentiary at Washington; and the Honorable Hitoshi Dauké, Shoshii, Third Class of the Imperial Order of the Rising Sun, Director of the Bureau of Fisheries, Department of Agriculture and Commerce;

His Majesty the Emperor of all the Russias, the Honorable Pierre Botkine, Chamberlain of His Majesty's Court, Envoy Extraordinary and Minister Plenipotentiary to Morocco, and Baron Boris Nolde, of the Foreign Office;

Source: Department of State Washington, Treaties and other International Agreement of the USA 1776–1949, Bevans, vol. I, Multilateral 1776–1917.

[1] Japan gave written notice of termination Oct. 23, 1940 (see art. XVI).

Who, after having communicated to one another their respective full powers, which were found to be in due and proper form, have agreed upon the following articles:

ARTICLE I

The High Contracting Parties mutually and reciprocally agree that their citizens and subjects respectfully, and all persons subject to their laws and treaties, and their vessels, shall be prohibited, while this Convention remains in force, from engaging in pelagic sealing in the waters of the North Pacific Ocean, north of the thirtieth parallel of north latitude and including the Seas of Bering, Kamchatka, Okhotsk and Japan, and that every such person and vessel offending against such prohibition may be seized, except within the territorial jurisdiction of one of the other Powers, and detained by the naval or other duly commissioned officers of any of the Parties to this Convention, to be delivered as soon as practicable to an authorized official of their own nation at the nearest point to the place of seizure, or elsewhere as may be mutually agreed upon; and that the authorities of the nation to which such person or vessel belongs alone shall have jurisdiction to try the offense and impose the penalties for the same; and that the witnesses and proofs necessary to establish the offense, so far as they are under the control of any of the Parties to this Convention, shall also be furnished with all reasonable promptitude to the proper authorities having jurisdiction to try the offense.

ARTICLE II

Each of the High Contracting Parties further agrees that no person or vessel shall be permitted to use any of its ports or harbors or any part of its territory for any purposes whatsoever connected with the operations of pelagic sealing in the waters within the protected area mentioned in Article I.

ARTICLE III

Each of the High Contracting Parties further agrees that no sealskins taken in the waters of the North Pacific Ocean within the protected area mentioned in Article I, and no sealskins identified as the species known as *Callorhinus alascanus, Callorhinus ursinus,* and *Callorhinus kurilensis,* and belonging to the American, Russian or Japanese herds, except such as are taken under the authority of the respective Powers to which the breeding grounds of such herds belong and have been officially marked and certified as having been so taken, shall be permitted to be imported or brought into the territory of any of the Parties to this Convention.

ARTICLE IV

It is further agreed that the provisions of this Convention shall not apply to Indians, Ainos, Aleuts, or other aborigines dwelling on the coast of the waters mentioned in Article I, who carry on pelagic sealing in canoes not transported by or used in connection with other vessels, and propelled entirely by oars, paddles, or sails, and manned by not more than five persons each, in the way hitherto practiced and without the use of firearms; provided that such aborgines are not in the employment of other persons or under contract to deliver the skins to any person.

Article V

Each of the High Contracting Parties agrees that it will not permit its citizens or subjects or their vessels to kill, capture or pursue beyond the distance of three miles from the shore line of its territories sea otters in any part of the waters mentioned in Article I of this Convention.

Article VI

Each of the High Contracting Parties agrees to enact and enforce such legislation as may be necessary to make effective the foregoing provisions with appropriate penalties for violations thereof.

Article VII

It is agreed on the part of the United States, Japan, and Russia that each respectively will maintain a guard or patrol in the waters frequented by the seal herd in the protection of which it is especially interested, so far as may be necessary for the enforcement of the foregoing provisions.

Article VIII

All of the High Contracting Parties agree to cooperate with each other in taking such measures as may be appropriate and available for the purpose of preventing pelagic sealing in the prohibited area mentioned in Article I.

Article IX

The term pelagic sealing is hereby defined for the purposes of this Convention as meaning the killing, capturing or pursuing in any manner whatsoever of fur seals at sea.

Article X

The United States agrees that of the total number of sealskins taken annually under the authority of the United States upon the Pribilof Islands or any other islands or shores of the waters mentioned in Article I subject to the jurisdiction of the United States to which any seal herds hereafter resort, there shall be delivered at the Pribilof Islands at the end of each season fifteen per cent (15%) gross in number and value thereof to an authorized agent of the Canadian Government and fifteen per cent (15%) gross in number and value thereof to an authorized agent of the Japanese Government; provided, however, that nothing herein contained shall restrict the right of the United States at any time and from time to time to suspend altogether the taking of sealskins on such islands or shores subject to its jurisdiction, and to impose such restrictions and regulations upon the total number of skins to be taken in any season and the manner and times and places of taking them as may seem necessary to protect and preserve the seal herd or to increase its number.

Article XI

The United States further agrees to pay the sum of two hundred thousand dollars ($200,000) to Great Britain and the sum of two hundred thousand dollars ($200,000) to Japan when this Convention goes into effect, as an advance payment in each case in lieu of such number of fur-seal skins to which Great Britain and Japan respectively would be entitled under the provisions of this Convention as would be equivalent in each case to two hundred thousand dollars ($200,000) reckoned at their market value at London at the date of their delivery before dressing and curing and less cost of transportation from the Pribilof Islands, such market value in case of dispute to be determined by an umpire to be agreed upon by the United States and Great Britain, or by the United States and Japan, as the case may be, which skins shall be retained by the United States in satisfaction of such payments.

The United States further agrees that the British and Japanese share respectively of the sealskins taken from the American herd under the terms of this Convention shall be not less than one thousand (1,000) each in any year even if such number is more than fifteen per cent (15%) of the number to which the authorized killing is restricted in such year, unless the killing of seals in such year or years shall have been absolutely prohibited by the United States for all purposes except to supply food, clothing, and boat skins for the natives on the islands, in which case the United States agrees to pay to Great Britain and to Japan each the sum of ten thousand dollars ($10,000) annually in lieu of any share of skins during the years when no killing is allowed; and Great Britain agrees, and Japan agrees, that after deducting the skins of their respective shares, which are to be retained by the United States as above pro-vided to reimburse itself for the advance payment aforesaid, the United States shall be entitled to reimburse itself for any annual payments made as herein required, by retaining an additional number of sealskins from the British and Japanese shares respectively over and above the specified minimum allowance of one thousand (1,000) skins in any subsequent year or years when killing is again resumed, until the whole number of skins retained shall equal, reckoned at their market value deter-mined as above provided for, the entire amount so paid, with interest at the rate of four per cent (4%) per annum.

If, however, the total number of seals frequenting the United States islands in any year falls below one hundred thousand (100,000), enumerated by official count, then all killing, excepting the inconsiderable supply necessary for the support of the natives as above noted, may be suspended without allowance of skins or payment of money equivalent until the number of such seals again exceeds one hundred thousand (100,000), enumerated in like manner.

Article XII

It is agreed on the part of Russia that of the total number of sealskins taken annu-ally upon the Commander Islands, or any other island or shores of the waters defined in Article I subject to the jurisdiction of Russia to which any seal herds hereafter resort, there shall be delivered at the Commander Islands at the end of each season fifteen per cent (15%) gross in number and value thereof to an authorized agent of the Canadian Government, and fifteen per cent (15%) gross in number and value thereof to an authorized agent of the Japanese Government; provided, however, that nothing herein contained shall restrict the right of Russia at any time and from time to time during the first five years of the term of this Convention to suspend altogether the taking of sealskins on such islands or shores subject to its jurisdiction, and to impose during the term of this Convention such restrictions and regulations upon the total number of skins to be taken in any season, and the manner and times and places of taking them as may seem necessary to preserve and protect the Russian seal herd, or to increase its number; but it is agreed, nevertheless, on the part of Russia that during the last ten years of the term of this Convention not less than five per cent (5%) of the total number of seals on the Russian rookeries and hauling grounds will be killed annually, provided that said five per cent (5%) does not exceed eighty-five per cent (85%) of the three-year-old male seals hauling in such year.

If, however, the total number of seals frequenting the Russian islands in any year falls below eighteen thousand (18,000) enumerated by official count, then the allowance of skins mentioned above and all killing of seals except such as may be necessary for the support of the natives on the islands may be suspended until the number of such seals again exceeds eighteen thousand (18,000) enumerated in like manner.

ARTICLE XIII

It is agreed on the part of Japan that of the total number of sealskins taken annually upon Robben Island, or any other islands or shores of the waters defined in Article I subject to the jurisdiction of Japan to which any seal herds hereafter resort, there shall be delivered at Robben Island at the end of each season ten per cent (10%) gross in number and value thereof to an authorized agent of the United States Government, ten per cent (10%) gross in number and value thereof to an authorized agent of the Canadian Government, and ten per cent (10%) gross in number and value thereof to an authorized agent of the Russian Government; provided, however, that nothing herein contained shall restrict the right of Japan at any time and from time to time during the first five years of the term of this Convention to suspend altogether the taking of sealskins on such islands or shores subject to its jurisdiction, and to impose during the term of this Convention such restrictions and regulations upon the total number of skins to be taken in any season, and the manner and times and places of taking them as may seem necessary to preserve and protect the Japanese herd, or to increase its number: but it is agreed, nevertheless, on the part of Japan that during the last ten years of the term of this Convention not less than five per cent (5%) of the total number of seals on the Japanese rookeries and hauling grounds will be killed annually, provided that said five per cent (5%) does not exceed eighty-five per cent (85%) of the three-year-old male seals hauling in such year.

If, however, the total number of seals frequenting the Japanese islands in any year falls below six thousand five hundred (6,500) enumerated by official count, then the allowance of skins mentioned above and all killing of seals except such as may be necessary for the support of the natives on the islands may be suspended until the number of such seals again exceeds six thousand five hundred (6,500) enumerated in like manner.

ARTICLE XIV

It is agreed on the part of Great Britain that in case any seal herd hereafter resorts to any islands or shores of the waters defined in Article I subject to the jurisdiction of Great Britain, there shall be delivered at the end of each season during the term of this Convention ten per cent (10%) gross in number and value of the total number of sealskins annually taken from such herd to an authorized agent of the United States Government, ten per cent (10%) gross in number and value of the total number of sealskins annually taken from such herd to an authorized agent of the Japanese Government, and ten per cent (10%) gross in number and value of the total number of sealskins annually taken from such herd to an authorized agent of the Russian Government.

Article XV

It is further agreed between the United States and Great Britain that the provisions of this Convention shall supersede, in so far as they are inconsistent therewith or in duplication thereof, the provisions of the treaty relating to the fur seals, entered into between the United States and Great Britain on the 7th day of February, 1911.[2]

Article XVI

This Convention shall go into effect upon the 15th day of December, 1911, and shall continue in force for a period of fifteen (15) years from that date, and thereafter until terminated by twelve (12) months' written notice given by one or more of the Parties to all of the others, which notice may be given at the expiration of fourteen years or at any time afterwards, and it is agreed that at any time prior to the termination of this Convention, upon the request of any one of the High Contracting Parties, a conference shall be held forthwith between representatives of all the Parties hereto, to consider and if possible agree upon a further extension of this Convention with such additions and modifications, if any, as may be found desirable.

Article XVII

The Convention shall be ratified by the President of the United States, by and with the advice and consent of the Senate thereof, by His Britannic Majesty, by His Majesty the Emperor of Japan, and by His Majesty the Emperor of all the Russias; and ratifications shall be exchanged at Washington as soon as practicable.

In faith whereof, the respective Plenipotentiaries have signed this Convention in quadruplicate and have hereunto affixed their seals.

Done at Washington the 7th day of July, in the year one thousand nine hundred and eleven.

[For the United States:]		[For Japan:]	
Charles Nagel	[SEAL]		
Chandler P. Anderson	[SEAL]	Y. Uchida	[SEAL]
		H. Dauke	[SEAL]
[For the United Kingdom:]		[For Russia:]	
James Bryce	[SEAL]	P. Botkine	[SEAL]
Joseph Pope	[SEAL]	Nolde	[SEAL]

---

[2] TS 563, *post.*

EXCHANGE OF NOTES RESPECTING BRITISH RESERVATION

*The Delegates of Great Britain to the President of the International
Fur Seal Conference*

WASHINGTON
July 7th, 1911

SIR,

The Delegates of Great Britain, in signing the treaty for the preservation and protection of the fur seals which frequent the waters of the North Pacific Ocean, are instructed to state that, while accepting the whole treaty on behalf of Great Britain and the Dominion of Canada, they are obliged to reserve for the present the assent of the other self governing Dominions within the British Empire so far as regards the words in Article III, lines 3 and 4: "and no sealskins identified as the species known as Callorhinus alascanus, Callorhinus ursinus, and Callorhinus kurilensis," because there has not been time to obtain the assent of those Dominions to these words, which were submitted to His Majesty's Government only a few days ago.

This reservation is made, not because His Majesty's Government think or have any ground for thinking that these Dominions are likely to object to the words in question, but solely because it has been impossible within the time to ascertain, conformably to the usual practice, whether they are prepared to undertake such obligations as the words impose. His Majesty's Government will consult these Dominions at the earliest possible moment with a view to obtaining their consent to the words for the present reserved.

We have the honour to be,
Sir,
Your most obedient Servants,

JAMES BRYCE
JOSEPH POPE

To

The Honorable CHARLES NAGEL
President of the Conference

———

*The President of the International Fur Seal Conference
to the Delegates of Great Britain*

July 7, 1911

The Right Honorable JAMES BRYCE, O. M.,
and
The Honorable JOSEPH POPE,
*Delegates of Great Britain to the
International Fur Seal Conference*

GENTLEMEN:

In reply to your note of today addressed to me, I have the honor to inform you that the Delegations of the United States and Japan have read and considered it, and that they regard the obstacles therein mentioned as so remote that they have decided to sign the North Pacific Sealing Convention with the understanding that the Governments of the United States, Japan and Russia are at liberty to await the acceptance by Great Britain of the Convention without the particular reservations mentioned in your note before proceeding with ratification.

I have the honor to be,

With the highest respect

CHARLES NAGEL
President of the Conference

NOTE OF WITHDRAWAL OF BRITISH RESERVATION

A Delegate of Great Britain to the Secretary of State

BRITISH EMBASSY
SEAL HARBOR, MAINE
July 18, 1911

DEAR MR. SECRETARY:

I have pleasure in informing you in confirmation of my telegram of to-day's date that my Government having just informed me that the Self-Governing Dominions of the British Empire (other than Canada) having been consulted by His Majesty's Government with regard to the words in Article III viz: "and no sealskins identified as the species known as Callorhinus alascanus, Callorhinus ursinus, and Callorhinus kurilensis", of the International Treaty, signed on July 7th at Washington "for the preservation and protection of the fur seals which frequent the waters of the North Pacific Ocean," have now expressed their assent to the words in question, their acceptance of which had been provisionally reserved at the time of the signature of the Treaty by the British Delegates to the Conference. I should therefore be very much obliged if you would cause this information to be conveyed to the Delegates who represented the United States at the Conference giving them to understand that the Treaty is now accepted in its entirety by His Majesty's Government on behalf not only of Great Britain and Canada but also of all the other British Dominions.

The whole Treaty, including the words in Article III above quoted, having now been thus accepted, the note of reservation addressed to the President of the Conference on July 7 by Mr. Pope and myself as British Delegates has now become ineffective and is hereby withdrawn by me on behalf of His Majesty's Government. Therewith also the note signed by the United States and Japanese Delegates at the same time explaining that they, while noting the reservation made by us, nevertheless signed the Treaty, has now become superfluous.

I have the honour therefore to request that you will have the goodness to communicate the above complete acceptance of the Treaty and withdrawal of the Note of Reservation to Mr. Secretary Nagel as President of the Conference, as it will no doubt be the wish both of the United States Delegates and of the United States Administration that the Treaty should be presented to the Senate of the United States at an early date.

With cordial congratulations on the successful issue of the Conference convoked by the United States and in the hope that the result of its deliberations may prove to be of benefit both to the nations more immediately concerned and to the world at large,

I have the honour to be, Dear Mr. Secretary,

Very faithfully yours,

JAMES BRYCE

P.S. I am sending a copy of this note to the Japanese Ambassador and to the Russian Charge d'Affaires in this country for the information of their respective Delegates.

> The Honourable
>   P. C. KNOX,
>   *Secretary of State,*
>   *etc. etc. etc.*

3

Transnational Cooperation Dilemmas

Diplomacy resembles chess. Each player must make his key moves in such a way as to anticipate the moves of his opponent. In the game of diplomacy, self-interest is the only sound basis on which to predict the reactions of the other nation. Thomas A. Bailey, *The Art of Diplomacy (1968)*.

3.1. INTRODUCTION

The card game discussed in Chapter 1 showed that there may be situations in which at least some countries behave in a way that harms the collective good. The fur seal story, told in Chapter 2, showed something similar. For forty years, too many seals were killed and by the wrong methods. This chapter exposes the fundamental forces that can cause collective destruction.

In both the card game and the fur seal case, the outcomes depended on the nature of the underlying problem, as specified by the *rules of the game*. In the card game, these rules described the rewards for every player. They also determined whether the players could communicate with one another, whether the actions taken by the players were publicly observable, and whether the parties were able to appeal to a third party for enforcement. In the fur seal story, the underlying problem was determined by a similar set of rules—and more, including the three-mile territorial limit and the feasibility of re-flagging. Also important was the biology and behavior of the fur seal. Recall that the sea otter was eliminated from the Pribilofs soon after the islands were discovered. The fur seal proved more resilient to the hunt, though it may have become extinct eventually were it not for the treaty.

As suggested by these examples, some rules, such as the fur seal's biology, are determined by nature. Others, like the three-mile limit, are human inventions, determined in a kind of meta game of international relations.

For both the card game and the fur seal story, the outcomes also depended on the *behavior* of the parties—that is, on how they *responded* to the incentives structured by the rules of the game. Some players in the card game handed in their red cards and some did not, even though every player faced precisely the same incentives. Something similar emerged from the telling of the fur seal story. After other approaches failed, the United States unilaterally prohibited its own citizens from sealing at sea, essentially handing in its red card. Canada did not reciprocate.

The outcomes we observe—the number of red cards handed in, the stock and culling rate of seals, the depositions of acidic compounds, and so on—all these outcomes depend on the interplay between these two forces: the rules of the game and the way that the players respond to these rules. This interplay *may* lead to a "tragedy of the commons," but it will not always do so. Sometimes the incentives to over-exploit are weak (in the acid rain game, emissions have been cut substantially by some countries, largely because of the damage these emissions cause at home) or even non-existent (recall that if every player in the card game got $5 for keeping her red card and $10 for handing it in, the incentives would promote full provision of the public good). At other times, as in the fur seal story, these incentives to over-exploit defeat most attempts to cooperate.

Behavior can also vary, and may depend on rules such as whether and how the parties can communicate. But behavior is more significantly shaped by the underlying incentive structure. Often, the incentives pull in different directions. They can make countries want to free ride, and they can make countries want to cooperate. Both behaviors were illustrated by the fur seal case. When incentives conflict, behavior can be complicated.

The purpose of this chapter is to expose these different incentives, to show how they are structured by the rules of the game of international relations, and to demonstrate how behavior responds to them.

3.2. TRANSNATIONAL EXTERNALITIES

In all the cases discussed thus far, unilateralism failed. It failed to get everyone to hand in their red cards. It failed to meet critical loadings of acidic depositions. And it failed to conserve the fur seal. Unilateralism failed in all these cases because of the underlying incentives. The outcome that any one country was able to realize depended not just on its own actions; it depended also on what *others* did. The actions taken by the players in these games of interdependence created, in the jargon of economics, transnational *externalities*.

In the fur seal case, the taking of seals by Canada and Japan reduced the stock of seals available to the United States and Russia. In the acid rain game, emissions of sulfur from tall stacks in Britain, Poland, and other countries increased the acidity of lakes in Sweden, Norway, and elsewhere on the continent of Europe. These are examples of *multilateral* externalities.

Many externalities are *bilateral*. Acid rain in North America is an example, but an even more instructive example is water conflict between the United States and Mexico.

When planning the Welton–Mohawk Irrigation Project in Arizona, just over the border from Mexico, US authorities omitted adequate provisions for drainage so that the benefit–cost ratio for the project—using only US figures—could justify construction (with the drainage provisions included, the benefit–cost ratio fell below one).[1] After the project was completed in 1961, and wastes were pumped into the Colorado River, the concentration of salts (total dissolved solids) on the Mexican side of the border jumped from 800 to 1500 parts per million. Mexico's marginal irrigated lands—a full 10 percent of the farm land in the Mexicali Valley—became infertile and

---

[1] The details of this case are from LeMarquand (1977).

soon had to be abandoned. A diplomatic row broke out between the two countries, and a meeting was soon arranged between Presidents Lopez Mateos and Kennedy to discuss the crisis. We shall learn in Chapter 5 how the diplomacy developed, but for now it is important only to understand how the problem arose in the first place.

The essential point is that the United States did not omit the drainage provisions with the *intention* of harming Mexico. It simply ignored the consequences of improper drainage for its southern neighbor, making pollution of the Colorado an externality rather than an act of aggression. Being disinterested in the consequences for Mexico may seem unneighborly (indeed, Mexico protested that "the essential part of the problem was not of a technical character but rather of a moral and judicial nature"[2]), but countries normally do act in their own interests. Had the United States been required to compensate Mexico for its losses, the outcome would have been different. The benefit–cost ratio for the project—still using only US figures, but now including the compensation payments—would have dropped. The project would not have been approved; the externality would have been internalized.

Of course, cross-border environmental destruction *is* sometimes driven by malicious intent—a potent example being the pollution caused by Iraq's destruction of Kuwait's oil wells during the Gulf War. But such actions are not externalities; they are acts of aggression. Externalities are not intended to cause harm.

And yet, as all the examples looked at thus far show, externalities *do* cause harm, and so can arouse strong emotions. They can even provoke threats to retaliate militarily, particularly when unfriendly countries are involved. Conflict over access to vital water resources is especially common. India and Pakistan nearly went to war when the waters of the shared Indus basin were diverted, following partition of the Indian subcontinent in 1947 (Kirmani 1990). Similarly, conflicts over access to the Jordan River and its associated ground water basins have triggered a string of military clashes in the Middle East going back at least to 1951. They also helped to spark the 1967 Arab–Israeli War (see Homer-Dixon *et al.* 1993; Fishelson 1995).

Even when externalities involve non-essential resources, normally congenial relationships can turn hostile. The fur seal conflict between the United States and Britain (Canada), created—in the words of the US Secretary of State, John Foster—a risk of "the horrors of a war between two kindred peoples" (see Gay 1987: 89). And clashes like this still flare up. In 1995, a Canadian gunboat fired shots across the bows of a Spanish fishing boat, the *Estai*, outside the 200-mile limit and forced the boat into port.[3] Spain's foreign minister, Javier Solana, accused Canada of "piracy on the high seas," and a Spanish gunboat was quickly dispatched to the Grand Banks. Canada meanwhile produced evidence that the *Estai* had been catching undersized halibut, and its ambassador to the European Union accused Spain of "crimes against conservation." After a cooling-off period, a settlement was negotiated, and a crisis averted. But this example, like the others, illustrates how easy it can be for transnational externalities to provoke an aggressive response.

[2] LeMarquand (1977: p. 30).   [3] See *The European*, March 17–23, 1995, pp. 2–3.

Use of the Colorado is an example of a *unidirectional* externality; drainage into this river by the United States harmed Mexico, but use of the river by Mexico did not affect the United States. Another example from the same continent, and one that is important in legal history, concerns the emissions of sulfur from a smelter in Trail, British Columbia earlier in the twentieth century. Unlike acid rain on the east coast, the emissions from the smelter were carried by the prevailing winds *south* over the border with the United States. As in the Colorado River case, Canada did not locate the smelter with the intention of harming the United States—the pollution was an externality, not an act of aggression—but nor did Canada have any incentive to take account of American interests in the matter.

Many international externalities are *reciprocal* in the sense that every country imposes externalities on all others that share a resource. Examples include global climate change and stratospheric ozone depletion. Every country emits greenhouse gases into the atmosphere and every country uses, or once used, ozone-depleting substances like chlorofluorocarbons (CFCs). All countries are also affected by, or at least have an expectation of being affected by, global emissions of these pollutants.

Unidirectional externalities are *asymmetric* by definition: if the upstream country dumps wastes into the river, the downstream country will be harmed; but if the downstream country pollutes the river, the upstream country will be unaffected. Reciprocal externalities need not be asymmetric, though they usually are, at least to some degree. Different countries will be affected in different ways by ozone deple-tion—depending, for example, on their distance from the poles. Similarly, coastal countries will be more affected by sea level rise than land-locked states, though even here there will be variability. For example, sea level has *fallen* in relation to the Alaskan coast as the melting of glaciers has made the land lighter (elsewhere in the United States, sea level has risen). The economies of some countries, particularly in the higher latitudes, may even benefit from climate change, at least in the medium term. And it is in the nature of both environmental problems that the damages each country suffers will not be proportional to its own share of global emissions. Small island states, for example, may be relatively the most affected by climate change, even though their emissions are among the least significant.

Externalities often affect production relationships. Excessive fishing has caused search costs to rise and yields to decline to the point where many important fisheries today are closed. Pollution of the Colorado River reduced crop yields in the Mexicali Valley, while emissions from the Trail Smelter harmed agriculture and forestry in Washington state.[4] Depletion of stratospheric ozone has increased the earth's expos-ure to ultraviolet-B radiation, which can damage crops and fisheries (directly and indirectly—by worsening smog, or ground level ozone pollution). An increase in the atmospheric concentration of greenhouse gases is expected to raise global mean temperature and sea level, affecting the productivity of climate-sensitive economic

---

[4] See Trail Smelter Arbitral Tribunal (1939). Other damages were claimed by the United States, but these were not awarded by the tribunal.

sectors like agriculture (in some areas, perhaps for the better), and also leading to coastal erosion, at least where shoreline defenses are lacking.

Externalities can also alter utility relationships. Only about a thousand giant pandas still live in the remote highlands in and near Szechuan province, and the extinction of this species would cause people in and outside of China to grieve. A great loss would be suffered, even though the panda has little use in production (though poaching for the panda's pelt may be more of a threat than bamboo die-off or habitat loss; see Schaller 1993). Concerns about the incidental killing of dolphins by modern tuna fleets, and the brutal means by which whales and seals are sometimes killed and domestic livestock reared and transported, are further examples, though in these cases utility depends on the manner in which individual animals are treated rather than on the chances of their species' survival.

Often, externalities impinge on both utility and production relationships. Though ozone depletion will alter production relationships, its most worrisome consequence is an increased incidence of skin cancer, a cause of both terrible suffering and premature death (US EPA 1988*b*). Global climate change will affect some production relationships, but it may also alter climate amenities (possibly, improving well-being in some regions) and impose hardship on people forced to migrate by climate change (see Cline 1992).

Although estimation of external effects is more difficult and controversial when utility relationships are altered (what does any of us lose by not being able to marvel at the sight of shoals of passenger pigeons darkening the skies over North America?), conceptually the distinction between externalities that affect production rather than utility relationships matters little; either way, unilateralism is likely to sustain only inefficient outcomes; superior, alternative outcomes will technically be within our reach and yet may not be gotten hold of. This is the dilemma of international environmental protection.

3.3. THE DILEMMA OF INTERNATIONAL ENVIRONMENTAL PROTECTION

Reciprocal externalities deserve special treatment for analytical reasons (unidirectional externalities are discussed further in Chapter 5). As we will see in Chapter 15, countries have not determined their greenhouse gas emission targets independently. They have made these choices after observing how others have chosen, or after forming expectations about how others will respond to their own choices. The calculus of revising targets and of deciding whether to meet them has similarly involved each country looking over its shoulder, as it were, to see what others are doing. This interdependence is what makes policy making a *game*. Formal analysis of these kinds of situations is essential to understanding how the dilemma of international environmental protection can arise—and why it is not so easily remedied. Let us now turn to it.

Here and throughout this book I shall take it that the primary players in games of international environmental relations are the countries themselves, as represented by their governments. States are certainly the primary subjects of international law.

To take a precedential example, in the *Trail Smelter* case, the damage suffered by the United States was caused by a private firm, but the tribunal hearing the case ruled that " … the Dominion of Canada is responsible in international law for the conduct of the Trail Smelter" (Trail Smelter Arbitral Tribunal 1941: 716–17). Furthermore, sovereignty designates states as the only players with unlimited rights to act in the international system. Only states can negotiate and ratify treaties, and only states are responsible for implementing them.

My formal analysis shall also assume that states are monolithic, unitary actors. This assumption, unlike the last, is made purely for reasons of convenience. It is an assumption that we know is untrue. States are represented at international negotiations by their governments, but governments are not imbued with a fixed set of preferences. A government's position on any given issue is rather determined by an internal negotiation, even if final decisions are made by the executive. Internal negotiations normally involve a variety of agencies or ministries, and the interests of *these* parties are in turn influenced by lobbyists representing the views of various associations, including grassroots environmental organizations and business groups. In democracies, the views of the electorate can also be expressed directly at the ballot box—extraordinarily, by a referendum; more routinely, by the election of representatives. And, of course, treaties must be ratified. Ratification may require a simple majority of the parliament already controlled by the executive or, as in the United States, a two-thirds majority of a politically independent legislature. Making matters even more complicated, governments change; and the views of incoming government may differ from the one it replaced—a problem especially for very lengthy negotiations. Europe, today, has added yet another layer to the process of treaty-making. The European Union prefers to negotiate with other countries as a block, but to do so all its member states (today, there are fifteen) must agree on a negotiating position before meeting with other countries. Finally, the process by which all these interests find expression isn't linear but rather reflects a feedback. Because parliament must ratify, for example, the executive has to take its views into account at an earlier stage of the negotiation.

The negotiation supergame is thus a huge and complex system, incorporating a rich and far-from-uniform set of domestic political institutions. Much is certainly lost in assuming that states are monoliths. But something is gained, too: the assumption allows us to obtain results that can be easily interpreted.[5]

The dilemma is often portrayed using the game shown in Figure 3.1(a) (the companion diagram, Figure 3.1(b), is discussed in Section 3.5). There are two players, labeled X and Y, each of which must choose a *strategy*, or a plan for how to act. For this game, the set of feasible actions is binary; the countries can only choose between playing Abate or Pollute. The game is played just once, meaning that each player has only one opportunity to act, and the players must make their choices simultaneously (put differently, each player must make its choice without knowing how the other country has chosen; see below). The actions that are *actually* chosen determine the

---

[5] I discuss the process of negotiation in more detail in Chapter 6.

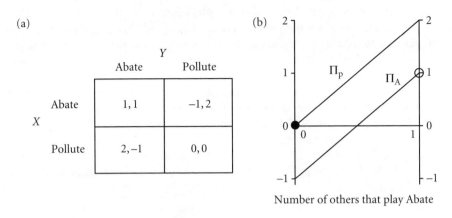

Figure 3.1. *The dilemma game*

outcome of the game. For example, if X plays Abate and Y plays Pollute, then the outcome of the game is (Abate, Pollute). In this game there are four feasible outcomes, the others being (Abate, Abate), (Pollute, Abate), and (Pollute, Pollute).

Associated with every feasible outcome is a *payoff* for each player. The payoffs for the game depicted in Figure 3.1(a) are shown in the different cells. Within each cell, the number on the left is X's payoff, and the number on the right is Y's. These payoffs are utility measures. They can be thought of as being expressed in monetary terms, although in this particular example this interpretation is not necessary; all that matters for this game is that each player be able to discern whether one outcome is preferred to another, and not whether one outcome yields a payoff precisely two or three times the size of another, or whether one player gains more or less than the other.

Self-interest dictates that each player prefer a larger payoff to a smaller one. It also requires that each player *not* care directly about the payoff received by the other country. In Figure 3.1(a), the outcome most preferred by X, (Pollute, Abate), is least preferred by Y and vice versa. However, X and Y both prefer (Abate, Abate) to (Pollute, Pollute).

To analyze this game, it is also important to be clear about what each player knows and does not know. I have already said that each player must act without knowing how the other will act. This makes the dilemma a game of *imperfect information*. I shall also take it that each player knows the choices that both parties may make, the payoffs associated with every outcome, and the preferences of the other player. This makes the dilemma a game of *complete information*. Finally, I shall assume that all of this is *common knowledge*: each player knows that the other player knows these things, each knows that the other knows that it knows these things, and so on.

So: how will the players choose? Consider player X's problem. Because of the interdependence that exists, player X, in deciding whether or not to abate its pollution, will wish to consider how the payoff it receives depends on player Y's choice. Suppose Y plays Abate. Then X receives a payoff of 1 by playing Abate and 2 by playing Pollute. Given Y's choice, X can do no better than to play Pollute. If Y plays Pollute, X gets a payoff of -1 if it plays Abate and 0 if it plays Pollute. Again, given that Y plays Pollute, X can do no better than to play Pollute, too. In other words, X's best strategy is to play Pollute whatever Y does; play Pollute is thus a *dominant strategy* for X. It is easy to confirm that the situation is entirely symmetric for Y; Y's best strategy is also to play Pollute whatever X does. Hence, there exists a unique equilibrium to this game: both players play Pollute. The outcome (Pollute, Pollute) is an *equilibrium* (formally, a *Nash equilibrium*) because neither player could do better by deviating unilaterally from this outcome. The equilibrium is unique because at least one player would choose to deviate unilaterally starting from any of the other three feasible outcomes.

The game depicted in Figure 3.1(a) is the famous "prisoners' dilemma" (PD).[6] The dilemma is that both countries play Pollute even though both would be better off if they both played Abate. The equilibrium is *inefficient*.

3.4. WHAT IS AN EQUILIBRIUM?

I have given the formal definition of an equilibrium (to be precise, a Nash equilibrium), but it is important also to have an intuitive understanding of the concept.

Consider a different game: the two-thirds game. Everyone in a class must choose an integer between 0 and 100. The student who guesses the highest integer which is not higher than two-thirds of the average of all guesses gets $100 (if there is a tie, the $100 is divided equally among all the winners). Obviously, your best guess in such a game depends on how you think others will guess—that is, there are no dominant strategies in this game. In actual experiments, people tend to start with fairly high guesses. In experiments conducted by Nagel (1995), for example, the median guess was 33. If the game is repeated, however, guesses tend to fall, suggesting that the original guesses cannot be an equilibrium.

The reason why people want to revise their own guesses downwards should be pretty obvious. If the average of everyone's guess is 25, say, and you guessed 30, then you would do better by lowering your guess to around 16—if, that is, you thought the other students would not revise *their* guesses. However, most people will probably anticipate that if *they* can gain by lowering their guess, then so can everyone else. Hence, if you were playing this game, you would probably want to guess even lower than 16. If you carry this logic further, you will find that there is a unique equilibrium

---

[6] The name derives from the following interpretation, described here by Luce and Raiffa (1957):

Two suspects are taken into custody and separated. The district attorney is certain that they are guilty of a specific crime, but he does not have adequate evidence to convict them at a trial. He points out to each prisoner that each has two alternatives: to confess to the crime the police are sure they have done, or not to confess. If they both do not confess, then the district attorney states he will book them on some very minor trumped-up charge such as petty larceny and illegal possession of a weapon, and they will both receive a minor punishment; if they both confess they will be prosecuted, but he will recommend less than the most severe sentence; but if one confesses and the other does not, then the confessor will receive lenient treatment for turning state's evidence whereas the latter will get 'the book' slapped at him.

for this game in which everyone chooses 0. In actual experiments, people do not get to this equilibrium the first time they play the game. They do not even get to this equilibrium the second time they play the game. However, as Nagel's (1995) experiments show, they do converge towards the equilibrium quickly if allowed to revise their choices.

An equilibrium is thus not the outcome that happens to be realized in a particular play of a game. An equilibrium is an outcome from which no player would prefer to deviate, given the choices made by the other players.

An equilibrium can be a situation that leaves everyone feeling contented. In the above guessing game, when everyone guesses 0, everyone wins. Moreover, the aggregate gain is maximized (with a fixed sum of $100 to share, this is a *zero sum game*) and everyone wins precisely the same amount, a situation that seems fair under these circumstances. So it is not only the case that no one could gain by deviating—say, by guessing 1 instead of 0. Everyone should also feel satisfied with the result.

An equilibrium need not have this character. In the PD game, though (Pollute, Pollute) is an equilibrium, it is not a situation in which the players will feel at ease. They will likely feel frustrated that they could not realize the more efficient outcome. If given time to work on the problem, the players will probably try to figure out a way to improve on the equilibrium. Every time I have played the card game, the students have wanted another chance to improve on the last round of the game.

In the fur seal case, behavior changed little except when the game was restructured, as when Russia monopolized the land hunt. Once pelagic sealing had begun, excessive harvesting became an equilibrium behavior—a situation that persisted for years. This was an inefficient equilibrium. It left all the players feeling frustrated. And this is why so much effort was devoted to trying to improve on the equilibrium. Eventually the parties succeeded, and the 1911 treaty established a new equilibrium. Throughout most of the life of the treaty, behavior was stable, with harvesting rates deviating little from the efficient level. The 1911 treaty did not make (Abate, Abate) an equilibrium of the underlying game. It couldn't do this because (Abate, Abate) is *not* an equilibrium of this game. The treaty rather *restructured* the game. In this new, transformed game, (Abate, Abate) *was* an equilibrium. The central challenge of international cooperation is to figure out how games like the PD can be restructured such that the mutually preferred outcome can be sustained as an equilibrium.

3.5. DIAGRAMMATIC REPRESENTATION

Figure 3.1(a) presents the dilemma game in customary (normal) form. Where countries are identical (that is, symmetric), as in Figure 3.1(a), games like this can also be represented diagrammatically.[7] Diagrammatic representation is especially useful in analyzing games involving more than two symmetric players (technically, the relationships should be depicted by a series of points rather than a line, but the line drawings are easier to follow, especially when N is large). However, in using the

---

[7] I got the idea of using this graphical representation from Schelling (1978).

diagrammatic representation from the start we shall be able to see how the more complex N-player games developed later relate to the more familiar two-player games.

The diagrammatic representation of the 2×2 dilemma game is shown in Figure 3.1(b). Here, the curve Π_A measures the payoff that either country receives by playing Abate and the curve Π_P measures either country's payoff to playing Pollute.[8] Since the two countries are identical, the calculus of choice is precisely the same for each player; and since this is a game, whether it is best for either player to play Pollute or Abate will in general depend on the other player's choice. The horizontal axis represents this choice. If the other country plays Pollute, the horizontal axis takes on the value 0. If the other plays Abate, the corresponding value is 1. More generally, the horizontal axis represents the number of the *other* countries (from the point of view of any country; remember, by assumption all countries are symmetric) that play Abate. As Π_P exceeds Π_A in Figure 3.1(b), whether or not the other country plays Abate, both countries can do no better than to play Pollute (again, play Pollute is thus a dominant strategy; in the diagram, this can be seen by noting that the two payoff curves never cross). The Nash equilibrium, (Pollute, Pollute), is shown by the solid dot. The outcome that maximizes the sum of the payoffs to both players—(Abate, Abate), or the *full cooperative outcome*—is identified by the open dot. Since, these dots do not overlap, we know that the equilibrium is inefficient.

3.6. DO PEOPLE REALLY BEHAVE THIS WAY?

You may already have noticed the connection between the game depicted in Figure 3.1 and the card game played in Chapter 1. Handing in your red card in the card game is like playing Abate in the dilemma game. Similarly, keeping your red card is like playing Pollute. The number of players differs between the two games, as do the monetary values. But the games are otherwise alike. For both games, each player can do no better than to keep his red card (play Pollute), whatever the other players do; and yet all the players are better off if every person hands in his red card (plays Abate).

However, though the incentive structures are similar, people behave differently when playing the card game than analytical game theory predicts. Recall that, in the classroom experiment, some people handed in their red cards, whereas, as just explained, analytical game theory predicts that no one would do so. Clearly, both approaches cannot be correct. And yet each seems to be telling us something.

As briefly noted in Chapter 1, we should not take the results of the classroom experiment *too* seriously. However, it remains true that even in "proper" experiments involving real money, some people play Cooperate (that is, Abate) rather than Defect (Pollute). The predictions of analytical game theory in this and in other contexts are not always confirmed by how people actually behave.

In a famous study carried out in New York City in 1968, almost half of all "lost" wallets left lying on the sidewalk were returned with the money (only about $5) still

---

[8] As already noted, these payoffs should be represented by points rather than curves since solutions in the interior of the figure are infeasible.

inside (see Frank 1988, for a discussion). The lost wallet game is like the PD in that it is a one-shot situation (the person who returns the wallet could not expect that her own wallet might someday be picked up by the owner of *this* wallet), and one in which the players cannot communicate. Self-interest should imply that the wallets will not be returned, and yet many are.

Most people, when told of this experiment, are not surprised—and nor was I. Hours after my wife left her purse on the London Underground, a woman called to tell us that she had found it. When she returned it to us later, I did not think to ask her *why* she returned the purse. I felt I knew the reason, because if our roles had been reversed my wife and I would have returned the purse to her. But I did ask the woman, who later became a friend, why she had not simply handed it in to the London Underground police. Her answer: she believed that *they* could not be trusted to return the purse. This is just to remind us that, while a substantial number of people return lost wallets, many do not and the people who return the wallets are aware of this.

However, the wallet game is unlike the PD in other respects, and we should be careful not to draw too much comfort from it. The payoff to the person who finds the wallet does not depend on what the owner of the wallet does, making the game more like the dictator game. In this game, two players can share a sum of money—say, $100. One player, however, decides how the money is to be shared. Analytical game theory predicts that the dictator should take the $100 for himself, leaving the other player with nothing. However, when I have played this game in the classroom, I find that most students do not behave in this way. The median response is usually 50–50.

Generosity may have its own rewards in these situations, but in the PD a person who plays Abate may be burned by the other player. In the PD, if you play Abate and the other player plays Pollute, you are worse off as compared with the situation in which both you and the other player play Pollute. So you might decide to play Pollute to avoid being taken advantage of. Moreover, if you play Pollute and the other player plays Abate, you will realize your highest possible payoff. So you have two motives for playing Pollute: "fear," or the motive of avoiding a big loss, and "greed," or the motive of reaping a large gain. Both of these motives have been shown to be important determinants of behavior (Dawes and Thaler 1988). That is, beliefs about how others will behave may affect individual behavior in the PD—even though, in its analytical form, play Pollute (keep your red card) is a dominant strategy.

As noted above, we cannot always expect real people to abide by the equilibrium behavior predicted by a game theory model in their first play of the game. But does repeated play cause people to converge towards the equilibrium in the PD game—as it does, for example, in the two-thirds game? It is a common finding of the experimental literature that cooperation starts out being relatively high in the first period of a repeated game (about 40–60 percent of players will cooperate), but deteriorates thereafter (Fehr and Gächter 2000a; Ostrom 2000). As noted in Chapter 1, I have observed a similar behavior in the classroom. The problem seems not just to get cooperation going. The problem is to keep it going despite free-riding by some players.

To sum up, though behavior, as revealed in experiments, does not conform precisely to the predictions of analytical game theory, it does seem that the incentives for free-riding in the PD are a strong attractor.

3.7 DO COUNTRIES BEHAVE THIS WAY?

And what of governments, the real players in games of transnational externalities? Do experiments with people tell us anything about how *governments* would behave in similar situations?

We do not know that they do, and we will probably never know. It is, of course, impractical to run experiments with real governments. The nearest we have come to doing this, to my knowledge, is a study by Peter Bohm (1997) of international emissions trading played by negotiating teams appointed by their countries' own energy ministries (the countries represented include Denmark, Finland, Norway, and Sweden). Two aspects of the experiment are especially relevant. First, the teams "included people whose rank and competence are representative of team members who would participate in real-world negotiations" (Bohm 1997: 13). Second, the experiment itself was designed "to mimic the incentives likely to confront decision makers in actual negotiations" (Bohm 1997: 37). The purpose of the experiment was to learn if countries would trade entitlements to pollute, and if their trading would conform to the prediction of microeconomics. Bohm found that these government players did trade, and that they exhausted 97 percent of the total gains from trade—almost perfectly conforming to the predictions of the reduced form model of competitive trading.

I have conducted many market games in the classroom, and also find that the gains from trade are nearly always nearly completely exhausted. So perhaps countries do not behave very differently from individuals. However, market games are very different from the PD. Would governments behave much the same as individuals have been observed to behave in PD games? Again, we do not know. But there is one study that adds an interesting twist to what we have learned so far. In an experiment using students who knew their "partner's" identity, Glaeser *et al.* (2000) found that students were more likely to cheat if their partner were of a different nationality.

In particular, Glaeser *et al.* (2000) played the following game. One student (the "sender") is given $15, and must decide how much to keep and how much to pass on to the other student (the "recipient"). Before making this decision, the recipient conveys a message to the sender about how he will behave subsequently. The sender then transfers some amount of money, which is then doubled by the experimenter. If the sender sends $12, for example, and thus keeps $3, the recipient actually gets $24. The recipient must then decide how much to return to the sender. For example, if the recipient keeps $15 and returns $9, the recipient gets $15 at the end of the game and the sender gets $12. Obviously, the aggregate gain is maximized when the sender sends the entire $15 to the recipient, but in sending money to the recipient, the sender risks losing the entire amount sent.

Glaeser *et al.* (2000) find that nationality has only a small and statistically insignificant effect on the amount sent. However, it has a large and highly significant effect on the amount returned. "People are much more likely to return low amounts if they are facing someone from a different country," Glaeser *et al.* (2000: 834) conclude. Notice that nationality was found to have little effect on *trust* (as indicated by the amount of money sent, perhaps influenced by the nature of the promise made by the recipient), but a pronounced effect on *trustworthiness* (as indicated by the amount returned as a fraction of the amount sent).

3.8. COMMUNICATION AND TRANSPARENCY

What gives rise to the the behavior predicted by analytical game theory? Is it just the payoffs of the PD that matter, or do the other rules of the game also matter?

In their informative book, *The New Sovereignty*, Abram Chayes and Antonia Chayes (1995: 144) claim that "the reason [for the] dilemma is lack of transparency. The conditions of the game specify that the parties cannot communicate with each other and that they have no information about each other's moves." If only the parties could talk about their problem and observe how the other player has chosen, or so this reasoning goes, the dilemma could be avoided.

From a purely analytical perspective, it is easy to see that play of this game may be preceded by any amount of discussion—and that the equilibrium will be precisely the same. For when the parties must make their actual choices, each will know that it can do better by reneging on a pledge to play Abate. Recall that the rules of the game specify that the game is played only once and is isolated from all other interactions. Hence, neither player can lose by reneging on a pledge to play Abate— or gain by fulfilling such a pledge. Individual rationality therefore dictates that both players play Pollute. From this perspective, communication will not remove the dilemma.

Nor will transparency make any difference. As the game is presently structured, each player, when deciding how to act, must make its choice without knowing how the other will move. However, suppose that the rules of the game require that player X move before Y and that X's choice be revealed to Y before Y must act (making the sequential game a game of perfect information). Then, whatever X does in Stage 1, Y will play Pollute in Stage 2. But, given that Y will play Pollute whatever X does, X can do no better than to play Pollute, too. Hence, even if the game were played sequentially, and the history of the game were public knowledge as the principle of transparency would presumably require, the equilibrium would remain (Pollute, Pollute).

These insights, however, are derived only from an analytical perspective. What about in real life? Here, as you would expect, a richer pattern of behavior can be observed.

Communication, for example, has been shown to help cooperation in experiments involving real people, especially if the players are allowed to meet face-to-face (Ostrom 1998). However, as Ostrom (1998: 7) points out, "communication alone is not a sufficient mechanism to assure successful collective action." Recall from the card game that even after a preliminary communication round, some students always hold on to their red cards. Experiments further show that when the stakes in a game are increased (so that players have more to gain from successful cooperation, but more to gain also from defection), the level of cooperation falls, even with face-to-face communication (Ostrom 1998).

Other experiments have found that, when the members of a *group* promise to cooperate, the extent of cooperation increases—provided that *all* the members of the group make such a promise (Dawes and Thaler 1988). One reason may be that, with universal promise-making, each player feels that there is a good chance that she will not be totally duped—that others, or at least some others, will play Abate, too. This way, a player who cooperates can be pretty sure of doing better as compared with the outcome in which she is the only player to cooperate. The "fear" factor mentioned earlier would be dampened. It might even be eliminated. However, the result that *all* members of the group must pledge to cooperate for promise-making to affect actual cooperation suggests a different explanation. It suggests that "universal promising creates—or reflects—group identity" (Dawes and Thaler 1988: 195).

Richard Benedick, the chief US negotiator in the ozone talks, refers to "spirit of Montreal," a kind of group identity that, according to Benedick (1998: 332), "reflected genuine feelings of solidarity and partnership to protect the ozone layer, in what was regarded as a noble and historic global movement." That the negotiators should identify with their collective mission, and not just their country's interests, is understandable. For the two do not entirely conflict. In the dilemma game, *all* players prefer (Abate, Abate) to (Pollute, Pollute). And as we shall see later, the incentives to cooperate in protecting the ozone were especially strong. The question is, did the spirit created at the meetings facilitate cooperation, or did an underlying incentive structure, already favorable to cooperation, nurture a collective spirit? I am inclined to favor the latter explanation, but the experimental evidence mentioned above suggests that the "spirit of Montreal" may have had some substantive effect.

As we shall see in Chapter 10, transparency is an essential ingredient of cooperation when countries are engaged in long-term relationships. However, the experimental evidence suggests that transparency is less important in settings more akin to the one shot PD. In one experiment, four individuals played the same game ten times consecutively (the game was repeated many times over among different groups of four individuals; see Fehr and Gächter 2000*a*). In each repeated game, the number of players, their payoffs, and the duration of the game were all common knowledge. Each player did not know the identities of the other players, but each player did know the aggregate provision of the public good at the end of each period (this again was common knowledge). And yet, even with this transparency, Fehr and Gächter (2000*a*) found that average contributions of the public good converged toward full free-riding. Knowing how the other players chose (in the aggregate) did not promote cooperation.

To sum up, though communication and transparency matter in situations involving real people, they do not overturn the basic insights of analytical game theory. Free-riding really is a problem.

3.9. SELF-ENFORCING AGREEMENTS

Recognizing that it is in their joint interests to play Abate, we might suppose that the two countries will negotiate an agreement which alters the payoffs in such a way that

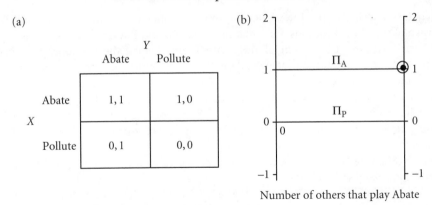

Figure 3.2. *A contractual resolution to the dilemma game*

each state's own interests compel it to play Abate. In considering such an agreement, we shall now have to take the payoffs in Figure 3.1 to be cardinal and not just ordinal. This means that the payoff which X or Y receives in the outcome (Abate, Abate) is not only greater than the corresponding payoff each gets in the outcome (Pollute, Pollute), but precisely one unit greater.[9] I shall further suppose that the payoffs in Figure 3.1 are measured in dollars, and that if X transfers \$1 to Y, X's payoff falls by \$1 and Y's rises by \$1.

Suppose that the parties reach an agreement which specifies that any country that plays Pollute must pay the other a fine equal to 2 (that is, \$2). This agreement changes the payoffs, and the revised game is shown in Figure 3.2. If Y plays Abate and X plays Pollute, X receives a payoff of 2 minus a fine of 2, or 0, and Y receives a payoff of -1 plus a fine of 2, or 1. The payoffs are reversed if X plays Abate and Y plays Pollute. If both parties play Pollute or if both play Abate, the payoffs are unchanged compared with Figure 3.1. Like the original dilemma game, the equilibrium to this adjusted game is unique. But it is otherwise very different. Player X will now play Abate whatever Y does, and Y will likewise play Abate whatever X does; play Abate is thus a dominant strategy in this game. By introducing the fine, the dilemma has been removed.

But this fixes things only if the contract is *binding* on both countries (otherwise the negotiation is just a particular expression of communication, and we already know that communication by itself cannot alter the equilibrium in this game, at least not from an analytical perspective). That is, a third party must be able to enforce the contract.

Third party enforcement is easy for most domestic conflicts. Indeed, the institutions of municipal government, including the courts and law enforcement agencies, exist partly to enable parties to resolve dilemmas of the type shown in Figure 3.1 (Axelrod 1984). However, there does not exist a super-national authority, or a World Government, that can enforce an agreement between countries. True, one country

---

[9] Cardinal utility functions can be derived from observing the choices which players make over lotteries; see, for example, Binmore (1994).

may take another to the International Court of Justice (ICJ), the principal judicial organ of the United Nations, for violating an agreement. But the Court will not hear the case without the consent of the accused; and even if the case goes to court, and the Court finds against the defendant, this party cannot be compelled to comply with the Court's decision. Indeed, despite the great abundance of international disputes, on average only about one substantive case comes before the Court each year. As Chayes and Chayes (1995: 202) have wryly noted, "the ICJ seems to be the only court in the world to have solved the problem of docket congestion." Even in the few cases that are heard, the Court's influence has been minimal. According to one legal expert (Shaw 1991: 672), "the record of compliance with judgments [of the ICJ] is only marginally satisfactory."

As noted in Chapter 1, the norms that govern relations between states require that international agreements be *self-enforcing*.[10] The agreement to impose a fine as a means of removing the dilemma is not self-enforcing. Knowing that it could not be forced to pay the fine, X's best strategy is to play Pollute. So is Y's. The only self-enforcing outcome in the game described in Figure 3.1 is (Pollute, Pollute).

3.10. INTRA- VS TRANSNATIONAL EXTERNALITIES

The concept of self-enforcement is fundamental to the analysis of international environmental relations, and marks the difference between intra- and transnational externalities. As we saw in the fur seal case, the excesses of intra-national harvesting were easily corrected by the state (whether Imperial Russia or the United States) having jurisdiction over its rookeries. Control of pelagic sealing in the high seas was another matter.

Rivalry between jurisdictions within a federal system is entirely different. The United States Constitution allows states to negotiate "compacts" concerning cross-border issues, subject to Congressional consent. Compacts are analogous to agreements between nation states, but disputes connected to compacts can be heard by the US Supreme Court, and rulings by the Court can be enforced by the federal government. Indeed, the federal government may itself *impose* an allocation upon states if they fail to reach agreement themselves. For example, the Boulder Canyon Project Act of 1928 conferred upon the Secretary of the Interior the authority to apportion the waters of the Colorado River at Hoover Dam and below among the three affected states—California, Arizona, and Nevada—in the event that they could not agree to a tristate compact (Muys 1976). Such higher order intervention is not possible in international relations.

---

[10] Even national institutions must be self-enforcing. An aggrieved party would only go to court if it believed that the court's judgement would not be arbitrary or corruptible and if the court's decision would be enforced by the executive. The accumulated case law is there to ensure consistency, and if for some reason a judgement seems not to be consistent with it, then the plaintiff (or defendant) may appeal to a higher court. Belief that the executive will enforce the court's ruling will depend on whether the executive has an incentive to do so. In democracies this incentive is the prospect that, if the executive does not fulfil its promises, it will be tossed out at the next election.

Though the distinction between intra- and transnational externalities has already been illustrated by the fur seal case, there is an even more powerful example. This is the "experiment" that took place when the Indian subcontinent was partitioned in 1947.

Disputes over access to the waters of the Indus Basin began in the early nineteenth century. In the colonial period, the Indus was under the jurisdiction of a single authority, the British raj, and conflicts were easily mended by the visible hand of central government, as Kirmani (1990: 201) explains:

[The] first major dispute was resolved in 1935 through arbitration by the Anderson Commission appointed by the central government. As the demand for irrigation water increased, a new dispute emerged and it was again resolved in 1942 by a new commission (the Rao Commission) appointed by the central government. The procedures followed to resolve the disputes on both occasions were similar. The central government had the responsibility and authority to settle disputes between the provinces; it appointed commissions comprising representatives of the provinces and chaired by a neutral expert to arbitrate; the commissions were given the powers to decide the issues if the parties failed to agree; the decisions of the commissions were final and binding; and the provinces succeeded in managing conflicts by following this system.

Partition divided the Indus basin between India and Pakistan, so that there no longer existed a central government capable of imposing or enforcing a settlement. As it happens, the waters feeding Pakistan's irrigation supplies were on the Indian side of the border, and a dispute arose in 1948 when India diverted these away from Pakistan. Although the canals feeding Pakistan's irrigation system were eventually reopened, relations between the two countries deteriorated when India claimed sovereign rights over the waters passing through its territory. Pakistan offered to settle the dispute by arbitration, but India refused, and (as noted earlier) it seemed for a time that the quarrel might lead to war. Fortunately, the parties stepped back from the brink, and a peaceful settlement was agreed. I shall describe the details of the agreement in Chapter 5, but for now we can simply note the difference that partition made. Conflict over the Indus was always present. What changed was that partition imposed a new constraint on how the conflict could be handled. Partition made it much harder to correct the externality of water diversion.

3.11. WHY ARE AGREEMENTS EVER KEPT?

I have so far argued that agreements to cooperate—that is, to play Abate—are kept only when enforced by a third party. Third party enforcement is plainly important. If it were not we would not rely on institutions like the courts so often in domestic situations. However, it is also true that agreements are kept even when the apparatus of the court is weak or non-existent.

One reason agreements are kept is that, in some situations, people care about the others affected by the agreement—a phenomenon Partha Dasgupta (2002) calls "mutual affection" (in the literature, this is sometimes also known as "pure altruism"). Mutual regard obviously applies within the family, but does it explain cooperation more generally? There is reason to think that it does not. Dawes and Thaler (1988) note that public contributions for the same activity reduce private contributions only slightly. If donors cared about the outcomes that their contributions supported, their contributions should fall by more—according to Dawes and Thaler (and I think they are overstating the case), they should fall to offset the public contributions.

Another reason agreements are kept has a social basis. If you believe others are disposed to being trustworthy, then you may be more inclined to reciprocate. This disposition to cooperate may be an acquired evolutionary trait, or it may be inculcated through social conditioning. It may also, as Dasgupta (2002) notes, apply exclusively to a group to which you feel some loyalty rather than to any and all situations. This last observation is confirmed by experimental evidence. In an experiment reported by Dawes and Thaler (1988), group identity raised cooperation from 30 to 70 percent (a range that is consistent with play of the card game reported in Chapter 1). When an alien group would benefit from a contribution, however, the level of cooperation fell below 30 percent. Indeed, the players in this setting behaved toward the alien group very much as the PD predicts they would. There is a suggestion here that the disposition to cooperate may be lower in international settings than in intra-national settings, even after controlling for all other differences.

A final reason why agreements are kept, noted also by Dasgupta (2002), is mutual enforcement. If the PD is repeated—if the players are engaged in a long-term relationship—then cooperation can be *made* to pay by ensuring that non-cooperation is punished. It is by this means, I believe, that treaties aspiring to overcome the PD can best be made self-enforcing. Chapters 10 and 11 are devoted entirely to the study of treaty enforcement by strategies of reciprocity.

3.12. COMMITMENT

Suppose that countries X and Y enter into an agreement to play Abate, and in so doing become jointly *committed* to playing Abate. Then, plainly, third party enforcement would not be needed to sustain the mutually preferred outcome as a self-enforcing agreement. So the reason that the outcome (Pollute, Pollute) is the equilibrium to the dilemma game is not just that states are sovereign. It is also that they are unable to commit to particular courses of action. Being unable to commit means that promises can be broken (and, as we shall see, that threats need not be carried out). But is this assumption appropriate?

It would certainly be wrong to assume that states could not *make* promises. But, as Schelling (1960) has taught us, declaring that one is committed is easy; being committed (i.e. keeping one's promise), or convincing others that one is committed, is much harder. In the dilemma game, it is in state X's interests to believe Y only when Y has no incentive to deceive X and X knows that Y has no incentive to go back on its word. However, in the PD, Y plainly does have an incentive to renege on its promise to X. An announcement by Y that it will Abate is therefore not *credible*. (Knowing this, Y is unlikely even to make such an announcement.) As Machiavelli (1947: 51), writing in 1513, advised his prince, "a wise leader cannot and should not keep his word when keeping it is not to his advantage." This is an injunction that most people obey.

In a study reviewed by Dawes and Thaler (1988), whether a person promised to play cooperate in the PD did not affect his decision actually to cooperate. However, the story told by this experiment has an added twist. As explained earlier, when *all* members promised to cooperate, the rate of cooperation did increase.

Of course, if governments were technically incapable of breaking a promise, then promises would be believed, and the ability to make a promise would have some force. But governments can break their promises. Moreover, they *do* break them when doing so is to their advantage (just as do the students in the trust game played by Glaeser *et al.* 2000). In 1959, Charles De Gaulle pledged not to negotiate with Algerian rebels until they agreed to lay down their arms, and yet began formal negotiations a year later without a cease-fire (Iklé 1967). In 1992, the British Government, led by the Conservatives, vowed to defend sterling's position in the Exchange Rate Mechanism come what may. Standing on the steps of the Treasury building in Whitehall, the Chancellor of the Exchequer, Norman Lamont, told the television cameras, "We are absolutely committed to the ERM." But only three weeks later Britain withdrew from the ERM, after the pound came under intense pressure. Currency dealers had reasoned (correctly) that the promise to defend the pound was not credible.

A more engaging example appeared in Dean Acheson's tribute to Harry Truman, published in the *New York Times* shortly after Truman's death in 1972.[11] Acheson, who was Secretary of State to President Truman, here recalls a private conversation between himself and the no-nonsense president:

On one occasion [Truman] cut me short in discussing an important presidential appointment, saying that he had already made up his mind and committed himself. When I continued to expostulate that he had not heard all the considerations he insisted that he had committed himself which, he said, ended the matter. Deciding to risk all, I suggested that it did not end the matter, since on the east front of the Capitol I had heard him commit himself to 'faithfully perform the duties of the office of the President of the United States' which surely required full hearing of the facts before making a decision. For a moment the famous Truman temper rose with his flush. Then he said calmly, 'Go ahead. You are quite right.' His final decision was the opposite of his 'commitment.'

Threats, like promises, must also be credible if they are to influence behavior. As we saw in the last chapter, when the United States lost its patience in the fur seal dispute, a bill reached the Senate floor calling for the complete destruction of the Pribilof herd in the event that Canada refused to order its sealers back to their ports. If Canada believed that the threat would be carried out, then it would almost certainly have been rational for Canada to do as the Americans asked, at least until a sealing agreement could be negotiated. However, in carrying out the threat, the United States would have hurt itself and not just Canada. Presumably, Canada could have seen through this. Presumably, too, the United States could have foreseen that Canada would reason that it would not be in the interests of the United States to carry out the threat. The threat was not credible. Perhaps this was why the bill did not pass.

---

[11] The paragraph was reprinted in *The Economist*, September 12, 1998, p. 6.

Credibility, however, is not enough. It must also be *public knowledge* that the threat is credible. In his first term in office, President Bill Clinton told the military junta in Haiti that US forces would invade the island unless the junta stepped aside and allowed the country's elected president to return to power. The threat was not believed, and Clinton dispatched planes to execute the invasion. Only then was the threat believed. President Clinton later recalled: "In Haiti I pretty much had to invade the country because [the junta] didn't believe me. When I finally had the planes in the air, they believed me and got out of there."[12]

Of course some government promises (and threats) *are* credible.[13] In many interactions states have no incentive to break a promise, and other states know this. This is sometimes true, for example, of coordination problems, discussed in the next chapter. It can also be true when interactions of the type shown in Figure 3.1 are repeated through time, as analyzed in Chapters 7 and 11, either because repetition enables one country to punish another for breaking its promise or because repetition allows countries to establish, and defend, a reputation for keeping their word. But these games are quite different from the one-shot dilemma game. In the one-shot dilemma game, a promise to play Abate is not credible.

3.13. STRATEGY

Where promises are not credible, a government may seek to alter the expectations that others have about how it will act by behaving strategically. A classical example is of the Corcyraean exiles and mercenaries who, in the fourth century BC, sailed for the island of Corcyra and, upon landing, burned their boats "so as to have no hope except in becoming masters of the country..." (Thucydides 1993).

Removing politics from the business of central banking is a more modern example. It is widely believed that independent banks are able to make monetary commitments credible, and there is some empirical support for this belief. Another example is the positioning of US armed forces in Europe during the Cold War. "When the Administration asked Congress for authority to station Army divisions in Europe in peacetime, the argument was explicitly made that these troops were there not to defend against a superior Soviet army but to leave the Soviet Union in no doubt that the United States would be automatically involved in the event of any attack on Europe" (Schelling 1966: 47). In other words, the stationing of US troops in Europe made credible the American promise to defend Western Europe in the event of a Soviet invasion.

Strategic maneuvering of this kind is prohibited by the rules of the dilemma game, though there is no reason why the potential for strategy should be ruled out in general, just as there is no reason why states should not be allowed to make promises.

Yet, simply allowing states the opportunity to behave strategically will not guarantee that the equilibrium will be altered. States may be unwilling to play a strategy that is unduly costly, and there may not exist a move that is both palatable and effective.

---

[12] *The Independent*, October 9, 1995, p. 13.
[13] To take a trivial example, in the dilemma game, the promise to Pollute is credible.

After sterling was withdrawn from the Exchange Rate Mechanism, the British government took only the tiniest of steps in the direction of independence (the Labour government has gone farther in establishing the Bank of England's independence but—and this is crucial—the changes that this government have made can be reversed as quickly as they were first adopted). The problem is that making the bank more independent means making it less democratically accountable. Similarly, the stationing of US forces in Europe did not stop the Soviet Union from erecting the Berlin Wall or from invading Hungary in 1956. In both of these cases, the Soviets calculated—rightly, it turned out—that Western commitment did not go so far as to warrant a call to arms in these instances.

A major theme of this book is that states must strategically manipulate their incentives if cooperation is to succeed. Strategy can make a difference, as was shown by the fur seal case. However, as suggested by the above example, strategy is not easy—and it cannot be relied upon to work every time.

3.14. WHALING CASE STUDY

The difficulty of making commitments and of using strategy to change incentives is nicely illustrated by the many attempts by the United States unilaterally to coerce whaling nations into conserving these great leviathans.[14]

The first legislative device intending to have this effect, the 1971 Pelly Amendment to the 1967 Fishermen's Protective Act, says that, if "the Secretary of Commerce determines that nationals of a foreign country, directly or indirectly, are conducting fishing operations [to include whaling] in a manner or under circumstances which diminish the effectiveness of an international fishery conservation program [including the International Convention for the Regulation of Whaling, or the ICRW], the Secretary of Commerce shall certify such fact to the President." Upon receipt of such certification, the Amendment adds, "the President *may* (emphasis added) direct the Secretary of the Treasury to prohibit the bringing or the importation into the United States of fish products of the offending country for such duration as he determines appropriate and to the extent that such prohibition is sanctioned by the General Agreement on Tariffs and Trade."

The credibility of the threat of trade sanctions was first tested in 1974, when Japan and the Soviet Union objected to the quotas that had been set for Antarctic minke whales by the International Whaling Commission (IWC), a body established by the ICRW. As instructed by the Pelly Amendment, the Commerce Secretary certified this behavior, but President Ford refused to order the embargo, "believing that the offending nations would abide by future IWC quotas and, more significantly, that *the embargo would harm American interests* (emphasis added)" (Ellis 1991: 440). The threat in the Pelly Amendment evidently was not credible—and that is perhaps why the amendment did not deter the Soviet Union and Japan from rejecting the IWC's quotas in the first place.

---

[14] I am drawing here from Ellis (1991).

The flaw in the Pelly Amendment is that it affords the president discretion. Potentially, the United States could secure for itself a higher payoff if the president were stripped of any discretion, for if the Soviet Union and Japan believed that the United States really would impose sanctions, then they might have obeyed the IWC decision (as we shall see later, whether the behavior of the USSR and Japan really would have been altered would also have depended on the magnitude of the punishment).

The 1979 Packwood–Magnuson Amendment to the 1976 Fishery Conservation and Management Act was intended to make up for this deficiency, to bind the president like Ulysses to the mast: "If the Secretary [of Commerce] issues a certification [that foreign nationals acted to diminish the effectiveness of the ICRW] with respect to any foreign country," the Amendment reads, "then each allocation [for fishing in US waters] ... *shall* (emphasis added) be reduced by the Secretary of State ... by not less than 50 percent." Furthermore, if certification is not terminated within a year of being issued, the Secretary of State "with respect to any allocation made to that country and in effect on such last day, *shall* (emphasis added) rescind, effective on and after the day after such last day, any harvested portion of such allocation; and may not thereafter make any allocation to that country...until the certification is terminated."

In binding the executive, the threat to impose the sanction became credible. At least this was the intention of the law. But when the Amendment was first triggered, the US executive found a way to wriggle out of its apparent commitment.

In 1982, the IWC recommended that whaling be indefinitely suspended. Japan objected to the moratorium (as did Peru, the Soviet Union, and Norway), and so should have had its quota to fish in US waters cut by the Packwood–Magnuson Amendment. But the Reagan Administration ignored its apparent statutory duty and instead offered Japan a second chance. In a bilateral agreement, the United States promised not to impose sanctions provided Japan withdrew its objection by April 1, 1985. American conservation groups sued the Secretaries of Commerce and State, and won their case in the lower court. The Supreme Court, however, reversed the lower court's ruling in 1986 by a close 5-to-4 majority. The bilateral agreement was thus allowed to stand; the Packwood–Magnuson Amendment was effectively set aside.

This was not the end of the story, however. After withdrawing its objection to the moratorium, as promised in the bilateral accord, Japan proceeded to carry out whaling for "scientific research." The IWC had rejected this rationale for whaling in 1987, but Japan objected to this decision—and so was not legally bound by it. Intent on defying the restrictions, a fleet of whaling vessels sailed from Japan in December 1987. After the first minke was killed, Secretary of Commerce Verity gave notice to President Reagan that "nationals of Japan are conducting whaling operations that diminish the effectiveness of the IWC's conservation program." The President had 60 days to act, and in April he announced that he had directed "the Secretary of State under the Packwood–Magnuson Amendment to withhold 100 percent of the fishing privileges that would otherwise be available to Japan in the US Exclusive Economic Zone." As Ellis (1991: 491) later noted, "this sounded drastic, but in fact it only eliminated 3000 metric tons of sea snails and 5000 tons of Pacific whiting." The lesson from this is clear: if threats are to alter behavior, they must be more than credible;

they must also, if carried out, harm the offending country severely. The discretionary Pelly Amendment, by the way, was not invoked in this instance. Indeed, no state has been sanctioned under the Pelly Amendment for failing to observe IWC regulations (see DeSombre 2000).

The main lesson to draw from this discussion is not so much that the Pelly and Packwood-Magnuson Amendments have been wholly impotent. The main lesson, I think, is that it isn't easy for a country to acquire commitment, even when doing so is to its advantage.

3.15. SOVEREIGNTY

If commitments cannot easily be entered into, and sovereignty is the other binding constraint, why not abolish sovereignty and install a World Government?

Technically, sovereignty can be eliminated, in much the same way that, technically, a central bank can be made independent. If the state of Massachusetts can recognize the authority of the US government in certain spheres, and the state of Kerala can recognize the authority of the government of India, then the United States and India can just as easily recognize the authority of a World Government. A World Government is feasible. That one does not exist reflects the choices that states have made. States have chosen not to be shackled by a higher authority, even though doing so could potentially remove the dilemma of international cooperation.

Why should citizens accept the authority of their national government but not that of a World Government? Put differently, why is the world configured as a collection of nation states, each having a government empowered to rule domestically, but each also accorded sovereign equality in international relations? This question is of a higher order than the ones that motivate this book, for I shall simply be taking it as given that the world is configured as a system of (interdependent) nation states. But it is easy to see that the organization of the world must itself be self-enforcing, and that what prevents global unification are the cultural differences that make the world a patchwork. In Nagel's (1991: 170) words: "The world as a whole contains cultural and national communities representing such radically diverse values that no conception of a legitimate political order can be constructed under which they could all live—a system of law backed by force that was in its basic structure acceptable to them all."

Of course, if a "legitimate" political order cannot be established, there remains the possibility of world domination. But even an "illegitimate" regime would need to be self-enforcing, and it is doubtful that it could be—especially as it would probably not be in the interests of any one country to maintain a global empire. Even in Renaissance Europe, unification was a tricky business, as Machiavelli counseled his prince:

... those states which by acquisition are joined to a hereditary possession of their conqueror are either of the same region and language or they are not. Where they are, it is very simple to keep them, especially when they have not been used to free government, and to possess them securely all that is needed is that the line of their own princes should become extinct. For in other matters, preserving their old ways and finding no difference in customs, men will live in quiet ... But when possessions are acquired in a province differing in language, customs, and laws, there are difficulties, and it takes great good luck and energy to keep them. (Machiavelli 1947: 3–4.)

3.16. INDEPENDENCE AND DOMINANCE

Suppose that one of the two players was a hegemon—unable to order the other state around, but capable of coercing it into embracing a regime of its choosing. Then, by arm-twisting or more subtle means, the hegemon could potentially coerce the other state into playing Abate. It might even enforce an outcome in which both itself and the other state played Abate. This, according to the theory of hegemonic stability, is the only means of sustaining international cooperation; at least in the theory's more extreme form, hegemonic dominance is both necessary and sufficient.[15]

But the hegemon's task is surprisingly difficult. Recall the unilateral policy of the United States, intent on punishing others for undermining the International Whaling Convention. By the rules of the treaty, signatories do not have to carry out the recommendations of the International Whaling Commission, and by the rules of international law whaling nations do not have to be parties to the treaty. So the US policy is not directed at enforcing compliance with either international law or with this specific agreement. The aim of the US policy is cruder: to coerce other nations into behaving as the *United States* would like them to behave.

Now, obviously, there is no reason to expect that an outcome that is perceived as being desirable to the United States will be good also for every other state. Environmental hegemony may not be collectively desirable. More interesting, however, is the question of whether, for good or ill, the United States is able to influence behavior abroad.

The United States certainly gets what it wants on some occasions. To get countries with large tuna fleets to protect dolphins, for example, the United States passed the International Dolphin Conservation Program Act in 1997. The law promised to lift trade restrictions against certain countries once they had ratified the Multilateral Dolphin Protection Agreement (negotiated in 1998), and so provided a strong incentive for a number of states to ratify.

However, the United States has found it remarkably difficult to alter the behavior of other states appreciably. Participation in the Dolphin Treaty remains low; many tuna-fishing states have yet to sign the agreement. And though the Pelly Amendment has been triggered more than a dozen times since 1974, sanctions have been applied only once—against Taiwan for violating its obligations under the Convention on International Trade in Endangered Species (CITES)—and even in this case the ban on imports of wildlife products was only partial.[16] The empirical record, at least as regards this particular issue, hardly endorses the claim that dominance is a sufficient condition for international cooperation.[17] Even a more comprehensive analysis of attempts by the one and only superpower to influence the behavior of others can find only limited success (DeSombre 2000).

---

[15] See Robert Keohane's (1984) description and analysis of this theory.

[16] The sanctions were lifted in 1995. See Jenkins (1996).

[17] See, however, Charnovitz (1994), who reckons that the Pelly Amendment may have influenced state behavior in some instances, even ignoring the Taiwan case.

Dominance is not necessary for cooperation either. All the parties to the North Pacific Fur Seal Treaty—the United States, Russia, Japan, and Great Britain (acting on behalf of Canada)—were great powers in 1911. Within this group there was no obvious hegemon. And yet the agreement succeeded in conserving the fur seal.

As Keohane (1984) has convincingly demonstrated, the reasons for international cooperation are not to be found in the theory of hegemonic stability. Coercion may be attempted. It may even succeed on occasion. So the theory of international cooperation should be capable of incorporating a hegemon. But the theory should not assume that a hegemon has both the wherewithal and the incentive to sustain cooperative outcomes under any and all circumstances. Nor should it assume that other countries will necessarily defer to the hegemon. Assertiveness by a dominant nation, and deference by others, are behaviors that the theory of international cooperation should explain rather than assume.

3.17. PREFERENCES AND INTERESTS

The dilemma game assumes that states have preferences over their own payoffs only, and do not care one way or the other about the consequences for other countries. Put differently, the dilemma game assumes that the preferences of a state coincide with its interests. Like the assumptions about commitment and sovereignty, this assumption about state preferences is partly responsible for the dilemma. But is the assumption reasonable?

It is certainly broadly consistent with the real world of international affairs. For example, when Secretary of State Warren Christopher urged President Clinton to submit the United Nations Convention on the Law of the Sea and its associated Agreement to the US Senate for its "advice and consent," he made a point of noting that "the interested Federal agencies and departments of the United States have unanimously concluded that our interests would be best served by the United States becoming a Party to the Convention and the Agreement." Two weeks later, the president wrote to the Senate, urging senators to ratify the agreement on the basis that it "advances the interests of the United States," both as a global maritime power and as a coastal state.

Political theorists of the "neoliberal" brand also equate a state's preferences with its self-interest. "Realists," however, contend that states care mainly about their survival and independence. To realists, states have preferences over payoff differences, not absolute levels.[18]

To contrast these opposing theories, suppose that the absolute payoffs of the game are as depicted in Figure 3.1 but that each country's preferences are over the *difference* between its own payoff and its rival's, and only over this difference.[19] Recasting

---

[18] See, for example, Stein (1990), Grieco (1990), and Milner (1992).

[19] Grieco (1990) specifies utility as an additive function of both absolute gains and the difference in gains. Under this set-up, state behavior will depend on the weights attached to these constituent elements. Here I take a rather extreme view of realism, and assume that states care only about the difference in gains.

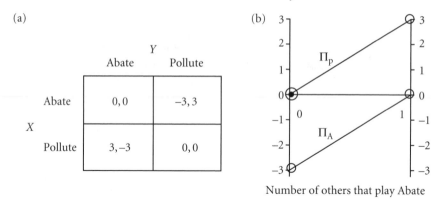

Figure 3.3. *The realist's dilemma game*

the payoffs as differences, we obtain the game shown in Figure 3.3. It can be seen immediately that if the players have preferences over their payoff differences, then the dilemma disappears. This is not because the dilemma has been removed but rather because, given the preference relation assumed by the theory, the dilemma was never there. If preferences are over differences in absolute payoffs, then dilemmas of the type we have been examining simply do not exist. Realists contend that countries " … often fail to cooperate even when they have common interests" (Grieco 1990: 4). But their assumptions really lead to the conclusion that states fail to cooperate because they do not have common interests. To realists, all games are zero sum.

Of course, some games *are* zero sum—the lost wallet, two-thirds, and dictator games being only three examples. Zero sum games are also common in the real world. In 1997, a deal was negotiated in Kyoto between the members of the European Union and over twenty other so-called "Annex I" countries. The European Union as a whole agreed to reduce its emissions of greenhouse gases by eight percent relative to the 1990 level, and the other Annex I countries also agreed to cap their emissions. Later, the European Union had to negotiate emission levels for each member state— percentage changes that would add up to the required eight percent overall reduction. The latter negotiation was a zero sum game. The negotiation would not affect environmental benefits for any country, since the aggregate emission level had already been chosen. It would only determine costs. If one member state accepted an emission ceiling that was one ton smaller, another could emit a ton more.[20] In a zero sum game, for every gain there is a loss, and for every loss a gain.

To interpret *every* interaction as a zero sum game, however, is to misunderstand the problem of cooperation. All the sealing nations gained from the Fur Seal Treaty, and every nation in the world has benefited from protection of the ozone layer. Kyoto was also negotiated with the expectation that every state could gain.

[20] To be precise, the game is zero sum provided that the emission reductions are achieved at overall minimum cost. The game of allocating entitlements to pollute is zero sum, once the total quantity of entitlements has been fixed, assuming that trading will equalize marginal abatement costs for all countries.

In Chapters 8 and 15, respectively, I shall provide estimates of the magnitude of the gains for ozone layer protection and global climate change mitigation.

There is yet another way of looking at this. To say that your country prefers outcomes which yield a lower payoff for others, holding fixed your country's own payoff, is really to say that your country takes pleasure in the suffering of others. Certainly, a "deviant" state may have preferences of this kind. But Schelling (1966: 2) argues—rightly, I think—that even in war, hurting is typically inflicted in order to coerce the harmed party into acting in a way which yields some advantage to the party causing the harm: "To inflict suffering gains nothing and saves nothing directly; it can only make people behave to avoid it. The only purpose, unless sport or revenge, must be to influence somebody's behavior, to coerce his decision or choice."

More fundamentally, preferences over payoff differences are incompatible with the concept of a transnational externality. By definition an externality arises where the action of one party affects the set of outcomes attainable by another, and where this effect is *not* taken into account by the party undertaking the action.

3.18. PREFERENCES AND MORALS

In contrast to political realists, some moral theorists argue that states ought to have positive regard for the well-being of others. Kant's Categorical Imperative, for example, enjoins us to "act only on that maxim through which you can at the same time will that it shall become a universal law." If one universalized the principle that states ought to pursue their own interests, regardless of the consequences for others, then as the dilemma game has taught us the consequence may be that every state's interests are harmed. Hence, this reasoning suggests that it would be inconsistent for states which care only about self-interest to wish to universalize the pursuit of self-interest.

But if Kantian states cannot endorse self-interest, what would they will to be a universal law? One possibility is that states may give emphasis to the act of cooperating rather than to the consequence. There is strong evidence showing that some people cooperate (play Abate, hand in their red cards) simply because they think it is the right thing to do. Moreover, and as explained earlier, public discussion of this motive (sometimes called "impure altruism") can promote cooperation by others (Dawes and Thaler 1988).

Kantian states might also follow Rawls (1972) and choose to play Abate or Pollute for the purpose of maximizing the lowest payoff received by any party. In the case of the dilemma game, application of the maximin rule yields the transformation shown in Figure 3.4. Here, there are two Nash equilibria.[21] Unlike the dilemma game, one of these is the Pareto efficient outcome (Abate, Abate).[22] Kantian states would want to coordinate on this outcome.

It happens that in this game coordination can be achieved provided the players can communicate before the game is played (recall that pre-play communication has no

---

[21] These are Nash equilibria in pure strategies. There also exists a mixed strategy equilibrium.

[22] Also unlike the dilemma game, there exists only one Pareto efficient outcome; in the dilemma game there exit three such outcomes, (Abate, Abate), (Abate, Pollute), and (Pollute, Abate).

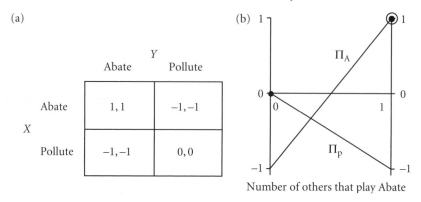

Figure 3.4. *Kantian transformation of the dilemma game*

effect on the equilibrium in the dilemma game, at least not from an analytical perspective). If country X intended to play Abate, then it would like Y to play Abate, and would urge Y to do so during the pre-play communication round. If, however, X intended to play Pollute, then it would prefer that Y play Pollute, and would communicate this to Y. Hence, pre-play communication would convey real information about each player's intentions. Once these intentions were known, each player could do no better than to play Abate.

However, the morality of choice in this game is not trivial when states care about *consequences*. How should a Kantian respond to a state that plays Abate? If the Kantian disregarded the consequences of its decision for itself, it would play Abate. However, if universality were interpreted to mean that the Kantian state should have regard for its own payoff as well as for the other player's, then these individual payoffs would be given by Figure 3.1, not Figure 3.4. If the Kantian state plays Pollute, its own payoff is higher and the other state's lower than if it played Abate. To the consequentialist, knowing which choice is morally superior requires a comparison of the worth of the gain to one state with the worth of the loss to the other (see Hardin 1988; Binmore 1994).[23] This thinking commends a utilitarian ethic.

Even if we accepted Kantian ethics, however, implementation of the Kantian solution would be infeasible unless states *were* Kantian. Yet, if states were Kantian, their interests would be consonant and international relations would be characterized by harmony rather than conflict. The problem of international cooperation would not exist.

Given that states are not Kantian, it is sometimes argued that parties may choose to *become* Kantian, if only because in being Kantian they can achieve the Pareto efficient outcome (Sen 1987). States may then elect to play Abate recognizing that, in Amartya Sen's (1987: 86) words, doing so "is better for the respective goals of all of us." As was explained earlier, when individuals identify with a group's collective welfare, cooperation can be increased. However, moral injunctions cannot be relied

---

[23] I should emphasize that I have tried here to isolate a moral problem. We shall see later that, in different situations, a state may act to advance its own interests and yet still satisfy moral principles.

upon to influence everyone, particularly in games like the PD in which there is a strong incentive not to cooperate. Furthermore, no player can commit to obeying a preference relation other than its own, just as no player can commit to a course of action that conflicts with its own interests.

Admittedly, it is extreme to assume that a state's preferences coincide *precisely* with its interests. For example, suppose that the payoffs to country X in Figure 3.1 are in dollar units while the payoffs to Y are in billions of dollars. The dilemma would still be there. But the moral implications would be very different. If X were to forego \$1 by playing Abate, Y would gain \$2 billion. To make the asymmetry even starker, suppose that X is rich and Y destitute. Would X really pass up the chance to enrich Y at next to no cost to itself? It would if it did not care at all about Y's utility, as the assumption that preferences coincide with self-interest implies. But we might suppose that X has a heart, and would sympathize with Emmerich de Vattel, the eighteenth century Swiss legal scholar, who argued that, while "in general, duties toward self prevail over duties towards others; ... this is only to be understood of duties which bear some proportion to one another. ... What idea should we have of a prince, or of a nation, who would refuse to yield the smallest advantage in order to gain for the world the inestimable blessing of peace?"[24]

If the situation described by Vattel were common to all problems of international relations, then the assumption that states have no regard at all for the well-being of others would be objectionable. It might be more reasonable to suppose that states had the preferences of a "minimal altruist" or what Kindleberger (1986) calls the "cheap Samaritan," and would behave in the manner commended by Vattel. However, the situations of interest to this book are not of this type. To provide international public goods will usually require more than cheap Samaritans.

In my formal analysis, I shall assume that a state's preferences coincide precisely with its interests, even though we know that behavior is more complicated than this. I make this assumption not because it is consistent with actual behavior. I make it because it allows the theory to produce sharp results. To show that countries can sustain at least partial cooperation even when they care only about self-interest is to show something significant. Of course, the theory would be equally sharp if we assumed that all states were, say, global utilitarians. But if this were the case, then the dilemma of international cooperation would not exist and nor would transnational externalities exist either. Any assumption about preferences between these extremes will produce a conflict between a state's nationalistic preferences and any impartial global preferences it may have (see Nagel 1991). (In situations like the one posed by Vattel the conflict should not be taken too seriously but in most situations it would need to be.) The assumption would inevitably be arbitrary.[25]

---

[24] From Vattel's *The Law of Nations or the Principles of Natural Law Applied to the Conduct and to the Affairs of Nations and of Sovereigns*, as quoted in Linklater (1990: 85).

[25] Alternatively, it might be assumed that states have preferences over the *equity* of a particular outcome—that is, the relative payoff they get—as well as the absolute payoff. Bolton and Ockenfels (2000) show that, with these preferences, there may exist multiple equilibria. It might be that no one will cooperate.

3.19. FULL COOPERATION AND SIDE PAYMENTS

Suppose that the constraint of self-enforcement did not bite—that, for the game described by Figure 3.1, any feasible outcome could be sustained by countries X and Y. Which outcome would they choose? Though the outcome (Abate, Abate) is strictly preferred by both players to the Nash equilibrium (Pollute, Pollute), the outcomes (Abate, Pollute) and (Pollute, Abate) are also Pareto efficient. So the answer is not obvious.

However, we can shrink the set of jointly preferred outcomes by allowing the countries that gain to compensate the losers. Such "side payments," as game theorists call them, need not be monetary (in the fur seal case, seal skins were exchanged). Cash payments are often paid, however (even in the fur seal case, money was exchanged), and it will usually be convenient to assume that side payments are paid in money.

To introduce money side payments, however, requires a further assumption: that each player's utility for money be linear (in the range of potential payoffs for the game). Suppose that, for every outcome of a game, each player can identify an amount of money such that this player would be indifferent between having this outcome and having this amount of money. Then, if utility were linear in money, and if appropriate utility scales were chosen for the players, the payoffs to both countries could be interpreted as money, and this money could be redistributed such that what appears as a gain for one party appears as a loss for the other, with the aggregate amount of money being constant.[26] Notice that under these assumptions we need not assume that an extra dollar is worth the same to X as to Y; we do not need to make international comparisons of utility to allow side payments (e.g. see, Luce and Raiffa 1957). If \$1 is transferred from X to Y, then we need only record that X loses \$1 worth of X-utility (measured in dollars) and that Y gains \$1 worth of Y-utility (measured in dollars).

If countries cooperate fully, and if side payments are allowed, then it is reasonable to assume that countries will seek to maximize their joint payoffs—and so will choose the full cooperative outcome over every other feasible outcome, as long as the constraint of self-enforcement can be ignored. In the dilemma game shown in Figure 3.1(a), the full cooperative outcome is (Abate, Abate). In Figure 3.1(b), this outcome is indicated by the open dot.

In this particular case, side payments would not actually be paid, because the full cooperative outcome is symmetric, and so are the two players. Consider, however, the version of the dilemma game shown in Figure 3.5. Here again, the players are symmetric. But the two full cooperative outcomes—(Pollute, Abate) and (Abate,

---

Or it might be that some countries will cooperate while others defect. Preferences of this kind are consistent with the behavior observed in actual experiments (see also the related approach of Fehr and Schmidt, 1999). But the predictions of these models are highly sensitive to the assumptions about preferences.

[26] To assume that utility is linear in money is to assume that the marginal utility for money is constant or, equivalently, that the elasticity of the marginal utility of consumption is zero. A recent review of the empirical evidence (Arrow *et al.* 1996) concludes that the elasticity of the marginal utility of consumption is positive and lies in the range 0.8–2.5. When an externality has a non-marginal effect on an economy, the assumption of linear utility should not be invoked lightly.

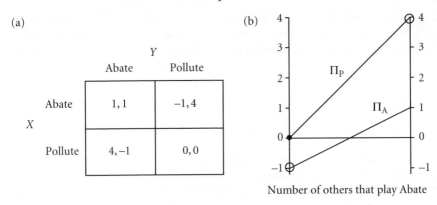

Figure 3.5. *Dilemma game 2*

Pollute)—are asymmetric, and choice of either would give the player required to play Abate a lower payoff than it could guarantee for itself by playing Pollute. In this case, side payments would be needed to ensure that the full cooperative outcome was acceptable to the two countries (of course, the problem of *sustaining* this agreement would still remain).

Consider a different example. Suppose ten students play the following sequential game known as the centipede game. The first student must choose between stopping the game or passing. If she stops the game she gets $10 and the other students get nothing. If she passes, she gets nothing and the $10 is passed to the second player. This second player can then either stop the game, in which case he would get $20 and the other students would get nothing, or pass. If he passes, the third player can get $30 by stopping the game or she can pass to the next player, and so on. There is a strong incentive in this game for the first player to stop the game and claim her $10. However, the aggregate payoff to the class is maximized if every student but the last passes.

If the students could negotiate an agreement, they would likely require that the first nine students pass, and that the total award of $100 be divided evenly among all the players. This way, each player would get $10. The $10 payment is compelling from three perspectives. First, it gives the first player what she could guarantee for herself by not participating in the agreement. Second, it gives all the other players more than they could guarantee for themselves by not having the agreement. Third, it gives all the players the same amount—an outcome that is especially appealing if there was no real reason why one student should be so lucky as to be chosen to go first. Notice, however, that side payments are only a necessary condition for ensuring that full cooperation is actually realized. The agreement must also be enforced. Without enforcement, the second player would have an incentive to stop the game and take $20. Moreover, the first player could anticipate that the second player would behave this way, and so she would be likely to stop the game and take $10.

Side payments are featured in Chapter 13. As suggested by these examples, we shall find that side payments can help to sustain cooperation when the underlying game is asymmetric (and only when it is asymmetric). Indeed, we shall find that side payments are especially helpful when the underlying game is *strongly* asymmetric. However, we shall also find that side payments can offer only limited help in promoting cooperation. The real challenge to international cooperation is not ensuring that everyone gains from an agreement. The real challenge is deterring free-riding.

3.20. THE *N*-PLAYER DILEMMA

The PD considered thus far involves two parties who must choose between two possible actions. Some situations of interest do involve only two countries, and we have already considered a number of such examples in this chapter. Some also involve binary choices, such as the choice of whether or not to carry out above ground testing of nuclear weapons. But most real situations involve more than two countries. Most also involve continuous choices. Global climate change, for example, is a game played by all countries and where the important choice variable is not whether to abate but by *how much* to abate.

Despite the obvious limitations of 2×2 games, international relations theorists rely on them to a remarkable extent. This may be because more complex games are technically harder to analyze, but Stein (1990) has argued that most international relations really are of the 2×2 type.[27] Simplifying is sometimes necessary. It can even be illuminating. However, the cost of simplifying must be acknowledged. Most international relations are not of the 2×2 type. Cooperation can be, and frequently is, partial—as the examples of the Helsinki and Oslo Protocols demonstrate. They also involve *at least* two countries. In some cases, as in the global treaties, they involve almost 200 countries. Analysis of 2×2 games had a certain logic during the Cold War when the concern was with superpower games of nuclear strikes. However, they are not suited to understanding contemporary problems of international relations, including trade, public health, and the fight against terrorism, not to mention environmental issues.

The reason I have begun by analyzing 2×2 games is simply to root my theory in familiar territory. What I shall show in this book is that it is relatively easy to extend the analysis of 2×2 games to continuous choices, a wider variety of strategies, repeated play, and many players. The only chapter in which the algebra gets at all complicated (in the sense of being messy, not difficult) is Chapter 13, and the reason is the assumption of asymmetry. As long as we can retain the assumption of symmetry, a lot can be learned from very simple analysis. Indeed, a lot can be learned from

---

[27] "Most basically," Stein (1990: 3–4) argues, "nations choose between cooperation and conflict, and such situations underlie the entire range of international relations from alliances to war." Later in his book, Stein (1990: 13) maintains that, "Like marriage, wars and alliances presuppose the existence of two interacting parties."

diagrams. Though many choices are continuous, there is one choice, a central focus of this book, that is binary. This is the choice of whether to be a party or a non-party to a treaty. The formal analysis of games in these richer environments begins in Chapter 7. Below, I simply extend my analysis of the one shot 2×2 game in just one dimension, by increasing the number of players.

Suppose, then, that there are N players ($N \geq 2$), that each has the same (linear) payoff function, and that each faces a binary choice of either polluting or abating. If a country pollutes, its payoff is Π_P; if it abates, it gets Π_A. Let z be the number of *other* countries that play Abate. The payoffs can then be written as

$$\Pi_P = a_P + b_P z, \qquad \Pi_A = a_A + b_A z, \qquad (3.1)$$

where a_P, b_P, a_A, and b_A are parameters. Setting $N = 2$, we see that the payoffs for the figures we have considered thus far depend on the parameter values in eqn (3.1).[28] For example, the dilemma game shown in Figure 3.1 is obtained by setting $a_P = 0$, $b_P = 2$, $a_A = -1$, $b_A = 2$.

Different versions of the situations we have considered thus far are drawn in Figure 3.6. Here, for concreteness, I assume $N = 100$. Thus, from the point of view of any player, there are 99 other players. The number of these other players that play Abate is shown on the horizontal axes of these figures. Obviously, the details of the figures depend on the parameter values that are chosen.[29] However, what is of interest to us here is more the general pattern than the details.

Figure 3.6(a) is a version of the dilemma game played by 100 countries. Irrespective of what the other players do, each country can do no better than to pollute. That this is so is indicated by the Π_P curve lying everywhere above the Π_A curve (just as in Figure 3.1(b)). The unique equilibrium is where all countries pollute, with each receiving a payoff of 0. The outcome which maximizes aggregate welfare is where all countries abate, with each receiving a payoff of 1. That the two payoff curves are parallel implies that the benefit of one more country playing Abate is precisely the same for every country. But this is not really important. It is more important that the curves do not cross. This makes play Pollute a dominant strategy.

Figure 3.6(b) is identical to 3.6(a) in that play Pollute is a dominant strategy. However, here, the equilibrium is efficient. An agreement requiring that every country play Abate would make every country worse off.

Figure 3.6(c) is the reverse of the dilemma game and is analogous to the 2×2 game depicted in Figure 3.2(b). In Figure 3.6(c), play Abate is a dominant strategy.

---

[28] I have normalized the payoffs such that each player gets a payoff of zero if no country plays Abate. This merely simplifies the mathematics. Notice that the payoffs corresponding to the figures shown earlier may also be compatible with non-linear payoff functions.

[29] The chosen parameter values in Figure 3.6 are as follows: in Figure 3.6(a), $a_P = 0$, $b_P = b_A = 2/99$, $a_A = -1$; in Figure 3.6(b), $a_P = 0$, $b_P = 2/99$, $a_A = -3$, $b_A = 2/99$; and in Figure 3.6(c), $a_P = 0$, $b_P = b_A = 1/99$, $a_A = 1$. Figure 3.6 (d) is discussed below.

Full cooperation requires that every country play Abate, but every country has a unilateral incentive to do so. Once again, no agreement is needed.

Of course, for all of these situations, it is not essential that the payoff curves be parallel. It only matters that they do not cross. We shall consider situations in which payoff curves cross in the next chapter.

Figure 3.6(d) depicts a PD in quadratic payoffs.[30] The important difference between this figure and Figure 3.6(a) is that full cooperation requires that 67 out of 100 countries play Abate. This figure is analogous to the game shown in Figure 3.5. The players are symmetric, but full cooperation requires that they behave asymmetrically.

Our primary concern is with situations in which unilateral behavior sustains inefficient outcomes. Plainly, the games described by Figure 3.6(b) and (c) are of no

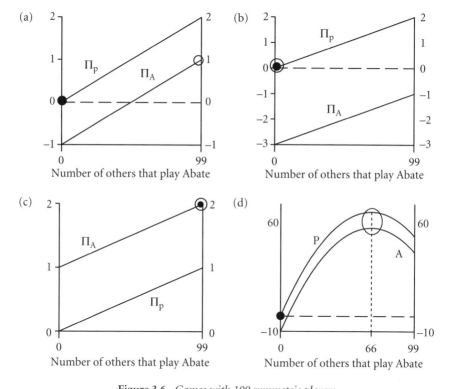

Figure 3.6. *Games with 100 symmetric players*
(a) 100-player prisoners' dilemma, (b) 100-player non-dilemma
(c) 100-player non-dilemma 2 (d) 100-player quadratic prisoner's dilemma

---

[30] To be specific, Figure 3.6(d) adds a quadratic term to eqn (3.1), yielding
$$\Pi_P = a_P + b_P z + c_P z^2, \quad \Pi_A = a_A + b_A z + c_A z^2,$$
where in the figure, $a_P = 0$, $b_P = b_A = 2$, $a_A = -10$, $c_P = c_A = -0.015$.

interest in this regard. Figures 3.6(a) and (d) are different. They describe situations in which unilateralism can be expected to make us all worse off compared to the potential of cooperation.

3.21. CONCLUSIONS

The prisoners' dilemma (PD) is a game of mixed motives. It describes a situation in which each of the players wants not to cooperate, but in which each also recognizes that if every player did that, the result would be bad all round. So, while the PD explains why unilateralism fails, it also explains why countries want multilateralism to succeed. As an approximation, the prisoners' dilemma describes the most difficult of all international cooperation problems, including global climate change. If this were an easy problem to solve, countries wouldn't have agonized over how to address it for the last decade.

Are the assumptions that underlie the analysis of the PD compatible with real behavior? The short answer is No. Real behavior is more varied than analytical game theory supposes. In this chapter I have tried to show that limited cooperation can occur even in situations when analytical game theory predicts that it will not. However, I have also shown that full cooperation is just one of two attractors, the other being free-riding. If free-riding is not as inevitable as the analytics supposes, it is also rarely if ever crushed. Usually it is the stronger of the two attractors.

PD-like games are common at all levels, and the incentive to cooperate has led to the creation of some ingenious institutions. Foremost among these is the nation state itself. The first obligation of the state is to defend its citizens from invasion. National defense is a public good, and the state uses its very visible hand to supply it. Most noticeably, it uses conscription in times of war (in some countries, even in times of peace). It also taxes the citizenry, to pay for their defense. Conscription is not a voluntary activity, and nor is paying taxes. If you decline to serve your country, or to pay your share of the tax burden, you are likely to be thrown in jail. Volunteerism may suffice to supply some public goods, but if it were dependable under any and all circumstances we would use it to supply the most important of all public goods, defense. That we do not suggests that free-riding is a very big problem.

Free-riding is especially problematic at the international level, where strong-arm solutions are not available. This is by mutual agreement. The citizens of a country bestow upon their government the authority to levy taxes and to draft soldiers. But states have not endowed a global government with anywhere near this kind of authority. This may be for good reason. But there is a price to pay. The provision of global public goods like climate change mitigation must rely on a kind of volunteerism. International cooperation may occasionally succeed but it would be a mistake to think that we can remedy every international environmental problem by this means when we consciously avoid using the same approach to supply important national public goods. And yet, as the example of the Fur Seal Treaty illustrates, international cooperation can, sometimes, succeed.

Actually, international cooperation succeeds fairly often for games that are unlike the PD—for problems not requiring enforcement. These kinds of problems, among others, are discussed in the next chapter.

4

Games with Multiple Equilibria

Trust is not a commodity in abundant supply among diplomats. Henry Kissinger, Diplomacy (1994)

4.1. INTRODUCTION

The students who play the card game discussed in Chapter 1 have a strong incentive to hold on to their red cards. This incentive is derived from the payoffs of the prisoners' dilemma (PD).

Imagine now a different card game, called *majority* 1 (or M1 for short). The mechanics of this game are the same as for the game described in Chapter 1: each student is given a red and a black card and is required to hand back one of these without anyone else knowing which card was handed in. What distinguishes this game from the PD are its payoffs. In this new game, each student gets $20 if she hands in her red card. If she keeps her red card (and so hands in her black card) she gets $0 provided a minority of students hand in a red card and she gets $30 if a majority of students hand in a red card (to avoid a tie, assume that there are an odd number of students). Suppose there are 35 students in the class. Then the equilibrium of this game will require that 18 students hand in their red cards, getting $20 each, and that 17 hand in their black cards, getting $30 each. The equilibrium would probably not be reached the first time the game is played, but in contrast to the game described in Chapter 1, it is likely that behavior will converge towards the equilibrium pretty quickly. This is because in this game there does not exist a tension between a player's individual interests and the group's collective interests; the equilibrium is efficient.

Like the PD, it appears that M1 has a unique equilibrium. However, the equilibrium of this game is unique only in terms of the *number* of students who keep or hand in their red cards. The equilibrium is not unique as regards the *identities* of the students who hand in or keep their red cards. If identities matter, there is a much large number of equilibria.

Moreover, though the equilibria of M1 are efficient, there may still exist a tension of sorts between the students who hand in their red cards and get $20 and the students who keep their red cards and get $30. The equilibrium attained in any play of the game may not seem fair. Why should some students get more money than others?

Now consider a different majority game, called M2. Again, the mechanics are the same as before. But now every student gets $10 for keeping the same card that the majority of students keep (and assume again that there are an odd number of students) and nothing for keeping the other card. It is certain (given that there are an odd number of students) that a majority of students will keep either their red cards or their black cards in a first round of play. It is likely (but not certain), however, that at least one student—and possibly many more—will be in a minority. This situation is not an equilibrium. If the cards were returned, and the students were allowed to play again, my guess is that they would all hand in the same card as did the majority in the first round—the play in the earlier round serving as a focal point for the second round. But even if they did not all hand back the same card as the majority did in the first round, we can be pretty sure that the students would quickly converge to a situation in which they all handed in the same color card. Again, one reason for this is that there is no conflict between a student's individual interests and the collective interests of the group.

M2 is a little like the two-thirds game discussed in Section 3.4. However, there is one important difference. In the two-thirds game, there is a unique equilibrium in which everyone guesses zero. In M2, there are *two* equilibria.[1] In one, everyone keeps her red card. In the other, all red cards are handed in.

Moreover, and in contrast to M1 and the PD, the equilibria of M2 are particularly compelling. They are not only efficient but fair. In M2, everyone receives the same payoff in either equilibrium.

This chapter considers games like these majority games: games for which there exist a multiple of equilibria. A common feature of these games is that the players do not have a dominant strategy. What it is best for each player to do depends on what he thinks others will do. This is very different from the PD. It happens that in the two majority games all the equilibria were efficient. However, this will not be true of the games studied in the rest of this chapter.

Though some games of transnational environmental policy happen to be like the majority games, the main reason for studying games with multiple equilibria is that a treaty may be able to change the rules of the game, transforming a PD game into a game more akin to the two majority games. I shall explain how a treaty can do this, and why countries should want to do this, in later chapters.

4.2. ALLOCATION GAMES

Virtually all treaty negotiations have a multiple of equilibria as regards the agreed allocation of resources.

In the Fur Seal Treaty negotiations, the parties had a strong incentive to ban pelagic sealing. Given the enforcement powers of the treaty, the pelagic sealing ban maximized the aggregate gain to all parties, and so could make every party better off as compared with a treaty that secured a smaller aggregate gain. To settle for anything other than a ban would essentially mean leaving money on the negotiating table—something that would be collectively wasteful. The sealing nations also had a strong incentive to allocate the aggregate gain among themselves in such a way that no party (or coalition of parties) could do better by walking away from the treaty. Again, the parties had a collective

---

[1] That is, there are two equilibria in pure strategies. There also exists an equilibrium in mixed strategies. In this equilibrium, each student hands in a black (red) card with probability one-half. The distinction between pure and mixed strategies is explained later in this chapter.

incentive to sustain full participation. However, as explained in Section 2.10.2, it is likely that the land kill could have been allocated in a number of ways, and still deterred non-participation. That is, the 15 percent share of sealskins given by the United States to Britain and Japan was not an inevitable feature of the negotiation. A 14 or 16 percent share—perhaps even a 20 percent share—would probably have been acceptable.

In the early 1990s, the European Community contemplated establishing a common carbon tax as a means of reducing greenhouse gas emissions. It was widely known that such a tax would prove much more costly for some member states than for others, and I was asked to prepare a simple analysis of this negotiation for the European Commission (Barrett 1992*d*). The formula I used in this analysis (the Shapley value from cooperative game theory) has a number of desirable properties. It gives a unique solution, and for this particular negotiation the solution not only made each country better off as compared with what it could get by walking away from the treaty; it also made each *coalition* of countries better off (technically speaking, the solution lay within the *core* of the game). However, it turned out that a number of allocations satisfied this last property (that is, the core was large), and though the calculated allocation was unique, it was not particularly compelling. It did not seem the kind of allocation on which real negotiators were likely to agree.

Curious about how actual people would negotiate this problem, I constructed a negotiation game based on this model (Barrett 1996), and organized a number of negotiations, both with students and real diplomats. The result: almost always, the parties negotiated an allocation that lay in the core. However, never was the agreed allocation equal to or even particularly close to the value calculated in my earlier study. Different negotiating teams settled on different final allocations. However, one allocation was agreed by several negotiating teams. This allocation reflected a compelling focal point in the negotiation. As explained in Chapter 2, the 15 percent allocation of seal skins in the Fur Seal Treaty was arrived at by a similar means.

Though much energy is expended in negotiating allocations—that is, in dividing up the pie—this aspect of negotiation should not be of prime importance. It is more important that a treaty be able to promote participation, enforce compliance, and stop leakage. Unless a treaty can do these things, there will be no pie for the parties to divide.

This, I think, should be the main lesson of the real European carbon tax negotiations. As will be discussed in more detail in Chapter 15, the tax was eventually abandoned—but not because of a failure to agree on a system of transfers. The tax was abandoned because it would have yielded little environmental benefit unless adopted by other countries.

4.3. CHICKEN: A DIFFERENT KIND OF DILEMMA

Figure 4.1 describes a game different from the PD—a game known as *chicken*.[2] Given that player *X* plays Pollute, player *Y* can do no better than to play Abate. However, if

---

[2] The game derives its name from the following narrative (Binmore 1992: 282–3):

The usual story that goes with Chicken concerns teenage virility rites. However, its strategic structure would seem equally well to represent the game played in grim earnest by middle-aged businessmen whose

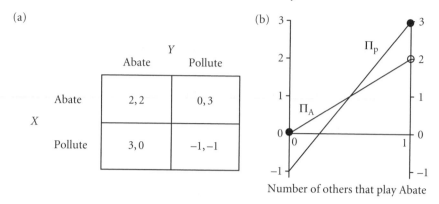

Figure 4.1. *Chicken game*

X were to play Abate, Y would play Pollute. In contrast to the PD, this game has *two* equilibria (in pure strategies), (Pollute, Abate) and (Abate, Pollute), and neither of these equilibria is Pareto-dominated. Starting from either of these equilibria, a move to the outcome (Abate, Abate) would make one of the players worse off. At the same time, the aggregate payoff in this game is highest when both players play Abate.

You may have noticed the similarity between this game and the M1 game discussed in Section 4.1; in both games, different players choose different actions in equilibrium. However, the equilibrium of chicken (or at least this version of chicken) does not maximize the aggregate payoff. This was not true of M1.

Note as well that if the chicken game were played sequentially, then there would exist a *unique* equilibrium (the same would also be true of M1). However, the equilibrium would depend on *which* player moved first. If X could move first, it would play Pollute. This is because X could reason backwards. It could see that, if it played Pollute, then Y would play Abate. Having the "first mover advantage" plainly allows X to realize its best possible payoff. As Schelling (1966: 117–118) has imaginatively put it, "The lady who pushes her child's stroller across an intersection in front of a car that has already come to a dead stop is in no particular danger as long as she sees the driver watching her: even if the driver prefers not to give her the right of way she has the winning tactic and gets no score on nerve." Of course, if the tables were turned and country Y could move first, then Y would also play Pollute, knowing that X would play Abate subsequently. In Schelling's example, if the car were moving and the driver did not meet the lady's gaze, then the stroller would likely remain on the

---

cars approach one another at speed along city streets that are too narrow for the cars to pass safely unless at least one driver slows down. If one player chickens out by slowing while the other continues to speed, the player who slows loses self-esteem and the other gains. If both slow, their initial levels of self-esteem remain unchanged. If neither slows, the consequences are unpleasant for both.

Notice that, in the game shown in Figure 4.1, full cooperation requires that both players play Abate. As suggested by the classical representation of the chicken game, this is not an essential feature of this game. However, it will prove important to later sections of this book.

sidewalk. To repeat, while sequential play of this game yields a unique equilibrium, the equilibrium actually reached depends on the order of play. This is not true of the PD.

Since the players can gain by moving first, each might try to pre-empt the other. For example, each player may tell the other player that it really will play Pollute, no matter what the other player does. Of course, in a game of complete information, the rhetoric of announcing an intention to play Pollute would have no effect. But if *X*'s payoffs were not known with certainty by *Y*, then *X* might be able to take actions that made *Y* *believe* that *X* really would play Pollute, no matter how *Y* chose (of course, *Y* would have a similar incentive if its payoffs were not known with certainty by *X*).

Negotiation games often do involve parties making threats with the intention of forcing the other side to back down. At the climate change negotiations held in The Hague in November 2000, the United States insisted on a flexible interpretation for the purpose of lowering the cost of participating, while Europe demanded a more rigid interpretation for the sake of the treaty's environmental integrity. In Bodansky's (2001: 48) words, "countries played a game of chicken, hoping that others would relent first." At least one side miscalculated, however, and by the time compromise proposals were offered, "there was insufficient time even to understand what others were suggesting, let alone engage in genuine negotiation" (Bodansky 2001: 48). A new negotiating session thus had to be scheduled. But before the parties could meet again, the new US President, George W. Bush, declared that the United States would not even play this game. Flexible or not, he was not interested in having the United States participate in the Kyoto Protocol. Somewhat ironically, at the next round of talks, Europe made substantial concessions on the issue of flexibility in order to secure the participation of countries like Japan, Canada, and Russia.

Chicken also creates incentives for parties to behave strategically. A country may want to make an irreversible investment in a preliminary round of play for the purpose of changing its payoffs in the chicken game, making play Pollute a dominant strategy. Plainly, maneuvering of this kind could diminish the aggregate payoff available to the two players. Far from creating incentives for countries to take "early action" to reduce their pollution emissions, chicken if anything creates incentives for countries to dig in their heels. The Rhine Chlorides case, discussed in Chapter 5, gives a real-world example of how decisions taken in a preliminary stage of a game may shape behavior in a subsequent stage—in this case, to the harm of the environment.

4.4. MIXED STRATEGIES

There is actually a third equilibrium to the chicken game—and one that is especially compelling because of its symmetry. In this equilibrium, countries play *mixed strategies*. Each country does not simply play Abate or Pollute (these are *pure* strategies); each rather plays Abate (and thus Pollute) with some probability. In the mixed strategy equilibrium of the game shown in Figure 4.1, each player plays Abate with probability one-half, yielding each player an *expected* payoff of 1 (see Appendix 4.1). The intuition is that, when the players move simultaneously, each is uncertain as to the strategy that will be chosen by the other player. This uncertainty is represented by a probability distribution over the other player's pure strategies (Binmore and Dasgupta 1986). In equilibrium, each player plays Abate with the same probability that the other player expects it to play Abate.

Think of a baseball game. Suppose that the pitcher has two different pitches he can throw—fast balls and change-ups. If the batter knew how the pitcher would throw next, he would adjust his batting accordingly, swinging early or late. The pitcher, of course, knows that the batter will behave in this way, and so will choose his pitches randomly. In doing so, the batter will not know how the pitcher will pitch on any given throw, though he probably will have a good idea about how often the pitcher is likely to throw a fast ball (change-up) for every hundred-or-so pitches. Each player is thus playing a mixed strategy, the pitcher in choosing his pitch, the batter in choosing the timing of his swing. On any given pitch, a particular ball will be thrown, and a particular swing of the bat will be chosen. But the strategy of how to pitch and the strategy of how to bat will obey a probability distribution.

4.5. CORRELATED STRATEGIES

The similarity to baseball, however, stops here. Baseball is a zero sum game. If the pitcher wins the batter loses and vice versa. This is not true of the game shown in Figure 4.1. In this game, the players have a collective incentive to avoid the outcome (Pollute, Pollute) and to promote the outcome (Abate, Abate) above the others. That is, the players of the chicken game could do better by *coordinating* their mixed strategies.

You can think of the mixed strategy equilibrium as being determined by two independent coin tosses.[3] Before choosing how to act, player X may toss a coin, deciding to play Abate if it comes up heads and Pollute if it comes up tails. Y may also base its decision on a coin toss. The mixed strategy equilibrium assumes that these coin tosses are independent. However, in the chicken game, the countries can obtain higher expected payoffs by coordinating their coin tosses—that is, by employing a *correlated strategy*.

Suppose, for example, that the players agree to toss a coin, and that they further agree that, if the coin comes up heads, then player X will play Pollute and player Y will play Abate. If the coin comes up tails, however, then player X will play Abate and player Y will play Pollute. Given these rules, X will play Abate if Y plays Pollute and Y will play Abate if X plays Pollute. Hence, each player receives an expected payoff of 1.5. This is greater than the expected payoff that the players would receive if they did not coordinate their randomizing problems (recall that this payoff is 1), and so we might suppose that the players will agree to coordinate.

Implementation of the correlated strategy by sovereign countries may be problematic, however. I have only shown that the players can gain by coordinating the coin toss *ex ante*. But the players do not choose to play Abate or Pollute until *after* the results of the toss are known. Unless the players can commit to carrying out the

---

[3] A coin toss may serve as a randomizing device here because the mixed strategy equilibrium requires that each player play Abate (Pollute) with probability one-half. This is not a general result, and in other situations a different kind of randomizing device will be needed.

agreement to make their choices on the basis of the toss, the "loser" of the coin toss has an incentive to ask that the coin be tossed again. Put differently, the loser of the coin toss would prefer to abandon the correlated strategy in preference to the mixed strategy equilibrium. The agreement to abide by the outcome of the coin toss is vulnerable to *renegotiation*; it is therefore not self-enforcing.

Moreover, though such an agreement could improve on the mixed strategy equilibrium, for the game shown in Figure 4.1 both players strictly prefer the outcome (Abate, Abate) to the correlated strategy equilibrium (a payoff of 2 beats a payoff of 1.5). Furthermore, (Abate, Abate) maximizes the aggregate payoff of the two players; they could not do better collectively than to play (Abate, Abate). However, as in the dilemma game, this mutually preferred outcome is not an equilibrium, and an agreement by both players to play Abate is therefore not self-enforcing in the chicken game. Once again our players face a dilemma. Even in games where the players have an incentive to coordinate—in the chicken game, by means of a coordinated coin toss—enforcement may be needed to sustain full cooperation.

4.6. TREATY PARTICIPATION

Though chicken is normally used in international relations as a model of confrontation or deterrence (the Cuban missile crisis is often illustrated by the chicken game; see Brams 1985), it serves a different purpose in this book. I shall show in later chapters how the PD can sometimes be transformed into a chicken game. In the transformed game, the principal choice of every state is not whether to play Pollute or Abate. The essential choice is whether to be a signatory or a non-signatory to a treaty that requires all parties to abate. This choice of whether to play Signatory or Non-signatory is sometimes (though not always, as will be discussed later) a game of chicken (see Carraro and Siniscalco 1993).

In a treaty participation game, whether a particular country participates often depends on the number of *other* countries that participate. Sometimes this decision depends on *which* other countries participate. The participation decision is thus not governed by dominant strategies. Though each country may prefer to be a free-rider, if too many countries do not participate, at least some countries may do better by participating. The participation game is thus a little like the M1 game discussed in the introduction to this chapter. In equilibrium, some countries participate and some free ride, just as some players hand in their red cards and others keep theirs.

The two sulfur protocols certainly reflect a situation in which states do not have dominant strategies. Substantial abatement by the Scandinavian countries has been necessitated by relatively weak abatement by upwind countries. Participation in these agreements may also reflect a kind of chicken game. However, a better example may be the Kyoto Protocol. When the United States rejected this agreement, the behavior of the other countries changed. To my surprise, Europe seemed more determined to make Kyoto succeed (even at the cost of allowing the treaty's environmental integrity to be compromised). At the same time, non-participation by the United States dulled the enthusiasm of other countries for ratification. Australia, for example, has hinted that it may not ratify Kyoto, given non-participation by the United States. For some countries at least, participation in Kyoto seems not to be a dominant strategy.

4.7. PURE COORDINATION

In some situations, the efficient outcome is self-enforcing, but so may be an inefficient outcome. These are pure *coordination* games.

Consider the game depicted in Figure 4.2.[4] In this game, it is in one country's interests to play Abate only if the other plays Abate; if the other plays Pollute, then one's own country can do no better than to play Pollute. Unlike the dilemma game, the outcome (Abate, Abate) in this coordination game is self-enforcing. However, so is the outcome (Pollute, Pollute).[5]

Again, you may notice the similarity between the coordination game and M2, discussed in section 4.1. In both games, there are two equilibria (in pure strategies). The important difference is that, in M2 both equilibria are efficient. This is not true of the coordination game shown in Figure 4.2.

As with chicken, if the pure coordination game were played sequentially, there would exist a unique self-enforcing outcome: (Abate, Abate). However, unlike chicken, the equilibrium of the sequential version of the coordination game does *not* depend on the order of moves. To see this, suppose that country X moved first. If X played Pollute, Y could do no better than to play Pollute. However, if X played Abate, Y would also play Abate. Obviously, the latter outcome is preferable to X (as well as to Y). Hence, if the game were played sequentially, we can expect that X would play Abate. So would Y, if the order of moves were reversed. The unique equilibrium in the sequential game is thus (Abate, Abate).

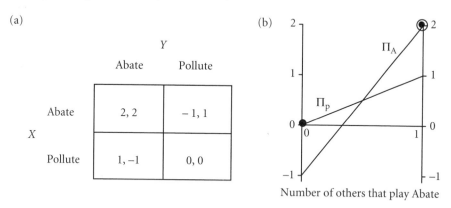

Figure 4.2. *Coordination game*

---

[4] This game is sometimes referred to as the "stag hunt" game, after a parable by Rousseau; see Binmore (1994).

[5] There also exists a mixed strategy equilibrium to this game, in which both players choose Abate with probability 0.5 and receive an expected payoff of 0.5. The calculation is similar to the one shown in Appendix 4.1.

Suppose, however, that the players must make their choices simultaneously (implying that information is imperfect). Then it might be argued that the outcome (Abate, Abate) is at least likely, given that this outcome is the unique Pareto-efficient outcome, and hence may serve as a focal point. In this situation, Sen's reasoning that individuals will pay attention to their collective interests and not just their individual interests seems especially compelling. Both players might play Abate, recognizing that to do so is better for their respective goals, and recognizing also that this outcome is an equilibrium.

However, if each player were unsure how the other player will behave, it may still be rational for each player to play Pollute. Each player can guarantee for itself a higher payoff by playing Pollute than by playing Abate. If X played Pollute, it could not get a lower payoff than 0. If it played Abate, however, then it might get a payoff of -1.

Would it make any difference if the players could communicate before making their choices? In the coordination game depicted in Figure 3.4, pre-play communication conveyed real information about each player's actual intentions, and therefore sufficed to coordinate behavior. This is not true of the game shown in Figure 4.2.[6] If X intended to play Pollute, it would prefer that Y play Abate, and hence would urge Y to do so. Since the same is true if X intended to play Abate, pre-play communication would leave the calculus of choice in this game unchanged. In this respect, the game shown in Figure 4.2 is akin to the PD. However, in contrast to the PD, each player in Figure 4.2 would choose to play Abate if it believed that the other player will play Abate.

Plainly, what each player requires is some assurance that the other player really will play Abate. Communication alone may not suffice for this purpose, at least not in one-shot situations, or situations in which mutual trust is absent. However, a treaty may help. As will be explained in Chapter 5, customary international law says that states must behave as they promise they will behave in an international treaty. As long as this customary law is habitually obeyed, or provided it is enforced in some kind of meta-game of international relations, the simple act of signing a treaty would suffice to provide the needed assurance.

Having mentioned this customary rule, you might think that it could just as easily be invoked to sustain full cooperation in the PD or in chicken. Could not both of the players sign an agreement to play Abate and rely on custom to enforce the agreement? It turns out that custom will not help remove the dilemma, and it could play only a minor role in chicken (where custom could steer countries toward one equilibrium rather than another). The reason, very briefly, is that states are free to participate in a treaty or not as they please. In the game shown in Figure 4.2, if one state is a party to an agreement requiring that participants play Abate, the other state will want to join, too. This is not true of either the PD or chicken.

---

[6] A different kind of coordination problem is described by the "battle of the sexes" game. In this game the equilibria in pure strategies are Pareto efficient, but these are asymmetric (because the players' preferences are asymmetric), and the symmetric mixed strategy equilibrium is not Pareto efficient. Farrell (1987a) shows that pre-play communication allows the players to improve on the mixed strategy equilibrium, but that the equilibrium with "cheap talk" falls short of sustaining perfect coordination.

4.8. AVIATION STANDARDS

The essential point, then, is that an efficient equilibrium of a coordination game can be sustained without the need for enforcement. An example is the setting of aircraft engine emission standards. Countries are free to set such standards as they please. However, the United Nations International Civil Aviation Organization (ICAO) was established under a 1944 treaty to coordinate aviation standards. Though parties have an obligation to adopt ICAO-recommended standards, compliance is voluntary. Nonetheless, compliance with ICAO standards is extraordinarily high.

In 1997, the US Environmental Protection Agency promulgated a rule for new aircraft emission standards for nitrogen oxides and carbon monoxide, in conformity with ICAO standards. According to the US EPA (1997: 4), the advantage of this rule is that it "will establish consistency between US and international standards, requirements, and test procedures." Consistency is desired for a number of reasons:

Since aircraft engines are international commodities, there is a commercial benefit to consistency between US and international emission standards and control program requirements. It would be easier for manufacturers to certify products for international markets since the US can certify engines for ICAO compliance. Emission certification tests meeting US requirements will also be applicable to all ICAO requirements. In addition to the economic benefit, this rule ensures that domestic commercial aircraft will meet the current ICAO standards, and thus, the public can be assured they are receiving the air quality benefits of the international standards. (US EPA 1997: 4.)

As indicated by the US EPA, the commercial incentives for standardization are overwhelming. Indeed, the commercial incentives are so strong that the US standards merely codify an accepted practice. As explained by the US EPA (1997: 5),

All engines covered by the new federal standards already meet ICAO standards or will meet them by the standards' effective dates. Manufacturers have already been developing improved technology in response to the ICAO standards. Therefore, there are no additional costs to be incurred by the aircraft industry as a result of this rule. In addition, the test data necessary to determine compliance are already collected by manufacturers during current engine certification tests. Thus, the regulations impose no additional burden on manufacturers.

The role of the state in this coordination game is thus more one of ensuring that the "right" standards are endorsed by the ICAO than in providing enforcement.

Though the setting of aviation standards is a coordination game, aviation emissions might be controlled by another means. Countries could, for example, set a cap on total aviation emissions. For environmental reasons, the latter approach is to be preferred; the environment is more affected by total emissions than by the emissions of individual aircraft. However, by selecting this instrument for policy, the game becomes more akin to a PD, at least as regards transboundary consequences; and a PD, by requiring enforcement, is harder for the international system to remedy. This hints at a major theme of this book. Strategic choice of the instrument of negotiation can alter the nature of the enforcement challenge. I develop this argument in more detail in Chapter 9, and apply it to a case study of ocean dumping.

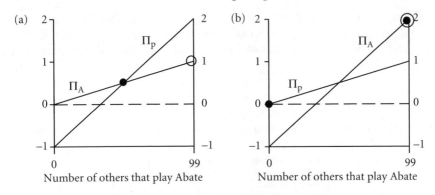

Figure 4.3. *Games with N = 100 symmetric players*
(a) 100-player chicken game, (b) 100-player coordination game

4.9. N-PLAYER GAMES

Figure 4.3 presents *N*-player versions of the chicken and coordination games.[7] To be specific, for the two games shown in this figure, there are 100 countries (or 99 other countries from the perspective of any particular country). The difference between these figures and the ones shown in Figure 3.6 are that the payoff curves cross. When payoff curves cross, countries do not have dominant strategies and there will exist a multiple of equilibria.

Figure 4.3(a) depicts the *N*-player chicken game. It appears from this figure that there exists a unique Nash equilibrium but this is not quite correct. In equilibrium, some countries play Abate and some play Pollute but as in the 2 × 2 version of the game, we cannot say *which* countries will play Abate and which will play Pollute in equilibrium; there are a multiple of pure strategy equilibria. There also exists a mixed strategy equilibrium in *which* every country behaves symmetrically *ex ante*, choosing to play Abate (Pollute) with the same probability. As in the 2 × 2 version of the chicken game, all the equilibria in Figure 4.3(a) are inefficient. As indicated by the open dot in Figure 4.3(a), the full cooperative outcome requires that every country play Abate. However, this outcome cannot be supported as an equilibrium.

I once played a game like this with playing cards in the classroom. As in the M1 game, each student would get $20 if she handed in her red card. If she kept her red card (and so handed in her black card) she would get $0 provided no more than 19 other students handed in a red card and she would get $30 if 20 or more other students handed in a red card (there were 37 students in the classroom). The equilibrium in pure strategies requires that precisely 20 students hand in a red card and, remarkably, when I played this game precisely 20 students did hand in a red card. (This surprised me. I had expected that it would take a few iterations to arrive at this

[7] For a discussion and analysis of particular kinds of chicken and coordination games, like the "best shot" and "weakest link" games, see Sandler (1998).

equilibrium.) When I asked the students how they had made their choices, some told me that they did not want to take a risk and so handed in their red cards. Others told me that they first made an educated guess about how the other students would choose—realizing that some wouldn't want to take a risk—and then made their choices accordingly. Essentially, these students played mixed strategies.

Figure 4.3(b) illustrates the *N*-player coordination game. As in chicken, the payoff curves cross, but here they cross in reverse direction (as in Figure 4.2(b)). There are two symmetric equilibria in pure strategies, one in which every country plays Abate and one in which every country plays Pollute (as in the two-player game, there is also a symmetric equilibrium in mixed strategies). Coordination in this case involves getting enough countries to play Abate, such that it becomes attractive for every country to play Abate. This is a tipping problem.[8] The M2 game discussed in Section 4.1 is also a tipping game—with the tipping point in this game occurring at the mid-point of the horizontal axis.

Again, I once played a game like this in the classroom. I told the students that each would get $20 if he kept his red card, but that each would get $0 if he handed in his red card and 19 or fewer other students did so and $30 if he handed in his red card and 20 or more other students did the same. There were 37 students in the classroom, and 25 handed in their red cards. If I played the game a second time, without allowing any time for discussion, my guess is that even more students would have handed in their red cards. In fact, I did play the game again, but before doing so I invited the students to discuss their problem. There seemed to be a unanimous opinion that no student could lose by handing in his red card, and in the next round 35 of the 37 students handed in their red cards. Two students had some doubt about how their peers would choose, and this helps explain why countries would want an international agreement to help them to coordinate. Communication may not suffice to sustain the mutually preferred outcome of a coordination game.

4.10. GEOGRAPHY AND COORDINATION

Figure 4.4(a) depicts a game in which nine countries, labeled I through IX, are located within a square.[9] The territory of each country is also a square, and these territories are shown by the solid lines. A transport network links the countries, and is shown by the broken lines. Country I is linked to Countries II and IV directly, but Country I can only connect with VII via an intermediary like IV.

Suppose that these countries have the usual binary choice; they may play Abate or Pollute. The payoffs each player gets are given by

$$\Pi_P = 0, \quad \Pi_A = -c + bz,$$

where *z* is now the number of *neighbors* to which a country is directly linked that play Abate. In Figure 4.4(a), four countries are directly linked to just two countries (these

---

[8] The seminal analysis of tipping is by Schelling (1978). For a more recent and informal discussion, see Gladwell (2000). Tipping is explored in greater depth in Chapter 9.

[9] My approach here is styled after a game studied by Peyton Young (1996).

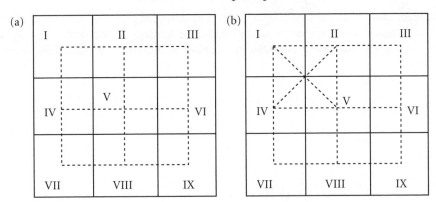

Figure 4.4. *Geographic coordination games*

are the countries on the corners), four are directly linked to three countries (these are the "middle" countries located along the perimeter of the square), and one is directly linked to four countries (this is the country located in the center of the square, Country V).

For this game, there are two interesting situations. Suppose $b = 1$ and $c = 1.5$. Then it is in the interests of a country to play Abate only if at least two of its directly linked neighbors play Abate. There are a number of possible equilibria. One is where every country plays Abate. Since every country is directly linked to at least two others, it is in the interests of every country to play Abate provided every other country plays Abate. Another equilibrium is where no country plays Abate. A third equilibrium is where Countries I, II, IV, and V play Abate and all the other countries play Pollute. Other equilibria also exist. However, it is more important to note that full cooperation requires that every country plays Abate, and that this is only one of many equilibria. To be sure of getting to this mutually preferred equilibrium, enough of the *right* countries must play Abate. Suppose, for example, that I, V, and IX play Abate. Then it is easy to see that all the other countries will play Abate. However, if Countries I and VIII played Abate, there would be no incentive for any other country to do so. It is not just the number of players that matters here. Even though the game is symmetric, the arrangement of the players also matters.

Suppose now that $b = 1$ and $c = 0.5$. Then a country will play Abate if and only if at least one directly linked neighbor plays Abate. In this case there are just two equilibria (in pure strategies), one in which every country plays Abate and one in which every country plays Pollute. Starting from a situation in which every country plays Pollute, only one country needs to play Abate for the entire system to shift to a new equilibrium in which every country plays Abate.

4.11. CATALYTIC CONVERTERS AND UNLEADED GASOLINE

An example of this situation is the spread of the use of catalytic converters and unleaded gasoline (see Heal 1999). These technologies are very close complements.

Catalytic converters only work in cars fueled by unleaded gasoline. Hence, a country wanting to reduce vehicle emissions by catalytic technology must establish a network of gasoline stations selling unleaded gas. Looked at differently, if unleaded gasoline were more widely available, the cost of requiring catalytic converters would be reduced.

Imagine that Country I unilaterally required that new cars be fitted with catalytic converters and at the same time ensured that unleaded gasoline was widely available. If people travel by car to other countries, then as the stock of cars fitted with catalytic converters increases in Country I, gas stations in Countries II and IV would have an incentive to offer unleaded gasoline. But, once unleaded gasoline became widely available in these countries, it would become more attractive for Countries II and IV to mandate the use of catalytic technology.

Suppose that Country I had a unilateral incentive to require that catalytic converters be used at home. Suppose, for example, that $c = -1$ for Country I. Then this country would require that catalytic converters be used irrespective of what its neighbors did. However, if I's neighbors had parameters $c = 0.5$ and $b = 1$, then they would require that catalytic converters be used, given that country I had adopted catalytic technology.

Suppose now that Country I also had parameters $c = 0.5$ and $b = 1$. Then all countries would be symmetric. Given that its neighbors did not adopt catalytic technology, Country I would not do so. However, imagine that the countries made their choices sequentially, with I moving first, II second, and so on. Then Country I would do better by playing Abate. For in doing so, Country I could be sure that II would play Abate (as will every other country in the chain). In this case, the decision by Country I to play Abate would be strategic. It would be rational for Country I to play Abate only because Country I could be sure that if it played Abate, then Countries II and IV would play Abate.

4.12. EUROPEAN INTEGRATION AND HARMONIZATION

As noted earlier, when $c = 1.5$ and $b = 1$, there exists an equilibrium in which Countries I, II, IV, and V play Abate but no other country does so. These four countries are better off when they all play Abate than when they all play Pollute, and so might coordinate their choices. Many of the environmental directives adopted by the European Union serve this purpose, ensuring that every country adopts the mutually preferred standard (or, under the Maastricht Treaty, the standard preferred by a qualified majority of members) when all (or at least a large enough number of members) can gain by harmonization.

Why do not all countries behave in this way? What is special about the European Union? Consider Figure 4.4(b). This is the same as Figure 4.4(a) with the exception that Countries I, II, IV, and V are more highly interconnected than are the other countries. Suppose now that every country has parameter values $c = 2.5$ and $b = 1$. Then it is in the interests of each country to play Abate only if at least three of its directly linked neighbors play Abate. There are now two equilibria in pure strategies. In one, every country plays Pollute. In the other, Countries I, II, IV, and V play Abate but all other countries play Pollute. Here, it makes sense for the more highly integrated countries to harmonize, but not for the other countries to do so. Closer integration thus provides the incentive for harmonization.

Notice that the countries in this example are interdependent as regards their technology choices, not their environmental quality levels; pollution is strictly local. Vehicle emissions do have trans-border effects, an example being the emission of nitrogen oxides, a precursor of acid rain. However, catalytic technology has spread primarily because of its advantages in reducing local pollution and for economic reasons.

4.13. HOW AUTOMOBILE STANDARDS ARE CHOSEN

The European Union is not the only region to have harmonized automobile emission standards. The United Nations Economic Commission for Europe has extended the EU's harmonization to much of the rest of Europe, and the United States, Canada, and Mexico are in the process of harmonizing vehicle emission standards under the North American Free Trade Agreement. The Aarhus Protocol on Heavy Metals (1998) requires parties to phase out the use of leaded petrol. And a global agreement has also been negotiated that creates a process by which global automobile standards can be established. This agreement, negotiated in 1998, has been ratified by important car producing states like the United States, Japan, the European Union, Canada, and Russia, and entered into force in August 2000.[10]

The incentive to harmonize automobile standards is not entirely due to network externalities. Harmonization can also lower fixed costs. As noted by Faiz *et al.* (1996: 2), "Development of a new emission control configuration typically costs vehicle manufacturers tens of millions of dollars per vehicle model, and takes from two to five years. By eliminating the need to develop separate emission control configurations for different countries, harmonization of emission standards can save billions of dollars in development costs."

But which country's standards will tend to be copied? Historically, standard-setting has been dominated by the United States (and the US federal standard has in turn be shaped by California). US standards are generally the most advanced in the world, and the US market is too large for foreign manufacturers to ignore. This means that a large number of foreign manufacturers tool up to satisfy US regulations. But having already incurred this cost, these companies can supply cars satisfying the US standards in their home markets at very low cost. Domestic regulators in these countries will therefore have little to gain and much to lose by setting a different standard at home.

Even countries that do not export to the United States have an incentive to adopt the same standards—or if not the same current standards than standards used previously by the United States. For example, Brazil adopted the 1975 US standards in 1992, the 1981 US standards in 1997, and the 1994–96 standards in 2000 (Faiz *et al.*

---

[10] The agreement is called the Agreement Concerning the Establishing of Global Technical Regulations for Wheeled Vehicles, Equipment and Parts which can be Fitted and/or Used on Wheeled Vehicles. See http:// www.unece.org/trans/main/welcwp29.htm.

1996). One reason for this is that the administrative costs of establishing technical standards are huge. The annual budget of the state of California's Mobile Source Program is $65 million, more than the entire environmental monitoring and regulatory budget of most developing countries (Faiz *et al.* 1996). Result: US standards have become the international standard.

As further evidence that it is the standard that is being adopted and not reduced emissions *per se*, most other countries only apply the US standards to autos as they roll off the assembly line, not throughout their lifetime as in the United States. The United States routinely tests whether vehicles comply with emission standards, and forces auto makers to recall thousands of cars each year for failing such tests. In many states, older cars are also routinely tested, and cars sometimes need to be refitted with new catalytic converters to earn a registration certificate. In Europe there is no such testing, and as a result, claims Faiz *et al.* (1996: 8), "manufacturers of such vehicles have little incentive to ensure that the emission control systems are durable enough to provide good control throughout the vehicle's lifetime."

What can be gained by an international agreement in this area? Recall from the previous section that there can be no guarantee that a decentralized system will choose the best standard.[11] The purpose of the global standards agreement is to "ensure that objective consideration is given to the analysis of best available technology, relative benefits and cost effectiveness as appropriate in developing global technical regulations."[12]

4.14. FAIRMINDED PREFERENCES

In recommending that Britain join the "Thirty Percent Club," the group of nations that had pledged to reduce their sulfur dioxide (SO_2) emissions 30 percent from their 1980 levels, the House of Commons Environment Committee (1984: lxxi) expressed a peculiar sentiment:

As our inquiry has progressed the stance of the United Kingdom has become increasingly isolated by its refusal to legislate to reduce SO_2 and NO_x emissions. Since our work began three West European countries have joined those already in the 30 percent club, and several Eastern European countries have committed themselves to reduce transfrontier emissions by 30 percent. SO_2 emissions in the United Kingdom have indeed fallen by 37 percent since 1970, but the levels of high-stack emissions which affect remote areas have not fallen. In 1970, when the 37 percent fall began, we were the largest emitter in Western Europe. In 1984, we are still the largest emitter. NO_x emissions have not fallen. In Western Europe only West Germany deposits more SO_2 in other countries than does the United Kingdom, and further significant reductions cannot be achieved by either without controls.

The Committee's concern in this passage appears to lie less with the net benefits to the United Kingdom of reducing its emissions—that is, less with self-interest—than with the fact that the United Kingdom had failed to conform to the majority behavior in Europe. Indeed, the Committee's evaluation did not even consider whether

---

[11] David's (1985) celebrated paper explains how the "wrong" standard may have been selected for the typewriter—and, now, the computer—keyboard.   [12] Article 1.1.5.

the other European countries were abating more than the United Kingdom simply because it was in *their* self-interest to do so (a view, as discussed in Chapter 1, that seems more consistent with the evidence). The Committee seemed rather to be arguing, "Because the other European nations are reducing their emissions, we should too."[13]

This expression of preferences is in keeping with Runge's (1984) claim that countries have preferences which reflect a kind of "fairmindedness." Essentially, countries are motivated by the desire, in Runge's (1984: 161) words, "not to be the odd man out." This implies that the dilemma in Figure 3.1 does not exist, that countries' preferences rather make the underlying game a coordination problem. In a fairminded world, there are no dominant strategy equilibria. Instead, each player will play Abate (Pollute) so long as it believes that the other will play Abate (Pollute).

If countries really did have such preferences, the implications would be profound. Sticks would not be needed to enforce international agreements. All that would be needed would be an agreement telling each country that it ought to play Abate.

Certainly, Runge's reasoning has superficial appeal. In contrast to the dilemma game, equilibria in the real world of international affairs often are not in dominant strategies. Instead, each country's choice of how to act often depends on how it expects others will act. Moreover, and contrary to what the dilemma game predicts, countries often do cooperate. Fairminded preferences can explain both of these observations.

However, this does not necessarily imply that countries actually have fairminded preferences. Even without fairminded preferences, there may exist equilibria that are not supported by dominant strategies. As we shall see later in this book, non-linear pollution damages and interdependent cost functions will have much the same effect. So will network externalities of the kind discussed earlier in this chapter. The observations that there may not exist dominant strategies and that countries will do better by coordinating their behavior are consistent with different underlying models. They do not point only in the direction of fairminded preferences.

Moreover, much evidence suggests that states do not have fairminded preferences. Look at it this way: when a country like Norway, which has a foreign policy that is as fairminded and morally commendable as any other country, stubbornly refuses to obey the policies recommended by the international whaling regime, we can be pretty sure that the assumption of fairminded preferences does not hold universally.

And it is as well to note that the recommendation by the House of Commons Environment Committee was rejected by the British government. As discussed in Chapter 1, the United Kingdom did not ratify the first sulfur protocol, and the reason is that the Thatcher-led government did "not intend to commit the country to expensive emission controls, especially when there [was] uncertainty about the environmental benefits to be achieved" both in the United Kingdom and in continental Europe (see Handl, 1986: 443). The British government was more interested in the consequences of its actions than in conforming.

---

[13] Importantly, the founders of the "Thirty Percent Club" *intended* to affect Britain's participation in this way. See Levy (1993).

An even more important example (because of the significance of the international agreement negotiated later) is the failure of a large number of countries to reduce their use of CFCs in the late-1970s (US EPA 1988*b*: 30576):

In 1978 the United States restricted the use of CFCs in aerosols. While several nations adopted similar restrictions (e.g., Sweden, Canada, Norway) and others partially cut back their use (European nations, Japan), there was no widespread movement to follow the United States' lead. Concerns existed then that other nations had failed to act because the United States and a few other nations were making the reductions thought necessary to protect the ozone layer. Similar concerns exist today that unilateral action could result in "free-riding" by some other nations.

Again, different explanations could account for the divergence in behavior. It may be that some countries would gain by reducing their use of CFCs unilaterally, whether or not other countries did so. Or it could be that, as in the chicken game, some countries could only gain by cutting back on CFCs when most others did not cut back their emissions. Whatever the reason, it is plain that fairmindedness was not the sole determinant of behavior.

In the theory developed later in this book, equilibria of the type that would be associated with fairminded preferences emerge as special cases when countries care only about their self-interest. As already noted, this is more in keeping with the way that states actually behave. Moreover, I shall show in Chapter 11 that even if countries insist on behaving symmetrically—on reaching a consensus on how *every* country should act—the cooperation that they would be able to sustain may fall far short of the mutually preferred level. Unanimity, even when it prevails, may not be capable of sustaining the level of cooperation predicted by fairminded preferences. Even to the extent that countries do conform, we should not be entirely satisfied with the consequences.

4.15. MORAL INJUNCTIONS

Instead of assuming that countries have fairminded preferences, we might suppose that they feel *morally obligated* to behave as others behave.[14] Consider again the PD game shown in Figure 3.1. It is plain that, if each country had to behave in exactly the same way, each would prefer that every country chose Abate over Pollute. Suppose, then, that *X* and *Y* obeyed a moral edict requiring that each country play Abate provided that the other did so, but that each was otherwise entitled to behave according to its self-interest. Then, clearly, there would be two equilibria in pure strategies. If *Y* played Abate, *X* would be morally obligated to play Abate, and if *X* played Abate, *Y* would bear the same moral obligation. By contrast, if *Y* played Pollute, *X* would be free of its moral obligation, and would thus choose also to play Pollute. Similarly, if *X* played Pollute, *Y* would not have to conform to the moral edict, and so would choose to play Pollute. Moral reasoning may thus transform the PD into a coordination game. The difference between this view of how countries behave and the assumption

---

[14] The approach I am taking here is similar to Sugden's (1984).

about fairminded preferences is that, when behavior is guided by moral reasoning there may be a tension between a country's interests and its moral conscience. Unless countries were ruled by their perceived moral duties, the outcome (Abate, Abate) might not be sustained as an equilibrium. There is no such tension in the assumption about fairminded preferences.

The morality of foreign policy *is* important, and has been since Woodrow Wilson's presidency. Most policy decisions need to be justified in moral terms and not only in terms of self-interest. Indeed, moral reasoning is often used to defend non-conformist behavior. In refusing to join the 30 Percent Club, for example, Britain argued that the outcome (Abate, Abate) was *not* manifestly the best outcome of the acid rain game. Similarly, Norway claims that it makes no sense to stop killing whales that are relatively abundant. Why, I once heard a Norwegian diplomat argue, should countries be free to kill tuna but not whales? Morally, the different policies seem inconsistent. More generally, though free-riding behavior is a commonplace, it is not something which the free-riders openly celebrate. Other reasons are given to justify non-participation, the uncertainty in the science being a particularly popular excuse. The problem with moral reasoning is that it can be twisted and manipulated. As Bailey (1968: 160) has put it, "An ingenious statesman, if he wishes, can usually find a moral cloak for selfish deeds."

The challenge for theory is thus not to select a single moral injunction and to let it govern all behavior. It would be more useful to determine the set of equilibria that might be sustained by the international system, and to then see how moral/fairness concerns can influence the selection of a particular equilibrium.

As will be demonstrated later in this book, the assumption of self-interest can sustain a variety of equilibria. For example, suppose that the dilemma game were repeated indefinitely. Suppose as well that the players adopt the strategy: play Abate in the initial period and thereafter make exactly the same choice as the other player in the previous round of play. Then it can be shown that, if one country plays this strategy, the other can do no better than to play the same strategy, and so (Abate, Abate) can be sustained as an equilibrium of the repeated PD (provided certain conditions hold; see Chapter 10). However, the conditions that allow (Abate, Abate) to be sustained as an equilibrium also allow other equilibria to be sustained. Suppose every player played the strategy, play Pollute in the initial period and thereafter make exactly the same choice as the other player in the previous round of play. Then (Pollute, Pollute) would be the equilibrium. Obviously, in this richer environment it matters a great deal how strategies are chosen. Moral reasoning, as well as concerns for fairmindedness, can be invoked in this selection process.

4.16. CONCLUSIONS

The one-shot PD studied in Chapter 3 is unusual partly because it has a unique equilibrium in dominant strategies. In many situations, countries do not have dominant strategies. This chapter has examined games with multiple equilibria.

The chicken game describes a situation in which, in equilibrium, symmetric countries behave differently. In Chapter 7 we shall see how a treaty can transform a PD into a chicken game. In this transformed game the choice becomes whether or not to participate in a treaty that requires all parties to play Abate. We shall find that, in equilibrium, some countries participate and some do not—that is, symmetric countries behave asymmetrically, just as in the chicken game.

The coordination game describes a situation in which every country wants to do what others are doing. In a coordination game, equilibria are symmetric but there are a multiple of equilibria. And it turns out that the PD games can also be transformed into a coordination game, either by requiring countries to choose a technology standard, as explained in Chapter 9, or by means of a trade restriction, as shown in Chapter 12.

The repeated version of the PD also has a multiple of equilibria. Concerns for fairness may play a role in selecting from among this set of equilibria. And, to sustain an equilibrium, it may also be necessary for each party to have some assurance about how the others will behave. If trust is in short supply, as the quote introducing this chapter implies, an international agreement may be needed—not only to coordinate but to enforce. Trust and fairness are also shaped by the background rules governing international behavior, rules that apply to all countries and a variety of circumstances. These rules are the subject of the next chapter.

Appendix 4.1. Calculation of Mixed Strategies

Consider the game shown in Figure 4.1, and suppose that player X plays Abate with probability $p_x \in [0,1]$ and that player Y plays Abate with probability $p_y \in [0,1]$. Of course, since both players face a binary choice, X and Y must play Pollute with probability $(1 - p_x)$ and $(1 - p_y)$, respectively.

Player X's *ex ante* payoff is

$$\Pi_x = p_x[2p_y + 0(1 - p_y)] + (1 - p_x)[3p_y - 1(1 - p_y)]$$

or

$$\Pi_x = (4p_y - 1) + p_x(1 - 2p_y). \tag{4A.1}$$

By inspection, you can see X will want to set $p_x = 0$ if $(1 - 2p_y)$ is negative and $p_x = 1$ if $(1 - 2p_y)$ is positive. If $p_y = 0.5$, X will not care how it chooses p_x.

Country Y's *ex ante* payoff can be shown to be

$$\Pi_y = (4p_x - 1) + p_y(1 - 2p_x). \tag{4A.2}$$

As above, it is easy to see that Y will want to set $p_y = 0$ if $(1 - 2p_x)$ is negative and $p_y = 1$ if this term is positive. If $p_x = 0.5$, Y will not care how it chooses p_y.

Suppose Y plays $p_y = 0$. Then from (4A.1) we know that X will want to set p_x as large as possible; that is, $p_x = 1$. From (4A.2), we can see that if $p_x = 1$, then Y will want to set p_y as small as possible; that is, $p_y = 0$. Hence, $(p_x = 1, p_y = 0)$ is an equilibrium. Equivalently, (Abate, Pollute) is an equilibrium. Using the same logic, it is easy to show that (Pollute, Abate) is also an equilibrium. These are the two equilibria in pure strategies.

Now let us derive the mixed strategy equilibrium. I noted that if $p_y = 0.5$, then X will not care how it chooses p_x. However, suppose X sets $p_x = 0.75$. Then, (4A.2) tells us that Y will want to set p_y as low as possible; that is, $p_y = 0$. However, (4A.1) tells us that if $p_y = 0$, then X will not want to set $p_x = 0.75$. Plainly, apart from the corner solutions, only if $p_x = 0.5$ and $p_y = 0.5$ will neither player be able to gain by deviating unilaterally. Hence, $(p_x = 0.5, p_y = 0.5)$ is the equilibrium in mixed strategies.

5

Customary Rights and Responsibilities

When Kansas and Colorado have a quarrel over the water in the Arkansas River
they don't call out the National Guard in each state and go to war over it. They bring
a suit in the Supreme Court of the United States and abide by the decision. There
isn't a reason in the world why we cannot do that internationally. President Harry
S. Truman, speech, Kansas City (1945)[1]

5.1. INTRODUCTION

The rules of the game determine whether cooperation is needed and is viable. Some
rules are given by nature. These include the direction of the prevailing winds, the fecun-
dity of a fishery, the migratory habits of the fur seal, and the uptake of carbon dioxide
by the oceans. Technology is also given, at least at any one time. Other rules, however,
can be manipulated by the players. A treaty, for example, changes the rules under which
countries exploit a resource (over time, a treaty can also change technology, by creating
incentives for innovation and diffusion). The rules that can be manipulated by treaties
are obviously of special interest to this book. But there are other human-made rules—
rules that are pretty much given at any one time but that evolve over longer periods of
time—that are also important. These are the rules of customary law. Custom often creates the need for a treaty. It also constrains what a treaty is able to do. At the same time,
an ineffective treaty system creates an incentive for custom to change.

In the case of the fur seal, custom determined that the United States did not have
exclusive rights to the seals beyond the three-mile limit (the tribunal that ruled on this
matter reached its decision by interpreting the custom). Custom also defined the territories of all the players in this game, including the three-mile limit. It determined that
third parties could not be excluded from sealing outside the three-mile limit (the treaty
had to get around this, by making entry unprofitable) and that reflagging was legal.
Custom said that a treaty could be negotiated, but it also told each country that participation in a treaty was voluntary—thus making it essential that the four-power treaty
promote participation. As suggested by the fur seal example, if the rules of custom had
been different, a treaty may not have been needed. Today, for example, customary law
recognizes the 200-mile Exclusive Economic Zone (EEZ). Had this existed a century
earlier, a treaty to protect the fur seal probably would never have been negotiated. It
would not have been needed. Recall that Russia's claim to a territorial limit half this size
was sufficient to give it total control of the waters near the seal's breeding grounds.

---

[1] Quoted in Rodes and Odell (1992: 163).

This chapter explains why custom is needed, how it is determined, and how, over longer periods of time, it can be changed. It also explains the role of custom in treaty negotiations.

5.2. VERTICAL vs HORIZONTAL LAW

Though nature pays no attention to lines drawn on a map, the institutions that can be used to correct an externality are *defined* by political boundaries. Local or intra-national externalities are the easiest to put right; they can be corrected by the state— by a legislature that creates law, a judiciary that settles legal disputes, and an executive that enforces the law. Transnational externalities can only be corrected by the inter-vention of two or more states. They are thus much harder to remedy.

To be sure, local externalities are not always corrected. Our national institutions can also fail. Some externalities are even *caused* by government intervention. A tragic example is the Aral Sea, once under the exclusive control of the Soviet Union. To turn the Central Asian desert into a major cotton-producing region, Soviet central planners diverted water from the Amu Darya and Syr Darya rivers for irrigation— shrinking the Aral Sea dramatically. Today, the Aral covers only about half the area it did forty years ago (see Figure 5.1). Once the world's fourth largest lake, it is now the eighth largest. But, though the USSR ruined the Aral, it also had the jurisdictional

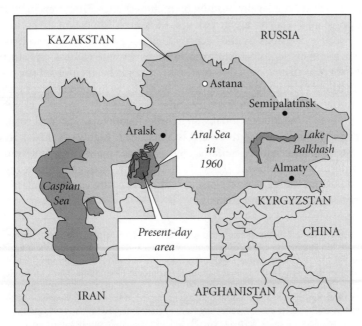

Figure 5.1. *Contraction of the Aral Sea*

Source: Matloff (1999). Reproduced with permission. © *The Christian Science Monitor* (www.csmonitor.com)

wherewithal to protect it. Indeed, a 1988 decree by the Soviet Central Committee ordered a cut in cotton production, and after the decree was implemented water began flowing into the Aral once again. We will never know, but the Soviets might have reversed the Aral's decline. In 1991, however, the Soviet Union was dissolved, and at a stroke restoration of the Aral Sea became a monumental institutional challenge. Today the Aral basin belongs to five countries: Kazakstan and Uzbekistan, which border the lake, and Kyrgyzstan, Tajikistan, and Turkmenistan, which control the waters that feed it. Technically, these five states can do whatever the Soviet Union could do. But they must act within the anarchic or horizontal international system, and this makes restoration of the Aral much, much harder.

Parties to a transborder externality cannot appeal to a World Legislature. The United Nations General Assembly may be stylistically similar to a parliament, but its resolutions are not legally binding on member states (and, to make matters worse, some states are not even UN members). Nor can the parties to a dispute depend on the World Court. As noted previously, the International Court of Justice (ICJ) can only decide cases that all sides to a dispute agree should be heard. Even if a dispute makes it this far, there is no World Executive with the authority to enforce the court's decisions. Though President Truman was right that international conflict *could* be resolved by the ICJ, states have chosen *not* to make decisions by the ICJ binding— and, indeed, the United States is among the countries that have decided in the past not to abide by ICJ rulings. Under the United Nations Charter, even decisions by the Security Council are not legally binding on member states. Situations in which international peace and security are at risk are, of course, important exceptions to this rule. But because decisions by the Security Council are subject to veto by any of its permanent members, enforcement even in these extreme cases is rare. In the UN's 55-year history, Security Council resolutions have only been enforced (by use of economic sanctions or military interventions or both, as in the actions that followed Iraq's invasion of Kuwait) on a few occasions.

And yet, though the international system lacks the hierarchical legal structure that characterizes our national institutions, it is nonetheless highly organized. In the horizontal system of international affairs, states at once make, interpret, and enforce rules of international behavior. They do this mainly through international agreements and custom.[2] Other sources of international law are also recognized, but they are subservient to treaties and custom.[3]

---

[2] Other sources of international law include general legal principles, like those expressed in the Stockholm and Rio Declarations; judicial decisions by the ICJ and other courts; and the interpretations of legal authorities like the International Law Commission. More controversial are the rules of "soft law," such as guidelines drawn up by the United Nations Environment Programme. These are not legally binding but "in the field of international environmental law have played an important role, by pointing to the likely future direction of formally binding obligations, by informally establishing acceptable norms of behavior, and by codifying or possibly reflecting rules of customary law" (Sands 1995: 103).

[3] Some legal scholars, for example, treat general legal principles as "a sub-heading under treaty and customary law and incapable of adding anything new to international law" (Shaw 1991: 84). Similarly, though the decisions of the ICJ may affect subsequent judgements, the doctrine of precedent, so important to the common law, does not exist in international law; the decisions of the ICJ have no legally binding force

5.3. DOMESTIC vs INTERNATIONAL LAW

Except where tyranny stifles civil and political freedoms, the law gives fullest expression to the values shared by its subjects, whether citizens in municipal law or states in public international law. It articulates what these subjects must and must not do, and to which rights they are entitled, both the positive rights allowing them to act as they please in some spheres and the negative rights prescribing how they may not be interfered with by others in other spheres. From this perspective, international and municipal law are alike.

From other perspectives, however, international and municipal law are very different. As a legal system expands to encompass a greater number of distinct communities, each with its own traditions and beliefs, the set of values shared by all its subjects inevitably shrinks. And this is why, as explained in Section 3.15, stronger international institutions have not been created. International law must somehow be accepted by theocratic as well as atheistic states, by autocracies as well as democracies, by poor as well as rich states, by superpowers and by weak states. No wonder international law is feebler than its domestic counterpart. With the differences between countries being so great, no country wants to cede an inch of authority to foreign powers.

Indeed, the great difference between international and municipal law is that international law must be accepted by *all* the parties to which it is meant to apply. The domestic laws of a democracy, by contrast, need only satisfy a majority (simple or otherwise). All persons are bound by their country's laws, whether they agree with them or not. True, the rights of minorities may be safeguarded. But these protections apply only to a restricted set of rights such as the right to vote, to free speech, to a fair and speedy trial, etc. They do not apply to every sphere of life. As mentioned before, paying tax is not an optional activity in any country; and nor is a term in the military voluntary when conscription is the rule. International law thus gives states much greater autonomy than municipal law gives its own legal persons.

A treaty is recognized as being legally binding on all its parties and *only* on its parties. Treaties are therefore analogous to contracts in domestic law. That is, treaties are *unlike* legislative acts. At the same time, treaties are not the same as contracts because contracts are written with the understanding that they will be enforced by a third party: the state. Treaties must be self-enforcing.

Customary law differs from domestic law in yet another way. Like legislation, customary law applies universally. However, unlike domestic law, custom is adopted by global consensus.[4] International law thus comes close to the ideal favored by Henry David Thoreau in his essay on civil disobedience. To Thoreau, "that government is best which governs not at all."

And yet states are not truly autonomous. The right of one country to act as it pleases may trample upon another's right not to be interfered with. States are interdependent

---

except as between the parties to which the decisions are meant to apply. Indeed, Article 38 of the Statute of the ICJ specifically refers to judicial decisions as being a "subsidiary means for the determination of the rules of law." The primary sources of international law are (in order) treaties and custom.

[4] As explained in a later footnote, however, custom may allow for exceptions.

and prefer constrained autonomy to lawlessness. Each state accepts constraints on its own freedom of action, realizing that this is the price to pay for having other states accept constraints on *their* behavior. Custom gives expression to this need for restraint. Treaties impose further constraints and apply them with greater specificity.

5.4. CUSTOM vs TREATIES

Constitutions and legislative acts, like treaties, are *formal* institutions. They are consciously and deliberately created and emerge from a rules-based process. Custom is different. Custom is an *informal* institution.[5] Custom is not created; it arises spontaneously; it consists of tacit arrangements (though these may become codified in treaties and related instruments[6]); and it evolves.[7] Custom is built from repeated interactions between states, a pattern of behavior that gives rise to reciprocal expectations about how states ought to behave.

Custom plays much the same role in international relations that it does in any society: it constrains behavior and coordinates expectations. In the domestic law of a modern, industrialized country, custom "is relatively cumbersome and unimportant and often of only nostalgic value" (Shaw 1991: 60). Why rely on custom when an accepted practice can be written down in the statute books? In more primitive societies, by contrast, custom substitutes for formal written rules and is thus relatively more important (North 1990).[8] Custom serves a similar function in international relations.

5.5. WHY STATES ADHERE TO CUSTOM

Of course, treaties and custom must both be self-enforcing. But treaties, being formal institutions, can mandate *specific* punishments for deviations from an agreed behavior, and rewards for adherence to it. Custom, by contrast, is enforced by informal mechanisms.

A state is prevented from deviating from customary law mainly by other states recognizing deviations as being unlawful (perhaps helped by an ICJ ruling confirming that the behavior is illegal). Deviations from custom are costly to the deviant. They must be defended—by the use of diplomatic, legal, and material resources if not also by use of force. Law breaking may also harm a state's reputation, making others reluctant to transact with it in the future. And a violation may invite others to deviate, if not from this custom then perhaps from others, when doing so serves *their* interests. The expectation that this could happen—that a single deviation could precipitate a

---

[5] See North (1990) for a discussion of formal and informal institutions.

[6] For example, the "no harm" principle, to be discussed later, has not only been affirmed by Principle 21 of the Stockholm Declaration; it has also been recognized in subsequent agreements, including the 1973 London Dumping Convention, the 1979 Geneva Convention on Long-Range Transboundary Air Pollution, the 1982 United Nations Law of the Sea Convention, the 1985 Vienna Convention for the Protection of the Ozone Layer, and the 1992 Convention on Biological Diversity.

[7] Sugden (1989) explains how "spontaneous order" may emerge in social situations.

[8] North (1990) is careful to add that informal rules can also be important to modern, Western societies.

general erosion in law abidance—may in turn make the original deviation seem threatening even to countries not harmed directly by it, and so provide an incentive for even these countries to challenge a deviant. Virtually every country objected to Iraq's invasion of Kuwait, and the reason is obvious. If the invasion went unchallenged, every state's sovereignty over its territory would be weakened. To a significant extent, deviations from custom sow the seeds of their own reversal.

Precisely for this reason, in the everyday world of international affairs, states do not calculate the gains and losses to a deviation from custom 24 hours a day. Unless a state has good reason to deviate, it simply behaves as others expect it to behave; it obeys the custom. Psychology—if it is permissible to use the term in the context of a state's behavior—adds an extra dose of inertia, making it that much harder for states to deviate. Legal scholars emphasize that states obey a custom because of "the psychological or subjective belief that such behavior is law" (Shaw 1991: 62). A state obeys a customary law not just because it is in its interests to do so. It obeys the custom because it feels legally obligated to do so. Customary law is thus to be distinguished from a norm or convention. It is a convention that diplomats should be exempt from having to pay parking fines issued by their host countries. The convention may be habitually obeyed but deviations are lawful.

Custom, like the common law, is a tradition-bound institution. But it persists because of the expectations of the players, not history.[9] Suppose circumstances change, so that a custom that previously served the international system reasonably well no longer does so. Then a unilateral deviation may win the approval of other states (so that the stigma of breaking the law fails to stick). And, if it does, then the initial deviation may trigger a chain reaction of deviations, leading to a change in the custom. Two hundred years ago, human rights issues were regarded as being solely within the national sphere of jurisdiction. Not so today. The customary law of state responsibility has changed; the custom has evolved.

5.6. HOW CUSTOM BECOMES ESTABLISHED AND EVOLVES

As mentioned previously, political borders determine whether and how transnational externalities become manifest. They are a part of the problem. They can also be a part of the solution. In the games studied in Chapters 3 and 4, the territories of each state were taken as givens. But in the bigger game of international affairs they are equilibrium outcomes.

In a domestic setting, the government assigns property rights. In the international system, custom must do so. A state's territory is not just where it says it is (some territories are disputed). It is where others recognize it to be.

The history of how the territorial sea came to be delineated illustrates how custom becomes established. It also shows how custom evolves. Today, the high seas belong to no country. Nationalization of the seas is a feasible option, however, and during the fifteenth to the seventeenth centuries, several states, including Denmark,

---

[9] Krugman (1991) emphasizes the importance of this distinction, though in a different context.

England, Genoa, Portugal, Spain, Turkey, Tuscany, and Venice, claimed sovereignty over huge sections of the oceans (Brownlie 1990: 233). These claims were abandoned, partly because the costs of enforcing them were deemed excessive. Instead, the notion of a closed sea gave way in the eighteenth century to an alternative allocation, one that is still recognized today: this is the customary principle of the freedom of the high seas.

But where does a coastal state's territory end and the high seas begin, at the high- or low-tide mark, or somewhere else? Deciding this is yet another task for custom. Initially, the territorial sea was determined by the so-called "cannon-shot" rule: the territory that a country could reasonably be expected to defend. This rule had the obvious attraction of a focal point. But it was also imprecise. Did it apply only where guns were actually in place? And, if so, what width should apply elsewhere? By the late 1700s an unambiguous uniform limit of one marine league (another obvious focal point) or three nautical miles was established, and this was accepted as custom well into the twentieth century.[10]

In the latter half of the twentieth century, a number of coastal states claimed rights beyond the three-mile limit for particular purposes, especially fisheries conservation. To protect its important cod fishery, for example, Iceland unilaterally extended its territorial limit from three to four miles, shortly after becoming independent of Denmark in 1950. Later, it extended the limit even farther—to 12 miles in 1958, to 50 miles in 1972, and to 200 miles in 1975 (Kurlansky 1997). The purpose of each successive claim was to exclude rival fleets. However, to be lawful, these claims needed to have the consent of other nations, and in this particular case the approval of other states was forthcoming. The 200-mile EEZ thus became a universal, customary standard.

The EEZ was an institutional response to the problem of scarcity caused by overfishing. However, it was an imperfect remedy. The EEZ excludes many productive fishing grounds, including a corner of the Grand Bank and all of the Flemish Cap. Technically, there is nothing to stop these areas from being nationalized. But even if the principle of freedom of the high seas were jettisoned, and all the world's oceans were nationalized, problems would remain. A number of fisheries straddle two or more jurisdictions. Ecology also intrudes. Though cod are bottom-dwelling demersal fish, they feed on pelagic species like capelin that move between the different EEZs, and between these zones and the high seas. The territories of *these* fishes obviously cannot be nationalized, and nor can the territories of migratory fish like tuna and marine mammals like whales be claimed. Similarly, though anadromous fish like salmon spawn in interior rivers, they spend much of their lives in the high seas where they may be caught by any nation (the same is true, in reverse, for catadromous fish like eels).

---

[10] To be sure, there were exceptions to this rule. Spain claimed a 6-mile limit, and Norway, Denmark, and Sweden each claimed a limit of 4 miles. Custom can tolerate such exceptions, provided they do not reflect opportunistic behavior. To take a related but more recent example, in deciding the *Anglo-Norwegian Fisheries* case, the International Court of Justice recognized Norway's claim to a procedure for measuring its territorial sea that differed from established custom. The reason is that Norway's procedure had its own logic, had been applied consistently by Norway, and had not previously been opposed by any other country.

The limit of the territorial sea was changed under a similar set of circumstances. In 1960, the United States and Canada proposed doubling the width of the territorial sea from three to six miles, and adding an exclusive fisheries zone extending a further six miles. Though their joint proposal was rejected by other states, the two six-mile limits, adding to a 12-mile band, became a focal point for future claims. Over time, countries began thinking of the 12-mile limit as a potential territorial limit, with an exclusive zone, not limited to fisheries, extending even farther out to sea. This new concept, like the 200-mile EEZ, was formalized in the Law of the Sea (LOS) Convention. But by the time the LOS treaty was finalized in 1982, as many as 25 states claimed territorial seas broader than 12 miles and 30 states claimed a narrower limit.[11] A consensus was still lacking. In the 1980s, expectations began to converge, however, and the limit of 12 nautical miles superceded the historic three-mile limit in customary law, even though the Law of the Sea Convention had not entered into force. To be sure, a few countries rejected the new limit. Even today, a few states claim jurisdiction to a wider territorial sea. However, these claims are not recognized by custom and thus have no authority.

Shaw (1991: 74–5) uses this example to explain how custom develops:

… one has to treat the matter in terms of a process whereby states behave in a certain way in the belief that such behaviour is law or is becoming law. It will then depend upon how other states react as to whether this process of legislation is accepted or rejected. It follows that rigid definitions as to legality have to be modified to see whether the legitimating stamp of state activity can be provided or not. If a state proclaims a twelve mile limit to its territorial sea in the belief that, although the three mile limit has been accepted law, the circumstances are so altering that a twelve mile limit might now be treated as becoming law, it is vindicated if other states follow suit and a new rule of customary law is established. If other states reject the proposition, then the projected rule withers away and the original rule stands, reinforced by state practice … .

Of course, what Shaw, a legal scholar, is describing here is custom as a spontaneous, self-enforcing institution.

As suggested by this example, to say that custom evolves is not to say that it changes slowly or incrementally. The evolution of custom is a little like the evolution of species. Some change is gradual. But there are instances in which, as suggested by the theory of punctuated equilibrium in paleontology, long periods of stability may be interrupted by sudden changes in custom. The three-mile limit was accepted as customary law starting around 1800 (Brownlie, 1990), and it persisted until fairly recently, when the three-mile limit quickly changed into a 12-mile limit, accompanied by a 200-mile EEZ.

5.7. WHY CUSTOM CHANGES

Like other institutions, custom changes as prices (including, in the case of non-marketed goods and services, shadow prices), preferences, and technologies change

---

[11] The numbers in this paragraph and the one that follows are taken from the "Commentary" submitted to the US Senate by President Clinton, when urging ratification of the Agreement Relating to the Implementation of Part XI of the United Nations Convention on the LOS.

(as will be explained in later chapters, treaties are revised for similar reasons).[12] Creation of the EEZ, for example, was an institutional response to a problem of scarcity.

Changes in technology play a similar role, as illustrated by the example of cod (Kurlansky, 1997). When plentiful, cod could be caught using weighted longlines—a technology still used today, though a modern longline will carry 5000–6000 baited hooks, many times more than was the norm a century ago. From the seventeenth century to the 1930s, longlines were dropped from two-man dories, the subject of Winslow Homer's best paintings. The quantity of fish that could be caught by this means depended on the time it took to travel to the best fisheries, and this was cut considerably by the invention, in New England, of the fast schooner. Later, steam power enabled trawlers to drag wide nets along the ocean bottom, without the need for bait. Sonar or spotter aircraft were used to locate larger schools, and trawlers increased in size, allowing even bigger nets to be dragged. Accompanying factory ships processed the catch at sea, and the invention of refrigeration allowed the fish to be kept fresh for longer, reducing the number of return journeys. Where the ocean floor was uneven, as off the elbow of Cape Cod, "rockhoppers" of up to three feet in diameter were attached to the nets, further increasing the range of the draggers. All these advances in technology lowered the cost of fishing, particularly in more distant waters, and in so doing hastened a collapse of the cod fishery.

Under a regime of open access, each country has little incentive to leave a fish in the sea. If it does so, the fish is likely to be captured by others. At best, the country that conserves the fish can expect to get back only a fraction of the total return on its investment in conservation. The larger share is likely to end up in another state's nets. But this also means that an alternative property rights arrangement could yield a conservation dividend. Increased scarcity, perhaps amplified by improved harvesting technologies, thus increases the incentives to innovate, by changing the system of property rights. The claim to an extended fishery zone or an EEZ is a response to this increase in scarcity. It is akin to the claim by the United States to the waters of the Bering Sea, and to the fur seals found therein. The difference is that the earlier claim by the United States was rejected by other states, which could only lose under this arrangement. Similarly, though Canada has claimed a 100 mile pollution-free zone along its Arctic coastline, this has not been accepted by its Arctic neighbor, the United States, and nor has it acquired international recognition (Shaw 1991: 363). Claims to an EEZ, by contrast, benefited a large number of coastal states, and so entered the canon of customary law.

Creation of the EEZ probably gave a huge boost to efficiency. Since most marine resources of commercial value lie within the EEZ, the creation of this new property right has essentially nationalized a large share of the ocean's resources. A few fishing areas lie outside the 200-mile limit, but most are contained within it. A similar pattern holds for most other coastal states.

Changes in technology can also lower the costs of monitoring and enforcing certain property rights. Vessels fishing for cod in the North Atlantic, for example, must

---

[12] See North (1990), who stresses the importance of changes in preferences and prices.

today be fitted with a new technology that signals their location via satellite. This new technology facilitates monitoring of area restrictions imposed by the North Atlantic Fisheries Organization. Without it, the area restrictions would be more costly to monitor—and, hence, less likely to be adopted in the first place.

5.8. THE CONTOURS OF JURISDICTION

The Coase theorem says that, for any initial allocation of property rights, a bilateral externality will be corrected by the parties themselves provided they are allowed to negotiate a reallocation of these rights and can rely on a third party to enforce such an agreement (Coase 1960). The state thus plays two roles in the Coase theorem. It assigns rights to a resource, and it enforces agreed redistributions of those rights.

In international affairs, the initial distribution of property rights is determined by custom. Custom also imposes a duty upon parties to an international agreement to comply. However, as I explain in Chapter 10, this duty to comply provides weak incentives in comparison with the domestic enforcement powers of the state.

Of the property rights assigned by custom, some are well specified, and some are ambiguous. And of the rights that are well defined, some give rights to individual states and some give rights to a community of states.

The property rights that are well specified include the territorial sea and the EEZ. Even in these cases, however, certain rights are shared. A coastal state may exclude foreign vessels from fishing in its territorial waters, but it cannot prevent foreign merchant ships from navigating through them; custom requires that all nations be allowed innocent passage. This is in contrast to a state's land and internal waters, where the home state has exclusive jurisdiction. The granting of innocent passage, a precondition for liberalized trade, reflects a compromise between the rights of coastal and maritime states. Similarly, within a country's EEZ other states have high seas freedom of navigation and rights of over-flight, the laying of cables, and so on.[13] The coastal state is only given exclusive rights to explore and exploit the natural resources found in the water (fish and certain minerals like bromine), on the seabed (cobalt, copper, and manganese), and in the subsoil (oil, gas, coal, and tin). And in contrast to the 12-mile limit, the 200-mile EEZ is not automatic; states must actually claim rights to the EEZ (or to fishery zones) for these to be recognized as existing in law. Many states have not done so. For some, like the 18 states that share the Mediterranean, there is little point. The Mediterranean is a shared resource.

Custom also recognizes the coastal state's jurisdiction over the resources—especially oil and gas—of the continental shelf, an area that may extend beyond 200 miles.[14] These rights, which inhere in the law and need not be claimed, do not

---

[13] States may also claim a "contiguous zone" beyond the 12-mile territorial limit for special purposes such as the enforcement of customs, immigration, and sanitary regulations. Many states do not claim a contiguous zone, and those that do often specify different ranges; 12 miles from the territorial limit is most common.

[14] Under the Law of the Sea Convention, a coastal state's rights to the continental shelf extend no farther than 350 nautical miles from shore or 100 miles from the point at which the sea depth reaches 2500 meters. See Brownlie (1990: 223).

include the resources of the seas above the shelf, and so, unlike the EEZ, exclude even demersal fisheries. Nonetheless, rights to the continental margin constitute a further nationalization of the ocean's commercially valued resources. Beyond the continental margin, however—a distance usually of not more than about 350 miles from shore—the rights of every state are the same. The resources of the high seas and its seabed belong to no state; custom says that they belong to every state.

Even here, however, there are differences. Fish and marine mammals found beyond the EEZ, where such a zone is claimed, are subject to the rule of capture. A tuna caught in the high seas belongs exclusively to the state that possesses it. The laws governing exploitation of the common heritage are different. If a state mines manganese from the deep sea floor, for example, all states are in principle entitled to a share of the benefit, though agreement on *how* this benefit is to be shared has only recently been settled (even today, details remain to be negotiated). The 1982 LOS Convention was rejected by the Reagan Administration, and later by Presidents George H.W. Bush and Clinton, largely because of the conditions it would have imposed on deep-sea mining, including royalty payments, production limits, and the transfer of technology. The 1994 Agreement Relating to the Implementation of Part XI of the LOS was negotiated to accommodate these concerns. It shifts control of deep-sea mining toward the countries most likely to bear the risk of investing capital in such an undertaking, and thus facilitated approval of the LOS by countries like France, Germany, Japan, and the United Kingdom. President Clinton asked the Senate to ratify the treaty, but it declined to do so, and the United States remains a non-party today.

Analogous property rights apply to the sky, atmosphere, and outer space. The sky above a state's territory, including its territorial sea, is recognized as being the exclusive property of the state—but only until you reach the upper atmosphere, something like 50–100 miles above the ground (just where space begins has not been decided legally). Airplane pilots must obtain permission of over-flight from the states they wish to fly over. The orbit of a satellite, by contrast, is chosen only by the state that puts it there. Other states are not recognized as having the authority to deny access.

The law of outer space is akin to that of the high seas. Not only do states enjoy the freedom of navigation in space, including the orbiting of satellites (even geostationary satellites), but the resources of space—the moon, the planets, and other objects—also cannot be appropriated by individual states. Moreover, the 1967 Treaty on the Exploration and Use of Outer Space, Including the Moon and Other Celestial Bodies stipulates that exploitation "shall be carried out for the benefit and in the interests of all countries ... and shall be the province of all mankind." Though this treaty is only binding on its parties, this avowal of rights validates an earlier General Assembly resolution which, though non-binding, was passed unanimously in 1963, and thus provides evidence of having been established as customary law (Shaw 1991: 329). Crucially, the important space countries, including the United States and the Soviet Union (today, Russia), are both parties to the 1967 Space Treaty.[15]

---

[15] The so-called Moon Treaty (the 1979 Agreement Governing the Activities of States on the Moon and Other Celestial Bodies) declares (in Article 11) that "the moon and its resources are the common heritage

In 1988, Malta proposed making the atmosphere a part of the common heritage, much like the resources of the seabed and outer space (Bodansky 1994). However, the idea failed to attract support, and so never became law. Though the legal status of the atmosphere is still developing (the first treaty on the atmosphere was signed only in 1979), as a practical matter the atmosphere is treated like the high seas. The Framework Convention on Climate Change refers to the climate as being of "common concern to humankind" only. The Vienna Convention does not even concede this much. It merely notes that "measures to protect the ozone layer from modifications due to human activities require international co-operation and action."

High seas fisheries are held in common by *all* states, and so are global common property resources. Access to other resources, however, is limited to a few states, and further entry can easily be barred. These *shared resources* include boundary waters (rivers, lakes, and small seas that form the border of two or more states), groundwater, regional "airsheds," and wildlife that either migrate between states or that inhabit an ecosystem that straddles two or more jurisdictions. Such resources are shared, and custom says that their use must be shared, and shared equitably, among the countries that have access to them.

Examples of shared water resources include the Aral Sea, which borders two countries and is shared by five; the Mekong River, which is shared by six countries; the brackish and shallow Baltic Sea, which is bordered by eight countries; and the Northeastern African aquifer, which is located under four countries. Other shared resources include the atmosphere over Europe, a medium for transporting acid rain emissions; the vincuna, whose habitat straddles five countries; and the lesser snow goose, a peerless formation flier which migrates between its winter home in northern California and its breeding grounds on the northern edge of continental Canada and on Wrangel Island in the Russian Arctic (Lopez, 1986).

Though rights to many resources are only vaguely specified in law, jurisdiction of the last continent, Antarctica, is a mess.[16] Australia, Argentina, Chile, France, New Zealand, Norway, and the United Kingdom all claim sovereignty over slices of Antarctica, each demarcated by lines of longitude drawn from the South Pole (see Figure 5.2). Inconveniently, the wedges claimed by Argentina, Chile, and the United Kingdom overlap and comprise a disputed territory.[17] And an additional slice, representing about one-seventh of the total area, remains unclaimed by any state.

---

of mankind" and that the benefits from exploitation of the moon's resources should be shared equitably between the parties to this agreement." The phrasing of this agreement is reminiscent of the LOS treaty, though the 1979 treaty has not been endorsed by any state having the capability to exploit the moon's resources, including the United States and Russia, and is thus not recognized by customary law.

[16] Unlike Antarctica, which is a continent, the Arctic is a frozen sea, an ice desert. Sovereignty over the Arctic is divided among the polar states: Canada, Denmark, Finland, Iceland, Norway, Sweden, Russia, and the United States. There are no overlapping claims, and no part of the Arctic is unclaimed.

[17] When its claim was challenged by Chile and Argentina, Britain offered to take the dispute to the World Court, but the offer was declined. In 1955, Britain applied to the Court unilaterally for arbitration, but Argentina and Chile said that the Court did not have jurisdiction in the matter, and the case was not heard (Shapley 1985). The dispute continues today.

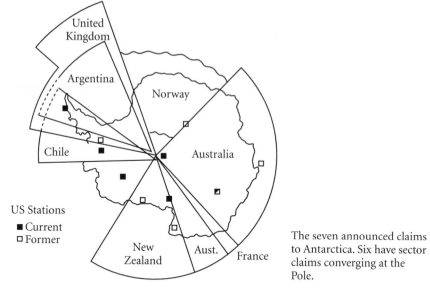

The seven announced claims
to Antarctica. Six have sector
claims converging at the
Pole.

Figure 5.2. *Sovereign claims to Antarctica*

Source: Shapely (1985: 68)

It is perhaps even more significant, however, that all of these claims are unrecognized by most other countries, including the United States, South Africa (a neighbor of Antarctica), and Russia, the former superpower. The latter three countries, however, are all members of the exclusive Antarctic club, and the rest of the world does not recognize *their* right to decide the fate of this continent. Some club-outsiders have proposed making Antarctica a world park, a territory held in common and off-limits to exploitation. Most of the parties to the Antarctic Treaty (discussed in Chapter 6) disagree, but they yielded to external pressure by banning mineral exploration for 50 years, starting in 1998, the year that the 1991 Antarctic Environmental Protocol entered into force. The current ban thus pushes aside the dispute between the members and non-members of the Antarctic club—for the time being anyway. Given current technologies and prices, however, exploitation of Antarctica is unprofitable in any case. The big question is whether the Antarctic Club will ban exploration and development should prices rise, and should technology become more congenial to the harsh conditions that prevail on this frozen continent. The answer isn't obvious, but it seems to me that a new regime for Antarctica will have to be inclusive, not exclusive. As noted in the preface, the existing regime lacks the legitimacy needed to make it stand in the long run.

5.9. SOVEREIGN EQUALITY

Being universal in application, custom helps define the rules of the game for every externality—rules that were taken as givens in the games studied in Chapters 3 and 4.

One such rule is that each state possesses the right to act. In the games studied previously, this right was expressed as the right to choose between playing Abate and Pollute. Rights like this one are derived from custom. Custom says that states are sovereign equals, meaning that each state possesses the right to manage its own affairs without fear of intervention by others. It also tells us that each state is held by others not to be bound by an international treaty to which it has failed to give its own consent. That is, the metagame of customary law decides that states are free to be signatories or non-signatories to a treaty as they please.

To recognize each state as possessing the same right to act is not, of course, to recognize that the actions of each state have the same *consequences*. If the United States ceases to emit CFCs, future depletion of the ozone layer will be materially affected. If the tiny island-state of Vanuatu does so, the change will go unnoticed. States are not symmetric; they have different payoff functions and action sets and much else besides. But states do have the same right to act. Indeed, having such a right is one of the most important aspects of statehood, the others being possession of a permanent population, a defined territory, and a government with the capacity to enter into relations with other states (Brownlie 1990). It is because international law recognizes every state as possessing the same right to act that both the United States and Vanuatu are allowed one vote in the United Nations General Assembly.

And yet, though countries are sovereign equals, some carry much greater weight in forming and sustaining custom (whether for good or ill). A customary law relating to the seas must have the support of the major maritime nations. Whether Vanuatu supports the 12-mile territorial sea is of little significance. It certainly will not affect whether this limit becomes a customary law. The support given by the United States, however, will be crucial. Similarly, a rule relating to the use of outer space must be approved by the space powers, the United States and Russia especially, or else have no chance of becoming customary law.

This imbalance is naturally resented by smaller states. But even a superpower must make concessions, and customary law is sometimes resented by big states like the United States, too.[18] Dissatisfaction is an inevitable consequence of both the diversity of state interests and the way in which custom is constituted. Customary law reflects how states behave, not abstract moral reasoning. Thus, there can be no presumption that the outcomes supported by custom are desirable, either from the perspective of particular countries or even in the aggregate.

5.10. TERRITORIAL SOVEREIGNTY

In 1895, US Attorney General Judson Harmon rejected Mexico's claim to the waters of the Rio Grande originating north of the border, arguing that "the fundamental principle of international law is the absolute sovereignty of every Nation as against all others within its own territory"(Caponera 1980: 7). As noted earlier, the right of a state to act is fundamental to the notion of sovereignty. Harmon was therefore only

---

[18] See, for example, Rabkin's (1998) critique.

affirming an established right. What invests Harmon's speech with historical significance is the fact that, only eleven years after it was delivered, the United States did an about-face, as it were, agreeing to share the disputed waters with Mexico.[19] I stress that this change of mind occurred without any threat of force. The concession by the United States was voluntary.

The US also conceded its right to act again in order to resolve the Colorado River dispute. In a 1973 agreement entitled The Permanent and Definitive Solution to the International Problem of the Salinity of the Colorado River, the United States pledged to limit salt concentrations at Mexico's Morelos Dam.[20] This was more than a gesture. To fulfil its pledge, the United States built the world's largest desalinization plant near Yuma, Arizona.[21] The plant cost $120m to build and over $16m annually to operate.[22]

Why did the United States acquiesce in these instances? One reason was that it was in its interests to do so. Suppose that the United States had *not* bowed to Mexico's demands. Then Mexico could have felt justified in ignoring pleas by the United States for assistance in resolving other crossborder disputes. Though the Colorado and Rio Grande Rivers flow south into Mexico, for example, the San Pedro and New Rivers flow north from Mexico into the United States, and the US would need Mexico's help in maintaining the quality of these waters (Utton 1988). It would also need Mexico's cooperation in resolving other crossborder problems, including illegal immigration, drug trafficking, and trade.

Failure to concede sovereignty over the Colorado might also have affected relations between the United States and third parties. Had the United States insisted that it had no obligation to maintain the quantity or quality of water flowing into Mexico, Canada would surely have felt justified in absolving itself from any responsibility to safeguard the waters flowing south of *its* border. As well, the United States was conscious that, had it not acceded to Mexico's request, then it would have been seen by others—especially by other developing countries—as having exploited its poorer neighbor. Relations between the United States and the South may thus have been damaged. Viewed in its proper context, the United States probably acted in its own interests when it retreated from the Harmon doctrine on these occasions.[23]

In its dispute with Pakistan over diversion of the waters of the Indus, India also invoked the Harmon doctrine, claiming "full freedom ... to draw off such waters as it needed" (Birnie and Boyle 1992: 219). Soon after asserting this right, however, India changed its mind, too. In signing the Indus Waters Treaty of 1960, India agreed to share the resource with its neighbor and rival. The difference between this dispute and the North American examples discussed above is that the specter of war hung

---

[19] This agreement was formalized in the 1906 Convention between the United States and Mexico concerning the Equitable Distribution of the Waters of the Rio Grande for Irrigation Purposes.

[20] To be more precise, this agreement was a minute of the International Boundary and Water Commission, the body set up under the Mexico–United States Boundary Waters Convention of 1889.

[21] This is not to say that the problems of salinity on the Colorado have gone away; see Utton (1988).

[22] See LeMarquand (1977: table 1, p. 37).

[23] See LeMarquand (1977). Mäler (1990) cites a study by Kneese which arrives at a similar conclusion.

over the Indus negotiations, a war that could have destabilized an entire region. Peaceful resolution of this dispute thus became the business of third party states.

To avert an armed conflict, a number of member countries asked the World Bank to broker an agreement between the two old adversaries. Though the hydrology of the basin recommended integrated management of the Indus, the World Bank proposed physically separating (that is, nationalizing) the two countries' water supplies so as to prevent the externality—and the attendant risk of a military encounter—from recurring. In particular, the Bank proposed allocating the three eastern rivers (the Ravi, Beas, and Sutlej) to India and the three western rivers (the Indus, Jhelum, and Chenab) to Pakistan. India agreed to construct the canals needed to divert the water, but Pakistan protested that the western rivers would be insufficient to replace the country's historic use of the eastern rivers, a claim that was later confirmed by a follow-up study. To remedy this situation, the World Bank amended its original proposal to include storage dams. However, India refused to pay for these, arguing that they were not needed and that its liability should in any case be based on the Bank's original proposal. The stalemate only ended when the Bank offered to pay for the replacement works itself, financed by Australia, Canada, Germany, New Zealand, the United Kingdom, Italy, and the United States (see Kirmani 1990).

5.11. THE "NO HARM" PRINCIPLE

It might seem from these cases that the allocation of rights to shared resources is *ad hoc*—that the United States and India forfeited their claims to territorial sovereignty because doing so happened to serve their interests on these occasions. In the details, the allocation of rights usually is *ad hoc*. But it is also governed by widely held beliefs about how rights ought to be allocated, beliefs that are enshrined in custom. For, though custom recognizes the right of an upstream state to act, it also recognizes the right of every downstream state not to be harmed.

In a famous decision, the arbitral tribunal set up by the United States and Canada under a 1935 convention to resolve the *Trail Smelter* quarrel explicitly acknowledged the right of a state not to be harmed. According to the tribunal, "no State has the right to use or permit the use of its territory in such a manner as to cause injury by fumes in or to the territory of another or the properties or persons therein, when the case is of serious consequence and the injury is established by clear and convincing evidence."[24]

This so-called "no harm" principle acquired special legitimacy when included in the 1972 Stockholm Declaration on the Human Environment. According to Principle 21, "States have, in accordance with the charter of the United Nations and the principles of international law, the sovereign right to exploit their own resources pursuant to their own environmental policies and the responsibility to ensure that activities within their jurisdiction or control do not cause damage to the environment of other States or of areas beyond the limits of national jurisdiction."[25]

---

[24] Trail Smelter Arbitral Tribunal (1941: 716).

[25] The Rio Declaration affirms the sovereign right of countries "to exploit their own resources pursuant to their own environmental *and developmental* policies" (emphasis added).

Though the second part of Principle 21—the part that validates the principle of territorial integrity or the right not to be harmed—has been emphasized by environmentalists and legal scholars, endorsement of the opposing principle of territorial sovereignty in the first part makes the entirety of Principle 21 a contradiction. Which part more often prevails in practice? Usually the first. As Björkbom (1988: 126), a Swedish diplomat, notes: "In theory and words [states] may subscribe to the famous Principle 21 of the 1972 Stockholm Declaration .... When it comes to practice and deeds, however, the second part of the principle is far too often disregarded."

When states do obey the "no harm" principle, the reason usually has less to do with the desire simply to adhere to the principle than with self-interest. Thus, while it is often noted that the arbitral tribunal deciding the *Trail Smelter* case based its decision on the "no harm" principle, it is less frequently recalled that Canada had accepted responsibility for past damages *before* the tribunal was convened. Canada and the United States share a long border, and the *Trail Smelter* was but one of many disputes that needed mending. Canada may thus have accepted responsibility in the expectation of a reciprocal gesture by the United States. Indeed, the arbitral tribunal acknowledged as much when it noted that, "while the United States' interests may now be claimed to be injured by the operations of a Canadian corporation, it is equally possible that at some time in the future Canadian interests might be claimed to be injured by an American corporation."[26]

One reason that the "no harm" principle is more usually disregarded is that the causes and consequences of many environmental problems are uncertain. The "no harm" principle is easily dodged if it is not known whether harm is being caused by a particular activity and whether a reduction or alteration in this activity would alleviate the harm. The *Trail Smelter* case was unusual in this respect. Recall the tribunal's reference to "clear and convincing evidence." The damage caused by the Trail smelter was real and measurable (the tribunal, after all, was charged with calculating the damage); cause and effect were manifest.[27] Where uncertainties loom large, however, "upstream" states can respond in different ways—for example, by pledging merely to fund research to reduce uncertainties, as the United States offered to do when Canada demanded that crossborder acid rain emissions be reduced.[28] (Recall that Canada responded in a similar manner to pleas by the United States to halt the pelagic seal hunt.)

Moreover, it is difficult to say what the "no harm" principle actually requires states to do. It might be interpreted as requiring that states not cause "serious" harm (as in the *Trail Smelter* decision), but when does a harm become serious? It may require that certain environmental thresholds not be exceeded or that critical loads be violated, but how are these levels to be established? "Harm" in this context is a murky

---

[26] Trail Smelter Arbitral Tribunal (1941: 685).

[27] Still, there were uncertainties, and the tribunal had to use its judgment, informed by mountains of evidence as well as expert testimony, as to the consequences of elevated levels of sulfur dioxide emissions.

[28] In this case, the United States' reluctance to abate its emissions was given some legitimacy by Canada's reluctance to reduce its own emissions. See McMahon (1988). Note, however, that the long-standing dispute was settled in the 1991 Canada–US Air Quality Agreement.

concept. The convention establishing the *Trail Smelter* tribunal asked that a regime for the smelter be designed that would prevent future damage, and the tribunal did so by prescribing permissible emissions of sulfur dioxide that varied with the growing season, the time of day, the turbulence, and the wind. Were these the "right" limits, preventing "serious harm" but going no farther than necessary? Presumably, opinions would differ on this question. Neither party contested the schedule, but both had agreed previously to be bound by the tribunal's decisions. In most cases, decisions like these will not be delegated. They will rather have to be negotiated. In pleading with their upwind neighbors to reduce their acid rain emissions, for example, Sweden, Norway, and Canada invoked both Principle 21 and the *Trail Smelter* decision, but they did not cling to these ideals, expecting or even hoping that the appropriate emission reductions would be easily and objectively determined. Rather they sought to bring their neighbors to the negotiating table, for the purpose of agreeing on *some* level of emission reductions.

The question of measurement aside, the "no harm" principle certainly has great normative appeal. However, it is as well to recall Coase's (1960) argument that the direction of an externality depends on the initial allocation of rights. If the upstream state has a right to pollute, the downstream state suffers the externality. If the downstream state has a right not to be harmed, however, then the upstream state suffers by being prevented from developing.

Recognizing this symmetry is important for reasons of efficiency as well as equity. Handl (1986) endorses the "no harm" principle partly based on the belief that it supports an efficient outcome. Though giving the right not to be harmed to the downstream party may (provided certain conditions hold) result in an efficient final allocation, Coase (1960) also showed that giving the right to pollute to the upstream party could result in precisely the same final allocation. Moreover, though efficiency insists that the upstream country internalize the damage that its own actions impose downstream, it also requires that the downstream country reduce its exposure to pollution. (The marginal cost of abatement upstream should equal the marginal cost of reducing exposure to damage downstream, which should in turn equal the marginal damage of exposure downstream.)[29] Enforcement of the "no harm" principle is thus not sufficient to guarantee efficiency. States must also be able to negotiate away from the initial allocation.

From an equity perspective, too, strict adherence to the "no harm" principle is not entirely satisfying. Its appeal depends on the identities of the upstream and downstream parties. Thus, while the United States paid the full cost of reducing the salinity of the Colorado River, Mexico has not had to pay the full cost of reducing the flow of pollution northwards. In a 1958 minute to the proceedings of the International Boundary and Water Commission (a body set up by the 1944 Water Treaty), Mexico agreed to pay for the operating and maintenance costs of joint sewage treatment

---

[29] Coase (1960) thus argued that, if the upstream party is to internalize the damages that its pollution causes downstream, then the downstream party should internalize the abatement costs that its own activities cause to be incurred upstream. See Baumol and Oates (1988) for a discussion of this "small numbers" case. See also Farrell (1987*b*) for a discussion of the role of information.

facilities. But it was only required to pay in proportion to its share of the sewage, adjusted for local wages; the United States agreed to bear all remaining costs. A 1967 minute further recognized that, if the sewage treatment facilities were expanded to satisfy the sanitation and health priorities of the United States, then the latter should bear a larger burden of the construction and development costs. And in a 1988 agreement on the expansion of treatment facilities on the border between Arizona and Sonora, Mexico was made to pay just 55 percent of the cost, even though it was responsible for 75 percent of the effluent requiring treatment (see Mumme 1994). These allocations conflict with the "no harm" principle and yet seem fairer, given the wide disparity in incomes between the two countries.

To summarize, international law recognizes the rights of both "upstream" *and* "downstream" states—that is, polluters as well as victims. There is nothing unusual about this. Principles often conflict in domestic settings, too. However, in domestic situations conflicting principles can be reconciled by *rules*. Indeed, Trail-smelter-like games are normally mediated by the state imposing an emission standard, one that protects the victims to a degree, but one that also allows the polluter to continue to emit some quantity of the pollutant without liability. The important difference between domestic and international disputes of this kind is that there is no third party that can independently develop a rule for settling every dispute. These must instead be resolved in a decentralized fashion. Since they cannot be imposed, they must be negotiated.

However, since it is really only the final allocation that determines efficiency, treaties tend not to negotiate an initial distribution of rights explicitly. The agreed initial allocation is more often implicit in the arrangements that may be made regarding side payments. I shall illustrate how custom helps shape property rights allocations in the penultimate section of this chapter.

5.12. CUSTOM AND CONTEXT

Customary principles do not so much define an initial allocation of property rights. They rather "play a significant role by setting the terms of debate, providing evaluative standards, serving as a basis to criticize other states' actions, and establishing a framework of principles within which negotiations may take place to develop more specific norms, usually in treaties" (Bodansky 1995: 119). Put differently, customary principles like the "no harm" principle provide a normative context to a negotiation.

In analytical game theory, context is irrelevant. But in experimental game theory it can make a big difference. Consider the Coase-like bargaining experiments conducted by Hoffman and Spitzer (1982, 1985). In these games, two or more people must bargain over a final allocation and a money side payment. One subject is chosen to be the "controller," the person who is entitled to move first and so claim an initial allocation. In some experiments, the controller is chosen by the flip of a coin. In other experiments, the controller is determined by winning a game of skill (specifically, a game of nim). From the perspective of analytical game theory, it should not matter how the controller is chosen. But in experiments with real people it does matter. The researchers discovered that "controllers were more likely to demand their individual maxima if the right to be controller was won in a game of skill and then reinforced by the experimenter" (Hoffman 1997: 421). By much the same reasoning, upstream states like the United States may choose not to demand full adherence to the Harmon doctrine because they recognize that their advantaged position was not earned or deserved—an observation reinforced by the existence of the customary "no harm" principle.

In another classroom experiment, I asked my students to negotiate a remedy to a unidirectional externality. There were two states, one upstream and one downstream. The upstream state polluted its downstream neighbor, and the two countries had an opportunity to negotiate an agreed level of pollution reduction. They could also negotiate a money side payment as part of the overall deal. The costs and benefits for pollution reduction were common knowledge, and I constructed the negotiation in such a way as to ensure that there was a unique, Pareto efficient outcome as regards pollution reduction, but not in terms of a money side payment. Implicit in the agreed money side payment was a perception as between the two players of the initial allocation of rights. If the students agreed that the upstream state should pay the downstream state for its residual damage, then the "no harm" principle would be validated by the negotiation. If the downstream state paid its upstream neighbor for the full cost of the agreed emission reduction, however, then the parties would be endorsing the principle of territorial sovereignty. Prior to the start of the negotiations, the students were told that the upstream state had claimed a right to use its waters as it saw fit and that the downstream state had claimed a right to receive unpolluted water.

Different groups of students were asked to play different versions of this negotiation. In one version of the game, students were told that the upstream state was five times richer on a per capita basis than the downstream state. In another version, I reversed these figures, making the downstream state richer. I also told some students about a previous agreement reached by the two parties. This agreement concerned an unrelated externality but suggested a precedent. In one of these negotiations, students were told that the upstream party previously paid the downstream country two-thirds of the compensation demanded by this party. In another version, I simply reversed these roles, telling the students that the downstream party had previously agreed to pay the upstream country two-thirds of the money demanded as compensation for reducing its pollution. In a fifth version of this negotiation game I provided no information at all about incomes and prior settlements.

Technically, the extraneous information about incomes and precedent should have made no difference to the negotiated outcomes. However, there were clear differences in the agreed side payments between the different cases.[30] If the upstream state were richer, it tended to get a smaller side payment. If the upstream state were poorer, it got a larger side payment on average. Similarly, the precedent of an earlier agreement influenced the average negotiated side payment. This illustrates the point made previously

---

[30] Three or four pairs of students negotiated each version of this game. In about four-fifths of the cases, the students agreed on the Pareto efficient allocation of pollution reduction. In a minority of cases, the students left money on the table, so to speak. In a game of complete information and common knowledge, this should not happen. Having run many experiments like this one before, I am confident that, with more experience, all the students would have agreed on the Pareto efficient final allocation.

that context seems to matter to the outcome of negotiations. And custom helps to shape context. If it doesn't unambiguously identify an allocation of rights, it does at the very least identify some allocations as being unlawful. Along with other pieces of information, it helps to restructure the set of outcomes that can be negotiated.

5.13. EQUITABLE UTILIZATION

Resolution of environmental disputes almost invariably demands mutual concessions, compromise, and give and take. Thus, concessions offered by the United States were matched by Mexico's acceptance of the right of the US to siphon off a quantity of the Rio Grande's waters. Mexico also agreed to accept water from the Colorado that was of poorer quality than could be obtained upstream, let alone poorer than it received in years past. Moreover, the 1973 Colorado River Treaty did not impose an absolute minimum threshold for the quality of the water reaching Mexico but a level determined relative to what was available at the Imperial Dam in California. A similar compromise underpinned the Indus settlement. Even in the *Trail Smelter* case the tribunal sought to impose an "equitable" regime for the future management of the smelter. The tribunal rejected a request by the United States that Canada pay a predetermined sum of money whenever sulfur dioxide concentrations exceeded a given level. The tribunal reasoned that "such a regime would unduly and unnecessarily hamper the operations of the Trail Smelter and would not constitute a 'solution fair to all parties concerned'" (Trail Smelter Arbitral Tribunal 1941: 726).

These decisions to balance the interests of the parties were not made arbitrarily. The negotiated settlements to the Rio Grande, Colorado, and Indus disputes all refer to the principle of "equitable utilization," suggesting that it was not just the circumstances of each case that promoted a compromise but customary law. At the same time, and as already indicated, it was also in the interests of these countries to comply with custom on these occasions. It is this mutual reinforcement that makes custom self-sustaining.

The problem here as before is that the customary principle is poorly defined. What exactly does "equitable utilization" require? Custom does not and cannot say. This is something that must instead be decided on a case-by-case basis, by negotiation.

Of course, negotiation is costly, and this is why governments define rights within their territorial boundaries and do not often leave these to be negotiated between the parties themselves. Ambiguity imposes transaction costs.[31] Such costs are an unavoidable burden imposed by the anarchical international system.

5.14. INDIVIDUAL vs COLLECTIVE RESPONSIBILITY

I shall show in later chapters that it becomes increasingly difficult to sustain full cooperation by means of a self-enforcing agreement when the number of countries that share a resource is larger. Here we can note a related observation: as the number of parties increases, the requirements of custom become progressively more vague,

---

[31] Even at the domestic level, Coase exaggerates by assuming that the initial allocation is chosen at zero cost. Property rights must usually be decided by a political process, providing opportunities for interested

and custom therefore becomes less influential. Moreover, and in contrast to an argument I made earlier in this chapter, this is true even if countries are symmetric. For a unidirectional externality involving just two countries, it is pretty obvious that mutual recognition of the "no harm" principle requires that the polluter state make concessions. But when the outcome depends on the actions of a sufficient number of countries, it is less clear what custom requires.

It is true that the responsibility not to harm other states, as articulated by the Stockholm Declaration, is unconditional; the Declaration does not say that a state must abate if and only if others abate. But, in general, the *consequences* of one state's behavior will depend on the behavior of others, and the Stockholm Declaration is above all else concerned with these consequences. Principle 21 says that states must not cause harm to other states or the global commons; it does not say that states must play Abate.

To see the significance of this distinction, suppose that there exists an environmental threshold such that, though all countries pollute the global environment, abatement by any country on its own would fail to improve environmental quality even by a little bit. To improve the environment, some minimum number of countries (two or greater) must reduce their emissions. Under these circumstances, a country that failed to play Abate could not be held to be individually responsible for the global pollution if not enough other states played Abate.

Even where abatement by each country *would* improve the environment, irrespective of the actions taken by others, the perceived responsibility of each country not to cause harm may depend on the behavior of others. Philosopher Russell Hardin (1988: 159) has made a similar observation about individuals. "If my responsibility for producing a particular result depends in part on what others have done," he says, "moral judgement of my action or inaction may turn not on whether the result is produced but on the 'fairness' of my action or inaction in the light of what others do." If a country pollutes the environment but by no more than any other country, then it may be seen to have behaved responsibly, or at least not to have behaved irresponsibly, whatever the consequences. The responsibility for collectively achieving more desirable outcomes is usually a collective responsibility.

Indeed, it is probably for this reason that customary law seeks not only to allocate rights but also to impose a duty upon states to cooperate (Shaw 1991). I should stress, however, that this is merely a procedural obligation. International law requires that states consult and negotiate in good faith. It does not require that they reach agreement, let alone that they sustain efficient outcomes. An upstream state has a duty to hear its neighbor's complaint. If it is unsatisfied with the terms being proposed, however, it can walk away from the negotiations and act pretty much as it pleases—subject, of course, to not causing harm downstream. What may prevent the upstream state from acting with impunity is not so much the "no harm" principle as the recognition that its own interests would be better served by compromise.

parties to dissipate the rents associated with improving the efficiency of resource utilization. For a discussion of this in a domestic context, see Anderson and Hill (1990). Skaperdas (1992) examines the allocation of rights in an anarchic setting, but one devoid of customary law or of an environment conducive to its development.

5.15. RHINE CASE STUDY

Let me now illustrate the central points of this chapter by telling another story, the Rhine chlorides case.[32] The dispute was eventually resolved by means of an international treaty, but the need for the treaty, and the design of the treaty—especially the agreed allocation of rights—were shaped by custom.

Sometimes known as the "sewer of Europe," the Rhine has been polluted by salts (as well as chemical and thermal wastes) since the 1930s. Figure 5.3 shows how the salt emissions were distributed in the 1970s. The bulk of chloride emissions originated in Germany and France; only about two percent entered from Switzerland.

The Netherlands is situated downstream of the other riparian states, and in this case was the sole victim; the upstream riparians were not affected by the chloride pollution. Though not a major risk to human health, salt can be tasted in drinking water. It can also damage water supply systems and lower the yields from irrigated agriculture. Salt pollution seriously harmed the Netherlands, which still takes about two-thirds of its freshwater from the Rhine. For many years, Dutch diplomats campaigned to get the upstream states to reduce their salt emissions, but it was not until the 1970s that these efforts came close to paying off.

At this time, about 40 percent of the salt pollution in the Rhine was emitted by a French state-owned potash mine, Les Mines de Potasse d'Alsace. This was also the only pollution source that could be easily controlled, and it was agreed early on in the negotiations that emission reductions needed to be concentrated at this mine (you can think of this as representing the full cooperative outcome). This left just two substantive issues to be resolved. Which countries should pay for the costs of cleaning up the pollution? and In what proportions should these payments be made? Strict adherence to the "no harm" principle would say that France and the other upstream states should pay for all the agreed clean up (plus further compensation). By contrast, the victim pays principle, or the Harmon doctrine, would require that Holland foot the entire bill. Custom could offer no more guidance than this, and in the end the states did just what you would expect—they struck a compromise.

Though the Netherlands was the victim, it was not entirely blameless.[33] The upstream riparians argued that sea water held back by Holland's famous dikes seeped into the Rhine delta. They also alleged that much of the chloride load in the Netherlands's groundwater was caused by North Sea salt water penetration. Pollution of these supplies was Holland's fault, and yet this pollution made it necessary for the Netherlands to draw more fresh water from the Rhine. Hence, while the upstream riparians admitted to polluting the Rhine, they also argued that the Netherlands's *need* for Rhine water was of its own making.

---

[32] I am drawing here from the excellent case analyses by LeMarquand (1977) and Bernauer (1996).

[33] As noted previously, the direction of an externality depends on the distribution of rights. If the downstream state has a right not to be harmed, it will put too many resources in harm's way, so to speak, forcing the upstream state to reduce its pollution even more or to compensate the downstream state for the increased damage. In this case, the actions of the downstream state harm the upstream state. The externality is reversed.

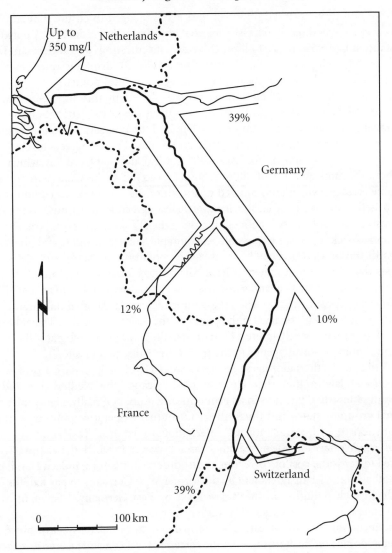

Figure 5.3. *Chloride emissions to the Rhine (from sources discharging more than 1 kg/sec)*
Source: Le Marquand (1977: 103)

Since custom could not offer an unambiguous allocation rule in this case, the parties had little alternative but to negotiate an allocation. In 1972, they agreed that emissions (by storage) at the French mine should be cut by 60 kilograms per second (kg/s), and they further agreed that the costs of this, estimated at FF 100 million, were to be shared according to the following formula: France and Germany were each to pay 30 percent; Switzerland was to pay 6 percent; and the Netherlands, the victim, was to pay 34 percent. In addition, all four states pledged to ensure that emissions from other sources did not increase. The goal of the emission reduction coupled with this stand-still provision was to limit chloride concentrations at the German–Dutch border to 200 milligrams per liter (mg/l), a limit value for drinking water established by the World Health Organization (and so an obvious focal point).

Why were the costs of the storage project shared in this way? According to Bernauer (1996: 210), the agreed allocation "reflects the relative contributions of the individual countries to the pollution problem and the intensity of their demand for chloride reductions." LeMarquand (1977) adds that France agreed to contribute toward the cost of abatement for reasons of "equity," and that Germany, which emitted about the same quantity of salt as France, agreed to pay the same share for much the same reason. Switzerland, situated upstream of the potash mine, could not possibly benefit from the project. But it nevertheless agreed to contribute to the effort for reasons of "solidarity", defined by the OECD's Principles on Transfrontier Pollution as seeking "as far as possible an equitable balance of rights and obligations as regards the zones concerned by transfrontier pollution." LeMarquand (1977: 119) suggests that Switzerland may also have contributed for moral reasons ("the Swiss feel it would be hypocritical and somewhat discriminatory to take advantage of their position as upstream riparian when these same obligations [to maintain water quality] apply under domestic law [with respect to the Swiss cantons]"). They also contributed for reasons of self-interest ("no doubt [the Swiss] also feel that solidarity on this issue could be advantageous to them on other subsequent issues").

Why did the Netherlands agree to pay as well? Handl (1986: 456), a professor of international law, argues that Holland paid because the Netherlands and the upstream states were "partners in an economically, if not politically, highly integrated regional group of states and thus subject to mutually operative political restraints uncharacteristic of a state's 'normal' international relations." To Handl, this was a special case. We have already noted other cases, however, in which the victim has contributed towards the cost of correcting transborder externalities. Indeed Handl gives yet another example: an agreement by the former West Germany to pay half the costs of reducing salt pollution in the Werra River by East Germany.[34] Payment by the victim-state is not the exception. It is rather the rule.

Agreement on how to allocate costs turned out to be relatively easy, but bigger problems loomed on the horizon. After the agreement was concluded, France revised its estimate of the cost of the storage project, increasing it by a factor of nearly five. Moreover, a feasibility study further suggested that the proposed solution of storing the wastes could contaminate groundwater. France also proposed that the other riparians not make the single lump-sum payment as agreed previously but instead contribute in the same proportions to the annual costs of storage—whatever these turned out to be. The other parties, however, refused to write a blank check.

After four more years of negotiation, a revised agreement was finally made ready for signing in 1976. The Convention on the Protection of the Rhine Against Pollution by

---

[34] See Mäler (1990) for a further discussion of the victim pays principle and its application in various cases.

Chlorides required that emissions be reduced by 20 kg/s in a first phase and by another 40 kg/s in subsequent phases. All these reductions were to take place "in French territory"—that is, at the potash mine. The agreement makes no mention of state responsibility, perhaps because of earlier court decisions that reflected conflicting views (see Kiss and Shelton 1997: 321). Implicitly, the parties accepted some sharing of rights.

The first phase reduction was to be achieved by injecting the dissolved salt into the subsoil, to a depth of 1800 meters, within eighteen months of the agreement entering into force. This was estimated to cost FF 132 million, and the parties agreed to share this cost according to the 1972 formula.

However, it was later discovered that, when the wastes were stored at times of low water flow, salt seeped into the groundwater, contaminating Germany's supplies. Germany therefore insisted that France close a facility that regulated emissions into the Rhine. Unfortunately for the Netherlands, however, closure of this facility increased emissions into the Rhine at times of low water flow, subtracting from the benefit of the 20 kg/s reduction.

To make matters worse, ratification of the agreement by France was delayed, ostensibly because of local opposition in the Alsace. In 1979, the agreement was actually withdrawn from the French parliament. Following more diplomatic pressures, the treaty was resubmitted in 1983 and ratified by the end of this year. This allowed it to enter into force in 1985, twenty years after negotiations began.

In 1987, however, a few weeks before deep injection of the mine's salt wastes was to begin, France announced that it would stockpile the salt wastes on land rather than inject it deep into the subsoil as previously agreed. France also insisted that the agreed reduction of emissions be cut back to 15 kg/s as a consequence of the closure of a French soda factory situated on a tributary of the Rhine. The other parties gave into these demands, even though their total contributions in terms of money were not reduced. They were impatient and wanted something—anything—to show for so many years of negotiations.

Of course, this only addressed the first phase of reductions. The 1976 agreement also required that emissions into the Rhine be reduced by an additional 40 kg/s. In 1991, after several more years of negotiations, a protocol to the 1976 agreement was signed, specifying a second phase of reductions. This involved stockpiling the salt on land, and later discharging the wastes into the Rhine subject to ensuring that the concentration of chlorides at the German–Dutch border stayed within the 200 mg/l limit agreed in 1972. The original agreement to reduce emissions by 60 kg/s was thus officially abandoned. The costs of implementing the new agreement were once again to be shared according to the earlier formula, though this time Switzerland was granted a one-off "credit" of FF 12 million, since its only major source of chloride emissions, a soda factory, was now closed. As a consequence of both the earlier French maneuver and the Swiss adjustment, the Netherlands was now paying a larger share of the cost of a project that yielded it a smaller benefit.

The 1991 agreement also required that the Netherlands reduce the concentration of salts in its IJsselmeer reservoir, which supplies Amsterdam with fresh water. Most of the salt pollution in the IJsselmeer entered from the Rhine. But brackish water was also pumped into the IJsselmeer for the purpose of reclaiming land from the North Sea. The agreement required that this water be diverted to the North Sea, with the costs again being shared according to the 30–30–34–6 formula.

Perhaps because of the long delays, perhaps because of the modest reductions being undertaken, the Netherlands had in the meantime modified its water supply system and irrigation techniques to reduce the damage caused by chloride pollution. As noted earlier, efficiency may demand some adaptation. But possibly too much was spent on adaptation in this instance. Given that emissions were cut back only slightly, the marginal costs of reducing damage by adaptation probably exceeded the marginal cost of reducing damage by reducing inflows.

Though concentrations at the German–Dutch border were kept within the 200 mg/l limit agreed in 1972, the Rhine agreements made little difference. The 15 kg/s emission reduction achieved by the first agreement reduced the total chlorine load of the Rhine by only four percent, and the emission flow adjustments effected by the second agreement were negligible, as the 200 mg/l threshold was rarely exceeded by this time. Emissions from the French potassium mine were falling, as output fell for reasons having nothing to do with the pollution abatement efforts (the mine is scheduled to be shut in 2004). Emissions from German coal mines also fell, because of cutbacks in production unrelated to the international agreements. As Bernauer (1996: 228) put it, "The outcome of the sixty years of effort is characterized by 'too little, too late,' that is, very small if any joint gains and very little impact on the environment."

5.16. CONCLUSION

Many of the rules of any particular cooperation game are determined by the metagame of customary law. Custom identifies the players, delineates their territories, and invests players with rights to act. It therefore helps determine the nature of a crossborder externality. However, custom also imposes responsibilities. It lets states decide for themselves whether they want to participate in international treaties, but it requires that states make sincere efforts to cooperate. It allows states to act as they please, but it also requires that states be good neighbors and "take adequate steps to control and regulate sources of serious global environmental pollution or transboundary harm within their territory or subject to their jurisdiction" (Birnie and Boyle 1992: 89). Custom cannot make countries abide by the decisions of the World Court, but it does compel countries to seek peaceful remedies to their crossborder conflicts.

The obligation to cooperate in good faith is perhaps the most important responsibility required by custom. Few of today's crossborder externalities can be corrected by custom alone. Particular disputes more often need to be resolved by negotiation, the result of which invariably becomes codified in a treaty. Custom helps to bring states to the negotiating table, even if it cannot make them agree. It directs states to seek an equitable solution, even if it fails to define precisely what this means. These details must rather be negotiated: slowly, frustratingly, line by line, and at considerable cost. I discuss how this is done in the next chapter.

6

International Environmental Agreements

We are every day, in one sense, accepting limitations upon our complete freedom of action... We have more than 4,300 treaties and international agreements, two-thirds of which have been entered into in the past 25 years... Each one of which at least limits our freedom of action. We exercise our sovereignty going into these agreements. Secretary of State Dean Rusk (1965)[1]

6.1. INTRODUCTION

Cooperative arrangements for managing shared environmental resources are typically codified in international environmental agreements (IEAs), variously referred to as treaties, conventions, protocols, covenants, compacts, agreements, charters, and acts.[2] IEAs differ from custom in that they are negotiated, written down in black and white, and legally binding only on the countries that consent to be bound by them.[3] If custom offers a general curative to transnational environmental problems, IEAs provide issue-specific remedies.

International environmental agreements address almost every kind of transnational environmental issue. They establish regimes for conserving marine mammals, such as whales and seals; fish, like tuna and salmon; biodiversity; migratory birds; and particular species of wildlife like the polar bear and vicuna. They obligate countries to preserve unique ecosystems like the Serengeti and the Galapagos Islands, and sites of cultural heritage, including the Pyramids and Hadrian's Wall. IEAs coordinate policies for preventing the spread of pests like the Mediterranean fruit fly and plant diseases like Dutch elm disease, and for controlling swarms of desert locusts, huge plagues of which can range over sixty or more countries. They impel countries to reduce pollution in regional and inland seas as well as in the high seas, by controlling run-off, setting emission standards, regulating tanker design, and establishing liability in the event of an oil spill. They create rules for managing Antarctica's mineral resources and marine life, including krill, whales, and penguins; they regulate civil nuclear power by requiring timely notification of a nuclear accident; they create organizations for managing shared river basins; and they establish common standards for safeguarding workers from toxic substances, asbestos, and other forms of

---

[1] Testimony before the Senate Foreign Relations Committee; from Ikenberry (2001: 22).

[2] According to Shaw (1991: 562), these identifying labels "refer to the same basic activity and the use of one term rather than another often signifies little more than a desire for variety of expression."

[3] Countries may also enter into a legally non-binding agreement, often referred to as an exchange of letters or a memorandum of understanding, the legal equivalent of a handshake.

pollution. IEAs protect animals from unkind "industrial" farming practices and scientific research, and they limit emissions of transboundary air pollutants and ozone-destroying chemicals. They promote the conservation of tropical forests, control or reverse land-use degradation ("desertification"), and regulate transboundary shipments of hazardous wastes and nuclear material. They ban nuclear weapons testing, and restrict the production and stockpiling of biological and chemical weapons. IEAs even regulate the use of outer space.

This chapter explains how IEAs get negotiated, and how the process of treaty negotiation affects treaty outcomes. It also examines a number of the important and common features of IEAs—features that the theory developed in subsequent chapters aims to explain.

6.2. ASCENDANCY OF THE ENVIRONMENTAL TREATY

The appendix to this chapter lists the multilateral IEAs that are either in force today or that could enter into force in the near future.[4] At least to my knowledge, this is the most comprehensive list of environmental treaties available.

Deciding which treaties to include and which to exclude is not obvious, however, and I make no claim to have gotten the classification right. The table excludes inland water navigation treaties, for example, and includes nuclear weapons test ban treaties, though a different arrangement could also be justified. The table leaves out "minor" protocols and amendments (footnotes to the table indicate the dates at which these were adopted), though good arguments could be made for including these.[5] The table also excludes treaties not intentionally designed to protect the environment but that have implications for environmental protection. Indeed, I refer to a number of such treaties in the text of this book.[6]

Even ignoring these issues of classification, the table is incomplete. It lists treaties for which it was relatively easy (for me) to obtain data—treaties written in English (with only one or two exceptions) and, more often than not, deposited with a multilateral organization. Other treaties must have escaped my search. Needless to say, the table will be out of date even before it is published.[7] My aim in presenting the table is not to be complete or current. The purpose, rather, is to give a sense of the scale and scope of these instruments.

Figure 6.1 uses the information from the table to show how use of the treaty instrument has increased over time. It charts the cumulative total of such IEAs,

---

[4] The appendix builds upon an earlier table, presented in Barrett (1991), which drew in turn from compilations by Kiss (1983) and Rummel-Bulska and Osafo (1991). As compared with these earlier lists, I have excluded (with a couple of exceptions, for reasons explained in the table's footnotes) agreements that are either no longer in force or that are not expected ever to enter into force. I have also added more treaties, many of which pre-date these earlier compilations.

[5] Amendments and protocols were only included in the table if they were given a name of their own.

[6] Examples include the standards agreements mentioned in Chapter 4.

[7] The data contained in the appendix were last updated in 2001. The data were obtained mainly from a variety of internet sources. Data for most treaties can be easily verified and updated using the internet.

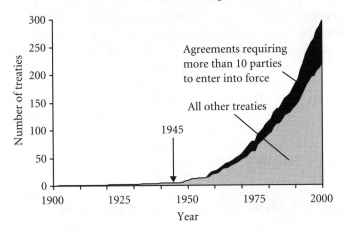

Figure 6.1. *Multilateral treaties currently in force by date of adoption*

sorted by their date of adoption. Thus, the 1911 North Pacific Fur Seal Treaty, discussed in Chapter 2, is excluded from Figure 6.1 (and from the table), since it is no longer in force. Similarly, though the first whaling convention was adopted in 1931, the convention in force today dates back to 1946, and only this last agreement is represented in the figure. Though by this construction Figure 6.1 slightly exaggerates the rate of increase in the number of multilateral environmental agreements, and understates the number of agreements existing earlier, the overall impression it leaves is broadly right: use of environmental treaties has increased significantly, especially since the Second World War. Only four of the 225 multilateral environmental agreements currently in force were adopted by 1945. And another 72 treaties adopted since 1945 could still enter into force (given time, most, but not all, of these treaties will enter into force).

Though environmental treaties are fairly modern institutions, their ancestry goes back a long way. The oldest international water agreement, at least to my knowledge, is a unilateral declaration granting freedom of navigation to a monastery, signed by Emperor Charlemagne in the year 805 (Food and Agriculture Organization 1978). The first North American IEA was a bilateral fisheries agreement between the United States and Canada (in those days, represented by Britain), signed in 1818—an agreement that also established the 49th parallel as the international boundary and provided for the restoration of property (including slaves) confiscated during the War of 1812. The first agreement on the conservation of nature—the Convention for the Protection of Birds Useful to Agriculture—was signed by eleven European nations in 1902. This is the oldest treaty listed in the appendix.

The growth in IEAs since 1945 coincides with the birth of our modern multilateral institutions, the United Nations (UN) being perhaps the most important. Moreover, multilateral IEAs are routinely negotiated under the auspices of the UN and its many agencies (or under regional organizations like the Council of Europe, which today comprises about forty states). For both reasons, it might seem that the UN system gave rise to the rapid growth in treaty negotiation, but this impression would be wrong.

What really explains the growth in IEAs is an increase in the demand for such institutions, not a more favorable supporting structure facilitating their supply. It was not until the middle of the twentieth century that transnational externalities became a pervasive fixture of international relations, helped by an increase in the scale of human activity (measured both at the intensive and extensive margins), an accumulation of previous environmental misdeeds, an increase in incomes in the industrialized countries, a change in preferences, and a more fragmented geo-political landscape. This last reason for the growth in IEAs is more important than is often recognized. As shown in Figure 6.2, the number of countries (approximated in the figure by UN membership) has increased several fold since 1945, mainly because of de-colonization and the break-up of the Soviet Union, and also as a result of civil war (Yugoslavia and Ethiopia being two recent examples).[8] As illustrated by the examples of the Aral Sea and the Indus Basin, fragmentation of the political landscape turns intra-national environmental problems into transnational conflicts, and thus creates a demand for treaty remedies. The UN system served as a helpful platform for resolving these conflicts of interdependence. It helped to reduce the transactions costs of treaty negotiations. But it was not the main cause of the growth in IEAs. It is probably better to think of IEAs and the UN institutions as arising contemporaneously, and as playing mutually supporting roles.

Figure 6.1 also distinguishes between the agreements requiring ten or fewer ratifications and those requiring more than ten ratifications to enter into force. Not only has the total number of agreements increased substantially, but the number of agreements requiring participation by a large number of countries has also increased. This matters. An important theme of this book is that cooperation is harder to sustain, the larger is the number of countries that contribute to or are affected by an externality. As suggested in Chapter 1, that a lot of agreements have been adopted does not mean that the world's shared environments are being adequately protected.

IEAs form a dense network of international alliances. Most countries will be a party to some bilateral agreements (usually with geographic neighbors), to a few "minilateral" agreements (often of a regional character), and to a number of global agreements.

International environmental agreements also overlap or are interrelated so that a particular environmental outcome may depend on more than one agreement. Bilateral agreements that provide for the exchange of whaling observers, for example, make these officials accountable to the International Whaling Commission (IWC), which was itself created by the International Convention for the Regulation of Whaling (ICRW). Whales are also protected by the Convention on International Trade in Endangered Species (CITES); and the harvesting of krill, the main diet of baleen whales in the Antarctic Ocean, is regulated by the Convention on the Conservation of

---

[8] Figure 6.2 only approximates the actual number of countries. Not every country is a UN member—Switzerland, for example, only joined in 2002. As well, even before the Soviet Union fell apart, Ukraine and Belorussia (today, Belarus) were UN members.

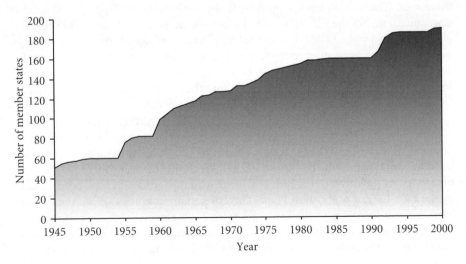

Figure 6.2. *Membership in the United Nations*

Antarctic Marine Living Resources, an agreement requiring close cooperation between its own commission and the IWC.

6.3. EU DIRECTIVES

The European Union (EU) has adopted several hundred environmental regulations, directives, and decisions (including amendments and revisions)—legislative measures that resemble IEAs but that need to be treated separately because they are negotiated and implemented in a unique institutional setting. For this reason, EU agreements are excluded from the table shown in the appendix.

Crucially, the European Commission can make decisions that are legally binding on member states, and under the Maastricht Treaty member states lose the veto as regards certain decisions by the Council of Ministers, including those relating to the environment. However, while the sovereignty of member states has been diluted, their essential rights remain intact. All the members of the EU can renegotiate the arrangements that are now in place, and every member is free to withdraw from the Union. The reason that the sovereignty of European member states has been eroded is not that these fundamental rights have been given away. Their sovereignty has been weakened because, through a succession of decisions, the incentive for members to exercise these rights has been reduced. The process of deepening has imposed costs on every member, and though these costs were willingly absorbed (presumably because they yielded an even greater benefit), they cannot be recovered later. It is because so many of the costs of integration are sunk that the incentive to withdraw has been muted. This is where the sovereignty of EU members has been compromised.

Indeed, largely because of the different institutional context, EU directives are of a different character than the IEAs listed in the appendix. The EU is more than a free trade area. The fundamental principle of the multilateral trading system is non-discrimination, but the EU seeks a deeper form of integration. It aims to create a single market, and most EU environmental legislation is designed to advance *this* aim, not to correct cross-border externalities. Lawnmower noise is hardly an issue for environmental diplomacy, and yet an EU directive prescribes maximum noise levels for lawnmowers. The reason, of course, is that the directive lets lawnmower manufacturers sell the same machines in Belgium and in Greece.

As well, the EU is hardly the ideal arrangement for correcting transnational externalities. Bilateral externalities are best resolved bilaterally, and multilateral externalities rarely fit neatly into the EU frame. The Rhine Chlorides Agreement, for example, includes Switzerland, which is not an EU member, while the majority of EU states are unaffected by pollution of the Rhine. Though acid rain emissions have been reduced by the EU's Large Combustion Plants Directive, many countries with a stake in this issue are non-members of the EU, and separate agreements (including the Helsinki and Oslo Protocols, discussed in Chapter 1) have been negotiated among this larger number of states, under the auspices of the UN's Economic Commission for Europe rather than the EU.

6.4. BILATERAL AGREEMENTS

The IEAs listed in the appendix also exclude bilateral agreements. This is partly because of the difficulty of compiling a comprehensive list of such agreements, but it is also because bilateral situations are special. For reasons explained in the next chapter, bilateral externalities are much easier to remedy than multilateral externalities. Though a few bilateral agreements are discussed in this book, my main concern lies with multilateral agreements.

To my knowledge, no one has counted all the bilateral environmental agreements in force today. However, this number is almost certain to be a multiple of the number of multilateral environmental agreements listed in the appendix. Surveys compiled by the Food and Agriculture Organization of the United Nations (1978, 1984) list 3707 agreements concerning the management of international water resources alone, most of which are bilateral (though many of these address navigational issues and only a fraction remain in force today). A report by the United States International Trade Commission (1991) identified seventy-four bilateral environmental agreements to which the United States was a party, out of a total of 170 IEAs in which the US had an interest of some kind. If the average country were a party to just ten bilateral IEAs, there would be about a thousand such agreements in total, more than three times the number of multilateral agreements.

6.5. THE PROCESS OF TREATY-MAKING[9]

The focus of later chapters is on explaining treaty *outcomes*. Such outcomes, however, do not come from the blue. They rather emerge from a *process*. Though I suppress

---

[9] This section expands on the discussion in Barrett (1998a).

the role of process in shaping treaty outcomes in subsequent chapters, this is only for analytical convenience. Process matters, and this section is intended to give a sense for why and how process matters to treaty outcomes.

The process of treaty-making is complex, and neither uniform nor linear, but for analytical purposes can be broken down into five stages: pre-negotiation, negotiation, ratification, implementation, and renegotiation. These different stages are discussed in turn below.

6.5.1. Pre-negotiation

Negotiations are normally preceded by a phase of pre-negotiation maneuvering. In the run-up to the Kyoto talks on climate change, for example, Australia claimed that it should be allowed to increase emissions, Europe argued for deep cuts, and the United States maintained that stabilization was more prudent. This is "cheap talk," and it is unlikely to have much effect on the outcome of negotiations in prisoners' dilemma (PD)-like games.[10] At the Kyoto negotiations, for example, Europe accepted smaller cuts in emissions than it had previously argued were needed, while the United States agreed to reduce rather than to stabilize its emissions. Australia got pretty much what it wanted—permission to increase its emissions. However, this outcome may not have been influenced by Australia's pre-negotiation announcements; it may rather have been determined by an assessment of Australia's real interests or perhaps by Australia's superior bargaining skill.

As discussed in Chapter 3, a country's public announcements are unlikely to influence the perceptions that others have about its true payoffs for the simple reason that others will know that it has an incentive to deceive them. Tactics of deception are also constrained by domestic politics. In democracies, elected representatives are prevented from falsifying their country's true preferences. If negotiators claimed publicly that they did not care about an environmental problem, hoping thereby to win concessions from other countries, there would almost surely be a domestic backlash. It is in the nature of a democracy that public sentiment is observable. Even for an autocratic state, interests can be discerned. It may not be credible for a dictator to profess indifference to a cross-border externality if that externality impinged on the economy's ability to produce an income for the ruling elite.

Forming a Negotiating Position

States are not monoliths, and their negotiators do not represent a single interest group. But, somehow, the preferences of the citizenry must be consolidated into a unitary negotiating position. In the United States, this requires an inter-agency agreement. For a cross-cutting issue like climate change, internal negotiations can involve a dozen or more government departments, including the Environmental Protection Agency and the Departments of State, Energy, Interior, and Treasury. Each of these government agencies, in turn, represents a variety of interests, and must forge a negotiating position of its own after being lobbied by trade associations,

---

[10] As explained in Chapter 3, cheap talk may matter in coordination games.

firms, environmental groups, and other non-governmental organizations (NGOs). By the time domestic negotiations end—and very often the president reconciles remaining differences—the team sent to negotiate with foreign governments is likely to be exhausted. But having agreed on what its country's interests are, and how it should conduct its negotiations, the official delegation must then negotiate with other states, and this will involve further give and take, and a reappraisal of both the country's interests and its negotiating strategy. Each round of intergovernmental negotiations thus initiates another round of intra-governmental negotiations. And so it goes on. For complex negotiations involving big stakes, the need to rebalance an internal position may necessitate sending a huge delegation. At the Kyoto Protocol talks, the US delegation exceeded fifty individuals. Hundreds more individuals, representing business groups and NGOs of various descriptions, also attended Kyoto, hoping to keep up the pressure on the government negotiators.

Coalition-building

Multiply the problems I have just noted by fifteen and you will get a sense of the coordination challenges faced by the EU. Not only must each of the member states arrive at its own position, in a manner like the one described above, but collectively all the fifteen states must agree on a common approach before negotiating as a bloc with other countries. Negotiating from a common position strengthens the EU's collective hand in negotiations. But the need to coordinate also makes it harder for the EU to negotiate effectively. A senior US diplomat told me that the EU was not even represented at some of the post-Kyoto negotiating sessions convened in The Hague in November 2000. Having failed to reach internal agreement on the way to move forward, the EU was unprepared to negotiate with other countries.

The EU is a permanent, formal arrangement, but other countries also find it convenient to form *ad hoc* coalitions before negotiations get underway. In the Montreal Protocol negotiations, the United States teamed up with Canada, Finland, Norway, Sweden, and Switzerland to comprise the "Toronto Group" of countries. In the climate negotiations, a number of coalitions were formed, including the "Umbrella Group," consisting of Australia, Canada, Japan, New Zealand, Norway, Russia, Ukraine, and the United States; the "Environmental Integrity Group," consisting of Mexico, the Republic of Korea, and Switzerland; and the "Alliance of Small Island States," comprising a number of small island nations. Other coalitions included the Less Developed Countries (LDCs), the G77-China, the Small Island Developing States (SIDS), and OPEC. As mentioned before, negotiating as a group confers a bargaining advantage. It may also be an efficient means by which countries sharing common interests can acquire information.

Strategic Behavior

The making of real commitments is different from an expression of intent. But as noted in Chapter 3, it is very hard for countries to make real commitments. A "commitment" to stabilize carbon dioxide emissions at 1990 levels, for example, is no such thing, if the pledge can be reversed at little or no cost. The European Community made such a declaration in 1990, but then failed to implement policies to achieve the target—signaling that it was *not* committed to the target. Anyway, it is hard to see how unilateral target-setting of this kind could be strategic—how it could affect the behavior of other nations, to the benefit of Europe—unless other countries could be expected to follow Europe's example, whether out of a sense of moral obligation or a preference to conform.[11] History teaches that leadership of this kind usually goes unrewarded.

Indeed, virtuous behavior can have the opposite effect intended. In the middle of the protracted Rhine chlorides negotiations, for example, a Dutch water company constructed a treatment plant to soften Amsterdam's drinking water. Anticipating future reductions in salt emissions, as promised by the 1976 agreement, the plant was designed to treat water with a low chloride content. If the upstream states reneged on their promise to reduce chloride emissions (and at the time the treatment plant was built, these countries had *not* invested in further storage), however, the water treatment facility would need to be re-engineered at considerable cost. The sunk investment in the treatment facility thus made the Netherlands more eager to reach an agreement to reduce salt emissions, and so weakened its bargaining position. Not surprisingly, the Netherlands got less than it wanted in the next round of negotiations (see Bernauer 1996).

Villainous behavior is sometimes better rewarded by pre-negotiation maneuvering. Countries may step up their exploitation of a shared resource, for example, or take other actions (including irreversible investments) to improve their post-negotiation payoff. Fortunately, however, these incentives to behave strategically can often be numbed. Thus, the climate change negotiations established 1990 as a baseline from which future emission reductions were to be negotiated—a baseline that current and future actions could not possibly alter.

6.5.2. Negotiation

Negotiations concerning complex, global issues are complicated affairs, and can involve well over 150 states. If only to reduce transactions costs, the parties that gather at such meetings can benefit by structuring the negotiations—by agreeing to divide the problem up in some fashion, perhaps, or by electing to negotiate in steps. This is why large-scale negotiations routinely start with an agreement on a process for collective decision-making.

Procedural Arrangements

Participants at the Third United Nations Law of the Sea (LOS) Conference first organized themselves into three committees, each concerned with a different issue and meeting separately but in parallel (see Sebenius 1984). The rules of procedure adopted by the conference required substantive issues to be decided by a two-thirds majority of the states participating in a negotiating session, and on a number of occasions

---

[11] For a demonstration of why behavior may not be copied, see Hoel (1991).

proposals put to the conference were blocked, usually by a coalition of land-locked countries. The negotiators worked from a draft text, commonly known as a "single negotiating text," which was reworked again and again as the negotiations progressed. When the final draft of the text was ready, nine years after the negotiations began, 130 nations voted to approve it, and the treaty was prepared for signature shortly thereafter. A number of important maritime nations, however, objected to the treaty, and declined to sign or ratify it. It was not until 1994, shortly before the LOS was to come into force, that a side deal was negotiated to win the approval of these crucial hold-outs.

The two-thirds rule adopted by the LOS Conference is actually one of two routes that can be taken for negotiating a major treaty. The other, as spelled out in Article 9 of the Vienna Convention on the Law of Treaties, requires the consent of all states participating in the drawing up of a treaty.

This "consensus" rule, the advantage of which is discussed in Chapter 11, was employed by the Intergovernmental Negotiating Committee (INC), a body created by a UN resolution to organize the negotiation of a first climate treaty. Like the LOS negotiations, diplomats negotiating the climate change agreement worked from a single negotiating text (which for most of the negotiations was littered with brackets), and divided the INC into separate negotiating groups. Unlike the Third LOS Conference, however, the INC faced a deadline: in a pre-negotiation maneuver, the General Assembly insisted that the Framework Convention on Climate Change be ready for signing at the United Nations Conference on Environment and Development in Rio de Janeiro in June 1992. The draft text submitted on the final day of the final negotiating session, just 15 months after the first session was convened, was approved without a formal ballot.

Committees, Agenda-setting, and Text-writing

Obviously, treaty negotiations have to start somewhere. But where? There will typically be many first drafts that would be acceptable at least to a majority of countries. But only one can be offered in a single negotiating text, and though it is technically possible to reverse the negotiations at a later time or even to throw the text out and start from scratch, in practice this rarely happens. So the first draft can have some influence on the nature of the agreement that is finally negotiated (see Raiffa 1982).

Similarly, committee arrangements can steer negotiations toward one outcome rather than another. For example, the order in which alternatives are put to a vote can alter a committee's final choice (see, for example, Riker 1986).

Committee chairmen determine the agenda and oversee preparation of the negotiating text, and so can shape a negotiation, whether for good or for ill. Senior negotiators can also guide a negotiation. We saw in Chapter 2 that President Taft's intervention helped to shift Japan's position, and thus clear the way for the Fur Seal Treaty to be adopted. Another president may not have written that letter. An even better example is the Treaty of Versailles negotiations. As John Maynard Keynes (1963: 34) tells it, "The President [Wilson], the Tiger [Clemenceau], and the Welsh witch [Lloyd George] were shut up in a room together for six months and the Treaty was what came out." In the field of environmental diplomacy, Benedick (1998) applauds the leadership of Mostafa Tolba, the Executive Director of the United Nations Environment Programme, in negotiating the Montreal Protocol; and Sebenius (1984) salutes the role played by Ambassador Tommy T.B. Koh of Singapore in guiding the LOS negotiations. The box on the next page shows how Raúl Estrada-Oyuela, Chairman of the Kyoto Protocol talks, was able to steer this particular negotiation.

Tactics

A diplomat's memoirs will emphasize not just the personalities of the individuals involved but the craft of statesmanship, especially in the exercise of *tactics*. John Maynard Keynes, who was a member of the British delegation to the Treaty of Versailles negotiations, later recalled a turning point at talks held in Paris on March 6, 1919. "The Delegates sat in a steep horseshoe with their advisers crowded behind them [Keynes sat behind the British Prime Minister, Lloyd George]. Inside the horseshoe was Clemenceau. In the middle of it facing the fireplace sat [Marshal] Foch. To the left of Foch were ranged in order the Japanese, the Italians, ourselves and the Americans, and on his other side facing us were the French" (Keynes 1949: 53). The British were especially keen to obtain immediate relief for German civilians, who were literally starving under the occupation. The French, however, blocked earlier attempts to provide relief. Keynes (1949: 59) continues:

The debate dragged on, but the French were losing ground. Suddenly a secretary hurried in with a sealed envelope for the Prime Minister [Lloyd George]. It contained another telegram from Plumer [General Plumer of the British forces] received whilst the Conference was in session. The Prime Minister read it out immediately in a sensational manner. 'Please inform the Prime Minister', the General telegraphed, 'that in my opinion food must be sent into this area by the Allies without delay .... The mortality amongst women, children and sick is most grave, and sickness due to hunger is spreading. The attitude of the population is becoming one of despair, and the people feel that an end by bullets is preferable to death by starvation .... I request therefore that a definite date be fixed for the arrival of the first supplies.' A considerable effect was produced; it became very difficult for the French to raise petty obstructionisms. I learnt afterwards that the whole thing had been stage-managed and that Plumer's telegram had been sent in response to a request from Paris, conveyed to him that morning in preparation for the afternoon.

Chance

Negotiations are also shaped by chance. Richard Benedick (1998) tells of a deadlock in the Montreal talks, and how it came to be broken. The negotiations became stuck on choice of a base year from which all negotiated reductions in chlorofluorocarbon (CFC) production and consumption were to be calculated. The United States and most other countries preferred 1986, while the Soviet Union insisted on 1990. As the negotiations were expected to finish in 1987, the majority of negotiators worried that a 1990 base year would create incentives for harmful strategic behavior. As discussed earlier, states might be tempted to increase their production and consumption in the 1987–90 period so as to establish a higher basis from which subsequent cuts would

Negotiation of the Compliance Article of the Kyoto Protocol

Only days before the Kyoto Protocol talks were scheduled to end, a "non-paper" by the Chairman of the Committee of the Whole, Ambassador Raúl Estrada-Oyuela of Argentina, split proposals for a compliance article into two alternatives:

Alternative A

"The Conference of the Parties serving as the meeting of the Parties to this Protocol shall, at its first session, in a manner that takes fully into account the need for compatibility with any procedures under Article 17, approve appropriate and effective procedures and mechanisms to determine and to address cases of non-compliance of Annex I Parties with the provisions of this Protocol, including through the development of an indicative list of consequences, taking into account the cause, type, degree and frequency of non-compliance. Any binding penalties for non-compliance under the procedures and mechanisms established under this Article shall be made available for the use of the clean development fund established under Article _."

Alternative B

"The Conference of the Parties serving as the meeting of the Parties to this Protocol shall, at its first session, approve appropriate and effective procedures and mechanisms to determine and to address cases of non-compliance with the provisions of this Protocol, including through the development of an indicative list of consequences, taking into account the cause, degree and frequency of non-compliance. Any procedures and mechanisms under this Article entailing binding consequences shall be adopted by means of an amendment to this Protocol."

The first version, reflecting the views of the G77 and China, limited compliance to the Annex I countries (that is, countries other than the G77 and China), and required that "any binding penalties" (read, financial penalties) be paid, effectively, to the non-Annex I countries.

Alternative B, reflecting the interests of the Annex I countries, did not limit compliance to the Annex I countries, and required that any binding compliance penalties be approved by an amendment—effectively, offering Annex I the means of avoiding enforcement.

In the event, Alternative B was adopted without alteration. But the Annex I countries got less than they wanted. Previously, the US proposed allowing parties to "borrow" emissions from a future control period as a way of staying in compliance, but Chairman Estrada managed to keep this wording out of the treaty. The EU and Norway requested that the agreement call for "prompt start" on compliance, but the Chairman made sure that these words were also left out of the final text.

Sources: The text is from FCCC/CP/1997/CRP.2, 7 December 1997. Information on Chairman Estrada's role is from FCCC/TP/2000/2.

be calculated. It turned out that the Soviets insisted on 1990 only because it coincided with the end of their five-year planning cycle, a problem that was easily remedied by adding a qualification to the treaty text. However, the reason for the Soviet's position only came to light on a chance event. During a break in the negotiations, the Soviet negotiator overheard Ambassador Benedick speaking in German. The Soviet negotiator knew German better than English, and was able to explain his position more clearly to Benedick in this language. From this point on, the negotiations proceeded more smoothly.

Leadership

Though personality, tactics, and chance help to determine the course of actual negotiations, I ignore them in later chapters because they cannot be neatly incorporated into a theory of international cooperation. They are important for understanding how a particular outcome came about but they tell us very little that is useful for policy.

To illustrate this point, consider the example of personality. Political scientist Oran Young (1994: 114) has emphasized the "leadership" qualities of negotiators, claiming that "efforts to negotiate the terms of international regimes are apt to succeed when one or more individuals emerge as effective leaders and that in the absence of such leadership, they will fail." This is true enough. But what is the implication for policy, that our representatives should be good leaders? Policy cannot make a person a good leader. It can only shape the rules for choosing representatives (or for deposing them), and alter the opportunity sets at their disposal. At any one time, we have to make do with the representatives we have. Better to show these individuals how they can do better—how they can use strategy, for example, to make treaties more effective—than to ask them to be better leaders, something they may not even be capable of.

As well, the circumstances that allow for leadership are in the main givens, and they are not always friendly to treaty-making. I believe Richard Benedick when he says that Montreal's success was due in part to the leadership shown by Mostafa Tolba. But Tolba also played a leading role in other negotiations that were not as successful. Presumably, his leadership talents were more or less constant in these different negotiations. What is more likely to account for the difference in outcomes are the fundamental forces that shape behavior—the kinds of incentives discussed in Chapters 3 and 4. These are the forces that leadership cannot alter but that strategy can sometimes restructure.

Transparency

There has been a trend in recent years of making negotiations more transparent and accessible to the media and NGOs. Superficially, this may seem to advance the cause of cooperation. However, it is as likely to have precisely the opposite effect.

States prefer to negotiate in private for good reason. Compromise is an essential lubricant to negotiation, and it would be extremely difficult for a country to compromise on its stated principles in full public view. Transparency can thus promote entrenchment of positions.

As negotiations have become more open, negotiators have found new ways of securing privacy. As interested parties of various descriptions are invited to one meeting, negotiators convene a closed meeting to get the real business done. The consequence of the increase in transparency has thus been a more burdensome process rather than a more effective one. As one negotiator told me, NGOs have acquired access, not influence. Many NGOs have come to the same conclusion, and are now thinking of scaling back their participation in conference negotiations.

The Convention-protocol Model

Negotiators can choose whether to negotiate a single agreement or to break a problem up, negotiating first a "convention" that aims to establish general principles, and only later negotiating follow-on "protocols" prescribing specific obligations in specific areas.[12] Examples include the Vienna Convention and its associated Montreal Protocol, the Framework Convention on Climate Change and its affiliated Kyoto Protocol, and the eight protocols negotiated under the umbrella of the Convention on Long-Range Transboundary Air Pollution (LRTAP). At one time, Canada proposed negotiation of a "Law of the Atmosphere," under which the issues of acid rain, ozone depletion, and climate change would be addressed by separate protocols (Bodansky 1994). This may have made sense from the perspective of the atmosphere. In complicated ways, all three issues are interrelated. However, the idea failed to catch on, probably because of the poor example set by the lengthy LOS negotiations.

To be eligible to sign a protocol, a state must usually have ratified its associated convention. Parties to a convention, however, are not obligated to be bound by any of its protocols. The decision not to link different aspects of an environmental problem—like the abatement of sulfur dioxide and nitrogen oxides in an acid rain agreement—can thus be strategic. Murdoch *et al.* (1997) argue that, had the LRTAP not provided for separate protocols to be negotiated for each of the different pollutants, smaller reductions in sulphur emissions would have been negotiated. They may be right, but in other situations linkage of separate issues can help countries cut a better deal overall (see Raiffa 1982). There is no theorem that says that linkage invariably helps or harms international cooperation. The effect depends on the issues that are linked and on the manner in which they are linked.

Delegation

The arrangements made between negotiators and their chief executives may also help determine treaty outcomes. After a verbal agreement was reached at the Non-Proliferation Treaty talks, the Soviet delegation handed the chief US negotiator, Arthur Goldberg, a new proposal (Zartman and Berman 1982). Goldberg refused to accept it, however. To the astonishment of the Soviets, Goldberg even refused to tell the President about the offer. "Don't you have to report it to Washington?" the Soviet negotiator asked. "No," replied Goldberg, "I don't have to report it to Washington. I'm authorized to negotiate and I see no point in reporting it to Washington." As matters turned out, Goldberg did report the offer to his government, but he knew it would be rejected out of hand. Indeed, he was pretty sure that the offer was made only to please the Romanians. "They knew we would not accept it," Goldberg said in an interview (Zartman and Berman 1982: 151). In this particular instance, delegation

---

[12] For a discussion of this convention-protocol approach, see Susskind (1994).

probably made little difference. But the outcome could have been otherwise. Goldberg could have lied, with neither Washington nor the Soviets being aware of the deception. Delegation of responsibility thus carries risks for the executive. The negotiator may strike a bargain that the executive does not like. This is one reason why agreements between countries need to be ratified.

6.5.3. Ratification

Treaties, being formal institutions, enter into law by means of formal procedures, the most important of which is ratification. Ratification, however, is preceded by other decisions that can be important on their own. Indeed, these other decisions can interact with the decision to ratify.

Signing, Acceding, and Ratifying

A state signals its intent to comply with an agreement by having one of its representatives sign it. For bilateral agreements, a signature is sometimes enough to establish a state's consent to be legally bound by a treaty. For multilateral agreements, however, a signature only indicates a state's intent to seek ratification; it does not impose a legal obligation for a state actually to ratify (Brownlie 1990).

Still, a signature is not a mere gesture. A country that signs a treaty is obligated to refrain from undermining its objectives. President Bill Clinton signed the Kyoto Protocol, which was subsequently denounced by his successor, George W. Bush. Bush declared that the United States would not become a party to the treaty, but Clinton's signature imposed a duty upon the United States not to interfere in the choices made by other countries to ratify and, should the agreement enter into force, to implement Kyoto.

Signing ceremonies usually mark the date at which a treaty is adopted (see the appendix). The Convention on Biological Diversity and the Framework Convention on Climate Change were signed by over 100 heads of state at the Rio Earth Summit in 1992, amid much fanfare. It is more usual, however, for IEAs to be signed by junior ministers or even civil servants in more ordinary surroundings. Normally, an agreement is open for signature for a fixed period, though after this time has lapsed provisions are usually made for eligible countries to accede at any time. Accession carries the same weight as ratification. However, countries that accede may not have participated in the negotiations.

While a signature is sometimes sufficient for an agreement to enter into force, it is more usual for IEAs to become legally binding only after being ratified. (Where a state's own constitution does not require ratification, an indication by this state of its acceptance or approval of a treaty is sufficient). Ratification safeguards against a country's negotiator deviating from her instructions and exceeding her authority.

Two-level Games

The process of ratification is for each state to determine, but normally requires the approval of a state's parliament. In the United States, ratification requires the approval of a two-thirds majority of the Senate, whereas in the United Kingdom approval by only a majority of MPs is required. This is a big difference. The two-thirds rule is a huge hurdle. And under the United States political system, the President does not "control" the Senate. It is rare for any political party to control two-thirds of the Senate's seats. Often, the President's party will not even control a majority of senators. Moreover, the President is not the leader of his party. A British Prime Minister with a comfortable majority can pretty much count on parliamentary approval of most treaties. In the United States, ratification can rarely be relied upon.

Of course, the President should be able to anticipate how the Senate will vote, and this expectation should in turn shape the treaty his Administration negotiates. Ratification thus provides a formal link between domestic and international politics, one that political scientist Robert Putnam (1988) describes as a two-level game. Though Putnam does not articulate the problem quite this way, the two-level game can be thought of as proceeding in stages. In Stage 1, the executives of every country negotiate an agreement. In Stage 2 the agreement comes before national parliaments for ratification. Negotiators are almost certain to look ahead and reason backwards, taking the requirements for ratification into account in Stage 1 (a point emphasized by Putnam).[13]

Parliamentary Pre-emption

Parliament might also try to pre-empt the executive. For example, parliament may move first by demanding that certain conditions be met for ratification (subject, presumably, to these demands being credible). Alternatively, it may require that particular conditions be satisfied if certain unilateral actions are to be avoided. The need for ratification allows parliament to play a role of its own on the international stage.

During the Montreal Protocol negotiations, the US Congress drafted legislation calling for trade restrictions to be imposed against nations that refused to accept their share of the common responsibility to reduce harmful emissions. According to Benedick (1998: 29), "US negotiators made certain that the implications of this threat were not lost on foreign governments, pointing out that there might be a price to pay for not joining in meaningful efforts to protect the ozone layer."

In the summer of 1997, the US Senate voted 95–0 in favor of a non-binding resolution rejecting a climate treaty that would restrict the emissions of industrialized countries but not developing countries and that would be a burden to the US economy. The resolution was intended as a shot over the bows of the Clinton Administration as it readied for the Kyoto talks. The Senate may also have hoped to alter the behavior of other countries at these negotiations. As matters turned out, however, the resolution had no such influence (see Chapter 15).[14] The treaty negotiated in Kyoto failed to satisfy the requirements that had been set by the Senate, and President Clinton never asked the Senate to ratify it. Perhaps this is the exception that proves the rule suggested by Putnam's analysis.

---

[13] Technically, the appropriate equilibrium concept to apply here is that of a subgame perfect equilibrium.

[14] A number of case studies examining the link between domestic and international politics in areas other than the environment are presented in Evans *et al.* (1993).

Openness

Instruments of ratification are usually deposited with one of the negotiating parties (the instruments of ratification to the North Pacific Fur Seal Treaty, for example, were deposited with the US government), or with the Secretary General of the UN (as in the case of the Framework Convention on Climate Change). A treaty's depository is responsible for informing parties of changes in the status of the treaty's membership. The 1969 International Convention on the Law of Treaties further requires that treaties be sent to the UN for registration and publication. International law thus ensures that treaties and their signatories are public knowledge.

I noted earlier that transparency may be injurious to treaty negotiations, but transparency of treaty *outcomes* is to be praised. At one time, secret treaties were common. The 1887 Reinsurance Treaty, for example, pledged Germany and Russia not to take sides with a "third Great Power" in a war involving one of the signatories. It also pledged both countries to "secrecy as to the contents and the existence of the present Treaty." Though such treaties were intended to build stability, they had the opposite effect. As Kissinger (1994: 166) explains, "Bismarck's machinations, which were intended to provide reassurance, over time had an oddly unsettling effect, partly because his contemporaries had such difficulty comprehending their increasingly convoluted nature. Fearful of being outmaneuvered, they tended to hedge their bets. But this course of action also limited flexibility, the mainspring of *Real-politik* as a substitute for conflict." The first of President Woodrow Wilson's Fourteen Points prohibits secret treaties; and international law prohibits them still today.

6.5.4. Implementation

Having entered into force, a treaty must be implemented. Implementation typically requires the passage of domestic legislation or the adoption of implementing regulations. Sometimes an IEA will actually require that domestic legislation be adopted to give domestic force to a treaty, though states are normally given substantial leeway in choosing the means for implementation. For example, the controls on CFCs mandated by the Montreal Protocol have been implemented in different countries by a variety of means—quotas, tradable permits, taxes, product regulations, and voluntary agreements.

Reporting

Many IEAs require parties to report data relating to their implementation—often, but not always, to a small administrative body set up under the agreement. For example, parties to the Montreal Protocol are required to provide the treaty's secretariat with data on production, imports, and exports of the substances controlled by the treaty.

Compliance with treaty reporting requirements varies widely. A study by the US General Accounting Office (1992) found that all but one of the seventeen parties to the Nitrogen Oxides Protocol submitted reports within a year of the agreement entering into force. By contrast, only 25 of the 104 parties to CITES submitted their reports as required in 1989.

Despite its many other successes, reporting has long been a problem for the Montreal Protocol. The GAO study cited above found that only fifty-two of the protocol's sixty-five parties submitted any consumption data for 1990, and only twenty-nine parties submitted a complete set of data that year. An *Ad Hoc* Group of Experts on the Reporting of Data found that the failure to report was often due to a lack of capacity to compile the required data in developing countries. Wanting to improve on this record, the parties offered technical assistance, financed by the Ozone Fund, and also threatened to withhold all related financial assistance if the failure to report persisted. In 1995, after the secretariat repeatedly but unsuccessfully tried to obtain data from Mauritania, the Implementation Committee recommended that the country be reclassified as a party not operating under Article 5 until it satisfied the treaty's reporting requirements. Among other things, this meant that Mauritania would be ineligible to receive financial assistance. Soon after the recommendation was made, Mauritania submitted the required data.

Verification

More problematic is verifying the accuracy of the data that are reported. Parties, after all, are asked to report on their *own* implementation (this being yet another expression of sovereignty), and must be tempted on occasion to mis-report.

Information recently made available by the Russian government shows that the Soviet Union systematically failed to report accurately the number of whales killed by its Antarctic whaling fleet in the 1960s, a deception carried out with the skilled assistance of the KGB (see Chayes and Chayes 1995). While the USSR reported to the IWC that it had killed 270 humpback whales in the 1961–62 season, the actual data reveal that just one of the fleet's four ships killed 1568 humpbacks that year. For the 1963–64 season, the Soviets reported killing 74 blue whales, while the true data reveal that a single ship killed more than 530 of these great leviathans. "The USSR's false reporting was so drastic and pervasive," writes Chayes and Chayes (1995: 155), "that some experts believe it accounts for the persistent inaccuracy of the IWC Scientific Committee's forecasts of whale populations, on which the catch limits were based."

Monitoring

Of course, the incentive for parties to deceive creates an incentive for others to monitor. The suspicion that certain whaling nations were violating IWC recommendations, for example, led to the creation of the International Observers Scheme in 1972. This established bilateral and trilateral agreements, by which means states whaling in the same oceanic region exchanged observers, based either on land or aboard ship. As matters turned out, the observers scheme proved an imperfect monitoring device. Only whaling states are represented by the observers scheme, and the design of the scheme may have promoted collusion among whaling states; since observers were swapped, each country might have been willing to overlook its partner's excess harvest on the understanding that its partner would reciprocate. Another problem was that the number of observers made available by a country was proportionate to the number of whaling vessels in its fleet. With bilateral exchanges, states with large fleets were thus incompletely monitored (Rose and Crane 1993). Finally, some states were not prepared to pay the costs of sending an observer (Lyster 1985). Monitoring by any state, of course, benefits *all* whaling states and is thus vulnerable to free-riding.

For all its faults, however, the observers scheme remains an outlier in international law. Most international agreements do not allow intrusive monitoring. An even more prominent exception is the Antarctic Treaty. This agreement allows unrestricted on-site inspections—probably because the treaty sets aside all territorial claims. More typical is the provision included in the Montreal Protocol, which authorizes the Implementation Committee "to undertake, *upon the invitation of the party concerned* (emphasis added), information-gathering in the territory of that party for fulfilling the functions of the Committee" (see Chayes and Chayes 1995: 187). Being protect-ive of their sovereignty, states are reluctant to accept on-site monitoring.

The alternative more often tried is to negotiate obligations that are easily monitored from a distance, even if they are less effective in correcting an externality. The Limited Test Ban Treaty prohibited above-ground and not underground nuclear testing because verification of underground testing by satellite observation and other off-site means was unreliable. Similarly, discharges of oil by tankers at sea are not regulated directly but by an agreement requiring that tankers be fitted with segregated ballast tanks. It is nearly impossible to monitor tanker discharges at sea, but it is easy to observe whether a tanker is fitted with segregated ballast tanks (see Mitchell 1993).

Rules, Discretion, and Administrative Bodies

Treaties sometimes tell the parties exactly what they are supposed to do and when. More often, however, they create a regime for managing a resource, and leave the details to be decided later, usually at regularly scheduled meetings of the parties. Decisions to continue the moratorium on commercial whaling, for example, are made at the annual meeting of the ICRW. Similarly, decisions to reconsider the ban on trade in African elephant ivory are made at the regular meetings of the CITES. Another important example is the Montreal Protocol, which fails to specify in detail how non-compliance should be handled (see Chapter 10). Suspected instances of non-compliance must instead be brought before an Implementation Committee, which reviews the evidence, and considers the circumstances that may have caused the non-compliance, before making recommendations regarding specific actions to be taken. Failure to specify a non-compliance rule *ex ante* may invite countries not to comply. However, the careful exercise of discretion may also prevent punishment of a country that is unable to comply for reasons beyond its control. Finding the right balance between commitment to a rule and flexibility is a familiar challenge to insti-tutional development (see, for example, Dixit 1996).

Flexibility is especially important to the management of high seas fisheries. Changes in agreed quotas and supplementary regulations are needed fairly frequently. Rather than negotiate these changes directly, fisheries agreements often delegate the task to a fisheries commission. But the commissions do not impose prescriptions. They rather facilitate management choices. Decisions about what to do are still made by parties. As Peterson (1993: 276) has found, "in no case have governments been prepared to transfer authority to make immediately binding decisions to an international fisheries commission."

As shown in Appendix 6.1, most IEAs have the support of an administrative organization. These are supposed to assist implementation by coordinating the collection and exchange of information submitted by the parties. Treaty secretariats are remarkably small organizations. Of the eight major IEAs examined by the US General Accounting Office (1992), the International Convention for the Prevention of Pollution from Ships has the largest secretariat—with a staff, in 1990, of just 20 and with a budget of only $3 million.

6.5.5. Renegotiation

Agreements can always be renegotiated, and negotiators can anticipate, in a world of certainty, whether an agreement may be vulnerable to renegotiation. Of course, it is precisely for this reason that diplomats can be expected to negotiate treaties that will not actually be renegotiated (just as they should negotiate treaties that will be ratified). Still, it is important to allow for the possibility that IEAs can be renegotiated (see Barrett 1994a, 1999a). As shown later in this book, recognition of this possibility can have a profound effect on the kinds of agreements that will actually be negotiated.

Uncertainty and Irreversibility

In an uncertain world, however, renegotiation may be triggered by unforeseen changes in the underlying relationships of the game, that is, by changes in the same parameters that cause custom to change: prices, preferences, and technology. Renegotiation may also be prompted by learning over time.

If implementation of a treaty could be reversed at zero cost, and if the environmental consequences of a treaty were also reversible, then negotiators could do no better than to behave myopically, negotiating an agreement in the current period that suited the background environment prevailing at this time, and only adjusting the agreement in subsequent periods if the background environment changed or if new information came to light. In this kind of world, history doesn't matter; the parties can do no better than to negotiate an agreement that suits the current period's background environment. Moreover, this would be true whether changes in the background environment were anticipated or whether they came as a total surprise.

If some costs had to be sunk in the course of implementing an agreement, however, or if the environmental consequences of earlier actions could not be costlessly reversed, then modifications to the treaty, reacting to unanticipated changes in the background environment, may need to bend to history. Renegotiation may improve matters starting from the existing state of affairs. But, with hindsight, it may have been better still if a different treaty had been adopted from the beginning. When shocks are unanticipated, countries can do no better than to follow a myopic rule, but they may nonetheless come to regret decisions taken earlier.

This is if changes are unanticipated. If the parties *know* that certain parameters will change in the future, and if earlier actions are irreversible, then far-sighted negotiators should deviate from the myopic rule in the initial negotiating period. For example, if the parties can anticipate that preservation of a unique environment would be favored over time, and that development would be irreversible, then they would want to deviate from the myopic rule. They would want to protect more of the resource in the near term than would otherwise be justified. Likewise, if there is uncertainty about the future background environment, and if the parties expect that this uncertainty will diminish with time, then countries may wish to negotiate an initial agreement that keeps future options open.[15]

To sum up, negotiation of a treaty may be linked to the need at some future date to renegotiate, a decision possibly complicated by irreversibilities. That is, there may be a need to negotiate a flexible treaty.

Mechanics of Renegotiation

Renegotiation can take different forms. A treaty may be entirely superceded by a new agreement, or it may be "adjusted" or "amended." Negotiated adjustments are binding on all the original signatories (though, as discussed later, parties may withdraw from a treaty at any time, after giving sufficient notice, and thus avoid having to comply with the adjustments). Amendments are different. Though all the original parties to an agreement must be invited to negotiate an amendment, and though these parties have the right to become parties to the amended agreement, they are not obligated to do so. Hence, a state may remain a signatory to the original agreement and not become a party to the amended agreement. Any state that accedes to the treaty after the amendments have come into effect, however, must become a party to the amended agreement and not just the original agreement. This is a requirement of international law.

The Montreal Protocol is a model of flexibility. It prescribes a sequence of obligations lasting in perpetuity, but one that could also be accelerated or decelerated, broadened or narrowed, strengthened or weakened as changes in science, technology, and treaty performance recommended. As matters turned out, the original treaty has undergone a number of transformations. It was adjusted in Vienna in 1995, amended in Beijing in 1999, and adjusted *and* amended in London in 1990, in Copenhagen in 1992, and in Montreal in 1997. A country that ratifies the Montreal Protocol today is joining a very different treaty from the one negotiated in 1987. The amendments to the Montreal Protocol are essentially separate agreements, and are listed this way in the appendix to this chapter.

6.6. DEFINING *N*

The parameter *N*, first introduced in Chapter 3, is the *potential* number of signatories to an IEA, or the number of countries that have reason to be at the negotiating table. These are the countries that either cause or are affected by an externality.

In principle, *N* is easy to calculate in the case of an IEA supplying a global public good such as ozone layer protection. It is equal to the total number of countries that exist.

---

[15] For analyses of these situations in a domestic context, see the classic papers by Krutilla (1967) and Arrow and Fisher (1974); see also Krautkraemer (1985) and Barrett (1992*a*).

But while the principle is straightforward in this case, the total number of countries in the world is a surprisingly shadowy figure. A few countries are recognized as existing by some countries but not by others. The former "homeland" of Bophuthatswana, for example, was granted independence from white-ruled South Africa in 1977, but its sovereignty was recognized only by South Africa. Taiwan, deemed a break-away province by China, has not claimed to be a separate state, though it did apply to join the GATT as a "customs territory." Palestine is not (yet) a state. And, yet, represented by the Palestine Liberation Organization, it has become a signatory to a number of regional Middle East agreements, including the Regional Convention for the Conservation of the Red Sea and Gulf of Aden Environment.

The EU poses a different problem for classification. It is a party to many IEAs, but to include the EU in N as well as its member states may be to double count. On the other hand, EU participation is not superfluous. Often, EU participation confers special privileges to member states. The Montreal Protocol, for example, allows unrestricted trading in "consumption entitlements" among EU members, a privilege not accorded to other parties. For both reasons, participation by the EU in the treaties listed in the appendix is indicated by an asterisk.

For the purposes of this book, it doesn't matter how many countries there are in the world *exactly*. The problems of global governance aren't very sensitive to the addition or subtraction of even a dozen countries. It is enough to know that the total number of countries is "large." What can matter are changes at a more micro scale. As shown in the next chapter, if the number of countries supplying a regional public good rises from two to three, the implications can be profound (more so than if N were to increase from, say, three to four).

In the theory developed later, I shall be taking N as given. Where the identities of countries matter, I shall be taking these as givens, too. Young (1994) has been critical of this approach, claiming that "the identity of the relevant participants in [the formation of international regimes] is seldom cast in concrete." He has also criticized what he calls "mainstream utilitarian accounts of international regime formation" for assuming that N, and the identities of the players, are, as it were, set in concrete (Young 1994: 94). I agree that N has been wrongly specified in particular applications (earlier I noted the tendency to assume $N = 2$, even in analyses of global games). But the number of players and their identities *can* be deduced. Moreover, they *must* be deduced by *any* theory that hopes to have something relevant to say on the subject.

The players in a game are simply the states that have the potential to act. If a game models negotiations as involving a set of X players (say, the countries that history tells us actually did negotiate), and yet this was preceded by a game involving a much larger set of Y players (with X being a subset of Y), the outcome of which determined X, then the negotiation game is a "subgame" of the larger game. Probably, the larger game should be the focus of inquiry.

When the North Pacific Fur Seal Treaty was negotiated in 1911, the fur seal was hunted by just four countries, and so it might seem obvious that N should be set equal to four in this case. However, as discussed in Chapter 2, fur seals spend much of their lives in international waters. In other words, *any* country could potentially hunt these animals. Indeed, costless reflagging of sealing vessels would make entry easy. Correct modeling of this game should therefore include every country as a player. Similarly, any analysis of a high seas fishery must consider N to be all the countries in the world. That is, our modeling of these kinds of problems must draw attention to the potential for entry, and of the need to deter entry by a treaty that limits participation.

6.7. PARTICIPATION RESTRICTIONS

N is defined by the nature of the problem being investigated. In the majority of cases, N is also the number of countries invited to participate in a negotiation.

When countries negotiate the provision of a global public good, no country can gain by restricting membership, and so all countries will be invited to negotiate. This explains why membership of the Vienna Convention for the Protection of the Ozone Layer is open to all countries (see the table in the appendix). Participation in the Montreal Protocol is restricted (again, see the table)—but only to parties of the Vienna Convention. Since any country can accede to the Vienna Convention, any country can join Montreal.

Where participation is restricted, the reason is usually that excluded parties have no opportunity to act, and no interest in the externality. Participation in the Niger River basin treaty, for example, is limited to the ten riparian states ($N = 10$ in this case). This is just as it should be.

6.7.1. Polar Bears

Participation is also restricted by the Agreement on the Conservation of Polar Bears, but this is a different kind of situation. Polar bears were previously hunted both for their skins and for sport (in Alaska, "aerial safaris," mostly in international waters, once accounted for 85–90 percent of the total number killed). In the 1950s it was thought that polar bears might become extinct. Unilateral policies to conserve polar bears would have been inadequate. Research showed that significant numbers of polar bears crossed international borders and earlier efforts to protect polar bears unilaterally had failed. As the Soviet member of the advisory body that helped prepare the way for multilateral negotiations put it, "Why should the USSR provide complete protection for the polar bear ... if they were only producing a larger crop for neighbouring nations?"[16]

Participation in the polar bear agreement was restricted to the five circumpolar states, Canada, Denmark/Greenland, Norway, the Soviet Union, and the United States. The treaty needed to include all these countries because they all have polar bear populations and a significant number of polar bears cross their shared boundaries. However, like the fur seal, polar bears may also be hunted in international waters. Indeed, negotiators of the five-party agreement feared that if they succeeded in conserving the polar bear, Japan and some European countries might initiate ship-based hunting (Fikkan *et al.* 1993).

[16] See Boardman (1981: 134).

Early drafts of the agreement anticipated the eventual need for a more comprehensive treaty, open to all nations to sign. However, the Soviets later insisted that the five-party agreement would be sufficient, and both they and the other negotiators believed that as long as the regime included the two superpowers and applied to all the polar bear states, entry by third parties would be deterred. As Fikkan *et al.* (1993: 138) put it, "the five signatories made rules for the entire area—territory clearly beyond their own national sovereignty—and expected non-signatories to comply."

In the event, a follow-on global agreement was never negotiated, even though the five-party agreement may not have been entirely effective in deterring entry. Polar bears were occasionally seen in Iceland, and there was some evidence that nationals of nine non-signatory countries may have been engaged in harvesting polar bears or in trading their skins (Boardman 1981). Unlike the Fur Seal Treaty, the polar bear agreement does not include an explicit mechanism for deterring entry. However, the economics of pelagic harvesting may have been unfriendly to entry in this case anyway. Entry would also have been deterred by changes in custom, especially the extension of the territorial sea to 12 miles, and the creation of the 200-mile Exclusive Economic Zone (EEZ). A further deterrent would have been entry into force of the CITES agreement in 1975 (the polar bear is listed in appendix II of CITES, and all five polar bear countries are also parties to CITES; see Lyster 1985), which restricts trade in polar bear products.

6.7.2. The Nile

Participation restrictions were uncontroversial in the cases of the fur seal and polar bear treaties, largely because excluded countries had not established a prior claim to these resources. In other treaties, participation restrictions can be controversial. Though the Nile was shared by nine countries (today, ten countries) at the time that the Nile Waters Agreement was adopted in 1959, the agreement was negotiated between just two riparians, Egypt and Sudan. Continued exclusion of the other riparians casts a cloud over the legitimacy of the regime, and a Nile-wide agreement is almost sure to be needed eventually. Indeed, informal talks on such an agreement have already begun.

6.7.3. Antarctica

Even more controversial, perhaps, are the participation restrictions in the 1959 Antarctic Treaty. Negotiations leading up to the signing of this treaty were limited to the twelve nations carrying out scientific research on Antarctica during the International Geophysical Year (July 1, 1957 to December 31, 1958): Argentina, Australia, Belgium, Chile, France, Japan, New Zealand, Norway, South Africa, the Soviet Union, the United Kingdom, and the United States. Other nations were excluded, and yet the fate of this continent should have been in every state's interests.

Under Article IX of the treaty, signatories were given the status of "consultative parties" only if they were one of the original twelve negotiating countries or a contracting party which had demonstrated "... its interest in Antarctica by conducting substantial scientific research activity there, such as the establishment of a scientific station or the despatch of a scientific expedition." Thus, the original twelve signatories formed a club, and set a high price for membership.[17]

In an early phase of the negotiations, the Soviets argued that all nations should be invited to the table. Though most of the other negotiating countries disagreed, many felt uncomfortable with the decision to exclude. According to Shapley (1985: 98), "New Zealand opposed inviting others but endorsed a principle of 'fair treatment' for non-parties. Norway preferred an 'open door' policy for other nations but wished to limit the conference to the twelve already there. Belgium said, 'There was no question of monopoly of the Antarctic continent,' and Australia agreed."

In November 1958, the United States tabled a draft article on the rights of non-participants. "The administrative measures which become effective pursuant to Article VII of the present Treaty," the draft began, "shall apply equally to all countries [that is, signatories *and* non-signatories] and shall be carried out in a uniform and non-discriminatory manner, with equal treatment being accorded to countries which are parties to the present Treaty and to countries not parties thereto, and to their respective nationals, so long as such countries and nationals respect the principles embodied in the present Treaty? (Shapley 1985: 98).

The chief US negotiator explained that it was "inherent in the US concept that fair treatment for all other countries should be provided in order to avoid the interpretation that the group was attempting to monopolize Antarctica for themselves" (Shapley 1985: 98–9). But, of course, other nations were excluded from participating in the negotiations, and in this sense the Antarctic twelve *were* monopolizing Antarctica. It is a basic principle of international law that states must consent to a treaty rule before they can be held to be legally bound by it. Article 34 of the Vienna Convention on the Law of Treaties reaffirms this principle, noting that "a treaty does not create either obligations or rights for a third state without its consent" (Shaw 1991: 579). The US proposal violated this principle, and was quickly abandoned.

Though entry to consultative status was costly, some countries were prepared to pay the price of admission. Brazil became the first country to join the Antarctic club, after it dispatched a used research vessel (purchased from Denmark, a non-consultative party) and a crew of 38 to Antarctica in 1982–83 (Shapley, 1985). Since then, more than a dozen countries have followed Brazil's lead.

In 1988, the consultative and contracting parties negotiated a new agreement, the Convention on the Regulation of Antarctic Mineral Resource Activities. This agreement was intended to establish a regime for mineral exploitation, one responsibility of which was "to keep under review the conduct of Antarctic mineral resource activities with a view to safeguarding the protection of the Antarctic environment in the interest of all mankind." With most countries being shut out of these negotiations, however, it was not obvious that this agreement could legitimately claim to represent the interests of *all* mankind. For reasons explained later, only six of the thirty-eight Antarctica Treaty parties signed the agreement, and the agreement is now almost certainly dead.

---

[17] Non-consultative parties do not have decision-making status.

In its place, the Antarctica Treaty club members negotiated another agreement (the 1991 Protocol to the Antarctic Treaty on Environmental Protection), which banned mineral exploitation for 50 years. This agreement thus postponed the decision of whether to allow mineral development or to impose a permanent ban, making Antarctica a World Park.[18] In leaving future options open, the agreement secured the acquiescence of third parties—for now. However, a cloud of illegitimacy still hangs over the Antarctic Treaty system.

6.7.4. Whaling

This experience might give the impression that inclusion is the best policy. However, inclusiveness raises problems of its own.

The ICRW was intended "to provide for the proper conservation of whale stocks and thus make possible the orderly development of the whaling industry." The objective, roughly put, was to reduce the rate of killing in the short run so as to build up the stock of whales, allowing a much larger sustainable catch in the long run. Membership to this agreement, however, was *not* restricted to the nations actively engaged in whaling, nor did the agreement include any provision for entry deterrence.

The treaty's original fifteen signatories all had interests in whaling as a commercial activity (Lyster 1985). Today, however, few of these signatories retain an interest in commercial whaling and most of the countries that acceded subsequently (for example, Switzerland) are also non-whaling nations. For this new majority of parties, whaling is an issue of preservation and animal welfare, not optimal sustained yield management. Austria joined the IWC in 1994 *to put a stop to whaling*. This clash in objectives, not to say values, explains why Iceland withdrew from the agreement in 1992, and why Iceland, Norway, Greenland, and the Faroe Islands established a splinter organization in 1992, the North Atlantic Marine Mammals Conservation Organisation.

This new treaty has an altogether different constitution. A country can accede to it only if all the existing parties give their consent, "a stringent requirement which reflects the desire to prevent entry by states which do not share a similar desire to allow the resumption of at least some commercial whaling ... ." (Sands 1995: 437). But though these countries may restrict participation, they cannot easily turn their backs on the claims expressed by the rest of the world. Every country has a potential interest in how whales are treated and in their preservation. The conflict exposed by the Whaling Convention cannot, in the long run, be addressed by a splinter treaty.

6.8. ENTRY INTO FORCE AND MINIMUM PARTICIPATION

As shown in the appendix, most multilateral agreements do not come into force until ratified by a minimum number of countries (of the 297 treaties listed in the appendix, only 9 do not specify a minimum of 2 or greater). Some agreements do not come into force until being ratified by *all* the parties at the bargaining table, an example being the North Pacific Fur Seal Treaty. Most multilateral treaties (especially treaties

---

[18] See Cameron (1996) regarding the campaign by non-governmental groups to make Antarctica a World Park, and the effect of this on the Antarctica Treaty system.

concerning global environmental problems), however, fix a minimum far short of the total number of negotiating countries. For example, though more than 100 countries participated in the negotiations on the Convention on Biological Diversity, only 30 countries needed to ratify the agreement for it to enter into force.

In some cases the countries that must ratify an agreement before it comes into force are named. For example, the International Whaling Convention specifies that the agreement must be ratified by the Netherlands, Norway, the Soviet Union, the United Kingdom, and the United States, as well as at least one other country, before entering into force. In other cases thresholds are specified. The Montreal Protocol would not enter into force until ratified by at least eleven countries "... representing at least two-thirds of 1986 estimated global consumption of the controlled substances ... " (mainly, CFCs).

Superficially, the need for minimum participation is almost obvious. It would not be in the interests of a country to be bound by a treaty until enough other states, and in some cases *particular* other states, were bound by these same obligations. Essentially, the "minimum participation clause" makes the obligations of each of its signatories a (non-linear) function of the total number of signatories. However, the minimum participation level can also serve a strategic purpose. As explained in the next chapter, it allows participation by each country to have a non-marginal effect on the environmental problem. As shown in Chapter 9, it may also serve to "tip" participation.

As indicated in the table in the appendix, the time taken to bring an IEA into force varies enormously. Some agreements never enter into force, while others enter into force immediately. It is hard to generalize. Entry into force doesn't even seem to depend strongly on the minimum participation level. It took 14 years for two of the East African marine treaties to enter into force, though only six ratifications were needed. By contrast, the Framework Convention on Climate Change entered into force in two years, despite having set a minimum participation level of 50.

Why might a treaty be negotiated but then never enter into force? The 1988 Convention on the Regulation of Antarctic Mineral Resource Activities provides an illustration. This treaty would only have come into force if ratified by sixteen of twenty Antarctic Treaty consultative parties participating in the negotiations, one of which was Australia (entry into force also required ratification by at least five developing countries and eleven developed countries). Six months after the agreement was open for signature, however, Australia announced that it would not sign the agreement, arguing that mining on Antarctica should be banned. As a claimant nation, Australia's rejection of the treaty was enough to kill it. Later, other claimants sided with Australia (and why not; given Australia's decision, none could gain by clinging to the treaty), and negotiation of an environmental protection agreement was soon underway. As noted earlier, this alternative agreement was adopted in 1991.

6.9. TREATY WITHDRAWAL

In addition to having the right *not* to become a party to a treaty, states also have the right to *withdraw* from a treaty to which they had previously acceded. This customary right is yet another expression of the principle of sovereignty.

Withdrawal, like accession, is a formal affair, and in most agreements the rights of accession and withdrawal are contained in separate treaty articles. Usually, multilateral agreements allow a party to withdraw upon giving written notification to the depository of the treaty. In many cases, a withdrawal can only take effect after a suitable period of time has elapsed following the withdrawing party's accession. Some global agreements, for example, require that a country be a party for at least three years before applying formally to withdraw. It also takes some time for an announcement of an intention to withdraw to take effect. Often a year's notice is required. These restrictions serve to make agreements more stable. They also make countries take their accession decisions seriously, and prevent countries from withdrawing on a whim or in the heat of the moment. Finally, they give the other signatories an opportunity to accommodate the concerns of a disgruntled party.

The threat of withdrawal (like the promise of accession) can be a powerful means of influencing the behavior of other countries, provided of course that the threat is credible. This is especially so if participation of the country threatening to withdraw is essential to the agreement's success. Indeed, an agreement can completely unravel if a key party withdraws, just as an agreement may never enter into force without a key player's accession. You may recall that Japan's announcement of an intention to withdraw from the Fur Seal Treaty caused the United States to offer to renegotiate. When Japan did finally withdraw, however, the agreement collapsed.

In most cases, a single withdrawal will not trigger termination of a treaty. It may, however, spark a renegotiation. Members of the ICRW can withdraw on six months' notice, and on a number of occasions members have withdrawn or have threatened to withdraw in order to put pressure on the IWC to relax its recommendations.

The freedom to accede and withdraw means that the number of signatories to an agreement can go up or down. Figure 6.3 shows changes in the membership of the ICRW over time. In the figure, the number of signatories at date t is equal to the number of signatories at date $t - 1$, less the number of withdrawals at date t plus the number of accessions at date t. Thus, at the end of 1979 there were 24 signatories to the ICRW, while in 1980 there were three accessions (China, Oman, and Switzerland) and one withdrawal (Panama), so that by the end of 1980 there were $24 + 3 - 1 = 26$ signatories.

This figure captures the essence of the self-enforcement problem. States have the right to accede to or withdraw from an IEA as they please (subject, of course, to any participation restrictions being met). This freedom plays a crucial role in the analysis to follow in subsequent chapters.

Though states do not often exercise their right to withdraw, having the right to do so can play a profound role in shaping a treaty, just as can the right to renegotiate. If a state can foresee that it will want to withdraw, it is as likely not to sign the treaty in the first place as to sign and withdraw later. Another reason withdrawals are rare is that the credible threat to withdraw may trigger renegotiation of a treaty. Probably the most important reason, however, is that most treaties do not require countries to restrict their behavior very much. Countries often do not withdraw because they have little to gain by withdrawing. Again, an exception is the Montreal Protocol. This

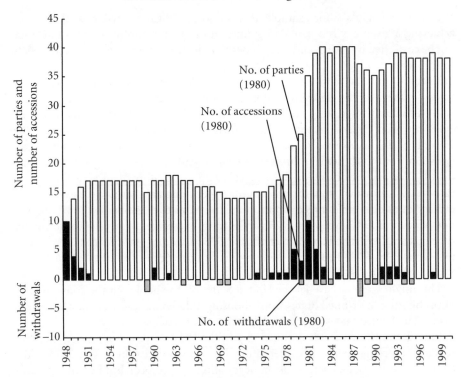

Figure 6.3. *Participation in the ICRW*

Source: Data supplied to the author by the IWC.

treaty restricts behavior but it restructures the incentives such that every party would be harmed severely by withdrawing.

6.10. BASIC OBLIGATIONS

All treaties impose basic obligations of some kind. The Helsinki Protocol requires parties to reduce their sulfur emissions by 30 percent. The Fur Seal Treaty banned pelagic sealing. These basic obligations are intended to correct the collective action problem that brought countries to the negotiation table in the first place.

Treaties like the Helsinki Protocol require that all parties bear exactly the same constraints. Other treaties, however, allow for even more diversity. An example is Helsinki's successor, the Oslo Protocol, which imposes different emission limits on different parties. Another example is the Kyoto Protocol. This treaty specifies different emission ceilings for different countries, with a range from -8 to $+10$ percent, relative to 1990 levels (some countries were not subject to *any* emission limits; see Chapter 15).

It is well known that uniformity can be undesirable for reasons of cost-effectiveness (Hoel 1992). If different countries have different marginal costs of compliance (in the case of the Helsinki Protocol, different marginal costs of reducing critical loads at certain "hot spots"), for example, then uniform obligations will raise the cost of achieving a given environmental outcome. However, non-uniform obligations may not be cost-effective either, and it turns out that the Kyoto limits are grossly cost-ineffective (Barrett 1998*b*). Cost-effectiveness, however, is usually better addressed by a different means: by allowing parties to reallocate their entitlements—that is, to trade—rather than by choosing uniform or non-uniform *ex ante* allocations.

A particularly interesting example of a treaty with non-uniform obligations is the 1988 Nitrogen Oxides Protocol, also known as the Sofia Protocol, a sister of the Helsinki and Oslo Protocols. The Sofia Protocol demands that signatories limit their emissions (or transboundary fluxes) of nitrogen oxides to a level no greater than that for 1987 "or any previous year, to be specified upon signature of, or accession to, the Protocol…" provided that, for any country specifying an alternative base year, the average of annual emissions or transboundary fluxes over the period 1987–96 does not exceed the 1987 level. Of the 25 parties to this agreement, only the United States specified an alternative base year, choosing 1978 instead of 1987. Since US emissions were greater in 1978, the US exception reduced the abatement required of the United States, at least in the short term.

This might seem to have let the United States off the hook, but the consequences of prohibiting the United States from choosing a different base year may have been worse. The United States may have decided not to participate at all.

Indeed, the United States declined to join the Helsinki Protocol precisely for this reason. According to the US International Trade Commission (1991: 5–73), "the United States played an active role in negotiating the protocol, but because the protocol did not credit the substantial progress the United States had already made in controlling sulfur dioxide emissions (reducing emissions by 24 percent since 1970), the United States elected not to participate." By contrast, the United States did become a party to the Sofia Protocol, helped by the provision allowing parties to choose an alternative base year. According to the International Trade Commission (1991: 5–73), "as with the sulfur dioxide protocol, credit for prior action was again a major issue in negotiating this protocol. The United States insisted on and finally achieved some credit for its progress in controlling nitrogen oxide emissions prior to the 1987 base year."

The economics literature has focused very much on cost-effectiveness, and this is an important issue. However, the primary concern of this book lies with increasing cooperation—and cooperation is defined more by participation and compliance than cost-effectiveness. True, cost-effectiveness interacts with these choices. Countries are less likely to participate in and comply with a treaty that is excessively costly. But cost-effectiveness is neither a necessary nor a sufficient condition for participation and compliance.

6.11. TRADE RESTRICTIONS

As shown in the appendix, about one in seven IEAs incorporate trade restrictions. What is not apparent from the table is that these trade restrictions serve different purposes.

Most treaties use trade restrictions as a direct means of achieving their objectives. Plant protection agreements are intended to prevent the introduction of pests and diseases, and so restrict imports. The Basle Convention is intended to stop hazardous wastes from being imported by parties not having consented to accept the waste, and so restricts exports. CITES bans trade in specimens and related products derived from the species listed in its appendices, restricting both imports and exports. CITES controls trade directly but only protects endangered species indirectly.

As described in Chapter 2, the trade restrictions in the North Pacific Fur Seal Treaty served a different purpose. They helped meet the aims of the treaty indirectly by deterring entry. The Montreal Protocol restricts trade for a similar reason. It aims to promote participation. This purpose of the Montreal trade restrictions is analyzed in detail in Chapter 12.

Trade restrictions are sometimes applied indirectly, without formal authority being given. The International Whaling Convention does not specify trade restrictions, but resolutions adopted by the IWC have sought to deter free-riding by urging parties to prevent both imports of whale products from non-parties and the transfer to non-parties of ships, gear, and expertise "necessary to the conduct of whaling operations in any form."[19] According to Rose and Paleokrassis (1996: 172), "these Resolutions were non-binding but were given significant force by the fact that they were mostly adopted unanimously by the major IWC nations, such as the US, the former USSR and Japan."

Trade restrictions may also be added to a treaty as it evolves. The International Convention for the Conservation of Atlantic Tunas does not incorporate trade restrictions, but the Inter-America Tropical Tuna Commission established by this treaty has recommended that restrictions be applied to a number of free-riding states, and these recommendations have been approved by treaty members. Whether the restrictions will work as intended is not yet clear. However, the evolution of this treaty is important. I discuss it in some detail in Chapter 12.

6.12. CONCLUSIONS

In contrast to custom, IEAs are specific remedies to specific transborder externalities. Each treaty is unique, but all IEAs share certain common features.

A typical treaty begins with a preamble in which the concerns of the parties are expressed and references are made to related agreements and declarations. It then provides definitions for the technical terms used in the treaty, and specifies basic provisions or obligations that all parties must satisfy. Most treaties also indicate how disputes are to be settled. They typically identify the treaty's depository; prescribe rules for making reservations and amendments, and specify the requirements for signature, accession, ratification, entry into force, and withdrawal. Some treaties create a supporting secretariat or administrative organization, describe how it should be constituted, and list its responsibilities. Many indicate when the treaty terminates, or

---

[19] See Rose and Paleokrassis (1996: 172).

when it must come up for renewal, or when a conference of the parties should meet and how its decisions are to be reached (by consensus, perhaps, or by a majority). Some include provisions for the reporting of data, and for monitoring and verifying compliance. A remarkably small number of treaties include enforcement mechanisms. Some incorporate an article on trade restrictions. A few provide for technical or financial assistance. If the treaty is an umbrella convention, it may indicate procedures for the adoption of protocols. Normally, a treaty concludes by indicating where and when it was adopted.

This chapter has described the process of treaty negotiation, and shown how this process can shape the kind of treaty that is ultimately negotiated. It has also discussed certain features of IEAs, including the conditions for entry into force and the possible application of trade restrictions. However, the chapter has not explained how a treaty can restructure the relationships among its parties (and between parties and non-parties). The quote that introduced this chapter implies that treaties restrain the behavior of participating countries. But how can treaties make a difference when participation is voluntary and compliance cannot be enforced by a third party? Essential to a treaty's success are the mechanisms that broaden and deepen cooperation. These important issues are taken up in the chapters that follow, beginning with the participation problem.

Appendix 6.1. Multilateral Environmental Agreements

Agreement	Date of adoption	Date of entry into force	Membership open (O) or restricted (R)	Minimum no. of ratifications	No. of signatories (*includes EU)	Provisions for trade restrictions	Created an administrative organization
Marine pollution—general							
International Convention for the Prevention of Pollution of the Sea by Oil (as amended[1])	1954	1958	O	10[2]	69	No	Yes
Amendments Concerning Tank Arrangements and Limitation of Tank Size	1971	Not yet in force[3]	R	46[4]	27	No	No
Amendments Concerning the Protection of the Great Barrier Reef	1971	Not yet in force[3]	R	46[4]	27	No	No
International Convention on Civil Liability for Oil Pollution Damage (as amended[5])	1969	1975	O	8[6]	64	No	Yes
International Convention Relating to Intervention on the High Seas in Cases of Oil Pollution Casualties	1969	1975	O	15	75	No	Yes
Protocol Relating to Intervention on the High Seas in Cases of Marine Pollution by Substances Other than Oil (as amended[7])	1973	1983	R	15	42	No	Yes

[1] In addition to the two amendments listed, two further amendments were negotiated in 1962 and 1969. This agreement was superceded by MARPOL 73/78. It is included here because of its historical significance.

[2] Including five states with at least 500,000 gross tons of tanker capacity.

[3] Although these amendments never entered into force, the substance of these amendments has been incorporated into MARPOL 73/78.

[4] Amendments come into force when accepted by two-thirds of the parties to the Convention for the Prevention of Pollution of the Sea by Oil.

[5] Agreement was amended by three protocols, negotiated in 1976, 1984, and 1992. The 1992 protocol is meant to supercede the 1969 convention, but the two agreements currently co-exist, because there are a number of parties to the 1969 convention that have not ratified the 1992 protocol.

[6] Including at least five states with at least one million gross tons of tanker capacity.

[7] This protocol was amended in 1991 and 1996.

Appendix 6.1. Continued

Agreement	Date of adoption	Date of entry into force	Membership open (O) or restricted (R)	Minimum no. of ratifications	No. of signatories (*includes EU)	Provisions for trade restrictions	Created an administrative organization
International Convention on the Establishment of an International Fund for Compensation for Oil Pollution Damage (as amended)[8]	1971	1978	R	8[9]	45	No	Yes
Convention on the Prevention of Marine Pollution by Dumping of Wastes and Other Matter (as amended)[10]	1972	1975	O	15	82	No	Yes
International Convention for the Prevention of Pollution from Ships[11]	1973	1983	O	15[12]	113	No	Yes
Protocol Relating to the International Convention for the Prevention of Pollution from Ships (as amended)[13]	1978						
Convention on Civil Liability for Oil Pollution Damage Resulting from Exploration for and Exploitation of seabed Mineral Resources	1977	Not yet in force	R	4	6	No	Yes
Convention on Conditions for the Registration of Ships	1986	Not yet in force	O	40[14]	17	No	No
International Convention on Oil Pollution, Preparedness, Response and Cooperation	1990	1995	O	15	55	No	No
Marine pollution—regional							
Convention on the Protection of the Marine Environment of the Baltic Sea Area (as amended)[15]	1974	1980	R	7	10*	No	Yes

Convention for the Protection of the Mediterranean Sea against Pollution[16] (as revised)[17]	1976	1978	R	6[18]	21*	No	Yes
Protocol for the Prevention of Pollution of the Mediterranean Sea by Dumping from Ships and Aircraft (as revised)[17]	1976	1978	R	6	21*	No	No
Protocol Concerning Cooperation in Combating Pollution of the Mediterranean Sea by Oil and Other Harmful Substances in Cases of Emergency	1976	1978	R	6	21*	No	No
Protocol for the Protection of the Mediterranean Sea against Pollution from Land-Based Sources (as amended)[19]	1980	1983	R	6	21*	No	No
Protocol Concerning Mediterranean Specially Protected Areas (as revised)[17]	1982	1986	R	6	21*	Yes	No
Protocol for the Protection of the Mediterranean Sea against Pollution Resulting from Exploration and Exploitation of the Continental Shelf and the Seabed and its Subsoil	1994	Not yet in force	R	Not specified	11	No	No
Agreement Concerning the Protection of the Waters of the Mediterranean Shores	1976	1981	R	3	3	No	Yes

8 Protocols were added in 1976, 1984, and 1992. The 1992 protocol was intended to replace the 1971 convention, but the two agreements currently operate in parallel.

9 Provided these states account for at least 750 million tons of "contributing" oil.

10 Amended in 1978 (twice), 1980, 1989, and 1993; superceded by protocol negotiated in 1996.

11 This agreement and the follow-on protocol together comprise MARPOL 73/78, which is considered to be a single legal instrument.

12 The merchant fleets of which constitute at least 50 percent of the gross tonnage of the world's merchant shipping.

13 MARPOL 73/78 was amended in 1984, 1985 (twice), 1987, 1989 (twice), 1990 (four times), 1991, 1992, 1994, 1995, 1996, and 1997. A protocol was also negotiated in 1997.

14 Provided these signatories account for at least 25 percent of total world tonnage.

15 Superceded by a 1992 convention of the same name.

16 Later renamed the Convention for the Protection of the Marine Environment and the Coastal Region of the Mediterranean.

17 Revised in 1995.

18 The Convention enters into force after the first of its protocols enters into force.

19 Amended in 1996.

Appendix 6.1. Continued

Agreement	Date of adoption	Date of entry into force	Membership open (O) or restricted (R)	Minimum no. of ratifications	No. of signatories (*includes EU)	Provisions for trade restrictions	Created an administrative organization
Kuwait Regional Convention for Cooperation on the Protection of the Marine Environment from Pollution	1978	1979	R	5	8	No	Yes
Protocol Concerning Regional Cooperation in Combating Pollution by Oil and other Harmful Substances in Cases of Emergency	1978	1979	R	5	8	No	No
Protocol Concerning Marine Pollution Resulting from Exploration and Exploitation of the Continental Shelf	1989	1990	R	5	8	No	No
Protocol for the Protection of the Marine Environment Against Pollution from Land-Based Sources	1990	1993	R	5	7	No	No
Convention for Cooperation in the Protection and Development of the Marine and Coastal Environment of the West and Central African Region	1981	1984	R	6	13	No	No
Protocol Concerning Cooperation in Combating Pollution in Cases of Emergency	1981	1984	R	6	13	No	No
Convention for the Protection of the Marine Environment and Coastal Area of the South-East Pacific	1981	1986	R	3	5	No	Yes
Agreement on Regional Cooperation in Combating Pollution of the South-East Pacific by Oil and Other Harmful	1981	1986	R	3	5	No	Yes

Treaty	Adopted	Entry into force	Status			Non-party	Party
Supplementary Protocol to the Agreement on Regional Cooperation in Combating Pollution of the South-East Pacific by Hydrocarbons or Other Harmful Substances in Cases of Emergency	1983	1987	R	3	5	No	Yes
Protocol for the Protection of the South-East Pacific Against Pollution by Land-Based Sources	1983	1986	R	3	5	No	Yes
Protocol for the Conservation and Management of the Protected Marine and Coastal Areas of the South-East Pacific	1989	1994	R	3	5	No	No
Protocol for the Protection of the South-East Pacific Against Radioactive Contamination	1989	1995	R	3	5	No	No
Regional Convention for the Conservation of the Red Sea and Gulf of Aden Environment	1982	1985	R	4	7[20]	No	Yes
Protocol Concerning Regional Cooperation in Combating Pollution by Oil and other Harmful Substances in Cases of Emergency	1982	1985	R	4	7[20]	No	Yes
Convention for the Protection and Development of the Marine Environment of the Wider Caribbean Region	1983	1986	R	9	23*	No	Yes
Protocol Concerning Cooperation in Combating Oil Spills	1983	1986	R	9	22	No	Yes
Protocol Concerning Specially Protected Areas and Wildlife to the Convention for the Protection and Development of the Marine Environment of the Wider Caribbean Region	1990	2000	R	9	15	No	Yes
Protocol on the Prevention, Reduction, and Control of Land-Based Sources and Activities	1999	Not yet in force[21]	R	Not specified	6	No	Yes

[20] Plus Palestine represented by the Palestine Liberation Organization.
[21] No signatory has yet ratified the protocol.

Agreement	Date of adoption	Date of entry into force	Membership open (O) or restricted (R)	Minimum no. of ratifications	No. of signatories (*includes EU)	Provisions for trade restrictions	Created an administrative organization
Agreement for Cooperation in Dealing with Pollution of the North Sea by Oil and Other Harmful Substances	1983	1989	O	9	9*	No	No
Convention for the Protection, Management, and Development of the Marine and Coastal Environment of the Eastern African Region	1985	1996	R	6	8*	No	Yes
Protocol Concerning Cooperation in Combating Marine Pollution in Cases of Emergency in the Eastern African Region	1985	1996	R	6	8*	No	Yes
Convention for the Protection of the Natural Resources and Environment of the South Pacific Region	1986	1990	R	10	15	No	No
Protocol for the Prevention of Pollution of the South Pacific Region by Dumping.	1986	1990	R	5	15	No	No
Protocol Concerning Cooperation in Pollution Emergencies in the South Pacific Region	1986	1990	R	5	15	No	No
Oslo Convention for the Prevention of Marine Pollution by Dumping from Ships and Aircraft (as amended)[22]	1972	1974	R	7	13	No	Yes
Paris Convention on the Prevention of Marine Pollution from Land-Based Sources (as amended)[22]	1974	1978	R	7	13*	No	Yes
Convention for the Protection of the Marine Environment of the North-East Atlantic	1992	1998	R	13[23]	16*	No	Yes
Accord of Cooperation for the Protection of the Coasts and Waters of the North-East Atlantic Against Pollution due to	1990	Not yet in force	R	5[24]	5*	No	No

Hydrocarbons or Other Harmful Substances Convention on the Protection of the Black Sea Against Pollution	1992	1994	R	4	6	No	Yes
Protocol on Protection of the Black Sea Marine Environment Against Pollution from Land-Based Sources[25]	1992	1994	R	4	6	No	No
Protocol on Cooperation in Combating Pollution of the Black Sea Marine Environment by Oil and Other Harmful Substances in Emergency Situations[25]	1992	1994	R	4	6	No	No
Protocol on Protection of the Black Sea Marine Environment Against Pollution by Dumping[25]	1992	1994	R	4	6	No	No
Marine fisheries							
Agreement for the Establishment of the Asia-Pacific Fishery Commission (as amended)[26]	1948	1948	R	5	21	No	Yes
Convention for the Establishment of an Inter-American Tropical Tuna Commission	1949	1950	R	2[27]	11	No	Yes
Agreement for the Establishment of a General Fisheries Council for the Mediterranean (as amended)[28]	1949	1952	R	5	24*	No	Yes
Agreement Concerning Measures for Protection of the Stocks of Deep Sea Prawns, European Lobsters, Norway Lobsters, and Crabs (as amended)	1952	1953	R	3	3	No	Yes
Convention on Fishing and Conservation of the Living Resources of the High Seas	1958	1966	O	22	57	No	Yes

[22] Superceded by the Convention for the Marine Environment for the North-East Atlantic, 1992. However, the Decisions, Recommendations and other agreements adopted under Oslo and Paris Conventions remain in force unless specifically terminated.

[23] Must be ratified by all the parties of the Oslo and Paris Conventions.

[24] Must include EEC.

[25] Protocol forms part of the convention.

[26] Amended in 1976, 1993, and 1996.

[27] Initially, the agreement would only come into force if signed by Costa Rica and the United States. Other states could accede upon the unanimous consent of the contracting parties. Costa Rica withdrew from the Convention in 1979.

[28] Amended in 1963, 1976, and 1997.

Appendix 6.1. Continued

Agreement	Date of adoption	Date of entry into force	Membership open (O) or restricted (R)	Minimum no. of ratifications	No. of signatories (*includes EU)	Provisions for trade restrictions	Created an administrative organization
Convention Concerning Fishing in the Black Sea (as amended)	1959	1960	R	3[29]	3	No	Yes
Agreement on the Protection of the Salmon in the Baltic Sea (as amended)	1962	1966	R	3	4	Yes[30]	Yes
Agreement Concerning Cooperation in Marine Fishing	1962	1963	R	3[29]	5	No	Yes
European Fisheries Convention (and Protocol)	1964	1966	R	8	12	No	No
Agreement on Reciprocal Access to Fishing in the Sakagerrak and the Kattegat	1966	1967	R	3	3	No	No
International Convention for the Conservation of Atlantic Tunas (as amended)[31]	1966	1969	O	7	35*	No[32]	Yes
Convention on Conduct of Fishing Operations in the North Atlantic	1967	1976	R	12	17	No	No
Convention on the Conservation of Living Resources of the South-East Atlantic[33]	1969	1971	0	4[34]	17	No	Yes
Convention on Fishing and Conservation of the Living Resources in the Baltic Sea and Belts (as amended)	1973	1974	R	4	6*	No	Yes
Convention on Future Multilateral Cooperation in the North-West Atlantic Fisheries[35]	1978	1979	R	6	18*	No	Yes
South Pacific Forum Fisheries Agency Convention	1979	1979	R	8	16	No	Yes
Convention on Future Multilateral Cooperation in North-East Atlantic Fisheries	1980	1982	R	7[36]	11*	No	Yes
Convention for the Conservation of Salmon in the North Atlantic Ocean	1982	1983	R	4[37]	8*	No	Yes

Agreement								
Nauru Agreement Concerning Cooperation in the Management of Fisheries of Common Interest	1982	Not yet in force	R	5	5	No	No
Constitutional Agreement of the Latin American Organization for Fishery Development	1982	1984	R	4	5	No	Yes
Eastern Pacific Tuna Fishing Agreement (with Protocol)	1983	Not yet in force	R	5	3	No[38]	Yes
South Pacific Fisheries Treaty	1987	1988	R	11[39]	12	No	No
Agreement on the Network of Aquaculture Centres in Asia and the Pacific	1988	1990	R	5	14	No	Yes
Convention for the Prohibition of Fishing with Long Drift Nets in the South Pacific (as amended)[40]	1989	1991	R	4	15[41]	Yes	Yes
Agreement Creating the Eastern Pacific Tuna Fishing Organization	1989	Not yet in force	R	4	5	No	Yes
Western Indian Ocean Tuna Organization Convention	1991	1992	R	3	4	No	Yes
Regional Convention on Fisheries Cooperation Among African States Bordering the Atlantic Ocean	1991	1995	R	7	17	No	Yes
Niue Treaty on Cooperation in Fisheries Surveillance and Law Enforcement in the South Pacific Region	1992	1993	R	4	17	No	No

29 Agreement came into force upon ratification by the original contracting parties.

30 Agreement requires that parties pass laws prohibiting the sale of salmon taken in contravention of the convention.

31 Protocols added in 1984 and 1992.

32 Trade sanctions were subsequently incorporated into this agreement.

33 A protocol of termination for this convention was adopted in 1990 but has not entered into force.

34 Provided these countries account for at least 700,000 metric tons of nominal catch in the designated area in 1968.

35 Supercedes the 1946 Convention for the Regulation of the Meshes of Fishing Nets and the Size Limits of Fish (as amended).

36 Provided these include at least three states exercising fisheries jurisdiction within the conservation area.

37 Provided these include at least two members of the West Greenland and North-East Atlantic Commissions and that at least one of the two members of each Commission exercises fisheries jurisdiction in the Commission area.

38 Agreement says that parties agree *not* to prohibit imports of tuna from other parties "as a result of any enforcement action by that Contracting Party consistent with this agreement, as long as such Party is acting in conformity with this Agreement."

39 Must include the United States plus ten island states to include the Federated States of Micronesia, Kiribati, and Papua Guinea.

40 Two protocols were added in 1990.

41 Plus Niue.

Appendix 6.1. Continued

Agreement	Date of adoption	Date of entry into force	Membership open (O) or restricted (R)	Minimum no. of ratifications	No. of signatories (*includes EU)	Provisions for trade restrictions	Created an administrative organization
Convention for the Conservation of Anadromous Stocks[42]	1992	1993	R	4	4	No	Yes
Convention for the Conservation of Southern Bluefin Tuna	1993	1994	R	3	3	No	Yes
Agreement for the Establishment of the Indian Ocean Tuna Commission	1993	1996	R	10	18*	No	Yes
Agreement to Promote Compliance with International Conservation and Management Measures by Fishing Vessels on the High Seas	1993	Not yet in force	O	25	19*	No	No
Convention on the Conservation and Management of Pollock Resources in the Central Bering Sea	1994	1995	R	4	6	No	No
Federated States of Micronesia Arrangement for Regional Fisheries Access	1994	Not yet in force	R	3[43]	7	No	No
Agreement for the Implementation of the United Nations Convention on the Law of the Sea Relating to the Conservation and Management of Straddling Fish Stocks and Highly Migratory Fish Stocks	1995	Not yet in force	O	30	25*	No	No
Protocol on the Conservation, Rational Utilization and Management of Norwegian Spring Spawning in the North-East Atlantic	1996	1996	R	4	4	No	No
Agreed Record of Conclusions of Fisheries Consultations on the Management of the Norwegian Spring Spawning Herring in the North-East Atlantic (including supplementary agreements)	1996	1997	R	5	5	No	No
Agreement for the Establishment of the Regional Commission for Fisheries	1999	Not yet in force	R	3	2	No	Yes

Agreement							
Agreement Concerning Certain Aspects of Cooperation in the Area of Fisheries (and Protocols)[44]	1999	Not yet in force	R	3	3	No	No
Agreement for the Establishment of the International Organization for the Development of Fisheries in Eastern and Central Europe	2000	Not yet in force	R	5	5	No	Yes
Framework Agreement for the Conservation of the Living Marine Resources of the High Seas of the South Pacific	2000	Not yet in force	R	4	4	No	Yes
International Convention for the Conservation and Management of Highly Migratory Fish Stocks in the Western and Central Pacific Ocean	2000	Not yet in force	R	10[45]	13	Yes	Yes
Convention on the Conservation and Management of Fishery Resources in the South-East Atlantic Ocean	2000	Not yet in force	R	3	9*	Yes	Yes
Marine mammal							
International Convention for the Regulation of Whaling (as amended)	1946	1948	O	6[46]	40	No	Yes
Agreement on the Conservation of Seals in the Wadden Sea	1990	1991	Not specified	3	3	No	No
Agreement on the Conservation of Small Cetaceans of the Baltic and North Seas	1992	1994	R	6	16*	No	Yes
Agreement on the Conservation of Cetaceans of the Black Sea, Mediterranean Sea, and Contiguous Atlantic Area	1996	Not yet in force	R	7[47]	16*	No	Yes

[42] Replaces the 1952 International Convention for the High Seas Fisheries of the North Pacific Ocean.

[43] The treaty is not subject to ratification and enters into force after being signed by Micronesia, Kiribati, and Papua New Guinea

[44] Two protocols are attached to this tripartite agreement.

[45] Must include three states situated north of, and seven states situated south of, the parallel marking 20°N latitude. In the event that, three years after the adoption of the treaty, no three states meeting the first criteria have ratified, then the convention shall enter into force following the 13th ratification.

[46] Must include The Netherlands, Norway, the USSR, the United Kingdom, and the United States.

[47] Comprising at least two Black Sea states and at least five Mediterranean states.

Appendix 6.1. Continued

Agreement	Date of adoption	Date of entry into force	Membership open (O) or restricted (R)	Minimum no. of ratifications	No. of signatories (*includes EU)	Provisions for trade restrictions	Created an administrative organization
Inter-American Convention for the Protection and Conservation of Sea Turtles	1996	Not yet in force	R	8	6	Yes[48]	Yes
Agreement on the International Dolphin Conservation Program	1998	1999	R	4	7	No	Yes
Cooperative Agreement for the Conservation of Sea Turtles of the Caribbean Coast of Costa Rica, Nicaragua, and Panama	1998	Not yet in force	R	3	0	No	Yes
Other marine							
Convention on the Continental Shelf	1958	1964	O	22	77	No	No
Convention on the High Seas	1958	1962	O	22	78	No	No
Convention on the Territorial Sea and the Contiguous Zone	1958	1964	R	22	73	No	No
Convention for the International Council for the Exploration of the Sea (as amended)	1964	1968	R	16[49]	7	No	Yes
United Nations Convention on the Law of the Sea	1982	1994	O	60	171*	No	Yes
Agreement Concerning the Preservation of Confidentiality of Data Concerning Deep Seabed Areas	1986	1986	R	1[50]	5	No	No
International Convention on Salvage	1989	1996	O	15	32	No	No
Agreement Relating to the Implementation of Part XI of the United Nations Convention on the Law of the Sea	1994	1996	O	40[51]	114*	No	No
Freshwater fisheries							
Convention Concerning Fishing in the Waters of the Danube (as amended)	1958	1958	R	4	4	No	Yes

Convention for the Establishment of the Lake Victoria Fisheries Organization	1994	1996	R	3	3	No	Yes
International rivers, lakes, and groundwaters							
Agreement Concerning the Regulation of Lake Inari by Means of the Kaitakoski Hydro-Electric Power Station and Dam	1959	1959	R	3	3	No	No
Protocol Concerning the Constitution of an International Commission for the Protection of the Mosel Against Pollution	1961	1962	R	3	3	No	Yes
Agreement Concerning the International Commission for the Protection of the Rhine Against Pollution (as amended)	1963	1965	R	5[52]	6*	No	Yes
Convention and Statute Relating to the Development of the Chad Basin (as amended)	1964	1964	R	4	5	No	Yes
Agreement Regulating the Withdrawal of Water from Lake Constance	1966	1967	R	3	3	No	No
Convention Concerning the Status of the Senegal River and Convention establishing the Senegal River Development Organization (as amended)	1972	1972	R	3	3	No	Yes
Convention on the Protection of the Rhine Against Chemical Pollution[53]	1976	1979	R	6	6*	No	Yes
Convention Concerning the Protection of the Rhine Against Pollution by Chlorides[53]	1976	1985	R	5	5	No	Yes
Agreement on the Establishment of the Organization for the Management and Development of the Kagera River Basin	1977	1978	R	3	4	No	Yes
Convention Relating to the Creation of the Gambia River Basin Development Organization	1978	1981	R	Not specified	4	No	Yes

[48] Agreement contains an article on trade measures but does not make proposals for their use.

[49] Agreement enters into force upon ratification by the original contracting parties.

[50] Enters into force for all parties upon signature.

[51] To include at least seven states referred to in paragraph 1(a) of Resolution II of the Law of the Sea, at least five of which must be "developed states."

[52] Agreement enters into force upon ratification by the original contracting parties.

[53] The 1963 agreement and the two 1976 conventions will be superceded by the 1998 Convention on Protection of the Rhine when this agreement enters into force.

Appendix 6.1. Continued

Agreement	Date of adoption	Date of entry into force	Membership open (O) or restricted (R)	Minimum no. of ratifications	No. of signatories (*includes EU)	Provisions for trade restrictions	Created an administrative organization
Agreement on Parana River Projects	1979	1979	R	3	3	No	No
Convention Creating the Niger Basin Authority	1980	1982	R	6	9	No	Yes[54]
Agreement on the Action Plan for the Environmentally Sound Management of the Common Zambezi River System	1987	1987	R	5	5	No	Yes
Convention on the Protection and Use of Transboundary Watercourses and International Lakes	1992	1996	R	16	30*	No	No
Protocol on Water and Health	1999	Not yet in force	R	16	36	No	No
Agreement on Joint Activities in Addressing the Aral Sea and Zone Around the Sea Crisis	1993	1993	O	Not specified	5	No	No
Agreement on the Preparation of a Tripartite Environmental Management Programme for Lake Victoria	1994	1994	R	3	3	No	Yes
Agreement on the Establishment of a Permanent Okavango River Basin Water Commission	1994	Not yet in force	R	3	0	No	Yes
Agreement on the Protection of the Rivers Meuse and Scheldt	1994	Not yet in force	R	3	2	No	Yes
Convention on Cooperation for Protection and Sustainable Use of the Danube	1994	1998	R	9	12	No	Yes
Protocol on Shared Water Course Systems in the Southern African Development Community Region	1995	1998	R	Two-thirds of the members of the SADC	13	No	Yes
Agreement on Cooperation for Sustainable Development of the Mekong River Basin	1995	1995	R	4	4	No	Yes

Agreement	Year	Date in force				No	Yes
Agreement Concerning the Trilateral Commission for the Development of the Riverbed Rio Pilcomayo	1995	Not yet in force	R	3	3	No	Yes
Agreement on Protection of the River Oder from Pollution	1996	Not yet in force	R	3	4*	No	Yes
Convention on the Collection, Storage, and Discharge of Wastes Resulting from Ships Navigating Along the Rhine and Other Inland Waters	1996	Not yet in force	R	6	6	No	Yes
United Nations Convention on the Law of the Non-Navigational Uses of International Watercourses	1997	Not yet in force	O	35	18	No	No
Air and atmospheric pollution							
Convention on Long-Range Transboundary Air Pollution	1979	1983	R	24	49*	No	Yes
Protocol on Long-Term Financing of the Co-operative Programme for Monitoring and Evaluation of the Long-Range Transmission of Air Pollutants in Europe	1984	1988	R	19[55]	38*	No	Yes
Protocol on the Reduction of Sulphur Emissions or Their Transboundary Fluxes by At Least 30 Percent	1985	1987	R	16	22	No	Yes
Protocol Concerning the Control of Emissions of Nitrogen Oxides or Their Transboundary Fluxes	1988	1991	R	16	29*	No	Yes
Protocol Concerning the Control of Emissions of Volatile Organic Compounds or Their Transboundary Fluxes	1991	1997	R	16	26*	No	Yes
Protocol on Further Reduction of Sulphur Emissions	1994	1998	R	16	28*	No	Yes
Protocol on Heavy Metals	1998	Not yet in force	R	16	36*	No	Yes
Protocol on Persistent Organic Pollutants	1998	Not yet in force	R	16	36*	No	Yes

54 Agreement reconstitutes the former River Niger Commission, now called the Niger Basin Authority.
55 Provided the aggregate of the UN assessment rates for these parties exceeds 40 percent.

Appendix 6.1. Continued

Agreement	Date of adoption	Date of entry into force	Membership open (O) or restricted (R)	Minimum no. of ratifications	No. of signatories (*includes EU)	Provisions for trade restrictions	Created an administrative organization
Protocol to Abate Acidification, Eutrophication and Ground-Level Ozone	1999	Not yet in force	R	16	31	No	Yes
Vienna Convention for Protection of the Ozone Layer	1985	1988	O	20	176*	No	No
Montreal Protocol on Substances that Deplete the Ozone Layer (as adjusted and amended)	1987	1989	R	11[56]	175*	Yes	No
London Amendment	1990	1992	R	20	144*	Yes	Yes
Copenhagen Amendment	1992	1994	R	20	115*	Yes	Yes
Montreal Amendment	1997	1999	R	20	48*	Yes	Yes
Beijing Amendment	1999	Not yet in force	R	20	2	Yes	Yes
United Nation Framework Convention on Climate Change	1992	1994	O	50	189*	No	Yes
Kyoto Protocol	1997	Not yet in force	R	55[57]	84*	No	Yes
Transportation of hazardous materials							
European Agreement Concerning the Carriage of Dangerous Goods by Road (as amended)	1957	1968	R	5	34	No	No
Agreement Concerning the Transboundary Movement of Hazardous Waste	1986	1986	R	3	3	Yes	No
Basel Convention on the Control of Transboundary Movements of Hazardous Wastes and their Disposal	1989	1992	O	20	142*	Yes	Yes
Ban Amendment	1995	Not yet in force	R	62[58]	22*	Yes	No
Basel Protocol on Liability and Compensation	1999	Not yet in force	R	20	13	No	No

Convention							
Convention on Civil Liability for Damage Caused During Carriage of Dangerous Goods by Road, Rail, and Inland Navigation Vessels	1989	Not yet in force	O	5	2	No	No
Bamako OAU Convention on The Ban of the Import into Africa and the Control of Transboundary Movement and Management of Hazardous Wastes within Africa	1991	1998	R	10	27	Yes	Yes
Regional Agreement on Transboundary Movement of Hazardous Wastes in the Central American Region	1992	1994	R	3	6	No	No
Convention to Ban the Importation into Forum Island Countries of Hazardous and Radioactive Wastes and to Control the Transboundary Movement and Management of Hazardous Wastes within the South Pacific Region	1995	Not yet in force	R	10	13	Yes	Yes
International Convention on Liability and Compensation for Damage in Connection with the Carriage of Hazardous and Noxious Substances by Sea	1996	Not yet in force	O	12[59]	8	No	Yes
Protocol on the Prevention of Pollution of the Mediterranean Sea by Transboundary Movements of Hazardous Wastes and their Disposal[60]	1996	Not yet in force	R	6	11	Yes	No
Rotterdam Convention on the Prior Informed Consent Procedure for Certain Hazardous Chemicals and Pesticides in International Trade	1998	Not yet in force	O	50	73*	Yes	Yes
European Agreement Concerning the International Carriage of Dangerous Goods by Inland Waterways	2000	Not yet in force	R	7	6	Yes	Yes

[56] Provided these states account for at least two-thirds of 1986 estimated global consumption of the controlled substances.

[57] To include countries located in Annex I which account for at least 55 percent of total carbon dioxide emissions for 1990 of the countries listed in Annex I.

[58] Three-fourths of the parties to the Basel Convention present at the time of adoption of the amendment.

[59] Including at least four states each with not less than two million units of gross tonnage.

[60] Protocol to the Convention for the Protection of the Marine Environment and the Coastal Region of the Mediterranean.

Appendix 6.1. Continued

Agreement	Date of adoption	Date of entry into force	Membership open (O) or restricted (R)	Minimum no. of ratifications	No. of signatories (*includes EU)	Provisions for trade restrictions	Created an administrative organization
Protocol on the Control of Marine Transboundary Movements and Disposal of Hazardous Wastes and Other Wastes[61]	1998	Not yet in force	R	5	6	No	No
Civil nuclear							
Convention on Third Party Liability in the Field of Nuclear Energy (as amended)	1960	1968	R	5	16	No	No
Convention Supplementary to the Paris Convention on Third Party Liability in the Field of Nuclear Energy (as amended)	1963	1974	R	6	14	No	No
Vienna Convention of Civil Liability for Nuclear Damage	1963	1977	O	5	35	No	No
Protocol to Amend the Vienna Convention	1997	Not yet in force	R	5	15	No	No
Convention Relating to Civil Liability in the Field of Maritime Carriage of Nuclear Material	1971	1975	O	5[62]	17	No	No
Convention on the Physical Protection of Nuclear Material	1980	1987	O	21	39[63]	Yes	No
Convention on Early Notification of a Nuclear Accident	1986	1986	O	3	97	No	Yes
Convention on Assistance in the Case of a Nuclear Accident or Radiological Emergency	1986	1987	O	3	95	No	Yes
Joint Protocol Relating to the Application of the Vienna Convention and the Paris Convention	1988	1992	R	10[64]	32	No	No
Convention on Nuclear Safety	1994	1996	O	22[65]	72[63]	No	No
Joint Convention on the Safety of Spent Fuel Management and on the Safety of Radioactive Waste Management	1997	Not yet in force	O	25[66]	42	Yes	No

Convention							
Convention on Supplementary Compensation for Nuclear Damage	1997	Not yet in force	R	5[67]	13	No	No
Nature and wildlife							
Convention for the Protection of Birds Useful to Agriculture	1902	1905	R	1[68]	10	Yes	No
Convention Relative to the Preservation of Fauna and Flora in their Natural State	1933	1936	O	4	10	Yes	No
Convention of Nature Protection and Wildlife Preservation in the Western Hemisphere	1940	1942	R	5	22	Yes	No
International Convention for the Protection of Birds[69]	1950	1963	O	6	15	Yes	No
African Convention on the Conservation of Nature and Natural Resources	1968	1969	R	4	43	Yes	No
Benelux Convention on the Hunting and Protection of Birds (as amended)	1970	1972	R	3	3	Yes	No
Convention on Wetlands of International Importance especially as Waterfowl Habitat (as amended)	1971	1975	O	7	124	No	Yes[70]
Protocol to Amend the Convention on Wetlands of International Importance Especially as Waterfowl Habitat	1982	1986	R	Two-thirds of the parties to Convention	60	No	No
Convention Concerning the Protection of the World Cultural and Natural Heritage	1972	1975	R	20	160	No	Yes

[61] Protocol to the Kuwait Regional Convention for Cooperation on the Protection of the Marine Environment from Pollution.

[62] Provided none of these five states has made a reservation.

[63] Includes EURATOM.

[64] To include at least five parties to the Vienna Convention and five parties to the Paris Convention.

[65] To include at least 17 states, each having at least one nuclear installation which has achieved criticality in a reactor core.

[66] To include at least 15 states having an operational nuclear plant.

[67] Each of these parties must possess at least 400,000 units of installed nuclear capacity.

[68] Enters into force for each party upon acceptance.

[69] Supercedes the 1902 Convention for those countries that ratify the 1950 Convention.

[70] The IUCN (World Conservation Union) acts as the *de facto* administrative body.

Appendix 6.1. Continued

Agreement	Date of adoption	Date of entry into force	Membership open (O) or restricted (R)	Minimum no. of ratifications	No. of signatories (*includes EU)	Provisions for trade restrictions	Created an administrative organization
Convention on International Trade in Endangered Species of Wild Fauna and Flora (as amended)	1973	1975	O	10	155	Yes	Yes
Agreement on Conservation of Polar Bears	1973	1976	R	3	5	Yes	No
Convention on the Game Hunting Formalities Applicable to Tourists Entering Countries in the Conseil d'Etente	1976	1977	R	5	5	Yes	No
Convention on Conservation of Nature in the South Pacific	1976	1990	R	4	6	No	Yes
Agreement on Joint Regulations on Flora and Fauna	1977	1977	R	None specified	4	Yes	No
Convention on the Conservation of Migratory Species of Wild Animals	1979	1983	O	15	75*	No	No
Memorandum of Understanding Concerning Conservation Measures for the Slender-billed Curlew	1994	1994	R	—[71]	21	No	No
Agreement on the Conservation of African–Eurasian Migratory Waterbirds	1996	1999	R	14[72]	32*	No	Yes
Memorandum of Understanding Concerning Conservation Measures for the Siberian Crane	1998	1999	R	2[73]	9	No	No
Memorandum of Understanding Concerning Conservation Measures for Marine Turtles of the Atlantic Coast of Africa	1999	Not yet in force	R	—[74]	9	No	No
Memorandum of Understanding on the Conservation and Management of Marine	1999	Not yet in force	R	2	0	No	Yes

Agreement							
Turtles and Their Habitats of the Indian Ocean and South-East Asia							
Memorandum of Understanding on the Conservation and Management of the Middle European Population of the Great Bustard	2000	Not yet in force	R	5[75]	3	No	No
Convention on the Conservation of European Wildlife and Natural Habitats	1979	1982	R	5[76]	44*	Yes	Yes
Convention for the Conservation and Management of the Vicuna	1979	1979	R	3	5	Yes	Yes
Protocol Agreement on the Conservation of Common Natural Resources	1982	Not yet in force	R	3	3	No	No
Benelux Convention on Nature Conservation and Landscape Protection	1982	1983	R	3	3	No	No
Protocol Concerning Protected Areas and Wild Fauna and Flora in the Eastern African Region[77]	1985	1996	R	6	8*	Yes	Yes
ASEAN Agreement on the Conservation of Nature and Natural Resources	1985	Not yet in force		6	6	No	Yes
Agreement for the Establishment of a Southern African Centre for Ivory Marketing	1991	1991	R	5[75]	5		
Agreement on the Conservation of Bats in Europe	1991	1994	R	3	21	No	No
Convention Concerning Protection of the Alps	1991	1995	R	3	9*	No	Yes

71 Enters into force upon signature of the range states; the precise number of signatories required is unspecified.

72 To include at least seven states from Africa and seven from Eurasia.

73 That is, two range states; there are a total of 12 range states.

74 Enters into force upon signature of the range states; the precise number of signatories required is unspecified.

75 All five must be range states.

76 To include at least four member states of the Council of Europe.

77 To the Convention for the Protection, Management and Development of the Marine and Coastal Environment of the Eastern African Region.

Appendix 6.1. Continued

Agreement	Date of adoption	Date of entry into force	Membership open (O) or restricted (R)	Minimum no. of ratifications	No. of signatories (*includes EU)	Provisions for trade restrictions	Created an administrative organization
Protocol for the Implementation of the Alpine Convention in the Field of Town and Country Planning and Sustainable Development	1994	Not yet in force	R	3	9*	No	No
Protocol for the Implementation of the Alpine Convention in the Field of Nature Protection and Landscape Conservation	1994	Not yet in force	R	3	9*	No[78]	No
Protocol for the Implementation of the Alpine Convention in the Field of Mountain Agriculture	1994	Not yet in force	R	3	9*	No	No
Protocol of Application of the Alpine Convention in the Field of Mountain Forests	1996	Not yet in force	R	3	8*	No	No
Protocol of Application of the Alpine Convention in the Field of the Protection of Soils	1998	Not yet in force	R	3	8	No	No
Protocol of Application of the Alpine Convention in the Field of Energy	1998	Not yet in force	R	3	6	No	No
Protocol of Application of the Alpine Convention in the Field of Tourism	1998	Not yet in force	R	3	8	No	No
Protocol of Application of the Alpine Convention in the Field of Transport	2000	Not yet in force	R	3	7	No	No
Convention on Biological Diversity	1992	1993	O	30	178*	Yes	No
Cartagena Protocol on Biosafety	2000	Not yet in force	O	50[79]	80*	Yes	Yes
Agreement on the Conservation of Biodiversity and the Protection of Prime Wilderness Areas in Central America	1992	1993	R	3	6	No	Yes

Name							
Lusaka Agreement on Cooperative Enforcement Operations Directed at Illegal Trade in Wild Fauna and Flora	1994	1996	R	4	9	Yes	No
Antarctica							
The Antarctic Treaty	1959	1961	R	12	44	No	No
Agreed Measures for the Preservation of Antarctic Flora and Fauna	1964	1982	R	All the Contracting Parties[81]	17	Yes[80]	No
Protocol to the Antarctic Treaty on Environmental Protection	1991	1998	R	26[81]	38	No	No
Convention for the Conservation of Antarctic Seals	1972	1978	R	7	17	No	Yes
Convention on the Conservation of Antarctic Marine Living Resources	1980	1982	O	8[82]	29*	No	Yes
Convention on the Regulation of Antarctic Mineral Resource Activities	1988	Not yet in force	R	16[83]	17	No	Yes
Plant protection							
Convention for the Establishment of the European & Mediterranean Plant Protection Organization (as amended)	1951	1953	R	5	34	No	Yes
International Plant Protection Convention (as amended)[84]	1951	1952	O	3	111	Yes	Yes
Plant Protection Agreement for the South-East Asia and Pacific Region (as amended)[85]	1956	1956	R	3	27	Yes	Yes
Agreement Concerning Cooperation in the Quarantine of Plants and their Protection Against Pests and Diseases	1959	1960	O	5	8	Yes	No

[78] Protocol forbids the capture, raising, cultivation, offer, sale, purchase, etc. of protected species.

[79] Must be parties to the Convention on Biological Diversity.

[80] Restrictions are imposed on the import of animals and plants to Antarctica.

[81] All the Consultative Parties of the Antarctica Treaty when the Protocol was adopted.

[82] All of which must have participated in the conference which created the convention.

[83] To include at least five developing countries and 11 developed countries.

[84] A revised text was negotiated in 1997, but this has not yet entered into force.

[85] Protocols to this convention added in 1991, 1994 (3), and 1996.

Appendix 6.1. Continued

Agreement	Date of adoption	Date of entry into force	Membership open (O) or restricted (R)	Minimum no. of ratifications	No. of signatories (*includes EU)	Provisions for trade restrictions	Created an administrative organization
International Convention for the Protection of New Varieties of Plants (as amended)	1961	1968	O	3[86]	46	No	Yes
Phyto-Sanitary Convention for Africa	1967	1974	R	Not specified	11	Yes	Yes
North American Plant Protection Agreement[87]	1976	1976	R	3	3	No	Yes
Agreement for the Establishment of the Near East Plant Protection Organization	1993	Not yet in force	R	10	11	No	Yes
Locust control							
Convention on the African Migratory Locust	1962	1963	R	6	16	No	Yes
Agreement for the Establishment of a Commission for Controlling the Desert Locust in the Eastern Region of its Distribution Area in South-West Asia (as amended)[88]	1963	1964	R	3	4	No	Yes
Agreement for the Establishment of a Commission for Controlling the Desert Locust in the Near East (as amended)[89]	1965	1967	R	3	13	No	Yes
Agreement for the Establishment of a Commission for Controlling the Desert Locust in North-West Africa (as amended)[88]	1970	1971	R	3	5	No	Yes
Agreement for the Establishment of a Commission for Controlling the Desert Locust in the Western Region	2000	2000	R	5	0	No	Yes
Forestry							
Agreement for the Establishment on a Permanent Basis of a Latin-American Forest Research and Training Institute	1959	1960	R	5[90]	13	No	Yes

International Tropical Timber Agreement[91]	1994	1997	R	28[92]	56*	No	Yes
Regional Convention for the Management and Conservation of the Natural Forest Ecosystems and the Development of Forest Plantations	1993	1993	R	4	6	No	Yes
Military							
Treaty Banning Nuclear Weapon Tests in the Atmosphere, in Outer Space and Under Water	1963	1963	O	3[88]	134	No	No
Treaty on the Prohibition of the Emplacement of Nuclear Weapons and Other Weapons of Mass Destruction on the Seabed and the Ocean Floor and in the Subsoil Thereof	1971	1972	O	22[94]	116	No	No
Convention on the Prohibition of the Development, Production, and Stockpiling or Bacteriological (Biological) and Toxin Weapons, and on their Destruction	1972	1975	O	22[94]	145	No	No
Convention on the Prohibition of Military or any other Hostile Use of Environmental Modification Techniques	1976	1978	R	20	79	No	Yes
South Pacific Nuclear Free Zone Treaty (as amended)[95]	1985	1986	R	8	10	No	No

86 Changed to five by the 1978 Amendment.
87 Has the status of a memorandum of understanding.
88 Amended in 1977.
89 Amended in 1977 and 1994.
90 Must include Venezuela.
91 The original agreement of 1983 was succeeded by a new agreement having the same name in 1994.
92 To include at least 12 producing states holding at least 55 percent of the votes accorded to this group of countries by the agreement and at least 16 consuming states holding at least 70 per-cent of the votes accorded to this group of countries by the agreement. Further provisions for entry into force are also provided.
93 The agreement came into force upon ratification by the original contracting parties.
94 To include the UK, the USSR, and the US.
95 Three protocols were added in 1986.

Agreement	Date of adoption	Date of entry into force	Membership open (O) or restricted (R)	Minimum no. of ratifications	No. of signatories (*includes EU)	Provisions for trade restrictions	Created an administrative organization
Convention on the Prohibition of the Development, Production, Stockpiling and Use of Chemical Weapons and their Destruction	1993	1997	O	65	175	No	Yes
Animal welfare							
European Convention for the Protection of Animals During International Transport	1968	1971	R	4	23	No	No
Additional Protocol	1979	1989	R	All parties to the Convention	23	No	No
European Convention for the Protection of Animals Kept for Farming Purposes	1976	1978	R	4	28*	No	Yes
Protocol of Amendment	1992	Not yet in force	R	All parties to the Convention	12	No	No
European Convention for the Protection of Animals for Slaughter	1979	1982	R	4	22	No	No
European Convention for the Protection of Vertebrate Animals Used for Experimental and Other Scientific Purposes	1986	1991	R	4	18*	No	No
Protocol of Amendment	1998	Not yet in force	R	All parties to the Convention	12	No	No
European Convention for the Protection of Pet Animals	1987	1992	R	4	17	Yes	No

Convention Concerning the Use of White Lead in Painting	1921	1923	R	2	62	No	No
European Agreement on the Restriction of the Use of Certain Detergents in Washing and Cleaning Products (as amended)[96]	1968	1971	R	3	10	No	No
Convention Concerning Protection Against Hazards of Poisoning Arising from Benzene	1971	1973	R	2	36	No	No
Convention Concerning Prevention and Control of Occupational Hazard Caused by Carcinogenic Substances and Agents	1974	1976	R	2	35	No	No
Convention Concerning the Protection of Workers Against Occupational Hazards in the Working Environment Due to Air Pollution, Noise, and Vibration	1977	1979	R	2	41	No	Yes
Convention Concerning Occupational Safety and Health and the Working Environment	1981	1983	R	2	34	No	No
Convention Concerning Occupational Health Services	1985	1988	R	2	19	No	No
Convention Concerning Safety in the Use of Asbestos	1986	1989	R	2	25	No	No
Convention Concerning Safety and Health in Construction	1988	1991	R	2	14	No	No
Convention Concerning Safety in the Use of Chemicals at Work	1990	1993	R	2	9	Yes	No
Convention on the Transboundary Effects of Industrial Accidents	1992	2000	R	16	26*	No	No
Convention Concerning the Prevention of Major Industrial Accidents	1993	1997	R	2	5	No	No
Safety and Health in Mines Convention	1995	1998	R	2	15	No	No

[96] Amended in 1983.

Appendix 6.1. Continued

Agreement	Date of adoption	Date of entry into force	Membership open (O) or restricted (R)	Minimum no. of ratifications	No. of signatories (*includes EU)	Provisions for trade restrictions	Created an administrative organization
Miscellaneous							
Treaty on Principles Governing the Activities of States in the Exploration and Use of Outer Space Including the Moon and Other Celestial Bodies	1967	1967	O	5[97]	80	No	No
European Convention on the Protection of the Archaeological Heritage[98]	1969	1970	R	3	25	No	No
Convention Establishing a Permanent Inter-State Drought Control Committee for the Sahel	1973	1974	R	3[99]	9	No	Yes
Convention on the Protection of the Environment Between Denmark, Finland, Norway, and Sweden	1974	1976	R	4	4	No	No
Agreement on an International Energy Programme	1974	1976	R	6[100]	20	No	Yes
Convention on the Protection of the Archaeological, Historical, and Artistic Heritage of the American Nations (Convention of San Salvador)	1976	1978	O	1	11	Yes	Yes
Treaty for Amazonian Cooperation	1978	1980	R	8	8	No	Yes
European Outline Convention on Transfrontier Cooperation Between Territorial Communities or Authorities	1980	1981	R	4[101]	33	No	No
Protocol	1995	1998	R	4	15	No	No
Second Protocol	1998	2001	R	4	11	No	No
Agreement on Transboundary Cooperation with a View to Preventing or Limiting Harmful Effects for Human Beings, Property, or the Environment in the Event of Accidents	1989	1989	R	2	4	No	No

Convention	Signed	In force		Threshold	Parties		
Convention on Environmental Impact Assessment in a Transboundary Context	1991	1997	R	16	33*	No	No
Treaty Establishing the African Economic Community	1991	Not yet in force	R	Two-thirds of OAU Member States	49	Yes	Yes
Convention on the Transboundary Effects of Industrial Accidents	1992	2000	R	16	30*	Yes	No
Convention on Civil Liability for Damage Resulting from Activities Dangerous to the Environment	1993	Not yet in force	R	3[102]	9	No	Yes
North American Agreement on Environmental Cooperation	1993	1994	R	3[103]	3	Yes	Yes
Agreement Establishing the South Pacific Regional Environmental Programme	1993	1995	R	10	26	No	
Convention to Combat Desertification in those Countries Experiencing Serious Drought and/or Desertification, Particularly in Africa	1994	1996	O	50	169*	No	Yes
Agreement Between Lithuania, Estonia, and Latvia on Cooperation in the Field of Environmental Protection	1995	1995	R	3	3	No	No
Convention on the Protection of the Environment Through Criminal Law	1998	Not yet in force	R	3	12	No	No

[97] Five must include the United States, the USSR, and the United Kingdom.
[98] Revised in 1992.
[99] One-half of original signatories.
[100] To account for at least 60 percent of the combined voting weight of the countries listed in Article 62.
[101] Provided at least two of these states share a common frontier.
[102] To include at least two member states of the Council of Europe.
[103] Enters into force with NAFTA.

Appendix 6.1. Continued

Agreement	Date of adoption	Date of entry into force	Membership open (O) or restricted (R)	Minimum no. of ratifications	No. of signatories (*includes EU)	Provisions for trade restrictions	Created an administrative organization
Convention on Access to Information, Public Participation in Decision-Making, and Access to Justice in Environmental Matters	1998	Not yet in force	R	16	40*	No	Yes
European Landscape Convention	2000	Not yet in force	R	10	18	No	No
Persistent Organic Pollutants Treaty	2000	Not yet in force		50			

7

The Treaty Participation Game

The global commons—the oceans, the atmosphere, outer space—belong to all the world's people. So, ruling out war, the only way to govern their use is through international agreements... [W]hen considering a treaty, the questions we must ask ourselves are: do the costs outweigh the benefits? Does signing a treaty amount to a net loss or a net gain in terms of our national interests? Frank E. Loy, Under Secretary for Global Affairs, US Department of State (1999).[1]

7.1. INTRODUCTION

How do you know whether a treaty succeeds in improving on unilateralism? In the case of the Fur Seal Treaty you could look at the stock of fur seals both before and after the treaty came into force and see a difference like night and day. In most cases the data do not tell such a convincing story. One person could look at the Montreal Protocol and conclude that it had no effect. Another person could reach the opposite conclusion.[2]

As indicated in Chapter 1, to see more requires a structured imagination. It requires a theory of international cooperation. This chapter begins to lay down the foundation for such a theory.

Following on from Chapter 3, I shall focus my attention in this chapter on public goods problems involving N countries (N can vary; the public good may be regional or global). In particular, I shall take the *underlying game* to be a prisoners' dilemma (PD). You will recall that these are the hardest situations for the international system to remedy. In other situations, countries will have strong incentives to supply a public good unilaterally. Alternatively, coordination will suffice to ensure that a public good is supplied—without the need for enforcement.[3] And in contrast to common property problems like the fur seal example, parties to a treaty seeking to supply a public good cannot gain by deterring entry. To the contrary, a key problem for international cooperation in the supply of public goods is how to broaden participation. This chapter focuses on the determinants of participation. Later chapters examine related aspects of the cooperation game.

---

[1] Doherty Lecture, University of Virginia Center for Oceans Law and Policy, Washington, DC, May 11, 1999.

[2] For the former view, see Murdoch and Sandler (1996). For the latter, see Tolba (1987).

[3] A game in which it is in the interests of one country to supply a public good unilaterally is a "best shot" game. A game in which supply by all countries is required for it to be in the interests of each country to supply the good is called a "weakest link" game. For a description and analysis of such games, see Sandler (1992).

7.2. RESTRUCTURING THE GAME

Taking the public good to be pollution clean-up, and recalling that the underlying game is a PD, we already know how the (one-shot) game will be played if countries are restricted to choosing between playing Abate and Pollute only: every country will play Pollute, even though every country would be better off if all countries played Abate. However, Chapter 6 tells us that countries can make other choices. They can negotiate an agreement that instructs signatories to play Abate provided certain conditions are satisfied. At the same time, sovereignty implies that every country is free to choose between being a signatory and a non-signatory to such a treaty. Sovereignty would thus seem to render every treaty impotent. However, we shall find that an international agreement can make a difference. It works by restructuring the relationships among the countries. Essentially, it changes the rules of the game.

Formally, the game will be modeled as follows: in Stage 1 every country chooses whether or not to sign a treaty; in Stage 2, the parties to the treaty choose jointly whether to play Abate or Pollute; and in Stage 3, the non-signatories choose independently whether to play Abate or Pollute.[4]

Though many treaties might be negotiated, I consider only international environmental agreements (IEAs) that can be sustained as an equilibrium within the anarchic international system. An IEA is an equilibrium if it is *self-enforcing*. This means that no signatory can gain by withdrawing unilaterally from the IEA and that no non-signatory can gain by acceding to it, given the terms of the treaty and the participation decisions of other countries. It means that signatories cannot gain collectively by altering the terms of the treaty, given the participation level and the decisions made by non-signatories. And it means that each non-signatory cannot gain by changing its decision of whether to play Abate or Pollute unilaterally, given the behavior of all other countries.

Actually, for this game structure, we can probably narrow the equilibrium concept just a little. Suppose that each player forecasts correctly in Stage 1 how the latter two stages of the game will be played, and so can calculate precisely the payoff it will get, given the choices made by the other players in Stage 1. Suppose further that, in Stage 2, signatories collectively choose their abatement levels having predicted correctly how non-signatories will behave in Stage 3.[5] Put differently, suppose that the players in Stage 1 can correctly forecast that the players in Stage 2 will correctly forecast how the players in Stage 3 will behave. Then the equilibrium will be especially compelling in the sense that the players' beliefs will be confirmed by the choices actually made in later stages of the game.

An important decision I do not model in this chapter is whether signatories actually undertake the abatement they agree to undertake—that is, whether they comply with the treaty they have signed up to. I simply *assume* that states *will* comply. This

[4] The approach used here draws from d'Aspremont *et al.*'s (1983) model of cartel stability, and was applied to treaty formation by Barrett (1992c, 1994a), Carraro and Siniscalco (1993), and Hoel (1992). The linear model used in this chapter appears in a slightly different form in Barrett (1999a).

[5] In the jargon of industrial organization, treaty signatories are "Stackelberg leaders."

would seem to be an important assumption, for without it even limited cooperation cannot be sustained as an equilibrium of the multi-stage game. But the assumption is needed because compliance can only be shown to be an equilibrium in a repeated game (unless one allows countries to commit to full compliance; see below). In Chapter 10, where international cooperation is modeled as a repeated game, I shall dispense with the assumption of full compliance and show that the main conclusions of this chapter remain unaltered. The assumption of full compliance thus turns out *not* to be important to the theory.

Here is another way of looking at the compliance issue. Recall that customary law requires full compliance by parties. Provided we assume that this custom is enforced outside the model, we can simply assume in this chapter that compliance will be full. In Chapter 10 I shall relax this assumption and show why the custom exists and why it is routinely obeyed. I shall also argue that it is of much less help than first appearances suggest.

The assumption of full compliance essentially means that signatories can be assumed to be capable of making binding commitments. Stage 2 can thus be modeled as a cooperative game. In such a situation, provided that the rules of the game and the payoffs of all players are common knowledge, it seems most likely that the signatories will maximize their aggregate payoff, taking as given the participation level.[6] That is, it seems reasonable to assume *collective rationality* on the part of treaty signatories.[7] To assume differently is to assume that negotiators leave money on the table at the conclusion of their negotiations. The Fur Seal Treaty is entirely consistent with this assumption. Given that all four players participated, they could do no better collectively than to ban pelagic sealing. Of course, this treaty also needed side payments to ensure that every player was made better off by being a signatory rather than a non-signatory. But in this chapter I assume that countries are symmetric, and as I shall show in Chapter 13, symmetric players cannot gain by using side payments.

Notice that my approach here is to blend the assumptions of individual and collective rationality. Individual rationality applies where sovereignty can be exercised—in the choice of whether to be a signatory or a non-signatory, and in the choice by non-signatories of whether to play Abate or Pollute. Collective rationality applies where decision-making is collectively undertaken—the decision by signatories as to what they should do (both in and out of the equilibrium). As we shall see, this approach goes some way towards reconciling the different approaches to analyzing problems of conflict and cooperation noted in Chapter 3. I stress, however, that this blending is not *ad hoc*. The rationality assumptions that underpin the theory can stand on their own two feet as it were. Moreover, they are compatible with the rules of international law.

---

[6] In Chapter 11 I make a different assumption. I fix the participation level and then let signatories choose collectively the abatement level that maximizes their joint payoff subject to ensuring that the agreement with participation given is self-enforcing.

[7] In later chapters—especially, Chapters 10 and 11—this concept will be developed further. In a static game, collective rationality means that cooperating states maximize their collective payoff, both on and off the equilibrium path.

7.3. AN EXPERIMENT IN TREATY PARTICIPATION

Since the analytical approach may seem divorced from the real world, let me begin by explaining how I introduce this topic in the classroom.

I start off by telling the students that a treaty has already been negotiated. The treaty says that signatories must play Abate, and the students are told that this requirement will be enforced externally (by custom perhaps). However, the treaty only comes into force if there are at least sixteen signatories (ratifying countries). Each student must fill out a form stating: (1) whether he will sign the agreement, (2) whether he will play Abate or Pollute if he signs the agreement and the agreement does not attract enough signatories to enter into force, and (3) whether he will play Abate or Pollute if he does not sign the agreement. Each student must choose without knowing how any of the other students have chosen. Let z be the number of *other* students who play Abate. Each student is told that she will get a payoff of $\Pi_P = z$ if she plays Pollute and a payoff of $\Pi_A = z - 14.5$ if she plays Abate. When I played this game there were twenty-nine students in the classroom.

Initially, ten students elected to sign the treaty. All the signatories said they would play Pollute if the agreement did not enter into force and all the non-signatories said they would play Pollute no matter what. This meant that every student got the same payoff: zero.

I then asked the students to discuss their problem out loud before choosing again.

One student said, "We should all sign the agreement."

"That is very well for you to say," replied another student. "But if everyone else signs the agreement, I'd do better by not signing."

"Yes, but if we all behaved that way, we'd all get nothing, and we can do much better than that," added another student.

"Surely," a fourth student said, "at least 16 of us should sign the treaty."

At this point I stopped the discussion and asked the students to make their choices again. This time, nineteen students chose to sign the treaty. Each of the signatories earned a payoff of $3.5, while each of the non-signatories earned $19.

I asked the students what they thought would happen if we played the game again. Most thought that the number of signatories would drop a little. I then asked what they thought would happen if the game were played many more times. The consensus seemed to be that the game would settle at an equilibrium in which there were exactly sixteen signatories.

Each student was asked to sign her sheet before handing it in. This way I could tell whether a student changed her mind between rounds. Nine of the nineteen students who voted "no" in the first round also voted "no" in the second round; the remaining ten first-round "no" voters changed their votes to "yes" in the second round. Only one of the original ten people who voted "yes" changed her vote to "no." This did not surprise me. It should have been plain at the end of the first round that too few students had voted "yes." The burden was plainly on the first round "no" voters to change their votes, and for the first round "yes" voters to vote "yes" a second time. Schelling's (1960) classroom games of focal points show that the status quo holds a strong attraction.

The underlying game that the students were playing was a PD. If the players were restricted to choosing between playing Abate or Pollute, a substantial number would probably play Pollute. I can say this with a little confidence because in the first round all the students said that they would play Pollute if the agreement did not enter into force.[8] The treaty, and especially the minimum participation clause, restructured the game. The Abate-or-Pollute game is a PD, but the Signatory-or-Non-signatory game is a game of chicken (see Chapter 4). The treaty changed the incentives facing the players.

Having seen this, the natural inclination is to propose raising the minimum participation level. With twenty-nine people in the classroom, it seems sensible to raise the minimum participation level to twenty-nine. This would effectively transform the game into a "weakest link" game—a game in which it is in each country's interests to supply the good provided all others supply it (see Sandler 1992). However, this proposal may not be credible. Indeed, the theory developed in this chapter suggests that the only credible minimum participation level for this game is precisely sixteen. I shall explain why in Section 7.15.

7.4. RESTRUCTURING THE TWO-PLAYER DILEMMA GAME

Let me now develop the analytical model. I shall begin with the easiest problem and show how the 2×2 dilemma game shown in Figure 3.1(a) can be restructured by an IEA.

To repeat, the game is played in stages:

Stage 1. All countries choose independently whether to be a signatory or non-signatory.
Stage 2. Signatories choose whether to play Abate or Pollute, with the objective of maximizing their collective payoff.
Stage 3. Non-signatories (if any) choose independently whether to play Abate or Pollute.

Since the game is played in stages, by the time Stage 3 arrives, the choices made in Stages 1 and 2 must be taken as given by the non-signatories. By assumption, these previous choices are common knowledge. However, since play Pollute is a dominant strategy of the one-shot game, every non-signatory will play Pollute in Stage 3 irrespective of how the preceding two stages were played. Notice that this means that the signatories do not have a strategic advantage in moving before non-signatories—they cannot influence the behavior of non-signatories. (We could even collapse the final two stages of the game into a single stage; see Section 7.17.)

---

[8] Interestingly, in the second round of the treaty participation game four students who signed the agreement said that they would play Abate even if the agreement did not enter into force. Of course, as discussed in Chapter 1, when I first played this game in the classroom, a fairly large number of students said that they would play Abate. However, by this point in the course, the students have a deeper knowledge of these games, and behave more in line with the analytical models.

Now consider the Stage 2 game. The behavior of the signatories will depend on the number of signatories. This number is determined in Stage 1, and is a given by the time Stage 2 arrives.

Suppose that just one country chooses to be a signatory in Stage 1. Then in Stage 2 this signatory will play Pollute. The sole signatory can look forward, and anticipate that the non-signatory will play Pollute in Stage 3; and, given that the non-signatory plays Pollute in Stage 3, the sole signatory can do no better than to play Pollute in Stage 2 (of course, even if the non-signatory played Abate in Stage 3, the sole signatory would choose to play Pollute in Stage 2). If both countries chose to be signatories in Stage 1, however, then they could do better *collectively* by playing Abate. In doing so, they would realize an aggregate payoff of 2. This is higher than the two players would realize (in aggregate) if either one or both of them played Pollute.

To summarize, the treaty will say that if there is just one signatory then it must play Pollute but that if there are two signatories then both must play Abate.

In Stage 1, the two players must choose independently whether to be a signatory or a non-signatory. Call one player X and the other Y and consider player X's choice first. When X decides how to play, it will consider how its payoff depends on Y's choice. So suppose Y plays Non-signatory. Then X will get a payoff of 0 whether it plays Signatory or Non-signatory. Assume for convenience that if a player is indifferent between playing Signatory or Non-signatory then it will choose to be a signatory. Then, given that Y plays Non-signatory, X will play Signatory. Suppose, however, that Y plays Signatory. Then X will get a payoff of 0 if it plays Non-signatory and a payoff of 1 if it plays Signatory. The latter payoff is strictly greater, and so X will certainly play Signatory given that Y plays Signatory. Hence, player X will choose to be a signatory in Stage 1 no matter what Y does. It is easy to see that Y will also choose to be a signatory. Play Signatory is thus a (weakly) dominant strategy for both players in Stage 1.

There is thus a unique equilibrium to the participation game: both countries become signatories to an IEA which requires that both countries play Abate. The IEA essentially transforms the game from the one depicted in Figure 3.1(b) to the one shown in Figure 7.1, where Π_s denotes the payoff to a signatory and Π_n the payoff to

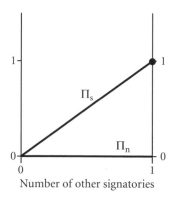

Figure 7.1. *Transformed 2-player dilemma game*

	Y	
	Abate	Pollute
Abate	B, B	D, A
Pollute	A, D	C, C

(X labels the row player; Y labels the column player)

Figure 7.2. *The generalized, symmetric 2-player dilemma game*

a non-signatory. In the transformed game, full cooperation is sustained by a self-enforcing IEA.

As noted earlier, the equilibrium treaty says that if there is one signatory then it must play Pollute but that if there are two signatories then both must play Abate. This is a little clumsy, but there is an alternative way of interpreting the equilibrium. This is that the self-enforcing IEA requires that *all signatories play Abate*, but that it only enters into force, and hence becomes legally binding on signatories, if *both players ratify*. Since this is how every bilateral agreement is written, this is the more natural interpretation.

I have thus so far worked with a specific example but it is easy to see that the main result holds under more general conditions. Consider the generic PD game shown in Figure 7.2. When restructured by a self-enforcing IEA, it is easy to show that there is a unique equilibrium to this game in which both countries are signatories and both play Abate, provided $A > B > C > D$ and $2B > A + D$.[9]

This result tells us that, for the two-player PD game, the values of the payoffs do not affect the ability of an IEA to sustain cooperation. I shall show below, however, that the two-player game is special. Bilateral cooperation is easy. Multilateral cooperation is harder, and depends on the values of the payoffs.

7.5. TRANSFORMING THE N-PLAYER DILEMMA GAME

Suppose now that there are N players, with $N \geq 2$. Let k denote the number of signatories, and let signatories be identified by the subscript s and non-signatories by the subscript n. Suppose further that the payoff functions are given by $\Pi_i = 2(Q_{-i} + q_i) - 3q_i$, where q_i is i's abatement and where Q_{-i} is the aggregate abatement by countries other than i; that is, $Q_{-i} = \sum_{j,j \neq i}^{N} q_j$. Finally, let $q_i \in \{0, 1\}$.

Then if i plays Abate it chooses $q_i = 1$. If i plays Pollute it chooses $q_i = 0$.

It is easy to confirm that these payoffs describe the game played in the previous section for the special case where $N = 2$. Of course we know that, for this special case, full cooperation can be sustained by a self-enforcing IEA.

---

[9] The latter condition ensures that the full cooperative outcome is symmetric.

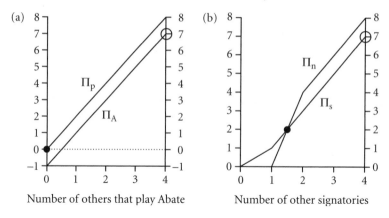

Figure 7.3. *Illustration of the linear, binary choice, N-player IEA*

If $N = 5$, however, then the dilemma game will appear as in Figure 7.3(a). For the transformed game, non-signatories will play Pollute in equilibrium. If there is only one signatory, it too will play Pollute (if this country plays Pollute it gets $\Pi_s = 0$; if it plays Abate it gets $\Pi_s = -1$). However, if there are two or more signatories, then they will each get a higher payoff if they all play Abate (e.g. if $k = 2$, each signatory gets $\Pi_s = 0$ if they both play Pollute and $\Pi_s = 1$ if they both play Abate). So the IEA will specify that signatories play Pollute if $k = 1$ and Abate if $k \geq 2$. Put differently, the IEA will require that signatories play Abate but that the agreement will only enter into force if signed (ratified) by at least two countries.

It remains to solve the participation decision—the Stage 1 game. This is shown in Figure 7.3(b). In equilibrium, $k^* = 2$; both signatories play Abate; and the three non-signatories play Pollute. The full cooperative outcome is *not* sustained as an equilibrium of this game. Indeed, full cooperation can only be sustained for these payoffs if $N = 2$. The result obtained in the previous section really is special.

7.6. A MORE GENERAL RESULT

To generalize even further, suppose the payoff functions for the N-player dilemma game are given by a special case of eqn (3.1). Suppose in particular that

$$\Pi_i = b(Q_{-i} + q_i) - cq_i, \tag{7.1}$$

where c is the cost to i of playing Abate and where b is the benefit i gets from the abatement by any country including itself.

Equation (7.1) is equivalent to (3.1) when $b_A = b_P = b$, $a_P = 0$, and $a_A = b - c$. Notice that we get $a_P = 0$ by simply normalizing payoffs—by rescaling every country's payoff such that every country gets a payoff of zero if no abatement is undertaken by any country. Hence, as compared to (3.1), eqn (7.1) imposes only one restriction. This is that, when country j plays Abate rather than Pollute, country i's payoff ($i \neq j$) increases by the same amount, whether i plays Abate or Pollute itself. This is a reasonable assumption. It ensures that the payoff curves in the underlying PD are parallel.

For eqn (7.1) to be a PD, three conditions must be satisfied. First, play Pollute must be a dominant strategy; that is, we must have $c > b$. Second, every country's payoff must increase in the number of others that play Abate. This implies $b > 0$. Finally, the Nash equilibrium must be inefficient. I shall strengthen this assumption slightly and require that the aggregate payoff for all countries be strictly increasing in the number of countries that play Abate.[10] This ensures that full cooperation will require that all countries play Abate. It is easy to show that this last condition will be satisfied if $N > c/b$.[11]

Signatories will play Abate provided the payoff they each get by playing Abate is at least as great as the payoff they each get by playing Pollute. The latter payoff is 0, since non-signatories always play Pollute. Hence, k signatories play Abate if and only if $-c + bk \geq 0$. Rearranging, signatories will play Abate if $k \geq c/b$. If this condition is not satisfied, signatories will play Pollute.

Notice that, if c/b is a non-integer, then signatories will be strictly better off when they choose to play Abate (assuming $N > c/b$), as compared to the non-cooperative outcome. Moreover, since $c > b > 0$ by assumption, and since k must be an integer, the self-enforcing IEA must consist of at least two countries. This generalizes the earlier result that full cooperation can always be sustained when $N = 2$.

Let k^0 be the smallest integer greater than or equal to c/b. Then we know that k^* must be at least as large as k^0. By the definition of k^0, signatories get a payoff of zero for $k < k^0$ and a payoff at least as large as zero for $k = k^0$.

Suppose now that there are k^0 signatories. Then it is easy to see that no other country will want to accede to the treaty. Doing so would obligate this country to play Abate without altering the behavior of any other signatory—or, indeed, any non-signatory. The assumption that play Pollute in a dominant strategy guarantees that, once there are k^0 signatories, no signatory will want to withdraw and no non-signatory will want to accede. The equilibrium agreement thus consists of $k^* = k^0$ signatories. In other words, k^* must satisfy

$$\frac{c}{b} + 1 \geq k^* \geq \frac{c}{b}. \tag{7.2}$$

This is a "linchpin equilibrium" in the following sense. If any signatory should withdraw, the agreement compels all the remaining signatories to play Pollute; the entire cooperative regime collapses.

This means that full cooperation can only be sustained as an equilibrium of this transformed game if signatories can do no better collectively than to play Pollute when

---

[10] We could let the aggregate payoff increase and then decrease in abatement—the Nash equilibrium would still be inefficient, but full cooperation would then require that only some countries play Abate. This would be an unusual case. See Figure 3.6(d).

[11] Let Q denote total abatement—that is, the total number of countries that play Abate. Then the aggregate payoff will be given by $\Sigma\Pi_i = Q(-c + bQ) + (N - Q)bQ = Q(-c + bN)$. Plainly, the aggregate payoff to all countries strictly increases in Q if and only if $N > c/b$.

$k = N - 1$ and Abate only when $k = N$. Typically, the equilibrium will only sustain an IEA with $k^* < N$ signatories. For example, the equilibrium of the underlying dilemma game shown in Figure 3.6(a), when transformed in the manner described above, has $k^* = 51$ signatories (though $N = 100$).[12]

7.7. VALUES MATTER

In contrast to the dilemma game, the equilibrium of the transformed game depends on the values of the parameters of the payoff functions and not just their ordering. Is the self-enforcing IEA able to improve much on the non-cooperative outcome? Denoting the payoff to each country under the full cooperative and non-cooperative outcomes by Π^c and Π^u, respectively, the total gain to cooperation is $(\Pi^c - \Pi^u)N = (-c + bN)N$. So the gain to cooperation is increasing in b and decreasing in c. By contrast, k^* is increasing in c and decreasing in b (ignoring integer problems). This means that, for N given, k^* will tend to be "large" ("small") when the total gain to cooperation is "small" ("large"). The international system is able to sustain less cooperation the greater is the potential gain to cooperation—that is, the greater is the need for cooperation.

We can illustrate this last observation by referring again to the game shown in Figure 3.6(a). The payoff to each country if all behave non-cooperatively—that is, if the equilibrium in unilateral policies is sustained—is $\Pi^u = \Pi_P(0) = 0$. The payoff each country gets if full cooperation is implemented is $\Pi^c = \Pi_A(N) = -c + bN = -101/99 + (2/99)*100 = 1$. The total gain to cooperation is thus $(\Pi^c - \Pi^u)N = (1 - 0)*100 = 100$. Suppose now that the value of parameter c is changed. If $c - b = 1.5$ (rather than 1), then we obtain $k^* = 76$ and $(\Pi^c - \Pi^u)N = (0.5 - 0)*100 = 50$.[13] Participation is increased (from 51 to 76), but the potential aggregate gain is smaller (dropping from 100 to 50).

Nonetheless, the gains *achieved* by an international treaty may be greater in absolute terms when cooperation appears weaker (that is, when participation is less full). For the examples given above, when $c - b = 1.5$ (and so $k^* = 76$), the aggregate payoff in equilibrium, $(N - k^*)\Pi_n(k^*) + k^*\Pi_s(k^*)$, is 38. By contrast, when $c - b = 1$ (and so $k^* = 51$), the aggregate payoff in equilibrium is 51. Since the payoff to non-cooperation is the same in both cases ($\Pi^u = 0$), these values represent the gains to cooperation achieved by international treaty.

Another important observation is that, in equilibrium, non-signatories get a higher payoff than signatories. Non-signatories free ride. Using the example in Figure 3.6(a) again, we find $\Pi_s(k^*) = -c + bk^* = 1/99$ and $\Pi_n(k^*) = bk^* = 102/99$. However, signatories do get a higher payoff than they would without the treaty ($\Pi^u = 0$). The transformed game—the game of whether or not to be a signatory to an IEA—thus bears a likeness to the chicken game (see Carraro and Siniscalco 1993). This can be seen by noting the similarity between Figures 7.3(b) and 4.3(a).

---

[12] For the PD described by Figure 3.6(a), $b = 2/99$ and $c = 101/99$; hence, $c - b = 1$.
[13] Here, $c = 1.5 + 2/99$ and $\Pi^c = (2/99 \times 100 - 1.5 - 2/99) \times 100 = 50$.

7.8. SUMMARY SO FAR

To sum up, by changing the rules of the game—by writing a treaty that specifies how each signatory should behave, conditional on the number of signatories—the equilibrium of the underlying dilemma game can be transformed. Full cooperation is virtually sure to be sustained when $N = 2$. For $N \geq 3$, however, full cooperation may not be sustainable. Often, some countries will cooperate and play Abate; others will free ride and play Pollute. Moreover, the equilibrium no longer depends on just the ordering of the payoffs; it depends also on the *values* of the payoffs. Since these values will vary from problem to problem, the equilibrium will also vary. In some cases, an IEA will be sustained by a large number of signatories. In other cases only a few countries will participate in the equilibrium IEA. For N given, the number of signatories to the self-enforcing IEA will be larger the smaller is the total gain to cooperation.

These results have important implications for international relations theory. This literature relies almost exclusively on the analysis of 2×2 games (when game theory is used at all) and yet we have seen that the results can be dramatically different when we increase the number of players from two to just three. Furthermore, in 2×2 PD games, the values of the payoffs are of no importance; only the preference ordering matters. Here we have seen that this is no longer true. Two different environmental problems, described by different payoff relations, result in different kinds of cooperative agreements, even though both are PD games. Finally, the international relations analysis of the PD game cannot explain why an international treaty might emerge or what its important features might be or whether it can make much of a difference. Here, the self-enforcing IEA emerges as an equilibrium, and we can see whether it makes any difference by comparing this equilibrium outcome to the non-cooperative and full cooperative outcomes. The PD game describes the underlying game; the IEA game describes the institution used to resolve it. Of course, these results have only been demonstrated for a special model. However, I shall show later that they are fairly robust.

7.9. SEQUENTIAL ACCESSION

The equilibrium in the participation game is unique with respect to the *number* of signatories. It is not unique with respect to the *identities* of the signatories. The only way it could be would be if the decision to be a signatory or a non-signatory were made sequentially.

To see this, consider again the game shown in Figure 7.3(b). Suppose that the choices made in Stage 1 are not made simultaneously. Suppose instead that Stage 1 is played in five periods, one each for the $N = 5$ countries. Label the countries 1, 2, 3, 4, 5, and assume that Country 1 chooses to be a signatory or a non-signatory in period 1, that Country 2 makes the same choice in period 2, and so on in succession. We know that if two countries have already signed the treaty, then another country will not sign. This is because $\Pi_n(2) > \Pi_s(3)$. Suppose, however, that when period 5 is reached, one country has already signed the treaty. Then Country 5 *will* sign since $\Pi_n(1) < \Pi_s(2)$. If, when period 4 is reached, no other country has previously signed the treaty, then Country 4 will also sign. Why? Because this country knows that if it signs, then Country 5 will sign, and Country 4 will therefore get $\Pi_s(2) > \Pi_n(1)$ (even if Country 5 does not sign, Country 4 cannot lose by signing).

Working backwards, we can expect that Countries 4 and 5 will sign the treaty and that Countries 1–3 will not sign. Suppose that Countries 1 and 2 did not sign the treaty. Then Country 3 knows that if it does not sign, Countries 4 and 5 will sign. By contrast, if Country 3 signed the treaty, then Country 4 would not sign and Country 5 would sign. Country 3 thus gets $\Pi_s(2)$ by signing and $\Pi_n(2)$ by not signing. Since $\Pi_n(2) > \Pi_s(2)$, Country 3 does better by not signing. Similarly, Country 2 would not sign, knowing that Country 3 would not sign and that Countries 4 and 5 will sign. In general, the agreement in which the first $N - k^0$ countries do not sign and the last k^0 countries do sign is thus the unique (subgame perfect) equilibrium of the sequential accession game.

This reasoning tells us that there is a "first-mover advantage" in the participation game (remember, the transformed dilemma resembles the chicken game, and as explained in Chapter 4 there is always an advantage to moving first in this game). Early movers are effectively able to commit to being free-riders. In a symmetric game, however, there is no obvious reason why countries should choose in succession. Simultaneous choice is the more reasonable assumption. Of course, with simultaneous choice it is impossible to predict which countries will sign and which will not. However, when countries are symmetric, this is of no importance. In Chapter 13 I dispense with the symmetry assumption and show how asymmetry can affect the order of play and the nature of the agreement that gets negotiated. In this set-up we will be better able to predict which countries will sign the self-enforcing treaty and which will not. Knowing the identities of the parties and non-parties will thus prove important.

7.10. CONTINUOUS CHOICES

The dilemma game assumes that choices about abatement are binary. Typically they will not be. In almost all cases, abatement is chosen along a continuum: countries can abate their emissions by 5 percent, or by 5.5 percent, or by 62 percent, and so on (alternatively, and indeed equivalently, countries can choose from a continuum of pollution emission levels[14]). Let us then consider a model in which abatement— or the provision of the public good—is continuous. To be specific, let q_i be chosen such that $q_i \in [q^{min}, q^{max}]$. Indeed, to make things easier, let $q_i \in [0, 1]$. We can think of feasible abatement as ranging between 0 and 100 percent.

By assumption, $c > b > 0$. Consider the equilibrium in unilateral policies. Taking as given the choices made by others, each country lowers its own payoff when it raises its abatement level even a little above 0. Hence, every country will play $q^u = 0$ in equilibrium. Indeed, play $q^u = 0$ is a dominant strategy for every country.

---

[14] To see the equivalence of these choices, let $\bar{e}_i$ be emissions (measured, say, in tons) in the absence of abatement and let e_i be actual emissions (also measured in tons). Denoting abatement by q_i (again, measured in tons), we have $q_i = \bar{e}_i - e_i$. Obviously, given $\bar{e}_i$, choice of e_i determines q_i and choice of q_i determines e_i. Diamantoudi and Sartzetakis (2001) argue that equivalence does not hold, but their model really shows that care must be taken to ensure that the feasibility constraints apply reasonably. This is not a problem for the linear model used here.

By assumption also, $bN - c > 0$. This means that the aggregate payoff strictly increases in aggregate abatement. So full cooperation will demand that every country play its maximal abatement level. That is, $q^c = q^{max} = 1$. The payoffs to playing these two strategies (i.e. $q^u = 0, q^c = 1$) are shown in Figure 7.4(b), using the functions illustrated in Figure 7.4(a). Here, $c = 2.5$, $b = 1$, and $N = 5$.

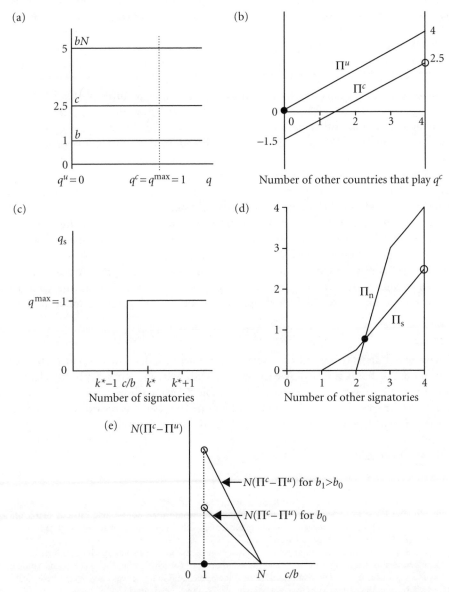

Figure 7.4. *Illustration of the linear IEA game in continuous choices*

Let us now analyze the self-enforcing IEA for this problem. Plainly, since $q^u = 0$ is a dominant strategy, non-signatories will play $q_n = 0$ irrespective of how many signatories there are and irrespective of the level of abatement chosen by these countries. Signatories, by contrast, will play $q_s = 0$ for $k < c/b$ (for then the joint net marginal benefit of abatement to signatories is negative) and $q_s = q^{max} = 1$ for $k > c/b$ (for then the joint net marginal benefit of abatement to signatories is positive); see Figure 7.4(c). Assuming that c/b is a non-integer, and letting k^0 denote the smallest integer greater than c/b, it is easy to show that the self-enforcing IEA is unique and consists of $k^* = k^0$ countries.[15]

The self-enforcing IEA is illustrated in Figure 7.4(d). If two or fewer other countries are signatories, another country gains by acceding. However, if three or more countries are signatories, a non-signatory loses by acceding. The self-enforcing IEA thus consists of three countries in this example. Non-signatories play $q_n^* = 0$ and earn a payoff of $\Pi_n(k^*) = 3$ (non-signatories get Π_n and from the perspective of each non-signatory three other countries are signatories). Signatories play $q_s^* = 1$ and earn a payoff of $\Pi_s(k^*) = 0.5$ (signatories get Π_s and from the perspective of each signatory there are two other signatories). All countries are better off compared to the equilibrium in unilateral policies (where each plays $q^u = 0$ and receives a payoff $\Pi^u = 0$). However, non-signatories do better than signatories; non-signatories "free ride" on the additional abatement undertaken by signatories.

By how much does the aggregate payoff increase with the self-enforcing IEA? We have $N(\Pi^c - \Pi^u) = N(-c + bN)$. This potential gain to cooperation is shown in Figure 7.4(e). The potential gain to cooperation is thus "large" when c/b is near 1 and b is "large." But it is precisely under these conditions that k^* is small relative to N. When k^* is large relative to N, the gain to cooperation is "small." That international cooperation cannot be achieved when it is most needed is already a familiar result.

7.11. ALTERNATIVE SPECIFICATIONS

I have relied up to this point on a very special linear model. The main attraction of this model is that it is relatively easy to work with; we can solve it without calculus. However, it represents only a special case. Table 7.1 shows how sensitive the results can be to the specification of the payoff function. The results as regards participation varies widely. Depending on the specification, the self-enforcing IEA consists of precisely two or three signatories, or it consists of from two to N countries, depending on parameter values.[16]

---

[15] The assumption that c/b is a non-integer is again made for convenience. If c/b is an integer then the self-enforcing IEA will consist of k^0 countries. Signatories would then not be made strictly better off. Moreover, because their joint marginal benefit of abatement will equal the marginal cost of abatement for *any* level of abatement, q_s will be indeterminant.

[16] For a more comprehensive and technical discussion of the importance of specification, see Barrett (2002b). Note also that a slight weakening in the assumption of collective rationality makes participation a more elastic variable. In a richer institutional setting, the participation rate can vary, and yet the basic qualitative result about the welfare gains to cooperation remains robust. See chapter 11.

Table 7.1. *Equilibrium number of signatories for various payoff functions*

Payoff function		k^*
Benefit of abatement	Cost of abatement	
bQ	cq_i	$k^* \in [2,N]$
bQ	$cq_i^2/2$	3
bQ	$c[(1-q_i)\ln(1-q_i)+q_i$	2
$b(Q-Q^2/2)/N$	$cq_i^2/2$	$k^* \in [2,N]$

Sources: Barrett (1994a, 1999a); see also Finus (2001).

Importantly, however, the linear model yields a qualitative result broadly compatible with the alternative models. A consistent finding is that an IEA is only able to improve substantially on the non-cooperative outcome when N is small. When N is large, an IEA is able to improve only marginally on non-cooperation. In this respect, the simple model I have been working with is quite robust.

7.12. WHY CANNOT IEAs HELP MORE?

Imagine a situation in which N is large, and suppose to begin that all countries cooperate fully. Sovereignty implies that a country can withdraw from such an agreement (or not join it in the first place). The only thing that would prevent this from happening would be if the other parties punished this country for not cooperating. Such a punishment must be large enough to deter the withdrawal, but it must also be credible. Credibility is a problem because, if the strategy space is limited to choice of a provision level, the only way that the deviant can be punished is for the other countries to reduce *their* provision of the public good. Doing so, of course, harms the countries that carried out the punishment as well as the deviant. It is this self-damaging aspect to the strategy of reciprocity that limits the credibility of the threat to punish.[17]

Stage 2 of the above model assumes that signatories choose a level of provision that maximizes their collective payoff for every feasible level of participation and not just for the equilibrium participation level. When a signatory deviates from the equilibrium by withdrawing, the level of participation falls, and the agreement tells the remaining signatories that they must lower their provision level. The new provision level chosen by the remaining signatories is not intended to harm the deviant (remember, in a one-shot model there can be no deviations). This choice is only a consequence of the assumption of collective rationality. However, the drop in abatement will have the effect of punishing the withdrawing country. Moreover, this "punishment" will be credible because,

---

[17] Of course, it is technically incorrect to speak of "deviations" and "punishments" in a one-shot setting. However, it will be instructive to pretend that we can give the model this dynamic interpretation. Beginning in Chapter 10 I shall develop a dynamic model in which deviations and punishments can be more legitimately analyzed.

given that a withdrawal has occurred, the remaining signatories really cannot do better in aggregate than by supplying the provision level prescribed by the treaty.

When N is large, and the gains to cooperation are large, a self-enforcing treaty cannot sustain a high participation rate and so is unable to make much of a difference. To see why, suppose that participation is full. Then, if one party withdrew from the agreement, the others collectively would not want to lower their abatement by much in response. To do so would hurt them too much. And, yet, it is precisely under these circumstances that the incentive to deviate unilaterally is great. A deviant will have a strong incentive to reduce its own abatement substantially when it withdraws. (Remember, when the gains to cooperation are large, the full cooperative abatement level is much bigger than the non-cooperative abatement level.) The deviant thus suffers little (in the form of reduced benefits) by withdrawing, and yet gains a lot (in the form of reduced abatement costs). The temptation to deviate will be hard to resist.

When N is large, and the gains to cooperation are small, a self-enforcing treaty may be able to sustain a high participation rate, but doing so will not make much of a difference—precisely because the gains to cooperation are small!

When N is small, the calculation will be different. A unilateral withdrawal may make the remaining signatories reduce their abatement substantially. By contrast, a deviant will not reduce its abatement by much since the full cooperative and non-cooperative abatement levels will not be far apart when N is small. Hence, when N is small, credible punishments will be large relative to the gains from deviating, and a self-enforcing agreement can therefore sustain something close to full participation.

7.13. NON-LINEAR PAYOFFS

The assumption of linear payoffs is important to this conclusion. Suppose payoffs were strongly non-linear. Then, if one country deviated, collective rationality may require

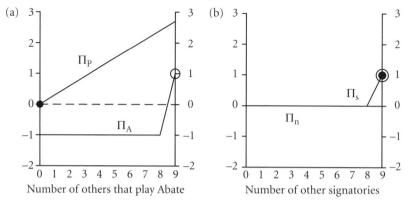

Figure 7.5. *Non-linear payoff game*
(a) Underlying game, (b) Treaty game

that the remaining signatories reduce their abatement by a lot, even when N is large and even when the gains to cooperation are large, making a deviation individually irrational. An example is shown in Figure 7.5(a).

However, though 7.5(a) resembles the PD, cooperation is rather easy to sustain for this special case. Because non-participation by just one country substantially harms all the other countries, these others have much to gain by enforcing an agreement to play Abate. To see this in the context of the model developed above, note that the self-enforcing agreement shown in Figure 7.5(b) requires that signatories play Abate and that the agreement come into force only if *all* countries participate.

7.14. CONSERVATION OF ANADROMOUS FISHES

The fur seal case exemplifies this kind of situation. If just one country failed to participate, there was little point in any of the other countries participating.

A more modern example is the Convention for the Conservation of Anadromous Stocks in the North Pacific Ocean. This agreement, which entered into force in 1993, was negotiated by the same countries that negotiated the Fur Seal Treaty—the United States, Canada, Japan, and Russia. It covers approximately the same geographic territory as the Fur Seal Treaty and resembles this agreement in a number of other respects. Like the pelagic sealing ban, it prohibits high seas fishing. The ban applies to anadromous fish at sea (six species of salmon and steelhead trout, fish that spawn in fresh water but that otherwise spend their lives in the sea). It also has a similar minimum participation clause. Like the Fur Seal Treaty, the Anadromous Stocks agreement could only enter into force after being ratified by all four parties. This reflects the belief that participation by each of the four countries was essential to the treaty's success.

Also, Like the Fur Seal Treaty, the Anadromous Stocks agreement needs to deter entry by third parties. The Fur Seal deterred entry by means of a trade restriction. Entry deterrence is harder for the Anadromous Stocks treaty to block. Though London had a monopoly in the processing of fur seal pelts, any state can process salmon. As a consequence, the payoff curves for the Anadromous Stocks Treaty cannot be made to cross in the manner shown in Figure 7.5(b).

This is not for lack of trying. Article IV of the Anadromous Stocks treaty instructs the parties to "cooperate in taking action, consistent with international law and their respective domestic laws, for the prevention by any State or entity *not* party to this Convention (emphasis added) of any directed fishing for, and the minimization by such State or entity of any incidental taking of, anadromous fish by nationals, residents or vessels of such State or entity in the Convention Area." To enforce this rule, Article III says that the parties "shall take appropriate measures ... to prevent trafficking in anadromous fish taken in violation of ... this Convention."

The main means of enforcing the agreement has been to patrol the waters of the Convention Area—by air, sea, and satellite—and to seize vessels suspected of undermining the treaty. Enforcement is relatively straightforward as regards the parties to the treaty. For example, when the US Coast Guard found six tons of salmon aboard the

Lobana, a Russian-registered vessel, the US returned the vessel, its catch, and its crew to Russia. The Russian authorities fined the captain and the owners of the *Lobana* and confiscated its nets and catch.[18]

Enforcing the agreement as against *non-parties* is more difficult. Seizures by parties to the Anadromous Stocks treaty depend on the consent of the flag state. This is why the parties have been encouraging countries like China and the Republic of Korea to accede to the treaty. Thus far, both countries have refused. However, China has entered into a bilateral agreement with the United States, facilitating the seizure of a number of Chinese-registered vessels.

At sea, anadromous fish are most conveniently caught by means of large scale driftnets. A single fishing vessel can set 10–35 miles of driftnet a night. The nets are typically set below the surface and allowed to drift overnight. Driftnets are indiscriminate killers, termed "walls of death" by environmentalists. A fisherman may set them to kill a particular species (like albacore tuna in the northeast Atlantic or swordfish in the Mediterranean or squid in the Pacific). But the nets will also ensnare a large number of "bycatch" species—including Pacific salmon. They also kill dolphins, sea turtles, and sea birds like the magnificent albatross. In the North Pacific, thousands of fur seals have been killed by driftnets (DeSombre 2000). Lost nets, sometimes called "ghost nets," are especially efficient killers. They can drift for weeks before washing ashore or sinking to the ocean bottom, burdened by the weight of their victims.

A number of legal instruments have been adopted to stop driftnet fishing. Most important is United Nations General Assembly Resolution 46/215, adopted in 1991, which imposes a moratorium on large-scale pelagic driftnet fishing on the high seas and "encourages all members of the international community to take measures, individually and collectively, to prevent large-scale pelagic drift-net fishing operations on the high seas." A number of seizures in the North Pacific have been undertaken in the name of enforcing this General Assembly resolution.

Efforts to protect Pacific salmon from third parties are further reinforced by related agreements, including the 1995 agreement on the Conservation and Management of Straddling Fish Stocks and Highly Migratory Fish Stocks (the Fish Stocks Agreement), and the Agreement to Promote Compliance with International Conservation and Management Measures by Fishing Vessels on the High Seas (the Compliance Agreement). The Fish Stocks Agreement says that the flag states of vessels that fish stocks regulated by a regional fishery organization should join the organization (or, short of that, apply the same restrictions as adopted by this organization). The Compliance Agreement also seeks to reduce the consequences of non-participation. It reminds flag states that, under international law, they have a duty not to undermine the effectiveness of international conservation measures.

However, as indicated in the appendix to Chapter 6, neither of these agreements has entered into force. Even if they did enter into force, they would have only limited effect if major fishing states did not accede to them. The need for these treaties arose

---

[18] Fisheries and Oceans Canada News Release NR-PR-00-47E, May 15, 2000.

because of the non-participation problem. However, their effect has in turn been limited by the freedom states have not to participate.

7.15. COLLECTIVE RATIONALITY

With full compliance, the only aspect of the games examined above that limits cooperation is the assumption of collective rationality. Relax this assumption and it is easy to show that any number of agreements would be self-enforcing, including the agreement that sustains full cooperation. To support full cooperation, you would only need to write an agreement saying that all parties must play Abate, and that the agreement only enters into force if ratified by all N countries.

This strategy for sustaining full cooperation is employed by economists Parkash Chander and Henry Tulkens (Chander and Tulkens 1994, 1997). They identify an agreement comprising all countries which has the property that, if one or more countries deviates from the agreement, the remaining signatories shut down the agreement and do not attempt to form another one; instead, they each behave as unilateralists and play non-cooperatively. This behavior by signatories—or the belief by each country that signatories will behave in this way—ensures that, under certain conditions, no country (and, in the Chander—Tulkens framework, no coalition of countries) can gain by deviating from full cooperation.

As already shown, there are circumstances in which this threat to revert to non-cooperative behavior, in the event of just one country failing to participate, will be credible. However, in most cases such an agreement will not be credible—at least not in the sense of being collectively rational.

So, is the assumption of collective rationality sensible? To appreciate the logic behind the assumption, consider the above agreement in more detail. The agreement is group rational for $k = N$. But suppose one country chooses not to be a signatory in the Stage 1 game. Then the agreement would require that the $N - 1$ signatories play Pollute in Stage 2 (of course, the sole non-signatory will also play Pollute in Stage 3). By the time Stage 2 is reached, the choice of this one country not to be a signatory has already been made and cannot be reversed; and, given this decision, it will not usually be credible for the $N - 1$ signatories to play Pollute in Stage 2. Maximization of their collective payoff will usually require that these signatories play Abate. Indeed, the country that chooses to play Non-signatory in Stage 1 could have foreseen that the threat to play Pollute if just $N - 1$ countries sign the agreement would not be credible. Hence the agreement specified above and fashioned after Chander and Tulkens will usually not be self-enforcing.

Here is another way of looking at the concept. Why do not Canada, Japan, Russia, and the United States scrap the Anadromous Stocks treaty and negotiate a new agreement, one that requires participation by China and Korea? The reason, presumably, is that the four countries that initiated the treaty would prefer their limited agreement to the alternative of no cooperation at all.

For much the same reason, it would not be credible to specify a minimum participation clause of twenty nine players in the experiment discussed in Section 7.3. If every student could commit not to renegotiate, then they could do no better than to set the minimum participation level equal to twenty nine. But when commitments of this kind are infeasible, credibility forces a reduction in the minimum participation level. By the concept of collective rationality used here, the only credible minimum participation level for this experimental game is sixteen players.

7.16. ALTERNATIVE PERSPECTIVES ON MINIMUM PARTICIPATION

The linear IEA says that signatories must play full abatement provided $k \geq k^0$, but that for any smaller level of participation signatories must play zero abatement.

There is another, more intuitive way of interpreting this result, as I noted in Section 7.3. This is for the agreement to require that signatories play full abatement—but that it only comes into force if signed by k^0 countries. k^0 can thus be interpreted as the minimum participation level for the self-enforcing IEA. In equilibrium, of course, the agreement would actually be signed by $k^0 = k^*$ countries.

The minimum participation level, k^0, is determined endogenously in this framework. Further, while the agreement specifies what this level is, signatories do not *choose* this level. Rather, signatories merely recognize that it is only optimal to play Abate if this minimum is satisfied.

Black *et al.* (1993) consider a different approach to sustaining cooperation, one which exploits minimum participation directly. They assume that an agreement becomes *binding* on parties provided the number of signatories exceeds some exogenously specified minimum. In assuming that the agreement is binding on parties, Black *et al.* essentially assume that signatories are committed to remaining as signatories. This, of course, countries cannot do. Sovereignty will not allow it.

In a game of complete information, the problem is familiar. All countries together could not do better than to specify that signatories must play Abate provided $k^* = N$ and that they must otherwise play Abate (an agreement reminiscent of the proposal by Chander and Tulkens). As noted previously, if countries could commit to playing this game, then the full cooperative outcome can be sustained. However, given that international law permits countries to accede or withdraw from an agreement as they please, commitment of this kind is infeasible. Therefore, in general the above agreement will not be self-enforcing.

However, Black *et al.* (1993) consider the more interesting case where there is incomplete information. Every country faces a binary choice; it can accede to the agreement or not as it pleases. Signatories must play an exogenously specified quantity of abatement and incur a cost c. The benefit to country i of abatement undertaken by any country (including i itself) is also a constant, but this benefit is known only to i. Calling this benefit b_i, Black *et al.* assume that $c > b_i$. Non-signatories thus choose not to abate. Signatories must abate whether or not their collective marginal benefit exceeds c.

Given a particular probability distribution for the benefit parameter, Black *et al.* then carry out a number of simulations showing how the expected aggregate payoff varies with the exogenously specified minimum participation level. They show that, for these simulations, the optimal minimum participation level is about 70 percent of the total number of countries. Depending on parameter values, this minimum participation level may result in expected aggregate payoffs vastly exceeding those in the non-cooperative outcome, or it may have very little effect.

In this model countries choose simultaneously whether or not to accede to the agreement, and the mechanism of a minimum number of signatories works only if countries are prohibited from revising this choice. However, the agreement would be extremely vulnerable to renegotiation. If the actual number of signatories fell short of the minimum participation level, countries would have an incentive to recalculate this level and choose again whether or not to accede (and, of course, all countries would know this when they chose their strategies in the first instance). Similarly, if the minimum level were exceeded, then (taking the choices of all other countries as given) each signatory would wish to withdraw from the agreement (and, again, this would be anticipated by all countries at the time they decided whether to accede to the agreement in the first place). Hence, only by chance would the agreement analyzed by Black *et al.* be self-enforcing. An agreement would only be self-enforcing if the actual number of signatories were equal to the minimum number specified by the agreement. This is essentially the problem we already examined in the transformed dilemma game, the only difference being that this game was one of complete information.

Carraro *et al.* (1998) take yet another approach to minimum participation. They assume complete information but allow countries to *choose* a minimum participation level. The difference between this approach and the stage game developed earlier is that the minimum participation clause is used strategically to manipulate the behavior of the players. In so doing it increases the level of participation.

To see why, suppose the minimum level is raised above k^*, the participation level determined by the IEA game studied in Section 7.6. Then participation will appeal to a larger number of states in Stage 1—for if the larger participation level is not reached, cooperation will fail entirely. You might think that this approach would favor setting the minimum participation level equal to N (as in the Chander–Tulkens framework), especially since information is complete in this game. However, remember that choice of a minimum participation level is being taken from the *ex ante* perspective. If an incomplete treaty were negotiated, each country stands a chance of being a non-signatory, and hence of being able to free ride. This is a chance every country would like to take, and so the players will not normally want to set the minimum participation level too high. Under plausible assumptions, Carraro *et al.* (1998) show that minimum participation will lie somewhere between k^* and N.

As I see it, the problem with this approach is that the treaty negotiated in this way is not self-enforcing. For suppose that actual participation fell short of the minimum level chosen in the preliminary stage of the game. In the Carraro *et al.* framework, cooperation must then be thwarted. But given that some countries have elected not to participate, we know from before that it will be in the interests of others to renegotiate and not to let cooperation slip through their hands. In other words, the threat not to cooperate unless the higher minimum participation level is achieved is not credible for $k > k^*$.

For reasons explained in Chapter 11, it can be argued that the collective rationality assumption used here demands too much credibility. Relaxing the assumption very slightly, however, changes the qualitative results obtained thus far by just a little. The results are, therefore, resonably robust.

7.17. ASYMMETRIC COMMITMENT

The stage game model allows signatories to make their choices before non-signatories—and yet, so long as non-signatories play dominant strategies in equilibrium, the choices made by signatories will have no effect on the choices made by non-signatories. As mentioned in Section 7.4, we could just as well collapse Stages 2 and 3 into a single stage.

When non-signatories do not play dominant strategies in equilibrium, however, it will matter whether signatories can make their choices before non-signatories. By choosing before non-signatories, signatories can effectively commit to playing particular strategies, an advantage denied to non-signatories. By choosing wisely, signatories can thus affect the choices made subsequently by non-signatories to their own advantage. Signatories have a strategic advantage in this set-up. When abatement is a *strategic complement*, signatories will have an incentive to abate *more* than they would if signatories and non-signatories made their abatement choices simultaneously. This is because additional abatement by signatories would impel non-signatories to abate more, to the benefit of every signatory. By contrast, when abatement is a *strategic substitute*, first-moving signatories would do better by abating *less* (see Barrett 1994a).[19]

Is it reasonable to allow signatories this opportunity to behave strategically?[20] As will be explained in more detail in Chapter 10, signatories and non-signatories are different before the law. International law obliges signatories to obey the treaties to which they belong. Individually, however, states are not required by international law to behave as they may have instructed *themselves* to behave. A country cannot commit to being a signatory, but given that it *is* a signatory it is expected to obey the commandments of this instrument. In the stage game, by the time Stage 2 comes around, signatories must take as given their earlier decision, and the decision by others, of whether to be a signatory or a non-signatory.

Why can a country not rely on others to enforce a unilateral declaration? There is, of course, the usual reason that enforcement may be costly to the countries carrying out the enforcement. However, there is also deeper reason. Suppose that at some date t, a state says that it will undertake an action at date $T > t$. Suppose further that at date $T - 1$ ($> t$) the state changes its mind and announces that it no longer wishes to undertake the action that it had pledged to undertake at date T. Then the question arises as

---

[19] See Bulow *et al*'s (1985) seminal paper on strategic complements and substitutes.

[20] Finus (2001) is inclined to respond "no". However, as explained below, signatories and non-signatories *are* asymmetric before the law.

to which country's wish should be enforced, the country that made the declaration at date t or the country that changed its mind at date $T - 1$. The answer isn't obvious.

As we shall see later, many industrialized countries, as well as the European Union as a collective, made "commitments" in the late-1980s to stabilize their carbon dioxide emissions. Very few of these countries adopted policies sufficient to suppress their emissions growth, however, and few succeeded in meeting their "commitments." What penalty will be imposed on countries that fail to stabilize their emissions? None. Other states are not obligated to punish a country for failing to fulfill a unilateral pledge—and, of course, this is partly why so many unilateral pledges to limit emissions growth have not been met. By contrast, and as explained in detail in Chapter 10, when Russia announced that it would not comply with the Montreal Protocol, the other parties to this agreement adopted measures that would bring Russia into compliance. Signatories and non-signatories really are different.

7.18. DEMOCRACY AND PARTICIPATION

I have thus far assumed that states are symmetric. But this was only for analytical convenience. States vary widely. They have different payoffs (the subject of Chapter 13). They also have different political institutions. The latter can be thought of as a mechanism for molding the preferences of the citizenry into a national payoff.

A liberal inclination may make you believe that more democratic countries are more likely to participate in an IEA. But this is far from obvious. True, less democratic regimes may hesitate to supply a public good that cannot provide the ruling elite with an income (Olson 1993). But in some cases the rulers can appropriate a large slice of the gains from cooperation. The regime established by the Russian czar for exploiting the fur seal is a prime example. Moreover, Levy (1995) speculates that autocratic regimes may care less about compliance, and so may be more inclined to participate. It seems that the effect of democracy on participation is an empirical question.

Congleton (1992) finds statistical support for the hypothesis that democracies were more likely to sign up to the Montreal Protocol. However, he measures participation in an early stage of the participation process. As noted before, virtually every country is a party to this agreement today. Participants include democracies like the United States and Great Britain and dictatorships like Cuba and North Korea. It is true that the vast majority of non-participants are undemocratic—examples include Iraq, Afghanistan, and Eritrea. However, these countries are either international outcasts or lacking an effective domestic government. Moreover, the result that democracies are more likely to participate is hardly robust. In a study of the Helsinki Protocol, Murdoch *et al.* (2002) find that more democratic countries were *less* likely to participate (recall from Chapter 1 that the United States and the United Kingdom did not sign this agreement, whereas the USSR did). Moreover, some agreements are negotiated exclusively by non-democratic regimes, an example being the Nile Agreement between Egypt and Sudan.

Fredriksson and Gaston (1999) take a different angle. They test the hypothesis that democratic governments are likely to sign up to an international agreement *sooner* than undemocratic governments. They find some support for the hypothesis, using data on ratification of the Framework Convention on Climate Change. However, I am not convinced that this tells us much. First, the Framework Convention really does not require that its participants do anything. Whether a country ratified the agreement more quickly would thus have no consequence for the global climate. Second, like the Montreal Protocol, almost every country became a party to the Framework Convention eventually.

Upon a little reflection, this ambivalence in the data should hardly come as a surprise. Observations about participation are not independent. As shown by the theory, participation is not a dominant strategy. One country's decision to participate depends on how many others participate (see also Chapter 9).

It might make more sense to determine whether democracies are more likely to reduce their emissions even in the absence of an international agreement. Murdoch and Sandler (1996) find that voluntary cutbacks in CFC emissions—actions that preceded entry into force of the Montreal Protocol—increase in the extent of political and civil freedoms. However, even this approach may not tell us much because emission choices may also not be in dominant strategies.

To know whether democracy affects the payoff to participating it is perhaps more useful to see whether democracy affects the provision of *local* public goods. For these problems, there is no interdependence and so countries *do* have dominant strategies. Barrett and Graddy (2000) find that freedoms do affect local pollution levels, especially when these affect human health directly. This suggests that more democratic regimes would be more inclined to provide global public goods, taking as given the behavior of other states.

One important implication of this is that the depth of cooperation sustained by international agreements may depend on the ability of the citizens of different countries to acquire information, to organize, and to demand environmental improvements from their representatives (whether elected or unelected). That is, protection of the global environment may be aided by *local* institutional reform and not just the design of better multilateral institutions.[21]

7.19. TREATIES AND CUSTOM

The focus of this chapter has been on the international treaty, a formal institution. Formal institutions are important, but they work best when supported by informal institutions. In a celebrated book, Putnam (with the assistance of Leonardi and Nanetti 1993) addressed the question of how it was that, after the Second World War, the north and south of Italy experienced very different rates of economic growth, despite having exactly the same formal institutions. The reason, he argues, is that the north had better informal institutions. People in the north read the newspapers; they voted; and, when public services fell short of expectations, they complained to their

---

[21] Using a similar reasoning, I have argued that trade-environment conflicts may be best resolved by local rather than multilateral reforms; see (Barrett 2000).

elected representatives. Informal institutions help determine how formal institutions are *used*. Use of our institutions, however, is a collective action problem of its own (why people bother to vote has long been a mystery for social scientists), and needs to be supported informally, at the domestic level by a culture of civic engagement.[22]

There is a similar need for support at the international level. Just as political institutions work better when the citizenry is engaged, and market institutions work better when there is a climate of trust, so treaties are more likely to succeed when countries feel a responsibility to participate in negotiations, to comply with treaties, to report honestly, to monitor others, and to enforce treaty obligations—behaviors commended by customary law. Successful international cooperation ultimately depends on more than just treaty design. It depends also on the support given to the treaty by state behavior.

7.20. CONCLUSIONS

In this chapter I have shown how an IEA can change the rules of the game of international cooperation by specifying how signatories must act, contingent on the level of participation. The behavior of signatories satisfies a compelling notion of collective rationality—with the implication that the threat by signatories to punish non-participation is credible. However, in harming non-participants, signatories to an IEA harm themselves, too. This limits their incentive to deter non-participation, with the consequence that participation may be less than full.

If only two countries share a resource, participation by both is needed to sustain a mutually more satisfying outcome—and since non-participation by one country makes non-provision of the public good by the other rational, free-riding is easily deterred. When the number of countries that share a resource increases, however, it will not always be in the interests of cooperating countries to deter non-participation.

The incentives to punish are related to the gains from cooperation. When the gains to cooperation are large, the incentive to free ride is great, and so stiff punishments are needed to deter free-riding. But stiff punishments are less credible when the gains to cooperation are large. In seeking to harm non-participants, cooperating countries shoot themselves in the foot.

Under certain circumstances, however, it will be possible to sustain full cooperation. Recall that the North Pacific Fur Seal Treaty has this feature. As outlined in Chapter 2, this agreement would only come into force if signed by all four parties. Moreover, if any party were to withdraw—as Japan did in 1940—the agreement would be terminated, with all four parties reverting to non-cooperative behavior. Since the remaining three parties did not establish an agreement of their own upon Japan's withdrawal, it appears that the threat was credible—though of course by the

---

[22] A follow-up study by Helliwell and Putnam (1995) confirmed Putnam's hypothesis that the difference in the performance of the north and south of Italy could be explained by measures of civic involvement. More recent treatments of the concept of "social capital" in domestic settings include Dasgupta and Serageldin (1999), Fukuyama (1999), and Putnam (2000).

time of Japan's withdrawal, all four parties were consumed by war. However, after the war, the treaty was negotiated anew—and this time, the treaty not only contained this same threat but made it more explicit. This suggests that the experience with the earlier treaty convinced all the parties of both the credibility and the utility of the threat. Recall that the history of fur seal exploitation taught the important lesson that anything short of a comprehensive agreement was largely a wasted effort.

This is what makes the Fur Seal Treaty unusual. As the Appendix to Chapter 6 shows, though all agreements specify a minimum participation level, the actual number of parties usually exceeds this minimum. The exceptions are mainly regional agreements—agreements concerning international river courses, closed seas, and regional ecosystems—for which N is small. Of course, it is precisely for these kinds of problems that full participation is vital to the success of a cooperation effort. If a resource is shared by only a few countries and just one chooses not to participate in an agreement seeking to protect it, the others will be materially affected. They will therefore have an incentive to punish non-participation severely. For a global resource, non-participation by just one country will normally affect all the others very little, making only small punishments credible.

Where actual participation exceeds the minimum participation level, the minimum participation clause is probably intended to coordinate behavior, as discussed in Chapter 9. However, cooperation may still be a problem. Cooperation and coordination are not mutually exclusive phenomena.

Though international cooperation can be sustained by an IEA, there is no guarantee that the best, institutionally feasible IEA will be negotiated. Given that the underlying game is a PD, non-cooperation will be an equilibrium. It may be possible to transform the situation, to sustain a measure of cooperation by restructuring the relationships among the countries that share a resource. But this will only result from conscious and deliberate reflection and careful diplomatic maneuvering. The theory developed here is thus best thought of as showing what is possible, what diplomats should aspire to achieve. It should make us marvel at the skill with which the Fur Seal and Montreal Protocol agreements were constructed. We have already learned how the Fur Seal Treaty succeeded. The full story of the Montreal Protocol's success will take longer to tell. The next chapter begins that story.

8

The Montreal Protocol

[T]he ozone agreement is, I believe, the beginning of a new era of environmental statesmanship—one that takes into account the complexities, the uncertainties, and the differences, in economic interest that in the past have limited concerted environmental action by nations. Mostafa K. Tolba, Executive Director, United Nations Environment Programme (1987)[1]

8.1. INTRODUCTION

If the theory begun in the previous chapter is to be of real utility, it must be able to explain the Montreal Protocol's success. To be more precise, it must be able to explain why Montreal *appears* to have been successful. "Success," of course, is an elusive concept in this context. As we do not know what the world would have done about stratospheric ozone depletion had countries pursued only unilateral policies, we cannot be sure whether Montreal really has made a difference. This again is something that the theory should be able to tell us.

Of course, I can do no more than show that the theory is not wrong. Moreover, there are other explanations for the Montreal Protocol's apparent success; and as I proceed, I shall distinguish my explanation from these. My assessment in this chapter will also be preliminary. I have only begun to build the theory of international cooperation. I limit my focus in this chapter to providing background and to showing the relevance of the theory presented thus far. As the theory is developed in later chapters, my explanation for the Montreal phenomenon will be rounded out. It will not be completed until Chapter 13.

The discussion of the Montreal Protocol, here and in later chapters, is selective. It is meant to complement, and not to substitute for, Richard Benedick's brilliant *Ozone Diplomacy*, an insider's view of the talks and of the underlying negotiation process (Benedick was the chief US negotiator at Montreal). I shall, in particular, emphasize aspects of this treaty that Benedick gives less weight to, re-framing features of the agreement to reveal their strategic roles. Whereas Benedick (1998: xi) provides "a case study of the diplomatic craft," one that can serve "as a paradigm for new diplomatic approaches to new kinds of international challenges," I come at this topic from the opposite direction. My approach is to build a theory from first principles, and to then apply the theory to Montreal and other cases. Whereas Benedick's book is rich in detail, the theory I develop in this book is sparse. Whereas Benedick describes the

---

[1] From Tolba (1987: 290).

twists and turns of this negotiation, the chance events that led negotiators down one path rather than another, the personalities of the negotiators and of those seeking to structure the negotiations, the relationships they developed and the effect these had in creating a "spirit of Montreal," my explanation stresses the more fundamental forces that shape a treaty. My view is that we can best understand these problems by looking at them from both of these perspectives.

8.2. BACKGROUND

In 1974, two chemists at the University of California, Mario Molina and Sherwood Rowland, published a scientific paper with astonishing implications (Molina and Rowland 1974).[2] Their paper suggested that stratospheric ozone could be destroyed by releases of chlorofluorocarbons (CFCs), a class of human made chemical discovered in 1928.

CFCs were an ideal chemical: highly stable, non-toxic, non-corrosive, non-flammable, and inexpensive to produce. Everyone knows CFCs were used as an aerosol propellent. But they were also used as a refrigerant, an insulator, and a solvent. They were found in asthma sprays, fire extinguishers (halons, a related compound), and styrofoam coffee cups. They were used for cleaning microchips, as a coolant in air conditioners, and as an insulator in refrigerators. They were so attractive that new uses for them were being found all the time.

When released, however, Molina and Rowland discovered that CFCs slowly make their way to the stratosphere, between 6 and 30 miles above the earth's surface. Long exposure to solar radiation causes the CFCs to break down and to release chlorine— and it is the chlorine, not the CFCs themselves, that is the problem. The Molina–Rowland theory, supported by preliminary experimental results, suggested that chlorine would destroy ozone.

The potential consequences of ozone depletion would be life-threatening and planetary in scale. Since stratospheric ozone absorbs harmful ultraviolet radiation, depletion of the ozone layer would allow more ultraviolet-B (UV-B) radiation to reach the earth. There would be more skin cancers and eye cataracts, lower yields in agriculture and fisheries, an accelerated deterioration of plastics used outdoors, and an increase in ground-level ozone (smog).[3]

---

[2] In 1995, along with Paul Crutzen, another researcher in this field, Molina and Rowland received the Nobel Prize for Chemistry.

[3] CFCs are also a greenhouse gas. However, depletion of stratospheric ozone has a negative effect on radiative forcing, partially offsetting the direct warming effect of CFC emissions. For this and other reasons, negotiators of the ozone and climate change agreements have tried to compartmentalize the two issues. But the separation is artificial; the problems are related. For example, in phasing out CFCs, Montreal increased the demand for hydrofluorocarbons (HFCs), a CFC-substitute that is also a greenhouse gas. The Kyoto Protocol aims to limit emissions of HFCs—but in the process would increase the costs of substituting for CFCs, and so, perhaps, undermine compliance with the Montreal controls. The two problems are also related in a different way. Though climate change would warm the atmosphere near the Earth's surface, it would cool the lower stratosphere and thereby accelerate the chemical processes that destroy ozone. Similarly, the atmospheric abundance of some greenhouse gases, as well as sulfate particles, can also affect the ozone layer.

The potential for damage was real enough: CFC use had increased substantially, and CFCs have long atmospheric lifetimes—lasting decades or centuries. CFCs were thus accumulating in the stratosphere. Even if all releases of CFCs were halted immediately, chlorine would continue to be released in the stratosphere for some time to come. If the theory were correct, some ozone depletion would be inevitable; and it would take a long time to reverse.

Exactly how much damage could CFCs cause—assuming that the Molina–Rowland hypothesis was correct? In 1976, the US National Academy of Sciences, in a follow-up study to the Molina–Rowland paper, predicted that releases of CFCs would eventually deplete stratospheric ozone by about seven percent: enough to pose a substantial risk.

Though the causal link between CFCs and stratospheric ozone depletion was still unproved, a number of countries unilaterally restricted consumption and production of CFCs beginning in the late 1970s (EPA 1988*b*): Belgium, Canada, Norway, Sweden, and the United States banned the use of CFCs in aerosols; the European Community (EC) adopted measures to reduce CFC use in aerosols by 30 percent from 1976 levels and also capped production capacity; the Netherlands required that a warning label appear on all aerosol products containing CFCs; Portugal banned CFC production and established CFC import quotas; Brazil capped production; Australia reduced CFC use in aerosols by two-thirds; and Japan reduced the use of CFCs in aerosols and discouraged increases in production capacity.

Some of these measures were largely symbolic. For example, European consumption of CFCs had already fallen 28 percent when, in 1980, the Community passed a directive requiring that consumption be cut by 30 percent from the 1976 level; and the Community's definition of "production capacity" actually allowed output to *increase* by more than 60 percent above the current level (Benedick 1998). A few of the measures, however, were significant and costly to implement. The US ban was especially important. The US was the biggest producer and consumer of CFCs, and its unilateral ban was enough to stabilize global CFC consumption—for a time.

However, because of growth in the use of CFCs for other purposes in the United States (the share of CFC-113, used as a solvent in the manufacture of computer chips, more than doubled from 1975 to 1982; see Haas 1992) and in other countries, global consumption of CFCs increased again in the early 1980s. Around this time, countries began to feel that unilateralism had begun to run its course, and that further action to protect the ozone layer would require international cooperation.

8.3. VIENNA AND MONTREAL

In 1977, at the request of the states that had already acted unilaterally to reduce CFCs, an International Conference on the Ozone Layer was convened by the United Nations Environment Programme (UNEP). The conference recommended that a global framework convention for the protection of the ozone layer be negotiated, and work on the treaty began right away.

From this time until the early 1980s, however, CFC consumption was declining, and predictions of eventual ozone depletion were revised downwards. Actual measurements of ozone levels also failed to show statistically significant losses. If anything, the unilateral actions taken in the late 1970s were perceived as having been an over-reaction. Though an international agreement was adopted in March 1985 (the Vienna Convention for the Protection of the Ozone Layer), it served only as a framework agreement; it did not require that any abatement be undertaken by signatories. Indeed, the Vienna Convention only mentions CFCs by name in an annex.

The greater achievement in Vienna was the adoption of a resolution to restart negotiations, with the aim of preparing a protocol by 1987 that would require real reductions in CFC emissions. The resolution also asked UNEP to convene workshops "to develop a 'more common understanding' of factors affecting the ozone layer, including *costs* [emphasis added] and effects of possible control measures [that is, *benefits*], a move which proved to be the springboard for the Montreal Protocol" (Benedick 1998: 45).

Just two months after Vienna, the British Antarctic Survey reported that, over the period 1977–85, the ozone layer over the Antarctic had been reduced by 40 percent.[4] This came as a shock; the loss in ozone recorded over Antarctica far exceeded earlier predictions.

It is a part of the folklore today that the discovery of the Antarctic ozone "hole" (a localized thinning of the ozone layer, an image of which is shown on the front cover of this book) was the catalyst behind Montreal.[5] Richard Benedick, however, emphatically rejects this perspective. He reminds us that cause and effect had not been established at this time. Moreover, it was unknown whether ozone depletion over the Antarctic implied anything for the other continents. Indeed, Benedick (1998: 20) recalls that "Antarctica was never discussed at the negotiations," which began in earnest in December 1986. The negotiators relied instead on the evidence from the global models of ozone depletion, and from the workshops held in the spring and fall of 1986 on possible alternatives to CFCs and on the environmental consequences of adopting particular controls. "It was generally accepted that changes in the ozone layer would pose serious risks to human health and the environment," Benedick (1998: 22) notes; "the point of contention among the participating governments was the extent of international action necessary to provide a reasonable degree of protection."

More important in Benedick's view than the ozone hole was a chance event of the kind discussed in Chapter 6. The EC is represented at international meetings by the EC presidency. Also influential is a committee comprising the current president and its immediate predecessor and successor. In January 1987, the presidency rotated—as it does every six months—and Belgium replaced the United Kingdom. Then, in July

---

[4] Interestingly, the data showing the dramatic depletion of ozone had been available since 1979. However, US satellites had been programmed to disregard data which fell outside the range of existing predictive models. When the satellites were reprogrammed to analyze all the data available, they revealed the same extent of depletion observed by the British ground-based facilities. The British team was so dumbfounded by their own discovery—possibly because it conflicted with US findings—that they checked and re-checked their own measurements, delaying publication by three years. See Benedick (1998) and Rowlands (1995).

[5] This view, incidentally, supports another hypothesis from international relations theory—that some kind of shock is needed to kick-start cooperation; see Young (1989).

1987, the United Kingdom was removed from the EC committee, and so lost its influence. The United Kingdom had opposed strong controls. Belgium, by contrast, was one of the countries to have acted unilaterally to ban CFCs in aerosols in the 1970s. When the Montreal talks began, the other committee members were Denmark and the Federal Republic of Germany, both of which were in favor of substantial cuts. To Benedick, this was a turning point. "It is likely," Benedick (1998: 36) writes, "that this serendipitous constellation, in the right place at the right time, contributed to the EC's finally accepting considerably stronger measures than it had espoused throughout the negotiating process."

Though the discovery of the ozone hole was not as important to the negotiations as is commonly believed, it did become a flashpoint for public attention. When the agreement was adopted on September 16, 1987, it was headline news.

8.4. BASIC OBLIGATIONS

I will not describe the process of negotiating Montreal—the preparation of a single negotiating text, the "capture" of European negotiators by industry, the role of UNEP's executive director, Mostafa Tolba, in steering the negotiations, and so on. As explained in Chapter 6, the negotiation process is important; it helps to give shape to a treaty. However, these and other aspects of the Montreal negotiations are vividly described in Benedick's book. Of more immediate relevance to the theory developed in Chapter 7 is the outcome: what was actually agreed. This is what I describe below. The appendix to this chapter contains the original agreement.[6]

The main achievement of the Montreal Protocol was to require that the production and consumption of a number of CFCs be cut by half (from their 1986 levels) by 1999 and that production and consumption of certain halons (compounds used in fire protection, another class of ozone-depleting substance) be stabilized at their 1986 levels.

Choice of 1986 as a base year was carefully calculated. It was intended to short-circuit incentives for unwelcome strategic behavior. Had a future year been chosen as the base, there would have been an incentive "to expand output substantially to establish a higher basis from which subsequent cuts would be calculated" (Benedick 1998: 82; see also the section on "Tactics" in Chapter 6). Even when using a historic base year, data were falsely reported to influence negotiations. West German industry understated consumption for 1986, hoping "that indications of lower growth relative to 1985 might influence the negotiators toward weaker controls" (Benedick 1998: 180). The deception back-fired. After Montreal, the West German consumption data were quickly "revised" upwards.

The Montreal restrictions applied to a basket of chemicals, each weighted by its "ozone-depleting potential." This formulation "gave countries an incentive to impose greater reductions on substances that were relatively more harmful to the ozone layer

---

[6] The current agreement, embodying the adjustments negotiated in London, Copenhagen, Vienna, Montreal, and Beijing, can be found at http:www.unep.org/ozone.

as well as those whose uses were less essential to them [that is, substances that were less costly to control]" (Benedick 1998: 78). In effectively creating emission "offsets," the weighted-basket provision lowered the overall cost of ozone protection.[7]

The Montreal Protocol was designed to be flexible, "to be reopened and adjusted as needed, on the basis of the periodically scheduled scientific, economic, environmental, and technological assessments" (Benedick 1998: 99). And, as matters turned out, Montreal *was* adjusted and amended—several times. It is still evolving today. Every revision strengthened the original controls, but the potential existed for the Montreal controls to be slackened. Though the Protocol required that all parties reduce their production and consumption of listed substances 20 percent from their 1986 levels, the decision to reduce these levels a further 30 percent could be reversed by a two-thirds majority of the parties, representing at least two-thirds of the total consumption of all parties. And further reductions could be made by "adjusting" the treaty at future meetings, ideally by consensus but if necessary by a two-thirds majority of the parties representing at least half of the total consumption of all parties. Such adjustments would, of course, be binding on all parties, even countries that opposed them. Broadening the agreement to include *new* substances, however, would require treaty amendments. As explained in Chapter 6, these would only be legally binding on the parties that had consented to be bound by them.

8.5. MINIMUM PARTICIPATION

Participation, the focus of Chapter 7, was a key talking point in Montreal. The United States was worried that it could, "in a situation analogous to its unilateral 1978 action, find itself bound to the obligations of an 'international' protocol while its major competitors were not" (Benedick 1998: 89). The Reagan administration thus insisted on "pushing for a proportion of consumption of 90 percent or higher as the trigger for entry into force and other actions" (Benedick 1998: 89).

As explained in Chapter 7, players in the prisoners' dilemma (PD) would collectively prefer to set a minimum participation level equal to 100 percent. Doing so would ensure that full cooperation was sustained. What prevents them from choosing this level is the recognition that the threat to cooperate only if this minimum participation level were satisfied would not be credible.

Indeed, most countries objected to the US proposal. They realized that, were they to require such a high participation level, an agreement requiring deep cuts in emissions would probably never enter into force. The demand for high participation would only serve to "weaken the protocol by extracting other concessions as the price for adherence" (Benedick 1998: 89). In particular, the 90 percent threshold would require approval by the Soviet Union and Japan as well as the EC. A lower threshold, by contrast, would require approval only by the EC (as well as the United States and its ozone allies, of course). Richard Benedick told me later that he preferred a lower threshold, so that responsibility for the treaty's entry into force would rest with

---

[7] As explained in Chapter 15, the Kyoto Protocol adopts a similar approach.

Europe. He also felt that if the lower threshold were satisfied and the treaty entered into force, Japan and the Soviet Union would eventually accede. With a high threshold, on the other hand, Japan and the USSR would have more leverage, and would likely insist on a weaker treaty.

The theory developed thus far cannot accommodate this kind of flexibility. Collective rationality, as defined in Chapter 7, prevents signatories from diluting their abatement in order to sustain a higher participation level. In Chapter 11, however, I shall weaken the assumption of collective rationality just a little, and show that there can indeed be a trade-off between breadth (in terms of participation) and depth (in terms of the extent of controls). In Chapter 12 I shall explain a different feature of this treaty: why, once the treaty entered into force, more countries would want to accede. This "tipping" effect is not a feature of the analysis developed in Chapter 7.

Richard Benedick also told me later that he was actually recalled to Washington during the Montreal talks, to explain to officials in the Reagan Administration that insistence on the 90 percent threshold would scuttle the treaty. President Reagan insisted that the United States needed the treaty, even if with a lower threshold, and so Benedick returned to Montreal with a more flexible mandate.

As agreed in Montreal, the Protocol would only enter into force after being ratified by at least 11 countries, making up at least two-thirds of global consumption of the controlled substances. This minimum participation clause provided only a mild incentive for participation. As discussed in later chapters, other features of the agreement proved more important to broadening participation. Consistent with the analysis in Chapter 7, however, the Montreal negotiators understood that the agreement might not attract universal participation.

As matters turned out, the Protocol easily crossed the minimum participation threshold, and entered into force on January 1, 1989, the earliest date allowed by the Protocol. At that time, the agreement consisted of 30 parties (including the EC), accounting for 83 percent of global consumption of the listed substances (Parson 1993).

Of course, the theory developed in Chapter 7 predicts that actual participation should exactly equal the minimum participation specified in the treaty. There are a number of reasons why actual participation exceeds the minimum for this treaty, some of which are discussed in later chapters, and one of which is explained below.

8.6. OZONE PAYOFFS

Chapter 7 suggests that the values of the payoffs determine the level of cooperation that can be sustained by a self-enforcing agreement.

The payoffs to the United States of abating ozone-depleting substances (ODSs), as understood around the time of the Montreal negotiations, were outlined in a report prepared by the US Environmental Protection Agency (EPA 1988*a*; see also EPA 1988*b*); see Table 8.1. Three scenarios were studied. The No Controls scenario assumed that all countries would do nothing to reduce emissions. The Montreal Protocol scenario assumed that the controls prescribed by the Montreal Protocol would be adopted by 94 percent of developed nations and 65 percent of developing

Table 8.1. *Predicted implications for the United States of the Montreal Protocol and of a unilateral ozone policy*

	No Controls	Montreal Protocol	Unilateral implementation of Montreal by the United States
Ozone depletion (percent)			
By 2000	1.0	0.8	0.9
By 2050	15.7	1.9	10.3
By 2100	50.0	1.2	49.0
Payoffs to the US (billions of 1985 $US)			
Benefits	—	3,575	1,373
Costs	—	21	21
Net benefits	—	3,554	1,352

Source: EPA (1988a).

nations, with all participating nations achieving 100 percent compliance. The Unilateral Implementation scenario assumed that the United States would undertake the Montreal controls unilaterally, and that no other country would do so.

The EPA study concluded that the Montreal Protocol would reduce the extent of ozone depletion from 50 percent under the No Controls scenario to only 1.2 percent under the Montreal Protocol scenario by 2100.[8] This suggests that the Montreal Protocol offered substantial environmental protection. However, the analysis presented in Chapter 7 suggests that the No Controls scenario is the *wrong* benchmark for evaluating the contribution of this agreement. The appropriate benchmark is the non-cooperative outcome. Countries might have undertaken substantial controls unilaterally (recall that fairly substantial unilateral policies had previously been enacted beginning in the late 1970s).

Table 8.1 also indicates that unilateral action by the United States, assuming no abatement by other countries, would dampen depletion significantly in the short run but have virtually no impact by the year 2100. Thus, while unilateral action by *all* countries might substantially reduce environmental damage, action by just one country—even one as large as the United States–would have little long-term effect (and, yet, for reasons explained later, would still be worth taking).

A key component of the benefit of ozone layer protection is the value of the illnesses and deaths by cancer that would be avoided. The effect on cancer incidence was determined by dose–response functions relating the change in the incidence of cancer to the predicted change in radiation exposure. The study found that more than 245 million cancers, including more than 5 million cancer deaths, would be avoided by the Montreal Protocol by the year 2165. These are large numbers.

---

[8] In fact, the EPA truncates depletion at 50 percent. The model employed by the EPA to evaluate ozone depletion indicated that depletion would exceed 50 percent in the No Controls case.

How were these avoided cancer cases valued? Non-fatal cancer cases were given a value equal to the cost of treatment. The value of avoided cancer deaths was equated to the "value of a statistical life," estimated by the EPA at $3 million. This is also a large number, though it is in keeping with values in the literature (see, for example, Viscusi 1998).[9]

Multiplying a large number of avoided cancer deaths by a large value for each death avoided implies a huge benefit to ozone layer protection. The present value benefit from avoided cancer deaths was estimated by the EPA to be in trillions of dollars. By contrast, all the other benefits estimated by the EPA added up to only a few tens of billions of dollars in present value terms. Though one can always fuss about details, the broad story told by the EPA analysis is that the public health effects of ozone depletion were paramount.

The costs of abatement depend on the ease with which non-ODS-using products can be substituted for ODS-using products, other substances and processes can be substituted for ODSs in the production of ODS-using products, and the current stock of ODSs can be reclaimed for future use. Costs also depend on the speed of substitution. Rapid substitution, forcing early obsolescence of the capital stock, would be especially costly. Innovation would require costly investments for R&D, but these investments would be justified by the expectation of lowering future substitution costs. Finally, costs would also depend on the policies used to implement the Montreal Protocol. If economic instruments were used instead of standards, for example, costs would likely be lower.

Though estimation of costs and benefits is never easy, it is the big picture that matters, and the story told by the EPA calculations is unusually clear. As Table 8.1 shows, the range of costs, in present value terms, is puny compared to the benefits.[10] Even unilateral implementation of the Montreal controls yields a benefit–cost ratio of 65 : 1—a figure that would tower over almost every other public investment made by the United States in 1988. The basic economics of ozone policy thus implied that, for the United States—and probably for most industrial countries—the benefit of acceding to the Montreal Protocol exceeded the cost by a wide margin, irrespective of the behavior of other countries.[11] Accession was a *dominant strategy* for the industrialized countries.

---

[9] Here is how you can think of the value of a statistical life. Suppose ozone depletion would increase the probability of a person getting a fatal cancer, and thus dying prematurely, by 1/10,000. Suppose also that the average person would be willing to pay $300 to avoid this additional risk. Under certain conditions, the value of this small change in the probability of premature death, $300, will equal 1/10,000 times the value of life—implying a statistical value of life equal to $300/(1/10,000), or $3 million. See Viscusi (1998).

[10] Benedick (1998: 103) notes that the CFC Alliance, an industry association which contended that Montreal was unjustifiably stringent, "initially predicted that costs of implementing the protocol in the United States would be in the range of $5–10 billion." Though the association later revised their estimate upwards, Table 8.1 shows that the justification for Montreal would be largely insensitive to variations in cost estimates.

[11] Using different data, Sprinz and Vaahtoranta (1994) conclude that the US interests in reducing ozone-depleting chemicals would be intermediate as compared with other industrialized countries. Note as well that the costs to most other industrialized countries of implementing Montreal should if anything be *lower* relative to the benefits than shown in Table 8.1. Recall that the United States reduced its consumption and production of CFCs substantially in the late 1970s by banning their use in aerosols. To implement Montreal, the United States would thus have to substitute for CFCs in other uses—primarily in air conditioning and

This may seem a puzzle. After all, the EPA's analysis shows that unilateral action by the United States would have little long-term effect on the ozone layer. So, how could the action be justified? There are two reasons. The first is that unilateral abatement by the United States would have a pronounced effect in the short-to-medium term. As shown in Table 8.1, unilateral implementation by the United States was predicted to cut ozone depletion by a third by 2050. And so long as costs and benefits are discounted, it is the short-to-medium term, not the long term, that matters. The EPA study assumed a discount rate of two percent, implying that a dollar of avoided damage 50 years from now is worth 2.6 times a dollar of avoided damage a hundred years from now in present value terms. The second reason that unilateral action would be justified is simpler. It is that the costs of implementing Montreal were low.

Of course, costs and benefits matter to the theory. But they matter to the real world, too. Estimates of the costs and benefits to the United States of ozone layer protection were instrumental in building support for a treaty within the US administration. According to Benedick (1998: 63):

A major break in the interagency debate came in the form of a cost–benefit study from the President's Council of Economic Advisers. The analysis concluded that, despite the scientific and economic uncertainties, the monetary benefits of preventing future deaths from skin cancer far outweighed costs of CFC controls as estimated either by industry or by EPA. This conclusion, which was based on the most conservative estimates and did not even attempt to quantify other potential benefits of preventing ozone layer depletion dismayed the revisionists [individuals within the administration who opposed negotiation of a strong treaty] and helped sway some administration officials who had been watching the controversy from the sidelines.

To sum up, the economics of ozone depletion favored unilateral implementation of the Montreal Protocol by rich countries. In Olson's (1965) terminology, the industrialized countries were "fully privileged."

8.7. MONTREAL SUCCESS?

This evidence suggests that Montreal may not have been successful after all (a conclusion also reached by Murdoch and Sandler 1996). But the analysis developed so far is incomplete.

After Montreal was negotiated, the costs and benefits of ozone protection changed. They changed partly because *the treaty changed*. The agreement in force today requires deeper, broader, and faster cuts in ozone-destroying chemicals than the agreement negotiated in 1987. Each successive tightening in the treaty would have increased costs more than benefits, lowering the benefit–cost ratio.[12]

---

refrigeration—and this would be more costly. When Montreal was negotiated, aerosols still accounted for over half of European production. Europe could thus implement Montreal more cheaply, largely by doing what the United States had done ten years before. An implication of this is discussed in the next chapter.

[12] I am implicitly assuming here that benefits and costs are non-linear, contrary to the assumptions of Chapter 7. Little is known about the shape of the ozone depletion damage function, though it is perhaps likely that the marginal benefit would fall—atmospheric models suggest that successive increases in abatement

The costs and benefits also changed because of learning *over time*. As explained later, for any given level of control, costs fell and benefits increased compared with earlier expectations. Moreover, while the EPA analysis assumes that abatement costs for the United States are independent of the actions undertaken by other countries (note how the cost estimates for the United States shown in Table 8.1 do not depend on whether other countries undertake the same controls), it is likely that each country's control costs would fall as other countries reduced their emissions. As explained in Chapter 9, this kind of interdependence makes cooperation even easier.

Two other features of the problem, however, were sure to frustrate cooperation. First, the parties worried that, as the Montreal Protocol controls came to bind on them, production of ozone-destroying chemicals might shift to non-parties—a phenomenon known as "trade leakage." In the limit, if leakage were severe enough, Montreal might only redistribute production, and thus have little environmental benefit even in the short-to-medium term. Substantial leakage would similarly render unilateralism impotent. This interdependence in trade was ignored by the EPA's cost-benefit calculations, but it was a real concern to the Montreal negotiators. One of the principal tasks of the agreement was to plug this potential trade leak—a subject I discuss in detail in Chapter 12.

Second, the agreement needed also to create incentives for developing countries with a less fortunate benefit–cost ratio to undertake abatement for the global good. Though the United States had a strong unilateral incentive to implement Montreal whether or not other countries did so (ignoring the leakage problem), it also had a strong incentive to ensure that other countries undertook the same controls. In the long run, remember, the EPA study showed that unilateral abatement by the United States would achieve little (and this without even allowing for leakage). Montreal would succeed in a meaningful sense only if developing countries also participated. Providing them with the needed incentive was another great challenge to the Montreal negotiators. I discuss it in Chapter 13.

8.8. KNOWLEDGE vs AUTHORITY

Are payoffs really this important to international cooperation? It is hard to know for sure, because of the usual counterfactual problem. And I would certainly agree that payoffs, representing state interests, are only part of the explanation for international cooperation successes and failures. But they are an essential part of the story, and any theory of cooperation that suppresses their importance is likely to mislead rather than inform.

Let me illustrate this point by contrasting the theory developed here with one that sees state behavior as being influenced by a cadre of scientific experts, an "epistemic

would bring about smaller increments in avoided ozone depletion; see EPA (1988a), exhibit 6-5. Marginal costs would very likely increase, as harder-to-substitute-for chemicals, or chemicals with a lower ozone-depleting potential were phased out. In Barrett (1994a), I show that, if the marginal benefit of abatement relation is steep, and if the marginal cost of abatement function is relatively flat, then a treaty will be signed by a large number of countries, but such a treaty will improve little on non-cooperation.

community" invested with the authority to impel "the national governments in which it is strongly entrenched to adopt convergent pollution control polices and support rigorous efforts at coordinated pollution control" (Haas 1990: 64–5).

Science certainly underpinned the measures negotiated in Montreal; and scientists were deeply involved in the Montreal process. But this is to be expected by the theory developed in this book. An understanding of the science is essential to defining, measuring, and evaluating payoffs. Political scientist Peter Haas, however, claims a much greater role for the epistemic community. He claims that it "substantially determined the outcome of the ozone negotiations" (Haas 1992: 189), and that it did so "through a combination of strategies ranging from persuasion of individuals and groups to the capture of various decision-making channels" (Haas 1992: 224). Rather than help to articulate a nation's interests, the epistemic community imposed its own. To Haas (1992: 188), the signing of the Montreal Protocol "ran contrary to US domestic particularistic interests, which oppose regulation, and also differed from a contemporary assessment of the aggregate national interest."

Richard Benedick's recollection of the negotiations is different. Far from directing the negotiations, Benedick says that scientists needed to be "drawn out of their laboratories and into the negotiation process;" far from steering the negotiations, scientists were made "to assume an unaccustomed and occasionally uncomfortable shared responsibility for the policy implications of their findings" (Benedick 1998: 5).

The claim that the United States signed the Montreal Protocol even though it harmed its national interest is also contradicted by Haas's own description of the situation:

The Office of Management and Budget (OMB), under the auspices of the Domestic Policy Council, convened a series of technical briefings from February through May 1987, concurrent with the international negotiations. Most of the scientific summaries were presented by epistemic community members who had briefed [Lee] Thomas, the EPA administrator, a year earlier. The OMB economists were swayed by the cost-benefit analysis presented by the President's Council of Economic Advisers (CEA), an analysis that was based on conservative economic estimates of human health effects from ozone depletion, was drawn from the EPA's extensive 1986 risk assessment study, and concluded that stringent regulations to prevent depletion of the ozone layer would be highly cost-effective. In preparing their analysis, the CEA members had included none of the ethical and ecological considerations that had encouraged the epistemic community to support stringent controls. Nevertheless, their findings based on economic considerations supported the community's position. In any case, the CEA members had been impressed and persuaded by the thoroughness of the epidemiological presentations during the policy review, and their reputation for economic professionalism helped overcome the Reagan administration's aversion to regulation. (Haas 1992: 219.)

Haas's reading of this situation is that the national interest—as reflected in the payoffs to the United States—supported the epistemic community's position, and that it was the community's authority rather than the economics that influenced the Reagan administration's decision to support the Montreal Protocol. Plainly, however, the facts, even as Haas presents them, are open to a different interpretation.

8.9. ACTIONS vs OUTCOMES

The analysis presented in Chapter 7 assumes that cause and effect is known, and known with certainty. And yet uncertainties about the relationships underlying payoffs often loom large. In the case of the Montreal Protocol, uncertainty pervades every link in the chain of knowledge needed to calculate payoffs—the relationship between emissions and chlorine loadings, between loadings and depletion, between depletion and skin cancers, and between skin cancers and welfare.

Do these uncertainties matter? In an important essay, economist Richard Cooper (1989: 181) concludes that they matter a great deal: "international consensus about practical knowledge, along with shared objectives, is a necessary condition for close international cooperation." Moreover, Cooper argues, uncertainties about actions and outcomes interact with costs and benefits: "So long as costs are positive and benefits are uncertain, countries are not likely to cooperate systematically with one another; and so long as sharply differing views are held on the relationship between actions and outcomes, at least some parties will question the benefits alleged to flow from any proposed course of action."

Uncertainties about the effects of actions on outcomes plainly matter. But Cooper's casting of the problem may be overly stark. The costs of implementing the Montreal controls, though small, were positive; and the benefits, though potentially large, *were* uncertain, as Richard Benedick has recently reminded us:

We seem to have forgotten that [the case for the Montreal Protocol] was completely theoretical. Measurements did not in fact record any thinning of the ozone layer (except over Antarctica, a seasonal occurrence which scientists at the time considered a special case, and for which there were numerous theories). There was, moreover, no evidence that CFCs were responsible. Finally, there was no sign of increased ultraviolet radiation actually reaching the Earth. (Benedick 1997.)

A lesson of Montreal is that cooperation can be sustained even when there is uncertainty about the effects of actions on outcomes. More important, perhaps, is a favorable benefit–cost ratio (this you will recall is an implication of the analysis in Chapter 7). Indeed, Cooper's analysis of the reasons for the success of the smallpox eradication campaign is consistent with this view.

Smallpox, a highly infectious and lethal disease which is estimated to have killed more people than plague, cholera, and war put together, was eradicated in 1977 by an international program of vaccination, surveillance, and quarantine coordinated by the World Health Organization (WHO). The demise of this deadly disease was certainly helped by scientific knowledge, particularly about such things as the effectiveness of the vaccine, the absence of a non-human host, and the immunity afforded by previous infection. But the economics of eradication also made it attractive for countries to cooperate:

A major incentive for a smallpox eradication program was that the estimated costs of eradication could be more than recouped by savings on vaccination and quarantines against its spread. The total cost of the smallpox eradication program to WHO and other international donors came to $112 million, plus perhaps an additional $200 million spent by the national governments of the countries in which smallpox was still found. WHO estimates that this $312 million one-time expenditure saved at least $1 billion a year in terms of vaccination programs, care of infected persons, and quarantine if smallpox existed on the scale it did in the late 1960s. Thus eradication of smallpox was not only an international public good in terms of the alleviation of suffering but it also offered a handsome return on investment by reducing precautionary expenditures worldwide. (Cooper 1989: 235.)

The eradication of smallpox stands alongside the Montreal Protocol as one of the great achievements of international cooperation. It was not just a consensus on the science that facilitated cooperation in these instances. An auspicious economic calculus helped, too. This is the central message of the theory developed so far.

8.10. LONDON NEGOTIATIONS

Shortly after the Montreal Protocol was signed, the science and economics of ozone protection took a dramatic turn. In 1988, the Ozone Trends Panel—a US-led research group involving more than 100 scientists from 10 countries—issued a comprehensive report concluding that the link between CFCs and ozone depletion was all but certain. The Panel also reported that the ozone layer over North America, Europe, the Soviet Union, China, and Japan had already been depleted by up to three percent (in the winter by as much as six percent). This was more than the models used to justify the Montreal controls predicted. The implication: Montreal needed to be renegotiated.

Only days after the Panel's report was released came more startling news: Du Pont, the world's largest producer of CFCs, announced that it intended to cease making these chemicals altogether (later Du Pont firmed up its pledge by announcing that it would phase out production by 2000). The company warned, however, that international cooperation was essential, and that participation in an agreement to phase out CFCs needed to be as broad as possible, to avoid production by other manufacturers relocating to non-signatory states (leakage).[13]

In 1989, the assessment panels set up by Montreal reported their findings. Chief among these was that, even if CFCs were phased out, the ozone layer would continue to be depleted by increased chlorine loading from carbon tetrachloride and methyl chloroform. Another problem was growth in the production of hydrochlorofluorocarbons (HCFCs), a substitute for CFCs. HCFCs were only less damaging to the ozone layer than the substances they replaced, and the new studies showed that HCFCs would also need to be phased out if chlorine concentrations were ever to return to their "natural levels." Even then, recovery of the ozone layer would take many decades because of the huge stock of long-lived CFCs already accumulated in the atmosphere.

---

[13] As explained in Chapter 9, this announcement may have been in Du Pont's self-interest. If the announcement made intervention by the US government more likely—and it probably did have this effect (and, moreover, could have been foreseen to have had this effect)—then Du Pont would have suffered losses in the CFC market. But a government-enforced CFC-ban would at the same time have created a market for CFC substitutes, and Du Pont was ahead of its rivals in substitute R&D, partly because of its reaction to the

Substitution away from CFCs proved easier and less costly than expected, partly because of dramatic advances in the development of alternatives. As the Panel for Technical Assessment reported to the first meeting of the parties to the Montreal Protocol in Helsinki in May 1989, by this time it was possible to phase out a number of ODSs by the end of the century. In February 1990, the US President's Council of Economic Advisers (1990: 210) topped even this announcement, reporting that a phase-out was not only feasible but cheap: "Preliminary estimates place the US costs of a phase-out of CFCs and halons by 2000 at $2.7 billion over the next decade if the schedule of intermediate reductions currently incorporated in the Montreal Protocol is maintained." (Note that the Council's estimate is many times smaller than the earlier estimate of the cost of meeting the much weaker Montreal target shown in Table 8.1.) The economic assessment panel set up by the Montreal process confirmed that the impression given by the EPA study applied more broadly: "the monetary value of the benefits of safeguarding the ozone layer," the report concluded, "is undoubtedly much greater than the costs of CFC and halon reductions" (see Benedick 1998: 133).

State behavior reflected this favorable economic calculus. By 1990, the 20 percent reduction in CFC use required by the Montreal Protocol for 1993 had already been met by "virtually all industrialized countries" (Benedick 1998: 172); and, though actions speak louder than words, eight industrial countries announced that they would reduce their use of CFCs unilaterally by much more than required by Montreal. The Montreal constraint did not seem to be biting on national policy-making. Rather, it seemed that cooperation needed to catch up to the accomplishments of unilateralism.

At the second meeting of the parties, held in London in June 1990, the Montreal Protocol was adjusted and amended. The adjustments accelerated and tightened the reduction schedules for the ODSs controlled by the Montreal Protocol, and would be binding on all the Montreal parties after entering into force in March 1991. The amendment increased the number of controlled substances from eight in the original treaty to twenty, including the original five CFCs and three halons, ten additional CFCs, methyl chloroform, and carbon tetrachloride. HCFCs were not controlled by the amendment, but a non-binding resolution was passed to indicate that these "transitional substances" should be phased out by 2020 if possible and by 2040 at the latest.[14] The amendment would enter into force after being ratified by at least 20 countries.

By the start of the London negotiations, 65 countries had signed the Montreal agreement. Importantly, more than 40 non-parties also attended the London meetings.

unilateral controls adopted previously by the United States. Through this chain of reactions, Du Pont may thus have gained financially from its phase-down; see Barrett (1992*b*). Du Pont may also have been motivated by a concern about losses—especially litigation in the event that a link between CFCs and skin cancers was proved (just think of the law suits filed against cigarette manufacturers). Officially, however, the company has maintained that its decision was based purely on the science, and this was confirmed to me in a private conversation with a former Du Pont executive closely involved in the decision.

[14] HCFCs were an important substitute for CFCs. If HCFCs were phased out too quickly, industry would have little incentive to invest in the equipment to produce and use them, and the cost of phasing out CFCs would therefore increase. A consequence could be an increase in the use of CFCs, especially by developing countries.

A major ambition in London was to increase participation, with the industrial country parties offering to pay developing countries for the "incremental costs" of complying with the agreement. The London Amendments came into force on August 10, 1992, by which time important developing countries like China and India had already acceded to the agreement. This was the greatest achievement of the London negotiations. It is the subject of a detailed assessment in Chapter 13.

8.11. COPENHAGEN NEGOTIATIONS

Even this amendment seemed insufficient not long after the diplomats had returned home from London. For the first time, significant increases in harmful UV-B radiation were recorded in Europe and Australia. More importantly, ozone loss was detected in the summer months—when more people are exposed to UV-B—over North America, Europe, Asia, South America, Australia, New Zealand, and the South Pacific. The EPA had now revised its earlier calculations, doubling its estimate of the number of US deaths from skin cancer by 2050 to 200,000. A World Meteorological Organization (WMO) and UNEP assessment published in 1991 predicted that a sustained 10 percent depletion would increase the number of non-melanoma skin cancers by 300,000 and the number of cataracts by almost 1.75 million each year.

Meanwhile, the costs of phasing out the listed chemicals continued to drop. For example, and "contrary to original expectations, demand for CFC-113 and [methyl chloroform] ... plummeted as electronics and aerospace companies developed an impressive variety of new 'no-clean' technologies and substitute solvents" (Benedick 1998: 201).

Reductions in costs were helped by the design of the agreement. Montreal did not limit the use of CFCs *per se*. It limited the production and consumption (defined as production plus imports minus exports) of these chemicals. It thus created a scarcity value for the existing stock of CFCs, and so provided incentives for their collection for subsequent re-use. This avoided the need to substitute prematurely for the existing stock of CFC-using capital and posed no additional risk to the environment—only released CFCs damaged the environment.

Measures adopted unilaterally continued to advance ahead of the adjusted Montreal controls and the London Amendment. A number of European countries brought forward the dates at which CFCs, halons, and other listed substances were to be banned. Du Pont announced that it would stop making CFCs by 1996, four years ahead of its earlier phase-down date. The US Senate passed a non-binding resolution supporting a quicker phase-out of CFCs by a 96–0 majority.

The Montreal Protocol was again renegotiated—this time at the fourth meeting of the parties, held in Copenhagen in November 1992. This time the dates by which the agreed phase-out of previously listed substances was to be completed were shortened in a further adjustment (CFCs were now to be phased out by 1996), and the number of substances controlled by the agreement was increased from twenty (under the London Amendments) to ninety-four by a new amendment. Importantly, these newly listed substances included the controversial HCFCs. Use of these was to be capped and subsequently phased out by 2030. By the time of the Copenhagen meeting, ninety-four countries had signed the Montreal Protocol. The Copenhagen Amendments entered into force on June 14, 1994.

8.12. RETURN TO VIENNA AND MONTREAL

Further adjustments to the Montreal phase-out schedules were made in Vienna in 1995, and a new amendment was negotiated, to include a scheduled phase-out for methyl bromide—a pesticide and fumigant, the only significant ozone-depleting chemical not yet regulated by the treaty. In a later renegotiation, held on the tenth anniversary of the Protocol once again in Montreal, the phase-out was brought forward to 2005. But by this time there was not much more that could be done to protect the ozone layer. Ozone depletion was expected to worsen through 2000, when the process of repair was predicted to begin, but this delay was caused largely by accumulation of CFCs emitted years before Montreal.

Instead, the negotiations entered a new phase. Concern among parties shifted from target-setting to effective implementation—how to increase participation, limit the growth in emissions by developing countries (as allowed by the original agreement), promote compliance, and control the emerging black market trade in CFCs. These issues are taken up in later chapters.

To prepare for the tenth anniversary meeting of the parties, Environment Canada commissioned a study titled *Global Benefits and Costs of the Montreal Protocol*. The results of the assessment are shown in Table 8.2. Benefits represent the damages avoided by eliminating ODSs. Costs reflect the full costs of implementing the phase-outs. As in the EPA study, no attempt was made to estimate what countries would have done had the agreement not been negotiated, entered into force, and implemented. Hence, these estimates reflect the net benefits of the phase-out schedules, not the net benefits of the agreement itself. In this sense, the title of the report is misleading.

Still, the results of the study are striking—and broadly compatible with the earlier EPA report. Costs are much higher, but of course the estimates shown in Table 8.2 are

Table 8.2. *Global benefits and costs of the Montreal Protocol phase-out, 1987–2060*

Health benefits	
Avoided cases of non-melonoma skin cancer	19,100,000
Avoided cases of melanoma skin cancer	1,500,000
Avoided cases of cataracts	129,100,000
Avoided skin cancer deaths	333,500
Monetized benefits	$459 billion
Costs	$235 billion
Net benefits	$224 billion + non-monetized health benefits

Source: ARC Research Consultants (1997).

for the entire world, not just the United States. They also reflect not only the original 1987 agreement but the subsequent amendments and adjustments. The monetary estimate of benefits is lower, but this excludes the human health benefits of ozone protection—the main component of the benefit figure shown in Table 8.1. The monetized benefit estimate in Table 8.2 is only for the avoided damages to fisheries, agriculture, and materials. The predicted number of avoided cancer cases is substantially lower compared with the earlier US study, but the time frame for this latest study is also a century shorter. It is remarkable that the Montreal phase-outs can be shown to be a good deal for the world, even when the principal benefit of the agreement and all the very long-term benefits are uncounted.

Figure 8.1 shows projections of the contributions of the different agreements in terms of stratospheric abundances. Once again, the "No Protocol" scenario presumes a kind of business-as-usual world, one that disregards the incentives for unilateral action to reduce loadings. So we cannot tell from the figure what Montreal and its amendments really will achieve. At the same time, the figure does indicate that the actions demanded by Montreal and its amendments (especially London and Copenhagen) will reduce abundances very substantially.

Figure 8.1 also shows that the later amendments mattered less than the first two. And yet the process of tightening the grip on ODSs continues. The last amendment, negotiated in Beijing in 1999, even imposes a new restriction, a phase-out of

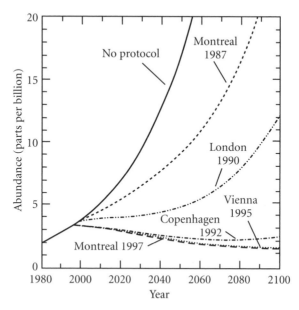

Figure 8.1. *Effects of international agreements on the abundance of ozone-depleting stratospheric chlorine/bromine*

Source: World Meteorological Organization (1998).

bromochloromethane. The new treaty thus increases the number of controlled substances to ninety-five.

8.13. CONCLUSIONS

As of this writing, participation in the Montreal Protocol is virtually full. Non-participants to this treaty include Afghanistan, Andorra, Bhutan, Eritrea, Guinea-Bissau, Iraq, and San Marino. These countries are either tiny or lacking an effective government or reluctant to engage in international affairs; one is an international outcast. In the short time between finishing the first draft of this book and making minor revisions, the number of parties increased from 175 (the number included in the table in Chapter 6) to 183. The countries acceding in this period of a few months include Cambodia, Cape Verde, Nauru, Palau, Rwanda, Sao tome and Principe, Sierra Leone, and Somalia. That even countries like these should accede to this agreement speaks to its great success. Participation in the related amendments is lower, but also increasing.

No other international agreement demands so much from so many parties as the Montreal Protocol and its related amendments, and we are already reaping the benefits. The abundance of ozone-depleting compounds in the atmosphere peaked in 1994 and is now declining.[15] The rate of decline in stratospheric ozone at mid-latitudes has slowed. The maximum extent of ozone depletion is expected to be realized in the next decade or so; and thereafter the ozone layer is expected to recover. By around 2050, the stratospheric concentration of ozone is expected to have returned to its "natural" (pre-1980) level.

I have heard environmentalists protest that the Montreal agreements do not go far enough. But even ignoring the Beijing controls, a complete and immediate global elimination of all emissions of ODSs would result in the stratospheric halogen loading returning to the pre-1980 values by the year 2033. Hence, Montreal gets us to the best-of-all feasible end states, though the journey takes 17 years longer than absolutely necessary. Even leaving aside the obvious point that an even faster phase-down would be costly and perhaps offer little in the way of added benefit, the achievements of the Montreal controls are truly outstanding. It may be correct to say that the glass is a few drops empty, but that should not blind us from seeing that it is almost completely full. In a world of mainly empty glasses, Montreal is an exception.

So *The Economist* newspaper was right to call the Montreal Protocol "a remarkable treaty" (Cairncross 1992). But we should be clear in understanding the sense in which the agreement is remarkable. The economics of ozone policy played a central role in shaping the course of negotiations, and a comparison of the benefits and costs of abatement would have commended substantial abatement by the industrialized countries even if an agreement had not been reached. The truly great achievement of this agreement was that it built even more cooperation upon this privileged edifice. The story of how it did this is told in the chapters that follow.

---

[15] The information found in this paragraph comes from the World Meteorological Organization (1998).

Appendix 8.1.

Miscellaneous No. 1 (1998)

Montreal Protocol

on

Substances that Deplete the Ozone Layer

Montreal, 16 September 1987

[The Protocol has not been ratified by the United Kingdom]

Presented to Parliament
by the Secretary of State for Foreign and Commonwealth Affairs
by Command of Her Majesty
January 1988

LONDON
HER MAJESTY'S STATIONERY OFFICE

APPENDIX 8.1 MONTREAL PROTOCOL
ON SUBSTANCES THAT DEPLETE THE OZONE LAYER

The Parties to this Protocol,

Being Parties to the Vienna Convention for the Protection of the Ozone Layer,

Mindful of their obligation under that Convention to take appropriate measures to protect human health and the environment against adverse effects resulting or likely to result from human activities which modify or are likely to modify the ozone layer,

Recognizing that world-wide emissions of certain substances can significantly deplete and otherwise modify the ozone layer in a manner that is likely to result in adverse effects on human health and the environment,

Conscious of the potential climatic effects of emissions of these substances,

Aware that measures taken to protect the ozone layer from depletion should be based on relevant scientific knowledge, taking into account technical and economic considerations,

Determined to protect the ozone layer by taking precautionary measures to control equitably total global emissions of substances that deplete it, with the ultimate objective of their elimination on the basis of developments in scientific knowledge, taking into account technical and economic considerations,

Acknowledging that special provision is required to meet the needs of developing countries for these substances,

Noting the precautionary measures for controlling emissions of certain chlorofluorocarbons that have already been taken at national and regional levels,

Considering the importance of promoting international co-operation in the research and development of science and technology relating to the control and reduction of emissions of substances that deplete the ozone layer, bearing in mind in particular the needs of developing countries,

Have agreed as follows:

ARTICLE 1

Definitions

For the purposes of this Protocol:

1. "Convention" means the Vienna Convention for the Protection of the Ozone Layer, adopted on 22 March 1985[1].

---

[1] Miscellaneous No. 13 (1985), Cmnd. 9652.

2.   "Parties" means, unless the text otherwise indicates, Parties to this Protocol.

3.   "Secretariat" means the secretariat of the Convention.

4.   "Controlled substance" means a substance listed in Annex A to this Protocol, whether existing alone or in a mixture. It excludes, however, any such substance or mixture which is in a manufactured product other than a container used for the transportation or storage of the substance listed.

5.   "Production" means the amount of controlled substances produced minus the amount destroyed by technologies to be approved by the Parties.

6.   "Consumption" means production plus imports minus exports of controlled substances.

7.   "Calculated levels" of production, imports, exports and consumption means levels determined in accordance with Article 3.

8.   "Industrial rationalization" means the transfer of all or a portion of the calculated level of production of one Party to another, for the purpose of achieving economic efficiencies or responding to anticipated shortfalls in supply as a result of plant closures.

ARTICLE 2

Control Measures

1.   Each Party shall ensure that for the twelve-month period commencing on the first day of the seventh month following the date of the entry into force of this Protocol, and in each twelve-month period thereafter, its calculated level of consumption of the controlled substances in Group I of Annex A does not exceed its calculated level of consumption in 1986. By the end of the same period, each Party producing one or more of these substances shall ensure that its calculated level of production of the substances does not exceed its calculated level of production in 1986, except that such level may have increased by no more than ten per cent based on the 1986 level. Such increase shall be permitted only so as to satisfy the basic domestic needs of the Parties operating under Article 5 and for the purposes of industrial rationalization between Parties.

2.   Each Party shall ensure that for the twelve-month period commencing on the first day of the thirty-seventh month following the date of the entry into force of this Protocol, and in each twelve-month period thereafter, its calculated level of consumption of the controlled substances listed in Group II of Annex A does not exceed its calculated level of consumption in 1986. Each Party producing one or more of these substances shall ensure that its calculated level of production of the substances does not exceed its calculated level of production in 1986, except that such level may

have increased by no more than ten per cent based on the 1986 level. Such increase shall be permitted only so as to satisfy the basic domestic needs of the Parties operating under Article 5 and for the purposes of industrial rationalization between Parties. The mechanisms for implementing these measures shall be decided by the Parties at their first meeting following the first scientific review.

3. Each Party shall ensure that for the period 1 July 1993 to 30 June 1994, and in each twelve-month period thereafter, its calculated level of consumption of the controlled substances in Group I of Annex A does not exceed, annually, eighty per cent of its calculated level of consumption in 1986. Each Party producing one or more of these substances shall, for the same periods, ensure that its calculated level of production of the substances does not exceed, annually, eighty per cent of its calculated level of production in 1986. However, in order to satisfy the basic domestic needs of the Parties operating, under Article 5 and for the purposes of industrial rationalization between Parties, its calculated level of production may exceed that limit by up to ten per cent of its calculated level of production in 1986.

4. Each Party shall ensure that for the period 1 July 1998 to 30 June 1999, and in each twelve-month period thereafter, its calculated level of consumption of the controlled substances in Group I of Annex A does not exceed, annually, fifty per cent of its calculated level of consumption in 1986. Each Party producing one or more of these substances shall, for the same periods, ensure that its calculated level of production of the substances does not exceed, annually, fifty per cent of its calculated level of production in 1986. However, in order to satisfy the basic domestic needs of the Parties operating under Article 5 and for the purposes of industrial rationalization between Parties, its calculated level of production may exceed that limit by up to fifteen per cent of its calculated level of production in 1986. This paragraph will apply unless the Parties decide otherwise at a meeting by a two-thirds majority of Parties present and voting, representing at least two-thirds of the total calculated level of consumption of these substances of the Parties. This decision shall be considered and made in the light of the assessments referred to in Article 6.

5. Any Party whose calculated level of production in 1986 of the controlled substances in Group I of Annex A was less than twenty-five kilotonnes may, for the purposes of industrial rationalization, transfer to or receive from any other Party, production in excess of the limits set out in paragraphs 1, 3 and 4 provided that the total combined calculated levels of production of the Parties concerned does not exceed the production limits set out in this Article. Any transfer of such production shall be notified to the secretariat no later than the time of the transfer.

6. Any Party not operating under Article 5, that has facilities for the production of controlled substances under construction, or contracted for, prior to 16 September 1987, and provided for in national legislation prior to 1 January 1987, may add the production from such facilities to its 1986 production of such substances for the purposes of determining its calculated level of production for 1986, provided that such facilities are completed by 31 December 1990 and that such production does

not raise that Party's annual calculated level of consumption of the controlled substances above 0.5 kilograms per capita.

7.   Any transfer of production pursuant to paragraph 5 or any addition of production pursuant to paragraph 6 shall be notified to the secretariat, no later than the time of the transfer or addition.

8. (a) Any Parties which are Member States of a regional economic integration organization as defined in Article 1(6) of the Convention may agree that they shall jointly fulfil their obligations respecting consumption under this Article provided that their total combined calculated level of consumption does not exceed the levels required by this Article.

   (b) The Parties to any such agreement shall inform the secretariat of the terms of the agreement before the date of the reduction in consumption with which the agreement is concerned.

   (c) Such agreement will become operative only if all Member States of the regional economic integration organization and the organization concerned are Parties to the Protocol and have notified the secretariat of their manner of implementation.

9. (a) Based on the assessments made pursuant to Article 6, the Parties may decide whether:

   (i) adjustments to the ozone depleting potentials specified in Annex A should be made and, if so, what the adjustments should be; and

   (ii) further adjustments and reductions of production or consumption of the controlled substances from 1986 levels should be undertaken and, if so, what the scope, amount and timing of any such adjustments and reductions should be.

   (b) Proposals for such adjustments shall be communicated to the Parties by the secretariat at least six months before the meeting of the Parties at which they are proposed for adoption.

   (c) In taking such decisions, the Parties shall make every effort to reach agreement by consensus. If all efforts at consensus have been exhausted, and no agreement reached, such decisions shall, as a last resort, be adopted by a two-thirds majority vote of the Parties present and voting representing at least fifty per cent of the total consumption of the controlled substances of the Parties.

   (d) The decisions, which shall be binding on all Parties, shall forthwith be communicated to the Parties by the Depositary. Unless otherwise provided in the decisions, they shall enter into force on the expiry of six months from the date of the circulation of the communication by the Depositary.

10. (a) Based on the assessments made pursuant to Article 6 of this Protocol and in accordance with the procedure set out in Article 9 of the Convention, the Parties may decide:

   (i) whether any substances, and if so which, should be added to or removed from any annex to this Protocol; and

(ii) the mechanism, scope and timing of the control measures that should apply to those substances;

(b) Any such decision shall become effective, provided that it has been accepted by a two-thirds majority vote of the Parties present and voting.

11.   Notwithstanding the provisions contained in this Article, Parties may take more stringent measures than those required by this Article.

ARTICLE 3

Calculation of Control Levels

For the purposes of Articles 2 and 5, each Party shall, for each Group of substances in Annex A, determine its calculated levels of:

(a) production by:

(i) multiplying its annual production of each controlled substance by the ozone depleting potential specified in respect of it in Annex A; and

(ii) adding together, for each such Group, the resulting figures;

(b) imports and exports, respectively, by following, *mutatis mutandis*, the procedure set out in subparagraph (a); and

(c) consumption by adding together its calculated levels of production and imports and subtracting its calculated level of exports as determined in accordance with subparagraphs (a) and (b). However, beginning on 1 January 1993, any export of controlled substances to non-Parties shall not be subtracted in calculating the consumption level of the exporting Party.

ARTICLE 4

Control of Trade with Non-parties

1.   Within one year of the entry into force of this Protocol, each Party shall ban the import of controlled substances from any State not party to this Protocol.

2.   Beginning on 1 January 1993, no Party operating under paragraph 1 of Article 5 may export any controlled substance to any State not party to this Protocol.

3.   Within three years of the date of the entry into force of this Protocol, the Parties shall, following the procedures in Article 10 of the Convention, elaborate in an annex a list of products containing controlled substances. Parties that have not objected to the annex in accordance with those procedures shall ban, within one year of the annex having become effective, the import of those products from any State not party to this Protocol.

4.   Within five years of the entry into force of this Protocol, the Parties shall determine the feasibility of banning or restricting, from States not party to this Protocol, the import of products produced with, but not containing, controlled substances. If

determined feasible, the Parties shall, following the procedures in Article 10 of the Convention, elaborate in an annex a list of such products. Parties that have not objected to it in accordance with those procedures shall ban or restrict, within one year of the annex having become effective, the import of those products from any State not party to this Protocol.

5.   Each Party shall discourage the export, to any State not party to this Protocol, of technology for producing and for utilizing controlled substances.

6.   Each Party shall refrain from providing new subsidies, aid, credits, guarantees or insurance programmes for the export of States not party to this Protocol of products, equipment, plants or technology that would facilitate the production of controlled substances.

7.   Paragraphs 5 and 6 shall not apply to products, equipment, plants or technology that improve the containment, recovery, recycling or destruction of controlled substances, promote the development of alternative substances, or otherwise contribute to the reduction of emissions of controlled substances.

8.   Notwithstanding the provisions of this Article, imports referred to in paragraphs 1, 3 and 4 may be permitted from any State not party to this Protocol if that State is determined, by a meeting of the Parties, to be in full compliance with Article 2 and this Article, and has submitted data to that effect as specified in Article 7.

ARTICLE 5

Special Situation of Developing Countries

1.   Any Party that is a developing country and whose annual calculated level of consumption of the controlled substances is less than 0·3 kilograms per capita on the date of the entry into force of the Protocol for it, or any time thereafter within ten years of the date of entry into force of the Protocol shall, in order to meet its basic domestic needs, be entitled to delay its compliance with the control measures set out in paragraphs 1 to 4 of Article 2 by ten years after that specified in those paragraphs. However, such Party shall not exceed an annual calculated level of consumption of 0·3 kilograms per capita. Any such Party shall be entitled to use either the average of its annual calculated level of consumption for the period 1995 to 1997 inclusive or a calculated level of consumption of 0·3 kilograms per capita, whichever is the lower, as the basis for its compliance with the control measures.

2.   The Parties undertake to facilitate access to environmentally safe alternative substances and technology for Parties that are developing countries and assist them to make expeditious use of such alternatives.

3.   The Parties undertake to facilitate bilaterally or multilaterally the provision of subsidies, aid, credits, guarantees or insurance programmes to Parties that are developing countries for the use of alternative technology and for substitute products.

ARTICLE 6

Assessment and Review of Control Measures

Beginning in 1990, and at least every four years thereafter, the Parties shall assess the control measures provided for in Article 2 on the basis of available scientific, environmental, technical and economic information. At least one year before each assessment, the Parties shall convene appropriate panels of experts qualified in the fields mentioned and determine the composition and terms of reference of any such panels. Within one year of being convened, the panels will report their conclusions, through the secretariat, to the Parties.

ARTICLE 7

Reporting of Data

1.   Each Party shall provide to the secretariat, within three months of becoming a Party, statistical data on its production, imports and exports of each of the controlled substances for the year 1986, or the best possible estimates of such data where actual data are not available.

2.   Each Party shall provide statistical data to the secretariat on its annual production (with separate data on amounts destroyed by technologies to be approved by the Parties), imports, and exports to Parties and non-Parties, respectively, of such substances for the year during which it becomes a Party and for each year thereafter. It shall forward the data no later than nine months after the end of the year to which the data relate.

ARTICLE 8

Non-compliance

The Parties, at their first meeting, shall consider and approve procedures and institutional mechanisms for determining non-compliance with the provisions of this Protocol and for treatment of Parties found to be in non-compliance.

ARTICLE 9

Research, Development, Public Awareness and Exchange of Information

1.   The Parties shall co-operate, consistent with their national laws, regulations and practices and taking into account in particular the needs of developing countries, in promoting, directly or through competent international bodies, research, development and exchange of information on:

(a) best technologies for improving the containment, recovery, recycling or destruction of controlled substances or otherwise reducing their emissions;

(b) possible alternatives to controlled substances, to products containing such substances, and to products manufactured with them; and

(c) costs and benefits of relevant control strategies.

2.   The Parties, individually, jointly or through competent international bodies, shall co-operate in promoting public awareness of the environmental effects of the emissions of controlled substances and other substances that deplete the ozone layer.

3.   Within two years of the entry into force of this Protocol and every two years thereafter, each Party shall submit to the secretariat a summary of the activities it has conducted pursuant to this Article.

ARTICLE 10

Technical Assistance

1.   The Parties shall, in the context of the provisions of Article 4 of the Convention, and taking into account in particular the needs of developing countries, co-operate in promoting technical assistance to facilitate participation in and implementation of this Protocol.

2.   Any Party or Signatory to this Protocol may submit a request to the secretariat for technical assistance for the purposes of implementing or participating in the Protocol.

3.   The Parties, at their first meeting, shall begin deliberations on the means of fulfilling the obligations set out in Article 9, and paragraphs 1 and 2 of this Article, including the preparation of workplans. Such workplans shall pay special attention to the needs and circumstances of the developing countries. States and regional economic integration organizations not party to the Protocol should be encouraged to participate in activities specified in such workplans.

ARTICLE 11

Meetings of the Parties

1.   The Parties shall hold meetings at regular intervals. The secretariat shall convene the first meeting of the Parties not later than one year after the date of entry into force of this Protocol and in conjunction with a meeting of the Conference of the Parties to the Convention, if a meeting of the latter is scheduled within that period.

2.   Subsequent ordinary meetings of the Parties shall be held, unless the Parties otherwise decide, in conjunction with meetings of the Conference of the Parties to the

Convention. Extraordinary meetings of the Parties shall be held at such other times as may be deemed necessary by a meeting of the Parties, or at the written request of any Party, provided that, within six months of such a request being communicated to them by the secretariat, it is supported by at least one-third of the Parties.

3.   The Parties, at their first meeting, shall:

(a) adopt by consensus rules of procedure for their meetings;

(b) adopt by consensus the financial rules referred to in paragraph 2 of Article 13;

(c) establish the panels and determine the terms of reference referred to in Article 6;

(d) consider and approve the procedures and institutional mechanisms specified in Article 8; and

(e) begin preparation of workplans pursuant to paragraph 3 of Article 10.

4.   The functions of the meetings of the Parties shall be to:

(a) review the implementation of this Protocol;

(b) decide on any adjustments or reductions referred to in paragraph 9 of Article 2;

(c) decide on any addition to, insertion in or removal from any annex of substances and on related control measures in accordance with paragraph 10 of Article 2;

(d) establish, where necessary, guidelines or procedures for reporting of information as provided for in Article 7 and paragraph 3 of Article 9;

(e) review requests for technical assistance submitted pursuant to paragraph 2 of Article 10;

(f) review reports prepared by the secretariat pursuant to subparagraph (c) of Article 12;

(g) assess, in accordance with Article 6, the control measures provided for in Article 2;

(h) consider and adopt, as required, proposals for amendment of this Protocol or any annex and for any new annex;

(i) consider and adopt the budget for implementing this Protocol; and

(j) consider and undertake any additional action that may be required for the achievement of the purposes of this Protocol.

5. The United Nations, its specialized agencies and the International Atomic Energy Agency, as well as any State not party to this Protocol, may be represented at meetings of the Parties as observers. Any body or agency, whether national or international, governmental or non-governmental, qualified in fields relating to the protection of the ozone layer which has informed the secretariat of its wish to be represented at a meeting of the Parties as an observer may be admitted unless at least one-third of the

Parties present object. The admission and participation of observers shall be subject to the rules of procedure adopted by the Parties.

ARTICLE 12

Secretariat

For the purposes of this Protocol, the secretariat shall:

(a) arrange for and service meetings of the Parties as provided for in Article 11;

(b) receive and make available, upon request by a Party, data provided pursuant to Article 7;

(c) prepare and distribute regularly to the Parties reports based on information received pursuant to Articles 7 and 9;

(d) notify the parties of any request for technical assistance received pursuant to Article 10 so as to facilitate the provision of such assistance;

(e) encourage non-Parties to attend the meetings of the Parties as observers and to act in accordance with the provisions of this Protocol;

(f) provide, as appropriate, the information and requests referred to in subparagraphs (c) and (d) to such non-party observers; and

(g) perform such other functions for the achievement of the purposes of this Protocol as may be assigned to it by the Parties.

ARTICLE 13

Financial Provisions

1. The funds required for the operation of this Protocol, including those for the functioning of the secretariat related to this Protocol, shall be charged exclusively against contributions from the Parties.

2. The Parties, at their first meeting, shall adopt by consensus financial rules for the operation of this Protocol.

ARTICLE 14

Relationship of this Protocol to the Convention

Except as otherwise provided in this Protocol, the provisions of the Convention relating to its protocols shall apply to this Protocol.

ARTICLE 15

Signature

This Protocol shall be open for signature by States and by regional economic integration organizations in Montreal on 16 September 1987, in Ottawa from 17 September 1987 to 16 January 1988, and at United Nations Headquarters in New York from 17 January 1988 to 15 September 1988.

ARTICLE 16

Entry into Force

1.   This Protocol shall enter into force on 1 January 1989, provided that at least eleven instruments of ratification, acceptance, approval of the Protocol or accession thereto have been deposited by States or regional economic integration organizations representing at least two-thirds of 1986 estimated global consumption of the controlled substances, and the provisions of paragraph 1 of Article 17 of the Convention have been fulfilled. In the event that these conditions have not been fulfilled by that date, the Protocol shall enter into force on the ninetieth day following the date on which the conditions have been fulfilled.

2.   For the purposes of paragraph 1, any such instrument deposited by a regional economic integration organization shall not be counted as additional to those deposited by member States of such organization.

3.   After the entry into force of this Protocol, any State or regional economic integration organization shall become a Party to it on the ninetieth day following the date of deposit of its instrument of ratification, acceptance, approval or accession.

ARTICLE 17

Parties Joining after Entry into Force

Subject to Article 5, any State or regional economic integration organization which becomes a Party to this Protocol after the date of its entry into force, shall fulfil forthwith the sum of the obligations under Article 2, as well as under Article 4, that apply at that date to the States and regional economic integration organizations that became Parties on the date the Protocol entered into force.

ARTICLE 18

Reservations

No reservations may be made to this Protocol.

ARTICLE 19

Withdrawal

For the purposes of this Protocol, the provisions of Article 19 of the Convention relating to withdrawal shall apply, except with respect to Parties referred to in paragraph 1 of Article 5. Any such Party may withdraw from this Protocol by giving written notification to the Depositary at any time after four years of assuming the obligations specified in paragraphs 1 to 4 of Article 2. Any such withdrawal shall take effect upon expiry of one year after the date of its receipt by the Depositary, or on such later date as may be specified in the notification of the withdrawal.

ARTICLE 20

Authentic Texts

The original of this Protocol, of which the Arabic, Chinese, English, French, Russian and Spanish texts are equally authentic, shall be deposited with the Secretary-General of the United Nations.

In witness whereof the undersigned, being duly authorized to that effect, have signed this Protocol.

Done at Montreal this Sixteenth day of September, One Thousand Nine Hundred and Eighty Seven.

[Here follow the signatures on behalf of:
Belgium
Canada
Denmark
European Economic Community
Egypt
Finland
France
Germany, Federal Republic of
Ghana
Italy
Japan
Kenya
Mexico
Netherlands
New Zealand
Norway
Panama
Portugal
Senegal
Sweden
Switzerland
Togo
United Kingdom
United States of America
Venezuela]

ANNEX A

Controlled Substances

Group	Substance	Ozone Depleting Potential*
Group I	$CFCl_3$ (CFC-11)	1·0
	CF_2Cl_2 (CFC-12)	1·0
	$C_2F_3Cl_3$ (CFC-113)	0·8
	$C_2F_4Cl_2$ (CFC-114)	1·0
	C_2F_5Cl (CFC-115)	0·6
Group II	CF_2BrCl(halon-1211)	3·0
	CF_3Br (halon-1301)	10·0
	$C_2F_4Br_2$ (halon-2402)	(to be determined)

*These ozone depleting potentials are estimates based on existing knowledge and will be reviewed and revised periodically.

9

Tipping Treaties

Look at the world around you. It may seem like an immovable, implacable place. It is not. With the slightest push—in just the right place—it can be tipped. Malcolm Gladwell, *The Tipping Point* (2000: 259)

9.1. INTRODUCTION

Treaties that sustain real cooperation must enforce participation. And, yet, most treaties do not incorporate enforcement mechanisms. They may include a minimum participation clause, but with the exception of bilateral and minilateral treaties, this minimum is usually exceeded; in equilibrium, it does not bite. This hints that treaties like this are trying to do something different. Their aim may be to coordinate state behavior.

As shown in Chapter 4, some games require only coordination. These are easy problems to remedy. My focus here is different. I shall show how situations that demand cooperation can be transformed into a game requiring only coordination. This strategic manipulation has an obvious advantage in that coordination games do not require enforcement measures. However, not all games can be transformed in this way. And there may be a cost to transforming a prisoners' dilemma (PD)-like game. The outcome that can be sustained by coordination may be welfare-inferior to the outcome that would be sustained were it not necessary for treaties to be self-enforcing. That is, the transformed coordination game may only be able to sustain a second-best outcome.

In PD games, players have dominant strategies. In the transformed games studied in Chapter 7, states do not have dominant strategies; whether a country signs a treaty or not depends on the number of others that sign. The transformed games studied here also do not have dominant strategies. The difference is that, in this chapter, the equilibria are symmetric. If there is a treaty, then all countries will sign it. Threshold effects are often important in these kinds of situations, and the minimum participation clause may serve a different purpose as compared with the games studied in Chapter 7. In coordination games, the minimum participation clause coordinates state behavior. It identifies the tipping point.

9.2. CONFORMING PREFERENCES

When you see countries behave in the same way, it may be tempting to conclude that they are doing so because they have a preference to conform. If this were true, however—if states cared only about conforming—then it would not matter what states did; the aggregate payoff would be maximized so long as all countries did the same thing. Non-cooperation would suffice to please everyone; there would be no prisoners' dilemmas, and no need to negotiate an environmental treaty.

The aim of international environmental agreements is usually to get countries to behave differently than they would if their strategies were chosen unilaterally. So suppose that countries have preferences over their conforming behavior *and* their interests, narrowly defined. Each country wants to do what the others do, but each would rather that all countries play Abate. Then treaties can play a role. Once a majority of countries contribute to the provision of a public good, say, the others, motivated partly by a preference to conform, may adopt the same behavior, with the consequence that every country participates and supplies the public good. The treaty aids the interests of each country by ensuring that the public good is supplied. But the treaty is *sustained* only by the preference to conform; there is no need for enforcement.

This assumption about preferences makes management of the transnational commons a coordination game. As discussed in Chapter 4, however, the hypothesis that countries are fairminded under any and all circumstances is rejected by the data. Many if not most treaties attract less than full participation. Even when we observe states seeking a symmetric outcome—one in which every state participates in a treaty, for example—we must be careful not to ascribe this to fairminded preferences. There may be another explanation. In Chapter 11 I shall show that it may be in the interests of countries to seek a symmetric outcome—a consensus treaty in which every country participates but in which participation must also be enforced. This result hints at something deeper. It is easy to *assume* that no country wants to be "the odd man out." But this only raises the higher order question of *why* countries should have such preferences. If we are inclined to want to conform, the reason may be that conforming often aids our interests. It does so in the model developed in Chapter 11.

9.3. PARTICIPATION BENEFITS

It is sometimes argued that international cooperation is particularly difficult to sustain because, in contrast to local commons problems, international cooperation requires unanimity or near unanimity (Ostrom *et al.* 1999). This is true of custom, and explains why customary law is so weak. It is also true of bilateral agreements; and as shown previously it is true of some minilateral agreements like the fur seal treaty. However, it is not true of treaties generally. Only rarely must every other country participate in a large-scale treaty for participation to be attractive to each country. Moreover, and as we have already seen, when unanimity is required, it often makes sustaining full cooperation *easier*, not harder.

An example that is sometimes given is eradication of an infectious disease (Sandler 1998). For highly contagious diseases, every state is pivotal to the success of a global eradication program. If every state eradicates the disease at home, the disease will be eradicated everywhere. But if just one state fails to eradicate the disease, the disease will continue to exist and will thus pose a risk to every country. The benefit to any state of eradicating the disease at home is thus highly non-linear. It may be near zero if $N - 2$ or fewer other states control the disease, but it may be huge if all the $N - 1$

other states control the disease. As long as the benefit of eradication to each country exceeds the costs of controlling the disease at home, coordination will suffice to eradicate the disease globally. Under these circumstances, global disease eradication is a "weakest link" game.

However, situations of this kind are exceptions. Even for disease eradication, coordination will rarely suffice (Barrett 2002c). First, and in contrast to the assumptions underlying the weakest link game, every country has some unilateral incentive to immunize its own population. Doing so will reduce the rate of infection at home, taking as given the immunization decisions of other countries. Second, as immunization increases abroad, the population at home becomes less vulnerable to infection. This is because the force of the infection is reduced by the reduction in the number of other countries that can spread the disease (Anderson and May 1991). The latter effect means that the marginal benefit of immunization at home *decreases* in the immunization efforts of other countries, precisely opposite the requirements of the weakest link game. Indeed, this is one reason why diseases persist. Just when we begin to bring a disease under control, we drop our guard; we stop immunizing. After a time we create a new population of potential hosts for the disease, enabling the disease to thrive once again.

To sum up: the benefits to each country of eradicating a disease at home *increase* (non-linearly) in the number of other countries that eradicate the disease, creating a positive feedback (at least after some threshold has been passed). Technically, eradication is a *strategic complement*. However, the benefits to each country of controlling a disease at home *decrease* in the extent of control undertaken by others (the benefits of control are prevalence-dependent), creating a negative feedback. Disease control is a *strategic substitute*.[1] As implied by this discussion, choice of the objective of an international program may affect behavior. Later we shall see that choice of an action or policy instrument may have a similar effect.

9.4. A VIRTUOUS FEEDBACK

I have thus far emphasized interdependence on the *benefit* side of the equation. Economist Geoffrey Heal (1993) has argued that interdependence can also be manifest on the *cost* side—that, in particular, as one country increases its abatement, the marginal cost of abatement for others may fall, making these countries want to increase their abatement. This creates a kind of virtuous feedback where abatement by one country begets abatement by others. It makes abatement a strategic complement.

Suppose Country X regulates the use of a pollutant. Then the industries relying on this pollutant must seek alternatives or else go out of business. Probably, they or their suppliers will undertake some R&D into alternative products and processes, to lower the cost of complying with the regulation. Eventually, some retooling will be required, and this will add to the cost of implementing the ban. All these costs must be taken into account by Country X before imposing the regulation. Once they have been incurred, however, these costs will be sunk, and so the technologies developed

---

[1] Again, see the classic paper by Bulow *et al.* (1985).

by X can be made available to Country Y at a relatively low cost (put differently, the fixed costs of substituting away from the polluting technology can be shared). The cost to Country Y of regulating the same pollutant will then be lower than it would have been had X not regulated its industry in the first place, even if X and Y would have faced the same cost *ex ante*. Regulation may thus become more attractive to Y. And if Y regulates the pollutant, it may pay industry to innovate some more, since the costs of the innovation will now be spread over a larger market. This may in turn lower the cost of the regulation to X, and X may possibly tighten its regulations in response, causing Y to tighten its regulation, and so on. At some point, Country Z may also find it attractive to regulate the same pollutant, and so the process may continue. As compared with the situation in which costs were independent, it is likely that more abatement will be undertaken in equilibrium. Indeed, as Heal shows, if the positive feedback is strong enough, full cooperation may not only be sustained as an equilibrium; it may be the *only* equilibrium. Under these circumstances, there would be no need for an international agreement.

As explained in Chapter 8, the United States had a strong incentive to undertake the Montreal controls unilaterally. So, probably, did every other industrialized country. However, interactions among the players gave the process an additional momentum. Recall that the United States banned chlorofluorocarbons (CFCs) in aerosols in 1978. European countries could comply with Montreal by doing the same thing, over a decade later (aerosols accounted for over half of European production, and the Montreal Protocol only required that production be cut by half). Europe had a second-mover advantage. It could learn from the earlier experience of the United States, and reduce its emissions for a fraction of the cost. As the representative of a European user group put it, "European industry is in the fortunate position of being able to introduce the alternative techniques developed [in the United States] without suffering the same degree of hardship" (Benedick 1998: 107).

For the US industry, the situation was different. Having already banned CFCs in aerosols, US firms had to cut back their use of CFCs in other areas—principally, in air conditioning and refrigeration. Even here, however, Montreal helped create a positive feedback, as Benedick (1998: 105) explains:

By cutting the market in half at a fixed date, the protocol was in fact tipping CFCs towards obsolescence. US negotiators had reasoned that, when substitutes were developed to such an extent, the remaining CFC market could probably not be sustained.

The expectation thus seems to have been that, as substitutes were developed for one use, the cost of substituting for CFCs in other uses would fall. However, the positive feedback created here depends on the threshold being passed. If the treaty cut CFC use by less than half, production may not have tipped. In fact, at an early stage of the negotiations, it was suggested that the treaty require an initial 20 percent cut in CFCs. The Toronto Group of countries argued forcefully for a bigger cut. As Benedick (1998: 65) later put it, "Since industry could easily achieve the 20 percent reduction with existing technologies for recycling and conservation ... , only the additional 30 percent requirement would provide any real incentive for development of substitutes to CFCs" (Benedick 1998: 65). Choice of a production limit was thus strategic. Whether it made sense on its own or not, its main virtue was in lowering the costs of making even bigger reductions. Choice of the 50 percent cut got the parties to the Montreal Protocol past the tipping point.

9.5. GOVERNMENT–INDUSTRY INTERACTIONS

I have so far focused on the international game of ozone protection. But a related game was also played at a different level, between governments and firms.

By providing CFC producers with the certainty that their sales were destined to decline, the protocol unleashed the creative energies and considerable resources of the private sector in search for alternatives. The treaty at one stroke changed the market rules and thereby made research into substitutes economically worthwhile. Stimulated by market incentives, industrial firms began deploying their resources to find solutions rather than to obstruct regulation. (Benedick 1998: 105.)

Firms will only invest in developing substitute technology if they believe that governments will reduce the demand for CFCs, and so create a demand for substitutes. But governments will only require a cutback in CFC use if they believe that substitutes will be available at an acceptable price. If governments knew the true costs of substituting away from CFCs, they would ban CFCs provided the benefits exceeded the costs. Their job would be easy.

However, the costs of substitution are private information. Industry has a better idea of their true value. And yet industry has little incentive to tell the government the truth. To avoid having to incur R&D costs, industry may want to convince government that substitution costs are high. Indeed, in 1975, Du Pont, the world's largest producer of CFCs, told the US Senate that restrictions on CFCs would cause "tremendous economic dislocation" (Benedick 1998: 31). Firms may even behave strategically, expending resources that signal to the government that substitution costs really are high. Knowing this, you might think that government should go ahead and regulate anyway. But of course the industry might be telling the truth; the costs of replacing CFCs might really exceed the benefits.

Credibility is another problem. Industry will only invest in finding substitutes if it believes that a market for substitutes really will exist. But this will depend in turn on whether the government's promise to restrict CFCs is credible. Suppose industry does not invest in finding substitutes. Then the restrictions will be more costly to implement, and the government may not want to implement the restrictions—in turn justifying the decision by industry not to invest in R&D.

This is more than a theoretical possibility. Previously, the state of California threatened to ban automakers from selling any cars in the state if they failed to sell a minimum number of "zero emission vehicles." If this threat were perceived to be credible, industry would surely produce and sell electric cars in California. Doing so would make business sense even if consumers did not want electric cars; it would be like paying an entrance fee for the privilege of supplying this huge market with the cars consumers did want. But industry could look forward and reason backwards. Suppose the industry did not make zero emission vehicles available. Would the California legislature really carry out its threat not to allow any automaker to sell new cars in the state? It almost certainly would not. The cost would be too high, politically as well as economically. As it happens, the automakers announced that they could not meet the legislature's target, and the legislature let the target slide. The cat and mouse game continues to be played today.

A threat is credible if the government is better off when it carries out the threat, given that industry has not made the investments needed to meet the government target. As demonstrated in Chapter 8, the benefits to the United States of restricting CFCs were perceived to be very high, making the promise by the United States to restrict CFCs unilaterally credible. Indeed, during the course of the negotiations leading up to Montreal, the US Congress debated legislation calling for "unilateral US measures in the event that the international negotiations failed."

Though the threat to regulate unilaterally was credible, the size of the market for CFC-substitutes depended on the outcome of the international negotiations. If these failed, and the United States acted unilaterally, the market for substitutes would be relatively small. The US industry would prefer that the regulations apply globally, for then the fixed costs of substitution could be spread over a much greater volume of sales. Global regulations would also create a level playing field. Indeed, bills reaching the floor of the US Congress calling for unilateral action included provisions for trade restrictions against nations that did not also restrict CFCs.

As noted in Chapter 8, when the Ozone Trends Panel concluded that the link between CFCs and ozone depletion was all but certain, Du Pont, the world's largest producer of CFCs, announced that it would increase R&D spending on substitutes and stop making CFCs by the end of the century. This was an extraordinary move, and one that had two positive knock-on effects.

The first was in accelerating the pace of the on-going negotiations. The Du Pont pledge was unconditional, but the company strongly urged governments to phase out CFCs world wide. When the main producer of a chemical says its product poses a risk to public health and should be banned, it is pretty hard for governments to defend a contrary policy. That Du Pont produced CFCs in several countries probably also helped.

The second knock-on effect was in impelling rivals to join Du Pont in supporting a phase out. Collectively, the CFC industry may have been better off if it had been allowed to continue producing CFCs. This way, the costs of R&D and new plant and equipment could be avoided. However, manufacturers of CFCs were thought to have an advantage in manufacturing CFC-substitutes. So the losers of a CFC-ban would also be the winners. Once Du Pont announced its intention to supply the market for substitutes, the status quo changed. Governments were more likely to require a cut in CFCs, and the money was to be made in the new markets, not the old. Given Du Pont's move, it became irresistible for Du Pont's rivals to change their behavior. Du Pont made its announcement in March 1988. By September of that year, the Alliance for Responsible CFC Policy—a coalition of US producer and user companies—announced its support for a phase-out. Later, European producers followed suit. A different kind of cascading behavior was thus triggered by the Du Pont announcement. All it took was for one company to "break ranks," as it were, and then every company had an incentive to reverse policy. The industry was tipped.

9.6. TREATY BANDWAGONS

Coordination becomes a problem if no country has an incentive to regulate unilaterally. For then threshold effects become important. Figure 9.1 gives an example of how interdependence in costs can make international environmental protection a coordination game (see Appendix 9.1 for details). Here, there are two symmetric equilibria in pure strategies. One is the familiar equilibrium in which every country plays Pollute. The other equilibrium is the full cooperative outcome in which every country plays Abate. Provided at least three countries play Abate, every country will play Abate. The challenge to the international system is not how to sustain full cooperation by means of an international agreement. This is easy. The problem is to get to the preferred equilibrium in the first place. This may require an international agreement to kick-start the process. For once the agreement gets at least three countries to participate, it will have created a bandwagon. Eventually, every country will participate.

To get the bandwagon going, the agreement needs to assure countries that they will cross the threshold—the point at which the two payoff curves cross, the tipping point. The way to do this is to require that every signatory play Abate and for the agreement to come into force, and therefore to be legally binding on signatories, only if a minimum number of countries has ratified the agreement; otherwise, signatories may act as they please. This way, becoming a signatory to the treaty becomes a (weakly) dominant strategy for every country; a country cannot lose by signing, but it will gain provided enough others sign. But then, once enough others sign, it will be in the interests of every country to sign. A kind of bandwagon will have been created.

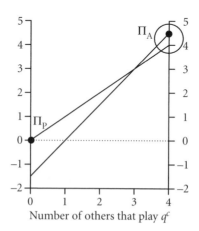

Figure 9.1. *A tipping treaty*

For the situation described in Figure 9.1, any minimum participation level of three or greater would suffice to get the bandwagon going.

I must emphasize that the treaty is providing a real service. It cannot be supposed that countries will be able to coordinate just by communicating. As explained in Chapter 4, so long as each player can guarantee for itself a higher payoff by playing Pollute than by playing Abate, we cannot be sure that the welfare-superior equilibrium will be sustained without an international agreement.

When an agreement only has to coordinate state behavior, actual participation will typically exceed the minimum participation level and enforcement mechanisms will be unnecessary. Most regional and global agreements do attract participation levels that exceed the minimum. Most also do not include enforcement mechanisms. But this does not mean that these treaties sustain full cooperation. Nor does it mean that most agreements need only coordinate state behavior. As explained in Chapter 1, some treaties may not help much. Being unsuccessful at negotiating an agreement that sustains real cooperation, negotiators may settle for one that expresses concern about a problem or that imposes obligations that countries were sure to meet anyway. Such a treaty would obviously not require any enforcement. It might include a minimum participation level, if for no other reason than that this is a boiler-plate clause in every multilateral agreement. And this minimum participation level may be chosen low enough to ensure that the agreement enters into force. But the environment may have been as well off had the agreement never been negotiated. A different kind of agreement, perhaps incorporating enforcement measures, may have helped more. Whether abatement is a coordination problem depends on whether abatement is a strategic complement and whether there exist threshold effects. These features in turn depend on the technology and economics of interdependence.

9.7. NETWORK EXTERNALITIES

Coordination is often a feature of games involving technology choices, as illustrated by the story told in Chapter 4 of the spread in the use of unleaded petrol and catalytic converters. In this example, there is no transnational environmental externality—the pollution is strictly local. But there is a transnational *network externality*, and this makes adoption of the technology standard a strategic complement.

Network externalities are common in many markets. A classic example is the telephone. The value to me of owning a telephone increases in the number of other people (with whom I want to communicate) who own phones. In the car example, the payoff to one country of requiring catalytic converters increases in the number of neighboring countries requiring catalytic converters. Use of the electric car and fuel cell technology also will only spread if there develops an expansive network of refueling stations.

Network externalities are not a feature of most environmental technologies. One country's demand for scrubbers (used to remove sulfur dioxide emissions from flue gases), for example, does not depend on the use of scrubbers by any other country. However, as explained below, it may be possible for countries to *create* a network externality and thus to promote adoption of a technology that may help to protect the environment.

9.8. OCEAN DUMPING CASE STUDY

When you think of oil being dumped at sea, you probably think of major tanker spills—accidents, like the *Exxon Valdez* and the *Torrey Canyon*. However, oil tankers deliberately and routinely discharge oil into the sea, and though the effect of each controlled release may be minuscule, the total effect of all such releases adds up to a significant environmental problem. Historically, for every ton of oil dumped into the sea by accident, another four tons is released deliberately.[2] In 1989, the year the *Exxon Valdez* ran aground, more than twelve times as much oil was released intentionally into the seas as was spilled by accident in Prince William Sound.

Intentional oil releases occur for several reasons. The most important is that a tanker designed only to carry liquids must carry sea water to provide ballast after a ship has completed an oil delivery. The ballast water mixes with the oil residues, and when the tanks are later pumped out before the next pick-up, the oil–water mixture enters the sea.[3] Sea water may also be used to clean the storage tanks before being refilled with a different grade of oil, and oil may also leak into a tanker's bilges. Technically, it is possible to separate the oil from these oil–water mixtures. But doing so is costly. To the tanker operator, who is unlikely to care much about the environmental consequences of his actions, dumping oil improves the bottom line.

9.8.1. Performance Standards

How should these deliberate discharges be controlled? Regulation began by doing the obvious—imposing quantitative limits on allowed releases, supplemented by more severe limits closer to shore and, later, outright bans in ecologically sensitive areas. At first, restrictions on discharges were imposed unilaterally. In the early 1920s, for example, Britain and the United States—great maritime powers with long and vulnerable coastlines—banned oil discharges within their three-mile territorial limits. This was as much as they could do. Under the rules of international law, foreign tankers could dump as much oil as they pleased outside the three-mile limit, and the coastal state could do nothing about it. This is why an international agreement was needed.

In 1926, an international conference on oil dumping proposed establishing a 50-mile zone from the shore, within which oil releases greater than 500 ppm were to be prohibited. The agreement was never signed, but it did put down a marker. Future negotiations would also focus on performance standards within particular zones.

A new round of negotiations began in 1935. The earlier 500 ppm standard was endorsed by the new agreement, but the zone within which this standard applied was

---

[2] See Mitchell (1993), especially table 5.1. Oil is also released from land-based sources and offshore production. And it is released naturally. Natural seepage is a significant problem in a number of areas, including the waters off Santa Barbara.

[3] Alien species may also be transported around the world, another transnational environmental problem. See Elton (2000).

extended to a possible 150-mile limit. Negotiators also considered requiring parties to provide reception facilities at their ports for oil–water mixtures, but the proposal was rejected. At the time, only seven of the negotiating countries had such facilities, and it was believed that others would not comply with the requirement. Much like the first sulphur protocol, it appears that negotiators were trying only to codify what states would have done without an agreement. In any event, Germany, Italy, and Japan rejected the agreement, and a conference at which the treaty was supposed to be signed was never held. Instead, the world began preparing for war.

In 1954, a new conference was convened. This time a 100 ppm standard was proposed within a 50-mile zone. The new standard was tougher than the restrictions proposed previously, but like these it only served to redistribute oil releases; it did nothing to reduce them. Moreover, like the earlier agreements, the new one included only the weakest of enforcement provisions. Ship masters were required to keep a record of all releases, and port states were allowed to inspect these, but verification was nearly impossible and only flag states could prosecute. By this time, however, the tanker trade had increased. Oil pollution became a commonplace on popular beaches, providing an incentive for governments to do *something*. And so, unlike the earlier agreements, the International Convention for the Prevention of Pollution of the Sea by Oil (or OILPOL) was signed and ratified by enough countries, including at least five major shipping states, to enter into force. Unfortunately, the enforcement provisions of the treaty meant that the agreement probably had no effect. According to Ronald Mitchell (1993: 203), a political scientist and author of a fascinating work on this subject, "Enforcement by flag states and beyond states' territorial waters of three miles was nonexistent despite the treaty's 50-mile zones." By not providing either the means or the incentives to enforce, the agreement improved little if at all on unilateralism. Three years after entering into force, a report by the Intergovernmental Maritime Consultative Organization (later renamed the International Maritime Organization) concluded that the treaty's greatest achievement was that it had "created a framework for further progress" (Mitchell 1994: 86).

In 1962, the agreement was amended to require that new tankers over a certain size be prohibited from discharging oil anywhere in the ocean. However, like the earlier agreements, there was no requirement that the port facilities needed to implement this new rule be provided. Nor was enforcement tightened.

In 1969, the agreement was amended again. This time, tankers were prohibited from releasing more than 60 L of oil per mile outside the 50-mile zone, a requirement that was easily met since only the rate of discharge needed to be controlled. The amendments also required that only "clean ballast" be discharged within the 50-mile zone, making detection of an oily sheen on the water evidence of a violation. Finally the agreement limited total discharges to 1/15,000 of a tanker's capacity, compliance with which could be verified simply by checking whether a tanker's cargo was clean. However, enforcement remained weak. Port inspections of cargo tanks were prohibited, and coastal states were still prevented from prosecuting violations by third parties occurring beyond the three-mile territorial limit. Anyway, the 1969 amendments did not enter into force until 1978, and by that time a different kind of regime had been created.

By the early 1970s, it was apparent that sovereignty, and especially the rights of flag states, made the performance standards approach ineffective. Negotiators began to look for another way to skin the cat of tanker pollution. Their attention turned to equipment standards.

9.8.2. Equipment Standards

The shift in direction began in 1972, when the United States passed the Ports and Waterways Safety Act. This required that the Coast Guard adopt equipment standards for tankers unilaterally by 1976 if an international agreement doing so had not been negotiated. Ships violating the US standards were to be barred from US waters.

Helped by this threat, another international conference was convened in 1973 to negotiate the International Convention for the Prevention of Pollution from Ships, known as MARPOL. The agreement tightened up the earlier performance standards a little but its more important contribution was in including new equipment standards. New tankers had to install segregated ballast tanks (to keep ballast water separate from the oil residues), and existing tankers had to do so within three years of the treaty entering into force. Compliance was to be verified by, among other means, regular port inspections. Parties were also authorized to detain ships that presented "an unreasonable threat of harm to the marine environment." Like the earlier agreements, there was no requirement that special port facilities be provided. But this time the need for such facilities was partially obviated by the new tanker equipment standard.

Ratification of this agreement proceeded slowly, and the United States became impatient. The United States even threatened unilateral measures—banning tankers without segregated ballast tanks from US waters—to coerce other states into taking action. It also proposed going much farther than the previous agreement, requiring that tankers have double bottoms or hulls to reduce the risk of accidental spills. Under pressure from the United States, a new conference was convened in 1978. This time, the parties agreed that new tankers over 20,000 tons must install segregated ballast tanks and crude oil washing facilities but that existing tankers over 40,000 tons needed only to install one of these technologies. The latter option was cheaper, and so was sure to be preferred. Indeed, rising oil prices made this technology attractive even without regulation. The new agreement absorbed the 1973 parent convention, and is now known as MARPOL 73/78. It entered into force in 1983.

The equipment standards radically changed the nature of the compliance problem. Compliance with the performance standards was virtually impossible to verify. Even aerial photos of an oil slick would not be accepted as legal evidence of a violation. Besides, even if a violation could be verified by the coastal state, only flag states could prosecute. Flag states have little incentive to do so. The actions of vessels registered under them harm only other coastal states, and why should a flag state care about *their* pollution? Moreover, prosecution by one flag state might only cause other ships flying the same flag to re-register with *another* flag state. So a flag state could justify its inaction by arguing that unilateral regulation would yield no environmental benefit. With flag states having little incentive to prosecute, coastal states had little incentive to monitor and verify. The prisoners' dilemma could not be shifted.

With the equipment standards, verification of compliance was a simple matter; the coastal state needed only carry out a quick inspection. Moreover, flag states did not have to enforce the agreement. Coastal states could do this themselves by banning ships from their ports—if not also by detaining them until they complied with the international standards.[4] No wonder Mitchell (1993) found that compliance with the performance standards was poor but that compliance with the equipment standards was perfect.

9.8.3. Strategic Analysis

Choice of the equipment standards restructured the relationships among the players. Recall the evidence from Chapter 3 suggesting that people are more inclined to play Pollute if they believe others will play Pollute, or if they are not assured that others will play Abate. With the performance standards, each operator could not be sure that his rivals were reducing their discharges, and so had an excuse for not limiting his own. With the equipment standards, matters were very different. "In contrast to discharge standards, each owner could be confident that no other owner could get away with an equipment violation (Mitchell 1993: 235)." At the very least, the equipment standards created a kind of level playing field. It made playing by the new rules seem fair.

My guess is that the incentives to adopt the equipment standards were even greater than suggested by Mitchell. Tanker transport is a network. The value to an owner of having a tanker of a particular design increases in the number of ports to which this tanker is allowed access. For example, there is little point in having a tanker with a huge draft if most ports are not deep enough to accommodate this design. As more states participated in the agreement, participation by others became more attractive—if for no other reason than to gain access to the ports of participating countries. Eventually, a tipping point would be reached; virtually every country would accept the new standard. You can think of it this way. Suppose that every other country is a party to the treaty. Then there would be little to gain by being a non-participant, and by allowing tankers registered under your flag to avoid the international standards. The non-participant's tankers would effectively be unable to make any deliveries to any foreign port. By extension, provided enough others participated in the agreement, it would be in the interests of every country to participate.

In this case, unilateralism would not have sufficed to tip the tanker market. As Mitchell (1993: 242) observes, "Industry would probably have responded to exclusively unilateral US requirements for SBT [that is, segregated ballast tanks] by equipping enough ships with SBT to service the US market, rather than equipping all ships with SBT." As illustrated in Figure 9.1, the *N*-player coordination game typically requires that several countries play Abate before it becomes attractive for every country to play Abate. For the tanker regulation game, the tipping point required substantial

---

[4] Other developments also aided compliance. For example, an increase in the price of oil increased the cost to tanker operators of their own releases. Mitchell (1993) explains how the first OPEC price shock of 1973 shifted the economics of crude oil washing. Before the price increase, washing was uneconomic from the perspective of the operators. After the increase, however, adoption of crude oil washing became a dominant strategy for the operators. For a more comprehensive discussion of the problem, see Mitchell (1993).

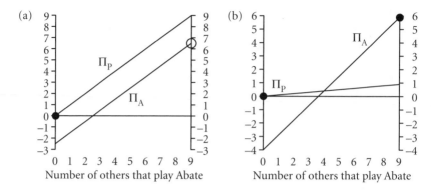

Figure 9.2. *Oil tanker regulation games*
(a) Performance standards game, (b) Equipment standards game

participation. MARPOL 73/78 would only come into force if ratified by at least fifteen countries making up at least half of the gross tonnage of the world's merchant shipping fleet. This substantial threshold seems to have been well chosen. As of September 2002, 121 countries have ratified the agreement. These signatories make up 96.4 percent of world tonnage.[5] Participation in this agreement is virtually full.

Figure 9.2 illustrates the two agreements, the old one (OILPOL) based on performance standards and the new one (MARPOL 73/78) based on equipment standards (the model underlying these figures is developed in the appendix to this chapter). OILPOL tried to shift the prisoners' dilemma game shown in Figure 9.2(a) in the manner described by Chapter 7 but failed. Recall that the model developed in Chapter 7 assumes that compliance is full.[6] With OILPOL, countries could sign the agreement and not worry about complying.

By refocusing on equipment standards, and thus by changing the rules of the game, MARPOL 73/78 was able to do much better. The equipment standards game is essentially a coordination game. It would look more like the game shown in Figure 9.2(b). Having chosen to negotiate equipment standards, the challenge became passing the tipping point—the point of intersection in Figure 9.2(b). This was the role played by the minimum participation clause.

Notice that, as drawn, the equipment standards game is not able to sustain the full cooperative payoffs. The payoff to all countries is maximized if every country plays Abate—and thus implements the performance standards. In Figure 9.2(a), this would give every country a payoff of 6.5. The equipment standards game only yields each country a payoff of 5.9. The reason is that, the model underlying these figures assumes that equipment standards are a more costly means of reducing oil pollution at sea (as well, the equipment standards may be less effective in reducing total oil releases). Of course, it is for this same reason that economists often reject the equipment standards approach. The usual advice given is that regulated parties should be

---

[5] See http://www.imo.org/imo/convent/summary.htm.
[6] The problems of monitoring and enforcing compliance are discussed in Chapter 10.

free to choose how to meet an environmental goal. However, in the international arena technology standards may have a *strategic advantage*. The maximum potential payoff may be beyond our reach, given the constraint of sovereignty. The payoff shown in Figure 9.2(b), attainable only by the use of technical standards, may be the best we can do.

The tanker case teaches two important lessons. First, the tanker market is not a network in the same sense as the telephone. It is technically possible for a tanker that is not fitted with segregated ballast tanks to service any port. However, the treaty was able to *create* a positive network externality by making it attractive for states to enforce the technical standard. Second, the case shows that the choice of *how* to regulate can be strategic. In the case of tanker regulation, one instrument of regulation (the performance standards)—indeed, the instrument that was the most natural choice—was entirely ineffective. It accentuated the dilemma-like quality of the PD game. An alternative and otherwise less appealing instrument (the equipment standards), by contrast, restructured the incentives in such a way that compliance was full and participation was increased. Though the difference might seem modest, the technical standard changed the rules of the game. It transformed the oil dumping game into a coordination game, and this made all the difference.

9.9. CONCLUSION

In the one-shot PD, states have dominant strategies. In some situations, however, this assumption will be violated. What each country does may depend on what others do. There are two kinds of interdependence. When one country plays Abate, others may be more or less inclined to play Abate. If others are more inclined to play Abate, then abatement is a strategic complement. If others are less inclined to play Abate, then abatement is a strategic substitute.

These payoff interdependencies will be a given for any problem. Sometimes we will be lucky and abatement by one country will cause others to abate. This may happen spontaneously. But if there are threshold effects, then an international agreement will be needed to ensure that the positive feedback gets the needed kick-start. The level of control adopted by a treaty must then be chosen strategically.

Even more importantly, the nature of the interdependence may depend on the action that is taken. That is, it may depend on the instrument of regulation. We are accustomed to thinking that instrument choice does not matter, or that it matters only under uncertainty.[7] In the anarchic international environment, however, instrument choice may make a big difference even under conditions of certainty. However, once again negotiators need to be alert to threshold effects. Not only must the instrument be chosen strategically. The level of minimum participation must be chosen strategically, too.

---

[7] See Weitzman's (1974) classic article showing that instrument choice may depend on uncertainty about the costs of control.

Appendix 9.1.

Derivation of Figure 9.1

Figure 9.1 assumes that payoffs are given by

$$\Pi_i(q_i; Q_{-i}) = b(q_i + Q_{-i}) - c\left(\frac{N - Q_{-i}}{N}\right)q_i$$

with $q_i \in \{0, 1\}$. Then, if $Q_{-i} = 0$, i will play $q_i = 0$ provided $c > b > 0$. Suppose, however, that $Q_{-i} = N - 1$. Then, since $N > c/b$ by assumption, i will play $q_i = 1$. Indeed, depending on the parameter values, if "enough" countries play Abate, then each will prefer to play Abate. To be precise, country i will play Abate provided

$$-c\left(\frac{N - Q_{-i}}{N}\right) + b > 0 \quad \text{or} \quad Q_{-i} > N\left(\frac{c - b}{c}\right).$$

The game illustrated in Figure 9.1 assumes $b = 1$, $c = 2.5$, and $N = 5$.

Derivation of Figure 9.2

Figure 9.2 assumes that payoffs take the form:

$$\alpha_i = b\left[N - (1 - q_i)(1 - \alpha t_i) - \sum_{j \neq i}](1 - q_j)(1 - \alpha t_j)\right] - cq_i - \gamma t_i + \beta]t_i - \delta 6 \sum_{j \neq i} t_j,$$

where α, β, γ, and δ are parameters (with non-negative values) and where t_i takes on a value of 1 if i adopts the segregated ballast tank (SBT) technology and a value of 0 if it does not. The parameter α takes on a value between zero and one; $\alpha = 1$ implies that the technology standard is just as effective in reducing emissions as the performance standard (assuming full compliance). The parameter γ is the cost of installing the SBT technology and the final term captures the network externality. This shows that if i does not adopt the technology, then it incurs a cost that increases in the number of countries that do adopt the technology—i's tankers are now shut out of these markets (of course, the environmental benefit to i of other countries adopting SBT is included in the bracketed term). Put differently, as long as δ is less than one, there is a benefit to i of adopting SBT that increases in the number of others that adopt SBT.

Notice that, so long as $t_i = 0$ for all i, the above game is identical to the game studied in Chapter 7. This is the prisoners' dilemma shown in Figure 9.2(a). By contrast, setting $q_i = 0$ for all i yields Figure 9.2(b). The network externality makes this game a coordination game. The games shown in Figure 9.2 assume $b = 1$, $c = 3.5$, $\alpha = 1$, $\gamma = 5$, $\beta = 1$, $\delta = 0.9$, and $N = 10$.

10

Compliance and the Strategy of Reciprocity

Speak softly and carry a big stick. President Theodore Roosevelt (1901)

10.1. INTRODUCTION

A measure of cooperation was sustained by a self-enforcing agreement in Chapter 7 only because signatories were assumed to comply fully with the agreement. If we were to drop this assumption, cooperation would unravel. The reason is that the collectively rational abatement level prescribed by the treaty is not individually rational. Each signatory could thus gain by reducing its abatement—even if only by a little—while none of the other signatories would have the opportunity to punish any such deviation. Given the chance, every signatory would thus deviate. Once we abandon the assumption of full compliance in the stage game, cooperation falls apart.

Of course, the analysis of Chapter 7 did rely on individual rationality as regards participation—the decision by signatories to remain within a treaty (as well as the decision by non-signatories to stay out). So Chapter 7 did not assume that states would comply with just *any* agreement. It merely assumed that signatories would comply with the agreements from which signatories did not want to withdraw unilaterally (and to which non-signatories did not want to accede unilaterally). This may seem a subtle distinction but it will prove important to the conclusions reached in this book about compliance and participation.

This chapter investigates the incentives for compliance, and the mechanisms needed to enforce compliance. It constructs a different kind of model from the one developed in Chapter 7, a model based on repeated interactions in which enforcement is endogenous. Nonetheless, the model developed here is compatible with the one developed previously. Indeed, the main conclusions of this chapter derive from a comparison of the results for the two models.

10.2. COMPLIANCE vs PARTICIPATION

As a practical matter, the assumption of full compliance adopted in Chapter 7 might seem innocent enough. States *do* tend to comply fully with their treaty obligations. Indeed, legal experts Abram Chayes and Antonia Chayes (1991: 311) introduce their analysis on compliance by noting that "international lawyers and others familiar with the operations of international treaties take for granted that most states comply with most of their treaty obligations most of the time." But we must be careful. The observation that states comply with the agreements to which they have acceded does *not* imply that they would comply with the agreements modeled in Chapter 7. These agreements require that states undertake more abatement than in the non-cooperative outcome. Most of the agreements listed in the Appendix 6.1 do not ask signatories to make such sacrifices.

The Chayeses (1991: 311) argue, however, that "states' behavior in entering into treaties suggests that they believe they are accepting significant constraints on future freedom of action to which they expect to adhere over a broad range of circumstances." So perhaps compliance can be relied upon even where treaties sustain real cooperation. But even this observation is consistent with a different reading of the evidence. The tipping treaties discussed in Chapter 9 constrain the behavior of their parties. But such treaties are self-enforcing in the sense that no party can gain by unilaterally failing to comply with them. The agreements modeled in Chapter 7 are of a very different stripe, and it would be wrong to assume that states would comply with *these* agreements just because they have complied with others.

Another way of looking at this is to consider the strategies that states choose rather than the outcomes that result from these choices. The agreements modeled in Chapter 7 do not incorporate non-compliance mechanisms, and nor, usually, do actual treaties. According to the Chayeses (1991: 313), "not only are formal enforcement mechanisms seldom used to secure compliance with treaties, but they are rarely even embodied in the treaty text." While this evidence would again seem to support the assumption of full compliance, the absence of explicit punishment mechanisms might only imply that particular agreements could do without them, rather than that the agreements modeled in Chapter 7 do not require them. Of course, it is also possible that actual treaties are sustained by *informal* enforcement mechanisms. But since such mechanisms are left out of the analysis of International Environmental Agreements (IEAs) in Chapter 7, one cannot be sure whether the agreements examined in this chapter could be sustained by informal mechanisms either.

It is widely accepted that compliance with actual IEAs is nearly full and that treaties rarely incorporate non-compliance mechanisms. What *is* now being disputed are the implications of these facts. The Chayeses (1991, 1993, 1995) conclude that such mechanisms are unnecessary, that even in their absence treaties are able to sustain something pretty close to full cooperation. More than that, they argue that sanctions are ultimately damaging to international cooperation. Political scientists George Downs, David Rocke, and Peter Barsoom (1996), by contrast, argue that international accords rarely improve much on the non-cooperative outcome and that they could only do so if they enforced compliance, either by means of treaty-based mechanisms (in their language, "centralized" enforcement) or by more diffuse means, building on international linkages, unilateral actions, and domestic law ("decentralized" enforcement). Put a little more crudely, the Chayeses advocate the "speak softly" approach to compliance, whereas Downs *et al.* counsel the need to "carry a big stick."

Who is right? The answer is not obvious because the analyses underpinning both views start from different premises. The Chayeses believe that the problems of free-rider deterrence and compliance enforcement can be decoupled. Downs *et al.* (1996) focus on the question of treaty compliance, though their analysis could be interpreted more broadly.[1]

In Chapter 7 we found that, even if compliance with international agreements were full, the anarchic international system might not be able to sustain efficient outcomes. This suggests that, even if the Chayeses were right that compliance can be upheld without the need for punishments or sanctions, their conclusion that (in the language of this book) full cooperation can be sustained may be way off the mark. It suggests, too, that Downs *et al.* may be right that agreements typically sustain less than full cooperation, but that they may be wrong that the reason for this is weak compliance enforcement. Deterrence of non-participation may be the greater problem.[2]

In this chapter I consider the deterrence of a generic deviation—one that could be interpreted as non-participation *or* as a failure to comply—and I shall obtain results that are consistent with the results given in Chapter 7. Since the model in Chapter 7 assumed that compliance was full, the theory developed here suggests that compliance enforcement is not the binding constraint on international cooperation. Participation—more generally, free-rider deterrence—is the greater problem (Barrett 1999*a*).

10.3. THE STRATEGY OF RECIPROCITY

Imagine that the one-shot prisoners's dilemma (PD) game is repeated, and suppose that, in a pre-play communication round, all players pledge to play Abate. In the one-shot prisoners's dilemma game, as we saw in Chapter 3, pre-play communication cannot shift the equilibrium. Whatever was agreed before play of the game, play Pollute will be a dominant strategy. If the game is repeated, however, a player can be punished for failing to fulfill its promise to play Abate. If a player deviated from the

---

[1] To be specific, their concern lies with the "depth of cooperation"—in the case of pollution, defined as "the reduction [required by a treaty] relative to a counterfactual estimate of the ... pollution level that would exist in the absence of a treaty" (Downs *et al.* 1996: 383). Unfortunately, they do not distinguish between the pollution levels of individual countries and the totals, or between the behavior of participants and non-participants. (In Chapter 11, I distinguish between "depth," meaning the abatement levels of treaty participants, and "breadth," meaning the level of participation.) Their formal analysis is of a two-player PD-like game, where "cheating can be limited or flagrant" (Downs *et al.* 1996: 384). Technically, non-participation isn't "cheating." Non-participation is legal. It is also practiced quite openly. As I argue later, however, non-participation involves a deviation from the cooperative level at least as large as any act of non-compliance. The Downs, Rocke, and Barsoom analysis does note that larger deviations can only be deterred using larger punishments, and so contains the seeds of the answers provided here. Since larger deviations from full cooperation are harder to deter, a treaty that can deter non-participation can deter non-compliance. Note, however, that the approach used by these authors differs substantially from my own. I incorporate specific requirements for credibility, including subgame perfection and collective rationality. I investigate an *N*-player game, and show that the two-player situation is a very special case. And my analysis of generic deviations from full cooperation (deviations that could be interpreted as acts of non-participation or non-compliance) are assessed relative to the game developed in Chapter 7 that focuses exclusively on the participation problem. It is by comparing these two solutions that I am able to conclude that non-participation is the binding constraint on international cooperation.

[2] Downs *et al.* (1996) only explicitly address the participation issue in the last paragraph of their paper, where they ask whether countries might want to limit participation in a treaty in order to deepen cooperation. This idea is developed formally in Chapter 11.

agreement by playing Pollute in some period T, say, the other player(s) could retaliate by playing Pollute in round $T + 1$ and perhaps thereafter. Though a player would gain in the short run by deviating, it could be made to lose in the long run. Provided players do not discount future payoffs too much, the full cooperative outcome of the one-shot game can be sustained as an equilibrium of the repeated game (I shall demonstrate this formally in Section 10.5).

That repeated play can sustain full cooperation as an equilibrium is well known. But the implications of this are not always appreciated. For in resolving one problem (that of allowing compliance to be an equilibrium behavior), the repeated version of the one-shot game throws up another. If the problem with the one-shot PD game is that cooperation can never be sustained as an equilibrium, the problem with the folk theorems for repeated games is that, under certain assumptions, *any* feasible outcome can be sustained as an equilibrium. I have already sketched how the full cooperative outcome could be sustained as an equilibrium of the repeated PD. It is even easier to see that the non-cooperative outcome can also be sustained as an equilibrium of this game. Suppose Country X plays Always Pollute. Then Country Y can do no better than to play Always Pollute. The strategy Play Pollute Always is thus an equilibrium.

In a sense, the theory of repeated games suggests that the problem of international cooperation is more one of choosing an equilibrium than of free-rider deterrence or compliance enforcement. Indeed, because IEAs can be negotiated openly (the rules of the game permit pre-play communication), even the equilibrium selection problem seems trivial. When all feasible outcomes can be sustained as an equilibrium of the repeated game, collective rationality dictates that the full cooperative outcome actually be selected, and pre-play communication helps to ensure that this outcome will actually be selected. If the one-shot PD compels one to ask how cooperation could *ever* be sustained, the theory of repeated games begs the question of why full cooperation is not *always* sustained.

One of the principal aims of this chapter is to show that this reasoning is wrong, that the full cooperative outcome cannot always be sustained by a self-enforcing agreement, even for very small discount rates. The reason is that the folk theorems for repeated games satisfy individual rationality but not collective rationality. Sovereignty makes individual rationality essential to any theory of international relations. But collective rationality is also important, not least because treaties are negotiated and their contents made public (see Chapter 6). We saw in Chapter 7 that collective rationality prevents the full cooperative outcome from being sustained as an equilibrium under the assumption of full compliance. I shall show here that collective rationality also prevents the full cooperative outcome from being sustained as an equilibrium when compliance is not assumed but is rather enforced by a strategy of reciprocity.

10.4. RECIPROCITY AND STATE SUCCESSION

More than just a little repetition is needed to sustain cooperation.[3] Consider repeated play of the PD. Suppose both countries know that the game will be played exactly

---

[3] Experiments by Fehr and Gächter (2000a) suggest that people may cooperate even in finite games, provided there exist opportunities to punish non-cooperators. However, the situation studied by Fehr and

twice and that this is common knowledge. Then, if one country failed to comply with an agreement to play Abate in the first round of the game, the other could punish it in the second period by playing Pollute. However, since the game will not be played a third time, neither player can be punished for failing to cooperate in round two. This means that neither player can do better than to play Pollute in round two, whatever happened in round one. The promise to play Abate in period two provided the other player played Abate in period one is thus not credible. Whatever the agreement may say, each player can do no better than to play Pollute in both periods.

Indeed, though this example supposed that the game was played twice, it is easy to see that, provided the game is played a *finite* number of times, both players know this number, both know that the other knows this number, and so on, the unique equilibrium is that both players play Pollute every period. Cooperation can only be sustained as an equilibrium if there *always* exists the prospect that non-compliance can be punished, as would be the case if the game were repeated infinitely often, or if the game were repeated a finite number of times but neither player knew precisely when it would end.

That states interact repeatedly is obvious. That their interactions should satisfy the above requirements, however, is less apparent. Stein (1983, 1990), for example, argues that indefinite repetition does not feature in international relations because states can disappear. Axelrod (1984: 188), by contrast, claims that "the good thing about international relations is that the major powers can be quite certain they will be interacting with each other year after year."

It is true that states can disappear—but this is not important to the theory. What matters to the theory is whether it is known in advance which states will disappear, and when. As long as there is a positive probability that a state will exist in the future, there remains a potential for reciprocity to do its work.

Even more importantly, though a state may disappear, its citizenry will not, and at a fundamental level relations between states are relations between the collective citizenry of states. Indeed, international law prohibits a new state from instantly disassociating itself from the relationships established by its predecessor. Where a new state is created by the merger of existing states (as when Tanzania was created by the union of Tanganyika and Zanzibar in 1964), the new state is required to assume the treaty obligations by which the former states were bound.[4] Where one state is divided into two or more new states, international law requires that these new states assume the treaty responsibilities of the former state. Similarly, when a new government takes power, whether by the bullet or the ballot box, the international obligations entered

Gächter differs from the focus of this chapter. In Fehr and Gächter's paper, the punishments are personalized. Each punishment harms only the person being punished and the person imposing the punishment. In the games examined in this chapter, punishments cannot be targeted in this way. The only way to punish is by restricting provision of the public good—an action that harms *every* player.

[4] The reunification of Germany is different. A new state was not created; rather, the former GDR was merged into the existing FRG. In this case, the treaties and agreements to which the FRG had been a party apply to the territory of the former GDR also. The responsibilities of the new Germany with respect to the treaty obligations of the former GDR are more problematic, but even here procedures were developed for effecting the succession. See Shaw (1991), pp. 626–7.

into by its predecessor must still be obeyed. Particular states can thus expect to inter-act in the future not least because international law endeavors to ensure that they *will* interact in the future.

10.5. TREATY- vs CUSTOM-BASED COMPLIANCE

Compliance by reciprocity can be treaty- or custom-based. An example of a treaty-based compliance mechanism is the one derived in Chapter 7: k states agree to abate their emissions indefinitely, and they further agree that, should any party fail to play Abate in any period, the treaty will thereafter terminate. This example is styled after the Fur Seal Treaty, but it is not essential that a treaty-based punishment be this severe. Nor is it necessary that the punishment mechanism be this explicit (see Keohane 1986). The essential feature of a treaty-based compliance mechanism is that it relies only on internal enforcement; non-parties play no role in enforcing compliance.

Custom-based compliance is different. As noted in Chapter 5, after a treaty enters into law, parties to the treaty automatically assume an *obligation* to comply with it. States are obligated to comply not just because they promised the other parties to the treaty that they would comply but because customary law says that they must comply.

How is this customary law, sometimes called the "compliance norm," sustained? Though custom is not enforced by specific penalties, it may be enforced via linkage with the many interdependencies that connect different states. Here is an illustration. Suppose Country Y contemplates violating a bilateral treaty it has concluded with X. It may be that X cannot punish Y in this particular instance, perhaps because X and Y will not interact again for a long time. Y then has no direct incentive to comply with the treaty. But in violating the treaty, Y would also be violating the compliance norm, and states other than X may be able to punish Y for this violation because *they* may be interacting with Y in the near future. Furthermore, it may be in the interests of these other states to punish Y, even if they were unaffected by the original violation. The rea-son is that, in failing to punish Y, they fail to assist X, and X may then reciprocate by failing to punish norm-violators that harm *these* countries in the future. Treaties are games, but they are also linked by an extended network, what might be called the Grand Game of International Relations. Even if compliance with a particular treaty cannot be sustained as an equilibrium when the interaction is viewed in isolation of all other interactions, it may be sustained as an equilibrium in a richer setting.[5]

But even this kind of enforcement might not be sufficient to sustain full coopera-tion, or anything approaching it. Keohane (1986) suggests that norms arising from *diffuse reciprocity* would need to go beyond the enforcement capabilities of specific reciprocity.[6] It would help, for example, if states complied with agreements not only because it was in their interests to do so but "in the interests of continuing satisfactory

---

[5] Kandori (1992) develops a model along these lines, and further considers instances in which defec-tions are observed only imperfectly.

[6] See also Keohane (1984) and Chayes and Chayes (1995). Elster (1989) provides arguments for why norms need not arise out of, or be compatible with, self-interest.

overall results for the group of which one is a part, as a whole" (Keohane 1986: 20). Suppose, for example, that states followed a rule like: if other states comply with an agreement (or at least if *enough* other states comply), then your state must comply.[7] This would certainly help. But suppose it was not in the interests of a state to comply. Then what? At this point, we might hope that the Chayeses (1993) were right in believing that states had a general propensity to comply with international agreements. For then we would not need to worry so much about incentives. And if the propensity to comply were sufficiently strong, it might even be concluded that states complied because they believed it was *right* to do so (with right superceding a state's interests), or because they had "internalized" the compliance norm; see Dasgupta (1993).

In my view we *do* need to think broadly about these matters. Though a state's foreign policy is primarily aimed at advancing the national interest, it is often justified in other terms. A state's policy may reflect what it perceives as being right and not just expedient. And states do not calculate whether compliance really is in their self-interests minute-by-minute. Barring a significant change in circumstances, states normally do what they agreed to do, what other states expect them to do, and what they in turn expect others to do: they obey the custom; they comply.

Suppose, then, that we made the very strong assumption that the compliance norm of custom has been internalized. Then what? The assumption would seem to make cooperation easy. However, it turns out that this assumption has absolutely no effect on the level of cooperation that can be sustained.

As Dean Rusk put it, a state exercises its sovereignty by going into an agreement—by choosing to participate. If a state anticipates that future compliance with the treaty will not be in its interests, then it will choose not to participate rather than to participate and not comply. Once in, a state accepts that its freedom of action is limited by the compliance norm. And if its interests become seriously compromised by a treaty, the likely outcome is a withdrawal, not non-compliance. Because international law recognizes the right of a state not to participate, the constraint of compliance need not bind at all. No wonder the compliance norm is habitually obeyed.

Countries can also avoid having to comply by more devious means, without violating the letter of the law. Restrictions on whaling imposed by the International Whaling Commission (IWC) led to an increase in the taking of whales by non-signatories (the so-called "pirate" whalers). Yet at least some pirate whaling was non-compliance by another name. Japan, for example, got around the IWC restrictions by re-registering its vessels under the flags of non-parties (Rose and Paleokrassis 1996). Chile became a pirate whaling nation in the 1950s, with Japanese financing, crews, and ships.[8] All these actions were legal.

If internalization of the compliance norm cannot assist cooperation, then clearly the compliance norm of customary law cannot bind. Treaty-based compliance mechanisms may be needed, but they too cannot bind. The binding constraint on cooperation is

---

[7] Keohane cites Sugden (1984), who tries to explain voluntary contributions for the supply of public goods as arising from the reciprocity principle that one should not free ride when others are contributing.
[8] Chile joined the ICRW in 1979, after the United States threatened Pelly Amendment certification.

deterring non-participation—more generally, free-riding. This, of course, was an assumption underlying my analysis in Chapter 7. At the same time, this analysis, being static, was unable to derive an explicit strategy for deterring non-participation. In the analysis to follow, I shall develop such a strategy—and prove the assertion that compliance is not the binding constraint on international cooperation.

10.6. GRIM TREATIES

Let me now show formally how cooperation can be sustained as an equilibrium without the assumption of full compliance.

Consider the infinitely repeated version of the one-shot PD game shown in Figure 3.1. Suppose that the two players negotiate an agreement in which they each pledge to play Abate and that they further agree that, should either player play Pollute in any period, then the treaty will be nullified and both countries will thereafter revert to playing Pollute forever. Can this "Grim" strategy sustain full cooperation as an equilibrium?

The answer depends on whether either country could do better by reneging. If both players comply fully with the agreement, each will receive a payoff of 1 each period. If one country cheats, it will get a one-off payoff of 2, which is greater than 1, but it will then get a payoff of 0 in each succeeding period, and 0 is less than 1. Whether cheating is rational thus depends on whether the short-term gain realized by cheating exceeds the long-term loss.

To compare payoffs realized at different times, let us weight future payoffs by a discount factor δ ($0 < \delta < 1$), such that the present value of the payoff realized at date t is the current value of the payoff multiplied by δ^t.

If both players comply fully with the agreement, then at time $t = 0$ each will earn $1 + \delta + \delta^2 + \delta^3 + \cdots$. A player that cheats in period T, however, will get $1 + \delta + \cdots + \delta^{T-1} + 2\delta^T + 0 + 0 + \cdots$. Compliance will only be in each country's self-interest if the former stream of payoffs is at least as great as the latter. It is a simple matter to show that this implies $\delta \geq 1/2$;[9] More generally, given the ordering of the payoffs in the one-shot PD game, the full cooperative outcome can be sustained as a subgame-perfect equilibrium of the infinitely repeated game provided the discount factor is sufficiently close to one; see Friedman (1971).

Let us now consider the infinitely repeated version of the one-shot game described by Figure 3.6(a). There are 100 countries. If they all cooperate fully they will each earn a per-period payoff of 1. If one player were to deviate, however, it would earn a payoff of 2 in the period in which it deviated, while the remaining 99 players would each get a payoff of only 0.98 in this period. Now suppose that the 100 countries negotiate a treaty in which they pledge to play Abate in the first period and every successive period provided no country played Pollute previously but that, should any player

---

[9] The payoff to complying fully with the agreement is at least as great as the payoff to deviating if $\delta^T + \delta^{T+1} + \cdots \geq 2\delta^T + 0 + \cdots$, or $\delta^{T+1} + \delta^{T+2} + \cdots \geq \delta^T$. Dividing both sides by δ^T yields $\delta + \delta^2 + \cdots \geq 1$. But the term on the left of this inequality can be rewritten as $\delta/(1 - \delta)$. Hence, complying fully with the agreement is individually rational if $\delta \geq 1/2$.

play Pollute in any period, every country will thereafter play Pollute forever. Can this agreement sustain the full cooperative outcome as an equilibrium?

The answer depends again on whether it is in the national interests of each of the parties to comply fully with the agreement. At date T, provided all other players comply with the agreement, each will get a present value payoff of $\delta^T + \delta^{T+1} + \delta^{T+2} + \cdots$ by complying, too. If a player should deviate, however, it would get a payoff stream of $2\delta^T + 0 + 0 + \cdots$. Given that the all others comply, each player could do no better than to comply, provided $\delta \geq 1/2$. It is a coincidence that this numerical result is identical to the result obtained earlier for the two-player game, but it is no coincidence that the qualitative results are the same. If players are sufficiently patient, the full cooperative outcome can be sustained as an equilibrium (in the sense defined above) by *any* number of players.

The Grim strategy calls for the complete dissolution of an agreement should any of its parties cheat. This is a severe punishment. But the strategy is feasible; international law allows it to be used. According to Article 60 of the Vienna Convention on the Law of Treaties, "a material breach of a multilateral treaty by one of the parties entitles … the other parties by unanimous agreement to suspend the operation of the treaty in whole or in part or to terminate it either: (i) in the relations between themselves and the defaulting State, or (ii) as between *all the parties* [emphasis added]" (Brownlie 1990: 618).

Do any agreements actually employ this strategy? Certainly, all bilateral treaties have this feature. So did the Convention on Conservation of North Pacific Fur Seals, in both its 1957 and 1976 versions. As explained previously, Article XII effectively requires that each of the parties play Grim.

The punishment of terminating an agreement is severe. But is it credible? It may not be because the countries that enforce the agreement harm themselves in the bargain. In the example above, defection by just one country reduces the per-period payoffs of each the other 99 parties from 1 to 0.98. In carrying out the threat to revert to playing Pollute forever, however, the per-period payoffs of each of these countries would fall to 0. Not only is the punishment disproportionate to the harm done by the defection (the punishment is never-ending), but the countries that comply fully with the agreement are harmed much more by their own act of enforcement than by the original act of non-compliance! As Shaw (1991: 596) has noted, "to render treaties revocable because one party has acted contrary to what might very well be only a minor provision in the agreement taken as a whole, would be to place the states participating in a treaty in rather a vulnerable position. There is a need for flexibility as well as certainty in such situations." But flexibility is no easy remedy either; flexibility can undermine the credibility of the threat to terminate a treaty.

10.7. CREDIBLE PUNISHMENTS AND INDIVIDUAL RATIONALITY

Notwithstanding the above criticisms, however, the Grim strategy *is* credible in the sense that it is subgame-perfect. If a country failed to comply with a treaty, and if all the other parties to the agreement obeyed the Grim strategy and punished the defection, it would be in the interests of each state to play Grim.[10]

By contrast, the more forgiving and certainly more famous "Tit-For-Tat" strategy is *not* subgame-perfect. Tit-For-Tat requires that each player begin by playing Abate and that each continue to play Abate so long as all the other players played Abate in the previous period. If, however, any player should play Pollute in any period, then each of the other players must play Pollute in the succeeding period. Only after the defector has played Abate should the other players return once again to playing Abate. (Moreover, should any country not return to playing Abate when required to do so by this strategy, then *this* country must be punished by the other parties; and so on.)

Consider again the game depicted in Figure 3.1. Suppose player Y plays Pollute in period T and then reverts to Tit-For-Tat. In reverting to Tit-For-Tat, Y must play the same move as did X in the previous round. So, in round $T + 1$, Y will play Abate. But if X is playing Tit-For-Tat then it must play Pollute in period $T + 1$ in order to punish Y for defecting. This means that Y will play Pollute in period $T + 1$, while X will play Abate in this period. And so on. Starting in period $T + 1$, if X plays Tit-For-Tat it will get $2\delta^{T + 1} - \delta^{T + 2} + 2\delta^{T + 3} - \delta^{T + 4} + \cdots$. But if X deviates and pretends that Y never cheated, it will get $\delta^{T + 1} + \delta^{T + 2} + \delta^{T + 3} + \cdots$. For discount factors near 1, the average per-period payoff of playing Tit-for-Tat is 1/2, while the average per-period payoff of deviating is 1. Rationality demands that X *not* implement the Tit-For-Tat strategy for sufficiently large discount factors.

That a single defection can, under Tit-For-Tat, result in an "unending echo of alternating defections" (Axelrod 1984: 176) is well known. But this is a criticism against the Tit-For-Tat strategy and not, as is sometimes claimed, every strategy of reciprocity.[11] There exists another forgiving strategy of reciprocity that can sustain cooperation without violating individual rationality. This is the "Getting-Even" strategy (see Myerson 1991).

Getting-Even demands that each country play Abate unless it has played Pollute less often than the other players in the past. Returning to the above example, suppose Y deviates from Getting-Even by playing Pollute in period T. Suppose further that Y thereafter reverts to Getting-Even—so that, in period $T + 1$, Y plays Abate. Country X, in playing Getting-Even, will play Pollute in period $T + 1$. But both players will thereafter play Abate. To see that this is subgame-perfect, notice that, if X plays Getting-Even, then it will get a present value payoff of $2\delta^{T + 1} + \delta^{T + 2} + \delta^{T + 3} + \cdots$. By contrast, if X deviates and plays Abate in period $T + 1$, then it will get $\delta^{T + 1} + \delta^{T + 2} + \delta^{T + 3} + \cdots$. Obviously, the former payoff exceeds the latter. It is easy to show that, for infinitely

---

[10] This requirement of credibility is essential. Thus, while Downs *et al.* (1996: 387) observe that states may be "unwilling or unable to pay the costs of enforcement," they make the mistake of arguing that "the only relevant criterion is that the punishment must hurt the transgressor state at least as much as that state could gain by the violation" (Downs *et al.* 1996: 386). This is one requirement, but it is not sufficient. At the very least, it must also be the case that the countries called upon to punish a violation be better off when doing so. This makes the threat to punish credible in the sense of being subgame perfect (individually rational). Even this is not enough, however. As noted in the next section, a treaty must also be collectively rational; for the two-player game examined by Downs *et al.*, this means that the treaty must be renegotiation-proof.

[11] See Chayes and Chayes (1995), p. 105.

repeated play of the game described by Figure 3.1, given that one player plays Getting-Even, the other can do no better than to play Getting-Even provided $\delta \geq 1/2$.

To summarize, we have identified two strategies of reciprocity that satisfy individual rationality: the unforgiving Grim strategy and the near-cousin of Tit-For-Tat, Getting-Even. But, though Getting-Even and Grim both satisfy this important property, they are otherwise very different strategies. Unlike Getting-Even, Grim imposes a disproportionate punishment. It therefore *seems* less compelling. We shall see below that it is.

10.8. CREDIBLE PUNISHMENTS AND COLLECTIVE RATIONALITY

The problem with the Grim strategy is that it is not *collectively* rational (again, see Myerson 1991).

Consider again infinitely repeated play of the game shown in Figure 3.1. Suppose a player deviates in period T. Then the average per-period continuation payoff for both players is 0. But if the players could re-start cooperation and re-institute the Grim strategy, each would get a payoff of 1 each period. No player has an incentive to deviate from a cooperation phase given that no other player deviates (Grim is individually rational). But collectively the players do have an incentive to deviate from a punishment phase. The threat to implement the Grim strategy punishment is credible from the perspective of each of the parties, but it is not credible from the perspective of *all* of them. It would only be credible if the parties could commit not to renegotiate the agreement. But countries cannot commit in this way. Treaty renegotiation is not only permitted by the rules of international law; renegotiation is a routine operation. An agreement to implement the Grim strategy, therefore, cannot be self-enforcing. Self-enforcing strategies must be renegotiation-proof.[12]

The Getting-Even strategy *is* self-enforcing because it is not only individually rational but also collectively rational. I have shown that Getting-Even is individually rational by showing that the strategy is subgame-perfect (for $\delta \geq 1/2$ in the above example). To show that it is collectively rational we need only show that the agreement employing the Getting-Even strategy is not vulnerable to renegotiation. So suppose that player Y deviates in period T. Then we know that X can do no better than

---

[12] There are several definitions of renegotiation-proof equilibria in the literature. Throughout this book I rely on the definitions in Farrell and Maskin (1989). For further contributions, see van Damme (1989) and Myerson (1991). I adopt the term "collective rationality"—used also by Myerson (1991)—for several reasons. First, it neatly expresses the contrast with individual rationality, another assumption underlying the theory. Second, it gives expression to the tension between individual and collective interests, not just in the underlying PD but in the treaty intending to improve on anarchy. Third, it applies equally to static and dynamic games. Finally, I use the term so as not to confuse my approach with the more conventional concept of a renegotiation-proof equilibrium. Farrell and Maskin (1989) limit their attention to two-player games, partly out of a concern for the formation of coalitions. The concept of collective rationality used here applies to N-player games, but embodies a rather strong assumption about coalitions. Concepts of coalition stability have been applied in different models of cooperation; see, for example, Finus (2001), Chapter 15.

to play Getting-Even in $T + 1$. If X plays Getting-Even it gets a payoff of 2 in period $T + 1$, and deviating can only yield a lower payoff. But given that X has no incentive to renegotiate, Y can do no better than to revert to Getting-Even (given that X plays Getting-Even, reversion is individually rational for Y for $\delta \geq 1/2$).

In this example it happens that the full cooperative outcome can be sustained as an equilibrium that is both subgame-perfect (individually rational) and renegotiation-proof (collectively rational). I show below, however, that this is a special result. Adding the assumption of collective rationality shrinks the set of feasible outcomes that can be sustained by a self-enforcing treaty. The possibility of renegotiation makes cooperation harder to prop up.

10.9. THE REPEATED N-PLAYER DILEMMA GAME

To generalize the repeated dilemma game, suppose that the per-period payoffs are given by eqn (7.1) with $N \geq 2$. Suppose also that b, $c > 0$ and $N > c/b$. Then, as explained in Section 7.4, the underlying game is a PD.

Under what conditions will Getting-Even sustain the full cooperative outcome of this game as an equilibrium? Suppose that all N countries agree to play Getting-Even—but that one such country (call it country j) deviates. To simplify the analysis, suppose that the discount rate is near zero (the discount factor is near one). Then, if j reverts to Getting-Even after having deviated, j will earn an average per-period payoff, $\Pi_j = -c + bN$. If j does not revert to Getting-Even, it will earn $\Pi_j = 0$. Play Getting-Even is thus individually rational provided $N > c/b$, which is true by assumption.

Is Getting-Even also collectively rational? If it is, then the countries other than j must not have an incentive to renegotiate the agreement. If these countries play Getting-Even in the punishment phase, country m, $m \neq j$, gets a payoff of $\Pi_m = b$. If these countries deviate collectively, however, then m will get $\Pi_m = -c + bN$. Play Getting-Even is thus collectively rational provided $b \geq -c + bN$ or

$$\frac{c}{b} + 1 \geq N. \tag{10.1}$$

Condition (10.1) tells us that the full cooperative outcome can only be sustained as an equilibrium of the repeated game if N is not too large.

Notice the connection between conditions (10.1) and (7.2). Both conditions give us the maximum number of countries capable of sustaining full cooperation by means of a self-enforcing agreement. The only difference is that condition (7.2) also tells how many countries would cooperate if N were greater than this maximal value. The one-shot game used in Chapter 7 tells us something about participation. The repeated game model developed above tells us something about enforcement. The two approaches should be seen as being complementary. I combine them in Chapter 11.

As developed above, the Getting-Even strategy requires that *all* the $N - 1$ others punish a single country for deviating. This may seem excessive, but our assumption about collective rationality means that these $N - 1$ others must choose an action that maximizes their collective payoff in a punishment phase. As long as b/c is a non-integer, the linear nature of the payoffs implies that these $N - 1$ others will either play Pollute or Abate. It will never be collectively rational for only some of these countries to play Pollute or Abate. Punishing a deviation will only be credible (in the sense of being collectively rational) if these $N - 1$ countries do better by playing Pollute; Indeed, this is precisely what condition (10.1) is telling us.[13]

Setting $b = 2$ and $c = 3$ reproduces the problem analyzed in the previous section. For these parameter values, condition (10.1) requires that $N \leq 5/2$. Hence, though two countries can sustain the full cooperative outcome as an equilibrium of the repeated game, as shown earlier, three or more cannot. For different parameter values, however, the maximal N that can sustain full cooperation can exceed two. For example, if $b = 2$ and $c = 5$, then the full cooperative outcome can be sustained as an equilibrium provided $N = 3$.[14]

To sum up, collective rationality limits cooperation in repeated games. It shrinks the set of outcomes that can be sustained by a self-enforcing treaty.

10.10. REPETITION WITH CONTINUOUS ACTIONS

Consider now repeated play of the game in continuous abatement choices, where country i must choose $q_i \in [0,1]$ in each of infinitely many periods. i's per-period payoff is given by eqn (7.1). Assume, as before, that $c > b > 0$ and $bN > c$. Then, as shown in Section 7.5, the Nash equilibrium of the one-shot game requires $q^u = 0$, while the full cooperative outcome demands $q^c = 1$.

Can the full cooperative outcome of the one-shot game be supported by an IEA if the game is repeated indefinitely? We already know that the full cooperative outcome can be sustained as a subgame-perfect equilibrium of the infinitely repeated game for sufficiently small discount factors. What we want to know is whether the agreement to punish non-compliance is renegotiation-proof.

Suppose Country j deviates. The other countries must then respond by punishing j. Following this punishment phase, the players revert to cooperation. Reverting to cooperation is rational for j provided the average payoff j obtains in the cooperative phase is at least as great as the maximal average payoff j can obtain during the punishment phase. Denote the value of j's abatement that maximizes its payoff in the punishment phase by q_j and let q_m^j be the abatement chosen by every country m, $m \neq j$, in this phase. Given q_m^j, and given that $b < c$, Country j can do no better than to play $q_j = 0$ in the punishment phase. Hence, j gets an average payoff of $b(N - 1)q_m^j$ in the punishment phase. In the cooperative phase, j gets a payoff of $\Pi_j = bN - c$ every period. Reverting to cooperation is thus in j's interests provided

$$b(N-1)q_m^j \leq bN - c. \qquad (10.2)$$

[13] For a proof, see the appendix to Barrett (1999a). [14] Of course, with these parameter values, we can only have a PD if $N \geq 3$.

Furthermore, compliance with the punishment outlined in the IEA would be group rational for the countries other than j provided

$$b\left[q_j^j + (N-1)q_m^j\right] - cq_m^j \geq bN - c, \tag{10.3}$$

where q_j^j is j's abatement during the punishment phase. For this problem, it is natural for us to take $q_j^j = 1$. Then eqn (10.3) becomes

$$q_m^j\left[b(N-1) - c\right] \geq b(N-1) - c. \tag{10.4}$$

There are two possibilities. Suppose $0 \geq b(N-1) - c$. Then any $q_m^j \in [0,1]$ satisfies eqn (10.4) (though group rationality demands $q_m^j = 0$ for $0 > b(N-1) - c$). Since eqn (10.2) is easily satisfied (e.g., by setting $q_m^j = 0$), the full cooperative outcome can thus be sustained by an IEA provided $0 \geq b(N-1) - c$. Suppose, however, that $0 < b(N-1) - c$. Then eqn (10.4) requires $q_m^j = 1$. But then eqn (10.2) cannot be satisfied since $b < c$ by assumption. Hence, the full cooperative outcome can only be sustained by a self-enforcing IEA if $c \geq b(N-1)$—that is, if, when one player deviates, the group rational abatement level of the $N-1$ other players is zero. This is precisely the same result obtained in Section 7.5. It is satisfied so long as condition (10.1) holds.

10.11. REPEATED GAMES AND COLLECTIVE CHOICE

The study of international relations draws liberally from the theories of repeated games and collective choice—and for good reason. The former theory teaches that cooperation between states can be sustained even by an anarchic, sovereignty-obsessed international system. The latter theory cautions that cooperation is likely to be restricted to only a few countries. Together, these theories tell us that there can be real cooperation, but that cooperation will be limited. These are important insights. They cut a middle-way between the more extreme alternatives: the realist view that meaningful cooperation is not even desirable and the liberal view that cooperation is easily sustained. But this alternative perspective is also built upon a shaky foundation: the theory of repeated games shows not just that cooperation can be sustained as an equilibrium but that it can be sustained by a *large* number of players (at least for sufficiently large discount factors). This conflicts with the teachings of collective choice theory.

This clash is hardly noticed in the literature, perhaps because Axelrod's (1984) famous treatment of repeated games considers interactions between just two players and Olson's (1965) equally-influential book on collective choice fails to explain precisely how a public good could be provided voluntarily except for a trivial case. The trivial case is of a "privileged group"—a group for which it is individually rational for at least one party to supply the public good unilaterally.

Olson reasons that cooperation could be sustained even by an "intermediate group"—"a group in which no single member gets a share of the benefit sufficient to give him an incentive to provide the good himself, but which does not have so many members that no one member will notice whether any other member is or is not helping to provide the collective good" (Olson 1965: 50). But Olson does not demonstrate formally how such a group could sustain cooperation. It is significant, however, that Olson should recognize the need to monitor or verify provision by other members of the group. For when a defection is detected, it can potentially be punished, and if it is credible for the other parties to punish a defection severely enough, the mere threat to punish may be sufficient to sustain cooperation. The problem, as I noted above, is that once reciprocity is built into the interaction, the folk theorems tell us that cooperation can be sustained as an equilibrium by a large number of countries (for sufficiently small discount rates). This is not the result Olson was looking for.

Of course, whether this conflict exists as a practical matter depends on how one decides whether a given number of players is "small." If the total number of countries in the world were "small," then cooperation should be easy. But then it is hard to see why the theory of collective action should be a mainstay of the international relations literature. Presumably, Olson's book has been influential because it tells a convincing story. We believe its conclusions, even if we have not seen the proof.

The analysis developed above reconciles the conflict in these literatures. It explains how cooperation could be sustained in non-trivial cases but also why it cannot be sustained when N is "large," even when players meet repeatedly and have very low discount rates. It also demonstrates that whether N is "large" or "small" in the sense defined above depends on the problem at hand. This is important. The total number of countries in the world is a "small" number *for some problems*. For other problems, however, even three countries may be too "large" a number to support full cooperation.

10.12. THE LIMITS TO COOPERATION

What puts the brake on cooperation? If a country cheats on a bilateral agreement, the other party will be severely affected, and will therefore have a strong incentive to punish the deviant severely—most likely by nullifying the treaty. As long as the agreement yielded each of the parties a gain, and as long as the parties do not discount the future too heavily, neither should ever deviate. Cooperation between two countries should not be a great problem.

Add just one more country, however, and the result could be different. For it may pay two countries to cooperate, even if the third country chooses not to cooperate. In such a situation, a unilateral deviation may not be punished very harshly—and so may not be deterred. Increase the number of countries with a stake in a resource and the problem of cooperation becomes amplified. This is why cooperation is harder to sustain as the number of countries that could potentially gain from cooperation increases.

Notice that this reasoning helps explain why reciprocity can be so effective in sustaining a "free trade" regime. Trade is a bilateral activity. If a party to the World Trade Organization "cheats," and thus harms another party, the state that is harmed can, after certain procedures are followed, retaliate. The retaliation is directed solely at the state that broke the trading rules. Others are not harmed by the punishment. Nor must other parties punish the offending state. Free trade is *not* a public good.

The credibility of a punishment depends on more than the number of parties. It depends also on the payoffs. Punishing a defection is more attractive the higher are the costs of abatement—for these costs are avoided in a punishment phase. By contrast, the greater are the benefits of abatement, the greater is the harm self-inflicted by the punishment of a defector. All of these factors determine the success of international cooperation—and they are all captured by condition (10.1). Notice, however, that the aggregate gains to cooperation are decreasing in the costs of abatement and increasing in the benefit of abatement. As demonstrated in Chapter 7, cooperation is especially elusive when it is needed most.

10.13. MONITORING AND COMMUNICATION

The above analysis assumes that actions can be monitored (and with zero detection lag). If actions cannot be observed, however, then cheating cannot be detected, and an agreement in which every party pledges to play Abate cannot be enforced. In contrast to the one-shot dilemma game (see Chapter 3), transparency is of fundamental importance in a repeated game.[15]

We can recall now the claim made by Chayes and Chayes (1995) that the dilemma in the dilemma game springs from the assumptions that the players cannot communicate and have no information about each other's moves. I showed in Section 3.8 that this reasoning cannot explain how the dilemma arises in the one-shot dilemma game. For the repeated dilemma game, however, matters are very different. It was presumably this game that the Chayeses had in mind.

Though the ability to monitor is essential to sustaining cooperation, monitoring need not be perfect. Even if moves can only be observed imperfectly, a degree of cooperation can often be sustained. Indeed, even if countries can only observe aggregate abatement (or emissions)—and even if *this* can only be observed imperfectly—a measure of cooperation can still be sustained under certain circumstances. The important difference is that, with imperfect monitoring, punishments are likely to be required in equilibrium (with perfect monitoring, no country will ever deviate in equilibrium, given that the threat to punish is credible). Errors will be inevitable. Punishments will sometimes be imposed even when no cheating has occurred; and they will sometimes not be imposed even when cheating has occurred.

The effect of communication is more complicated. As we learned in Chapter 3, communication will not shift the equilibrium of the one-shot PD. Communication is important in the repeated game because it can help get cooperation going in the first place. However, communication also makes the assumption of collective rationality more compelling—and this assumption makes cooperation *harder* to sustain, not easier.

To see why, suppose that the players can communicate prior to the start of play but that they cannot communicate thereafter. Suppose, further that the players agree to

---

[15] Of course, in a repeated game, when a player chooses an action in period t, it does not know how the other players will choose in period t, but it does know how everyone acted in every previous period, and is able to make its own actions contingent on the history of the game.

play Grim in the pre-play communication phase, and that in some future period one player deviates. What will the other players do? If they could communicate, they would very likely rewrite the agreement to play Getting-Even. If they could not communicate, however, it is more likely that the players would act as the agreement instructed them to act; they would play Grim. This suggests that, if communication were impossible, the players may be more inclined to write Grim into their agreement in the first place. Grim, after all, can sustain more cooperation than Getting-Even. Being unable to communicate after an agreement has entered into force is a near-equivalent to being committed not to renegotiate.

10.14. FUR SEAL COMPLIANCE

The main feature of the theory outlined above is that a strategy of reciprocity is needed to enforce both participation and compliance. Deterring non-participation, however, is the more challenging task. A mechanism capable of deterring non-participation can also be relied upon to deter non-compliance.

Recall from Chapter 2 that the Fur Seal Treaty has this same feature. The punishment mechanism in Article XII of both the post-war versions specifies that any act of non-compliance can lead to the complete dissolution of the treaty, just as can a withdrawal. The agreement further requires that the parties meet to consult on an alleged deviation, providing an opportunity for the kinds of managerial fixes commended by Chayes and Chayes (1995). Formal and informal mechanisms for enforcement need not be mutually exclusive.

Of course, the agreement does not specify Getting-Even exactly. But it does require that the parties "consult together on the need for and nature of remedial measures," should a violation occur. Such "remedial measures" could conceivably require that the injured parties be compensated in the manner suggested by Getting-Even as a condition for re-establishing a cooperative phase.

The Fur Seal Treaty created a gain from cooperation by deterring pelagic sealing, and this is what needed to be monitored. As noted in Chapter 2, the treaty required that the states with breeding populations (the United States, Japan, and Russia) keep watch over their seals throughout their territory and in the high seas. It might seem curious that the agreement would require that this be done. But notice that knowledge of a violation is itself a public good. This did not matter in the formal analysis of this chapter, but only because I assumed that monitoring was costless (if provision of a public good is costless, free-riding is not a problem). Monitoring of the fur seal populations would be expensive, and each party might prefer that the others do the monitoring.[16]

What would happen if a violation were detected? The enforcement procedures of the treaty permitted the seizure of suspected sealing vessels, even ones caught in

---

[16] Of course, the United States monitored pelagic sealing long before the Fur Seal Treaty was negotiated, and probably had a unilateral incentive to do so after the treaty entered into force. However, under the terms of the Fur Seal Treaty, the United States would only get a fraction of the increased harvest, and so would get only a fraction of the benefit of monitoring.

international waters and registered under the flag of another party. This kind of action is precisely what Britain and Canada had previously objected to, but the treaty requires that seized ships and crews be returned to the authorities of their *own* country for trial (the United States had previously sought to try foreign nationals in US courts).

As noted in Section 2.10.4, trial at home was facilitated by the requirement that each of the parties adopt domestic legislation making pelagic sealing by nationals illegal and subject to punishment.[17] Domestic legislation is easy to observe and, once passed, hard to change for the purpose of opportunistic gain. Provided that the judiciary of each of the parties was independent and could be expected to conduct a proper trial of any alleged violation, no party could gain by cheating (it is almost as if the treaty facilitated a commitment by each party to punish itself for a treaty violation detected by others).

But the Fur Seal Treaty did more than ensure that deviations would be punished. It also reduced the incentive to deviate. In giving the pelagic sealing nations (Canada and Japan) a share of the land-based harvest, pelagic sealing became more costly. Reductions in the population of seals would force a reduction in the land-based harvest, to the cost of the pelagic sealing nations which obtain a share of the harvest (the loss would be significant, remembering the relative efficiency of land-based killing). The pelagic nations were also given money to compensate their sealers for the loss of their livelihood. The United States agreed to pay Canada and Japan $200,000 each for this purpose. The money was intended to take the sealing vessels out of action, or to refit them for an alternative use.[18] If these costs, once incurred, were sunk, there would be an added incentive for pelagic sealing not to be revived.

The Fur Seal Treaty is consistent with this analysis in one more respect: just as the punishment mechanisms outlined earlier are never used in equilibrium, so (to my knowledge) the punishment provisions of the Fur Seal Treaty were never activated. Being severe and credible, and being recognized as having these qualities, no party could gain by deviating.

10.15. COMPLIANCE WITH THE MONTREAL PROTOCOL

Montreal is another "success"—and not just because it required huge cuts in emissions. It is a success because the negotiated cuts have actually been achieved. As with the Fur Seal Treaty, compliance with the Montreal Protocol has been virtually full.

This may not seem like a great achievement. After all, the analysis in Chapter 8 implies that the industrialized countries would have wanted to comply with Montreal for nationalistic reasons. The developing countries, being compensated for incremental costs, would have had little incentive to "cheat."

---

[17] Another treaty that expressly requires that domestic legislation be passed in order to implement an agreement is the Nitrogen Oxides Protocol. This agreement requires that parties apply national emissions standards to major new stationary sources and/or source categories and to new mobile sources based on the "best available technologies which are economically feasible."

[18] The money had to pass through the hands of the pelagic governments before reaching the sealers. Canada awarded its sealers just $60,663, whereas Japan paid out $560,000 (Gay 1987).

But after Montreal was negotiated, the upheavals in central and eastern Europe changed the calculus of compliance. Where there were previously nine parties from this region, by 1996 there were twenty-seven states—and some of these were slow to ratify Montreal and its amendments, often for understandable reasons. For example, a mission by the Protocol's Technology and Economic Assessment Panel to Azerbaijan found that the country was unable to ratify "because the State Committee for Ecology did not have resources to translate the protocol into Azeri, and in any case had no access to the only existing copy in the country" (Benedick 1998: 277). Many of these newly created states also lacked an effective government capable of implementing the controls. Moreover, central planning had distributed production of CFCs in a way that made no sense to the new order (aerosol production in the Soviet Union, for example, was concentrated in Latvia and Lithuania; see Benedick 1998). Finally, with the economies of this region convulsing, ozone protection must not have seemed a priority.

And yet Montreal did not adjust to the changed status of these countries. In 1992, Russia and other economies in transition asked for their burdens to be eased—for the other parties to recognize that they now belonged to a new category of country, to be distinguished from the industrialized and developing (Article 5) countries. However, when the Netherlands proposed an amendment to the Protocol, effectively formalizing this request, developing countries objected, and there was little support among the industrialized countries of the West for a change. This failure to renegotiate—to let the former communist countries comply with easier targets and timetables—invariably forced non-compliance onto the agenda of the Protocol's Implementation Committee.

Of course, the transition economies always had the option of withdrawing from the agreement. However, we shall see in Chapter 12 that the Protocol imaginatively and effectively deterred non-participation. Though the former communist states may no longer have had an incentive (or perhaps even the wherewithal) unilaterally to protect the ozone layer, withdrawing from the agreement would have made them even more worse off. Being deterred from withdrawing, and with the other parties refusing to renegotiate, non-compliance may have seemed an alluring outlet, especially as the penalty for non-compliance was unspecified. The original text of the Montreal Protocol deferred design of a non-compliance mechanism to a later meeting of the parties.

Indeed, it was not until non-compliance actually threatened to be a problem years later that a mechanism for punishing it was finally drawn up. Richard Benedick, who introduced the non-compliance article into the text, later justified deferment of the elaboration of the non-compliance mechanism, saying that if the matter had been forced in Montreal, the negotiations would likely have become stalled on "controversial legal fine points" (Benedick 1998: 270). It is as well to note, however, that non-compliance may have become a problem not only because of the changes in eastern and central Europe (changes that the negotiators in Montreal could not have anticipated), and the failure of Montreal to adjust to them, but also because an effective mechanism for punishing non-compliance had not been specified earlier. The omission must surely have raised at least a little doubt in the minds of some governments as to whether non-compliance would be punished harshly. It may even have given some countries the impression that non-compliance would not be punished at all.

At the fourth meeting of the parties—held in 1992, when the Dutch proposal was snubbed and by which time the parties knew that some of the former communist countries were unlikely to implement Montreal fully—the parties to Montreal agreed to an "indicative list of measures that might be taken by a meeting of the parties in respect of non-compliance with the Protocol." These included: (1) assistance, including "technology transfer and financial assistance"; (2) "issuing cautions"; and (3) "suspension ... of specific rights and privileges under the Protocol ... including those concerned with industrial rationalization, production, consumption, trade, transfer of technology, financial mechanism and institutional arrangements." These procedures mirrored the mechanisms in the Fur Seal Treaty, in that they included both carrots and sticks—and were imprecise as to how particular violations would be treated.

In 1995, the Technology and Assessment Panel formally confirmed that a number of the former Soviet republics were unlikely to comply with Montreal; and, though Russia had not formally submitted a report to the protocol's secretariat indicating that it expected to exceed its quotas, its public declarations were interpreted as being equivalent in effect.[19] The treaty's non-compliance procedure was thus finally put to the test.

Two other expected situations of non-compliance were easily remedied. When it became apparent that Belarus and the Ukraine were unlikely to comply with the 1996 restrictions, a deal was reached with the Implementation Committee in which financial assistance for implementing a post-1996 phase-out program would be provided so long as these states agreed to certain restrictions on the export of controlled substances (the purpose being to prevent trans-shipment, as neither Belarus nor the Ukraine manufactured CFCs). This was renegotiation through the back door.

Russia's impending non-compliance was a more formidable challenge. The Implementation Committee offered Russia essentially the same deal that it had struck with Belarus and Ukraine, and Russia accepted. But at the seventh meeting of the parties, held in Vienna in December 1995, an amendment was added, forbidding Russia from exporting controlled substances to Article 5 parties. This infuriated the Russian delegation. Russia's environment minister even warned that, if the recommendations were approved, "the process of replacing ODS [ozone depleting substances] will significantly lose momentum ... , measures to strengthen export controls will not be taken, there will be a trend towards illegal production of ODS by producers and the use of these products by consumers. There will be another incentive (over and above those already existing) for autarky, which will be deliberately exploited by the corresponding political forces" (Brack 1996: 104).

The other parties were unmoved by this threat. Indeed, not a single country voiced support for the reservations; Venezuela (a CFC producer) even argued that the trade restrictions against Russia should be strengthened further. This was too much for the

---

[19] The Protocol's non-compliance procedure, adopted in Copenhagen in 1992, allows possible situations of non-compliance to be reported to the secretariat by parties that expect not to comply, or by parties that suspect others of not complying. The secretariat may also, on its own initiative, report concerns about possible non-compliance to the Implementation Committee.

Russians. "At the last session of the meeting, the Russian delegation denounced these provisions, stated that the Federation retained its right to consider all circumstances and draw the corresponding conclusions with regard to further compliance, and left the hall" (Brack 1996: 104).

Evidently, the other parties believed that the restrictions were in their interests. Some of the amendment's sponsors (India especially) hoped that the restriction would protect their export markets (Benedick 1998). For others, the proposal had the appeal of at least dampening the black market trade, as well as providing Russia with an incentive to comply (obviously, once Russia was back on track, the sanctions would no longer be needed or indeed justified). But though the other parties would be better off with the restrictions than without them, given that Russia accepted their terms, suppose Russia carried out its threat not to comply. What then?

The Montreal apparatus never actually spelled out the consequences of Russia's non-compliance (indeed, Russia had not actually failed to comply at the time that the amendment was tabled). It merely renegotiated the terms of its compliance. But, surely, if the parties were prepared to restrict Russian trade as a deal for compliance, they would at the very least impose the same restrictions if Russia refused the offer. My interpretation of the situation is that, from the perspective of all the other parties as a collective, the restrictions were a dominant strategy. In other words, these countries would have been better off imposing the restrictions whether or not Russia acquiesced. The amended deal was renegotiation-proof.

But, given this, was Russia's threat not to comply credible? If Russia refused the offer, it would undoubtedly face trade restrictions. It would also lose funding, though it would be free to supply CFCs to its own market. If it accepted the offer, it would still face trade restrictions; but these would be lifted once Russia was in compliance, and the promised funding would lower the cost to Russia of complying.

It seems that Russia was better off accepting, for it soon shifted its position. In February 1996, the Russian environment minister wrote a conciliatory letter to the executive secretary of the Ozone Secretariat. The minister acknowledged "the current concern in the international community regarding possible deliveries of ODS from Russian sources during the period in which they are being phased out" and promised to take steps "toward solving the problems of control within our borders." The Implementation Committee responded by noting that "the Russian Federation had by its actions taken important steps to comply with [the above decision of the conference of the parties] and towards achieving full compliance with the control measures of the Protocol," and it said that it would "consider favorably additional steps to expedite financial assistance" as regards implementing the phase-out, thus approving plans by the Global Environment Facility to subsidize substitution of CFCs in Russia by a further $35 million ($8.6 million had previously been awarded).[20]

As in the case of the Fur Seal Treaty, and indeed the theory outlined earlier, enforcement of the Montreal compliance mechanism is a collective responsibility. All parties (excluding members of the Commonwealth of Independent States) were

---

[20] See the March 1996 report of the Implementation Committee (UNEP/OzL.Pro/ImpCom/13/3).

expected to restrict their trade in the controlled substances with Russia. Failure to do so would itself have constituted a violation and presumably invited punishment by the other parties. In this respect, the compliance mechanism worked out by the Montreal parties resembles the theory outlined earlier in the chapter. The important difference is that, as in the case of the Fur Seal Treaty, the parties to the Montreal Protocol were able to make use of an expanded strategy space, including compensating payments and trade restrictions, not to mention moral suasion. These strategies are the subject of later chapters.

10.16. CONCLUSIONS

The compliance mechanisms used in the North Pacific Fur Seal Treaty and the Montreal Protocol are unusual. As noted in the introduction to this chapter, most IEAs make no provision for non-compliance. What this means is open to different interpretations. It may mean that such mechanisms are unnecessary—that compliance can be secured by other means or that most agreements try only to coordinate state behavior. However, it may mean that such mechanisms *are* needed, and the fact that they are rarely used only implies that most agreements sustain only non-cooperative outcomes. These possibilities were outlined in the introduction to this chapter.[21]

The theory developed here teaches that, for PD-type problems, non-compliance mechanisms are needed if cooperation is to be sustained by international treaty. Moreover, the examples of the Fur Seal Treaty and Montreal Protocol support this claim—and I should add that the Chayeses (1995) do not consider the evidence provided by these cases.

The Chayeses (1995: 32–33) argue that "sanctioning authority is rarely granted by treaty, rarely used when granted, and likely to be ineffective when used." The real problem with sanctions, they say, is that their use "entails high costs to the sanctioner" (Chayes and Chayes 1995: 33). This last observation hits the bulls-eye and has been a focus of this chapter. But as Downs et al. (1996) argue, it would be wrong to conclude from this that the absence of sanctions is to be cheered. The fact that sanctions are rarely embodied in treaty texts need not mean that they are unhelpful in sustaining cooperation. Their absence may rather signal that the imposition of sanctions is not credible. Possibly, the failure to incorporate sanctions is a missed opportunity for sustaining cooperation. Similarly, the fact that sanctions are rarely used does not mean that they are ineffective. To the contrary, game theory teaches that if the sanctions are severe and credible, then they will never be invoked. The mere threat to impose them would be sufficient to ensure full compliance. Finally, the observation that sanctions are likely to be ineffective when used is also open to a different interpretation: perhaps sanctions are used only when they are likely to be ineffective. Compliance with the Montreal Protocol may have been even less of a problem had the agreement initially specified punishments for non-compliance. As it is, the (implicit)

---

[21] For a broader, but also less pointed, discussion of compliance with international environmental agreements, see Weiss and Jacobson (1998).

threat to impose trade restrictions against Russia seems to have been enough to sustain full compliance.

This chapter suggests as well that the literature's concern about compliance has been misplaced. Free-riding is the bigger problem. You can think of it this way: If a country really is intent on not complying with a treaty, it can simply withdraw from the treaty. Doing so releases the country from all its obligations, both under treaty law and custom. Compliance, therefore, cannot be a problem for the international system so long as non-participation can be deterred.

The models analyzed in Chapter 7 assumed that parties complied fully with the self-enforcing IEA, and yet these agreements typically could not sustain full cooperation because they could not deter free-riding. This chapter has done away with the assumption of full compliance and yet has obtained results identical to the results of Chapter 7. This suggests that free-rider deterrence is the real constraint on international cooperation, not compliance.

The Fur Seal Treaty and Montreal Protocol have deterred free-riding, but not through the strategy of reciprocity outlined in this chapter. They did so by linking environmental controls (the ban on pelagic sealing, the reduction in ODS emissions) to trade measures. I consider this strategy of linkage in Chapter 12.

Before turning to this subject, however, I want to return to the participation problem. Here and in Chapter 7, cooperation was limited by the requirement that parties choose a level of abatement that maximizes their aggregate payoff. This limits the ability of signatories to punish defections—and so it ultimately limits participation. In the next chapter I relax this assumption.

11

The Depth and Breadth of International Cooperation

There is no durable treaty which is not founded on reciprocal advantage, and indeed a treaty which does not satisfy this condition is no treaty at all, and is apt to contain the seeds of its own dissolution. Thus the great secret of negotiation is to bring out prominently the common advantage to both parties of any proposal, and so to link these advantages that they may appear equally balanced to both parties. François de Calliéres, *De la Maniere de Negocier Avec les Souverains* (1716).[1]

11.1. INTRODUCTION

To this point, the theory suggests that participation is *the* problem of international cooperation. But the data sometimes tell a different story. Many agreements sustain close to full participation. Some are even negotiated on the basis that the best deal should be reached, subject to participation being full or nearly so. According to a Swedish diplomat (Kjellen 1994: 151), who took a leading role in negotiating the Framework Convention on Climate Change, "a major objective of the negotiation was to have all the big players sign the convention during the Earth Summit at Rio."

This is a different way of looking at international cooperation. In Chapters 7 and 10, parties to a treaty were assumed to choose abatement levels so as to maximize their joint payoff, *taking the number of parties and their identities as given*. The diplomat quoted above, however, suggests that the abatement levels prescribed by a treaty may be chosen *subject to a participation constraint*.

If countries could have it both ways—if they could choose the abatement levels that maximized their joint payoff *and* ensure that participation was full—then full cooperation would always be sustained. But if the constraint of self-enforcement binds, we can't have it both ways. Something has to give. Either participation must be less than full *or* signatories must choose abatement levels that fall short of maximizing their collective payoff.

Indeed, Kjellen readily blames the feebleness of the Framework Convention (discussed in detail in Chapter 15) on the overriding desire for consensus. "If we were to reach consensus," he says, "there could be no commitments on targets and timetables in the final agreed text." This hints at a trade-off. Countries can reach a consensus around a weak agreement, or they can negotiate a more potent but incomplete agreement. When negotiating the Framework Convention on Climate Change, the lead

---

[1] Calliéres was a French diplomat. The quote from his book is from Freeman (1997: 7).

negotiators evidently chose the consensus option. That is, they chose to negotiate a treaty that was "broad but shallow."

The Montreal negotiators chose differently. At one point in the negotiations, as noted in Chapter 8, the US Government proposed making entry into force conditional on a minimum participation level of at least 90 percent of global consumption. However, according to Benedick (1998: 89), "When the United States proposed this percentage at Montreal, the reaction was almost universally negative; only the Soviet Union supported 90 percent. Many observers feared that such a requirement could hold the treaty hostage to Japan or the Soviet Union, which might then weaken the protocol by extracting other concessions as the price for adherence."

Now, as noted earlier, participation in the Montreal Protocol is nearly full today. And the treaty is also as deep as they come—almost as deep as the feasibility constraints allow. So in this particular case, countries were able to have their cake and eat it too. The reasons for this are the subjects of the next two chapters. This chapter focuses on the trade-off between depth and breadth—a trade-off that was apparent in 1987, even if it didn't ultimately constrain cooperation in this particular case.

The potential virtue of a "narrow but deep" treaty, as compared to a "broad but narrow" treaty, was noted previously by Downs *et al.* (1996: 399):

One possible strategy is to restrict regime membership to states that will not have to defect very often. The idea is that whatever benefit is lost by excluding such states from the regime will be more than made up by permitting those that are included to set and also enforce a deeper level of cooperation .... This may be a reason, quite different from the large-n coordination concerns of collection action theory, why many deeply cooperative regimes have a limited number of members and why regimes with a large number of members tend to engage in only shallow cooperation. Is this trade-off real? Must states sometimes choose between aggressively addressing an environmental ... problem and trying to create a community of states? We do not know.

This chapter inquires into this apparent trade-off between the depth and breadth of cooperation. We shall see that the trade-off highlighted above is real. But we shall also find that it will not always be better to negotiate a "narrow but deep" treaty. Contrary to the conjecture made by Downs *et al.* (1996), a "broad but shallow," consensus treaty is often to be preferred.

This conclusion adds a twist to the story told thus far. The story to this point has been that participation was the binding constraint on cooperation. This chapter shows that, even if participation is full, cooperation may be less than full. Participation may be a necessary condition for sustaining full cooperation, but it is not sufficient.

We often think of agreements as being weak or shallow when countries are asymmetric and a consensus can only be reached around some "lowest common denominator." But treaties need not be diluted to sustain a consensus among asymmetric countries. As explained in Chapter 3, transfers in money or in kind can always be used as a sweetener, to make participation attractive to a cross-section of countries. The Fur Seal Treaty provides a striking example of the utility of side payments. In this chapter I continue to assume that countries are symmetric—and yet we shall still find that the parties to an agreement may need to lower their provision levels in order to entice others to accede. The reason is that, by lowering the payoff to cooperating, a consensus treaty makes the threat to punish non-cooperators more credible. Since cooperators have less to gain from ignoring a deviation and continuing to cooperate, they have less to lose by punishing deviations.

Whether a threat is credible depends on the perceived rationality of the players. A threat may be credible for one concept of rationality but not for another. We saw this in the previous chapter when contrasting the assumptions of individual and collective rationality. The threat to play Grim is credible if agreements need only be individually rational but not if they must be collectively rational.

The rationality assumptions made to this point make it especially difficult to sustain a consensus agreement when N is large. The reason is that the assumption of collective rationality used thus far demands that cooperating countries impose small punishments when N is large (large punishments are not credible), and small punishments are not enough to deter deviations. This chapter weakens the concept of collective rationality used previously, and shows that it is possible to sustain a treaty that is either "broad but shallow" or "narrow but deep" (or anything in between). Note, however, that the weaker assumption of collective rationality is not made just to obtain this flexibility. As I shall explain later in the chapter, the assumption can stand on its own two feet, as it were.

The main lesson of this chapter is that a consensus treaty shifts the constraint of self-enforcement. Rather than reduce participation, it reduces each party's provision of the public good as compared with the full cooperative outcome. One virtue of a consensus treaty is that it is "fair"—it requires that all symmetric countries make the same sacrifice to protect the shared environment. It turns out, however, that the consensus treaty may also make every country better off as compared with the incomplete treaties we have examined thus far. Equity and efficiency may thus be mutually reinforcing.

11.2. WEAKENING THE ASSUMPTION OF COLLECTIVE RATIONALITY

As in Chapter 10, I use the repeated game framework in this chapter and rely on the concept of collective rationality. Like Farrell and Maskin's (1989) definition of a renegotiation-proof equilibrium, from which this concept is derived, collective rationality is compatible with two different kinds of punishments. The self-enforcing treaties studied in the previous chapter might best be called *strongly collectively rational* (SCR). For these treaties, the countries called upon to punish a deviating country would collectively prefer to impose the prescribed punishments than revert to cooperation or play an alternative, feasible punishment. A *weakly collectively rational* (WCR) treaty narrows this choice. For these treaties, the countries called upon to punish a unilateral deviation would collectively prefer to comply with the treaty than to ignore the deviation and revert to cooperation. In other words, a WCR treaty cannot be rewritten after a deviation has occurred. It can only be obeyed or ignored.

An example best illustrates the difference between the concepts. Suppose that a country withdraws from an agreement seeking to supply a public good, or fails to accede to this agreement in the first place. Suppose, too, that the countries that *are* parties to the agreement (or that remain as parties) are required by the treaty to punish this free-rider. Since self-enforcing agreements must be individually rational, we know that each such party will impose the punishment prescribed by the treaty, given that all other parties do so. But punishing is self-damaging to all these countries collectively, and there is nothing to stop these countries from contemplating their collective situation and proposing a change in the treaty. If these countries can only choose between imposing the prescribed punishment or not, and they cannot do better collectively except by imposing the punishment, then the treaty is WCR. If, however, these countries can choose to impose different punishments than required by the treaty, but cannot gain by doing so, then the treaty is SCR. As suggested by this example, all SCR treaties are WCR, but the reverse is not true. SCR treaties are more credible. Indeed, that is why I relied on this concept in earlier chapters.

11.3. ALTERNATIVE APPROACHES

Weakening the rationality assumption is one way to get a consensus agreement, but it is not the only way.

An alternative is to make different assumptions about the beliefs of the players. Recall that Chander and Tulkens (1997) show in a static game that a consensus agreement can sustain full cooperation if the parties believe that, in the event that one of them should deviate, the agreement will be nullified and all the other parties will thereafter behave non-cooperatively. However, as explained in Chapter 7, this only begs the question of *why* countries might hold such beliefs—especially as they are unlikely to be confirmed by how states actually behave.

Another approach is to alter the payoffs of the players. In a static game, Hoel and Schnieder (1997) add to each country's payoff a cost for not cooperating that increases in the number of countries that do cooperate. This can be interpreted as a penalty for not conforming, or for deviating from the customary law requiring states to cooperate. It has the consequence that, if enough other countries participate, then each will be inclined to participate. If the cost of not conforming is big enough, the underlying game will not be a prisoners' dilemma (PD); it will rather be a coordination game. As we learned in Chapter 4, the full cooperative outcome is easy to sustain for these kinds of games. It is important to note as well that, within the Hoel–Schnieder framework, the penalty imposed on non-conformers does not cost the cooperators a penny. Nor is imposition of the penalty willful. The mechanism that triggers the punishment is hard-wired into the treaty. The assumption about payoffs is thus equivalent to an assumption about preferences: countries prefer to conform.

Of course, customary international law requires that countries make an effort to cooperate. It also requires that they comply with the agreements they sign up to. So the alteration of payoffs modeled by Hoel and Schnieder may be looked at as a kind of shorthand way of incorporating custom into the theory.[2] However, this approach

---

[2] This is not how Hoel and Schnieder (1997) interpret their assumption.

suffers from a familiar problem: the adjustment is *ad hoc*. How do we know the magnitude of the penalty that must be paid for not obeying the custom? We should also be wary of making a punishment automatic and costless as regards the countries called upon to carry it out. As this book has repeatedly emphasized, cooperation often fails because punishing non-cooperators is costly to the countries required to implement the punishments. Threats are easy to make but they need not be carried out. Moreover, we can expect that they will *not* be carried out so long as doing so harms the countries asked by a treaty to punish non-cooperators.

This would not matter if we interpreted Hoel and Schnieder's assumptions about payoffs as reflecting a preference to conform (see Section 4.14). But how is one to know the strength of this preference? Adjustments for conforming preferences must also be *ad hoc*. Moreover, to assume that countries have "fair-minded" preferences merely helps to ensure that, in equilibrium, countries will tend to conform (once again, the game is not a PD; it is a coordination game). This is not very illuminating. Furthermore, this approach does not address the higher order question of where these preferences come from. Nor can it tell us why countries conform in some cases but not in others. In 2001, President George W. Bush rejected the Kyoto Protocol, despite the support given to this treaty by virtually all other countries and the administration that preceded him. This kind of behavior is a repudiation of the notion that countries would prefer to conform, even if at the expense of the national interest.

The approach taken here has an advantage over these alternatives. I shall show that it may be in the *interests* of countries to conform.

11.4. CONCEPTS

Let me now provide a more formal description of the alternative concepts of collective rationality.[3]

Suppose that there are k signatories to a self-enforcing agreement and that each signatory gets a payoff of Π_s every period in a cooperative phase. Suppose further that non-signatories behave non-cooperatively. Indeed, suppose that they have a dominant strategy: to play q^u. As in earlier chapters, the latter assumption is a simplification; it allows us to ignore strategic interactions between signatories and non-signatories. To simplify matters even more, assume $q^u = 0$. Given every other country's behavior, non-signatories cannot do better than to play zero abatement.

A self-enforcing agreement must be able to deter unilateral deviations. So suppose one party to the treaty—call it j—deviates by failing to comply. Suppose as well that this deviation is observed perfectly and instantaneously and that it is common knowledge. The deviation will then trigger a punishment phase. During this phase, the treaty tells j to play q_j^i every period (you can think of this as a way for j to make amends for its willful deviation). The treaty also instructs the other $k - 1$ signatories to supply Q_{-j}^j of the public good in this phase (the purpose being to punish j for cheating).

---

[3] My analysis here and in the next few sections draws from Barrett (2002a).

Now consider the incentives that this treaty creates for both j and all the other signatories collectively. For discount factors very close to one, country j cannot lose by obeying this strategy provided

$$\max_{q_j} \Pi_j(q_j; Q^j_{-j}) \leq \Pi_s. \tag{11.1}$$

In words, given that the other $k - 1$ signatories provide Q^j_{-j} of the public good in the punishment phase, the maximum payoff that j can secure for itself in the punishment phase is no greater than the payoff it could get by complying with the treaty and thus re-establishing cooperation. That is, if eqn (11.1) holds, then j can do no better than to play q^j_j. Country j will therefore prefer to comply.

When push comes to shove, the $k - 1$ other parties to the agreement must also prefer to carry out their side of the bargain and supply Q^j_{-j} of the public good in the punishment phase. They will prefer to do this provided

$$\Pi_m(Q^j_{-j}; q^j_j) \geq \Pi_s \tag{11.2}$$

holds for every signatory m, $m \neq j$. If condition (11.2) is satisfied, then each signatory m does at least as well when all signatories other than j supply Q^j_{-j} in the punishment phase as when they ignore the deviation and continue to cooperate (notice that if condition (11.2) is satisfied for every signatory then it will also be satisfied for the summation of all the $k-1$ aggrieved signatories as a group). Condition (11.2) thus makes the threat to impose the punishment credible in the WCR sense of the term.

Condition (11.2) must be strengthened for a SCR treaty. For this kind of treaty it must not be possible for the countries other than j collectively to do better by choosing any feasible alternative to Q^j_{-j} (or, equivalently, q^j_m) in a punishment phase. That is, for a SCR treaty, Q^j_{-j} must be the solution to

$$\max_{Q_{-j}} \sum_{m, m \neq j} \Pi_m(Q_{-j}; q^j_j) \geq (K-1)\Pi_s. \tag{11.3}$$

It is easy to see that if condition (11.3) is satisfied then (11.2) will be satisfied but that the reverse need not be true. In general, SCR treaties are more credible than WCR treaties. Up to this point I have implicitly assumed that collectively rational punishments must be SCR.

11.5. BINARY ACTIONS

If actions are binary—if countries must choose either to play Pollute or Abate—then the WCR assumption makes no difference. Precisely the same number of countries can sustain a self-enforcing agreement whether condition (11.2) or (11.3) must be obeyed. The reason is that the binary choice cuts off any room for maneuver. The deviant must be punished. Assuming that the symmetric enforcing countries behave symmetrically, they must play $Q^j_{-j} = 0$. This will only be optimal from the perspective of condition (11.3) if $b(k - 1) - c \leq 0$. Obviously, we must have $q^j_j = 1$ in a punishment phase, and so condition (11.2) requires $b \geq bk - c$. These two requirements are equivalent. Both concepts also require that eqn (11.1) be satisfied. Because play

Pollute is a dominant strategy, eqn (11.1) requires that $q_j^i = 0$. Since $Q_{-j}^j = 0$, and Π_s = $bk - c$, eqn (11.1) requires $bk - c \geq 0$. Both requirements together imply that a self-enforcing agreement must satisfy eqn (7.2). Full cooperation can only be sustained if eqn (10.1) is satisfied.

11.6. CONTINUOUS ACTIONS

If actions are continuous (abatement by each country must lie *between* 0 and 1), there is a difference between WCR and SCR treaties, but the difference is trivial.

Because payoffs are linear, condition (11.3) will tell the enforcing countries to play zero abatement in the punishment phase provided $b(k - 1) < c$ (if $b(k - 1) = c$, then any level of abatement will be optimal). This is the same requirement as when actions are binary, and so the self-enforcing agreement will be the same as above.

Punishing a deviant only pays for the parties to a WCR treaty if $b(k - 1) \leq c$. However, condition (11.2) then requires $[c - b(k - 1)](1 - q_m^j) \leq 0$ and this will be satisfied for any feasible q_m^j. So a WCR and a SCR treaty can sustain precisely the same level of cooperation. The only difference is that the WCR treaty can do this while imposing smaller punishments.

The difference between WCR and SCR treaties only makes a difference when we consider the possibility that countries may negotiate by consensus.

11.7. CONSENSUS TREATIES

If N is small enough, we needn't compromise between choosing a high level of abatement and sustaining wide participation. However, if N is sufficiently large, the constraint of self-enforcement will bite. Thus far, the constraint has limited participation. I now consider whether it might limit cooperative abatement levels instead.

Since, for a sufficiently large N, a consensus treaty must require that less of the public good be supplied in a cooperative phase, we can only obtain a consensus treaty in general if actions are continuous.

A consensus treaty must satisfy eqn (11.1). If the treaty is WCR, condition (11.2) must also be accommodated. In the previous section I assumed that the signatories would play $q = 1$ in a cooperative phase and solved for the value of k capable of sustaining this payoff. Here, I turn things around. I set k equal to N and solve for the maximum payoff that can be sustained by a self-enforcing agreement. Denote this payoff by $\overline{\Pi}_s$.

Equation (11.1) requires

$$b(N - 1)q_m^j \leq \overline{\Pi}_s. \tag{11.4}$$

If condition (11.4) holds, then for discount factors close to one, the deviant cannot lose and may gain by re-establishing cooperation. The LHS of condition (11.4) is the best payoff j can get by continuing not to comply. The RHS of condition (11.4) is the average payoff j will get if it plays the strategy allowing a new cooperative phase to become established.

Similarly, condition (11.2) requires

$$b\left[q_j^j + (N-1)q_m^j\right] - cq_m^j \geq \overline{\Pi}_s. \tag{11.5}$$

If condition (11.5) holds, each of the $N-1$ countries called upon to punish j cannot do better than by carrying out their threat. Given that j plays q_j^j, the others are no worse off, and may be better off, playing q_m^j as opposed to ignoring the deviation and reverting to the cooperative phase without punishing j.

Setting $q_j^j = 1$ and rearranging, conditions (11.4) and (11.5) require

$$\frac{\overline{\Pi}_s - b}{b(N-1) - c} \leq q_m^j \leq \frac{\overline{\Pi}_s}{b(N-1)}$$

or

$$\overline{\Pi}_s \leq \frac{b^2(N-1)}{c}. \tag{11.6}$$

The RHS of eqn (11.6) is the maximum payoff that can be sustained by a self-enforcing, consensus agreement.

It might seem strange that this maximum value should be increasing in N. Remember, however, that the payoff to full cooperation is increasing in N, too. The ratio of the former payoff to the latter can be shown to be decreasing. Equation (11.6) thus tells us that, if the payoff each country realizes in the cooperative phase is lowered by enough relative to the full cooperative payoff, then a consensus agreement can be made WCR for *any* N. Lowering the payoff to cooperation reduces the incentive to renegotiate and thus makes more credible the threat to punish unilateral deviations.

It can now be seen why a SCR treaty cannot in general sustain a consensus. If N is large enough, the SCR concept requires that the countries other than j play $q_m^j = 1$ in a punishment phase. This is no punishment. Hence, for N large enough, a SCR consensus treaty does not exist.

11.8. CREDIBILITY vs FAIRNESS

This raises an important question: is it more plausible for treaties to be WCR or SCR? The answer is not obvious. SCR treaties are more credible. But that does not mean that they are more likely to be negotiated. Suppose that there was a fixed cost to negotiating or renegotiating a treaty. Then a deviation may trigger a simple response: the parties to the treaty either carry out the requirements of the treaty or they do not. Renegotiation, being costly, may not be undertaken.

However, there is a more compelling reason for supporting the WCR assumption. The extra credibility of an SCR treaty can only be obtained at the cost of reduced flexibility. An agreement backed up by credible threats is compelling, but so is an agreement that is perceived to be "fair." Suppose that the players held strong beliefs that all countries should play their part—that the equilibrium for symmetric players should itself be symmetric. Strict adherence to the SCR concept would require that this concern for fairness take a back seat to credibility. But why should credibility outweigh concerns for fairness?[4]

To be clear, I am not arguing that agreements should be fair from an abstract, moral perspective (though that may also be true). My point, rather, is that an agreement is more likely to be self-enforcing if it is perceived by its parties to be fair. As law professor Daniel Bodansky (1999: 603) puts it, "whether international environmental regimes are perceived as legitimate will play an important role in their long-term success."

The behavior of real people suggests that concerns for fairness often dominate credibility. Consider, for example, the ultimatum game. In this game, two people have a fixed sum of money to divide—say, $100. One person, the Proposer, is able to make a proposal for how to divide the money. The other person, the Responder, can either accept or reject the proposal. If the proposal is rejected, both players get nothing. If the proposal is accepted, both players get the amounts specified by the proposal. If the Proposer were to look forward and reason backward, she would offer $99 (assuming that the proposal must be in whole dollar increments). She would make this offer because she would know that the Responder would prefer to get $1 than nothing, and so would accept the proposal. (Why offer a 98–2 split when you know that a 99–1 split will be accepted?) However, in experiments with real people, most offers are in the range of 40–50 percent ($ 40–50). Proposals offering less than 30 percent of the total money available are almost always rejected. Almost never does a Proposer offer less than 20 percent or more than 50 percent. I stress that these are common findings. It has been observed in countries as diverse as Indonesia, Russia, Japan, Israel, the United States, and several European countries (see Fehr and Gächter 2000*b*). It has also been observed in seventeen vastly different primitive societies (Henrich *et al.* 2001). The reason: low offers seem unfair.

One reason low offers may seem unfair is that these games do not explain why one party should be the Proposer and the other the Responder; it just happens that one party *is* the Proposer and the other the Responder. But why should the party chosen to be the Proposer be so lucky?

Here's another way in which a sum of money can be divided. The Proposer chooses a division, and the Responder chooses which piece of the division he wants. Obviously, in this situation, the Proposer will propose a 50–50 allocation, and it will not matter which piece of the sum the Responder chooses. This allocation mechanism results in a fair allocation. In particular, it results in an allocation that is *envy-free*, meaning that neither player prefers the other person's allocation to her own. It also results in an allocation that is *role-neutral*, meaning that the equilibrium payoffs do not depend on how the roles are assigned to the two players.[5]

My guess is that the players in the ultimatum game recognize that the 50–50 split is the fair allocation, and that, moreover, each recognizes that the other player

---

[4] Binmore (1998) makes a different criticism. He argues that a negotiated equilibrium should resist demands for renegotiation *on* the equilibrium path, but that it is unreasonable to demand that negotiated agreements be renegotiation-proof *off* the equilibrium path, too. By this reasoning, also, WCR treaties are more appealing.

[5] See Young (1994) for a discussion of fair allocation processes.

recognizes the 50–50 split as being the fair allocation. The Responder will punish deviations from this fair allocation, and the Proposer can anticipate this response (this explains why the Proposer offers more than $1). However, the Responder has only a very blunt punishment to hand: he can only accept or reject. If the Responder could impose a separate penalty in whole dollar increments, he might choose a value that was broadly proportional to the deviation from the 50–50 division. Being able only to wield his blunt weapon, however, he will only punish deviations that deviate *enough* from the fair division.

In the ultimatum game, concerns for fairness upset the subgame perfect equilibrium. The theory tells us that the threat to punish offers below, say, 40 percent, should not be credible; and yet, based on how real people play this game, the threat *is* credible. A similar logic may support a WCR consensus treaty. The threat to impose the WCR sanctions against a deviant may not be credible in the SCR sense. However, if the WCR sanctions are perceived as being necessary to enforce an inherently fair allocation, then they may be credible in a different sense. When push comes to shove, the players in this treaty game may carry out their threat rather than renegotiate, to sustain the outcome they perceive to be fair.

There is yet another way of looking at this. Experimental evidence suggests that, when given the opportunity to punish a free-rider, cooperating players will take it, even if imposing a punishment is self-damaging (Fehr and Gächter 2000*a*). The reason given by these authors is that the cooperating players dislike being made a "sucker." This suggests that the WCR assumption may be reasonable after all. Collectively, all the cooperating countries may feel that they have been treated unfairly by the free-rider, and they may be willing to punish this country even though doing so is, strictly speaking, irrational. Essentially, emotions override rationality.[6]

Having made this argument, it might be tempting to weaken the collective rationality assumption even further. After all, the full cooperative outcome is a symmetric outcome with symmetric players, and this "fair" outcome can be sustained as a subgame perfect equilibrium, a concept only a bit less credible than WCR punishments. However, for reasons given in Chapter 10, subgame perfection is too weak a requirement for international agreements. It suppresses the collective nature of the negotiation enterprise. The WCR concept strikes a kind of compromise.

Even if you believe that the SCR concept has special merit, there is virtue in considering the WCR alternative. Doing so allows us to test robustness. It also allows us to examine the implications of negotiation by consensus. If the SCR concept is believed to be more appropriate, then in general countries will be unable to sustain consensus agreements. This is important to know. If, however, the WCR concept seems compelling, partly because it is better suited to sustaining a consensus, then we have learned an important lesson: agreements sustaining full participation may not sustain full cooperation. This, too, is important to know.

---

[6] Note that Fehr and Gächter (2000*a*) make a peculiar assumption. They assume that when player *i* punishes deviant *j*, only *i* and *j* are harmed; the other cooperating players are unaffected. This can't happen in a public goods game where strategy sets are limited to choice of a provision level.

11.9. "BROAD BUT SHALLOW" vs "NARROW BUT DEEP"

If we accept the relevance of the WCR concept, cooperation can be manifest in a number of ways. Parties to an agreement may maximize their collective payoff, taking their participation as given; or they may instead decide that participation must be full, and maximize their collective payoff subject to meeting the constraint of self-enforcement (as discussed later, intermediate outcomes are also sustainable). What are the implications of these alternatives?

Let k^* denote the number of signatories to a (possibly) incomplete treaty. For the linear model in continuous actions, k^* is the largest integer not greater than $(b + c)/b$. Now, if N happens not to exceed k^*, then it seems pretty obvious that full cooperation will be sustained. Suppose, however, that $N > k^*$. Then a partial agreement may be formed, with $k = k^*$ signatories. This, of course, was a prediction of Chapter 7.

Of course, if there are k^* signatories, and if $N > k^*$, then there must be $N - k^*$ non-signatories. In keeping with Chapter 7, assume that these non-signatories behave non-cooperatively, setting $q_n = 0$. Signatories will of course play $q_s = 1$. Denote the payoff to a non-signatory by $\Pi_n(k^*; N)$ and the payoff to a signatory by $\Pi_s(k^*; N)$. Upon substituting we get $\Pi_n = bk^*$, $\Pi_s = bk^* - c$.

From eqn (11.6) we know that a consensus treaty can support a payoff of $\overline{\Pi} = b^2(N - 1)/c$. So, which kind of agreement will countries prefer to negotiate, a "narrow but deep" partial agreement or a "broad but shallow" consensus treaty?

Put yourself in the shoes, so to speak, of a signatory to a partial agreement. Broadening participation gets non-participants to supply more of the public good, which helps you. Moreover, since the abatement by each party is lower for a consensus treaty than a partial treaty, your costs fall. This is all for the good. However, your country would lose to the extent that other signatories to the partial agreement reduce *their* abatement under the consensus alternative. Taken together, it isn't obvious which kind of agreement signatories to a partial agreement will prefer. However, for the linear model it is easy to confirm that signatories to a partial agreement will always prefer the consensus alternative. To be precise, it can be shown that $\overline{\Pi}(N) > \Pi_s(k^*; N)$ for $N > k^*$.[7] In other words, the signatories to a partial agreement consisting of k^* countries will *always* prefer a consensus treaty.

What about the non-signatories to the partial agreement? Since these countries free ride, it might seem that they would prefer the status quo. If a consensus agreement were negotiated, these countries would now have to incur a cost for abatement. Moreover, the signatories to the partial agreement would lower their provision of the public good as participation increased, and this would harm the non-signatories to a partial agreement. On the other hand, however, the *other* non-signatories to the partial agreement would have to supply some of the public good if a consensus agreement

---

[7] Suppose that this claim is false. Then, upon substituting, we must have $b^2(N - 1)/c \leq bk^* - c$. The RHS of this inequality is increasing in k^* and k^* cannot exceed $(b + c)/b$. Hence, if the inequality holds for $k^* = (b + c)/b$ then it will hold for any k^*. Substitution and a little algebra shows that this implies $N \leq (b + c)/b$. Since k^* is the largest integer not greater than $(b + c)/b$, this implies $N < k^*$. By assumption $N > k^*$. Hence, the claim must be true.

were formed instead, and this would benefit each such non-participant. Upon reflection, non-signatories to a partial agreement may be better off with a consensus agreement provided N were sufficiently greater than k^*. Indeed, it can be shown that $\overline{\Pi}(N) \geq \Pi_n(k^*;N)$ for $N \geq (ck^* + b)/b$.[8] Since $b < c$ by assumption, N must be at least two countries greater than k^* for non-signatories to prefer a consensus agreement.

Now imagine that all countries around the negotiation table can look forward and calculate the implications of negotiating a partial vs a consensus agreement. As the negotiations get underway, no country knows whether it will be a signatory or a non-signatory to a partial agreement (this will be true so long as countries must choose to be a signatory or a non-signatory independently—that is, without knowing how the others have chosen—as assumed in Chapter 7). If a partial agreement is negotiated, each party can expect to get a payoff of $\hat{\Pi} = \left[k^*\Pi_s + (N-k^*)\Pi_n\right] \div N$. This payoff is obviously less than Π_n and so a consensus agreement is more likely to be preferred by all countries from this *ex ante* perspective. Indeed, it can be shown that, from this *ex ante* perspective, all countries will prefer the consensus alternative provided $N \geq (c/b)^2$.[9]

Notice that there is no time inconsistency problem here. *Ex ante*, all countries would rather that there be a consensus agreement provided $N \geq (c/b)^2$. *Ex post*, no country could gain by deviating since the consensus treaty is self-enforcing.

Consider an example. Suppose $N = 99$, $b = 2$, and $c = 15$. Then an incomplete CR treaty will consist of eight signatories—and from an *ex ante* perspective all countries will prefer to negotiate by consensus. However, if $b = 2$, and $c = 131$, then an incomplete CR treaty will consist of 66 signatories—and, from an *ex ante* perspective, all countries will prefer this treaty to a consensus. A consensus treaty will be preferred only when an incomplete CR treaty would attract participation by a small fraction of countries.

To sum up, if agreements need only be WCR, countries may prefer to negotiate by consensus. A consensus treaty will appear especially attractive when non-participation in a partial agreement would be substantial. Consensus agreements are not only fair; from the perspective of the negotiating table, they hold the prospect of making every country better off as compared with the partial agreement alternative. With WCR treaties, participation will be either full or nearly full. As explained earlier, this result is more compatible with the treaties listed in the Appendix 6.1.

---

[8] Upon substituting, $\overline{\Pi}(N) \geq \Pi_n(k^*;N)$ implies $b^2(N-1)/c \geq bk^*$, which upon rearranging proves the claim.

[9] A consensus agreement will be preferred to a partial agreement if $\overline{\Pi} \geq \hat{\Pi}$. Upon substituting we get $b^3N^2 - b[b^2 + c(b + c)]N + c^2(b + c) \geq 0$. The LHS of this inequality is quadratic. Let $\underline{N}$ and $\overline{N}$ denote the two values of N for which the quadratic term equals zero. By inspection, the inequality holds for $N \geq \overline{N} \geq \underline{N}$. Solving the quadratic yields $\underline{N} = (b+c)/b$ and $\overline{N} = (c/b)^2$. Since $\overline{N}$ is the largest integer less than or equal to $(b+c)/b$, and since $\underline{N}$ and $\overline{N}$ need not be integers, it follows that $\underline{N} \geq \overline{N}$. But the proposition holds for $N > \overline{N}$. Hence, $\overline{\Pi} \geq \hat{\Pi}$ only holds for $N > \overline{N}$ if $N \geq \overline{N}$ or $N \geq (c/b)^2$.

11.10. INTERMEDIATE AGREEMENTS

I have thus far considered two extreme treaties. In one, a subset of countries chooses a per-country abatement level with the objective of maximizing the collective payoff of the group, without any regard for the need to deter free-riding. In the other, all N countries choose an abatement level for each country with the objective of maximizing their collective payoff, subject to ensuring that the agreement is self-enforcing. The former kind of agreement is compelling by the logic developed in Chapter 7. The latter kind is compelling from the perspective developed in this chapter. However, it should be obvious that any agreement between these extremes can also be sustained as a self-enforcing treaty—provided such agreements need only be WCR. To be precise, an agreement consisting of *any* number of countries can always be sustained as a WCR treaty.

This last observation is important because in the real world it may be pretty clear which countries should participate in a treaty and which need not do so. That is, "fairness" may be context-dependent. In the Montreal Protocol negotiations, it was agreed that the industrialized countries had to reduce their emissions more, and faster, than developing countries. Similarly, in the climate change negotiations, it was accepted from the start that the industrialized countries needed to move first, partly because they were more able to do so by virtue of their incomes and partly because they were more responsible for the historic build-up of greenhouse gases. The WCR concept allows the burden of cooperation to be carried by such a "focal" group of countries.

11.11. INCREASING MARGINAL COSTS

There is one more reason why a consensus may be supported. If marginal abatement costs increase in the level of abatement (as in the payoff functions shown in the second and last rows of Table 7.1), then the total abatement achieved by any incomplete treaty can always be achieved at lower cost by widening participation. The reason is that the signatories will be abating more than the non-signatories and, since marginal abatement costs are increasing, the cost of abating at the margin must be greater among signatories than non-signatories. Holding total abatement constant, a slight redistribution in abatement away from signatories and toward non-signatories will therefore lower costs. This reduction in costs provides a strong, additional incentive for widening participation. Indeed, it can be shown that, *if marginal abatement costs are increasing, countries will always prefer to negotiate by consensus* (Barrett 2002a).

Though I have assumed throughout the analytical chapters of this book that marginal costs are constant (or, equivalently, that abatement is binary), they are more likely to be increasing. As we shall see in Chapter 15, marginal costs increase very steeply for climate change mitigation. For reasons of fairness, countries agreed in Berlin in 1995 that a climate protocol must limit the emissions of the industrialized countries only. However, because marginal costs increase steeply, there will be a tension between limiting emission reductions for reasons of fairness and wanting to widen participation in order to lower the total cost. The Kyoto Protocol tries to resolve this tension by requiring emission reductions only by the industrialized countries, as agreed in Berlin, *and* by allowing these countries to meet these by reducing emissions within the developing countries (by means of the so-called Clean Development Mechanism or CDM). Essentially, industrialized countries can offset their own emissions by reducing emissions in developing countries. The problem is that, as explained in Chapter 15, the CDM is likely to be costly to administer, and so may not help much in lowering costs.

The US Senate and the administration of George W. Bush have criticized Kyoto for imposing emission ceilings on industrialized countries but not on developing countries. The reason, as far as I can tell, is not that they think Kyoto is unfair. The reasons are that a partial agreement would be environmentally ineffective (emissions may relocate to developing countries) and costly.

Leaving aside the problem of environmental effectiveness, discussed in the next chapter, the challenge is how to reconcile concerns for fairness with concerns for cost effectiveness. One possibility is to require that developing countries limit their emissions (this helping to achieve cost-effectiveness), with the industrialized countries paying directly for the cost (achieving a fair outcome). This approach, adopted by the Montreal Protocol, is analyzed in Chapter 13. Another possibility is for the developing countries to agree to limit their emissions, with the final distribution of abatement being determined by emissions trading. It is easy to show that, if the developing countries are offered a large enough initial allocation of emission entitlements, then they can be made no worse off by acceding, and would actually be made better off by trading (as would the industrialized countries).[10] As explained in Chapter 15, this is the arrangement Kyoto made for the economies in transition.

So the preference for consensus, inspired by a collective desire to lower costs, can accommodate concerns for fairness by means of side payments or by carefully chosen initial allocations of tradeable emission entitlements. However, the problem remains that either kind of agreement needs to be enforced. As shown in this chapter, expanding the breadth of cooperation may necessitate a sacrifice in the depth of cooperation. Montreal was able to have it both ways. It sustains virtually full participation *and* requires huge cuts in emissions. Kyoto, we shall learn in Chapter 15, is not so lucky.

11.12. CONCLUSIONS

The main result of Chapter 7, that participation may be substantially less than full, sits rather awkwardly next to the facts. So, too, does the notion that agreements satisfying full participation will typically sustain full cooperation. Countries often seek to agree by consensus; and free-riding, is not as common as the theory developed in

---

[10] For analyses of emissions trading cast within an international negotiating framework, see Barrett (1992*e,f,g*). Note, however, that these analyses put the enforcement problem to one side. The aim is to determine allocations of emission entitlements that would be "acceptable" to a wide variety of countries, representing different interests as regards climate change. As explained in Chapter 15, though negotiations may focus on initial allocations and the design of trading and related "flexible" mechanisms, the real problem lies with enforcement.

Chapters 7 and 10 predicts. At the same time, agreements arrived at by consensus are notoriously weak. The theory developed in this chapter provides an explanation for this.

It is true that some important treaties are incomplete. But it is not obvious that free-riding is the reason for non-participation. Iceland, an active whaling nation, withdrew from the Whaling Convention in 1992 only after other parties objected to a resumption of whaling on animal welfare rather than conservation grounds. Though Afghanistan and Eritrea have yet to sign the Montreal Protocol, the reason is not that they aspire to free ride.

Indeed, countries feel rather uneasy about being identified as a free-rider (recall the reaction, noted in Section 4.14, of the House of Commons Environment Committee to Britain being labeled the "dirty man of Europe"). They seem rather to be inclined to join in with other states, to help form a consensus. There are many reasons for this. States may have a preference to conform. They may have to pay a price for failing to conform. They may be persuaded that, for moral reasons, they ought to cooperate provided enough others do so. Or, from the *ex ante* perspective, states may realize that it is in their interests to negotiate by consensus. In this chapter I have emphasized this last explanation.

I have also shown that self-enforcement can assert itself in different ways. It may be manifest in under-provision as well as non-participation. That a treaty sustains full participation may thus be no reason to cheer; consensus treaties may still fall far short of full cooperation. Related to this, I have shown that countries may need to moderate their demands (in terms of per-country provision) not just because of the "lowest common denominator" effect usually associated with the need to accommodate heterogeneous countries, but also because moderation may be necessary to make wider participation self-enforcing.

Of course, the exception, once again, is Montreal. The next chapter explains how this agreement was able to sustain full participation, even while requiring very deep cuts in emissions.

12

Trade Leakage and Trade Linkage

The use of trade measures in [multilateral environmental agreements] has been and will continue to be an effective tool for achieving important environmental objectives.
Non-paper by the United States Government (1996), submitted to the Committee on Trade and Environment, World Trade Organization (September 11, 1996)

12.1. INTRODUCTION

The theory developed thus far tells us that it is especially hard for the international system to supply *global* public goods. The punishments needed to deter free-riding, or to sustain efficient provision levels, will not usually be credible when the number of countries is very large. And yet I have also argued that the Montreal Protocol sustains full cooperation, or something very close to it. So how was Montreal able to do this? As explained in Chapter 8, a favorable cost–benefit ratio helped. But so did strategy. This chapter and the next emphasize how the treaty manipulated the incentives to sustain full cooperation. This chapter stresses the importance of sticks; the next chapter emphasizes the need for carrots. It is really the combination of the two instruments that makes Montreal a success.

Of course, we have already examined the utility of sticks, and the problem of making sticks credible. And we have learned that credibility limits the level of international cooperation that can be sustained. But we have thus far restricted choice of sticks to choice of pollution abatement (reciprocity). This chapter considers the advantage in expanding the strategy space—in letting countries use instruments other than strategies of reciprocity for deterring non-cooperation. In particular, the focus of this chapter is on the use of trade restrictions.

Trade restrictions can do two things. They can be used both to punish countries that do not cooperate and to correct for a loss in the "competitiveness" of the countries that do cooperate. And it turns out that there is an intimate connection between these different purposes. Concerns about a loss in "competitiveness" help to make the threat to punish, and punish severely in some cases, credible. At the same time, trade restrictions are not a ready cure-all for every cooperation problem. They need to be dispensed with great care.

12.2. ISSUE LINKAGE

The problem with reciprocity is that it loses its strength as the number of countries supplying a public good increases. This is because, when limited to choosing provision levels as punishments, enforcement is self-damaging. To do better, parties have to enrich the strategy space. They need to link participation to some other action.

Linkage probably seems the obvious remedy. But it is a mistake to think that linkage is a quick fix. It is even a mistake to think that linkage will always be beneficial. Linkage can hinder as well as aid cooperation. Whether linkage will assist cooperation depends on the issues that are linked, and the manner in which they are linked.

The example of whaling best illustrates this point. After the ban on commercial whaling came into effect in 1986, Iceland appealed to the International Whaling Commission (IWC) for permission to carry out limited whaling for "scientific purposes." The IWC rejected Iceland's application, and Iceland objected to the IWC's decision in turn. The United States threatened to certify Iceland under the Pelly Amendment, banning imports of fish products from Iceland. We learned earlier how threats like this often fail the credibility test. But in this case credibility was not the problem; the problem was linkage.

At the IWC's 1987 meeting, Iceland's representative defended "the sovereign right of Iceland to pursue its own science without interference from either the IWC or the United States" (Ellis 1991: 475). He also threatened "to oust US forces from the NATO base at Keflavik if the United States persisted in hamstringing Icelandic research whaling" (Ellis 1991: 475). This sufficed to tilt the balance of the negotiations Iceland's way. At the IWC's 1989 meeting, Iceland offered to cap its 1989 harvest (for scientific purposes) at sixty-eight fin whales. It also announced that it would abstain from whaling in 1990 and had no plans to resume whaling thereafter. This announcement was welcomed by the United States, which promptly dropped its threat to impose sanctions.

Iceland's linkage of the IWC and NATO was deliberate, but linkage can be unavoidable. Indeed, linkage is sometimes so obvious that it need never even be discussed openly. At the IWC's 44th Annual Meeting, held in Glasgow in 1992, Norway announced that it would resume commercial whaling. At first, the United States and the European Union protested. But as Norway entered into membership talks with the European Union, Europe hushed any criticism of Norway's whaling policy. US objections to Norway's policy were also silenced after Norway succeeded in getting Israel and the Palestine Liberation Organization to sign a peace accord (Rose and Paleokrassis 1996).

So, what kinds of linkage *are* beneficial to cooperation? Cesar and de Zeeuw (1994) offer an abstract example. They analyze the linkage of two asymmetric, two-player prisoners' dilemma (PD) games. When considered in isolation, the full cooperative outcomes of these games cannot be sustained by a self-enforcing agreement. (The reason for the failure of cooperation is the assumed strong asymmetry.) However, when these games are linked—and it is crucial that the games be mirror images of each other—then the linked game will be a symmetric PD and, invoking the logic of Chapter 10, it is easy to show that the full cooperative outcome of this linked game can be sustained by a self-enforcing treaty.[1]

---

[1] Hauer and Runge (1999) link a one-shot PD environmental game to a one-shot coordination "trade liberalization" game. Unsurprisingly, they find that, if the gains from coordination are large enough, the linked game becomes a coordination game, too. Linkage then helps resolve the environmental dilemma without compromising the coordination problem.

It is not essential that the linked games be *precise* mirror images of each other. As long as the combined game is sufficiently symmetric, linkage will help to sustain cooperation (see Folmer *et al.* 1993). But knowing this does not help all that much. Linkage assists cooperation here only because the games being linked are asymmetric. Cesar and de Zeeuw (1994) do not show how linkage can help in symmetric games—the focus of this book thus far. Moreover, they rule out the use of side payments. As explained in Chapter 3, side payments may be needed to make cooperation individually attractive in asymmetric settings; and as I shall show in Chapter 13, side payments can boost cooperation when countries are strongly asymmetric. Finally, the Cesar–de Zeeuw analysis is limited to the special, two-player situation and does not specify, as a practical matter, the kind of issue that one might want to link to the resolution of a crossborder externality.

12.3. LINKAGE TO COOPERATIVE R&D

In these respects, a paper by economists Carlo Carraro and Dominico Siniscalco (1994) is more helpful. These authors link two symmetric, N-player games: a PD-like game (akin to the model shown in the second row of Table 7.1) and a cooperative Research and Development (R&D) agreement (R&D is assumed in this model to reduce both the production costs of firms and the emission/output ratio). Though protection of the shared environment is taken to be a public good, Carraro and Siniscalco assume that non-parties can be excluded from enjoying the fruits of cooperative R&D. This last assumption is crucial. Compared to the stand-alone environmental agreement, it ensures that linkage to R&D increases the benefit–cost ratio for accession. The effect can be striking: whereas the PD-like game can sustain cooperation among only three countries, Carraro and Siniscalco show that the linked game can sustain full cooperation in a self-enforcing agreement even when $N = 100$.

This is not a general result, however, and nor is this kind of linkage a common feature of actual treaties. For sure, international agreements routinely encourage cooperation in R&D. But in no case, so far as I am aware, do they seek to deprive non-signatories of the fruits of this cooperation, and only if they did would linkage with R&D cooperation increase participation in the Carraro–Siniscalco framework. The reason for this may be that signatories are technically unable to prevent their R&D from spilling over to non-signatories, or it maybe that signatories are unable to commit to denying non-signatories access to their R&D. The latter possibility is particularly interesting.

Though I do not know of a real world example that illustrates the Carraro–Siniscalco result, I can cite a counterexample: the Montreal Protocol.

The Montreal Protocol is superficially consistent with the Carraro–Siniscalco model. Article 9 of the agreement requires that parties "cooperate ... in promoting ... research, development, and exchange of information on," among other things, the "best technologies for improving the containment, recovery, recycling or destruction of controlled substances or otherwise reducing their emissions ..." Cooperation is also to be extended to R&D in "possible alternatives to controlled substances, to products containing such substances, and to products manufactured with them ... ."

But non-parties to the Montreal Protocol are allowed easy access to this R&D. Though signatories are discouraged from exporting technologies for producing and using controlled substances, and are to refrain from subsidizing such exports, the agreement explicitly exempts from these restrictions "products, equipment, plants or technology that improve the containment, recovery, recycling or destruction of controlled substances, promote the development of alternative substances, or otherwise contribute to the reduction of emissions of controlled substances."

That the Montreal Protocol makes no attempt to prevent or even to discourage signatories from passing on the fruits of their R&D to non-signatories suggests that the threat to restrict access to such knowledge may not be credible. Carraro and Sinsicalco *assume* that signatories withhold such knowledge from non-signatories, rather than show that they would *choose* to do so (though it is possible that states would choose to do so in their model; this would need to be checked). They therefore assume, implicitly, that signatories can commit to keeping their innovations secret.

My guess is that signatories to the Montreal Protocol could probably gain more by doing precisely the opposite as suggested by Carraro and Siniscalco—they would probably gain most by *sharing* their R&D with non-parties. As explained in Chapter 9, if the fruits of the R&D carried out by the first countries to sign the agreement are made widely available, the cost to other countries of acceding to the agreement may fall. The sharing of R&D may thus create a kind of bandwagon—a process that would benefit the first countries to sign and thus earn them a return (in the form of increased global reductions in emission) on their earlier investment. Under these circumstances, the refusal to share R&D would not be credible.

Indeed, though developing countries eventually received financial assistance in exchange for participation (the subject of the next chapter), Benedick (1998: 266) argues that "much or most of technology transfer and ODS phaseout in the developing world would probably take place even in the absence of the [Multilateral Fund], as a response to market factors and international competition. These forces became particularly powerful after the accelerated phaseout in the North generated a wave of attractive and affordable new technologies and alternatives."

12.4. TRADE LEAKAGE

Like R&D spillovers, international trade is automatically linked to environmental protection. But the effect of trade on cooperation is very different. If signatories to an environmental agreement reduce their pollution emissions, comparative advantage in the pollution-intensive industries is likely to shift to non-signatories, with the consequence that global emissions may fall by less than the reduction undertaken by signatories—a phenomenon known as *trade leakage*. In contrast to R&D spillovers, trade linkages may exacerbate free-riding.

A careful analysis by economists Brian Copeland and Scott Taylor (2000) shows that leakage may be negative—or, put differently, that abatement may be a strategic complement because of the trade mechanism. The effect of trade leakage described above might be called the production relocation effect. However, there will also be two other effects. Abatement would push up the cost of the polluting good in international markets, causing consumers to substitute cleaner goods. There would also be an income effect. Non-parties that specialized in producing the polluting good would get a higher price for their output, and thus realize a gain in income. If the environment were a normal good—if people were willing to pay more to protect the environment as they became richer—then these non-parties specializing in producing the polluting good would cut back on their pollution. Non-parties specializing in producing clean goods, by contrast, would experience a fall in income, and may therefore pollute more. When you add up all these effects, leakage could be either positive or negative (i.e. abatement could be a strategic substitute or a strategic complement). The sign (positive or negative) and magnitude of leakage is an empirical question.

Many of the negotiators at Montreal feared that the production effect of leakage would dominate—so much so that leakage would effectively make non-parties "pollution havens." They apparently had reason to worry. According to Benedick (1998: 248),

India, in particular, had embarked on a policy of expanding domestic production and export markets in the South, where it anticipated outstanding commercial opportunities as the North phased out CFCs. Indeed, in 1988, a year after the Montreal Protocol was signed, India had purchased an entire CFC plant from an American chemical company. In addition, India established three new CFC manufacturing plants during 1991 ....

India claimed that this expansion was needed to satisfy domestic demand, but Benedick (1998: 248–9) says that this could not have been true. "[M]ost of India's fivefold increase in CFC production from 1986 to 1993," he says, "was exported to other developing nations—and this output represented only about half of its recently expanded capacity, which was clearly oriented toward future sales."

12.5. POLICIES TO LIMIT LEAKAGE

In theory, signatories can correct for trade leakage by adjusting their border taxes. A simple example explains the logic.[2] Suppose that pollution arises from one sector only and is regulated by means of a pollution tax. Then, leakage could be neutralized by supplementing the pollution tax with a tariff on imports from non-signatories and a subsidy on exports from signatories to non-signatories.

Stiffer border tax adjustments could even *reverse* trade leakage by shifting pollution-intensive production toward signatories—that is, toward countries that have a lower emissions–output ratio.[3] In other words, border taxes could be used as an instrument of strategy. For sure, this would be a second-best policy; it would be better if participation in the treaty were full. But, being unable to impel others to participate, use of second-best instruments may be the best option available to the parties to an international agreement.

---

[2] I consider here only trade leakage in goods markets. For an analysis of trade leakage in the market for traded fuels, see Hoel (1994).

[3] I am ignoring here the optimal tariff that would accompany these adjustments. See Markusen (1975).

This is for a textbook economy. In a more realistic setting, calculation of the optimal border tax adjustment would strain the computing capabilities of even a well-funded secretariat. Where production of goods in two or more sectors causes pollution, for example, the analysis must take account of distortions between and not simply within sectors. Michael Hoel (1996) shows that in these more realistic settings even the *sign* of the border tax adjustment cannot be determined without a detailed analysis of the workings of the domestic and international economies.

Even ignoring these practical difficulties, border tax adjustments may clash with the multilateral trading rules of the World Trade Organization (WTO), incorporating the General Agreement on Tariffs and Trade (GATT). There are two main problems.

The first is that, if some parties to the WTO are not also parties to the environmental agreement, then the adjustments would violate the non-discrimination principle of the WTO; some WTO members would be subject to different tariff arrangements than others.

For sure, exemptions may be allowed. Article XX of the GATT allows parties to take measures "necessary to protect human, animal or plant life or health" or "relating to the conservation of exhaustible natural resources," and a legal expert from the GATT Secretariat advised negotiators to the Montreal Protocol that the trade restrictions in this agreement would satisfy Article XX (Benedick 1998). Others within the GATT had a different view, however, and the GATT Secretariat later criticized the discriminatory nature of the Montreal Protocol trade restrictions on the basis that they were unnecessary, that other, more GATT-consistent measures could have been taken. I shall return to this criticism later, but it is as well to point out here that, whatever a legal interpretation may recommend, no member of the GATT/WTO has challenged the trade restrictions in the Montreal Protocol. The parties to this agreement have thus voted with their feet, as it were, and endorsed the discriminatory trade restrictions in the Montreal Protocol. In the anarchical international system, this is more significant than a legal opinion.

The second problem with the use of border tax adjustments is that, if they were based on the manufacture of the traded good (in the trade jargon, with the "production or processing methods" or PPMs), rather than on the characteristics of the traded good itself, then otherwise identical products would be subject to different border taxes. Such a differentiation is currently prohibited by the trading rules. Of course, the parties to the WTO could always renegotiate this agreement to allow for differentiation of this kind. But doing so would create tremendous practical problems.

Indeed, though Article 4 of the Montreal Protocol allows parties to restrict trade in products made using ozone-depleting substances, such as electronic components made using chlorofluorocarbons (CFCs) as a solvent, the Ozone Secretariat was advised in 1993 that such a restriction would be impossible to implement (Van Slooten 1994). Trace residues are hard to detect, especially where CFCs have been used as solvents. Moreover, since ozone-depleting substances (ODS) are bound to be used indirectly, if not directly, in the manufacture of most traded goods, a wide interpretation of the clause would need to include nearly all trade. Brack (1996) claims that the costs to signatories of a blanket import ban would exceed the environmental benefits (put differently, the threat to impose a total ban would not be credible).

Could a cruder but easier-to-calculate instrument work nearly as well as the appropriate border tax adjustment? Probably not. Hoel (1996) has demonstrated that a pollution tax differentiated by sector would be even harder to calculate than the optimal border tax adjustment. For example, Hoel shows that there is no simple relationship between fossil fuel intensity and the optimal sector-specific carbon tax. Moreover, the available empirical evidence suggests that crude sectoral differentiation may be ineffective. Oliveira-Martins *et al.* (1992) find that, if energy-intensive industry in Europe were exempted from having to pay a carbon tax, then leakage would be unaffected and the predicted output losses for the energy-intensive sector would be virtually unchanged.

It would seem, then, that we have reached an impasse. Though trade leakage could undermine the supply of global public goods, the policies needed to correct for trade leakage may well be impractical, illegal (in the sense of violating the existing multilateral trade agreements), or ineffective. In most instances (there may be exceptions), leakage cannot be corrected using second-best policies.

However, recall that leakage is only a problem if participation in an international environmental agreement (IEA) is incomplete. If participation is full, then leakage will be zero by definition. So, if leakage cannot be corrected directly by the use of tariffs, differentiated taxes and the like, perhaps it can be neutralized indirectly by policies that punish non-participation and thus deter free-riding in the bargain. This roundabout way of correcting leakage is a hallmark of the Montreal Protocol.

12.6. TRADE RESTRICTIONS IN THE MONTREAL PROTOCOL

The Montreal Protocol bans trade between signatories and non-signatories in the substances (like CFCs) controlled by the treaty. It also bans imports from non-signatories of products containing these substances—goods like refrigerators and air conditioners. The treaty leaves open the possibility that signatories may also ban imports from non-signatories of products *made using* the listed substances (like computers, the circuits of which may be cleaned using CFCs), but as noted previously implementation of this ban would pose a number of practical problems and trade in such products has not been restricted. Signatories have retained the option to restrict trade in these products in the future, however, and according to Van Slooten (1994) the threat to do so has provided some incentive for countries to participate in the Protocol (see also Brack 1996). But the two-way ban on trade in ozone-depleting chemicals has almost certainly had the greater effect on behavior, and it is this policy that I consider in detail below.

A trade ban is a blunt instrument for controlling leakage—blunter, certainly, than the appropriate border tax adjustment (a trade ban is like a very, very high tariff). But, as noted earlier, leakage can be controlled indirectly by deterring non-participation, and this is what the negotiators intended the trade ban to do. According to Benedick (1998: 54), the United States first proposed including trade restrictions in the treaty "to create incentives for nations to adhere to the protocol and simultaneously to protect US industry against unfair competition from countries not submitting themselves to the treaty's requirements."

Of course, in deterring non-participation, the trade ban would simultaneously deter free-riding and thus do what a strategy of reciprocity perhaps could not do: sustain full cooperation. In Benedick's (1998: 91) words, the restrictions were "critical, since they constituted the only enforcement mechanism in the protocol." Recall the central message of this book: cooperative agreements to protect the shared environment must be self-enforcing. A mechanism must be built into a treaty to restructure incentives. In the Montreal Protocol, this was the principal role played by the trade restrictions.

How can trade restrictions succeed where more conventional strategies of reciprocity fail? The answer is not obvious. Trade restrictions have a familiar feature: they hurt the countries that impose them as well as those on the receiving end. So there must have been something special about the ozone depletion problem that made the threat to impose trade restrictions credible.

12.7. LINKING ENVIRONMENTAL PROTECTION TO TRADE

To learn more, it will be helpful to link the model of international cooperation developed in Chapter 7 to a model of international trade. Doing so will allow us to illustrate the effect of trade leakage and trade linkage on international cooperation.

We normally think of trade as arising from differences between countries—differences in endowments, perhaps, or technologies. However, up to this point I have assumed for analytical convenience that countries are symmetric. Fortunately, I can retain the assumption of symmetry and still incorporate a model of trade (symmetry, recall, has the advantage in letting us show graphically how a treaty can transform incentives). Moreover, I can do this without having to resort to *ad hoc* modeling (e.g. by specifying leakage and the gains-from-trade exogenously). I will, however, have to rely on a very special model of trade. My analysis in this chapter will thus be even more illustrative than were previous chapters.[4]

The trade model used here is partial and so the analysis ignores general equilibrium effects. In particular, the consumption effect of trade noted earlier is ruled out by assumption. Moreover, the environmental benefit of abatement is assumed to be independent of income. These assumptions mean that leakage is only associated with a production effect. By construction, leakage is positive in this model.

As the model is tailored to fit the ozone depletion problem, I assume: (1) that the environmental agreement may only restrict trade in goods directly linked to the environmental problem,[5] (2) that the industry producing these goods is imperfectly competitive,[6] and (3) that the industry's output is homogeneous (though a number of substances are

---

[4] The model presented here is a slightly simpler version of the one presented in Barrett (1997a). The important difference is that I assume here that abatement is binary.

[5] Chang (1995) calls such policies "direct trade interventions." They are to be distinguished from restrictions on goods unrelated to the environmental problem, which Chang calls "pure trade sanctions."

[6] According to Haas (1992), when the Montreal Protocol was being negotiated, CFCs were produced by only 17 companies operating in 16 countries. Calculations by the US EPA (1988b) show that the Protocol's controlled substances were produced by only seven companies in the United States in 1986, and that one company—Du Pont—accounted for 54 percent of this total. See also Parson (1993).

controlled by the treaty, each is a commodity). Finally, I borrow from Brander (1981) and Brander and Krugman (1983) the assumption that firms segment the global market, choosing destination-specific output levels. This means that a company like Du Pont does not choose a total output level, letting the market decide how it should be distributed around the world. Instead, it chooses a level of output to produce and ship to each market. An implication of this assumption is that, provided transport costs are low enough (and I assume for simplicity that transportation costs are zero), every firm will serve every market under a regime of free trade. In this setting, the gains from trade derive mainly from increased competition and are manifest in lower prices and thus a higher consumers' surplus (producer profits will also be affected).

Though this construction captures a number of important features of stratospheric ozone protection, I must emphasize that other approaches might be taken and that the results obtained here may not hold generally. This caution is all the more important in that I make a number of simplifying assumptions and only solve even this special model numerically. My purpose, to repeat, is to illustrate how the Montreal Protocol was able to sustain full participation.

12.8. THE UNDERLYING FREE TRADE GAME

The novelty in this game, as compared with earlier chapters, is that I now introduce a new set of players: firms. Governments have the authority to regulate their own manufacturers of CFCs, but in doing so they can be expected to take into account how firms will "react" to their regulatory interventions. Firms thus choose last in this game.

The model is developed in Appendix 12.1. Here I provide a summary. As before, there are N symmetric countries. A single firm resides within each country (so that there are also N symmetric firms), firm location is fixed, and entry of new firms is somehow restricted. Each firm produces a joint product: a homogeneous traded good and a public bad, ozone depletion. Production of the traded good is costly and depends on whether the firm is allowed to produce CFCs (play Pollute) or whether it is required to substitute away from these chemicals (play Abate). Firms choose their origin-specific output levels simultaneously (i.e. each firm makes this choice without knowing how its rivals have chosen), while their governments decide whether they must play Pollute or Abate. Firms take these decisions as given (they are made in the preceding stages of the game).

Note that there is one important difference between this model and the ones developed in previous chapters. Here, a country's emissions are variable; they depend on whether the country lets its firm play Pollute and on the output level chosen by the firm. The output level of each firm depends in turn on the output levels of the other firms. If other firms produce more, prices will be lowered, and it will be in each firm's interests to scale back production. In other words, destination-specific output levels are strategic substitutes.

To begin, assume that there exists a regime of free trade and that all countries must choose simultaneously whether to require their firms to play Pollute or Abate. In doing so, each country will take account of how its choice will affect firm behavior

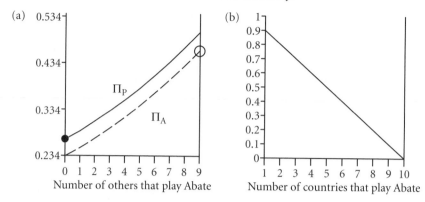

Figure 12.1. *The underlying free trade game.*
(a) Underlying free trade game, (b) Leakage rate

and, therefore, global emissions. Each country will also take account of how its choice will affect the profits of its firm and the consumers's surplus realized by its citizenry.

The game is illustrated in Figure 12.1. In this example, $N = 10$, $b = 0.025$, and the cost to each country of playing Abate exceeds this benefit (I will explain this cost below). In this game, no matter how many others play Abate, each country can do no better than to play Pollute. There is thus a unique equilibrium in which every country plays Pollute and gets a payoff $\Pi_P(0) = 0.269$. Every country would be better off, however, if each played Abate. Every country would then get $\Pi_A(9) = 0.462$.

This underlying game looks almost identical to Figure 3.6(a). But it is actually very different from the PD games examined previously in this book. Leakage is an important feature of this game. When a country plays Abate, its firm is required to use the more costly substitutes for CFCs, and its best response to this regulation is to reduce output. Crucially, the output of the $N - 1$ other firms also changes. In equilibrium, these other firms increase their outputs (remember, output is a strategic substitute). If these firms are allowed to pollute, this increase in output will increase emissions. This is the leakage effect—which, by construction, is positive in this model. As one country reduces its emissions, other countries increase theirs.

Figure 12.1(b) shows the magnitude of leakage for the game modeled in Figure 12.1(a). The leakage rate is defined here as the increase in the emissions of all polluting countries divided by the reduction in the emissions of a country that plays Abate. If the firms in polluting countries did not adjust their outputs, leakage would be zero. In the example shown in Figure 12.1, the leakage rate is positive and falls (linearly) as the number of countries that play Abate increases. This is because, as more countries play Abate, there are fewer left that can play Pollute. Note, however, that a different model of trade would yield a different leakage relation.

How does this model compare with the underlying game developed in Section 7.4? It is easiest to think of this earlier model as taking place in a world with perfect competition and without trade (and so without trade leakage). As explained in Appendix 12.1, in this world, the cost of abatement for each country would be a constant $c = 0.034$.

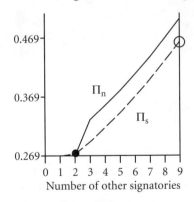

Figure 12.2. *Self-enforcing IEA for the free trade game*

12.9. THE SELF-ENFORCING IEA WITH FREE TRADE

The first three stages of the free trade game constitute the stage game modeled in Chapter 7: in Stage 1, countries choose simultaneously whether or not to be signatories to an IEA, and in Stages 2 and 3, respectively, signatories and non-signatories choose to play Abate or Pollute. The new twist is a fourth stage in which firms—the manufacturers of the CFCs—choose their segmented outputs. The solution to this last stage is given in Appendix 12.1. The solutions to the other stages of the game are found by following the procedures outlined in Chapter 7.

The self-enforcing agreement for the example given by Figure 12.1 is shown in Figure 12.2. The equilibrium agreement consists of $k^* = 3$ signatories (Stage 1 is solved for using condition (7.2)). Each signatory plays Abate (it pays signatories collectively to play Abate in Stage 2 provided $k \geq 3$). Non-signatories play Pollute (play Pollute is a dominant strategy for non-signatories in the Stage 3 game). In equilibrium, $\Pi_s(3) = 0.272$ and $\Pi_n(3) = 0.330$. The self-enforcing agreement thus improves only marginally on the equilibrium in unilateral policies.

It is interesting to compare this result with the situation in which competition is perfect and there is no trade. Then, as explained above, $c = 0.034$ and $b = 0.025$. We know from Chapter 7 that this implies that there will be $k^* = 2$ signatories in a self-enforcing IEA. Trade thus increases participation in the IEA. This is because of trade leakage. Leakage reduces the benefit to playing Abate. Play Abate is only collectively rational if a greater number of countries cooperate. Note, however, that while leakage increases k^*, it reduces the emission reductions achieved by each signatory. Having a greater number of signatories does not imply that the agreement is more successful.

12.10. TRADE BANS, COORDINATION, AND MINIMUM PARTICIPATION

Suppose now that trade between signatories and non-signatories is banned (remember, the model is a partial equilibrium model, and so the ban is limited to trade in CFCs).

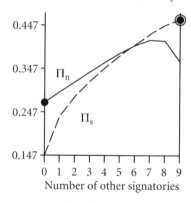

Figure 12.3. *Self-enforcing IEA with trade ban*

Suppose also that non-signatories play Pollute and that signatories play Abate. Then we obtain the payoffs shown in Figure 12.3.

This is a radically different picture. When the number of other countries that sign the agreement is low, every country prefers to be a non-signatory. When the number of other countries that sign the agreement is large, every country prefers to be a signatory. There are two (stable) equilibria here. In one, every country is a non-signatory and no abatement is undertaken. In the other, participation in the IEA is full, and all countries abate their emissions. The ozone layer is fully protected.

The trade restrictions make all the difference. Signatories suffer tremendously from a trade ban when participation is low. Not only are they harmed by the usual free-riding, but they must also endure a substantial loss in the gains from trade. When participation is high, however, the tables are turned. The benefit that non-signatories derive from free-riding is overwhelmed by the loss they suffer in being unable to trade with the majority of other countries. The trade restriction transforms the underlying PD game not into a chicken game, as observed in Figure 12.2, but into a coordination game, as shown in Figure 12.3 (compare this figure to Figure 4.3(b)).

In this coordination game, there are two equilibria (in pure strategies). The equilibrium in which every country is a signatory is superior in welfare terms, but how can countries coordinate on the mutually preferred equilibrium?

This is an easy problem. All that is needed is a minimum participation clause. For the game shown in Figure 12.3, the critical threshold is $k = 6$. If the treaty only entered into law if ratified by six or more countries, then no country could lose by ratifying when four or fewer other countries had already ratified, and every country could gain by ratifying when five or more others had already done so. Participation would be tipped.

Trade restrictions are also tied to a minimum participation clause in the Montreal Protocol. To become legally binding on parties, the agreement had to be ratified by at least eleven countries accounting for at least two-thirds of the 1986 level of global consumption of the controlled substances. As noted by Benedick (1998: 89–90), "In effect, to become binding, the protocol would have to be ratified by the United States and at least four of the six other large consumer countries (France, the Federal Republic of Germany, Italy, Japan, the Soviet Union, and the United Kingdom), or by the United States and the [European Community] as a unit." Moreover, according to Benedick (1998: 90), the *intention* of the minimum participation clause was to "provide a sufficient critical mass to increase the pressure on any potential large holdouts to join the treaty." This "critical mass" is the tipping point identified in Figure 12.3. With trade restrictions, as Benedick (1998: 243) observes, "the more nations that joined the protocol, the more uncomfortable it would be for a country to remain on the outside."

As noted in Section 8.5, the attempt by the United States to set a minimum participation rate of 90 percent failed. In Figure 12.3, all that is needed to tip cooperation is a high enough minimum participation rate. So why was the two-thirds hurdle preferable to the 90 percent threshold? There are, I think, two reasons. The first is that the 90 percent threshold would have given bargaining power to the USSR and Japan. If the two-thirds hurdle were satisfied and the treaty entered into force, then it probably would have been in the interests of the USSR and Japan to join—if only to avoid the trade restrictions. However, if the 90 percent threshold were not satisfied, entry by the USSR and Japan would decide *whether* the treaty entered into force—and, thus, whether the trade restrictions applied. With enough asymmetry, these countries might prefer that the treaty not enter into force. At the same time, these countries would know that their accession would greatly benefit other countries. Hence, the USSR and Japan might have used the higher threshold to obtain concessions. This was the fear noted in Section 8.5.

The other reason is that the power of the trade restriction in tipping participation was at this time unclear. As noted below, the trade restrictions were only given teeth in 1990. The tipping effect really gathered strength after this time.

12.11. THE CREDIBILITY OF TRADE RESTRICTIONS

The analysis is not quite finished. Figure 12.3 assumes that: (1) non-signatories play Pollute, (2) signatories play Abate, and (3) signatories ban trade with non-signatories. For the analysis to hold up, we must be sure that, if these assumptions were dropped, the same outcomes would be sustained as equilibria. That is, we must be sure that it is actually in the interests of non-signatories to play Pollute and that it is actually in the interests of the signatories to play Abate and to enforce a trade ban.

Simulation shows that, given that trade between signatories and non-signatories is banned, every non-signatory can do no better than to play Pollute, irrespective of how the other non-signatories behave and irrespective of whether signatories play Abate or Pollute. Moreover, given that non-signatories play Pollute, and given that trade between signatories and non-signatories is banned, simulation also shows that signatories do better collectively by playing Abate provided $k \geq 2$ (since trade with non-signatories is banned, abatement by signatories cannot promote trade leakage). Finally, given that non-signatories play Pollute and signatories play Abate, simulation shows that signatories are better off with a trade ban provided $k \geq 3$.

Suppose, then, that we are at the welfare-preferred equilibrium in Figure 12.3. Withdrawal by any country would then be irrational because of the trade ban. Suppose, however, that a country withdrew from the agreement anyway. Then we know that the remaining signatories would carry out their threat to ban trade. That is, the threat to restrict trade with non-participants is credible. It is, of course, because of this that no country will free ride in equilibrium. And because no country will free ride, trade will not actually be restricted in equilibrium.

What makes the threat to ban trade credible? Ignoring the effect of the trade ban on the environment, it can be shown that, if $k = 9$, signatories gain by banning trade. Though their producers are not permitted to export to the free-riding country, the ban increases the price of CFCs within signatory markets and this more than compensates. Though consumers' surplus in signatory countries is lowered by the ban, firm profits rise and the combined effect makes banning trade marginally attractive to signatories. I must emphasize that this result need not hold every time; and that it will not hold for other models of trade (see Barrett 1999c). Very often, a trade restriction will be self-damaging.

However, the more important effect of the trade ban in this example is on the environment. Given that nine countries participate, the trade ban lowers the emissions of the free-riding state substantially (the free-rider's output falls almost 60 percent), by plugging the trade leak. Even if signatories would otherwise lose by banning trade, if leakage were believed to be substantial, banning trade would be in the interests of signatories. Ironically, *while leakage frustrates unilateral efforts to protect the shared environment, it assists multilateral cooperation.* It makes imposition of the trade restriction credible.

This insight is crucial. Benedick (1998: 91) says that the objective of the trade restrictions "was to stimulate as many nations as possible to participate in the protocol, by preventing nonparticipating countries from enjoying competitive advantages and by discouraging the movement of CFC production facilities to such countries." The above analysis teaches not just that trade restrictions would plug the trade leak but that the threat to impose trade restrictions was actually made credible by the real worry that leakage would be severe.

12.12. TRADE RESTRICTIONS IN THE MONTREAL PROTOCOL—AGAIN

The game described by Figures 12.1–12.3 bears a likeness to the Montreal Protocol. Very few countries are non-parties to this agreement, and none can be described as a free-rider. So participation in this treaty is virtually complete.

Is this because of the trade restrictions? We cannot be sure, of course, because the counterfactual is missing; we do not know what Montreal would have achieved without the trade restriction. However, a South Korean diplomat once confided to me that his government had acceded in order to avoid trade restrictions (see also Benedick 1998: 244), and there is some evidence that other countries—like Taiwan,

Myanmar and even Japan—acceded for the same reason (see Brack 1996).[7] Indeed, Benedick (1998: 243) claims even more for the trade restrictions:

The pace of ratification by developing countries accelerated markedly after the 1990 London decisions put teeth in the trade restrictions. From mid-1990 until mid-1993, when trade restrictions applying to non-parties entered into force, the number of developing-country parties more than doubled, to nearly 70. It was surely no coincidence that although only 4 of the 13 larger developing countries … for which trade was critical—Brazil, Mexico, Nigeria, and Venezuela—had ratified before the London Amendment, all the remaining 9—Algeria, Argentina, China, Indica, Indonesia, Iran, Saudi Arabia, South Korea, and Turkey—joined by early 1993, before the trade restrictions became fully effective.

I was also told by an executive of a major CFC manufacturer that the trade sanctions were needed to gain industry's support for the Montreal Protocol, and so influenced participation by industrialized countries. Without trade restrictions, leakage would have shrunk the market for CFC-substitutes and thereby reduced the incentives to develop effective substitutes. Benedick (1998: 91) claims that a consensus emerged among the countries negotiating the Montreal Protocol that the trade measures "were indispensable to the protocol's effectiveness".

It might seem obvious that the trade restrictions in the Montreal Protocol should be welcomed. But, as mentioned previously, they may possibly violate the multilateral trading rules, and were criticized by the GATT Secretariat. This is important, because if the multilateral trading system prohibited the use of trade restrictions in multilateral environmental agreements, protection of the global environment may become even harder.

12.13. THE MULTILATERAL TRADING RULES

Linkage between trade and the environment cuts in both directions. Just as trade restrictions may be needed to protect the environment, so restrictions on environmental policy may be needed to safeguard a liberalized trading regime. If either trade or the environment were to take priority, the treaties in one area would need to bend to the rules established by a treaties in the other. Yielding to just one of these concerns, however, without having regard for the other, would almost certainly be welfare-damaging. And yet, where neither issue dominates, the rules established by different treaties may clash. As noted earlier, the Montreal Protocol collides with the GATT/WTO rules in two areas: first, in discriminating between parties to the GATT/WTO; and, second, in restricting trade in products based on their manufacture.

As it happens, the collision has injured neither regime. Trade in "like products" has not actually been restricted, and nor has the "most favored nation" principle actually

---

[7] Taiwan is not a signatory to the Montreal Protocol because of its unusual international status. However, Taiwan has complied with the requirements of the treaty, and the Montreal Protocol explicitly exempts non-parties from the trade restrictions if they are determined by the parties to be in full compliance and have submitted data verifying their compliance. Taiwan has satisfied both of these requirements, and so has avoided the trade penalty.

been violated. Participation in the Montreal Protocol is virtually full, and so parties to the GATT/WTO have not been subjected to the trade restrictions. In addition, no party to the GATT/WTO has complained officially about the trade restrictions in the Montreal Protocol. This result is entirely compatible with the theory outlined above. In Figure 12.3, all countries strictly prefer the regime with trade restrictions; none, therefore, has an incentive to object to their inclusion.

But, though neither regime has been injured by the apparent incompatibility between the Montreal trade restriction and the multilateral trading rules, the GATT Secretariat has argued that the trade restrictions against non-parties were unnecessary (GATT 1992: 25):

> ... the parties to the Montreal Protocol ... could have structured the Protocol in such a way that it reduced consumption of CFCs in the participating countries by the target amount, without the necessity of including provisions for special restrictions on trade with non-parties. Since, however, the drafters had other goals as well, including that of providing compensation to CFC producers in the participating countries (by allowing them to receive extra profits from selling the diminishing quantity of CFCs), trade provisions which discriminate against non-participants were included in the Protocol.

The Secretariat is mistaken here on two counts. The first is to assume that signatories would want only to limit consumption at home. As noted earlier, signatories wanted also to reduce trade leakage. They may also have wanted to reduce emissions abroad by altering the terms of trade (see Uimonen and Whalley 1997). Finally, and most importantly, they certainly wanted to deter free-riding. The Secretariat's criticism does not address the question of how free-riding could be deterred without the use of trade restrictions. As demonstrated earlier in this chapter, a simple strategy of reciprocity may not have succeeded as well as the trade restrictions.

The Secretariat is also wrong in concluding that the restrictions were aimed at filling the pockets of the CFC producers in signatory countries. The proposal to restrict trade between parties and non-parties was first tabled by the United States. The United States recognized that the Montreal Protocol would increase the profits of its CFC manufacturers by restricting the quantity of CFCs that could be traded. But the US government did not allow these manufacturers to reap the surplus sown by the treaty; instead, it taxed the windfall.

A GATT panel ruling from the celebrated tuna-dolphins case raises an additional concern—whether trade restrictions should be allowed when their purpose is to change the environmental policies of other states (non-parties, in the context of the Montreal Protocol restrictions). According to the 1994 ruling (GATT 1994):

> If ... Article XX were interpreted to permit Contracting Parties [to the GATT] to take trade measures so as to force other Contracting Parties to change their policies ... , the balance of rights and obligations among Contracting Parties, in particular the right of access to markets, would be seriously impaired. Under such an interpretation the General Agreement could no longer serve as a multilateral framework for trade among Contracting Parties.

The problem with this argument is that it puts trade above the environment. The claim that trade restrictions should not be used to alter the environmental policies of other countries may be valid where there are no crossborder externalities.[8] But where the environment is transboundary, and where trade restrictions can be used to correct them, a prohibition on their use may mean that the shared environment cannot be safeguarded. It is wrong to assert that trade liberalization must take priority over all other international affairs, just as it is wrong to insist that environmental protection is more deserving than other claims on the international system.

12.14. SEA TURTLE PROTECTION

The more recent ruling of the WTO appellate body on the shrimp-turtles case is kinder to the environment. The appellate body struck down a decision by the original panel hearing this case, finding that a trade restriction imposed by the United States to protect sea turtles was permitted under Article XX (WTO 1998). A concern of the WTO in this instance, as in the tuna-dolphin case that came before it, was the unilateral nature of the US action.

Under a law passed in the 1980s, the United States required shrimpers to fit their nets with "turtle excluder devices" or TEDs. These prevent the turtles from being drawn into the deep end of the net, and provide a means of escape. But TEDs are costly. They also reduce a shrimper's productivity. And as a unilateral measure, the US law puts US commercial interests at a competitive disadvantage. Potentially, unregulated foreign shrimpers could undercut their US rivals, forcing them out of business. It is even possible that the US law may offer no protection for the endangered sea turtles, which can migrate for thousands of miles, weaving in and out of the Exclusive Economic Zones (EEZs) of coastal countries as well as the high seas. It may rather serve only to change the nationalities of the shrimpers, much as the unilateral and bilateral restrictions on pelagic sealing encouraged entry by third parties. The leakage rate for sea turtle protection could be very great. This is why the United States banned shrimp imports from countries not using TEDs, provoking a complaint to the WTO by India, Malaysia, Pakistan, and Thailand.

The United States helped negotiate the Inter-American Convention for the Protection and Conservation of Sea Turtles, which mentions TEDs as a measure that can be taken to protect sea turtles. However, the appellate body could find no evidence that the United States tried to negotiate similar treaties with other WTO members against whom the US trade restrictions were applied. Hence, the appellate body ruled against the United States not because sea turtle protection could not qualify under Article XX. It ruled against the United States because the US law was applied "in a manner which constitutes arbitrary and unjustifiable discrimination between members of the WTO, contrary to the requirements of the chapeau of Article XX" (WTO 1998: 75).

---

[8] For example, it is often claimed that weaker environmental standards confer a competitive advantage and that fair trade demands countervailing remedies that level the playing field of international competition. In Barrett (1994*b*), I identify instances in which a country may want to weaken its environmental policy for reasons of competitiveness, but I argue that these cases are special and that countervailing measures are more likely to be welfare-reducing than welfare-enhancing. See also Bhagwati and Srinivasan (1996), Esty (1994), Rauscher (1997), and Uimonen and Whalley (1997).

Questions still remain, however. How would the WTO respond to a complaint from a non-party to an environmental agreement, against whom trade restrictions had been applied, when this non-party participated in the negotiation of the environmental agreement but chose not to ratify? Or suppose negotiations stall, and an impatient player in the negotiation imposes trade restrictions anyway. Could the restrictions be justified on the basis that the country imposing them engaged in "serious, good faith negotiations"?

The answers to these questions are not obvious. On the one hand, trade restrictions can help sustain international environmental cooperation, and so should be permitted. On the other hand, trade restrictions could potentially be applied unfairly. Use of trade restrictions would seem to be justified when the environmental agreement they are meant to sustain is fair. But how is one to know what constitutes a "fair" agreement?

12.15. THE MORALITY OF STICKS vs CARROTS

Fairness has not been an issue thus far in this chapter. I have taken countries to be symmetric, implying that all non-parties are free-riders. Imposing trade restrictions against free-riders is morally defensible. But suppose that some of the countries that emit the pollutant do not benefit from abatement. The countries that do benefit from abatement would want these other countries to reduce their emissions, and may be inclined to impel them to do so by threatening to impose trade restrictions. Aggregate welfare may even be increased if all countries abated their emissions. But fairness may demand that the countries unaffected by the pollution not be forced to reduce their emissions. This is especially true if the countries unaffected by the pollution are substantially poorer than the countries wanting their emissions to be reduced. Though trade restrictions may succeed in impelling poor countries to cut their emissions, the result may be unfair.

As mentioned in Chapter 8, the Montreal Protocol compensates developing countries for the "incremental costs" of complying with the agreement. I shall demonstrate in the next chapter that the offer to pay compensation also served to increase participation in this agreement. But, since the Montreal Protocol uses both the threat of trade restrictions and compensating payments to increase participation, the question arises which measure had the greater effect. Benedick believes that the trade restrictions deserve most of the credit. "It is probable," he writes, "that in the sober aftermath of London, the trade provisions, linked with access to modern technology, proved even more important than the ozone fund in motivating developing countries to join the protocol" (Benedick 1998: 243).

He may be right (we will never know for sure), but there is reason to believe that each instrument was rendered more effective by the existence of the other. Twum-Barima and Campbell (1994) note—correctly, I think—that trade restrictions may not have been enough to encourage countries with large domestic markets like China and India to accede; for this, the Multilateral Fund was needed. But there is also another reason that the Fund was needed. In making the agreement fair, the compensating payments invested the threat to impose trade restrictions with moral legitimacy.

As explained in the previous chapter, experiments show that people do not always behave according to their interests (as narrowly defined). In the ultimatum game, people often refuse offers which appear derisory, even when doing so harms their interests. They seem to be guided as much by their principles as by their interests. The trade restrictions examined in this chapter pose no problem for principle because of the assumption of symmetry. In the real world example of the Montreal Protocol, however, the credible threat of sanctions may not have been enough to sustain full participation. The accompanying use of carrots may have been needed to legitimize the threat to impose trade restrictions. This would seem to be the kind of information a future WTO panel would need to consider in judging whether a trade restriction intended to enforce a multilateral agreement should be allowed to stand.

12.16. CONSERVATION OF BLUEFIN TUNA AND SWORDFISH

As shown in Chapter 6, many international agreements incorporate trade restrictions. But as noted in Chapter 6, trade restrictions are usually an objective of such agreements, not a means of enforcement. The Convention on International Trade in Endangered Species, for example, is essentially a trade agreement.

In fact, few agreements besides the Montreal Protocol use multilateral trade restrictions to enforce cooperation.[9] An exception is the convention establishing the International Commission for the Conservation of Atlantic Tunas (ICCAT).

ICCAT aims to maintain populations of tuna and "tuna-like fishes" (including swordfish) in the Atlantic and adjacent seas (including the Mediterranean) "at levels which will permit the maximum sustainable catch."[10] Like all fisheries agreements, however, it has been hampered by two problems: non-participation and non-compliance.

To aid enforcement, ICCAT members are required to monitor the tuna and swordfish fishing activities of both parties and non-parties. They must also assist in collecting data on landings and trans-shipments, and in reporting vessels suspected of violating the Commission's recommendations, whether they fly the flag of a party or a non-party. When given permission by a ship's master, authorities like the US Coastguard are encouraged to board pelagic fishing vessels registered with non-parties and collect information on the ship's activities. Parties are also urged to record data on the fishing vessels of non-parties that enter their ports, to photograph these vessels, and to interview their crews. They are further to discourage their own nationals from associating with the activities of non-parties which could undermine the effectiveness of ICCAT measures. ICCAT also promotes satellite surveillance.

Effective monitoring is a precondition for effective enforcement but it is not sufficient. ICCAT must also impel non-parties to conform with the Commission's

---

[9] Surprisingly, given the history of the sea turtles case, the Inter-American Convention for the Protection and Conservation of Sea Turtles does not incorporate trade restrictions.

[10] Only by coincidence will the maximum sustainable catch be the most desirable rate of harvest. See Dasgupta (1982) and Clark (1976).

recommendations. The Secretariat encourages all non-parties to accede to the agreement, or at the very least to become a "cooperating party," meaning "a non-Contracting Party that does not hold membership in ICCAT as a Contracting Party but voluntarily fishes in conformity with the Conservation decisions of ICCAT." The aim is to identify and then isolate the rogue fishing states. The Secretariat writes to the authorities of these states asking them "to rectify their fishing activities so as not to diminish the effectiveness of the ICCAT conservation programs and to advise the Commission of actions taken in that regard."

Though the treaty does not mention the use of trade measures, it does ask parties "to set up a system of international enforcement," and in the mid-1990s ICCAT adopted resolutions recommending that parties "take non-discriminatory trade restrictive measures" against non-parties. This ultimately led to bans on the import of Atlantic bluefin tuna and swordfish from a number of countries, including Belize and Honduras. A ban against Panama was threatened, but when Panama acceded to the agreement in 1998, the threat was withdrawn. Becoming a member is not an easy means of escape, however. Equatorial Guinea is an ICCAT party, but after it failed to comply with ICCAT recommendations on catches, the Commission adopted a recommendation by the Compliance Committee to ban imports of bluefin tuna from this country. This recommendation and the letter by the Commission chairman to the Government of Equatorial Guinea make interesting reading and are reproduced in Appendixes 12.2 and 12.3, respectively to this chapter.[11] Since the restrictions on Equatorial Guinea were imposed, a number of other countries (both parties and non-parties) suspected of violating ICCAT conservation measures have been identified. They may become the target of trade restrictions in the future.

The threat to impose trade restrictions by the cooperating members of ICCAT was obviously credible (the restrictions were imposed!). But more than credibility is required to deter non-compliance and non-participation. Trade restrictions must also hurt the target countries severely. The ICCAT trade restrictions will have some effect. They will shrink the size of the market available to the violating countries. But ICCAT has only thirty-five parties, and so there remains a large market in which violating states can sell their catch. My guess is that the current participation level is well below the tipping point. The trade restrictions may ultimately have little effect. We shall have to wait and see.

My feeling is that this may be an area where an evolution in customary law could help. The essential problem lies with the ability of countries to undermine the objective of fisheries conservation. A treaty was negotiated in 1993 to put a stop to this. The Agreement to Promote Compliance with International Conservation and Management Measures by Fishing Vessels on the High Seas says that all states have an obligation not to undermine the effectiveness of international conservation measures—an obligation that extends even to those agreements to which a country is not a party. However, the Compliance Agreement has not entered into force, and would

---

[11] The recommendation is from Annex 5–10 and the letter is from Appendix 8 of Annex 8 of the proceedings of the Sixteenth regular meeting of the Commission. See http://www.iccat.es.

only apply to its parties in any event. It is not enough. What is really needed is a general condemnation of countries that undermine multilateral efforts to conserve fish stocks. At the same time, of course, application of such a customary obligation would necessitate rules for conservation treaties that are widely perceived to be fair.

12.17. CONCLUSIONS

It is tempting to conclude from the example of the Montreal Protocol that the global environment would be better protected if only the threat of trade restrictions were incorporated into every multilateral environmental agreement. Such a conclusion is both wrong and dangerous—wrong because the Montreal Protocol is very likely a special case; dangerous because the unwise use of trade restrictions to enforce international agreements may only succeed in damaging the international trading regime.

This brings us back to the subject of linkage. Where trade restrictions cannot deter free-riding, countries will inevitably search for other punishments—trade sanctions, perhaps, or a withdrawal of development assistance or exclusion from a collective security pact. These punishments, if actually implemented, may help to promote cooperation. But virtually every punishment will harm signatories as well as non-signatories, and may thus fail the credibility test. Even if they are credible, they may, like the ICCAT restrictions, be so feeble as to be unable to change behavior. These are the fundamental obstacles to sustaining international cooperation. We have seen here that these obstacles were overcome in the case of the Montreal Protocol. But this may be the exception that proves the rule that free-riding is difficult to deter, especially as regards the provision of global public goods.

Appendix 12.1. The Trade Model

Let inverse demand in country i be linear and given by $p(x^i) = 1 - x^i$, where x^i is consumption of the good in country i.

Firm j's costs are also linear and are given by $C(x_j, q_j) = \phi q_j x_j$, where x_j is total output by firm j and q_j is the abatement standard for firm j. Abatement is binary; that is, $q_j \in \{0, 1\}$. Firm j takes q_j as given and so takes unit costs as given and constant. Transport costs are zero. Emissions by firm j (and thus country j) are $x_j(1 - q_j)$. If country j plays $q_j = 1$, then emissions by j will equal zero; if j plays $q_j = 0$, then emissions by j will equal firm j's output.[12]

Firms are assumed to choose their outputs for each market simultaneously. Specifically, firm j takes its own abatement standard, the standards imposed on other firms, and the segmented outputs of other firms as given and chooses a quantity to produce and ship to market i, x^i_j, so as to maximize

$$\pi_j = \sum_{i=1}^{N} (1 - x^i - \phi q_j) x^i_j. \tag{12A.1}$$

The first order conditions (for an interior solution) require that every firm increase output so long as the gain in revenue exceeds the corresponding increase in costs. Formally, this requires

$$1 - x^i - x^i_j - \phi q_j = 0 \quad \text{for all } i, j. \tag{12A.2}$$

It is easy to confirm that eqn (12A.2) is also sufficient and that the solution is unique. I shall restrict choice of parameter values such that firms produce positive quantities in equilibrium.

Since the players are symmetric, all firms required to abate will produce the same output in equilibrium, as will all firms allowed to pollute. Let $x_A(x_P)$ denote the output of a firm that abates (pollutes), and let z represent the number of other countries that play Abate. Country j takes z as given but can anticipate how the market for CFCs will "respond" to its own choice of whether to play Abate or Pollute. If j plays Pollute, eqn (12A.2) becomes

$$N - [zx_A + (N - z)x_P] - x_P = 0,$$
$$\tag{12A.3a}$$
$$N - [zx_A + (N - z)x_P] - \phi N - x_A = 0.$$

If j plays Abate, eqn (12A.2) becomes

$$N - [(z + 1)x_A + (N - z - 1)x_P] - \phi N - x_A = 0,$$
$$\tag{12A.3b}$$
$$N - [(z + 1)x_A + (N - z - 1)x_P] - x_P = 0.$$

Consider now the decision facing country j. j's net benefits are the sum of firm j's profits and the consumer surplus realized by the citizens of j, less the environmental damage suffered by country j. Pollution is assumed to be a pure public bad and aggregate emissions are given by $\sum_{i}^{N} = x_i(1 - q_i)$. Marginal environmental damage for each country is a constant, b. Given the demand specification, consumer surplus for country j is $(x^j)^2/2$. j's payoff is thus

$$\Pi_j = \pi_j + (x^j)^2/2 - b\left[\sum_{i=1}^{N} x_i(1 - q_i)\right]. \tag{12A.4}$$

---

[12] The important assumption here is that emissions are proportional to output. We can then normalize so that emissions are equal to output when abatement is nil.

Upon substituting (12A.3) into (12A.4), country j can calculate the payoff it will get, given the behavior of both firms and the other governments. To be specific, country j can calculate $\Pi_A(z)$ by substituting (12A.3a) into (12A.4). It can also calculate $\Pi_P(z)$ by substituting (12A.3b) into (12A.4). Non-signatory j will play Pollute provided $\Pi_P(z) > \Pi_A(z)$; otherwise, j will play Abate.

How does this model compare with the one developed in Chapter 7? It is easiest to think of this earlier model as taking place in a world with perfect competition and autarky. The cost of playing Abate is then the reduction in consumers' surplus associated with the higher cost of production when emissions must be abated. If a country plays Pollute, its consumers' surplus is $1/2$. If it plays Abate, its consumers' surplus falls to $(1 - \phi)^2/2$. The cost of playing Abate is then $\phi(1 - \phi/2)$. This is a constant. It can be thought of as being equivalent to the cost term c used in Chapter 7. For the example shown in Figure 12.1, $c = 0.034$.

**Appendix 12.2. RECOMMENDATION BY ICCAT REGARDING
EQUATORIAL GUINEA PURSUANT TO THE 1996
*RECOMMENDATION REGARDING COMPLIANCE IN
THE BLUEFIN TUNA AND NORTH ATLANTIC
SWORDFISH FISHERIES***

RECOGNIZING the authority and responsibility of ICCAT to manage populations of tuna and tuna-like species in the Atlantic Ocean, and its adjacent seas, at the international level;

EXPRESSING CONCERN with regard to the over-fished status of bluefin tuna in the Atlantic Ocean;

NOTING the obligation of all Contracting Parties to comply with ICCAT conservation and management measures;

RECOGNIZING that effective management of bluefin tuna stocks cannot be achieved unless all Contracting Parties comply with ICCAT conservation and management measures;

RECALLING the actions of the Commission over many years in calling upon Equatorial Guinea to comply with ICCAT conservation and management measures for Atlantic bluefin tuna;

RECALLING the Commission's *Resolution for an Action Plan to Ensure the Effectiveness of the Conservation Program for Atlantic Bluefin Tuna*, adopted in 1994 to ensure effective conservation of Atlantic bluefin tuna;

RECALLING FURTHER the 1996 *Recommendation Regarding Compliance in the Bluefin Tuna and North Atlantic Swordfish Fisheries*, which provides for the possibility of imposing import restrictions, consistent with each Contracting Party's international obligations;

CONSIDERING the import data and other compelling information submitted by ICCAT Contracting Parties for 1997, 1998, and 1999, which reveal significant exports of Atlantic bluefin tuna by Equatorial Guinea, despite the fact that, for those years, Equatorial Guinea has had a catch limit of zero for both east and west Atlantic bluefin tuna stocks;

MINDFUL of the repeated efforts of the Commission to express its concerns to, and seek the cooperation of, Equatorial Guinea over the past several years;

NOTING with concern the fact that Equatorial Guinea has not responded to the expressions of concern from the Commission and has reported no bluefin tuna catch data; and

FURTHER NOTING that this Recommendation does not prejudice the rights and obligations of Contracting Parties based on other international agreements; Therefore,

THE INTERNATIONAL COMMISSION FOR THE CONSERVATION OF ATLANTIC TUNAS (ICCAT) RECOMMENDS THAT:

a Contracting Parties take appropriate measures, consistent with provisions of the 1996 *Recommendation Regarding Compliance in the Bluefin Tuna and North Atlantic Swordfish Fisheries* to the effect that the import of Atlantic bluefin tuna and its products in any form from Equatorial Guinea be prohibited, effective from the time this Recommendation enters into force.

b The Commission again call upon Equatorial Guinea, as a Contracting Party to ICCAT, to comply with all the ICCAT conservation and management measures.

c The Commission encourages each Contracting Party, Non-Contracting Party, Entity and Fishing Entity to participate in efforts to ensure the sustainability of marine living resources in the Convention Area, as called for in the International Plan of Action for the Management of Fishing Capacity.

Appendix 12.3. LETTER TO EQUATORIAL GUINEA Pursuant to the Application of ICCAT'S 1996 *Recommendation Regarding Compliance in the Bluefin Tuna and North Atlantic Swordfish Fisheries and the 1998 Resolution Concerning the Unreported and Unregulated Catches of Tunas by Large-Scale Longline Vessels in the Convention Area*

At its 1999 meeting, the International Commission for the Conservation of Atlantic Tunas (ICCAT) reviewed the fishing activities of vessels of Contracting Parties under its *Recommendation Regarding Compliance in the Bluefin Tuna and North Atlantic Swordfish Fisheries*, adopted in 1996. This Recommendation was previously supplied to you as an ICCAT Contracting Party and is enclosed for your convenience.

The subject Recommendation provides that if any Contracting Party exceeds its catch limit during any two consecutive management periods, the Commission will recommend appropriate measures, which may include trade restrictions. Any trade measures authorized will be import restrictions on the subject species and consistent with each Party's international obligations. In addition, the trade measures will be of such duration and under such conditions as the Commission may determine.

The Commission has been concerned about the fishing activities of vessels flagged by Equatorial Guinea for several years and has made a number of efforts to communicate these concerns to your country and to seek your collaboration in addressing them. On February 26, 1999, the Commission sent a letter to Equatorial Guinea requesting you to take the necessary action to ensure that your flag vessels do not fish for bluefin tuna since your country does not have a quota allocation for either stock of bluefin tuna. In agreeing to send this letter, the Commission noted specifically that trade data collected through the Bluefin Tuna Statistical Document (BTSD) Program indicated vessels flagged by your country were harvesting Atlantic bluefin tuna, although no catch data had been reported to ICCAT. In that letter, the Commission referenced the *Recommendation Regarding Compliance in the Bluefin Tuna and North Atlantic Swordfish Fisheries* and indicated that this Recommendation provides for the use of trade restrictive measures against ICCAT Contracting Parties to ensure compliance.

At its 1999 meeting, the Commission took note of BTSD statistics that indicate vessels of Equatorial Guinea are continuing to harvest considerable quantities of Atlantic bluefin tuna outside ICCAT's quota regimes and that your country has not reported any such harvests to the Commission. In addition, your government has not responded to the Commission's correspondence or concerns. Therefore, pursuant to the terms of paragraph 3 of the *Recommendation Regarding Compliance in the Bluefin Tuna and North Atlantic Swordfish Fisheries*, the Commission adopted the enclosed Recommendation at its 1999 meeting that requires Contracting Parties to take appropriate measures to the effect that the import of Atlantic bluefin tuna and its products in any form from Equatorial Guinea is prohibited.

In a separate action, the Commission also reviewed the fishing activities of various ICCAT Contracting Parties, Non-Contracting Parties, Entities, and Fishing Entities under its *Resolution Concerning the Unreported and Unregulated Catches of Tunas by Large-Scale Longline Vessels in the Convention Area*, adopted in 1998. This Resolution is also enclosed for your convenience. The 1998 Resolution calls upon ICCAT Contracting Parties, Cooperating Non-Contracting Parties, Entities and Fishing Entities to collect, examine and submit to ICCAT import and landing data and associated information on imported frozen tunas and tuna-like fish products. Based on an annual review of these and other data, ICCAT will identify those Contracting Parties, Non-Contracting Parties, Entities and Fishing Entities whose large-scale longline vessels have been fishing for tuna and tuna-like species in a manner which diminishes the effectiveness of ICCAT conservation and management measures. ICCAT will request identified Contracting Parties, Non-Contracting Parties, Entities and Fishing Entities to take all necessary corrective actions, and will review those actions at its subsequent annual meeting. If the actions taken are not sufficient, ICCAT will recommend effective measures, if necessary including non-discriminatory trade restrictive measures on the subject species.

The information available to ICCAT at its 1999 meeting included landings and import data submitted by Contracting Parties, as well as other information. Enclosed please find a list of large-scale longline vessels compiled from these data, many of which are believed to have fished for tuna and tuna-like species in the ICCAT Convention Area. A number of these vessels are registered in Equatorial Guinea.

Based on this information, ICCAT identified Equatorial Guinea in accordance with paragraph 2 of its *Resolution Concerning the Unreported and Unregulated Catches of Tunas by Large-Scale Longline Vessels in the Convention Area*, as a Contracting Party whose large-scale longline vessels have been fishing tuna and tuna-like species in a manner which diminishes the effectiveness of ICCAT conservation and management measures. Accordingly, ICCAT hereby requests the Government of Equatorial Guinea to take all necessary measures to ensure that its large-scale longline vessels do not continue to diminish the effectiveness of ICCAT conservation and management measures, including, if appropriate, the revocation of vessel registration or fishing licenses of the large-scale longline vessels concerned.

At its 2000 meeting, the Commission will review information concerning the fishing activities of your country's vessels and consider any actions that may have been taken to control these activities. If it is determined Equatorial Guinea has not taken appropriate steps to control its vessels, the Commission can, as described above, recommend that Contracting Parties take non-discriminatory trade restrictive measures on the subject species, consistent with their international obligations, to prevent those longline vessels from continuing the fishing operations that diminish the effectiveness of ICCAT conservation measures.

Thank you for your prompt attention to these matters.

Commission Chairman

13

The Side Payments Game

When cooperation is not voluntarily forthcoming, positive incentives are the best way to achieve sustained inter-governmental cooperation. GATT Secretariat, "Trade and the Environment," (1992: 36)

13.1. INTRODUCTION

I have assumed thus far that countries are symmetric when they obviously differ widely. Some countries are affected more (in absolute or relative terms) by an environmental problem than are others, and some degrade the shared environment by more than do others. These asymmetries often dominate negotiations and they sometimes seem to be the main obstacle to a successful outcome. In this chapter I shall show that asymmetries are important, but that they are not an insurmountable barrier to successful cooperation. To the contrary, they may make cooperation easier.

I have also assumed thus far that cooperation can only be sustained by the credible threat to punish free-riders. To many this will seem too negative a perspective. Carrots can be, and sometimes are, used in place of, or along with, sticks. Would not it be better, as the GATT Secretariat suggests, to construct positive incentives for participation in an international treaty?

In this chapter, I relax these assumptions. I shall show that carrots *can* promote cooperation—but *only* if countries are sufficiently asymmetric. I shall also show that carrots only help if coupled with the use of effective sticks. As the lawyer–economist Howard Chang (1995) has argued, the "carrots only" approach advocated by the GATT Secretariat is unable to resolve a transnational PD.

What exactly is a "carrot"? It is sometimes thought of as the obverse of a stick. Consider the analysis in Chapter 7. Suppose that an agreement consists of k^* parties. If one party withdrew from such a treaty, all the others would punish the deviant by playing Pollute instead of Abate.[1] This is a stick. Now suppose that there were $k^* - 1$ parties. Then, if one country acceded, the other parties would reward this country by playing Abate. This might be called a carrot. When looked at in this way, sticks and carrots are different sides of the same coin.

This is not how the term is used here. In this chapter, a carrot is a new instrument, introduced by enlarging the strategy space (just as trade sanctions were introduced

---

[1] Since I am referring to a one-shot model, there are no opportunities for parties to react. The language used here and elsewhere in this chapter is once again meant to assist intuition.

in the last chapter). It is represented by a money side payment. You can think of it as an inducement or a compensating payment.[2]

To the non-economist, the offer of a "side payment" may sound like a kick-back, an under-the-table bribe, or a back-hander, but this is not how the term should be interpreted. It is better thought of as an incentive payment needed to make a country undertake an obligation that it would otherwise be unwilling to accept. The Fur Seal Treaty made participation by the pelagic sealing nations acceptable because of side payments, paid partly in cash and partly in kind (the share of the annual harvest). There was nothing vulgar or unseemly about these side payments. They were instrumentally essential; without them, a deal would never have been agreed; the fur seal would never have been saved. Moreover, fairness demands that these side payments be paid. In refraining from harvesting seals at sea, the pelagic nations created a gain to cooperation. They deserved to get a share of this gain. In the analysis that follows we shall find that side payments are of a similar character: they are both instrumentally helpful in sustaining cooperation and essential in supporting a fair outcome.

13.2. SIDE PAYMENTS WITH SYMMETRIC PLAYERS

It might seem obvious that side payments should be able to increase participation, but Carraro and Siniscalco (1993) have shown that side payments can only aid cooperation if the parties to an agreement can commit to remaining as signatories.[3] As noted in Chapter 3, countries cannot commit to remaining within an agreement. The rules of international law allow countries to withdraw from an international treaty, at least after giving sufficient notice; and, as if to reaffirm this freedom, nearly all treaties include an explicit provision for withdrawal. So the Carraro–Siniscalco result really tells us that side payments cannot help.

This is surprising because we know that side payments *are* a feature of some international agreements, the Fur Seal Treaty included. So something must be awry with the Carraro–Siniscalco analysis.

To learn what it is, we must first understand the reason Carraro and Sinsicalco obtain this result. Consider again the simple model analyzed in Section 7.5. The payoff functions of the players are given by $\Pi_P = 2z$ and $\Pi_A = -1 + 2z$, where z is the number of other countries that play Abate, $\Pi_P(z)$ is the payoff that a country gets by playing Pollute (given that z other countries play Abate), and $\Pi_A(z)$ is the payoff that a country gets by playing Abate. As shown in Section 7.5, the self-enforcing agreement for this game consists of $k^* = 2$ signatories. Each signatory plays Abate in equilibrium; if $N \geq 3$, each non-signatory (and there will be $N - 2$ of these) plays Pollute.

Denote the payoffs to signatories and non-signatories by $\Pi_s(k)$ and $\Pi_n(k)$, respectively. For this example, $\Pi_n(2) = 4$ and $\Pi_s(2) = 1$. Non-signatories do better because they free ride. But notice that $\Pi_s(3) = 3$. The two signatories to the self-enforcing

---

[2] Of course, even here, the coin of a side payment has two sides: the money can be given as a reward for participating in an agreement, or withheld as a punishment for not participating.

[3] Carraro and Siniscalco (1993) also consider the possibility that a subset of non-signatories may commit to paying the remaining non-signatories to cooperate.

agreement would gain if one more country acceded; their aggregate payoff would rise from 2 to 6, for a gain of 4. Any country that acceded, however, would lose in the bargain; its payoff would fall by 1 (that is, from $\Pi_n(2) = 4$ to $\Pi_s(3) = 3$). Since the gain to the two signatories exceeds the loss to an acceding country, there is a gain from trade. A deal can be made.

Suppose that the two signatories offered to pay a non-signatory a money side payment of 2, as an inducement to accede. A non-signatory that took up this offer would increase its payoff by 1, and so would accept. Moreover, the signatories offering the payment would also gain. Their individual payoffs would rise from 1 to 2. Everyone would be better off (including any remaining non-signatories; their payoffs would rise from 4 to 6).[4]

However, once there are three parties to the treaty, each of the two original signatories—the countries that promised to make the payment—would do better by withdrawing, taking the participation of the other signatories as given. In staying in the agreement, a signatory would get a payoff of 2. Taking as given the behavior of all the other players, however, it could calculate that, if it withdrew unilaterally, the number of signatories would fall back to two. The country that withdrew would thus get a payoff of 4. This is more than it would get by staying in the agreement, and so the agreement with side payments cannot be self-enforcing.

This result easily generalizes. We know that $\Pi_s(k^* + 1) > \Pi_s(k^*)$. The signatories to a self-enforcing agreement gain when another country accedes. We also know that $\Pi_s(k^* + 1) < \Pi_n(k^*)$. Unless compensated, every non-signatory loses by acceding. Provided $k^*[\Pi_s(k^* + 1) - \Pi_s(k^*)] > [\Pi_n(k^*) - \Pi_s(k^* + 1)]$, however, signatories can compensate a non-signatory for acceding and still be better off. The problem is that, once this payment is made, the original signatories will get a payoff strictly less than $\Pi_s(k^* + 1)$, and yet we know that $\Pi_s(k^* + 1) < \Pi_n(k^*)$. So each of the original signatories would do better by withdrawing unilaterally from the agreement with side payments, taking as given the participation decisions of all other countries. An agreement with side payments cannot be self-enforcing. The only way that side payments can be made to work is if the original signatories can commit to remaining as signatories; and this, of course, they cannot do. This is Carraro and Siniscalco's main result.

There may be another reason why the offer of side payments in this context would not work. Recall that the countries are symmetric by assumption. Though they may recognize that they would do better by paying a non-signatory to accede, the original signatories may recoil at the thought of getting a lower payoff than another, otherwise identical signatory. Just as a Responder in the ultimatum game may reject an offer that makes it better off, so a signatory may decline to pay another country to accede. Such a payment would amount to an additional reward to free-riding behavior, something that cooperating countries may be unable to countenance. The treaty incorporating side payments would thus be neither envy-free nor role-neutral.

---

[4] The original signatories only need to offer a side payment of 1 to get a non-signatory to accede. I suggest the larger side payment of 2 because it increases the payoff of all the three countries by 1 each. However, the results are not sensitive to the particular offer that is made.

As noted earlier, however, side payments *are* sometimes offered. Moreover, the intent in offering them is often to increase participation.[5] In the Fur Seal Treaty, as noted previously, side payments were needed to induce the pelagic nations to participate. In the Montreal Protocol, discussed in detail later in this chapter, side payments were used to compensate developing countries for participating. Notice, however, that in both of these cases, the countries that offered the side payments were different from the countries that accepted them. In the fur seal case, the countries offering the side payment had their own breeding populations, and so could kill the seals on land—an option that was unavailable to the pelagic sealing nations. In the case of the Montreal Protocol, the countries offering the payment were rich and benefitted most from ozone layer protection; the countries accepting the payments were poor and benefitted less. The problem with the Carraro–Siniscalco analysis is that it assumes that countries are symmetric.[6] In doing so, this work seems to have overlooked the context in which side payments can succeed.

Asymmetry also changes the perceptions as regards fairness. An agreement to transfer money as a means of securing greater participation can be envy-free if the players paying the money are different from the countries receiving it. Moreover, the roles played by the players would be determined by history or geography or some other such factor; they would not be determined arbitrarily.

13.3. COOPERATION AMONG ASYMMETRIC COUNTRIES

Asymmetric games of international cooperation are notoriously difficult to work with and must usually be solved numerically. Here I simplify by assuming that there are only two types of country and that, as in Section 7.6, each country faces a binary choice (to Abate or to Pollute) and receives a payoff that is a linear function of the choices of all other countries. These simplifications give us everything we need (the underlying game is an asymmetric prisoners' dilemma) while at the same time allowing us to obtain sharp analytical results.[7]

There are N countries, N_1 of which are of type 1 and N_2 of which are of type 2 ($N = N_1 + N_2$). If any country of type i ($i = 1,2$) plays Pollute (Abate) it gets a payoff Π_P^i (Π_A^i), where

$$\Pi_P^i = \alpha_i(b_1 Z_1 + b_2 Z_2), \quad \Pi_A^i = -c + \alpha_i(b_1 Z_1 + b_2 Z_2); \qquad (13.1)$$

where Z_i represents the *total* number of type i countries that play Abate ($N_i - Z_i$ type i countries thus play Pollute); where, after normalizing, $\alpha_2 = 1$ and $\alpha_1 \in [0,1]$; and where $b_2 \geq b_1 > 0$.

According to eqn (13.1), every country benefits at least as much when one more type 2 country plays Abate as when one more type 1 country does so; each type 2

---

[5] In some cases, like the Rhine Chlorides agreement, discussed in Chapter 5, side payments reflect an implicit allocation of rights.

[6] Carraro and Botteon (1997) extend this earlier paper for a special case of asymmetry.

[7] The analysis presented here draws from Barrett (2001*a*).

country benefits at least as much as each type 1 country from the abatement under-taken by any country; and a country's own net benefit of abatement, $-c + \alpha_i b_i$, is at least as high for a type 2 country as for a type 1 country. Payoffs are normalized such that countries of either type get a payoff of zero if no country undertakes any abate-ment (in the context of eqn (3.1), this means setting $a_P = 0$).

In applying this framework to stratospheric ozone depletion, we can think of type 1 countries as being "poor" and type 2 countries as being "rich." The rich countries use far more ozone-depleting substances, so that abatement by a rich country will improve the environment by more than may abatement by a poor country ($b_2 > b_1$). The poor benefit less from global abatement than the rich (i.e. $\alpha_2 > \alpha_1$), however, because depletion is less near the equator, and because people with darker skin are less likely to get skin cancer.

If abatement is a prisoners' dilemma (PD) game, two further conditions must hold. First, play Pollute must be a dominant strategy for every country; that is,

$$c > b_2. \tag{13.2a}$$

Second, the aggregate payoff of all N countries must strictly increase in Z_1 and Z_2:

$$\alpha_1 N_1 + N_2 > c/b_1. \tag{13.2b}$$

Assume that these conditions are satisfied. Then we know that all N countries will play Pollute in equilibrium, but that all N countries would be strictly better off if every country played Abate instead. This is a familiar situation. What we want to know is this: if the strategy space were enlarged to accommodate side payments, could a welfare-superior outcome be sustained by a self-enforcing agreement?

13.4 COOPERATION WITHOUT SIDE PAYMENTS

Consider to begin the solution to the participation game without side payments. In particular, suppose that, in Stage 1, all countries choose simultaneously to be a sig-natory or a non-signatory; that, in Stage 2, signatories choose jointly whether to play Pollute or Abate (i.e., signatories behave cooperatively); and that, in Stage 3, non-signatories simultaneously and independently make the same choice (i.e, non-signatories behave non-cooperatively).

Solving the game backwards, it is obvious by eqn (13.2a) that all non-signatories must play Pollute in equilibrium. The first two stages of the game, however, are a bit harder to solve.

Let k_i denote the number of signatories of type i. Then it can be shown (see Appendix 13.1) that, in equilibrium, signatories will play

$$Z_i^* = 0 \quad \text{if } c/b_i > \alpha_1 k_1 + k_2, \quad Z_i^* = k_i \text{ if } c/b_i < \alpha_1 k_1 + k_2. \tag{13.3}$$

Conditions (13.3) are consistent with the results obtained previously for symmet-ric countries. With symmetry, $\alpha_1 = 1$ and $b_1 = b_2$. Conditions (13.3) say that if $c > bk$ then signatories should play Pollute but that if $c < bk$ then signatories should play Abate. This is the same result as was obtained in Chapter 7.

It remains to solve the Stage 1 game. Three types of equilibria are possible (for $k_1 + k_2 > 0$):[8]

$$c/b_1 + \alpha_1 > \alpha_1 k_1^* > c/b_1, \quad k_2^* = 0 \quad \text{for } \alpha_1 N_1 > c/b_1 \tag{13.4a}$$

$$k_1^* = 0, \quad c/b_2 + 1 > k_2^* > c/b_2 \quad \text{for } N_2 > c/b_2 \tag{13.4b}$$

$$c/b_2 + \alpha_1 > \alpha_1 k_1^* + k_2^* > c/b_1, \quad \alpha_1 k_1^* + \alpha_1 k_2^* b_2 / b_1 > c/b_1. \tag{13.4c}$$

These are "linchpin" equilibria in the sense that, if any signatory were to withdraw from these equilibrium agreements, *all* the remaining signatories would play Pollute. We solved for similar equilibria in Chapter 7. Here, however, asymmetry adds a new dimension. Depending on the parameters of the problem, the self-enforcing agreement (assuming one exists) may comprise a subset of type 1 or type 2 countries only or a combination of both types of country.[9] It will consist of one type of country if countries are strongly asymmetric. It may consist of both types of country if countries are weakly asymmetric.

13.5. EXAMPLES

The following examples illustrate the qualitatively different kinds of equilibria that can be sustained as self-enforcing treaties. In all of these examples, let $N_1 = N_2 = 50$, $c = 100$, and $b_2 = 6$. An equilibrium is characterized by a pairing $\{k_1^*, k_2^*\}$.

Example 1. Suppose, to begin, that the two types of country are strongly asymmetric. Suppose, in particular, that $b_1 = 3$ and $\alpha_1 = 0.5$. Then, there exists just one equilibrium, $\{0, 17\}$, yielding an aggregate payoff of 5950 (for comparison, the full cooperative outcome yields an aggregate payoff of 23,700). This equilibrium satisfies eqn (13.4b). The equilibria defined by eqn (13.4a) and eqn (13.4c) do not exist.

Example 2. Suppose now that the asymmetry is weaker. In particular, suppose that $b_1 = 3$ and $\alpha_1 = 0.75$. Then there exist two equilibria, $\{45, 0\}$ and $\{0, 17\}$. These equilibria satisfy eqn (13.4a) and eqn (13.4b), respectively, and support aggregate payoffs of 7312.5 and 7225, respectively (the aggregate payoff in the full cooperative outcome is 29,375).

Example 3. If $\alpha_1 = 0.9$ and $b_1 = 5.9$, then the two types of country are more similar, and there now exist six equilibria:$\{19, 0\}, \{18, 1\}\}, \{17, 2\}, \{16, 3\}, \{15, 4\}$, and $\{0, 17\}$.

---

[8] To see that eqn (13.4a) is an equilibrium notice that, by eqn (13.3), any country that accedes to the agreement will be required to play Abate. The accession would not change the behavior of the incumbent signatories, however, and eqn (13.2a) ensures that under these circumstances such an accession would make the acceding country worse off. Now consider a withdrawal. If a signatory withdrew from the agreement unilaterally, the remaining $k_1^* - 1$ signatories would be required to play Pollute by eqn (13.3).The constraints on k_1^* given in eqn (13.4a) ensure that a withdrawal by any type 1 signatory would make the withdrawing country worse off. The other types of equilibria can be solved for using the same procedure.

[9] Notice that, if eqn (13.4a) holds, then $k_1^* \in \{2, \ldots, N_1\}$since, by eqn (13.2a), $c > \alpha_1 b_1$; if eqn (13.4b) holds, then $k_2^* \in \{2, \ldots, N_2\}$ and, if eqn (13.4c) holds, then $k_1^* \in \{1, \ldots, N_1\}$and $k_2 \in \{1, \ldots, N_2\}$ since $\alpha_1 k_1^* + k_2^* > c/b_1, c/b_2 > 1$ and since eqn (13.4c) is feasible by eqn (13.2b). As in the symmetric model analyzed in Chapter 7, the self-enforcing agreement consists of at least two signatories.

The aggregate payoffs associated with these equilibria range from 7990 for $\{0, 17\}$ to 8787.5 for $\{15, 4\}$.

Example 4. Finally, suppose that the two types of country are nearly symmetric. In particular, suppose that $\alpha_1 = 0.99$ *and* $b_1 = 5.95$. Then there exist 18 equilibria, each with $k_1^* + k_2^* = 17$ (the equilibria are thus $\{0, 17\}, \{1, 16\}, \{2, 15\}, \ldots, \{16, 1\}$, and $\{17, 0\}$). Aggregate payoffs range from 8364.4 for $\{17, 0\}$ to 8449 for $\{0, 17\}$ (full cooperation yields an aggregate payoff of 49,521.25).

If countries were symmetric, with $b = 6$ and $c = 100$, the self-enforcing agreement would consist of seventeen signatories. All the equilibria for Example 4 also consist of seventeen signatories. This example thus tells us that the model developed in Chapter 7 is robust with respect to the assumption of symmetry. If countries are just a little asymmetric, the equilibrium number of signatories will be the same as when countries are perfectly symmetric.

13.6. EQUILIBRIUM SELECTION

As just shown, when countries are asymmetric there will typically exist a multiple of equilibria. Which equilibrium will be selected? If the choice of whether to be a signatory or a non-signatory were made simultaneously, we could not say. However, if one type of country could commit to being a non-signatory, or pre-empt the other type of country, then there would exist at most one equilibrium. Suppose, for example, that type 1 countries could commit in this way. Then the equilibrium in all of the above examples would be $\{0, 17\}$. The same equilibrium would be sustained if the decision of whether to be a signatory or a non-signatory were made sequentially, with the type 1 countries choosing first, and with all past choices being publicly observable (see Section 7.9).

A coordinating norm would suffice to establish such an order of play. For example, there might exist a norm that the rich should be first to take on the responsibility of protecting the global environment. After all, by assumption the rich countries contribute more to the problem, and benefit more (in absolute terms) from cooperation.

There is a special class of problem, however, for which we need not rely on a norm to select the equilibrium. For Example 1, there is a unique equilibrium. The rich cooperate and the poor do not. This situation is characterized by strong asymmetry. I examine it below.

13.7. STRONG ASYMMETRY

Upon a little reflection, you will probably see that the model supporting the equilibrium in Example 1 is inappropriate. The type 1 countries are effectively side-lined in this game, and yet the type 2 signatories can gain if the type 1 countries also play Abate. The rules of the game should allow the type 2 countries to transact with the type 1 countries; that is, the type 2 countries should be allowed to pay the type 1 countries to accede to an agreement requiring them to play Abate. Of course, as we learned earlier, simply allowing countries to make side payments does not mean that any more cooperation will be sustained. But, as we shall now see, this is not true when countries are strongly asymmetric.

Consider the following game: in Stage 1, every type 2 country chooses to be a signatory or a non-signatory; in Stage 2, type 2 signatories collectively choose (i) whether to play Abate or Pollute *and* (ii) a money side payment m to be paid to every type 1 country which agrees to accede to the agreement and play Abate; in Stage 3, every type 1 country chooses to be a signatory or a non-signatory, under the conditions laid down above; and in Stage 4, all non-signatories of whatever type choose to play Abate or Pollute.

As above, we solve the game backwards. Since, by eqn (13.2a), play Pollute is a dominant strategy, all non-signatories will play Pollute in equilibrium. To solve the Stage 3 game, note that every type 1 country will take m, z_2, and the number of *other* type 1 countries that play Signatory (Abate) as given. Accession for any type i country is rational provided

$$m \geq c - \alpha_1 b_1. \tag{13.5}$$

By assumption, $c > b_2 > \alpha_1 b_1$; so the payment needed to make accession by a type 1 country individually rational is strictly positive.

If eqn (13.5) is satisfied, it will be in the interests of every type 1 country to accede; otherwise, it will not be in the interests of any type 1 country to accede. Assuming that side payments are not rationed, and denoting an equilibrium of this side payments game by two stars, we have:[10]

$$Z_1^{**} = k_1^{**} = 0 \quad \text{if } m < c - \alpha_1 b_1, \quad Z_1^{**} = k_1^{**} = N_1 \quad \text{if } m \geq c - \alpha_1 b_1. \tag{13.6}$$

In Stage 2, type 2 signatories take k_2 as given. By assumption, they choose to $Z_2 \in \{0, \ldots, k_2\}$ to maximize their aggregate payoff,

$$\Pi^s = Z_2(-c + b_1 Z_1 + b_2 Z_2) + (k_2 - Z_2)(b_1 Z_1 + b_2 Z_2) - m Z_1. \tag{13.7}$$

Assuming for simplicity that c/b_2 is a non-integer, the solution requires

$$Z_2^{**} = 0 \quad \text{if } k_2 < c/b_2, \quad Z_2^{**} = k_2 \quad \text{if } k_2 > c/b_2. \tag{3.18}$$

Type 2 signatories must also choose a money side payment m to maximize eqn (13.7). By assumption, type 2 signatories anticipate correctly that, if m satisfies (13.5), then $Z_1^{**} = N_1$; otherwise $Z_1^{**} = 0$. Type 2 signatories only lose by offering more than $m = c - \alpha_1 b_1$. They gain by offering $m = c - \alpha_1 b_1$ if and only if the payoff

---

[10] With rationing, not all type 1 countries will accede. I do not consider this possibility here, for the maths would then become even more cumbersome. Moreover, rationing is not an essential part of the story I wish to illuminate. The industrial country parties to the Montreal Protocol established a total budget to be spent on compensating developing countries for their participation, implying that side payments were rationed. However, the industrial countries specified a total ceiling only to be sure that their financial commitment was not open-ended. As more money was needed, the budget was increased. The industrial countries have shown a willingness to compensate *every* developing country for their participation.

they get by offering this side payment to all type 1 countries exceeds the payoff they get by not offering it. A little algebra shows that this implies

$$m^{**} = 0 \quad \text{if } k_2 < c/b_1 - \alpha_1, \qquad m^{**} = c - \alpha_1 b_1 \quad \text{if } k_2 \geq c/b_1 - \alpha_1. \tag{13.9}$$

It remains to solve for k_2^{**}. Recall that this analysis was motivated by the special case where b_2 was substantially greater than b_1, so that eqn (13.4c) does not hold. This implies that $c/b_1 > c/b_2 + \alpha_1$; and this in turn implies:

$$Z_2^{**} = 0, \quad m^{**} = 0, \quad Z_1^{**} = k_1^{**} = 0 \quad \text{if } k_2 < c/b_2 \tag{13.10a}$$

$$Z_2^{**} = k_2, \quad m^{**} = 0, \quad Z_1^{**} = k_1^{**} = 0 \quad \text{if } c/b_1 - \alpha_1 > k_2 > c/b_2 \tag{13.10b}$$

$$Z_2^{**} = k_2, \quad m^{**} = c - \alpha_1 b_1, \quad Z_1^{**} = k_1^{**} = N_1 \quad \text{if } k_2 > c/b_1 - \alpha_1. \tag{13.10c}$$

Two types of agreements can thus be sustained (for $k_1 + k_2 > 0$):

$$k_1^{**} = 0, \quad c/b_2 + 1 > k_2^{**} > c/b_2 \quad \text{for } c/b_1 - \alpha_1 > N_2 > c/b_2. \tag{13.11a}$$

$$k_1^{**} = N_1, \quad c/b_1 + 1 - \alpha_1 > k_2^{**} > c/b_1 - \alpha_1 \quad \text{for } N_2 > c/b_1 - \alpha. \tag{13.11b}$$

The new result is eqn (13.11b). Provided b_1 is not too small, the equilibrium agreement will consist of $k_2^{**} + N_1$ signatories, each of which plays Abate, with the type 2 signatories compensating the type 1 signatories by an amount $c - \alpha_1 b_1$ each. Notice that the provision of side payments increases participation in the equilibrium treaty by both type 1 *and* type 2 countries. Strong asymmetry "ratchets up" the co-operation problem from one of supplying the public good directly to one of paying others to supply the good. According to eqn (13.11b), participation by type 2 countries depends on the parameter values for type 1 countries, not type 2 countries. More type 2 countries participate in the agreement with side payments because it is only jointly optimal for the required payments to be offered if the cost can be spread over a large enough number of type 2 countries.[11]

For Example 1, where the two types of country are strongly asymmetric, the equilibrium agreement with side payments is {50, 33}, and the aggregate payoff is 17,800, or almost three times as large as in the earlier game. *Changing the rules of the game to allow side payments can thus have a dramatic effect on the equilibrium when countries are strongly asymmetric.*

13.8. FAIRNESS

The assumption that the type 2 signatories can make a take-it-or-leave-it offer to the type 1 countries may seem jarring. Why shouldn't type 1 signatories receive a share of the surplus created by their participation? Fairness may require that type 1 signatories receive such a share. Perhaps more importantly, and as we learned previously,

---

[11] In contrast to this approach, Hoel and Schneider (1997) assume that signatories offer side payments to *every* non-signatory, irrespective of their type. They find that side payments reduce the number of signatories that pay others to abate (in the context of this model, they find that the number of type 2 signatories falls when side payments are offered). In the model developed here, this wouldn't happen; type 2 signatories wouldn't offer side payments to type 2 non-signatories.

experimental studies have found that derisory offers in ultimatum games are often rejected.[12]

The side payment game, however, is not the same as the ultimatum game. The ultimatum game, you may recall, is a two-player game. The game we are analyzing is played by $N \geq 2$ players. If there were three or more players, there would be a difference between the *incremental* gain (the gain that a type 1 country gets by accepting the offer) and the *total* gain received by type 1 players (the gain received by a type 1 player when the offer to pay side payments is made to, and accepted by, *all* type 1 players), provided $\alpha_1 > 0$ and $N_1 \geq 2$. The decision of whether to accede would be guided by the incremental gain. But the decision to accept the offer as regards fairness would more likely be guided by the total gain. A zero incremental gain would presumably be acceptable provided that the total gain in equilibrium were large enough.

Indeed, type 1 signatories may gain *more* than type 2 signatories under this arrangement. In Example 1, a type 1 signatory gains 121.5 by the offer of side payments whereas a type 2 signatory gains just 96.8. Though considerations of fairness do not play an explicit role in the side payments game, the equilibrium may nonetheless be fair. If it is, then the offer of side payments will be especially compelling.

13.9. COST SHARING

If countries are weakly asymmetric, as in Examples 2–4, then the sequence of moves just considered no longer seems appropriate. At the same time, the assumption that side payments cannot be paid seems excessively harsh. Even when countries are strongly asymmetric, as in Example 1, it is not obvious that the game analyzed above is the only alternative to the game without side payments. Let us then treat countries as being symmetric as regards their accession decision but allow them to share the burden of public good provision.

In particular, suppose that signatories adopt the Chander–Tulkens (1994) cost-sharing rule. As compared with some alternatives studied in the literature, the Chander–Tulkens rule has a number of advantages: it belongs in the core (more precisely, the α- and γ-core; see Chander and Tulkens 1994), it has a unique solution, and it is simple.[13] The rule requires that each signatory bear a share of the total cost

---

[12] The ultimatum game is presented and discussed in Section 11.8. See also Ostrom (1998) both for a summary of the literature and a discussion of the implications.

[13] Alternative cost-sharing rules include the Nash bargaining solution, used by Carraro and Siniscalco (1993), and the Shapley value, used by Barrett (1997b) and Carraro and Botteon (1997). Both of these approaches have the virtue of yielding unique solutions. But they are otherwise very different. The Nash bargaining solution is compelling in two-player games, but it loses its appeal in situations with more than two players because it takes no account of coalitions. The Shapley value recognizes that coalitions may form, but it assigns a payoff to each country based on the average over all possible coalitions and this value may not lie in the core of the game.

of providing the public good equal to that country's share of the total benefit to all signatories. After cancelling terms, this rule gives signatory i the payoff

$$\Pi_s^i = \frac{-c\alpha_i (Z_1 + Z_2)}{\alpha_1 k_1 + k_2} + a, (b_1 Z_1 + b_2 Z_2). \tag{13.12}$$

Since maximization of the joint payoff of signatories is unaffected by intra-treaty money transfers, the abatement choices of signatories are still given by (13.3). Furthermore, equilibria (13.4a) and (13.4b) are unchanged by the offer of side payments. The equilibria given by eqn (13.4c) do change—though only slightly—when side payments are on offer. The solution for these equilibria are derived in Appendix 13.1.

Let us now examine how application of this cost-sharing rule affects the equilibria for Examples 1–4.

Example 1. In this case, the equilibrium agreement consists of both types of country but with the "poor" paying the "rich" to play Abate![14]

The distributional aspects of this result are peculiar, but does the cost-sharing rule at least increase cooperation? It certainly increases participation. It can be shown that there exist sixteen different equilibria. The solution requires $17.17 > 0.5 \, k_1^* + k_2^* > 16.67$, and so k_1^* must be an even number. The sixteen equilibria are, then, $\{2, 16\}, \{4, 15\}, \ldots, \{32, 1\}$. There are seventeen signatories in the equilibrium without side payments, and so the Chander–Tulkens cost-sharing rule increases participation by from one to sixteen countries.

However, this increase in participation is of no real benefit; the maximum aggregate net benefit resulting from the application of cost-sharing is only 5600—an amount strictly less than the aggregate net benefit without cost-sharing (5950). The problem is that cost-sharing increases participation by increasing the number of type 1 countries that participate while *decreasing* the number of type 2 countries that participate. Type 1 countries contribute less to the problem, and so contribute less to the solution than type 2 countries.

Perhaps even more importantly, type 2 signatories actually do worse with cost-sharing as compared to the equilibrium agreement without side payments. Though type 1 signatories share the cost of abatement by the type 2 signatories, there are fewer type 2 signatories undertaking abatement and thus less abatement being undertaken in aggregate.

From a number of perspectives, then, application of the Chander–Tulkens cost-sharing rule may yield a very unappealing outcome when countries are strongly asymmetric.

Is this also true when countries are weakly asymmetric? Consider again the other examples:

Example 2. Once again there are sixteen equilibria, ranging from $\{1, 16\}$ to $\{21, 1\}$.[15] However, the largest aggregate net benefit that can be sustained by side

---

[14] In this case, of the four conditions for an equilibrium consisting of both types of country, only condition (13A.3a) is satisfied. [15] In this case, only condition (13A.3c) holds.

payments is only 6800. This again is lower than the aggregate net benefit without cost-sharing.

Example 3. For this example there again exist sixteen equilibria, ranging from $\{1,16\}$ to $\{18,1\}$.[16] The largest aggregate net benefit that can be sustained is still 8787.5 for $\{15,4\}$.

Example 4. In this case, there are again sixteen equilibria, ranging from $\{1,16\}$ to $\{16,1\}$, just as was the case without side payments.[17] The application of cost-sharing makes no difference.

The message of this analysis is clear: allowing for side payments when all countries choose simultaneously to be a signatory or a non-signatory is not able to sustain any additional cooperation. Indeed, the analysis provides a compelling explanation for why the kind of cost-sharing rule proposed by Chander and Tulkens (1994), which in their cooperative framework seems so appealing, is virtually never used in the real world.

13.10. THE MONTREAL PROTOCOL

I have thus far emphasized the methodological differences between my analysis and the earlier literature. More important, however, is that the results reported here, in contrast to these earlier results, are consistent with the design of the Montreal Protocol.

The negotiators of the original, 1987 agreement eschewed side payments. Developing countries played only a minor role in these negotiations. The industrialized countries stood to gain the most from ozone layer protection, and the objective of the 1987 negotiations was to ensure their participation. At the time, this seemed a great challenge, though with hindsight, perhaps, it was not that difficult. As explained in Chapter 8, the industrialized countries had strong incentives to reduce their production and consumption unilaterally; that is, for these countries, the inequality in eqn (13.2a) was probably reversed. Later, as the terms of the agreement were strengthened, the costs of participation by these countries increased relative to the benefits, and it is possible that the constraint of self-enforcement eventually came to bite on these countries. However, as explained in Chapter 12, the credible threat of imposing trade restrictions would have helped to secure full participation by these countries. Rather than "ratchet up" the cooperation problem, as in the case studied earlier in this chapter, the real cooperation problem for the industrialized countries was to provide incentives for developing countries to accede to the treaty. Once the trade restrictions were put in place in the original Montreal Protocol, this was the biggest remaining task for international cooperation.

Consistent with the theory developed here, the original treaty was amended in 1990 to include a provision for compensating developing countries for the "incremental costs" of their participation. The parties agreed on the total compensation

---

[16] For this example, ten equilibria satisfy eqn (13A.3b). These range from $\{5,13\}$ to $\{18,1\}$. The equilibrium that sustains the highest aggregate net benefit is $\{15,4\}$. Six more equilibria satisfy (13A.3d). These are $\{1,16\}$, $\{2,15\}$, $\{3,14\}$, $\{11,7\}$, $\{12,6\}$, and $\{13,5\}$. The latter set of equilibria at best sustain an aggregate net benefit of 7520.   [17] For this example, only eqn (13A.3b) holds.

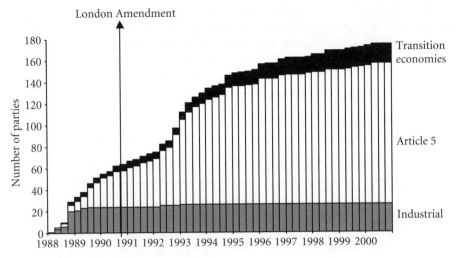

Figure 13.1. *Ratification of the Montreal Protocol*

Source: http://www.unep.org/ozone/ratif.shtml.

required for an initial period ($160–$240 million for 1991–93), given assumptions about participation, and then apportioned this cost according to the United Nations assessment scale, the obvious focal point. Apportionment was not a question for the analysis presented earlier in this chapter for the simple reason that all rich countries were assumed to be symmetric.

Soon after the amendment was negotiated, the number of developing country parties to the Montreal Protocol shot up. Today, as noted previously, participation in the agreement is virtually full. Of the 175 parties to the treaty (excluding the European Community), 130 qualify to receive assistance from the Protocol's Multilateral Fund.

Figure 13.1 charts the time path of ratification. I have distinguished here not only between the Article 5 countries and the industrial countries, but also between these countries and the European economies in transition.[18] This last group is special for several reasons.

Though Figure 13.1 shows that participation by the economies in transition increased over time, this was not because the Protocol extended its geographic reach, as is true of the increase in participation by developing countries. It was because the territory of the old Soviet Union and its satellites fragmented after the agreement was negotiated.[19]

When Montreal was negotiated, it seemed that the Berlin wall would stand forever and that the Soviet Union was as durable as any state. These countries participated

[18] Some countries that you might think of as being in transition are classified as Article 5 countries. These include Albania, Georgia, Kyrgyzstan, and Romania.

[19] The figure reflects participation from today's perspective. Though unification of the two German states in 1990 reduced the number of parties by one, Figure 13.1 only shows participation by one Germany — and the date of Germany's ratification is shown as the date that the Federal Republic ratified.

in the negotiations on a par with the industrial countries of the West. They not only had to meet the same production and consumption limits but they also agreed to contribute in the same proportions (i.e., according to the UN scale of assessments) to the Multilateral Fund. When the old order of Central and Eastern Europe crumbled, these countries were unable or unwilling to fulfil the promises they had made in Montreal and London. As discussed in Chapter 8, they struggled to comply with the treaty's production and consumption limits. They could hardly be expected to pay substantial sums to the Protocol's Fund.

As shown in Figure 13.1, some developing countries ratified the treaty before compensating payments were negotiated. Indeed, Mexico was the first country to ratify Montreal. This seems to refute the theory developed earlier. But, as always, great care must be taken in holding history up to the light of a highly abstract model.

Mexico was a CFC producer. So were many of the other important developing countries that ratified before London, including Brazil and Venezuela (though Brazil only ratified Montreal after negotiations for the London Amendment had begun). These countries would have been affected by the Protocol's trade restrictions. Moreover, the treaty's emission constraints did not bind on the vast majority of developing countries at this time; developing countries were given a ten-year extension to comply with the industrial country limits. Finally, the continued participation of these developing countries was not inevitable; and the terms of the agreement could also have changed. Indeed, in the negotiations leading up to London, Mexico proposed easier production and consumption ceilings for developing countries. This was intended as a bargaining chip—Mexico also introduced a draft amendment saying that "the obligation [of Article 5 parties] ... to comply with ... the control measures ... will be subject to the transfer of technologies and financial assistance." The decision to participate in the 1987 agreement may thus have been tactical.

An important focus of the negotiations was whether contributions to the Fund should be mandatory or voluntary (the theory developed earlier suggests that they should be mandatory). Developing countries wanted them to be "legally enforceable" (Benedick 1998: 153), but some industrial countries demurred. The agreed text simply says that "The Multilateral Fund shall be financed by contributions from [industrial countries] in convertible currency... etc. on the basis of the United Nations scale of assessments." It does not prescribe an explicit penalty for failing to contribute to the Multilateral Fund, but since the scale is expressed in percentages to two decimal points, the London Amendment did "convey the impression of at least a tacit commitment" (Benedick 1998: 187). This language seems to have been enough; over the period 1991–95, compliance with this aspect of the treaty was nearly full. Of the total arrearage in payments, 99 percent was attributable to just seven transition economies transition, for whom special conditions applied because of their economic collapse (Benedick 1998: 262).

Perhaps most importantly, the Montreal Protocol compensates only for incremental costs. Moreover, according to Benedick (1998), this was not even a contested issue, suggesting that the offer to pay incremental costs was perceived to be fair. This may be because the developing countries also stood to gain from ozone protection.

In other words, it appears that $\alpha_1 > 0$ for the type 1 poor countries. According to Benedick (1998: 151–52),

Even though harmful ultraviolet radiation would cause relatively greater incidence of skin cancer among lightly pigmented populations, all people are susceptible to suppression of the immune response system and to eye cataracts. Indeed, poorer general health conditions and medical facilities increase the risks for populations in developing countries from these prospective health threats. Similarly, productivity declines in agriculture and fisheries would have a disproportionate impact on the developing world, where many already subsist at the margin and food shortages are common. In addition, damage to materials, plastics, paints, and buildings from increased ultraviolet radiation would be more severe in the tropics than elsewhere.

There were, to be sure, problems to be resolved in defining what "incremental cost" meant and in creating an effective administrative structure. Another problem was how to use the Fund to lower production and consumption at a time when the Protocol allowed developing countries to *increase* these levels in the short-to-medium run. Finally, countries almost certainly exaggerated their claims to the Fund's resources. However, all these problems have been managed reasonably well.

Through February 2001, a total $1.22 billion has been granted to the Multilateral Fund by thirty two industrialized countries. The Executive Committee that manages the Fund has approved the expenditure of $1.19 billion, to support about 3460 projects and activities in 124 developing countries (as noted before, 130 developing countries qualify to receive financial assistance). These investments are expected to reduce the consumption (production) of ozone-harming chemicals by more than 142,000 (39,000) tons.[20]

Having been classed as industrial countries in 1987, the European transition countries were ineligible for Multilateral Fund assistance. But following the political and economic changes that convulsed these countries, assistance for compliance was provided by a different institution, the Global Environment Facility (GEF), set up previously to help developing countries protect the shared environment. So far, the GEF has authorized the expenditure of $125 million (with an additional $112 million of co-financing) to assist a number of transition economies to comply with the Montreal Protocol, including Belarus, Bulgaria, the Czech Republic, Hungary, Poland, Russia, Slovakia, Slovenia, and Ukraine.[21]

By any reasonable standard, these are substantial achievements. Had Montreal not embraced countries like India and China, the agreement would have fallen far short of sustaining full cooperation. Preventing the non-compliance or withdrawal of the European transition economies was equally essential. At the same time, the expenditure of just over $1 billion is really a pittance when compared to the cost–benefit figures shown in Chapter 8. Indeed, as this chapter has shown, this is why the offer of side payments proved so successful.

---

[20] See the web page for the Secretariat of the Multilateral Fund for the Implementation of the Montreal Protocol, http://www.unmfs.org/general.htm.
[21] See http://www-esd.worldbank.org/mp/publications/q&a.htm.

13.11. BIODIVERSITY CONSERVATION

Biological diversity is depleted for many reasons. Individual species are harvested directly, sometimes to the point of extinction; and, as we have seen, many treaties, starting with the Fur Seal Treaty, address this kind of problem. Pollution is another cause of biodiversity loss, and is also addressed by a number of international agreements. Species are also transported, often unwittingly, to new ecosystems, which they sometimes dominate with dramatic effect. Hawaii is a tropical paradise, but as ecologist E.O. Wilson (2002: 44) explains, it is "highly synthetic: the vast majority of plants and animals easy to find originated somewhere else." According to Wilson (2002: 44), of the 1935 flowering plant species in Hawaii today, 902 are alien. "Ancient Hawaii," Wilson (2002: 44–5) says, "is a ghost that haunts the hills, and our planet is poorer for its sad retreat." Biological invasions—externalities associated with globalization and international trade—are addressed by a number of agreements, including the plant protection agreements, the Convention on Biological Diversity and Biosafety Protocol (as applied to living modified organisms), and the Sanitary and Phytosanitary Agreement under the World Trade Organization.

The greatest threat to biological diversity, however, is habitat destruction, especially the clearance of tropical forests. Again, a number of treaties protect habitat, including the Ramsar Convention, which protects wetlands, and the Berne Convention which protects the habitat of European wildlife. But only one treaty offers a comprehensive approach to biodiversity conservation. This is the Biodiversity Convention.[22]

Habitats especially deserving of preservation are now being identified. Called "hotspots," these habitats contain a dense concentration of endemic species. A recent analysis by Myers *et al.* (2000), identifies twenty-five habitats that the authors guess harbor 44 percent of all plant species and 35 percent of vertebrates on just 1.4 percent of the Earth's land surface. These areas, rich in endemics, are also highly threatened. Most are in the tropics; the leading hotspots are all located in developing countries. Biodiversity is valued globally—for its existence and for the genetic information encoded within it, among other reasons.[23] But these global public good aspects of biodiversity are valued especially highly by the rich countries. Global biodiversity conservation is thus marked by a strong asymmetry. As in protection of the ozone layer, the rich countries would like the poor to provide a service. In this case, biodiversity conservation.

This asymmetry is acknowledged by the Biodiversity Convention, which also emphasizes the need for *in-situ* conservation. Article 8 requires parties to establish a system of protected areas for biodiversity conservation, and Article 20 instructs developed country parties to provide "new and additional financial resources to enable developing country Parties to meet the agreed full incremental costs to them of implementing measures which fulfill the obligations of this Convention … ." This language is very much akin to the text of the Montreal Protocol. In the sense defined above, the problem is similar, too. But so far, very little money has been raised and allocated for this purpose.[24]

---

[22] In addition to habitat protection, the Biodiversity Convention promotes the sustainable use of biodiversity and "the fair and equitable sharing of the benefits arising out of the utilization of genetic resources … ."

[23] Dasgupta (2001) provides a synthesis of the economic and ecological value of biodiversity conservation.

[24] For a preliminary analysis of biodiversity as a global cooperation problem, see Barrett (1994c). Small amounts of money is also earmarked toward global biodiversity conservation by the Global Environment Facility.

13.12. CONCLUSIONS

This chapter has obtained a number of results, some negative and some positive. The important negative result is that side payments on their own have little effect on international cooperation. Side payments make the recipients more inclined to participate, but they lower the payoffs of the donor countries, and so make them less inclined to participate. They do not on their own fundamentally alter the cooperation problem. In particular, they do not make punishments for free-riding any more credible.

The important positive result of this chapter is that strong asymmetry between players changes the rules of the game, and thereby enables side payments to sustain a vastly superior outcome compared to the agreement without side payments. In a sense, strong asymmetry does much the same thing as commitment in Carraro and Siniscalco's (1993) paper, although the "commitment" made possible by strong asymmetry is of a different type than they consider. Strong asymmetry means that some countries can only lose by acceding to an agreement that eschews side payments. With strong asymmetry, countries do not *choose* to be committed to any particular course of action; the payoffs of the game simply ensure that these countries *are* committed to being non-signatories. Schelling (1960) has taught us that this is a vital distinction.

The real advantage of strong asymmetry is that it is not arbitrary like the assumption of commitment can be (though countries cannot easily enter into commitments, countries *are* asymmetric). Moreover, analysis of the equilibrium with strong asymmetry does not need to appeal to cooperative game theory and its many alternative solution concepts. So the predictions of the model developed here deserve to be taken seriously—all the more so, perhaps, because they are consistent with the example of the Montreal Protocol.

More than this, the model also tells us that the Montreal Protocol is a special case. When negotiating the side payments in this agreement, the United States insisted that it be "without prejudice to any future arrangements that may be developed with respect to other environmental issues" (Benedick 1998: 184), and these exact words were later imprinted in Article 10 of the London Amendment. The theory developed here not only explains how side payments came to be important to the Montreal Protocol but also why they cannot be a general solution to the problem of international cooperation. This, too, is something that the earlier literature has been unable to explain. Indeed, the theory developed here provides an answer to the puzzle of why side payments are not used more often.

As noted in the last chapter, the Multilateral Fund also helped to make the agreement fair. On their own, trade restrictions might have deterred non-participation by the developing countries, but such an outcome would not have been fair. Side payments not only helped to increase participation. They also legitimized the threat to impose trade restrictions. It is really the combination of carrots and sticks that succeeded in protecting the earth's ozone layer.

Appendix 13.1

Derivation of (13.3). Since non-signatories will play Pollute, the aggregate payoff of signatories, Π^s, can be written as:

$$\Pi^s = [(\alpha_1 k_1 + k_2)b_1 - c]Z_1 + [(\alpha_1 k_1 k_2)b_2 - c]Z_2. \tag{13A.1}$$

Maximization of Π_s with respect to z_i requires

$$Z_i^* = k_i, \quad \text{if } \alpha_1 k_1 + k_2 > c/b_i$$

$$Z_i^* \in \{0, k_i\}, \quad \text{if } \alpha_1 k_1 + k_2 = c/b_i \tag{13A.2}$$

$$Z_i^* = 0, \quad \text{if } \alpha_1 k_1 + k_2 < c/b_i$$

for $i = 1, 2$. Assuming for simplicity that c/b_i is a non-integer so that (13A.2) holds with strict inequality, the solution requires that *all* signatories of type i play either Abate or Pollute. There are three kinds of equilibria: either $Z_1^* = Z_2^* = 0$ or $Z_1^* = 0, Z_2^* = k_2$ or $Z_1^* = k_1, Z_2^* = k_2$. Note that $Z_1^* = k_1, Z_2^* = 0$, though feasible, cannot be an equilibrium. This means that, in an agreement consisting of both types of country, if it is optimal for type 1 signatories to play Abate then it must be optimal for type 2 signatories to play Abate.

Derivation of the Conditions for Equilibria Consisting of Both Types of Country Based on the Chander–Tulkens Cost-sharing Rule. Suppose to begin that $\alpha_1 k_1 + k_2 > c/b_1$. Then a type 1 country won't accede if $\alpha_1(b_1 k_1 + b_2 k_2) > -c\alpha_1(k_1 + 1 + k_2)/[\alpha_1(k_1 + 1) + k_2] + \alpha_1[b_1(k_1 + 1) + b_2 k_2]$ or $c/b_1 > [\alpha_1(k_1 + 1) + k_2]/(k_1 + 1 + k_2)$, which holds by the model's assumptions. Similarly, a type 2 country won't accede, since $c/b_2 > (\alpha_1 k_1 + k_2 + 1)/(k_1 + k_2 + 1)$.

Upon a withdrawal from an equilibrium agreement, two possibilities must be considered. Either all the type 1 signatories must play Pollute or all the signatories of both types must do so. If neither of these conditions were satisfied, then a withdrawal from the agreement would always be individually rational.

Consider first the former possibility. For a withdrawal by a type 1 signatory, $c/b_1 > \alpha_1(k_1 - 1) + k_2 > c/b_2$ and for a withdrawal by a type 2 signatory, $c/b_1 > \alpha_1 k_1 + k_2 - 1 > c/b_2$. A unilateral withdrawal by a country of either type will then cause all the remaining type 1 signatories to play Pollute if $c/b_1 + \alpha_1 > \alpha_1 k_1 + k_2 > c/b_2 + 1$. Given this, a type 1 signatory would not withdraw if $\alpha_1 k_1 + k_2 > c(k_1 + k_2)/(b_1 k_1)$; and a type 2 signatory would not withdraw if $\alpha_1 k_1 + k_2 > c(k_1 + k_2)/(b_1 k_1 + k_2)$. Taken together, these conditions yield:

$$c/b_1 + \alpha_1 > \alpha_1 k_1^* + k_2^* > (c/b_1)(1 + k_2^*/k_1^*), \quad \alpha_1 k_1^* + k_2^* > c/b_2 + 1 \tag{13A.3a}$$

Now suppose that a withdrawal impels all signatories to play Pollute. Then we have $c/b_2 + \alpha_1 > \alpha_1 k_1 + k_2$. Withdrawal by a type 1 signatory will therefore be irrational if $\alpha_1 k_1 + k_2 > c(k_1 + k_2)/(b_1 k_1 + b_2 k_2)$. Since the RHS of this inequality cannot exceed c/b_1, and since we are considering the case where $\alpha_1 k_1 + k_2 > c/b_1$, we know that a type 1 signatory will not withdraw from this agreement. A similar calculation shows that a type 2 signatory will not withdraw either. This yields:

$$c/b_2 + \alpha_1 > \alpha_1 k_1^* + k_2^* > c/b_1 \tag{13A.3b}$$

There remains one other possibility: there may exist equilibria in which countries of both types are signatories but only type 2 signatories play Abate. This requires

$$c/b_1 > \alpha_1 k_1^* + k_2^* > c/b_2. \tag{13A.4}$$

A type 1 country would prefer not to accede to this agreement if either of the following holds:

$$c/b_1 - \alpha_1 > \alpha_1 k_1^* + k_2^* > c/b_2 - \alpha_1 \tag{13A.5a}$$

$$c(k_1^* + k_2^* + 1)/b_1(k_1^* + 1) - \alpha_1 > \alpha_1 k_1^* + k_2^* > c/b_1 - \alpha_1. \tag{13A.5b}$$

A type 2 country would not want to accede if either of the following hold:

$$c/b_1 - 1 > \alpha_1 k_1^* + k_2^* > c/b_2 - 1, \quad c(k_2^* + 1)/b_2 - 1 > \alpha_1 k_1^* + k_2^* \tag{13A.6a}$$

$$c(k_1^* + k_2^* + 1)/(b_1 k_1^* + b_2) > \alpha_1 k_1^* + k_2^* > c/b_1 - 1. \tag{13A.6b}$$

A type 1 signatory would be strictly worse off by withdrawing from agreement (13A.4) if

$$c/b_2 + \alpha_1 > \alpha_1 k_1^* + k_2^* > c/b_2. \tag{13A.7}$$

Finally, a type 2 signatory will prefer not to withdraw if either of the following hold:

$$c/b_2 + 1 > \alpha_1 k_1^* + k_2^* > c/b_2. \tag{13A.8a}$$

$$c/b_1 + 1 > \alpha_1 k_1^* + k_2^* > c/b_2 + 1, \quad \alpha_1 k_1^* + k_2^* > k_2^* c/b_2. \tag{13A.8b}$$

Notice that (13A.8b) and (13A.7) cannot both be satisfied. Since (13A.7) must be satisfied, this means that (13A.8a) must hold. But if (13A.7) holds, then (13A.8a) will hold, too. In addition, (13A.5b) and (13A.6a) cannot both hold. So there exist three possible types of equilibria. One satisfies (13A.4), (13A.5a), (13A.6a), and (13A.7). This is given by:

$$c/b_2 + \alpha_1 > \alpha_1 k_1^* + k_2^* > c/b_2, \quad c/b_1 - 1 > \alpha_1 k_1^* + k_2^*,$$

$$(c/b_2)(k_2^* + 1) - 1 > \alpha_1 k_1^* + k_2^*. \tag{13A.3c}$$

The second possible kind of equilibrium satisfies (13A.4), (13A.5a), (13A.6b), and (13A.7), and the third satisfies (13A.4), (13A.5b), (13A.6b), and (13A.7). However, the conditions needed to sustain these last two types of equilibria can be combined to yield:

$$c/b_2 + \alpha_1 > \alpha_1 k_1^* + k_2^* > c/b_2, \quad c/b_1 > \alpha_1 k_1^* + k_2^* > c/b_1 - 1,$$

$$c(k_1^* + k_2^* + 1)/(b_1 k_1^* + b_2) > \alpha_1 k_1^* + k_2^*. \tag{13A.3d}$$

If (13A.3a) or (13A.3b) holds, then the self-enforcing agreement will require that both types of signatory play Abate. If (13A.3a) is satisfied, a unilateral withdrawal will trigger only the type 1 signatories to play Pollute. If (13A.3b) holds instead, then a withdrawal would impel all the signatories to play Pollute. Conditions (13A.3c) and (13A.3d) are relevant only for equilibria in which type 2 signatories play Abate and type 1 signatories play Pollute.

14

Summary

This completes my presentation of the theory. I will not attempt to summarize all of the book's conclusions, only the ten most important conclusions for treaty-making:

1. *The principal task of a treaty is to restructure incentives.* A treaty is negotiated because countries are dissatisfied with the status quo. To induce a change in behavior requires a change in incentives. A treaty like the Helsinki Protocol that simply obligates countries to meet an emissions target does not restructure incentives and so will not change behavior.[1] Unless a treaty changes incentives, countries are likely only to agree to a target they felt confident they would meet anyway.

2. *Compliance needs to be enforced, but participation is the binding constraint on international cooperation.* For the reason previously mentioned, the fact that most countries comply with most treaties most of the time is no reason to think that substantial cooperation is being achieved.[2] At the same time, punishing only non-compliance will not sustain real cooperation either. The reason is that countries can easily avoid such punishments by not participating. A treaty that sustains real cooperation must deter non-compliance *and* non-participation.[3] The latter is harder to achieve; it requires more substantial punishments, and these will generally be less credible. Participation should therefore be a main focus of any treaty negotiation.

3. *Regional or minilateral environmental problems are easier to remedy than global environmental problems.* This is not a new idea, but I think I have given a clearer explanation for why the result holds. I have also shown that whether a given number of countries is "large" or "small" depends on the problem at hand.[4] A corollary is that treaties seeking to manage common property resources effectively must deter entry.

4. *The means by which a treaty tries to change behavior is a strategic choice.* The instrument for changing behavior may be a quantitative limit—on emissions, say, or fishing catch. Alternatively, it may be a policy or measure—a technology standard (use of a turtle excluder device) or a common emissions tax, or a subsidy for R&D, or a trade restriction. Such instruments can be strategic substitutes or strategic complements. That is, some instruments will induce a positive feedback (as your country does more, others do more), some a negative feedback (as your country does

---

[1] At least not materially. See Levy (1993, 1995). See also Chapter 1.

[2] See Downs *et al.* (1996). See also Chapter 10.

[3] This is demonstrated in Barrett (1999*a*) and in Chapter 10.

[4] Olson's (1965) classic study argues that cooperation becomes harder as the number of players increases. In Barrett (1994*a*), I showed that there are circumstances in which even a large number of players can sustain high levels of cooperation. This is also demonstrated in Chapters 7 and, in different ways, in Chapters 10–13.

more, others do less).[5] Some instruments are also easier to monitor and verify than are others.[6]

5. *There is a trade-off between the depth and breadth of cooperation, and choice of the right balance is strategic.* Having chosen an instrument for changing behavior, negotiators must set a level for it—the value of an emission limit, say, or the magnitude of the common tax, or the choice of a technology standard (e.g. a vehicle emissions limit). In general, choice of an instrument level (the depth of cooperation) affects the participation level (the breadth of cooperation) that can be sustained, and vice versa. The credibility of the mechanism needed to enforce a given level of participation decreases in the depth of cooperation, and so negotiators may need to choose between having a "narrow but deep" treaty and a "broad but shallow" treaty. The incentives to negotiate a "broad but shallow" treaty are especially strong when cost-effectiveness favors spreading provision of a public good over a large number of countries.[7]

6. *Linkage of instruments can be a strategic choice.* Linkage can serve different purposes. It can facilitate agreement (you scratch my back and I will scratch yours) or it can change incentives. The latter purpose of linkage is strategic. For example, pollution clean-up may be linked to cooperative R&D.[8] Alternatively, choice of a quantitative limit on CFCs may be linked to a ban on trade between parties and non-parties. The latter combination may transform a prisoners' dilemma game into one requiring coordination, making cooperation—both deep and broad—easier to sustain. Though the trade ban may limit trade leakage—the worry that emissions may rise in non-cooperating countries as emissions are reduced in cooperating countries—leakage may in turn render the threat to restrict trade credible.[9] Use of trade restrictions for treaty enforcement is not an instant cure-all, appropriate for any and all environmental problems. But nor should trade restrictions be forbidden as a general rule.

7. *The minimum participation level of a treaty is a strategic choice.* This level determines when and whether a treaty enters into force, and it plays different roles depending on the chosen instrument. If the instrument for changing behavior is a strategic substitute or has a neutral effect on behavior (as your country does more, the behavior of other countries is unaltered), the participation level that can be sustained by a treaty will likely have an upper limit and setting a higher minimum participation level will only result in a treaty not entering into force.[10] If the instrument is a strategic complement, however, then there is likely to exist a threshold or tipping point, and provided the treaty gets countries over this threshold, participation is likely to tip.[11] Actual participation will thus exceed the minimum participation level, possibly by a large margin.

---

[5] In Barrett (1994*a*), pollution abatement is a strategic substitute. In Heal (1993), it is a strategic complement. See also Chapters 7 and 9.

[6] See Mitchell's (1993, 1994) interesting study of oil pollution at sea. See also Chapter 9.

[7] These ideas are developed in Barrett (2002*a*) as well as Chapter 11.

[8] See Carraro and Siniscalco (1994) and the discussion in Chapter 12.

[9] The transformation is shown in Barrett (1997*a*), and the credibility of the linkage is discussed in Barrett (1999*c*). Both issues are discussed in Chapter 12.

[10] A number of papers find limits on participation in a treaty, including Barrett (1992*c*, 1994*a*), Carraro and Siniscalco (1993), and Hoel (1992). See also Chapter 7.

[11] The classic article on tipping is by Schelling (1978). Tipping treaties are discussed in this book in Chapters 4 and 9.

8. *The offer of side payments can be a strategic choice.*   Side payments—transfers in money, in kind, or in technology—play three roles in a treaty. They may reflect an implicit agreement about property rights, as in the example of the Rhine Chlorides Treaty. They may be needed to ensure that the countries which would otherwise lose by participating, gain by participating, as in the North Pacific Fur Seal Treaty.[12] And they may redefine the cooperation problem. In the London Amendment to the Montreal Protocol, side payments play all three roles. The treaty differentiates between rich and poor nations, acknowledging their "common but differentiated responsibilities." It also makes participation in the interests of developing countries, by paying for the incremental costs of their compliance. Finally, the London Amendment ratchets up the cooperation problem. It not only requires that the rich countries reduce their emissions; it also requires that the rich countries pay developing countries to reduce *their* emissions. It is this last role of side payments that is strategic.[13]

9. *Treaties are often able to sustain only a second-best outcome.*   Treaty negotiators need to come to a realistic assessment of the outcome that can be supported by the available mechanisms. Only then should they negotiate the details. If they try to negotiate a treaty that is both deep and broad, for example, and only later worry about whether credible enforcement mechanisms can sustain this level of cooperation, their effort may fail. Though it is not necessary for a treaty to be right in every detail from the very start, it is essential to build sustainable supporting mechanisms (compliance and participation enforcement, especially) from the beginning. Ultimately, these supporting mechanisms will determine what a treaty is able to do. Details—such as the levels at which the chosen instruments are set—can be changed later. Indeed, uncertainty about science and technology is likely to favor negotiation of a flexible treaty.[14]

10. *Customary law determines whether a treaty is needed and what a treaty is able to achieve.*   Recognition of the freedom of the high seas necessitated the North Pacific Fur Seal Treaty, while the establishment of the 200-mile Exclusive Economic Zone almost a century later nationalized a large share of the ocean's commercial resources, obviating the need for other treaties. Treaty failures may also cause custom to change. I speculate in Chapter 12, for example, that inadequacies in the current treaty system—inadequacies that may be impossible to overcome by means of treaties alone—may necessitate a new customary law forbidding countries from undermining fishery conservation agreements by reflagging and other means. Though custom is not "made" in the same way that a treaty is made, it is something that can be shaped by behavior over a longer period of time.

As indicated by the entire text that precedes this chapter, I am not claiming that every feature of this theory is radical and new. The theory makes use of many contributions

---

[12] See the discussion on side payments in Mäler (1990, 1991). Chander and Tulkens (1992, 1994, 1997) devise formulas for allocating side payments—formulas that have a number of desirable properties. See also Chapter 13.

[13] The strategic role of side payments is analyzed in Barrett (2001*a*) and in Chapter 13.

[14] The importance of flexibility, a hallmark of the Montreal Protocol, is discussed in Benedick (1998).

made by many researchers representing different disciplines over a period of many years. What I have done is to pull these many disparate ideas together, and to combine and package them in a coherent fashion.[15] There is an intimate connection between each of the chapters, and a consistent approach is used throughout. As well, I have tried to connect the theory to practice—and practice to the theory. Indeed, knowledge of the statecraft of treaty-making has played a major role in shaping the theory.

My aim has been to provide a theory of treaty-making, with an emphasis on strategy, not negotiation skills, that can help practitioners. My aim also has been to build a platform on which other researchers can build (and, where appropriate, disassemble and rebuild). Admittedly, it is unusual for a book to have both aims, but this is an applied subject. The theory of international cooperation has to provide an approach for the conduct of policy, or otherwise it is of no use. And practitioners need to think deeply about these problems. They are hard, and it is no good to pretend otherwise. The problems addressed by this book are too important.

In the next chapter, I demonstrate how the theory can be used to improve treaty-making. My focus is the most difficult environmental treaty negotiation ever attempted.

---

[15] Barrett (2002*b*) and Michael Finus (2001) offer more formal treatments of the subject. See also the survey article by Ulrich Wagner (2001).

15

Global Climate Change and the Kyoto Protocol

The pages of history are filled with stories of important and worthy international efforts that took years to triumph, and suffered many setbacks along the way. Some said the superpowers would never limit their nuclear arsenals–but they did. Some said we would never rid the world of smallpox; that we would never join together to take action to fix the ozone hole in the atmosphere. But we did.

Likewise, I am confident that world efforts to fight global warming will continue. I am equally confident that the United States will continue to be a leader in this fight. We will not give up. The stakes are too high; the science too decisive; and our planet and our children too precious. Frank E. Loy, Under Secretary for Global Affairs and Head of the US Delegation to the COP6 negotiations, speaking after the negotiations held in The Hague collapsed on November 25, 2000.

15.1. INTRODUCTION

There is a joke—told, I think, by President Ronald Reagan—that the economist, having seen something work in practice, tries to show how it could be made to work in theory. It might be argued that this is all that I have done in this book, but I hope that I have shown much more.

I began this book by demonstrating that it is not even obvious how to tell whether a particular agreement really "works." I have presented a theory capable of explaining why the more obvious successes of international cooperation have worked—and in the course of doing so I have also explained why other treaties have failed. The theory is simplistic but it also makes sharp predictions.

It shows, for example, that there is not a magic formula for success, and that different environmental problems must be approached in different ways. It also shows that enforcement is critical. It cautions against the view that countries can solve the enforcement problem simply by appealing to a state's responsibilities, by exhortation, by naming and shaming, and by offering assistance. These measures may be helpful; and, diplomatically, they may be necessary; but they will not suffice for remedying the hardest cooperation failures. To address these, countries must be able to make credible threats both to deter free-riding and to enforce compliance. The problem is that the threats needed to sustain full cooperation will not always be credible. In hurting the countries that fail to cooperate, the countries seeking to enforce an agreement typically injure themselves—and this is an outcome they would rather avoid. If there is one aspect of my approach that distinguishes it from the rest of the literature it is that I have taken the constraint of self-enforcement very, very seriously. Every important result in this book springs from the assumption of state sovereignty.

Though I have emphasized successes like the Montreal Protocol and the Fur Seal Treaty, international cooperation more often fails. On occasion, this is due to bungled diplomacy. More upsetting, however, is the lesson that there may not exist a silver bullet solution to every crossborder environmental problem. And, yet, a more positive message also emerges from this work. We might do better if we acknowledged that the constraint of sovereignty is not easily disarmed or pushed aside. If we took this constraint more seriously, we might approach cooperation problems differently. Though we may be unable to sustain a first best, we might improve on unilateralism. We might sustain a kind of second best.

Since I began writing this book, an unprecedented amount of diplomatic energy has been spent on the latest global environmental threat: climate change. As explained later in this chapter, the treaty negotiated to deal with this problem—the Kyoto Protocol—was consciously styled after Montreal (see Table 15.1 for a comparison of the two treaties). This was for obvious reasons. Climate change became a political issue shortly after Montreal was negotiated. And, like ozone layer protection, climate change mitigation is a global public good. It was natural to think that the remedy that worked for the ozone layer could be made to work, after a little rejigging, for the global climate. Upon closer examination, however, it turns out that these problems are very different (Barrett 1999*b*). Montreal was the wrong model, and the Kyoto Protocol is unlikely to sustain meaningful cooperation.

This is not for the reasons usually given—that Kyoto will do little to moderate climate change, that monitoring of the agreement will be imperfect, that its mechanisms are too complicated, and that its implementation will be too costly—though these criticisms are also valid. The main strike against Kyoto is the most crucial of all: the agreement fails to solve the enforcement problem.

Indeed, enforcement did not even attract the full attention of diplomats until quite late in the process—at the negotiating session held in The Hague in November 2000, almost three years after the Kyoto framework was first negotiated. At later sessions held in Bonn and Marrakech in 2001, an enforcement mechanism was agreed, but as I shall explain later, it has a number of design faults. This would not matter that much if a better enforcement mechanism could be devised, but it is not obvious how the Kyoto framework could be enforced effectively. However, if the negotiators had reflected on the need for enforcement and on the difficulty of devising an effective enforcement mechanism earlier in the process, they may have negotiated a different kind of treaty—one that sustained more cooperation. The need to do this is a central message of this book.

How could a treaty of such importance fail to address the enforcement problem earlier? Both before and after Kyoto was negotiated (the essential plan of Kyoto was mapped out years before the treaty was negotiated in late 1997), I put this question to actual negotiators and academics playing supporting roles. And always I received the same unsatisfying response: Enforcement was something that was best addressed later, I was told. You cannot solve every aspect of this problem in one stroke. Better

Table 15.1. *A comparison of the Montreal and Kyoto Protocols*

	Montreal	Kyoto
Quantitative emission limits:		
–for industrialized countries	Yes.	Yes.
–for developing countries.	Yes.	No.
Emission offsets.	Yes; subtracts from production the amount destroyed.	Yes; subtracts from gross emissions removal by sinks.
Comprehensive treatment of gross emissions.	Yes; trade-offs allowed within ODS categories.	Yes; limitation applies to an aggregate of six pollutants.
Non-uniform emission limits.	Yes; developing countries have different limits, though limits are uniform within country categories.	Yes; limits are country-specific, and economies in transition allowed to use an alternative base year.
Permanent emission limits.	Yes.	No; limitation only for 2008–12; future limitations by amendments.
International trading in emission entitlements.	For purposes of "industrial rationalization"; EC treated as a bubble.	Yes.
Intertemporal trading in emission entitlements.	No.	Yes; emission limits over the period 2008–12 must be met *on average* and additional reductions can be credited to the next control period.
Joint implementation.	No; not needed since all signatories subject to emission ceilings and trading is already allowed.	Yes, between Annex I countries and, through the CDM, between Annex I and non-Annex I countries.
Reporting requirements.	Yes.	Yes.
Verification procedure.	Yes.	Yes.
Side payments.	Yes; pays incremental costs for developing countries, and the Global Environment Facility (GEF) offers assistance to economies in transition.	Transfers would be effected by trading and the CDM. Funds are also made available by the Convention through the GEF; and Kyoto establishes an adaptation fund.
Compliance procedure and mechanism.	Yes, though specific punishments are not mandated.	Yes, though mechanisms with "binding consequences" can only be adopted by amendment.
Free-rider deterrence mechanism.	Yes; trade restrictions with non-parties in ODSs and products containing ODSs, plus the threat to ban trade in products made using ODSs.	No, with the possible exception of the minimum participation clause.
Leakage prevention mechanism.	Yes; in the form of trade restrictions between parties and non-parties.	No.
Minimum participation for entry into force.	Ratification by at least 11 countries making up at least two-thirds of global consumption of ODSs in 1986.	Ratification by at least 55 countries, accounting for at least 55 percent of total Annex I CO_2 emissions for 1990.

to build a framework and then, over time, give it the support it needs to develop. The reason Kyoto failed to address the enforcement problem at an early stage is that the negotiators and others involved in shaping this agreement believed it could be added on later. This, in my view, was a mistake. And I hope that this book has shown that it is a mistake that could have been foreseen when the negotiations first commenced.

Of course, a climate treaty does need to evolve. As explained in Section 1.9, a treaty addressing a problem of such complexity and about which so much is uncertain needs to be flexible; it needs to be able to adapt to new knowledge; and it needs to add in procedures over time that assist implementation. But as also explained in Chapter 1, these changes must be built on a firm foundation. And this, to my view, is Kyoto's main flaw. It provides a framework but not a foundation. That is, Kyoto fails to restructure the climate game.

The theory told in this book offers a different perspective than the one embraced by the Kyoto negotiators: the negotiators should have begun by asking what kind of enforcement was practicable, and then designed an architecture to suit this foundation. International cooperation in this area, as in others, must strategically manipulate the incentives states have to participate in and to comply with a treaty. Kyoto does not do this.

No one, not even the people most involved in negotiating the Kyoto Protocol, believe it to be perfect. But the flaws in this agreement have been tolerated for the simple reason that, in the words of John Prescott, the British Deputy Prime Minister, Kyoto has been "the only game in town."[1] So it will not suffice only to criticize Kyoto. I must rather take the joke that introduced this chapter to heart and propose a plausible alternative to Kyoto. The purpose of this chapter, and the final task of this book, is thus not only to use the theory to expose Kyoto's flaws but to demonstrate how the theory can help in constructing a superior treaty design.

Let me be clear about this. The theory does not point to a single solution. It only guides design. It prompts us to ask critical questions. More important than the specifics of my proposal is the thinking that lies behind it.

My proposal is given in this chapter's penultimate section, but first I need to give some background to this important and vexing environmental problem, beginning with the science.

15.2. CLIMATE SCIENCE

Pick any spot, and monitor the weather over a 24-hour-period. It is likely that the temperature will be cooler in the evening than in the day. The skies may be clear or cloudy, the air humid or dry. It may rain or snow, be calm or blustery. Over the course of a week, the weather will be even more variable. Over an entire year it will change more still. Now move from this spot, perhaps further inland, or nearer to the coast, or to a higher altitude, or to a different latitude. The weather will change again—and

---

[1] G. Lean, "UK To Go It Alone on Global Warming," *The Independent*, 2001 April 1.

the further you move from where you are, the greater (likely) will be the change. Even small changes in time and location can reveal a dramatic change in the weather.

The global climate is different. It is a measure of the earth's *average* weather—an average calculated over both space and time. The global climate is less variable and more stable than the weather. Some years may be warmer than others, and some may be wetter, but changes in the global climate are generally tiny compared to changes in the weather.

And yet the global climate isn't fixed. Even when the climate is stable it varies around some mean. And the climate can also shift—to a new mean; possibly to a new variance. Indeed, the climate has changed in this way in the past, and it will do so in the future whether a climate treaty succeeds or fails. Over the last two and a half million years, the earth's climate has oscillated between warmer and cooler periods (the last cool period was the so-called Little Ice Age, which ended about 1650), largely due to interactions between the atmosphere and the oceans, variability in the heat output of the sun, and volcanic eruptions. The worry now, however, is that the climate may be changing for a different reason: the accumulation of greenhouse gases in the atmosphere, caused by human activities. This new disturbance might best be called *human-induced* global climate change.

The atmosphere is rich with gases that trap the sun's heat, especially water vapor and carbon dioxide (CO_2). These create a natural "greenhouse effect," keeping the earth about 34 °C warmer than it otherwise would be, a temperature difference that is needed to support life. Human activities have increased the concentration of these gases in the atmosphere. Today, they are about 30 percent higher than they were before the industrial revolution.

By how much should this increase in the concentration of greenhouse gases warm the earth? In 1896, Svante Arrhenius, a Swedish chemist, tried to answer this question. He figured that a doubling in CO_2 concentrations would increase mean global temperature by about 5 °C (Rowlands 1995: 66). In hindsight, this was a remarkable calculation. A century's advancement in atmospheric science and generous application of the world's most powerful computers produces only a slightly different estimate. The best guess today is that a doubling in CO_2 concentrations would increase mean global temperature by about 1.5–4.5 °C.

Is this prediction being realized? It is impossible to know for sure. Mean global temperature has risen by about 0.3–0.6 °C since the late-nineteenth century. But this change could reflect natural variability. Knowing whether the increased concentration of greenhouse gases is causing the warming is like trying to determine whether the Helsinki Protocol made any difference to European acid rain. To answer both these questions requires a counterfactual that we do not have. To prove that human-induced climate change was real, you would have to construct another earth with an atmosphere identical to our own except for holding atmospheric concentrations of greenhouse gases to their pre-industrial level. Then you would have to take measurements of, say, global mean temperature over a long period of time for both earths and compare the data. Only then could you be sure that the increased concentration of greenhouse gases really was changing the earth's climate.

Obviously, this kind of experiment cannot be done. The best that atmospheric scientists can do is to create a computer model of the earth and its climate system, just as I have used simple theoretical models to determine the effects of a treaty on environmental protection. When the Intergovernmental Panel on Climate Change (IPCC) claims that human-induced climate change can be detected in the climate record what they mean is that their models show that it is unlikely that the earth would have warmed like it has in the last century were it not for the increase in atmospheric concentrations. Essentially, the models are supplying the needed counterfactual. The important point to make here is that this approach can't be conclusive. You can show that a model is not wrong; you cannot prove that it is right. Nevertheless, the IPCC felt sufficiently sure of the relationship to declare, in its 1995 report, that "the balance of evidence suggests a discernible human influence on global climate;" and in its follow-on report, issued in 2001, the IPCC strengthened this assessment, claiming that "most of the observed warming over the last fifty years is likely to have been due to the increase in greenhouse gas concentrations."[2]

This uncertainty about the past may seem substantial, but it is nothing compared to the uncertainty about the future. The IPCC has not changed its basic prediction that a doubling in CO_2 concentrations would increase mean global temperature by about 1.5–4.5 °C. But its predictions for mean global temperature change a century ahead have varied. The first, second, and third assessment reports (issued in 1990, 1996, and 2001, respectively) predicted temperature changes of 2–5 °C, 1–3.5 °C, and 1.4–5.8 °C, respectively, by 2100 (the latest report also predicts that sea level will rise about half a meter by 2100, mainly because of thermal expansion). These variations are fairly large; and, remarkably, these changes are mainly due to a pollutant that is not even a greenhouse gas: sulfate aerosols.

These tiny particles, emitted primarily from coal burning, are a little like volcanic dust. They reflect light away from the earth and so have a cooling effect. The first assessment report took no notice of aerosols. But after determining that the relatively cool temperatures observed in 1992 and 1993 were due at least in part to Mt Pinatubo's eruption, climatologists added sulfates to their models. The effect was striking. The models now came much closer to replicating the earth's climate history. They also predicted a reduced rate of warming. This is the main reason that the IPCC's second assessment report predicted a smaller change in mean global temperature.

Why did the third assessment report predict a larger change as compared with the previous report? The main reason is that the latest IPCC report assumes that the developing countries will reduce their emissions of sulfur dioxide, a potent local pollutant, in line with the kinds of cuts made previously by industrialized countries. This seems a reasonable assumption, but it is noteworthy that changes in our understanding of just one piece of the climate puzzle could cause such a substantial change in our prediction of future climate change.

---

[2] IPCC (2001: 10). Note that the expression "likely" is a judgmental estimate, defined by the IPCC to mean a 66–90 percent chance; see IPCC (2001: 2).

Indeed, other aspects of the climate are much less well understood. A number of feedbacks, some positive and some negative, could cause sudden jumps. The IPCC predictions for changes in global mean temperature are relatively small. However, they may mask bigger regional changes and the potential for very big changes, even if only with very small probability.

The phenomenon most discussed in this regard is the circulation of the North Atlantic—sometimes referred to as the thermohaline circulation. The Gulf Stream carries warm, salty water from the southern Atlantic Ocean northwards, along the eastern shore of the United States up to the elbow of Cape Cod and thence over to the seas between Greenland, Iceland, and Norway. Here, the frigid air cools the surface water, causing the dense, salty water to sink into the deep ocean. This sinking creates a kind of vacuum, and the warm, salty water from the Gulf of Mexico rushes in to fill it. It is by this means, scientists think, that the Gulf Stream conveyor belt is powered, in the process sending warm air over the continent of Europe. London, England and Battle Harbor, Newfoundland are both near 52° latitude, but London is about 10 °C warmer on average—due partly to the winds that blow warm air from the Atlantic over the British Isles.

Human-induced climate change might alter this system. Greater snow melt feeding the rivers that empty into the North Atlantic would lower the density of the surface waters, causing the conveyor belt to weaken (fresh water is lighter than salt water, which explains why small island nations can obtain fresh water from wells). A wave of positive feedbacks might then be set off. If the surface waters were to cool enough (and less salty water freezes at a higher temperature), sea ice would form, putting a lid over the ocean. This would result in even less cooling of the surface, and so weaken the Gulf Stream even more. The sea ice would itself increase the albedo (reflectivity) of the ocean surface, resulting in more cooling. And this greater cooling would in turn leave more of the surface of Europe covered in snow, increasing the albedo of the earth's surface, and so reinforcing the cooling effect. It is possible that the northern extent of the Gulf Stream (the so-called North Atlantic Drift) might even switch off. Europe might get cooler, not warmer (but note that Europe is predicted to be warmer as a result of climate change at least through 2100; see IPCC 2001). The term "global warming" implies a general warming everywhere, but plainly this is not inevitable. "Climate change" is the better term.

A "flip" in regional climate is not the only possibility. The climate might also become less stable. A warm summer might cause the sea ice to melt, cooling the North Atlantic's surface waters, and so starting up the conveyor belt again. Warmer air over the continent could then trigger a new influx of fresh water, forcing the Gulf Stream to weaken once more, and so on in a kind of cycle. Perhaps the *average* climate will not change very much. Perhaps the bigger effect will be an increase in temperature *variation*.

These kinds of changes are not just theoretical. Flips have already been found in the climate record. According to Adams *et al.* (1999: 20), "There is evidence from the study of ocean sediments that deep-water formation in the North Atlantic was diminished during the sudden cold Heinrich events and other colder phases of the last [130,000] years ... " An IPCC Workshop on Rapid Non-linear Climate Change (IPCC 1998: 6) also found evidence in the palaeoclimatic data "that an increase in the surface freshwater flux into the North Atlantic, could lead to a significant weakening or even a complete collapse of the [thermohaline circulation, or THC]," and that this could be "triggered by warming and increased precipitation associated with increasing greenhouse gas concentrations." The latest IPCC assessment report is no more encouraging. Though "current predictions using climate models do not exhibit a complete shut-down of the [THC] by 2100 ... [after this time the THC] could completely, and possibly irreversibly, shut-down in either hemisphere if the change in radiative forcing is large enough and applied long enough" (IPCC 2001: 16).

Though this uncertainty about the Gulf Stream is large, there are many other features of the climate system, including the dynamics of the Southern Ocean, that are *less* well-understood. Uncertainty is a central feature of climate change. Indeed, it is as well to recall that scientists were concerned about the prospect of global *cooling* in the early 1970s (Rowlands 1995). Further research can reduce the uncertainties, but it cannot eliminate them.

This is important for understanding the international negotiations. One reason often given for the failure to build an effective climate regime is uncertainty about the science. As noted in Chapter 8, however, the science of ozone depletion was also uncertain at the time that the Montreal Protocol was negotiated, and yet this did not block negotiation of an effective treaty. Uncertainty may not be the real reason that the climate change talks have taken so long and achieved so little. Uncertainty may rather be masking a more fundamental obstacle.

15.3. CLIMATE NEGOTIATIONS

The so-called anthropogenic greenhouse gases include not only CO_2, but also methane, nitrous oxide, hydrofluorocarbons, perfluorocarbons, sulfur hexafluoride, and (tropospheric) ozone (all but the last of these gases are controlled by the Kyoto Protocol). Halocarbons, including CFCs and HCFCs, are another kind of greenhouse gas, though it is now known that the direct warming effect of these gases is partly offset by a cooling effect caused by the reduction in stratospheric ozone. Partly for this reason, but mainly because these substances are already being controlled by the Montreal Protocol, the climate negotiations have focused on the other gases, especially CO_2, which accounts for about 80 percent of the aggregate warming potential (Nordhaus 1994). The key challenge for these negotiations has been to decide by how much these emissions should be reduced.

15.3.1. Toronto Targets

In 1988, participants at a semi-political conference on climate change recommended that, as a first step, CO_2 emissions should be reduced 20 percent from the 1988 level by 2005. As the conference was held in Toronto, this target became known as the "Toronto target." Though the 20 percent figure was plucked from the air, the idea that climate policy should be directed at meeting a *target* coupled with a *timetable* has had a lasting influence on the negotiations. It dominated negotiations up to the Kyoto meeting, and it remains the most fundamental feature of this agreement. The idea of setting targets and timetables really began a few months before, however, in another Canadian city. In setting targets and timetables for reducing emissions, the Montreal Protocol served as the model, or focal point, for climate change diplomacy. This turned out to be a mistake. As Richard Benedick (2001*a*: 13), who participated in the Toronto conference, later recalled, the Toronto participants (and Benedick takes co-responsibility for their decision) "took precisely the wrong lesson from the ozone experience."

15.3.2. Unilateral Targets

Following publication of the IPCC's interim first report in May 1990, a number of OECD countries announced their intention to reduce CO_2 emissions, and nearly all of these unilateral pledges were expressed in Toronto-like terms.[3] Some, including Austria, Denmark, Italy, and Luxembourg, pledged to meet the Toronto target precisely. Others, like New Zealand, set a goal of meeting the target by 2000 rather than 2005. Some countries set a goal of stabilizing their CO_2 emissions at the 1989 level by 2000 (Norway) or at the 1990 level by 2000 (Finland, Switzerland, United Kingdom) or to reduce emissions 3–5 percent by the year 2000 (the Netherlands). Germany, helped by reunification, set the most ambitious target: a 25–30 percent reduction in CO_2 emissions from 1987 to 2005. Australia aimed to reduce its emissions of *all* greenhouse gases not controlled under the Montreal Protocol (that is, not only CO_2, but also methane and nitrous oxide), while the United States and Canada pledged to stabilize their emissions of all greenhouse gases, *including* those covered by the Montreal Protocol. France and Japan set targets for stabilizing CO_2 emissions at the 1990 level by 2000 in *per capita* terms (allowing emissions to increase as population increased), while Spain promised only to limit *growth* in its CO_2 emissions to 25 percent. Finally, some countries did not set a national target at all. They rather agreed to play a part in achieving a collective target, the most important being the one announced by the European Community (EC) in October 1990. The EC target aimed to stabilize Community-wide emissions at the 1990 level by 2000, a target to which all its member states were collectively bound. Members of the European Free Trade Association, including Iceland and Sweden, in turn negotiated a separate agreement in which they pledged jointly to meet the EC target.

It is interesting to recall that the initial, unilateral responses to the emerging science of ozone depletion were mainly action-based, not target-based. The United States, for example, banned the use of CFCs in aerosols; it did not set a specific target for production and consumption. The EC did set a target but, as explained in Chapter 8, the EC target was more akin to the Helsinki 30 percent club target; the EC target was chosen because it was going to be met anyway. This would not be true of most of the greenhouse gas targets pledged in the early 1990s. Indeed, very few of these pledges were actually fulfilled.

---

[3] The International Energy Agency (1992) has compiled a comprehensive listing of climate change policies, and I am drawing here from this report.

The main reason for this is that only a few countries implemented policies to meet their targets. And this lack of action reflected the fact that no country was truly committed (in the sense explained in Chapter 3) to meeting its target. In some cases, the target was specified merely as a goal, but even where the targets were intended to be more than this there were problems. Targets were to be met unilaterally in some cases, but in other cases achievement of a target was conditional on other countries taking similar action. Though New Zealand set an ambitious goal of reducing its CO_2 emissions 20 percent from the 1990 level by 2000, it simultaneously insisted that any policy adopted should have a net benefit for New Zealand. These more cautious declarations reflected an awareness that a game was being played—a game broadly compatible with the prisoners' dilemma (PD).

The history of the European Community's target is especially telling. When the target was agreed in 1990, no decision was made as to how it would be met, and as it was a collective target, no country was individually responsible for meeting it. A collective policy was needed, and the European Commission proposed a mix of measures to include an energy conservation program and a carbon/energy tax. The tax, which was to be set at a rate equivalent to $3 per barrel of oil, rising over time to $10 per barrel, probably would have sufficed to meet the stabilization target.[4] But in May 1992, shortly before the Rio Earth Summit convened, the Community announced that its tax policy was to be conditional on other OECD countries (especially the United States and Japan) adopting the same policy themselves. As the chances that the United States would do so were nil, this meant that Europe was not prepared to implement the policy needed to achieve its own target.

Conveniently for European politicians, conditionality shifted the blame for inaction to the United States, which was heavily criticized for not adopting a CO_2 emissions target of its own. But the first Bush Administration studied the problem, and concluded that the nation's interests would be ill-served by targets. The President's Council of Economic Advisers (1990), in arguing the administration's case, cited a study predicting that the Toronto target, if extended to the year 2100, would cost the United States between $800 billion and $3.6 trillion. The Council noted that this was 35–150 times greater than the cost of complying with the Montreal Protocol, and argued that the benefits did not seem to justify the cost. The report concluded that the "highest priority in the near term should be to improve understanding in order to build a foundation for sound policy decisions. Until such a foundation is in place, there is no justification for imposing major costs on the economy in order to slow the growth of greenhouse gas emissions."[5] This comparison with Montreal is relevant. I shall return to it later in this chapter.

15.3.3. Rio

Because of the refusal by the United States to accept a target, the final text of the Framework Convention on Climate Change, which was signed by over 150 countries

---

[4] See Barrett (1992d). Note, however, that with (carbon-intensity neutral) economic growth the tax would have to be progressively increased over time if the emission ceiling were to be met indefinitely.

[5] Council of Economic Advisers (1990: 223).

at the Rio Earth Summit in June 1992, did not specify precise targets for any country.[6] Article 4 of the agreement says that developed country parties recognize "that the return by the end of the present decade to earlier levels of anthropogenic emissions of carbon dioxide and other greenhouse gases" would be desirable. It also urges parties to devise policies "with the aim of returning individually or jointly to their 1990 [emission] levels." But it does not require that any party meet any target. Indeed, it is precisely for this reason that the agreement was signed by so many countries (as of September 2002, by 189 countries, more than any other international environmental agreement; see Appendix 6.1) and came into force so quickly (in March 1994).

15.3.4. Berlin

Like many treaties, the Framework Convention initiated a process that included annual meetings called Conferences of the Parties (COPs). At the first of these, held in Berlin in 1995, the parties (including the United States, under a new administration) agreed that the industrialized parties should set emission limits within specified time-frames, such as 2005, 2010, and 2020, and that these should be incorporated within a protocol, possibly to be ready for signing by the end of 1997. This is where the idea of Kyoto was given birth.

It is worth noting that by this time most countries had still not devised, let alone implemented, effective policies for meeting their earlier "commitments." Some countries, like Norway, Finland, and Australia, conceded that they did not expect to meet their targets (Grubb 1995). Other countries were on course for meeting their targets, but this was because of a fortuitous confluence of circumstances—in the case of Germany, reunification; in the case of Britain, privatization of the coal and electric utility industries, hastening a substitution of natural gas for coal. Most importantly, the European Union signally failed to adopt a collective policy sure of meeting its collective target. In a letter to the chairman of the European Parliament's environment committee, leaked on the eve of the Berlin conference, Jacques Santer, the president of the European Commission, conceded that "a single tax ... applicable in all member states [was] no longer conceivable".[7] Evidence supplied to the European Commission suggested that at most three of the EU's fifteen member states—Germany, the United Kingdom, and tiny Luxembourg—would stabilize their own CO_2 emissions at the 1990 level by 2000.[8]

In the summer of 1997, the US Senate protested against the Berlin Mandate (and the Clinton administration's endorsement of it), voting 95–0 in favor of a resolution that the United States should not be a signatory to an agreement that: (1) would require that the industrialized countries reduce their greenhouse gas emissions, unless the agreement imposed similar obligations on developing country parties; and (2) would harm US economic interests. It is worth recalling, by the way, that the Senate voted by a similar margin (96–0) in favor of a non-binding resolution supporting a *faster* phase-out of CFCs than prescribed by the Montreal Protocol and the

---

[6] For an excellent discussion and analysis of this convention, see Bodansky (1993).
[7] *The European*, March 17–23 (1995: 1).   [8] *Ibid.*

London Amendment. This is one of many indicators pointing to a huge difference between these two global problems.

15.3.5. Kyoto

A two-thirds majority of the Senate would be needed to secure ratification by the United States, and so the Senate's views needed to be heeded this time. They were not. The agreement negotiated in Kyoto in December 1997 imposed quantitative emission ceilings on the industrialized countries only. It did not impose any such ceilings on developing countries like China and India, though a mechanism was included in the treaty that could support emission reductions in developing countries through the back door as it were (the Clean Development Mechanism, discussed later in this chapter).[9]

Immediately after the negotiations ended, a number of Republican Senators demanded that the agreement come up for ratification immediately so that they could vote it down. President Clinton, however, having disregarded the Senate's earlier advice, declined to seek its consent. He knew that he could not get a two-thirds majority. And yet he signed the treaty anyway in November 1998.

Some countries not only signed but ratified the agreement soon after its adoption. As of March 2001, 33 states had ratified Kyoto. However, only one of these countries belong to the so-called "Annex I" group of countries—the countries that are obligated by the treaty to limit their emissions. The other ratifying countries—almost half of which were small island states—are not required by the treaty to limit their emissions. Why did so few industrialized countries ratify to this point?

15.3.6. The Hague

Remarkably, the main reason is that Kyoto was at this time still an unfinished document. Key issues were left unsettled in Kyoto, including the rules governing the calculation of an Annex I party's assigned amount of emissions, the so-called "flexible mechanisms," and compliance. These issues were still being negotiated in November, 2000 in The Hague, at the same time that the ballots for the US presidential election were being recounted in Florida. The unresolved issues are of little importance to the non-Annex I countries, for the treaty will not restrict their emissions. Indeed, and as I shall explain later, Kyoto will also not *really* limit the emissions of a substantial number of industrialized countries. But for the other countries—for Australia, Canada, the European Union, Iceland, Japan, New Zealand, Norway, Switzerland, and the United States—the unresolved issues would determine both the costs and the benefits of participation. It would be irresponsible for these countries to ratify an agreement when it was not even known what they were agreeing to.

Another reason for the slow pace of ratification may have been the realization by the other Annex I countries that there was little to gain, and perhaps much to lose, by building a regime that ultimately failed to secure the support of the United

---

[9] Depledge (2000) gives an article-by-article, official history of the negotiations.

States—the world's only superpower and the biggest emitter of CO_2 (in 1998, the United States emitted almost 65 percent more CO_2 than the European Union). In many ways, the post-Kyoto stalemate was reminiscent of the standoff that existed in 1992, when the European Community declined to implement policies to reduce its own emissions, proposing instead a multilateral remedy (a carbon-energy tax) contingent on US approval—an approach that stood no chance of succeeding.

15.3.7. Bonn/Marrakech

In March 2001, President George W. Bush rejected the Kyoto Protocol, effectively withdrawing the United States from the Kyoto process.

The manner in which this decision was communicated, perhaps even more than the decision itself, irked other world leaders, especially in Europe. It is possible that, had the style of his rejection been different, the response of other countries may have been different. Had he shown sincere interest in addressing the climate change problem and not implied that, because the science is uncertain, little action was justified; had he acknowledged the responsibility of the United States as the world's leading polluter, and not just complained about the cost of Kyoto to the United States; had he said that the aims of Framework Convention, negotiated under his father's administration, were worthy, but that Kyoto was not obviously the best device for realizing those aims—had he said all of this, and had he done so first by communicating directly and in private to the other leading countries on this issue, the response by these countries may have been different. By the time President Bush denounced the treaty, support for Kyoto even within Europe was already showing signs of fracturing (Benedick 2001*b*). It is possible that at least some other countries would have welcomed a fresh approach. However, in rejecting the treaty in the way that he did—and, crucially, in doing so without offering an alternative—President Bush only reinforced the view that Kyoto had to be the only way forward; and he only made other signatories, especially members of the European Union, *more* determined to conclude the negotiations and bring the treaty into force.

With the United States a declared non-participant, ratification by most of the remaining Annex I countries became essential to the treaty's entry into force. And so, at the negotiations held in Bonn in July 2001, the Europeans conceded on many issues that, only a few months before, they had been unwilling to yield to the United States. In particular, they made a generous allowance for "sinks"—credits for the absorption of carbon dioxide by forests, cropland management, and revegetation—and retreated from an earlier insistence that most emission reductions be achieved domestically rather than through international trading.

Japan, with a large share of Annex I emissions, now became a pivotal player. As the EU environment minister, Margot Wallström, admitted before the Bonn meeting, "We are fully aware of the fact that we will have to look at how to keep Japan on board in order to keep the Kyoto process alive."[10] And so Japan was offered a sweetener: a

---

[10] "Pronk Urges Japan to be Independent of US in Climate Policy," *The Japan Times* Online, June 13, 2001.

credit for its carbon sinks. According to Benedick (2001*b*), the concessions given to Japan in Bonn effectively lowered its required emission reduction from six to just one percent. Canada also was accommodated. It was now effectively allowed to *increase* its emissions by five percent (Benedick 2001*b*).[11] Of course, a more generous allowance for sinks would lower the price of allowance trading, harming countries like Russia. But Russia's participation was also essential to the treaty's entry into force, and so Russia was also given a concession, after a delay, at the seventh Conference of the Parties, held in Marrakech in November 2001—a huge quantity of

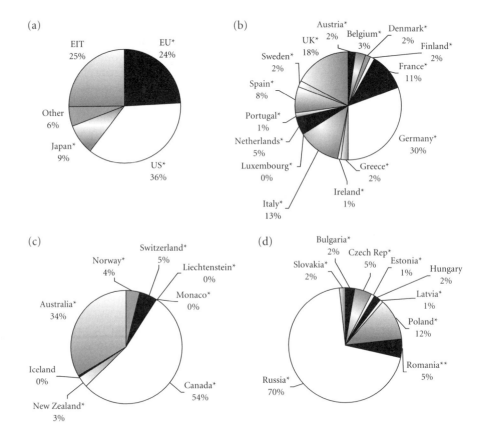

Figure 15.1 *Shares of Kyoto Protocol Annex I 1990 CO_2 emissions*
(a) Shares of 1990 Annex I CO_2 emissions, (b) Member state shares of 1990 EU CO_2 emissions, (c) Shares of other Annex I 1990 CO_2 emissions, (d) Shares of total EIT CO_2 emissions

[11] Australia was given a concession earlier. Article 3.7—the so-called "Australia clause"—allows a country to include net positive land-use emissions in calculating their base year emissions. For Australia, this is calculated to have increased base year emissions by 19 percent, making achievement of the Kyoto target much easier. See Victor (2001: 63).

forest credits that essentially added to its already huge quantity of "hot air." At both of these meetings, an agreement was also reached on a compliance mechanism—discussed at length later in this chapter.

Today, the Kyoto Protocol is substantially complete. The institutions created by the treaty will have to be developed, and the treaty will need to be superceded by subsequent agreements, specifying emission limitations for future periods. But there is no longer a reason for the Annex I countries to delay ratification.

15.4. PROSPECTS FOR KYOTO'S ENTRY INTO FORCE

Will Kyoto enter into force? To do so, it must be ratified by at least fifty-five countries, accounting for at least 55 percent of the total CO_2 emissions for 1990 of the thirty-eight Annex I countries—the industrialized countries subject to emission ceilings and listed in Figure 15.1. The first trigger for entry into force has already been met. As of September 2002, 94 countries have ratified Kyoto. But most of these countries belong to the non-Annex I group of countries—the countries that are *not* subject to an emissions ceiling—and they have nothing to lose and something to gain by ratifying Kyoto. The second trigger for entry into force has not been met yet.

As of September 2002, the Annex I ratifying countries make up only 37.1 percent of total Annex I emissions. Given non-participation by the US, entry into force depends on Russia ratifying the agreement. But even Russia's participation is not sufficient to satisfy the second trigger. Another moderately large country (Canada, Poland, or Australia) must also ratify. Alternatively, at least two small Annex I countries must ratify (Switzerland, Estonia, New Zealand, Liechtenstein, and Monaco).

Though Australia has said that it would not ratify,[12] and other countries have given mixed messages, at the second earth summit, held in Johannesburg in August–September 2002, Russia and Canada both pledged to ratify. It would thus seem that Kyoto will enter into force. We shall know for sure around the time that this book is published.

However, even if Kyoto enters into force (and these pledges to ratify may not be fulfilled), victory for the treaty cannot be declared. Like all the other transition countries, Russia has nothing to lose by ratifying, given its hot air. And Canada, already given generous credits in Bonn/Marrakesh, announced after the Johannesburg summit that it would unilaterally claim a further thirty percent credit for exports of "clean" energy (hydropower and natural gas) to the United States.[13] This last

---

[12] See, for example, "Australia: Kyoto Climate Accord is Defunct," *The Washington Post*, April 16, 2001, p. A13.
[13] See, for example, Steven Chase, "Liberal MPs Threaten to Withdraw Kyoto Votes," *Globe and Mail*, September 13, 2002, p. A4.

manoeuvre hints at even worse to come. If a country like Canada can claim credits in violation of the agreement and get away with it, more deceitful ways of breaking with the agreement can easily be found by other countries.

Even without any cheating or Enron-inspired emissions accounting, entry into force may make little difference. With all the concessions already given thus far, with the generous rules for emissions trading, and with the United States a non-participant, the treaty could end up having no effect at all on global emissions (Buchner *et al.* 2001).

Of course, if Kyoto does not constrain emissions, countries like Russia will have little reason to sell their surplus entitlements (Manne and Richels 2001). They may thus choose to bank these for a subsequent control period (2013–2017, say). This would make it necessary for many of the other Annex I countries to undertake real reductions. However, we cannot be sure that they would respond in this way. They might play with the accounting rules, or withdraw, or just plain fail to comply. The latter possibility is taken up later in this chapter.

It is worth recalling the experience with Montreal. The Montreal Protocol entered into force on January 1, 1989, the earliest date allowed by the treaty. If ratification of Kyoto had proceeded as quickly, the Kyoto Protocol would have entered into force in March 1999. Of course, and as explained in Chapter 8, entry into force of the original Montreal Protocol was helped by a favorable cost–benefit ratio for the main producers and consumers of CFCs. However, Montreal also created a foundation for building in greater and greater sacrifices, by these and other countries. As explained later in this chapter, Kyoto fails to do this. The real problem with Kyoto is not that it starts off achieving little. The real problem is that it doesn't provide a structure for both broadening and deepening cooperation over time.

The theory suggests that part of the explanation for Kyoto's failure is to be found in the payoffs. I turn to these below.

15.5. IMPACTS, DAMAGES, ADAPTATION

The *impacts* of climate change include physical and ecological effects: erosion of shoreline; possible bleaching of coral reefs; changes in disease prevalence due to an improved climate for disease vectors; damage from more extreme weather events; and so on. Different impacts are likely to be measured in different units. Shoreline losses, for example, might be measured in miles or square miles, whereas changes in disease prevalence would be measured in mortality, years of life lost, or disability-adjusted lost years. Knowing the individual impacts is important. But we also need a sense of the *aggregate* impact, and this can only be obtained by putting the different measures of impacts in a standard metric. This is normally done by attaching economic values to the impacts. These values are called *damages*.

Calculation of damages requires an understanding both of the expected effects of climate change on economic and ecological systems as they exist now *and on how these systems can be expected to adjust or adapt to climate change*. Forest ecosystems, for example, may move toward the poles. Similarly, farmers are sure to change the crops they grow and the date of first planting. Adaptation, especially by economic systems, is likely to limit the impacts of climate change. This is especially true if you think of the potential for technological change. Biotechnology, for example, may engineer new crop varieties that perform better in an altered climate. Similarly, new pesticides and vaccines may prevent malaria from becoming re-established in areas like the Southern US and Europe. Ecological systems are generally slower to adjust than economic systems, and so are more vulnerable. The same may be true of the economies of developing countries. In the American Midwest, farmers already harvest their wheat using huge, air-conditioned combines; in Ethiopia they still use hand tools.

Adaptation reduces damages, but is also costly. An efficient response to climate change would thus minimize the sum of damage and adaptation costs (I consider mitigation below). Put differently, efficient adaptation will balance the benefits of small changes in adaptation—measured as reductions in damage—with the associated costs. In a market economy, much adaptation can be expected to be done automatically. Ignoring subsidies, farmers, for example, could be expected to reap nearly all the gains from adaptation (of course, farmers may still be worse off as a consequence of climate change; adaptation only reduces damages). The exceptions to this market-led adaptation are local public goods like dikes and sea walls. These would almost certainly need to be provided by the state. Crucially, however, adaptation will not normally require international cooperation. Adaptation by poor countries may be funded in part by the rich, but this assistance is a side payment—an important and justified one, as explained later in this chapter.

An essential feature of climate change is that it may actually *benefit* some sectors of some economies, at least in the medium run (for a doubling in CO_2 concentrations, say). For example, the IPCC's third assessment report predicts increases in mean stream flow in the high latitudes and Southeast Asia, but decreases in Central Asia, the Mediterranean, Southern Africa, and Australia. Recent estimates compiled by Nordhaus and Boyer (2000) show losses to agriculture in tropical countries like Brazil and India, but gains in the northern temperate climates of Canada and Russia. Seasonal effects will also vary. Warmer temperatures would increase the demand for air conditioning in the summer, but reduce the demand for space heating in the winter. Finally, the increased concentration of CO_2 may amplify plant growth (a phenomenon known as the "CO_2 fertilization"), giving a boost to agriculture and forestry nearly everywhere. Notice the contrast with stratospheric ozone depletion. This would harm some countries more than others but it would not benefit any country or economic sector.

Estimates of the damages (including adaptation costs) to the United States of a doubling in CO_2 concentrations, expressed as a percentage of Gross Domestic Product (GDP), are shown in Table 15.2. With two exceptions, the estimates are very similar (although these total figures mask substantial variability in particular categories of damage like forest loss). The Titus study is at the high end, but this analysis assumes that mean temperature will rise 4 °C, whereas most of the other studies assume an increase closer to 2.5 °C (recall that the IPCC predicts a mean global

Table 15.2. *Selected estimates of total climate change damage and* CO_2 *abatement costs for the United States (Percent of GDP)*

Damage study	$2 \times CO_2$ damage	Cost study	Abatement cost	
			Stabilization	20% cut
Cline	1.1%	Jorgenson–Wilcoxen[1]	0.6%	1.7%
Fankhauser	1.3%	Edmonds–Reilly[1]	0.4%	1.1%
Tol	1.5%	Manne–Richels[1]	0.7%	1.5%
Nordhaus (1994)	1.0%	Martin–Burniaux[1]	0.2%	0.9%
Titus	2.5%	Rutherford[1]	0.2%	1.0%
Mendelsohn–Neumann (1999)	−0.1%	Goulder[1]	0.3%	1.2%
Nordhaus–Boyer (2000)	0.5%	Jorgenson *et al.* (2000)	1.25%	NA

[1] Cost estimates are from a study by the Energy Model Forum of Stanford University, which ran 14 different cost models using common assumptions and standardizing for the emission reduction scenarios shown above.

Sources: IPCC (1996), tables 3.4 and 4.1.4; Nordhaus (1994), Nordhaus and Boyer (2000), and Jorgenson *et al.* (2000).

temperature increase of 1.5–4.5 °C for a doubling in CO_2 concentrations). Mendelsohn and Neumann (1999) are at the low end. They conclude that the United States would benefit on balance from a 2.5 °C increase in temperature, due largely to gains in agriculture and forestry.

These estimates may be the best available, but it is worth underlining that they are highly uncertain. To derive them, you have to start with the science, which is uncertain, add in the impacts, which are uncertain, predict adaptation responses, which are uncertain, and then value all these changes—adding another layer of uncertainty, and one that is particularly large in the case of effects (like biodiversity loss) that are not priced by the market. And, as speculative as even these estimates may be, much less is known about the damages that might be suffered by countries other than the United States. Also important is whether the changes are gradual or sudden—slow changes imply smoother and less costly adjustment. Finally, the extent of climate change is likely to be key. The common wisdom is that damages are likely to be non-linear (Nordhaus and Boyer 2000). This means that, if climate change proves to be one percent greater than expected, damages would likely increase by more than one percent.

15.6. MITIGATION COSTS

Climate change can be mitigated by reducing atmospheric concentrations of greenhouse gases—by reducing emissions and by sucking CO_2 out of the atmosphere, a process known as "sequestration." Growing trees eat CO_2, and carbon is also stored in the soils and the oceans. Just as damages can be reduced by adaptation, so mitigation can be achieved most efficiently both by limiting emissions and by sequestering CO_2. The two activities together limit *net* emissions.

Estimates of the costs of reducing CO_2 net emissions in the United States, expressed as a percentage of GDP, are shown in the right hand column of Table 15.2. Here again there is broad agreement among all the studies cited.

However, as with the estimates of damages, estimates of mitigation costs are uncertain and controversial. A number of people believe that mitigation costs could be very low, that some quantity of net emission reductions could be obtained for free or even at a negative cost. This is possible. It requires that people behave irrationally or that there exist structural or regulatory barriers to energy efficiency. There is some evidence that people do behave irrationally, and regulatory barriers also exist. However, the so-called "bottom-up" models that produce optimistic estimates of mitigation costs assume that irrational behavior and regulatory obstacles can be corrected at no cost. The evidence cautions against such optimism. Sweden is as environmentally conscious as any country. It also has adopted the world's highest carbon tax (International Energy Agency 1992). And, yet, Sweden's CO_2 emissions *increased* from 1990 to 1998.[14] If reducing emissions were cheap and easy, it is belied by this evidence.[15] Interestingly, Sweden's carbon tax is not the kind advocated by economists. Industrial polluters are offered a tax break relative to households, partly to defend their international competitiveness. A better designed tax would be more efficient at lowering Sweden's emissions, but it has little chance of becoming law.

15.7. BENEFIT-COST ANALYSIS

Table 15.2 tells us that the total damages (including adaptation costs) from climate change for the United States are of about the same magnitude as the total cost of reducing emissions 20 percent from the 1990 level.[16] This implies a very different cost-benefit ratio than for ozone protection. But the difference is even greater than suggested by comparing Tables 15.2 and 8.1. For the *benefits* of reducing CO_2 emissions would be substantially smaller than the total damages of a doubling in CO_2 concentrations.

The reason for this is that the benefits are the damages *avoided* by a policy or action, and it simply is not possible to avoid all climate change damages. We have been increasing the concentration of greenhouse gases for more than two centuries,

[14] According to the web page of the Climate Change Secretariat, Sweden's CO_2 emissions increased from 55,443 to 56,953 Gg over this period.

[15] It is sometimes argued that there may exist a "double dividend" to reducing emissions by means of a carbon tax. Such a tax would not only reduce emissions, but (depending on the tax and the pre-existing distortions) provide a revenue base that would allow inefficient taxes to be reduced; see Goulder (1995). An improvement in the efficiency of public finance would certainly be welcomed. But my view is that, unless we can explain why the potential (second best) efficiency gains to tax reform remain unexploited, and develop a theory that can explain how introduction of a carbon tax could lead to an improvement in the tax code, it would be imprudent to associate the "double dividend" with global climate change policy.

[16] Note that these estimates of damages and costs are independently derived. As explained in the next paragraph, the 20 percent cut in emissions cannot eliminate climate change damage.

Table 15.3. *Selected estimates of global marginal abatement benefit and global CO₂ marginal abatement cost ($US per ton C)*

Benefit study	Marginal benefit	Cost study[2]	Marginal cost	
			Stabilization	20% cut
Ayres & Walter	$30–$35	Jorgenson-Wilcoxen	$20	$50
Nordhaus	$6.8	Edmonds–Reilly	$70	$160
Cline	$7.6–$154	Manne–Richels	$110	$240
Peck & Teisberg	$12–$14	Martin–Burniaux	$80	$170
Fankhauser	$22.8	Rutherford	$150	$260
Maddison	$8.25	Cohan–Scheraga	$120	$330

[1] For most studies, the marginal benefit increases over time. The estimates presented here correspond to the period 2001–10.

[2] Cost estimates are from the Energy Models Forum simulations; see Table 15.2.

Source: IPCC (1996), tables 3.11 and 4.1.4.

and it is not technically feasible to return atmospheric concentrations to pre-industrial levels in the short term. Some climate change is virtually guaranteed to occur no matter what we do now. All we can hope to do is dampen the effects.

Table 15.3 provides estimates of the marginal benefit from reducing net emissions. This is defined as the present value reduction in future damages (including adaptation costs), associated with a one ton reduction in CO₂ net emissions today. To convert damages into marginal benefits requires a number of assumptions, perhaps the most important being the rate of discount. The benefits of reducing emissions today will only be felt decades, even centuries, into the future. The more the future is discounted, the lower will be the benefit of reducing emissions today. For example, Nordhaus (1991, 1994) discounts future benefits at a rate of about 4–5 percent, while Cline (1992) employs a discount rate of about 2 percent, and this difference in discounting explains most of the difference in their estimates of marginal benefits. (For purposes of comparison, the EPA's analysis of the benefits of abating ozone-depleting substances employed a 2 percent discount rate.)[17]

Full cooperation requires that countries reduce their emissions up to the level at which the global marginal benefit of abatement equals the marginal cost (if the marginal benefit exceeded marginal cost, one more ton of abatement would increase benefits by more than costs and so increase the aggregate payoff). Though the estimates vary widely, the evidence presented in Table 15.3 suggests that a 20 percent cut

[17] Choice of the appropriate discount rate is a contentious and complicated subject; see the papers in Weyant and Portney (1999). The rate is normally derived exogenously, based either on market returns or utility-related considerations. However, for a problem like climate change, the discount rate should be determined endogenously. That is, future consumption will depend in part on climate change damages and the actions taken to mitigate these, and so the discounting of consumption needs to reflect this; see Dasgupta *et al.* (1999).

Table 15.4. *Global climate policy costs and benefits (billions of $US 1990)*

	Optimal policy in 2005	Global stabilization	$2 \times CO_2$ concentration limit
Benefit	$283	$1512	$681
Cost	$92	$4533	$1365
Net benefit	$192	−$3021	−$684
Benefit–cost ratio	3.08	0.33	0.50

Source: Nordhaus and Boyer (2000), table 7.3.

from 1990 levels is almost certain not to be justified. It is not even obvious that stabilization of CO_2 emissions could pass a benefit–cost test.

What level of mitigation would be justified? For many years, Yale economist William Nordhaus has produced estimates of the optimal climate policy. His latest estimates are presented in Table 15.4. These show that full cooperation yields a benefit–cost ratio (as compared with the base case in which nothing is done to reduce emissions) of just $3:1$. This requires that a carbon tax be set at about $9/ton C in 2005, rising to just under $13/ton C in 2015. This is a very modest tax. It would reduce global emissions by just over 5 percent in 2015 relative to the business-as-usual level and by 11 percent by 2100.

It is interesting to compare these results with the benefit–cost estimates for ozone protection. According to Table 8.1, the benefits to the United States alone of the Montreal Protocol exceed $3.5 trillion in present value. Hence the *damages* from ozone depletion to the United States would exceed this value (the Montreal Protocol still allows some depletion). The damages to the *world* would be greater still, since no country can gain from ozone depletion. Nordhaus and Boyer (2000) estimate that the total global damages from climate change would be close to $4 trillion in present value. Obviously, both sets of estimates are subject to substantial error, but the basic message is that ozone depletion may be the more serious environmental problem. One reason for this is that ozone depletion kills people. Current studies do not show climate change to be as deadly.

However, the bigger difference between the two environmental problems is that climate mitigation is much more costly than substitution for ozone-depleting chemicals. Nordhaus and Boyer (2000, table 7.4) estimate that the optimal climate program would yield the United States a net benefit of just $22 billion. The net benefit in present value terms to the entire world of the optimal climate program is just $192 billion. This is less than the global net benefit of ozone layer protection given in Table 8.2—and it must be remembered that this estimate excludes the most important category of benefit—avoidance of skin cancers and cataracts. If you add the benefits, including health benefits, for the United States only ($3,575 billion from Table 8.1) to the global monetized benefits ($459 billion from Table 8.2), and divide by the global cost of phasing out all ozone-depleting substances ($235 billion from

Table 8.2), you get a benefit–cost ratio of over 17 : 1. Adding the health benefits to the rest of the world would raise this ratio substantially. Hence, not only do the economics of ozone layer protection recommend elimination of all ozone-destroying emissions (i.e. 100 percent abatement), but the benefit–cost ratio of this ambitious objective far exceeds the benefit–cost ratio to the more modest climate policy (demanding just 5 percent abatement in the short run and 11 percent in the long run). The economics of ozone and climate policy are really very different.

15.8. ECONOMICS OF THE KYOTO PROTOCOL

What are the economics of the Kyoto Protocol? Does Kyoto offer a benefit in excess of the cost? Does it approximate full cooperation?

According to an analysis undertaken by the Clinton Administration, the marginal cost to the Annex I countries of implementing Kyoto would range from $14 to $23/ton C (Clinton Administration 1998). This lies close to the expected marginal benefit of mitigation (see Table 15.3), implying that Kyoto is indeed a good deal for the world.

However, this analysis rests on a key assumption: that the Kyoto emission limits are met in a globally cost-effective manner. To achieve an overall emission target at minimum cost, marginal costs must be equalized over all polluters (if marginal costs were $20 for one country and $15 for another, the total cost of limiting emissions could be reduced by $5 if the latter country reduced its emissions by an extra ton while the former reduced its abatement by this same amount), and Kyoto's "flexible mechanisms" are meant to effect this outcome.

15.8.1. FLEXIBLE MECHANISMS

If trading in the allowances given to Annex I countries were perfect, all gains from trade would be exhausted, and marginal abatement costs would be equalized among these countries.[18] The non-Annex I countries are not obligated to reduce their emissions, and so their marginal mitigation costs will be near zero. However, the Clean Development Mechanism (CDM) is intended to bring marginal costs between Annex I and non-Annex I closer together. It allows an Annex I country to offset its emissions by undertaking abatement within a non-Annex I country. For example, a US company might convert a power station in China from coal to natural gas, claiming credit for the associated savings in greenhouse gas emissions. If the CDM also worked perfectly, trading would essentially be extended to the non-Annex I countries, and marginal abatement costs would be equalized everywhere—an assumption in the Clinton Administration's analysis.[19] Relying on this assumption, the Clinton Administration calculated that the total costs to the United States of implementing

---

[18] In addition to trading, Kyoto also allows Annex I countries to make project-based trades: an approach referred to as "joint implementation."

[19] For a more detailed critique of the Clinton Administration analysis, see Hahn and Stavins (1999).

Kyoto would be about \$7–\$12 billion a year (Clinton Administration 1998). For comparison, George W. Bush's global climate change initiative budgets \$4.5 billion in total climate-related spending in 2003. Not a big difference, it would seem. However, President Bush claims that the Kyoto Protocol would have cost the United States up to \$400 billion (Bush 2002).

There are good reasons for thinking that the Clinton Administration substantially underestimated costs. Though its analysis assumes that the market for emission entitlements would be perfect, up to the meeting in The Hague, Europe insisted that trading be "supplemental to domestic actions," implying that trading would be restricted. This would have increased compliance costs (though it might also increase environmental benefits since it would limit transactions in "hot air;" see below). As matters turned out, the agreement reached in Bonn only requires that "a significant effort" be made for achieving emission reductions domestically. However, it is unlikely that international trading would be perfect.

The rules for operating the CDM are also problematic. Because non-Annex I parties do not face an emission ceiling, incentives are created for "paper trades." The non-Annex I seller would gain by not having to do anything. The Annex I buyer would gain by not having to pay much for complying. The losers would be the other countries. But precisely because the other countries would lose from paper trades, they will want to monitor such transactions very carefully. This is why Kyoto requires that parties ensure "transparency, efficiency and accountability through independent auditing and verification of project activities." However, certification of CDM transactions will entail transactions costs, and these will limit CDM trading. The Clinton Administration's analysis of the CDMs assumes zero transactions costs.

What would have been the actual costs of implementing Kyoto for the United States? It is impossible to say for sure, but the Clinton Administration estimated that, without Annex I trading and the CDM, both marginal and total costs would increase by a factor of about ten.[20] At this level of cost, Kyoto would not be a good deal, either for the Annex I countries or for the world as a whole.

The assumption that there will be no international arbitrage, either through emissions trading or the CDM, may be extreme. However, analyses like the one by the Clinton Administration assume that emission reductions will be achieved cost-effectively at home, and this is almost certain not to happen either. Cost-effective domestic implementation would require a uniform carbon tax (or, equivalently, a perfectly competitive market in domestic emissions trading, encompassing all of the country's sources). Even the countries that have adopted a carbon tax vary the tax rate by sector (energy-intensive export industries are often exempt from paying the tax). Similarly, the domestic trading systems designed thus far are not models of market efficiency. The United Kingdom's trading program, for example, relies on voluntary participation, and Denmark's is limited to the power sector (Rosenzweig *et al.* 2002).

Moreover, the costs of implementing Kyoto will depend on the time frame. If less time is allowed for implementation, costs will rise. Manne and Richels (1998)

---

[20] Nordhaus and Boyer (1998) and Manne and Richels (1998) obtain similar estimates.

estimate substantial savings to a gradual transition to the Kyoto targets, with marginal costs falling by a factor of ten or more in 2010 (short lead times require that capital be retired early, and this is costly). Kyoto's design, however, fixes the end-date at 2008–12. Delays in negotiating the final agreement, and in bringing it into force, have shortened the available implementation time, and so will increase implementation costs. This will, in turn, discourage ratification.

15.8.2. Hot Air and Minimum Participation

Though emissions trading will lower overall costs, by design it will also lower the environmental benefit of the treaty. As explained previously, the emissions of the economies in transition (EIT) are substantially below their allowed levels. According to David Victor (2001, Figure 2.1), the EIT will have a surplus of about 6 billion tons of CO_2 over the period 2008–12. The other Annex I countries, by contrast, will have a deficit about 10 billion tons over the same period (assuming full participation and before taking account of the Bonn/Marrakech agreements). In the aggregate, and assuming full participation, the Kyoto constraints would bind—that is, marginal costs would be positive even with "hot air" trading. But emissions trading with the EIT will also cut the reduction in emissions achieved by Kyoto by some 40 percent. This is one reason why Europe wanted to limit the extent of trading.

Of course, participation will not be full with the United States a declared non-participant. And the concessions given in Bonn/Marrakech will limit the overall reduction in emissions achieved by Kyoto even further. These changes will lower the costs of implementing Kyoto. But, as mentioned before, they will also limit the benefit.

The Annex I countries that can trigger Kyoto's entry into force account for about 56 percent of global CO_2 emissions.[21] The second trigger for entry into force only requires that enough of these countries, making up just 55 percent of this total amount, ratify the agreement. This means that the treaty can enter into force when the countries that must actually limit their emissions account for just 31 percent of global emissions.

In fact, the problem is even worse than this. Recall that, with the United States a non-participant, entry into force will require ratification by the economies in transition, including Russia. But the Kyoto limits will not bind on these countries, and so Kyoto will only demand reductions by the remaining Annex I parties—the European Union and Japan, and Norway—plus the other Annex I countries that ratify. These countries make up only about 19 percent of global emissions. Small reductions in emissions by such a small part of the problem over such a short period of time will make little difference to the climate. Global emissions will continue to rise, even if Kyoto enters into force.

---

[21] The list of countries, shown also in Figure 15.1, is from FCCC/CP/1997/7/Add.1. The data on CO_2 emissions are from Nordhaus and Boyer (2000), table 3.1. Note that the trigger list of countries excludes a few countries that had not submitted data on their 1990 emissions by the time the Kyoto Protocol was being negotiated. Most importantly, the list excludes Ukraine, which accounts for just under two percent of global emissions, according to the Nordhaus and Boyer (2000) data.

15.8.3. LEAKAGE

Even this may overstate what Kyoto can accomplish. If Kyoto succeeds in reducing the emissions of these Annex I countries, the consequence may be to *increase* the emissions of other countries—including the non-Annex I parties—because of leakage. Will leakage be severe? We do not know; the literature that is available offers conflicting evidence on the magnitude of leakage for climate change.[22] But so long as leakage is positive (and, in the case of climate change, leakage will be compounded by the workings of the international energy market—a reduction in CO_2 emissions by Annex I parties would depress the world price of traded, carbon-intensive fuels, and so increase consumption of these fuels by other countries), it will dampen the environmental benefit of Kyoto.

Leakage is certainly a political worry, though it is usually expressed as a concern about a loss in competitiveness rather than in environmental effectiveness. In the debate that preceded the vote on the Byrd–Hagel Senate Resolution, Senator Byrd, a co-sponsor of the resolution, criticized the climate negotiations for not capping the emissions of developing countries: "I do not think," he said, "the Senate should support a treaty that requires only half the world—in other words, the developed countries—to endure the economic costs of reducing emissions while the developing countries are left free to pollute the atmosphere and, in so doing, *siphon off American industries* (emphasis added)." And after President George W. Bush rejected Kyoto, the European Commissioner for the Environment, Margot Wallström, when asked if the European Union should proceed without the United States, responded: "Why should we put European business and European companies under such pressure and let American Companies off the hook? Why should they play by other rules than European companies?"[23]

It was, of course, this same concern that led to Kyoto being negotiated in the first place. Recall that Europe set a collective target for reducing emissions back in 1990, and proposed meeting this target by means of a carbon/energy tax. Recognizing that this minilateral policy would have little environmental benefit, and that leakage could damage European competitiveness, Europe made adoption of this policy conditional on Japan and the United States adopting the same tax—which, of course, never happened. Kyoto was meant to fix this problem, but it has proved to be the wrong solution. It has not fundamentally changed the incentives; Kyoto has not restructured the game.

15.9. KYOTO ENFORCEMENT

How would Kyoto enforce compliance? Article 18 says that procedures and mechanisms for compliance should be determined by the parties at their first meeting and

---

[22] Estimates of the magnitude of leakage for climate change vary widely. In the case of a unilateral reduction in carbon emissions by the European Union, estimated leakage rates range from 2 to 80 percent (see Fisher *et al.* 1996). That is, for every 100 tons of carbon abated by the EU, global emissions could fall by from 20 to 98 tons. This is a big range. If the 80 percent figure is right, leakage would render unilateral abatement virtually impotent.

[23] S. Castle and P. Peachey, "Europe Struggles to Contain Fury at Bush's Betrayal," *The Independent*, March 30, 2001.

should include "an indicative list of consequences." Though the treaty postpones the design of a compliance mechanism, the Montreal Protocol also put off the decision of how to enforce compliance. Like Kyoto, Montreal only required that compliance enforcement mechanisms be determined by the parties at their first meeting.

However, there are two important differences between these agreements. The first is that, according to Article 18 of the Kyoto Protocol, compliance "procedures and mechanisms ... entailing binding consequences" must be approved by amendment. As required by Article 20, an amendment would require approval of at least three-fourths of the parties present and voting at the meeting of the parties. Moreover, the compliance amendment would only be binding on the parties that ratified the amendment, provided at least thee-fourths of the parties to Kyoto also ratified the amendment.

Since this is a crucial point, and one that has been little noticed, let me emphasize that the Kyoto Protocol expressly prohibits compliance enforcement with "binding consequences" except by means of an amendment. Since any party could decline to ratify a compliance amendment, it can avoid being punished for failing to comply. Montreal did not provide such an easy means of escape.

The second difference between the compliance provisions of the two treaties is that, from the beginning, Montreal included a measure for promoting participation—the trade restriction. Kyoto provides no comparable incentive. The minimum participation clause does provide a small incentive for countries to participate: the Annex I country whose ratification just makes Kyoto enter into force has an incentive to participate, for in ratifying the agreement this country would benefit from the abatement undertaken by the other Annex I parties. However, participation by any more Annex I countries would have no effect on the abatement undertaken by others. The minimum participation clause in Kyoto is not a tipping point. It is more like a linchpin.

However, it is unlike the linchpin equilibrium studied in Chapter 7. Since compliance cannot be enforced, the ratifying party that triggers entry into force could not be sure that its participation really would change the behavior of any of the other parties. These other countries could not comply and still avoid "binding consequences."

When I pointed out this fundamental weakness to a European negotiator before the meeting in The Hague, I received a cold response. "We will deal with the compliance problem later," he said. "But how?" I asked. "We are working on it," he said.

15.9.1. Compliance Negotiations

In fact, negotiators on all sides recognized the need for effective compliance, and a US negotiator told me that this was the issue on which there was the most agreement in The Hague. Though an agreement on compliance could not be reached at this conference, a proposal tabled by the president of COP6, Jan Pronk, the Dutch Environment Minister, received broad support. This required that a party that failed to comply with its emission limitation obligations in the first control period, reduce its emissions by *more* than required otherwise in the second control period. This extra reduction was meant to make up for the non-compliance and penalize the delay in reducing emissions. The "penalty" for non-compliance proposed by Pronk would begin at 1.5 and then rise by 0.25 "after the subsequent commitment period if the Party concerned is not in compliance at the end of the subsequent control period" (Pronk 2000).

An example might make the proposal clearer. According to the emissions data given in Kyoto's annex, the US emitted 4,957,022 Gg of CO_2 in 1990. By agreement, emissions must fall to 93 percent of this level by 2008–12. This means that US emissions over this period must not exceed 4,610,030 Gg annually. Suppose, however, that the United States falls short of this target, emitting an average of 4,710,030 Gg per year. Then the United States will have exceeded its emission limitation by 100,000 Gg per year, or by 500,000 Gg in total. According to the Pronk proposal, the United States would have to reduce its emissions in the next control period (2013–17) by an additional 750,000 Gg (1.5 times the 500,000 Gg shortfall), on top of the reduction needed to comply with the limits set for this control period. Essentially, the penalty for not controlling in the current period is a tighter emission limit in the next period.

As with the original approach of setting targets and timetables, there was broad agreement with the Pronk approach. Countries only disagreed about the magnitude of the penalties.[24] The response by the so-called "Umbrella" group of countries (including Australia, Canada, Japan, and the United States) merely suggested a change in the penalties, with the United States bearing a penalty of 1.3, Japan of 1.1, Australia of 1.0 (no penalty), and with Canada accepting a graduated penalty that increased to 1.3 (none of these penalties would be escalated in a future control period). The G77 and China—countries that are not bound by Kyoto to any emission limit—proposed an increase in the penalty for non-compliance to 2.0, and adding a penalty of 0.5 *per year* for as long as the party is in non-compliance (and, why not, since these countries would be exempt from the penalties![25]). After receiving these responses, Pronk revised his earlier proposals, but only in the details. His compromise proposal (Pronk 2001) established a graduated penalty, beginning at 1.1, and then rising to 1.5 and 2.0 in steps, with each step based on the size of the discrepancy between actual and allowed emissions.

In Bonn, a classic compromise was worked out, with countries agreeing to a fixed penalty of 1.3—ironically, the value advocated earlier by the United States, before it effectively withdrew from the negotiations. More important than the value, however, is the design of the enforcement mechanism. It is remarkable that countries should have debated the value of the penalty rate when the mechanism itself was so obviously flawed.

15.9.2. Design Faults

There are, in particular, five problems with the compliance mechanism agreed in Bonn.

---

[24] These responses are contained in FCCC/CP/2001/MISC.1.

[25] As noted by Daniel Bodansky (2001), Kyoto not only exempts the non-Annex I countries from having to meet an emission limit. It also allows these countries to have a say in determining the rules that would apply to other countries.

First, the punishment prescribed by this mechanism is forever delayed. If a party fails to pay its penalty in the second control period (presumably, 2013–17), it is assigned a new penalty for the third control period (with the penalty rate in future commitment periods to be determined by an amendment), and so on. A punishment that is always delayed is never carried out.

Second, the magnitude of the penalty depends not just on the compliance failure and the penalty rate, but on the emission limit for the follow-on control period. Importantly, this emission limit must be accepted by the party in non-compliance (otherwise this country will not participate in the next control period). If a country has any reason to think that it will not meet its first commitment period emission limit, it will insist on a generous emission limit for the next period, weakening if not wiping out the effectiveness of the penalty.

Third, the proposal relies exclusively on self-punishment. Using the framework developed in Chapter 11, it can be shown that, by abating more in a punishment phase than in a cooperative phase, the non-complying country aids enforcement. By increasing its own abatement, it makes punishment by the other parties more attractive and, thus, more credible. But this is only one ingredient of an effective strategy of reciprocity. The other parties must actually punish the party that failed to comply. Put differently, compliance with the compliance mechanism must itself be enforced, and the compliance mechanism agreed in Bonn and Marrakech fails to do this. A country that fails to comply with its emission limitation obligations can avoid paying a penalty by failing to comply with the compliance provision itself.

Fourth, the agreement reached in Bonn/Marrakech ignores the participation problem. If the compliance penalty worked as intended, it would increase the costs of participation for a country that did not comply, making non-participation by this country, either by withdrawal or by failure to ratify an amendment establishing a future control program, *more* attractive. Alternatively, a country that believed it might not comply with a given emission ceiling will make its participation conditional on being assigned a more generous emission ceiling (just as Japan and Canada won concessions in Bonn). As shown in Chapter 10, compliance and participation are joint problems requiring a joint solution.

Finally, and as mentioned previously, the compliance mechanism agreed in Bonn/Marrakech is not (legally) binding. It could only be made (legally) binding by means of an amendment, and the countries most likely not to comply will also be the countries least likely to approve of such an amendment.

I should note that Kyoto does not rely entirely on the penalty rate for enforcement. The agreement also suspends the right of the party not in compliance to sell emission credits; requires that the party explain why it was in non-compliance; and demands that it provide a plan for complying in the future. The latter two requirements especially are of the type that would be recommended by the so-called managerial approach to compliance advocated by Chayes and Chayes (1993, 1995). However, the negotiators obviously perceived these measures to be inadequate. Otherwise, why would they also want to incorporate a compliance penalty?

15.9.3. Summary

To sum up, the focus of the Kyoto negotiations was on the setting of targets and timetables. When the treaty was first negotiated, little attention was given either to compliance or participation. In a sense, the treaty at this time resembled the Helsinki Protocol. It specified targets and timetables without restructuring the game.

In contrast to Helsinki, however, the targets and timetables agreed in Kyoto required real emission reductions by some countries. To take an example, the United States is required to reduce its emissions seven percent from the 1990 level by 2008–12. Because US emissions have been rising, achievement of the Kyoto limits would require a reduction in emissions in 2008–12 of about 30–35 percent from the business-as-usual level (Bodansky 2001). For this particular problem, this is a substantial level of reduction–too substantial for the US Senate; and too substantial for President George W. Bush, as we now know.

The environmental ambition of the 1997 agreement created pressures for change; in the language of Chapter 10, Kyoto was not renegotiation-proof. Non-participation by the United States was the most dramatic consequence of the original design, but this decision set in motion other changes, especially generous allowances for sinks credits for particular countries whose ratification was needed to bring the treaty into force. Having attempted to do more, Kyoto eventually had to retreat toward Helsinki-type emission ceilings—limits that would not be very costly to meet but that also would not alter behavior very much.

Reading the newspapers, you would think that President Bush's rejection of the treaty was the spoiler. But it is very unlikely that Kyoto would have been ratified by the US Senate even if Kyoto-friendly Al Gore had been elected president. As this became increasingly clear, a number of people began to think that the Kyoto targets needed to be renegotiated. Richard Benedick (2001*b*: 5), for example, even proposed "a new, tailor-made protocol article applying to the 'special circumstances' of the United States" *after* President Bush rejected the treaty. Easier-to-meet targets would obviously have helped. But this need to renegotiate emission limits even before the treaty enters into force points to a fundamental flaw in the Kyoto approach of setting targets and timetables. Without strong enforcement, the treaty is incapable of sustaining a cooperative climate policy, except by allowing parties to do little more than they would have done without a treaty.

Daniel Bodansky (2001) has proposed an alternative to renegotiation of the Kyoto targets. He believes that the problems with the treaty could have been addressed by incorporating a "safety valve" in the negotiations held at The Hague. A safety valve would allow polluters to purchase emission allowances at a fixed price—ensuring that the price of allowances would not exceed this price. If abatement turned out to be inexpensive, the binding constraint would be the quantity of emissions established by the targets and timetables. If abatement turned out to be expensive, the binding constraint would be the escape valve price. When there is uncertainty about abatement costs—and there is for climate change—this hybrid approach is superior to a plain cap-and-trade approach.[26] The safety valve would also aid compliance and participation by limiting marginal compliance costs. However, it would not eliminate the compliance/participation problem. Bringing the Kyoto Protocol more in line with the policies commended by cost–benefit analysis is only a necessary condition for successful cooperation. To sustain full cooperation also requires effective enforcement.

15.10. TRADE RESTRICTIONS

So, how could the Kyoto Protocol be enforced? The obvious alternative to the approach agreed in Bonn is the use of trade restrictions. After all, trade restrictions enforced the Montreal Protocol, and Kyoto is in many ways a similarly styled treaty.

To be effective, trade restrictions would need to be severe (so that, when imposed, behavior will be changed) and credible (meaning that, given that a country chooses not to participate, or not to comply, the cooperating countries are better off for imposing the restrictions). It would be easy enough to make trade restrictions severe. The manufacture of virtually all goods releases greenhouse gases, and a restriction in trade in all goods would be even more severe than the Montreal restrictions. But restricting trade in all goods between parties and non-parties would probably not be credible. Even if leakage were severe—and as noted earlier, it is not obvious that it would be—the cost–benefit figures shown earlier suggest that countries would gain relatively little environmentally from a trade restriction. They would, by contrast, have much to lose by restricting all trade.

More limited trade measures would be more credible. Indeed, border tax adjustments (BTAs) are the most effective means of neutralizing trade leakage. But imposing BTAs would require calculating the CO_2 emitted in the manufacture of every traded good (how much CO_2 was emitted in the production of this book, including all the computer time spent writing it?), and this would be costly and impractical. Recall from Chapter 8 that the parties to the Montreal Protocol considered restricting trade in goods manufactured using CFCs, but decided that it would be impossible to do so. Even when Europe was thinking of imposing a common carbon tax, the Commission did not make BTAs a feature of its tax proposal. Instead, it exempted the energy using industries from having to pay the tax, to address concerns about leakage. This diluted the power of the tax in reducing emissions, and helped kill the idea of imposing a common tax.

A rough approximation of the appropriate BTA may seem a practical alternative. However, as explained in Section 12.5, crudely calculated BTAs work less well at correcting leakage. They are also susceptible to political manipulation: a convenient tool for protectionism.

Even carefully calculated BTAs are prone to manipulation, either for reasons of improving the terms of trade or for enhancing climate mitigation (a higher tax adjustment would shift carbon-intensive production toward the cooperating countries,

---

[26] Roberts and Spence (1976) explain the superiority of the mixed regulatory system; see also Dasgupta (1982). For an application to climate, see Pizer (1999).

increasing the effectiveness of the treaty). The latter motive may seem desirable, but if non-parties believe that climate mitigation is a poor investment for them or that the treaty incorporating the BTAs was unfair to them, then the interests of these countries may be harmed by application of the BTAs. As explained in Chapter 12, trade restrictions should only be used to enforce "fair" treaties.

Finally, application of trade restrictions to the climate change problem would strain the multilateral trading system. BTAs would violate the principle of not restricting trade based on production and process methods. They may also violate the non-discrimination principle of the World Trade Organization (WTO). Of course, the WTO also allows exceptions for the purpose of environmental protection. So the use of trade restrictions in the Kyoto Protocol would expose a tension between the interests of liberalized trade and environmental protection, and between the participants and non-participants of the Kyoto Protocol. Montreal created a milder problem for the trading system. As mentioned above, it did not implement the trade restriction that would have violated the rule on production and process methods. It had also secured the participation of most of the GATT members, and all of the large ones. And it addressed a problem that harmed all states, and yet was relatively inexpensive to ameliorate.

15.11. KYOTO ALTERNATIVES

To sum up, the Kyoto Protocol is a poorly designed treaty. It may not enter into force. It may enter into force but not be fully implemented. Or it may enter into force and be fully implemented, but only because the parties would have undertaken the emission reductions required by the treaty anyway. Kyoto does not restructure the game of climate change mitigation in a way that will change international behavior materially. More importantly, Kyoto does not provide the supporting incentives needed to effect a change in behavior over time.

Can Kyoto be improved upon? A number of alternatives to Kyoto have been proposed, and these are summarized in Table 15.5.

I shall not comment in detail on these proposals.[27] The most important observation is that few of these proposals address the compliance/participation problem directly. Many will lower costs, in some cases by incorporating a safety valve/escape clause. But as noted previously, this kind of approach does not address the compliance/participation problem directly. The proposals by Aldy *et al.* (2001) and Nordhaus (1998) recommend application of trade restrictions as a means of enforcement. However, and as noted above, there are reasons to be cautious about using trade restrictions in a climate change treaty.

David Victor's (2001) proposal is different from all the others in addressing the enforcement problem directly—and creatively. Recognizing the limitations of international enforcement, Victor emphasizes the importance of domestic enforcement, arguing that the advanced industrial democracies could be relied upon to enforce

---

[27] For a fuller discussion of these proposals, see Barrett and Stavins (2002).

Table 15.5. *Proposals for alternatives to Kyoto*

Author(s)	Proposal
Aldy *et al.* (2001)	International cap-and-trade system coupled with a safety-valve, implemented by an international agency making additional permits available at a fixed price, the proceeds from which would finance R&D and abatement in developing countries.
Benedick (2001*b*)	United States to develop a modest domestic cap-and-trade system. A relatively small number of leading polluting countries to coordinate policy measures. Expansion in state-funded energy R&D, financed by a small carbon tax. Technology targets and technology transfer to developing countries, financed as foreign aid rather than through a trading system.
Bradford (2001)	All countries allocated permits corresponding to their business-as-usual emissions path. An international authority is given funds for purchasing such permits, with individual contributions based on criteria like per capita income and the expected benefits from climate change mitigation.
Cooper (1998, 2001)	Agree internationally on a set of actions, especially a common carbon tax, rather than targets. Developing countries allowed to phase-in the tax. Revenues to be retained by governments.
Hahn (1998)	Rather than develop a single system, allow experimentation with a number of different approaches, including cap-and-trade systems, coordinated measures, a carbon tax, and so on.
McKibbin and Wilcoxen (1997, 2000)	Establish a permit price by international agreement every ten years. Each country issues emission permits (permits that last a year) and emission endowments (permits that last in perpetuity). Developing countries given surplus endowments in early years, creating some incentive for long-term emission reductions.
Nordhaus (1998, 2002)	Harmonized carbon tax, with the level of the tax established by benefit-cost analysis, and implemented by an international voting mechanism. Developing countries participate after their per capita incomes pass a threshold. Compliance promoted by countervailing duties applied to imports from non-participating countries.
Schelling (1998, 2002)	Like the Marshall Plan, countries focus on mutually agreed actions, without international enforcement.
Schmalensee (1998)	Begin with a broad but shallow treaty, rather than with Kyoto's narrow but deep approach, and build in depth over time.
Stavins (2001)	A global approach, in which developing countries take on "growth targets," triggered by per capita income; with targets for all countries becoming more ambitious over time; and with international trading, perhaps supplemented by a safety-valve.
Stewart and Wiener (2001)	Modify Kyoto by enabling participation in a cap-and-trade system by developing countries, with targets for all countries tightened over time. Trading and CDM rules to be simplified. Compliance to be enforced by financial penalties imposed by the Compliance Committee.
Victor (2001)	Trading accompanied by a safety-valve. Developing countries to participate in trading system by adopting growth targets. Compliance promoted by buyer liability rule for permit trading.

international obligations. However, a treaty that limited participation to these countries only would be ill-suited to the climate mitigation problem, which demands a global remedy. Victor argues that the way around this problem is to change the rules for international emission trading by incorporating "buyer liability." Under this arrangement, if the seller of a permit did not reduce its emissions as promised, the buyer could not claim the emission credit. This arrangement would aid enforcement, Victor argues, because the buyers would be private entities in the liberal democracies, and their obligations, spelled out in domestic implementing legislation, could be reliably enforced by domestic institutions. Victor is right that domestic enforcement can help—we saw this most clearly in the case of the Fur Seal Treaty. But it can only help if the country participates in the treaty in the first place. As I have repeatedly argued, compliance and participation are linked problems and need to be considered jointly. Buyer liability does not solve the participation problem, and so cannot, on its own, solve the compliance problem. Looked at differently, enforcement of Kyoto would be problematic even if trading were prohibited. Turning the tables on liability does not change this basic fact.

Thomas Schelling's (1998, 2002) proposal is characteristically singular in its approach. It explicitly eschews international enforcement. It would also abandon the targets and timetables approach, relying instead on the implementation of policies and measures—that is, on actions rather than outcomes. Schelling would invite countries to pledge to adopt policies and measures, and open these to international review. The policies and measures proposed might create a kind of yardstick by which countries would be judged—providing a small incentive, perhaps, for mitigation beyond the non-cooperative level. Without international enforcement, however, his proposal cannot effect substantial mitigation. Essentially, his proposal would only improve on unilateralism by appealing to the kind of "tote board diplomacy" highlighted by Levy (1995), and noted in Chapter 1.

What we need, it seems to me, is an approach that gets around the enforcement problem, but that also provides a long-term solution to what is, after all, a long-term problem. Richard Benedick's (2001*b*) proposal has the same aim and shares common features with my own proposal, which is outlined below.[28]

15.12. THE LONG-TERM SOLUTION

In the very long term, scarcity will force us to substitute away from fossil fuels, whether we do anything to mitigate climate change or not. A climate mitigation policy needs to accelerate this substitution—and it must do so even while substantial quantities of fossil fuels remain ready to be tapped, at relatively low cost. In the short term, natural gas can be substituted for oil and coal, nuclear power may possibly be substituted for fossil fuels, and energy can be conserved. In the long run, however, new technologies will be needed, and the development of these will require substantial R&D.

---

[28] See also Barrett (2001*b*).

Like Montreal, Kyoto is meant to provide a "pull" incentive for R&D. In capping emissions, Kyoto raises the cost of polluting, and so creates a demand for carbon-saving technologies, just as Montreal created a demand for CFC substitutes. The difference between the two situations, as already shown, is that the cost of substituting for CFCs was low. The cost of climate change mitigation will be much higher, and this matters. When the costs of supplying a global public good are high, the incentive not to participate is high, and the burden on enforcement very great. If the treaty cannot support that burden, the result will be very weak incentives for innovation and diffusion of new technologies.

If the enforcement problem could be solved, what kinds of technical progress would we require? As indicated in a report by Battelle (2001), nearly all commercial energy is either converted into electricity for stationary uses or refined and processed for mobile uses. Basically, emissions must be cut in power plants and in automobiles. More radical possibilities also exist, but any climate mitigation policy has to contend with the fact that our economies have developed around these technologies. We have a huge installed base of equipment that runs on electricity. And our economies are automobile-based. Just as climate change damages will be high because our economies have been designed to suit our current climate, so mitigation costs will be high if we move away from our existing economic structure. Here as in other areas, our history will to some extent determine our future.

For power plants, there are two basic paths. One involves substituting away from fossil fuels. The other involves carbon capture and sequestration.

Alternatives to fossil fuels exist today. They include hydro, nuclear, solar, and wind power. But each of these alternatives has problems of its own (whether economic, environmental, or safety-related). R&D needs to address these concerns.

Carbon capture is a technology that "scrubs" the flue gases of a power plant using chemical processes to remove CO_2. The captured CO_2 must then be put somewhere—it must be sequestered—and there are a number of ways in which this might be done.[29] One is to liquify the CO_2 and inject it deep into the ocean. Water at depths greater than a thousand meters is cool and dense, and would not reach the surface for centuries. CO_2 can also be injected into the ground, in depleted oil and gas wells, coal mines, and salt domes. Carbon capture and sequestration has the advantage of allowing fossil fuels to be burned. Special interests in old energy would be protected. And, in allowing fossil fuels to be consumed, the prices of these fuels would be raised. High prices would in turn discourage non-participants from increasing their emissions, squeezing shut one of the important channels of trade leakage.

However, both storage remedies may also cause environmental damage. Ocean storage would raise the pH level, possibly harming zooplankton and bacteria. Underground storage could leak, returning CO_2 to the atmosphere. Worse, a massive leak could kill. CO_2 is heavier than air, and a sudden release would displace oxygen, suffocating everything in the neighborhood of the release.

Note that both means for reducing CO_2 emissions pose risks. In reducing one risk—the risk of climate change—we create others. Substitution of nuclear power

---

[29] See United States Department of Energy (1999) and Herzog *et al.* (2000).

creates risks to safety both in the short- and long-term because of the need to store the wastes. Carbon capture and storage poses similar risks. It is easier to be *for* climate change mitigation until one has considered the consequences of effecting the mitigation—not just in terms of dollars and cents but in terms of risks. Risk–risk trade-offs are a familiar feature of environmental regulation (see Viscusi 1998). They need to be incorporated in our decision-making.

A number of alternatives already exist for the conventional automobile. One is the electric car. If CO_2 emissions can be eliminated from power production, electric cars would, at a stroke, eliminate CO_2 emissions from automobiles. Another possibility is the fuel cell, especially the type fueled by hydrogen. The production of hydrogen fuel, however, would itself increase CO_2 emissions unless produced by non-carbon energy sources like nuclear power or fossil fuel energy accompanied by CO_2 separation and capture.

Mitigation can also involve sequestering the CO_2 already in the atmosphere—and, here again, there are a number of alternatives. The approach most often discussed, and already embodied within the Kyoto framework, is forest, plant, and soil sequestration. Photosynthesis fixes CO_2, and stores it in the biomass and the soil. Some sequestration by this means is already economic (see Stavins 1999). But sequestration can also be enhanced technologically. Genetic engineering could potentially augment the natural bioconversion process, and make CO_2 biomass storage more durable. An even greater source of sequestration is the oceans. Phytoplankton in the surface waters fix CO_2, and by means of the "biological pump" much of this gets stored in the deep ocean, where it is slowly mineralized by bacteria. Some areas of the ocean contain little phytoplankton and, as a consequence, fix little CO_2. The reason is often a deficiency of iron. Fertlizing these areas with iron could promote phytoplankton growth—and, hence, CO_2 sequestration.

These approaches also entail new risks. If carried out on a large scale, genetic engineering and iron fertilization could change the structure of important ecosystems. Another problem with sequestration is measurement—not only measurement of how much CO_2 is sequestered by a particular action, but also of whether an action would have occurred anyway. In the discussion to follow, I focus on the other alternatives.

15.13. A TECHNOLOGY-CENTERED APPROACH

As noted before, Montreal was the wrong model for a climate treaty. A better model may be the MARPOL treaty. This agreement, discussed in Chapter 9, abandoned the approach tried earlier that set quantitative emission limits but without the ability to monitor or enforce them. Instead, MARPOL imposed a technology standard (segregated ballast tanks). In my view, a climate agreement needs to do something similar.

15.13.1. Research and Development

But a climate treaty must also help create the kind of technological breakthroughs discussed above. As already noted, the kind of "pull" incentive created by Kyoto can only be supported by strong enforcement. And a "pull" incentive is not always sufficient to effect a change in technology. Commercial innovation often builds on government-funded research. For example, drug and vaccine development typically builds on the basic research done by the National Institutes of Health in the United States and similar institutes in other countries. Basic research needs to be a part of any climate program. Remarkably, however, all the while that Kyoto has been negotiated, government-funded energy R&D decreased. Ironically, it decreased the most in the countries most (vocally) committed to Kyoto (Battelle 2001). This situation needs to be reversed.

The knowledge obtained from basic research is a public good, and would best be supplied cooperatively. Examples of "big science" collaborative research include the International Space Station, governed by an international agreement involving the United States, Russia, Canada, Japan, and the European Space Agency, and the new Large Hadron (particle) Collider, funded by Europe, the United States, Japan, and Canada. However, the research required for climate-centered technological break-throughs requires a broader base of support. From this perspective, a better model for R&D cooperation may be the Consultative Group on International Agricultural Research (CGIAR), funded by twenty-one industrialized nations, nineteen developing countries, several foundations, and nearly a dozen international organizations.

Richard Benedick (2001*b*) also stresses the need for R&D. However, he believes more can be achieved, at least in the near term, by agreements involving a smaller number of countries rather than a global treaty—an approach that also finds some support in game theory (Carraro *et al.* 2002). However, for reasons of legitimacy, it would be hard to defend an exclusionary treaty. And the problem itself demands a global remedy. As explained in Chapter 11, a problem like climate change is better addressed by a broad-based agreement. At the same time, the Kyoto Protocol has been justly criticized not only for exempting developing countries from having to bear similar obligations as industrialized countries but for allowing developing countries to shape the kinds of obligations only industrialized countries are expected to bear. As suggested by Daniel Bodansky (2001), this approach gives representation without taxation. An effective climate change treaty must be global, but it must also be fair—and from the perspective of all countries, both poor and rich.

Consistent with the approach outlined in Chapter 11, financing of collaborative R&D should be contingent, with each country's contribution to the global R&D fund depending on: (i) an agreed total expenditure level, assuming full participation; (ii) a share for each country determined by its circumstances (shares may be based on the UN scale of assessments or on measures of each country's historic contribution to greenhouse gas concentrations or perhaps on historic or current emissions); and (iii) the other countries contributing. The last component is especially important. It ensures that, if country i accedes, then all the other parties will increase their funding by a specified amount. Alternatively, if i withdraws, the others will lower their funding.[30] This creates an incentive to participate. It builds in a strategy of reciprocity. The

---

[30] This proposal is reminiscent of Guttman's (1978) proposed "matching mechanism" for the supply of public goods.

proposal also imposes a cap on the *total* financial obligation of every country. In contrast to Kyoto and a cap-and-trade system with a safety valve, parties to the R&D protocol would know the maximum total cost of participation before deciding to ratify.

Having financed the required R&D, the agreement needs also to create incentives for commercializing the technologies that can be developed from this knowledge. In contrast to basic research, commercialization is best done by the private sector. This requires a "pull" incentive.

15.13.2. Technology Standards

A pull incentive is normally best provided by the price mechanism, and Kyoto creates such a mechanism indirectly, by putting a "shadow price" on emissions. In limiting emissions, Kyoto imposes an implicit price penalty on carbon—and so creates an incentive for reducing carbon emissions. However, as explained previously, Kyoto's weak enforcement creates only a weak incentive for innovation. Somehow, a better pull incentive needs to be created.

Following the MARPOL example, this could be done by mandating standards. Standards are adopted for many reasons. First, and as explained in Chapters 4 and 9, when there are network effects, demand for a technology will depend on the number of others that use it or that can be expected to use it. Network effects can be direct (with the demand for a new fuel cell technology depending on the availability of refueling stations) or indirect (with the demand for the technology depending on the availability of replacement parts and service). Second, where there are switching costs, buyers may be reluctant to purchase a technology that locks them in, making them an orphan of a failed technology.[31] Finally, where there are substantial economies of scale, costs will be lower with technological specialization.

The setting of standards often creates a tipping effect. If enough countries adopt a standard, it may become irresistible for others to follow, whether because of network effects, cost considerations (as determined by scale economies), or lock-in.

Standards can be open or proprietary. Standards protocols should prescribe open standards, which promote competition. A relevant example of an open standard is the vehicle emission standard that created the market for the catalytic converter.[32]

Open standards are public goods. No country can be excluded from using them, and no country's use of a standard reduces the availability of the standard to others. But how should open standards be chosen, by the market or by governments? Governments are not always good at picking standards. They often pick a standard to protect a national champion, for example, but proprietary standards only yield a return if they get diffused—and, by their very nature, they tend not to be. At the same time, *de facto* standards determined by the market place are often not very good either. The free market may select the "wrong" standard[33]; or it may force companies to bring a technology to market too early—that is, before it is perfected; or it may

---

[31] Possibly for this reason, electric cars in the United States are leased rather than sold.

[32] An example of a proprietary standard is the Windows® operating system.

[33] This is the so-called QWERTY problem; see David (1985).

prevent any one standard from attaining the market share needed for it to tip; or it may allow a single proprietary standard to dominate, depriving users of variety. A hybrid system relying on committees comprising both government and industry representatives may be best (Farrell and Saloner 1988). The standards agreement for automobiles discussed in Section 4.13 was negotiated with substantial input from industry, as were the production and consumption limits of the Montreal Protocol.[34] A public–private partnership for climate change mitigation technologies is also needed.[35]

Standards protocols should be non-exclusionary. They are intended to promote wide adoption of a technology. Since all countries will be affected by the protocols, all should have a say in their design.

Standards also need to evolve. The standards protocols and the collaborative R&D protocol should thus be mutually reinforcing, with the R&D protocol helping to identify new standards, and with the standards protocols suggesting future directions for R&D.

The main advantage in this approach is its strategic effect on behavior. Provided that the minimum participation level were set appropriately, a strong incentive would be created for more and more countries to participate. It is likely that the tipping point would have to include Europe, Japan, and the United States at a minimum.

Tipping would also be helped by an almost automatic trade restriction. In prescribing a new standard, parties would essentially be banning imports of technologies that failed to meet the standard, just as many countries today effectively ban imports of cars not meeting their domestic vehicle emission standards and power plants not meeting their prescribed emission standards. The minimum participation level would thus not only ensure a large market for the new technology but a shrinking market for the old technology. Note that, in contrast to trade restrictions applying to a Kyoto-type agreement, trade restrictions based on standards are legal.[36] They would also be easy to administer.

Another advantage of this approach is that compliance would be easy to monitor and verify. As explained in detail by Victor (2001), monitoring of the sources and sinks controlled by the Kyoto Protocol is difficult and subject to considerable uncertainty. Effective monitoring will often require intrusive inspections—an approach not usually welcomed by the anarchic international system. Monitoring of standards agreements, by contrast, is relatively easy. And as explained in Chapter 4, compliance enforcement is almost unnecessary. Once enough countries adopt a standard, none will have an incentive to break from it.

Though the agreement to effect a technological transition needs to be global, the developing countries should not be expected to pay all their costs. These should

---

[34] See also Funk and Methe's (2001) case study of how global industry standards were established for mobile telecommunications.

[35] This should include technology *users* as well as producers. The interests of producers and consumers are not always consonant.

[36] Technical standards must conform to the rules of the Agreement on Technical Barriers to Trade. Note that some kinds of standards would not be allowed. For example, the WTO has ruled against the Corporate Average Fuel Economy standards adopted by the United States. However, it is relatively easy to design a standard that achieves the environmental aim while at the same time complying with the requirements of the multilateral trading system.

rather be financed by a multilateral fund, akin to the Montreal Protocol's fund, with contributions to the fund being based on arrangements similar to the R&D fund. Compensation based on incremental costs would reduce transfers as compared with emissions trading, and thus promote participation by industrialized countries. As with the Montreal Protocol's Multilateral Fund, the effect of these transfers would be to "ratchet up" the cooperation problem (see Chapter 13).

15.13.3. In the Short Term

The best thing we can do in the short run is to invest in a long-term technological transition, but further actions could also be taken. Policies and actions are more important than targets and timetables, and countries could develop a system of pledge-and-review akin to Schelling's (1998, 2002) proposal. The pledges would be unilaterally-based, but declared within a multilateral framework. One of the problems with Kyoto is that it has deflected attention from what countries can and should do on their own to mitigate climate change. This approach would shift the short run focus back to the country level. It would be enforced by domestic institutions only. These policies and measures could be incorporated in another protocol.

15.13.4. Adaptation Assistance

Finally, given that the climate is almost certain to change no matter what we do, in the medium run and in the long run, consideration needs to be given for the industrialized countries to assist the developing countries in adaptation. An adaptation fund was incorporated into the Kyoto Protocol in Bonn, financed by a tax on CDM transactions and voluntary contributions, and something like it needs to be incorporated in an alternative climate change treaty. An acknowledgment needs to be made, in my view, that the industrialized countries are mainly responsible for the accumulation of greenhouse gases; and that, while cost–benefit analysis may not commend a radical climate change policy given current knowledge, developing countries should not be made to bear the cost associated with a more modest approach.

15.13.5. Summary

To sum up, the proposal sketched here acknowledges that a climate treaty needs to think about the long run and the technological transition that will reduce greenhouse gas concentrations, as instructed by the Framework Convention. It would involve collaborative R&D in developing new technologies, follow-on protocols establishing technology standards, a multilateral fund to help spread the new technologies to developing countries, a short-run system of pledge-and-review, and a further protocol for adaptation assistance.

To be sure, the proposal outlined here is not of an ideal climate treaty.[37] Like the technology-based treaty examined in section 9.8.3, it is unable to sustain full cooperation, mainly because it is not fully cost-effective. On paper, Kyoto appears

---

[37] For a preliminary evaluation of this proposal, which first appeared as Barrett (2001*b*), see Buchner *et al.* (2002).

superior. But the Kyoto approach cannot be supported by the international system. Though the technology-based approach has a number of weaknesses, it recognizes that the constraint of self-enforcement must be obeyed; that incentives need to be built into the treaty such that, the more some countries do to mitigate climate change, the greater is the incentive for others to do more; that mitigation must be done globally if it is to be effective; and that, though developing countries have a responsibility to reduce their emissions, industrialized countries have a responsibility to assist them in making the required technological transition as well as in adapting to the climate changes that will occur in any event. Though the proposal suggested here is not a first best, it may be better than the alternatives in satisfying the requirements I laid out in the preface to this book: that a treaty be individually rational, collectively rational, and fair.

Finally, let me state again that the value in this proposal lies less in its details than in the thinking that lies behind it. Kyoto incorporated enforcement as an after thought. My proposal begins by asking what kinds of behavior can be enforced. As this book has shown, this is the better way to approach international cooperation problems.

15.14. CONCLUSIONS

Coming from an economist, my proposal must seem especially curious. The usual prescription suggested by economics is for the state to establish an environmental outcome (justified by cost–benefit analysis, of course), leaving it to the market to decide how best to achieve this outcome. This is how Kyoto was designed.

Kyoto actually had two role models, the Montreal Protocol, as noted previously, and the US Clean Air Act amendments. As explained in Chapter 1, the latter policy set a national ceiling for SO_2 emissions, allocated a share to every major polluting plant, and allowed these pollution entitlements to be traded. It has been a successful program. But a climate treaty has to be implemented within the anarchic international system, and this makes all the difference. The total volume of SO_2 permits is fixed by the US Congress, whereas the total volume of Kyoto permits depends on the participation level. And, of course, Kyoto cannot be enforced in the same way as a US law can be. Yes, the US government can enforce a *domestic* law implementing Kyoto. But it cannot make other countries comply let alone participate.

The usual aversion to standard-setting stems from a domestic model of regulation, one that can rely on the strong arm and visible hand of the state for enforcement. International agreements need to be self-enforcing, and so must restructure incentives. This requires strategic thinking, and the proposal for incorporating standards protocols derives from a strategic approach to treaty-making, one that is styled to suit the climate problem (different environmental problems, as I have repeatedly argued, will have different, usually second best, international remedies). That the theory should recommend an approach so contrary to conventional reasoning confirms my motivation for writing this book in the first place.

References

Adams, J., Maslin, M., and Thomas, E. (1999). "Sudden Climate Transitions During the Quaternary." *Progress in Physical Geography*, 23(1): 1–36.

Aldy, J. E., Orszag, P. R., and Stiglitz, J. E. (2001). "Climate Change: An Agenda for Global Collective Action." prepared for conference on The Timing of Climate Change Policies, Pew Center on Global Climate Change, Washington, DC.

Anderson, R. M. and May, R. M. (1991). *Infectious Diseases of Humans: Dynamics and Control.* Oxford: Oxford University Press.

Anderson, T. L. and Hill, P. J. (1990). "The Race for Property Rights." *Journal of Law and Economics*, 33: 177–97.

ARC Research Consultants (1997). *Global Benefits and Costs of the Montreal Protocol on Substances that Deplete the Ozone Layer.* Ottawa: Environment Canada.

Arrow, K. J. (1951). *Social Choice and Individual Values.* New York: John Wiley.

Arrow, K. J. and Fisher, A. (1974). "Preservation, Uncertainty, and Irreversibility." *Quarterly Journal of Economics*, 87: 312–19.

Arrow, K. J., Cline, W. R., Mäler, K.-G., Munasinghe, M., Squitieri, R., and Stiglitz, J. E. (1996). "Intertemporal Equity, Discounting, and Economic Efficiency," in J. P. Bruce, H. Lee, and E. F. Haites (eds) (1996), *Climate Change 1995: Economic and Social Dimensions of Climate Change.* Cambridge: Cambridge University Press, 125–44.

Axelrod, R. (1984). *The Evolution of Cooperation.* New York: Basic Books.

Bailey, T. A. (1968). *The Art of Diplomacy: The American Experience.* New York: Appleton-Century-Crofts.

Baland, J.-M. and Platteau, J.-P. (1996). *Halting Degradation of Natural Resources: Is there a Role for Rural Communities?* Oxford: Clarendon Press.

Barrett, S. (1991). "Economic Analysis of International Environmental Agreements: Lessons for a Global Warming Treaty," in OECD, *Responding to Climate Change: Selected Economic Issues.* Paris: OECD.

—— (1992a). "Economic Growth and Environmental Preservation." *Journal of Environmental Economics and Management*, 23: 289–300.

—— (1992b). "Strategy and the Environment." *Columbia Journal of World Business*, 27: 202–8.

—— (1992c). "International Environmental Agreements as Games," in R. Pethig (ed.), *Conflict and Cooperation in Managing Environmental Resources*, Berlin: Springer-Verlag.

—— (1992d). "Reaching a CO_2 Emission Limitation Agreement for the Community: Implications for Equity and Cost-Effectiveness." *European Economy*, Special Edition No. 1, 3–24.

—— (1992e). "'Acceptable' Allocations of Tradeable Carbon Emission Entitlements in a Global Warming Treaty," in UNCTAD (ed.), *Combating Global Warming: Study on a Global System of Tradeable Carbon Emission Entitlements.* New York: United Nations, 85–113.

—— (1992f). "Transfers and the Gains from Trading Carbon Emission Entitlements in a Global Warming Treaty," in UNCTAD (ed.), *Combating Global Warming: Study on a Global System of Tradeable Carbon Emission Entitlements.* New York: United Nations, 115–25.

—— (1992g). *Convention on Climate Change: Economic Aspects of Negotiation.* Paris: OECD.

—— (1994a). "Self-enforcing International Environmental Agreements." *Oxford Economic Papers*, 46: 878–94.

Barrett, S. (1994*b*). "Strategic Environmental Policy and International Trade." *Journal of Public Economics*, 54: 325–38.

—— (1994*c*). "The Biodiversity Supergame." *Environmental and Resource Economics*, 4: 111–22.

—— (1996). "European Carbon Tax," in A. R. Beckenstein, F. J. Long, M. B. Arnold, and T. N. Gladwin (eds), *Stakeholder Negotiations: Exercises in Sustainable Development*. Chicago: Irwin, 69–91.

—— (1997*a*). "The Strategy of Trade Sanctions in International Environmental Agreements." *Resource and Energy Economics*, 19: 345–61.

—— (1997*b*). "Heterogeneous International Environmental Agreements," in C. Carraro (ed.), *International Environmental Negotiations*. Cheltenham, UK: Edward Elgar.

—— (1998*a*). "On the Theory and Diplomacy of Environmental Treaty-Making." *Environmental and Resource Economics*, 11: 317–33.

—— (1998*b*). "Political Economy of the Kyoto Protocol." *Oxford Review of Economic Policy*, 14: 20–39.

—— (1999*a*). "A Theory of Full International Cooperation." *Journal of Theoretical Politics*, 11(4): 519–41.

—— (1999*b*). "Montreal v. Kyoto: International Cooperation and the Global Environment," in I. Kaul, I. Grunberg, and M. A. Stern (eds), *Global Public Goods: International Cooperation in the 21st Century*. New York: Oxford University Press, 192–219.

—— (1999*c*). "The Credibility of Trade Sanctions in International Environmental Agreements," in P. Fredriksson (ed.), *Trade, Global Policy, and the Environment*, World Bank Discussion Paper No. 402, 161–72.

—— (2000). "Trade and Environment: Local versus Multilateral Reforms." *Environment and Development Economics*, 5: 349–59.

—— (2001*a*). "International Cooperation for Sale." *European Economic Review*, 45: 1835–50.

—— (2001*b*). "Towards a Better Climate Treaty." *Policy Matters*, 01–29, Washington, DC: AEI-Brookings Joint Center for Regulatory Studies. Reprinted in *World Economics*, 3(2): 35–45.

—— (2002*a*). "Consensus Treaties." *Journal of Institutional and Theoretical Economics*, 158(4), forthcoming.

—— (2002*b*). "The Theory of International Environmental Agreements," in K.-G. Mäler and J. Vincent (eds), *Handbook of Environmental Economics*. Amsterdam: Elsevier, forthcoming.

—— (2002*c*). "Global Disease Eradication. "Invited paper, European Economics Association Conference, Venice, Italy, August.

Barrett, S. and Graddy, K. (2000). "Freedom, Growth, and the Environment." *Environment and Development Economics*, 5: 433–56.

Barrett, S. and Stavins, R. (2002). "Increasing Participation and Compliance in International Climate Change Agreements." mimeo, Johns Hopkins University and Harvard University.

Battelle (2001). *Global Energy Technology Strategy: Addressing Climate Change*. Washington, DC: Battelle.

Baumol, W. J. and Oates, W. E. (1988). *The Theory of Environmental Policy*. Cambridge: Cambridge University Press.

Behring Sea Arbitration (1893). *The Case of the United States Before the Tribunal of Arbitration*. No. 6, March, London: HMSO.

Benedick, R. E. (1997). "The UN Approach to Climate Change: Where Has it Gone Wrong?" Resources for the Future, Weathervane, http://www.weathervane.rff.org/pop/pop4/benedick.html.

—— (1998). *Ozone Diplomacy: New Directions in Safeguarding the Planet*, enlarged edition. Cambridge, MA: Harvard University Press.

—— (2001*a*). "Contrasting Approaches: The Ozone Layer, Climate Change, and Resolving the Kyoto Dilemma," in E. D. Schultze *et al.* (eds), *Global Biogeochemical Cycles in the Climate System*. San Diego: Academic Press for Max Planck Institute for Biogeochemistry, 317–31.

—— (2001*b*). "Striking a New Deal on Climate Change." *Issues in Science and Technology Online*, Fall issue.

Bernauer, T. (1996). "Protecting the Rhine River Against Chloride Pollution," in R. O. Keohane and M. A. Levy (eds), *Institutions for Environmental Aid*. Cambridge, MA: MIT Press, 201–32.

Bhagwati, J. and Srinivasan, T. N. (1996). "Trade and the Environment: Does Environmental Diversity Detract from the Case for Free Trade?" in J. Bhagwati and R. E. Hudec (eds), *Fair Trade and Harmonization, Vol. 1, Economic Analysis*, Cambridge, MA: MIT Press, 159–223.

Binmore, K. (1992). *Fun and Games: A Text on Game Theory*. Lexington: D.C. Heath & Co.

—— (1994). *Game Theory and the Social Contract, Volume I: Playing Fair*. Cambridge, MA: MIT Press.

—— (1998). *Game Theory and the Social Contract, Volume 2: Just Playing*. Cambridge, MA: MIT Press.

Binmore, K. and Dasgupta, P. (1986). "Game Theory: A Survey," in K. Binmore and P. Dasgupta (eds), *Economic Organizations as Games*. Oxford: Basil Blackwell.

Birnie, P. W. and Boyle, A. E. (1992). *International Law and the Environment*. Oxford: Clarendon Press.

Björkbom, L. (1988). "Resolution of Environmental Problems: The Use of Diplomacy," in J. E. Carroll (ed.), *International Environmental Diplomacy: The Management and Resolution of Transfrontier Environmental Problems*. Cambridge: Cambridge University Press, 123–37.

Black, J., Levi, M. D., and de Meza, D. (1993). "Creating a Good Atmosphere: Minimum Participation for Tackling the 'Greenhouse Effect.'" *Economica*, 60: 281–93.

Boardman, R. (1981). *International Organization and the Conservation of Nature*. London: Macmillan.

Bodansky, D. (1993). "The United Nations Framework Convention on Climate Change: A Commentary." *Yale Journal of International Law*, 18: 451–558.

—— (1994). "Prologue to the Climate Change Convention," in I. M. Mintzer and J. A. Leonard (eds), *Negotiating Climate Change: The Inside Story of the Rio Convention*. Cambridge: Cambridge University Press.

—— (1995). "Customary (and not so Customary) International Environmental Law." *Indiana Journal of Global Legal Studies*, 3: 105–19.

—— (1999). "The Legitimacy of International Governance: A Coming Challenge for International Environmental Law?" *American Journal of International Law*, 93: 596–624.

—— (2001). "Bonn Voyage: Kyoto's Uncertain Revival." *The National Interest*, Fall Issue, 45–55.

Bohm, P. (1997). *Joint Implementation as Emission Quota Trade: An Experiment Among Four Nordic Countries*. Copenhagen: Nordic Council of Ministers.

Bolton, G. E. and Ockenfels, A. (2000). "ERC: A Theory of Equity, Reciprocity, and Competition." *American Economic Review*, 90(1): 166–93.

Brack, D. (1996). *International Trade and the Montreal Protocol*. London: Royal Institute of International Affairs.

Bradford, D. F. (2001). "Succeeding Kyoto: A No-Cap but Trade Approach to GHG Control: Version 02a." mimeo, Princeton University and NYU School of Law.

Brams, S. J. (1985). *Superpower Games: Applying Game Theory to Superpower Conflict*. New Haven: Yale University Press.

Brander, J. (1981). "Intra-Industry Trade in Identical Commodities." *Journal of International Economics*, 11: 1–14.

Brander, J. A. and Krugman, P. R. (1983). "A 'Reciprocal Dumping' Model of International Trade." *Journal of International Economics*, 15: 313–23.

Brenton, T. (1994). *The Greening of Machiavelli: The Evolution of International Environmental Politics*. London: Royal Institute of International Affairs.

Brownlie, I. (1990). *Principles of Public International Law*. Oxford: Oxford University Press.

Buchner, B., Carraro, C., and Cersosimo, I. (2001). "On the Consequences of the US Withdrawal from the Kyoto/Bonn Protocol." mimeo, Fondazione Eni Enrico Mattei.

Buchner, B., Carraro, C., Cersosimo, I., and Marchiori, C. (2002). "Back to Kyoto? US Participation and the Linkage between R&D and Climate Cooperation." Climate Change Modelling and Policy Unit, Fondazione ENI Enrico Mattei, Venice, Italy.

Bulow, J., Geanakoplos, J., and Klemperer, P. (1985). "Multimarket Oligopoly: Strategic Substitutes and Complements." *Journal of Political Economy*, 93: 488–511.

Burtraw, D., Krupnick, A., Mansur, E., Austin, D., and Farrell D. (1997). "The Costs and Benefits of Reducing Acid Rain." Discussion Paper 97-31-REV, Resources for the Future, September.

Bush, G. W. (2002). "President Announces Clear Skies and Global Climate Change Initiatives." speech given to the National Oceanic and Atmospheric Administration, Silver Spring Maryland, February 14.

Cairncross, F. (1992). "Survey of the Environment." *The Economist*. May 30.

Cameron, J. (1996). "Compliance, Citzens and NGOs," in J. Cameron, J. Werksman, and P. Roderick (eds), *Improving Compliance with International Environmental Law*. London: Earthscan, 29–47.

Caponera, D.A. (1980). *The Law of International Water Resources*. Legislative Study No. 23, Rome: FAO.

Carraro, C. and Botteon, M. (1997). "Burden Sharing and Coalition Stability in Environmental Negotiations with Asymmetric Countries," in C. Carraro (ed.), *International Environmental Negotiations*. Cheltenham, UK: Edward Elgar.

—— Buchner, B., Cersosimo, I., and Marchiori, C. (2002). "Prospective Climate Regimes: A Theoretical and Empirical Assessment." Climate Change Modelling and Policy Unit, Fondazione ENI Enrico Mattei, Venice, Italy.

—— and Siniscalco, D. (1993). "Strategies for the International Protection of the Environment." *Journal of Public Economics*, 52: 309–28.

—— (1994). "R&D Cooperation and the Stability of International Environmental Agreements." Nota di Lavoro 65.94, Fondazione Eni Enrico Mattei, Milan, Italy.

Carraro, C., Moriconi, F., and Oreffice, S. (1998). "α-Rules and Equilibrium Endogenous Coalitions." mimeo, University of Venice and Fondazione ENI. E. Mattei, December.

Cesar, H. and de Zeeuw, A. (1994). "Issue Linkage in Global Environmental Problems." Nota ke Lavoro 56.94, Fondazione Eni Enrico Mattei, Milan, Italy.

Chander, P. and Tulkens, H. (1992). "Theoretical Foundations of Negotiations and Cost-Sharing in Transfrontier Pollution Problems." *European Economic Review*, 36: 288–99.

—— (1994). "A Core-Theoretic Solution for the Design of Cooperative Agreements on Transfrontier Pollution." *International Tax and Public Finance*, 2: 279–93.

—— (1997). "The Core of an Economy with Multilateral Environmental Externalities." *International Journal of Game Theory*, 26: 379–401.

Chang, H. F. (1995). "An Economic Analysis of Trade Measures to Protect the Global Environment." *Georgetown Law Journal*, 83: 2131–213.

Charnovitz, S. (1994). "Encouraging Environmental Cooperation through the Pelly Amendment." *Journal of Environment and Development*, 3: 3–28.

Chayes, A. and Chayes, A. H. (1991). "Compliance Without Enforcement: State Regulatory Behavior Under Regulatory Treaties". *Negotiation Journal*, 7: 311–31.

—— (1993). "On Compliance." *International Organization*, 47: 175–205.

—— (1995). *The New Sovereignty*. Cambridge, MA: Harvard University Press.

Clark, C. W. (1976). *Mathematical Bioeconomics*. New York: Wiley.

Coase, R. H. (1960). "The Problem of Social Cost." *Journal of Law and Economics*, 3: 1–44.

Cline, W. R. (1992). *The Economics of Global Warming*. Washington, DC: Institute for International Economics.

Clinton Administration (1998). "The Kyoto Protocol and the President's Policies to Address Climate Change: Administration Economic Analysis." White House, Washington, DC, July.

Congleton, R. D. (1992). "Political Institutions and Pollution Control." *Review of Economics and Statistics*, 74: 412–21.

Cooper, R. N. (1989). "International Cooperation in Public Health as a Prologue to Macroeconomic Cooperation," in R. N. Cooper, B. Eichengreen, C. R. Henning, G. Holtham, and R. D. Putnam (eds), *Can Nations Agree?* Washington, DC: Brookings Institution.

—— (1998). "Toward a Real Treaty on Global Warming." *Foreign Affairs*, 77(2): 66–79.

—— (2001). "The Kyoto Protocol: A Flawed Concept." Nota di Lavoro 52.2001, Fondazione Eni Enrico Mattei, Venice, Italy.

Copeland, B. R. and Taylor, M. S. (2000). "Free Trade and Global Warming: A Trade Theory View of the Kyoto Protocol." mimeo, Department of Economics, University of British Columbia.

Council of Economic Advisers (1990). *Economic Report of the President*. Washington, DC: U.S. Government Printing Office.

d'Aspremont, C. A., Jacquemin, J., Gabszeweiz, J., and Weymark, J. A. (1983). "On the Stability of Collusive Price Leadership." *Canadian Journal of Economics*, 16: 17–25.

Dasgupta, P. (1982). *The Control of Resources*. Cambridge, MA: Harvard.

—— (1993). *An Inquiry into Well-Being and Destitution*. Oxford: Clarendon Press.

—— (2001). *Human Well-Being and the Natural Environment*. Oxford: Oxford University Press.

—— (2002). "Social Capital and Economic Performance: Analytics," in E. Ostrom and T.-K. Ahn (eds), *Social Capital: A Reader*. Cheltenham, UK: Edward Elgar, forthcoming.

—— and Serageldin, I. (eds) (1999). *Social Capital: A Multifaceted Perspective*. Washington, DC: World Bank.

—— Mäler, K.-G., and Barrett, S. (1999). "Intergenerational Equity, Social Discount Rates, and Global Warming," in J. P. Weyant and P. R. Portney (eds), *Discounting and Intergenerational Equity*. Baltimore: Johns Hopkins University Press, 51–77.

David, P. (1985). "Clio and the Economics of QWERTY." *American Economic Review*, 75(2): 332–37.

Dawes, R. M. and Thaler, R. H. (1988). "Cooperation." *Journal of Economic Perspectives*, 2: 187–97.

Depledge, J. (2000). "Tracing the Origins of the Kyoto Protocol: An Article-by-Article Textual History." United Nations Framework Convention on Climate Change, FCCC/TP/2000/2.

DeSombre, E. R. (2000). *Domestic Sources of International Environmental Policy: Industry, Environmentalists, and US Power*. Cambridge, MA: MIT Press.

Diamantoudi, E. and Sartzetakis E. S. (2001). "Stable International Environmental Agreements: An Analytical Approach." mimeo, Department of Accounting and Finance, University of Macedonia, Greece.

Dixit, A. K. (1996). *The Making of Economic Policy: A Transaction-Cost Politics Perspective*. Cambridge, MA: MIT Press.

Downs, G. W., Rocke, D. M., and Barsoon, P. N. (1996). "Is the Good News About Compliance Good News About Cooperation?" *International Organization*, 50: 379–406.

Elliot, H. W. (1887). *Our Arctic Province: Alaska and the Seal Islands*. New York: Charles Scribner's Sons.

Ellis, R. (1991). *Men and Whales*. London: Robert Hale.

Elster, J. (1989). "Social Norms and Economic Theory." *Journal of Economic Perspectives*, 3: 99–117.

Elton, C. S. (2000). *The Ecology of Invasions by Animals and Plants*. Chicago: University of Chicago.

Esty, D.C. (1994). *Greening the GATT: Trade, Environment, and the Future*. Washington, DC: Institute for International Economics.

Evans, P. B., Jacobson, H. K., and Putnam, R. D. (eds) (1993). *Double-Edged Diplomacy*. Berkeley: University of California Press.

Faiz, A., Weaver, C. S., and Walsh, M. P. (1996). *Air Pollution from Motor Vehicles: Standards and Technologies for Controlling Emissions*. Washington, DC: World Bank.

Farrell, J. (1987a). "Cheap Talk, Coordination, and Entry." *Rand Journal of Economics*, 18: 34–9.

—— (1987b). "Information and the Coase Theorem." *Journal of Economic Perspectives*, 1: 113–29.

Farrell, J. and Maskin, E., (1989). "Renegotiation in Repeated Games." *Games and Economic Behavior*, 1: 327–60.

Farrell, J. and Saloner, G. (1988). "Coordination Through Committees and Markets." *RAND Journal of Economics*, 19(2): 235–52.

Fehr, E. and Gächter, S. (2000a). "Cooperation and Punishment in Public Goods Experiments." *American Economic Review*, 90(4): 980–94.

—— (2000b), "Fairness and Retaliation: The Economics of Reciprocity." *Journal of Economic Perspectives*, 14(3): 159–81.

Fehr, E. and Schmidt, K. M. (1999). "A Theory of Fairness, Competition, and Cooperation." *Quarterly Journal of Economics*, 114(3): 817–68.

Fikkan, A., Osherenko, G., and Arikainen, A. (1993). "Polar Bears: The Importance of Simplicity," in O. R. Young and G. Osherenko (eds), *Polar Politics: Creating International Environmental Regimes*. Ithaca: Cornell University Press, 96–151.

Finus, M. (2001). *Game Theory and International Environmental Cooperation*. Cheltenham: Edward Elgar.

Finus, M. and Tjøtta, S. (2001). "The Oslo Protocol on Sulfur Reduction: The Great Leap Forward?" mimeo, Department of Economics, Institute of Economic Theory, University of Hagen, Germany.

Fischbacher, U., Gächter, S., and Fehr, E. (2000). "Are People Conditionally Cooperative? Evidence from a Public Goods Experiment." Institute for Empirical Research in Economics, University of Zurich, Working Paper No. 16.

Fishelson, G. (1995). "Addressing the Problem of Water in the Middle East," in S. L. Spiegel and D. J. Pervin (eds), *Practical Peacemaking in the Middle East, Vol. II: The Environment, Water, Refugees, and Economic Cooperation and Development*. New York: Garland, 117–37.

Fisher, B. S., Barrett, S., Bohm, P., Kuroda, M., Mubazi, J. K. E., Shah, A., and Stavins, R. N. (1996). "An Economic Assessment of Policy Instruments for Combatting Climate Change," in Intergovernmental Panel on Climate Change, *Climate Change 1995: Economic and Social Dimensions of Climate Change*. Cambridge: Cambridge University Press, 397–439.

Folmer, H., van Mouche, P., and Ragland, S. (1993). "Interconnected Games and International Environmental Problems." *Environmental and Resource Economics*, 3: 313–35.

Food and Agriculture Organization (1978). *Systematic Index of International Water Resource Treaties, Declarations, Acts and Cases by Basin*, Legislative Study No. 15. Rome: FAO.

—— (1984). *Systematic Index of International Water Resource Treaties, Declarations, Acts and Cases by Basin, Vol. II*, Legislative Study No. 34, Rome: FAO.

Frank, R. H. (1988). *Passions Within Reason: The Strategic Role of the Emotions*. New York: Norton.

Fredriksson, P. G. and Gaston, N. (1999). "The Importance of Trade for Ratification of the 1992 Climate Change Convention," in P. G. Frederiksson (ed.), *Trade, Global Policy, and the Environment*. World Bank Discussion Paper No. 402, Washington, DC: World Bank, pp. 173–89.

Freeman, C. W. Jr (1997). *The Diplomat's Dictionary*. Washington, DC: United States Institute of Peace Press.

Friedman, J. (1971). "A Noncoooperative Equilibrium for Supergames." *Review of Economic Studies*, 38: 1–12.

Fukuyama, F. (1999). *The Great Disruption: Human Nature and the Reconstitution of Social Order*. New York: Touchstone.

Funk, J. L. and Methe, D. T. (2001). "Market- and Committee-Based Mechanisms in the Creation and Diffusion of Global Industry Standards: The Case of Mobile Communication." *Research Policy*, 30: 589–610.

Fur Seal Arbitration (1895). *Proceedings of the Tribunal of Arbitration at Paris*. Washington, DC: Government Printing Office.

Gay, J. T. (1987). *American Fur Seal Diplomacy: The Alaskan Fur Seal Controversy*. New York: Peter Lang.

General Agreement on Tariffs and Trade (1992). "Trade and the Environment," in *International Trade 1990–91*. Geneva: GATT.

—— (1994). *Report of the Panel, United States-Restrictions on Imports of Tuna*. GATT Doc. DS29/R.

Gladwell, M. (2000). *The Tipping Point: How Little Things Can Make a Big Difference*. Boston: Little, Brown & Company.

Glaeser, E. L., Laibson, D. I., Scheinkman, J. A., and Soutter, C. L. (2000). "Measuring Trust." *Quarterly Journal of Economics*, 115: 811–46.

Goulder, L. H. (1995). "Environmental Taxation and the Double Dividend: A Reader's Guide." *International Tax and Public Finance*, 2: 157–83.

Grieco, J. M. (1990). *Cooperation Among Nations: Europe, America, and Non-Tariff Barriers to Trade*. Ithaca: Cornell University Press.

Grubb, M. (1995). "The Berlin Climate Conference: Outcome and Implications," *Briefing Paper no. 21*. London: The Royal Institute of International Affairs.

Guttman, J. M. (1978). "Understanding Collective Action: Matching Behavior." *American Economic Review*, 68: 251–55.

Haas, P. M. (1990). *Saving the Mediterranean: The Politics of International Environmental Cooperation*. New York: Columbia University Press.

—— (1992). "Banning Chlorofluorocarbons: Epistemic Community Efforts to Protect Stratospheric Ozone." *International Organization*, 46: 187–224.

Hahn, R. W. (1998). *The Economics and Politics of Climate Change*. Washington, DC: American Enterprise Institute.

Hahn, R. W. and Stavins, R. N. (1999). *What Has the Kyoto Protocol Wrought? The Real Architecture of International Tradeable Permit Markets*. Washington, DC: AEI Press.

Handl, G. (1986). "National Uses of Transboundary Air Resources: The International Entitlement Issue Reconsidered." *Natural Resources Journal*, 26: 405–67.

Hardin, R. (1988). *Morality within the Limits of Reason*. Chicago: University of Chicago.

Hauer, G. and Runge, C. F. (1999). "Trade-Environment Linkages in the Resolution of Transboundary Externalities." *The World Economy*, 22: 25–39.

Heal, G. (1993). "Formation of International Environmental Agreements," in C. Carraro (ed.), *Trade, Innovation, Environment*. Dordrecht: Kluwer.

—— (1999). "New Strategies for the Provision of Global Public Goods: Learning from International Environmental Challenges," in I. Kaul, I. Grunberg, and M. A. Stern (eds), *Global Public Goods: International Cooperation in the 21st Century*. New York: Oxford University Press, 220–39.

Helliwell, J. F. and Putnam, R. D. (1995). "Economic Growth and Social Capital in Italy." *Eastern Economic Journal*, 21(3): 295–307.

Henrich, J., Boyd, R., Bowles, S., Camerer, C., Fehr, E., Gintis, H., and McElreath, R. (2001). "In Search of Homo Economicus: Behavioral Experiments in 15 Small-Scale Societies." *American Economic Review*, Papers and Proceedings, 91: 73–8.

Herzog, H., Eliasson, B., and Kaarstad, O. (2000). "Capturing Greenhouse Gases." *Scientific American*, February.

Hoel, M. (1991). "Global Environmental Problems: The Effects of Unilateral Actions Taken by One Country." *Journal of Environmental Economics and Management*, 20: 55–70.

—— (1992). "International Environment Conventions: The Case of Uniform Reductions of Emissions." *Environmental and Resource Economics*, 2: 141–59.

—— (1994). "Efficient Climate Policy in the Presence of Free-Riders." *Journal of Environmental Economics and Management*, 27: 259–74.

—— (1996). "Should a Carbon Tax be Differentiated Across Sectors?" *Journal of Public Economics*, 59: 17–32.

Hoel, M. and Schnieder, K. (1997). "Incentives to Participate in an International Environmental Agreement." *Environmental and Resource Economics*, 9: 153–70.

Hoffman, E. (1997). "Public Choice Experiments," in D.C. Mueller (ed.), *Perspectives on Public Choice: A Handbook*. Cambridge: Cambridge University Press, 415–26.

Hoffman, E. and Spitzer, M. L. (1982). "The Coase Theorem: Some Experimental Tests." *Journal of Law and Economics*, 25: 73–98.

—— (1985). "Entitlements, Rights, and Fairness: An Experimental Examination of Subjects' Concepts of Distributive Justice." *Journal of Legal Studies*, 14: 259–97.

Homer-Dixon, T.F., Boutwell, J.H., and Rathjens, G.W. (1993). "Environmental Change and Violent Conflict." *Scientific American*, February, 38–45.

House of Commons Environment Committee (1984). *Acid Rain*. vol. 1, London: HMSO.

Ikenberry, G. J. (2001). "Getting Hegemony Right." *The National Interest*, No. 63, 17–24.

Iklé, F. C. (1967). *How Nations Negotiate*. New York: Praeger.

Intergovernmental Panel on Climate Change (1996). *Climate Change 1995: Economic and Social Dimensions of Climate Change*. Cambridge: Cambridge University Press.

—— (1998). *Report of the IPCC Workshop on Rapid, Non-linear Climate Change*. IPCC Secretariat.

—— (2001). *Summary for Policymakers: A Report of Working Group I of the Intergovernmental Panel on Climate Change*. IPCC Secretariat.

International Energy Agency (1992). *Climate Change Policy Initiatives*. Paris: OECD.

International Trade Commission (1991). *International Agreements to Protect the Environment and Wildlife*. Washington, DC: United States International Trade Commission.

Jenkins, L. (1996). "Trade Sanctions: Effective Enforcement Tools," in J. Cameron, J. Werksman, and P. Roderick (eds), *Improving Compliance with International Law*. London: Earthscan.

Jorgenson, D. W., Goettle, R. J., Wilcoxen, P. J., and Ho, M. S. (2000). *The Role of Substitution in Understanding the Costs of Climate Change Policy*. Washington, DC: Pew Center on Global Climate Change, September.

Kandori, M. (1992). "Social Norms and Community Enforcement." *Review of Economic Studies*, 59: 63–80.

Keohane, R. O. (1984). *After Hegemony: Cooperation and Discord in the World Political Economy*. Princeton: Princeton University Press.

—— (1986). "Reciprocity in International Relations." *International Organization*, 40: 1–27.

Keynes, J. M. (1949). *Two Memoirs*. London: Rupert Hart-Davis.

—— (1963). *Essays in Biography*. New York: Norton.

Kindleberger, C. P. (1986). "International Public Goods without International Government." *American Economic Review*, 76: 1–13.

Kirmani, S. S. (1990). "Water, Peace and Conflict Management: The Experience of the Indus and Mekong River Basins." *Water International*, 15: 200–5.

Kiss, A. and Shelton, D. (1997). *Manual of European Environmental Law*. Cambridge: Cambridge University Press.

Kiss, C. (1983). *Selected Multilateral Treaties in the Field of the Environment*. Nairobi: United Nations Environment Programme.

Kissinger, H. (1994). *Diplomacy*. New York: Touchstone.

Kjellen, B. (1994). "A Personal Assessment," in I. M. Mintzer and J. A. Leonard (eds), *Negotiating Climate Change: The Inside Story of the Rio Convention*. Cambridge: Cambridge University Press.

Krautkraemer, J. A. (1985). "Optimal Growth, Resource Amenities and the Preservation of Natural Environments." *Review of Economic Studies*, 52: 153–70.

Krugman, P. (1991). "History versus Expectations." *Quarterly Journal of Economics*, 106: 651–67.

Krutilla, J. V. (1967), "Conservation Reconsidered." *American Economic Review*, 57: 777–86.

Kuran, T. (1998). *Private Truths, Public Lies: The Social Consequences of Preference Falsification*. Cambridge, MA: Harvard University Press.

Kurlansky, M. (1997). *Cod: A Biography of the Fish that Changed the World*. New York: Penguin.

LeMarquand, D. G. (1977). *International Rivers: The Politics of Cooperation*. Vancouver: Westwater Research Centre, University of British Columbia.

Levy, M. A. (1993). "European Acid Rain: The Power of Tote-Board Diplomacy," in P. M. Hass, R. O. Keohane, and M. A. Levy (eds), *Institutions for the Earth: Sources of Effective International Environmental Protection*. Cambridge, MA: MIT Press, 75–132.

—— (1995). "International Co-operation to Combat Acid Rain." *Green Globe Yearbook*.

Linklater, A. (1990). *Men and Citizens in the Theory of International Relations*, 2nd edn. London: Macmillan.

Lopez, B. (1986). *Arctic Dreams: Imagination and Desire in a Northern Landscape*. London: Macmillan.

Luce, R. and Raiffa, H. (1957). *Games and Decisions*. New York: John Wiley.

Lyster, S. (1985). *International Wildlife Law*. Cambridge: Grotius.

Machiavelli, N. (1947). *The Prince*. Arlington Heights, IL: Harlan Davidson.

Mäler, K.-G. (1990). "International Environmental Problems." *Oxford Review of Economic Policy*, 6: 80–108.

Mäler, K.-G. (1991). "The Acid Rain Game II." mimeo, Stockholm School of Economics.

Manne, A. S. and Richels, R. G. (1998). "The Kyoto Protocol: A Cost-Effective Strategy for Meeting Environmental Objectives?" mimeo, Stanford University and Electric Power Research Institute.

—— (2001). "US Rejection of the Kyoto Protocol: The Impact on Compliance Costs and CO_2 Emissions." paper presented at the Stanford University Energy Modeling Forum Meeting on Burden Sharing and the Costs of Mitigation, Snowmass, Colorado, August 6, 2001.

Markusen, J. R. (1975). "International Externalities and Optimal Tax Structures." *Journal of International Economics*, 5: 15–29.

Matloff, J. (1999). "Optimism Rises, with Water, in Bid to Revive Aral Sea." *Christian Science Monitor*, February 5; http://www.csmonitor.com/durable/1999/02/05/p8s2.htm.

Matthiessen, P. (1978). *Wildlife in America*. New York: Penguin.

McKibbin, W.J. and Wilcoxen, P.J. (1997). "A Better Way to Slow Global Climate Change." *Brookings Policy Brief*, No. 17, Washington, DC: Brookings Institution.

—— (2000). "Moving Beyond Kyoto," *Brookings Policy Brief*. No. 66, Washington, DC: Brookings Institution.

McMahon, M. S. (1988). "Balancing the Interests: An Essay on the Canadian–American Acid Rain Debate," in J. E. Carroll (ed.), *International Environmental Diplomacy*. Cambridge: Cambridge University Press, 147–71.

Mendelsohn, R. and Neuman, J. E. (1999). *The Impact of Climate Change on the United States Economy*. Cambridge: Cambridge University Press.

Milner, H. (1992). "International Theories of Cooperation Among Nations." *World Politics*, 44: 466–96.

Mirovitskaya, N. S., Clark, M., and Purvey, R. G. (1993). "North Pacific Fur Seals: Regime Formation as a Means of Resolving Conflict," in O. R. Young and G. Osherenko (eds), *Polar Politics: Creating International Environmental Regimes*. Ithaca: Cornell University Press, 22–55.

Mitchell, R. (1993). "Intentional Oil Pollution of the Oceans," in P.M. Haas, R.O. Keohane, and M. A. Levy (eds), *Institutions for the Earth: Sources of Effective International Environmental Protection*. Cambridge, Mass: MIT Press.

—— (1994). *Intentional Oil Pollution at Sea: Environmental Policy and Treaty Compliance*. Cambridge, Mass: MIT Press.

Molina, M. J. and Rowland, F. S. (1974). "Stratospheric Sink for Chlorofluoromethanes: Chlorine Atom-Catalysed Destruction of Ozone." *Nature*, 249: 810–12.

Mumme, S. (1994). "Enforcing International Environmental Agreements: Lessons from the U.S.-Mexico Border." *Journal of Environment and Development*, 3: 71–89.

Murdoch, J.C. and Sandler, T. (1996). "The Voluntary Provision of a Pure Public Good: The Case of Reduced CFC Emissions and the Montreal Protocol." *Journal of Public Economics*, 63: 331–49.

—— (1997). "Voluntary Cutbacks and Pretreaty Behavior: The Helsinki Protocol and Sulfur Emissions." *Public Finance Review*, 25: 139–62.

—— and Sargent, K. (1997). "A Tale of Two Collectives: Sulphur versus Nitrogen Emission Reduction in Europe." *Economica*, 64: 281–301.

—— and Vijverberg, W. P. M. (2002), "The Participation Decision Versus the Level of Participation in an Environmental Treaty: A Spatial Probit Analysis." *Journal of Public Economics*, forthcoming.

Muys, J. C. (1976). "Allocation and Management of Interstate Water Resources: The Emergence of the Federal-Interstate Compact." *Denver Journal of International Law and Policy*, 6: 307–28.

Myers, N., Mittermeier, R. A., Mittermeier, C. G., da Fonseca, G. A. B., and Kent, J. (2000). "Biodiversity Hotspots for Conservation Priorities." *Nature*, 403: 853–8.

Myerson, R. G. (1991). *Game Theory: Analysis of Conflict*. Cambridge, MA: Harvard University Press.

Nagel, R. (1995). "Unraveling in Guessing Games: An Experimental Study." *American Economic Review*, 85(5): 1313–26.

Nagel, T. (1991). *Equality and Partiality*. Oxford: Oxford University Press.

National Oceanic and Atmospheric Administration (NOAA, 2000). *The Setting of the Annual Subsistence Harvest Take Ranges of Northern Fur Seals on the Pribilof Islands for the Period 2000–2002*. Draft Environmental Assessment, Juneau, Alaska, June.

Nordhaus, W. D. (1991). "To Slow or not to Slow: The Economics of the Greenhouse Effect." *The Economic Journal*, 101: 920–37.

—— (1994). *Managing the Global Commons*. Cambridge, MA: MIT Press.

—— (1998). "Is the Kyoto Protocol a Dead Duck? Are There Any Live Ducks Around? Comparison of Alternative Global Tradable Emissions Regimes." mimeo, Department of Economics, Yale University.

—— (2002). "After Kyoto: Alternative Mechanisms to Control Global Warming." paper prepared for a joint session of the American Economics Association and the Association of Environmental and Resource Economists, Atlanta, Georgia, January 4, 2001.

Nordhaus, W.D. and Boyer, J. (1998). "Requiem for Kyoto: An Economic Analysis of the Kyoto Protocol." paper prepared for the energy Modeling Forum meeting, Snowmass, Colorado, August 10–11.

—— (2000). *Warming the World: Economic Models of Global Warming*. Cambridge, MA: MIT Press.

North, D. C. (1990). *Institutions, Institutional Change and Economic Performance*. Cambridge: Cambridge University.

Oliveira-Martins, J., Burniaux, J.-M., and Martin, J. P. (1992). "Trade and the Effectiveness of Unilateral CO_2-Abatement Policies: Evidence from GREEN." *OECD Economic Studies*, No. 19, 123–40.

Olson, M. (1965). *The Logic of Collective Action*. Cambridge, MA: Harvard.

—— (1993). "Dictatorship, Democracy, and Development." *American Political Science Review*, 87(3): 567–76.

Ostrom, E. (1990). *Governing the Commons: The Evolution of Institutions for Collective Action*. Cambridge: Cambridge University Press.

—— (1998). "A Behavioral Approach to the Rational Choice Theory of Collective Action." *American Political Science Review*, 92(1): 1–22.

—— (2000). "Collective Action and the Evolution of Social Norms." *Journal of Economic Perspectives*, 14(3): 137–58.

Ostrom, E., Burger, J., Field, C. B., Norgaard, R. B., and Policansky, D. (1999). "Revisiting the Comons: Local Lessons, Global Challenges." *Science*, 284: 278–82.

Parson, E. A. (1993). "Protecting the Ozone Layer," in P. M. Haas, R. O. Keohane, and M. A. Levy (eds), *Institutions for the Earth*. Cambridge, MA: MIT Press, 27–73.

Paterson, D. G. and Wilen, J. (1977). "Depletion and Diplomacy: The North Pacific Seal Hunt, 1886–1910." *Research in Economic History*, 2: 81–139.

Peterson, M. J. (1993). "International Fisheries Management," in P.M. Haas, R.O. Keohane, and M. A. Levy (eds), *Institutions for the Earth*. Cambridge, MA: MIT Press.

Pizer, W. A. (1999). "Choosing Prices or Quantity Controls for Greenhouse Gases." Climate Change Brief No. 17, Washington, DC: Resources for the Future.

Pronk, J. (2000). "Note by the President of COP6," Climate Change Secretariat, November 23.

—— (2001). "New Proposals by the President of COP6." Climate Change Secretariat, April 9.

Putnam, R. D. (1988). "Diplomacy and Domestic Politics: the Logic of Two-Level Games." *International Organization*, 42: 427–60.

—— (2000). *Bowling Alone: The Collapse and Revival of American Community*. New York: Simon and Schuster.

Putnam, R.D., Leonardi, R., and Nanetti, R.Y. (1993). *Making Democracy Work: Civic Traditions in Modern Italy*. Princeton: Princeton University Press.

Rabkin, J. (1998). *Why Sovereignty Matters*. Washington, DC: American Enterprise Institute.

Raiffa, H. (1982). *The Art and Science of Negotiation*. Cambridge, MA: Harvard University Press.

Rauscher, M. (1997). *International Trade, Factor Movements, and the Environment*. Oxford: Clarendon Press.

Rawls, J. (1972). *A Theory of Justice*. Oxford: Oxford University Press.

Riker, W. H. (1986). *The Art of Political Manipulation*. New Haven: Yale University.

Roberts, M. J. and Spence, M. (1976). "Effluent Charges and Licenses Under Uncertainty." *Journal of Environmental Economics and Management*, 5: 193–208.

Rodes, B. K. and Odell, R. (1992). *A Dictionary of Environmental Quotations*. Baltimore: Johns Hopkins University Press.

Rose, G. and Crane, S. (1993). "The Evolution of International Whaling Law" in P. Sands (ed.), *Greening International Law*. London: Earthscan.

Rose, G. and Paleokrassis, G. (1996). "Compliance with International Environmental Obligations: A Case Study of the International Whaling Commission," in J. Cameron, J. Werksman, and P. Roderick (eds), *Improving Compliance with International Environmental Law*. London: Earthscan.

Rosenzweig, R., Varilek, M., Feldman, B., Kuppalli, R., and Janssen, J. (2002). *The Emerging International Greenhouse Gas Market*. Washington, DC: Pew Center on Global Climate Change, March.

Rowlands, I. H. (1995). *The Politics of Global Atmospheric Change*. Manchester: Manchester University Press.

Rummel-Bulska, I. and S. Osafo (eds) (1991). *Selected Multilateral Treaties in the Field of the Environment*, vol. 2. Cambridge: Grotius.

Runge, C. F. (1984). "Institutions and the Free Rider: The Assurance Problem in Collective Action." *Journal of Politics*, 46: 154–81.

Sandler, T. (1992). *Collective Action: Theory and Applications*. Ann Arbor: University of Michigan Press.

—— (1998). "Global and Regional Public Goods: A Prognosis for Collective Action." *Fiscal Studies*, 19(3): 221–47.

Sands, P. (1995). *Principles of International Environmental Law*. Manchester: Manchester University Press.

Schaller, G. B. (1993). *The Last Panda*. Chicago: University of Chicago Press.

Schelling, T. C. (1960). *The Strategy of Conflict*. Cambridge: Harvard University Press.

—— (1966). *Arms and Influence*. New Haven: Yale University Press.

—— (1978). *Micromotives and Macrobehavior*. New York: W.W. Norton.

—— (1998). *Costs and Benefits of Greenhouse Gas Reduction*. Washington, DC: American Enterprise Institute.

—— (2002). "What Makes Greenhouse Sense?" *Foreign Affairs*, 81(3): 2–9.

Schmalensee, R. (1998). "Greenhouse Policy Architecture and Institutions," in W. D. Nordhaus (ed.), *Economics and Policy Issues in Climate Change*. Washington, DC: Resources for the Future.

Schmalensee, R., Joskow, P.L., Ellerman, A. D., Montero, J. P., and Bailey, E. M. (1998). "An Interim Evaluation of Sulfur Dioxide Emissions Trading." *Journal of Economic Perspectives*, 12: 53–68.

Scott, A. D. (1955). "The Fishery: The Objectives of Sole Ownership." *Journal of Political Economy*, 63: 116–24.

Sebenius, J. K. (1984). *Negotiating the Law of the Sea*. Cambridge: Harvard University Press.

Sen, A. (1987). *On Ethics and Economics*. Oxford: Blackwell.

Shapley, D. (1985). *The Seventh Continent: Antarctica in a Resource Age*. Washington, DC: Resources for the Future.

Shaw, M. N. (1991). *International Law*. Cambridge: Grotius Publications.

Skaperdas, S. (1992). "Cooperation, Conflict, and Power in the Absence of Property Rights." *American Economic Review*, 82: 720–39.

Sprinz, D. and Vaahtoranta, T. (1994). "The Interest-Based Explanation of International Environmental Policy." *International Organization*, 48(1): 77–105.

Stavins, R. N. (1998). "What Can We Learn from the Grand Policy Experiment? Lessons from SO$_2$ Allowance Trading." *Journal of Economic Perspectives*, 12(3): 69–88.

—— (1999). "The Costs of Carbon Sequestration: A Revealed-Preference Approach." *American Economic Review*, 89(4): 994–1009.

—— (2001). "President Bush's Withdrawal from the Kyoto Protocol Provides Opportunity for Meaningful Action." *Boston Globe*, April 4.

Stein, A. A. (1983). "Coordination and Collaboration: Regimes in an Anarchic World," in S.D. Krasner (ed.), *International Regimes*. Ithaca: Cornell University Press.

—— (1990). *Why Nations Cooperate: Circumstance and Choice in International Relations*. Ithaca: Cornell University Press.

Stewart, R. B. and Wiener, J. B. (2001). "Reconstructing Climate Policy: The Paths Ahead." *Policy Matters*, 01–23, Washington, DC: AEI-Brookings Joint Center for Regulatory Studies, August.

Sugden, R. (1984). "Reciprocity: The Supply of Public Goods through Voluntary Contributions." *Economic Journal*, 94: 772–87.

Sugden, R. (1989). "Spontaneous Order." *Journal of Economic Perspectives*, 3: 85–97.

Susskind, L. E. (1994). *Environmental Diplomacy*. Oxford: Oxford University Press.

Swedish Environmental Protection Agency (1999). *Facts About Swedish Policy: Acid Rain*. Stockholm: Swedish Environmental Protection Agency, November.

Thucydides (1993). *History of the Peloponesian War*. London: Everyman.

Tolba, M. K. (1987). "The Ozone Agreement—and Beyond," *Environmental Conservation*, 14(4): 287–90.

Trail Smelter Arbitral Tribunal (1939). "Decision." *American Journal of International Law*, 33: 182–212.

—— (1941). "Decision." *American Journal of International Law*, 35: 684–736.

Twum-Barima, R. and Campbell, L. B. (1994). *Protecting the Ozone Layer through Trade Measures: Reconciling the Trade Provisions of the Montreal Protocol and the Rules of the GATT*. Geneva: United Nations Environment Programme.

Uimonen, P. and Whalley, J. (1997). *Environmental Issues in the New World Trading System*. London: Macmillan.

United States Department of Energy (1999). *Carbon Sequestration Research and Development*. Washington, DC: US Department of Energy.

United States Environmental Protection Agency (1988a). *Regulatory Impact Analysis: Protection of Stratospheric Ozone*. Washington, DC: EPA, August.

United States Environmental Protection Agency (1988*b*). "Protection of Stratospheric Ozone; Final Rule." *Federal Register*, 53: 30566–602.

—— (1997). *Adopted Aircraft Engine Emission Standards*. EPA 420-F-97-010, Washington, DC: EPA, April.

United States General Accounting Office (1992). *International Agreements are Not Well Monitored*. Washington, DC: U.S. GAO.

United States Government (1996). Non-paper on Multilateral Environmental Agreements, WTO/CTE/W129, September 11.

United States International Trade Commission (1991). *International Agreements to Protect the Environment and Wildlife*. Washington, DC: USITC Publication 2351.

Utton, A. E. (1988). "Problems and Successes of International Water Agreements: The Example of the United States and Mexico," in J. E. Carol (ed.), *International Environmental Diplomacy*. Cambridge: Cambridge University Press, 67–83.

van Damme, E. (1989). "Renegotiation-Proof Equilibria in Repeated Prisoners' Dilemma." *Journal of Economic Theory*, 47: 206–17.

Van Slooten, R. (1994). "The Case of the Montreal Protocol," in *Trade and Environment: Processes and Production Methods*. Paris: OECD, 87–90.

Victor, D. G. (2001). *The Collapse of the Kyoto Protocol and the Struggle to Slow Global Warming*. Princeton: Princeton University Press.

Viscusi, W. K. (1998). *Rational Risk Policy*. Oxford: Clarendon Press.

Wade, R. (1987). "The Management of Common Property Resources: Finding a Cooperative Solution." *World Bank Research Observer*, 2: 219–34.

Wagner, U. J. (2001). "The Design of Stable International Environmental Agreements." Journal of Economic Surveys, 15(3): 377–411.

Weyant, J. P. and Portney, P. R. (eds.) (1999). *Discounting and Intergenerational Equity*. Baltimore: Johns Hopkins University Press.

Weiss, E. B. and Jacobson, H. K. (1998). *Engaging Countries: Strengthening Compliance with International Environmental Accords*. Cambridge, MA: MIT Press.

Weitzman, M. L. (1974). "Prices vs. Quantities." *Review of Economic Studies*, 41: 477–91.

Wilson, E. O. (2002). *The Future of Life*. New York: Alfred A. Knopf.

World Meteorological Organization (1998). *Scientific Assessment of Ozone Depletion: 1998*. WMO Global Ozone Research and Monitoring Project, Report No. 44, Geneva.

World Trade Organization (1998). *United States-import Prohibition of Certain Shrimp and Shrimp Products*. Report of the Appellate Body, WT/DS58/AB/R, Geneva: World Trade Organization.

Young, H. P. (1994). *Equity*. Princeton: Princeton University Press.

—— (1996). "The Economics of Convention." *Journal of Economic Perspectives*, 10: 105–22.

Young, O. R. (1989). "The Politics of International Regime Formation: Managing Natural Resources and the Environment." *International Organization*, 43: 349–75.

—— (1994). *International Governance: Protecting the Environment in a Stateless Society*. Ithaca: Cornell University Press.

Zartman, I. W. and Berman, M. R. (1982). *The Practical Negotiator*. New Haven: Yale University.

Index